Natural Computation

Natural Computation

Whitman Richards, editor

A Bradford Book
The MIT Press
Cambridge, Massachusetts
London, England

This book was printed and bound by Halliday Lithograph in the United States of America.

Library of Congress Cataloging-in-Publication Data

Natural computation / edited by Whitman Richards.
   p. cm.
   "A Bradford book."
   Includes bibliographies and index.
   ISBN 0-262-18132-0. ISBN 0-262-68055-6 (pbk.)
   1. Perception -- Mathematical models.   2. Artificial intelligence.   3. Human information processing -- Mathematical models.   I. Richards, Whitman.
BF311.N35   1988
152.1--dc19   88-15892
                                                   CIP

Contents

Preface

The key event which raised our level of understanding of symbolic processing by biological systems was David Marr's arrival here at the A.I. Lab in 1973. This was two years after he had received his Ph.D. in Neurophysiology at Trinity College, having completed a theoretical study of the cerebral neocortex. Around this time I recall a racquets friend of mine—a physicist also from Cambridge—asking what I thought about Marr's work. Somewhat embarrassed, for I had given Marr's papers only a superficial glance, my reply was evasive. Prompted by his inquiry, however, I reexamined the two published works—one on the cerebral cortex and the other on the cerebellum—and promptly went back to my psychophysical experiments. What relevance did these papers have to what I was doing? I think my reaction was typical of many. Yet today, in light of the advances in computational vision that have been made over the past ten years, I wonder how much we have missed.

It was not until 1974 that I really began to interact with Marr, who needed a bangboard to try out his ideas on stereopsis. At the same time (over gin and tonics) he would raise questions about the significance of my experimental inquiries, eventually opening new doors, leading me to appreciate the value of what he was about. Marr brought together two things: the formal but machine-driven approach of the A.I. community and the knowledge of biological systems provided by psychology and neurophysiology. At first this union existed only in Marr himself plus a select few and was not present in the community. For example, when Stuart Sutherland came by on one of his perennial visits to M.I.T., he gave two talks, one to the A.I. Lab and the other to the Psychology Department. The first was entitled "Why A.I. should talk to Psychology"; the second was "Why Psychology should talk to A.I."!

By 1976, however, Marr's stature among a few influential forces (e.g. Marvin Minsky!) had reached the point where a faculty appointment seemed proper. H.-L. Teuber, who had created a novel and unique department here, supported this move. Consequently we pressed for an appointment in Psychology, or more appropriately Brain Science. Following the usual custom, Marr gave a "job talk", which was an extension of his 1976 paper on the Early Processing of Visual Information. It was very poorly received. Today, of course, this work is regarded as classic. My point is that in only ten years, Marr's approach that integrated computational (A.I.-ish) and biological approaches to understanding perceptual (and motor) systems became accepted and well established. Indeed, the standard demanded of the scientist studying perception now is much higher than it was only a decade ago, thanks to Marr.

There were, of course, several other key players in this development. These include the members of Marr's group and his supporters, particularly Patrick Winston and later Michael Brady. Within this original group, Shimon Ullman and Tomaso Poggio were the next most powerful intellectual forces. Not surprisingly, their papers are cited frequently here and elsewhere, and their contributions provide a framework for many of the articles collected in these selections.

Another group of key players that helped fertilize the ground and bring about the growth and acceptance of Marr's ideas were those who funded our collaborative efforts here at M.I.T. Sally Sedelow at NSF and Jack Thorpe at AFOSR must be given special acknowledgement, for they were the first to accept and later jointly fund our first proposals in 1975 entitled "Computational Algorithms for Visual Processing". These studies continued for many years under the project direction of Eamon Barrett, Howard Resnikoff, Ed Weiss and Y.-T. Chien at NSF and Genevieve Haddad and John Tangney at AFOSR. During this period DARPA also provided considerable support through the A.I. Lab and its facilities, and more recently Bill Vaughan's "Inference from Images" program has been most helpful.

Since Marr's book on Vision appeared in 1982, there have been considerable advances and also divergences in our individual outlooks on the nature of the perceptual process. These Selections in Natural Computation represent my point of view, developed over the past seven years as I taught and learned from my students here at M.I.T. It is a view expressing how modern psychophysics should study perceptual and motor systems. Recently some have accused me of being a neo-Gibsonian. I must admit some guilt, for I believe Gibson was on the right track when he stated that "perception is direct". I share the spirit of this claim if interpreted to mean that our analysis of any perceptual process should be directed at understanding how high-level inferences can be made directly from reasonable lower-level inputs, such as the "primal-sketch primitives", rather than getting bogged down with excessive intermediate sensory apparatus. In retrospect, it is a bit of a shame that adequate computational facilities were not available in Gibson's time, in order that his original ideas could be tested rigorously as Marr demanded. Another missing ingredient was that the nature of the inference process was not understood to the extent it is today. Shimon Ullman deserves special credit for this latter advance, which was triggered by his deep analysis of "the recovery of structure from motion", and which became the springboard for the "Observer Theory" now being proposed by Bennett, Hoffman, & Prakash.

Finally, I wish to thank my colleagues and students, family and friends for helping me bring together the intellectual framework for this book, and to William Gilson for patiently formatting these selections. I hope they will offer the intent reader a broad, new perspective for psychophysics.

I

Introduction to Natural Computation

The Approach

W. Richards

Massachusetts Institute of Technology

1.0 What Is Natural Computation?

A classic problem of perception, long recognized by philosophers, and explicitly stated by Descartes (Crombie, 1964), is that biological systems have available through their senses only very limited information about the external world. Yet these systems make strong assertions about the actual state of the world outside themselves. These assertions are of necessity incomplete. Clearly, a replica of an object and its qualities cannot be embodied within the brain. How can an incomplete description, encoded by neural states, be sufficient to direct the survival and successful adaptive behavior of a living system (or machine)? Why are such representations so reliable when they are based on information that is so incomplete?

The answers to these kinds of questions is the domain of Natural Computation. For example, how can a jumble of incoming auditory sense data be processed to yield a reliable statement about the location and nature of one sound source among many? Clearly, we make such assertions with confidence every moment of our lives from complex samples of the world reflected in the peripheral pattern of neural activities. Because these data are of necessity incomplete, they are potentially subject to many interpretations (as illusions illustrate). The major task of Natural Computation is a formal analysis and demonstration of how unique and correct interpretations can be inferred from sensory data by exploiting lawful properties of the natural world.

2.0 Three Levels of Analysis

Several difficult steps are involved in this analysis, and for clarity it is imperative to know which step one is embarking on (Marr, 1976, 1982). For example, when we ask "How do we see?", the question is somewhat ambiguous. Do we mean, "What kinds of neurons and circuitry underlie the process of seeing?" Or do we mean, "What types of computations are involved—digital, analog, statistical, parallel or serial?" Or, lastly, are we referring to "the kinds of information about the world in which the brain takes an interest?" An understanding of the perceptual process in its entirety demands answers to all three questions.

To sharpen these distinctions further, I will elaborate an example given by Marr & Poggio (1977). Consider the simple pocket calculator. What constitutes an understanding of its operation? Suppose a child experimented with the device and developed a hunch that for any three buttons M, N and $\times$, where M and N are "number" buttons, then the sequence $M \times N$ or $N \times M$ produced the same display. Does this generalization about the behavior of the device (along with

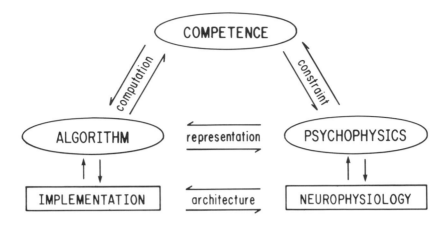

Figure 1 Understanding either a physical or biological system entails several levels of analysis.

other similar observations) represent a complete understanding of the machine?

The answer is no. We cannot understand the calculation without appreciating that it is an embodiment of an arithmetic—a formal system of axioms and deduction rules. It is the constraints at this more abstract level which give rise to the observed regularities in the behavior of the device. Understanding a perceptual system is similar. We can not claim to understand its function simiply by recording its performance. We must also understand the concepts that are to be embodied in the perceptual machine—our brains. Then we can ask how these concepts—such as the notion of an arithmetic—can be implemented using neural hardware.

Let me now elaborate further with two specific examples. Recall that a countless number of appropriately chosen pairs of narrow-band lights will appear the same color as "white". The rules underlying these equivalences depend upon the fact that our visual transducers have one of only three different absorption spectra.

Similar equivalences can be constructed using textures. For example, in Figure 2 a texture of randomly oriented lines is seen to match similar lines having only three orientations. Think of such constraints upon our own eyes as analogous to the constraints embodied in the calculator that allow $N \times M$ to equal $M \times N$. Where did these constraints come from? Why are three different color receptors (or orientations) and not 12 or 20 sufficient for color vision (or texture)? If we can not answer such questions, then we can not claim to comprehend fully the processing of spectral or textural information. It is this level of analysis that we would wish to stress most in this book, for too easily we slip into a discussion of mechanism and lose sight of the goals and constraints that underlie solutions to perceptual problems. Because we are attempting to understand the formal properties of the conceptual structure which underlies a behavior, we identify this level of analysis as developing a theory of the competence of the system.

Let us return again to our pocket calculator. Assume that we have understood

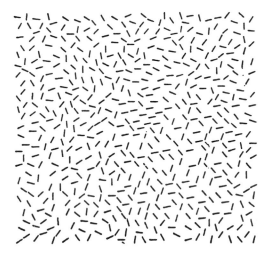

Figure 2 A texture of randomly oriented lines can be matched by similar lines having only three orientations. This is a texture analog of trichromatic vision. Limitations of this kind clearly shed light on the mechanisms of perception. However a deep understanding of the perception should recognize why the structure of the world permits such shortcuts in information processing. (From Riley, 1977).

(or proposed) a particular arithmetic. Do we now understand the calculator? Clearly not, for we have not shown how our proposed arithmetic is actually instantiated in the machine. (Note that once we do this, we will implicitly capture the properties and behavior of the number-world.) At this stage we must now ask how a number is to be represented and how the operations of interest are executed. Again consider multiplication as an example. We probably will elect a binary or octal representation for the numbers but certainly not Roman numerals! Immediately we see that a decision about a scheme for multiplication (or division, or whatever) influences our choice of number

system. Representation and algorithm are intimately coupled. The problems at this level—such as theoretical limits upon the speed and convergence of any particular algorithm or recipe for carrying out a computation—should be treated in their own right, independently of the deductive system set up for numbers. As illustrated in Figure 1, the level of representation and algorithm is a particular computational embodiment of a competence.

Finally, there is still at least one other level of analysis, namely that which studies the mechanism carrying out a computation. A particular algorithm may be implemented in several ways, such as via vacuum tubes, transistors, solid-state

Figure 3 In one part of the pattern the small squares are assigned only one of three gray levels. This region is hard to distinguish from the balance of the pattern which is built up of checks having any one of 64 gray levels, randomly assigned. Why are such limitations not serious handicaps to perception? (Riley, 1977).

materials or neurons. Here, although we are interested primarily in neural mechanisms, it will be useful to run our algorithms first on a computer to check for the consistency and completeness of a particular information processing scheme.

3.0 Method

Our levels of understanding illustrated in Figure 1 serve as the framework for studying a perceptual feat. Specifically, we recommend that a problem in Natural Computation be analyzed as follows:

Step 1 Goal and Givens.

Begin by considering the goals of the biological system. Specifically, what property or events in the world should be captured? Is there any evidence that Man can indeed extract the desired information? If so, what hints can be obtained from psychophysics regarding the sensory data or primitives used in the computation?

Step 2 Theory of Competence.

Given the information processing goal, and the available sense data, develop a theory to show how a reliable and accurate representation can be computed. What plausible natural constraints are required to yield a unique representation or interpretation of the data?

Step 3 Representation and Algorithm.

Having now determined the constraints and general strategy for achieving the perceptual goal, a particular form of representation is chosen and a formal computational procedure (algorithm) is devised for interpreting the available input data correctly.

Step 4 Implementation and Mechanism.

Lastly, the algorithm is implemented in a computer and its structure and behavior are compared with psychophysical or neurophysiological evidence. If a correspondence between the biological and computational implementations is not found, then the source of incompatibility is determined and the analysis reinitiated at the appropriate step.

For many, the principle aim is to understand the human perceptual system. Here, the success of one's understanding can be gauged by a comparison of the behavior of the surrogate machine with psychophysics. This is a kind of Turing Test. To the degree that the successes and failures of the machine implementation match the psychophysical successes or failures (illusions), then the behavior is understood. Note that discrepancies between the machine's behavior and ours can occur at any of the three levels shown in Figure 1. Perhaps the most embarrassing case is at the level of competence, where either the given sense data were improperly chosen, or, more seriously, where inappropriate axioms or postulates about the world model were made at the outset. A proper theory of competence is essential to understanding perception, yet it is the most neglected area of study.

4.0 Theory of Competence: An Example

Algorithms and Mechanisms have immediate appeal to perceptual scientists because there is the feeling that one is dealing with tangible results—i.e. directly observable behavior, which if mimicked or modeled, is considered understood. But

	Natural Computation Approach	Mathematical Formalism
Step 1	*Identify the Goal and the Givens.* What is the desired representation? What data are available?	Define the domain and range of the function.
Step 2	*Show theoretically how a reliable representation can be computed.* What are the natural constraints that will force the unique interpretation?	Find a unique mapping (function).
Step 3	*Design a particular algorithm that correctly interprets the available input information.*	Describe a procedure for computing the function.
Step 4	*Test whether the primate visual system uses the particular algorithm.* (If not, identify which step above is incompatible and reiterate.)	Identify relation between the elements of the procedure and their biological (machine) implementation.

Table 1 Steps in a Computational Analysis (from Richards, 1979).

if one were to duplicate a Model T down to the last nut and bolt, would we really understand its operation? When the engine began to "diesel" or "backfire" would we realize why? Trying to understand the competence of a biological system from its structure is even more elusive, because often these mechanisms are adaptations of previously existing hardware (Dumont & Robertson, 1986). Consequently their performance can be a significant corruption of an ideal implementation, masking the true goal of the computation. The competence of a biological system is thus exceedingly difficult to infer from its performance. But without a theory for the competence of a system, we really do not have a theory of perception.

Understanding the competence of the human perceptual system is largely a mathematical exercise, grounded in penetrating insights into the structure of the world. It is truly a *psycho-physics*, for it demands an understanding of the physical world as well as a knowledge of our own cognitive goals and capabilities. Because this level of analysis is the most difficult to grasp, an example is provided:

Step 1: Goals and Givens.

Consider a tiled floor as illustrated in Figure 4. Is angle ACB a right angle? Perceptually, this is an easy judgement to make: the answer is yes. Yet when this tesselation is projected onto the image plane of your retina, the corresponding angle acb is probably not a right triangle.

Furthermore, notice that an infinity of angles can produce the same retinal image. ACB is only one of many possible alternatives. How, then, can you tell whether the 2D image acb arises from a right triangle in the 3D world?

1

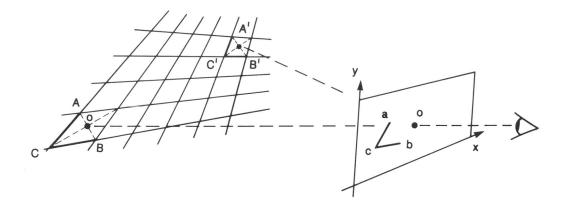

Figure 4 Points ABC in 3D project into the xy-image plane as a, b, c. Is angle ACB a right angle? (Note that given only abc, there are an infinity of possible triangles that will produce an identical image. Most of these imaged triangles will not be right triangles.)

Step 2: Theory of Competence.

To answer this question, we must first explore the mapping of right triangles ACB in 3D onto the 2D image plane. When a right triangle is projected onto the image plane, will its image be an arbitrary triangle? If not, what relations will be preserved in the projection? Are these relations sufficient for us to infer that the imaged angle could only have arisen from a right triangle? If not, are there a restricted set of useful conditions where we can be assured that in 3D the angle acb is a right angle? Generally, because we have gone from a higher to a lower dimension, some constraints must be introduced that will allow us to recover the information lost in the projection. We will introduce three: First, we assume that the tiled pattern

on the floor is stable and that the floor is horizontal. Second, we assume that the viewer is standing erect on the floor, and can only sense whether his viewing angle to the vertical is constant as he swivels his eye right to left (i.e. he can not measure absolute angles, but can sense changes in his up-down view). Third, we will use parallel (orthographic) projection rather than perspective projection. Given these conditions, we now consider the behavior of a circle circumscribed about triangle ABC in 3-space.

The circle about ABC in 3D projects into an ellipse in the 2D image plane. The equation for this ellipse has the following form:

$$ax^2 + by^2 + cxy + dx + ey + 1 = 0 \qquad (1)$$

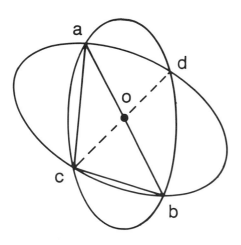
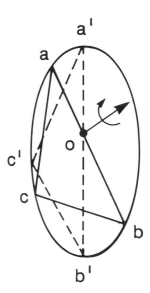

Figure 5 A single view of a right triangle can have an infinity of possible circumscribed ellipses (left). Two views of identical right triangles, confined to lie in a plane, yield a unique circumscribed ellipse.

If triangle ABC is indeed a right triangle, with angle ACB the right angle, then the midpoint of AB is the center of the circumscribed circle (see Figure 5). Let o be the projection of this midpoint. Then d, the fourth corner, lies in the projection of the circumscribed circle, where $co = od$. Taking the origin of the image plane coordinates at O, we have four sets of (x, y) values, corresponding to the points a, b, c, d. Substituting into equation (1) we obtain four equations in five unknowns. Hence a single view of a triangle does not provide enough information to tell whether it is a right triangle or not. The ambiguity is illustrated in Figure 5 (left) by showing two different ellipses that pass through the image points a, b, c, d. (If you claim to be able to make this judgment with one view, then other constraints or assumptions have been introduced!)

Let us now swivel our eye or camera slightly to the right to obtain a second view of the tiling on the floor. Our second view will produce a second set of points $a'\, b'\, c'$, as illustrated in Figure 5 (right). We now have six equations (or eight if point d' is added) in only five unknowns. If these points all lie on the same ellipse, then because the equations are linear the solution is unique. If points O and O' coincide and points d and d' do not lie on this unique ellipse, then the angle ABC and $A'\, B'\, C'$ can not be right angles. Two orthographic views of the tiled tessellation on the horizontal floor, one a rotation of the other, suffice to determine whether that pattern can have a right angle. Given our constraints, these are minimal conditions necessary for this competence.

Whether the observer elects to use this particular competence is another matter. If so, he might have a "built in" interpretation rule to the effect that "if I am standing on a horizontal floor and see two views of a pattern such that the vertices can be interpreted reliably as the projections of a right triangle, then I will assert that the intersections are at right angles". Such an assertion rests on assumptions. If they are wrong, then the perceiver will err![1]

5.0 Observer Mechanics[2]

5.1 False targets

What chance does the perceiver have of being correct in his assertion about seeing right angles? We know that an infinity of triangles will project into any given image ellipse. For example, in Figure 6, two triangles abc and $a'\,b'\,c'$ are inscribed in an ellipse satisfying the right-triangle reconstruction given in the previous section. However, in this case it is clear that both acb and $a'\,c'\,b'$ can not be right angles belonging to the same tesselated surface. These false targets are easily eliminated from image information. However, now consider the inscribed triangles pqr and $p'\,q'\,r'$. Do these arise from a rectangular grid? Unfortunately, given any regular tessellation of a grid, such as one created by parallelograms, there is always a unique right-angle interpretation for some non-horizontal plane. This is a second kind of false target which can not be identified from image information alone. Recall that

the observer does not know the viewing angle to the surface, and hence the inclination of the plane of the grid is a free variable. For a non-rectangular grid, the tessellations of a parallelogram will also fit within an ellipse. Now, because an ellipse in 3D projects into an ellipse in the 2D image plane, the observer following our inference rules might incorrectly conclude pqr is the projection of a right triangle. And because there are many more ellipses than circles, we have the very undesirable condition that the number of such inappropriate pairs of views greatly exceeds the number of cases where the two triangles are inscribed in a circle. Of course, some of these we can reject immediately. But the number of incorrect possibilities is still much greater than those correct. Where have we gone wrong?

5.2 A "kind" world

The problem illustrated in Figure 6 may be summarized as follows. Given any regular tessellation, there will *always* be a unique right angle solution for two views of the pattern, and some (unknown) inclination of the plane of the tiling. Moreover, this space of false targets is much greater than the space of "correct" targets! So most of the time, our inference will be wrong, assuming all angles and inclinations are equally likely.

The only escape from this difficulty would be if the distribution of plane sur-

---

[1] Note that this issue is entirely separate from the observer's ability to measure the x, y coordinates of the points abc, $a'\,b'\,c'$. We assume accurate data, and hope that our solution is stable to perturbations in the data. (This can be explored by computer simulation.) If the condition of solution stability is not met, then our theory for competence is not a very practical one.

[2] This section is based on a monograph by Bennett, Hoffman & Prakash (1988), who address in detail the issues discussed here.

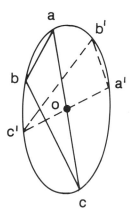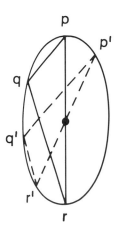

Figure 6 Inscribed triangles abc and $a'b'c'$ satisfy the solution for reconstructing a right triangle in 3D projected into a 2D image. Yet angles abc and $a'b'c'$ both can not be projections of a right angle from the same tesselated surface such as that illustrated in Figure 4. In this case, the inscription rule offered in Section 4 (Figure 5) is obviously incomplete. However, in the right panel, pqr and $p'q'r'$ satisfy the inscription conditions, but here represent the projections of a tesselation of a non-horizontal grid of parallelograms. How do we exclude this second type of false target?

faces in the were biased in our favor. If horizontal surfaces were more populous than other inclinations, then when the conditions of our solution are met, we would have a high chance of interpreting the tessellation correctly. This is a "kind" world. It is a world with structure; it is a world that is not arbitrary. The success of our perceptual inference thus requires that our interpretation rules and goals be commensurate with the structure of the world. If they are not, or if the world were chaotic without structure, then perception could not succeed. Further discussion of such important preconditions for perceiving is given in a recent book called *Observer Mechanics* by Bennett, Hoffman & Prakash (1988). It is mandatory reading for any serious student of perception.

5.3 Fundamental hypothesis: natural modes

The consequence of the above discussion of perceiving the simple right angle is enormous. If the world were just a collection of random events, perception would not be possible. Indeed, there would be nothing to perceive! The success of a perceptual act is intimately coupled with the observer's ability to build internal representations whose assumptions reflect the proper structure and regularities present in the world. Discovering these regularities and understanding how they underlie perception is the objective of a theory of competence. Fundamental to perception is thus the notion that there is indeed structure in the world. This is our fundamental hypothesis given that perception is generally successful. Events and structures in the world must be clustered in a multi-dimensional space (Bobick & Richards, 1986, 1988; Marr, 1970). As a result of natural selection and environmental pressures, as well as physical and architectural constraints imposed on development of new structures, nature adopts only a few of the many possible solutions to each problem it encounters (Mayr, 1984; Stebbins & Ayala, 1985). We see evidence for the modality of natural structures every day of our lives, but it is so ingrained that this modality seems quite natural. Animals are not asymmetric and arbitrary, but are symmetric. Plants grow toward the light. Fish and whales, although biologically quite different, look similar because their particular body design is efficient for locomotion through fluids. Even chaotic systems, such as turbulence or clouds, are not arbitrary structures but exhibit modal behavior (Levi, 1986). Our fundamental hypothesis about the world is thus the following:

Principle of Natural Modes: Structure in the world is not arbitrary and object properties are clustered about modes along dimensions important to the interaction between objects and environments.

Perception is impossible without some such underlying principle. However, given a world exhibiting structure, the perceptual process becomes potentially comprehensible. One goal of Natural Computation is to understand what types of modal structures and regularities provide the most useful constraints upon our observations.

6.0 What's New?

Natural Computation clearly has antecedents (Gibson, 1961; Helmholtz, 1925; Johansson, 1964; Longuet-Higgins, 1972; Yilmaz, 1967). However, no one before Marr (1976) clearly distinguished three levels at which biological information processing can be understood, and used each level to aid in understanding the other. Marr's integration of the understanding of the mechanism, the algorithm and the theory of competence is unique. Ullman's (1979) analysis of the recovery of structure-from-motion was the first study to provide a complete analysis of a competence and to carefully distinguish this analysis from its embodiment in the algorithm he designed to carry out the computation. With the exception of Horn (1974), Land & McCann (1971) and Longuet-Higgins (1978), no predecessor had ever completed a rigorous, computational analysis and at the same time showed how a formal procedure (algorithm) could be designed to effect a proposed solution. This concrete step is very important because it links competence to performance, as expressed by the mechanism of the biological system. It also provides an demonstration that a theory of competence is in fact plausible, practical, and has no unforeseen "flaws". Clearly, the advent of computer technology has allowed us this distinct advantage. However, the attraction of this new tool should not overshadow the need to begin first with an understanding of why the computation should take place at all, and how this competence can be achieved in principle.

Acknowledgments: John Rubin and Donald Hoffman's comments were greatly appreciated.

References

Bennett, B.M., Hoffman, D.D. & Prakash, C. (1988) *Observer Mechanics*. Forthcoming. See *Proc. Int. Conf. on Computer Vision*, 1987.

Bobick, A. & Richards, W. (1986) Classifying objects from visual information. MIT A.I. Lab. Memo 879.

Crombie, A.C., (1964) Early concepts of the senses and the mind. *Sci. Amer.*, 210(May):108–116.

Dumont, J.P.C. & Robertson, R.M. (1986) Neuronal circuits: an evolutionary perspective. *Science*, 233:849–853.

Gibson, J.J. (1961) Ecological optics. *Vision Res.*, 1:253–262.

Helmholtz, H. von (1925) *Treatise on Physiological Optics*. New York: Dover.

Horn, B.K.P. (1974) Determining lightness from an image. *Comp. Graphics & Image Proc.*, 3:277–299.

Johansson, G. (1964) Perception of motion and changing form. *Scand. J. Psychol.*, 5:181–208.

Land, E.H. & McCann, J.J. (1971) Lightness theory. *J. Opt. Soc. Am.*, 61:1–11.

Levi, B. (1986) New global formalism describes paths to turbulence. *Physics Today*, 39(4):17–18.

Longuet-Higgins, H.C. (1972) Making sense of music. *Proc. Roy. Inst.*, 45:87.

Longuet-Higgins, H.C. (1978) The perception of music. *Interdisiplinary SW Rev.*, 3:148–156.

Marr, D. (1970) A theory for cerebral neocortex. *Proc. Roy. Soc. Lond. B*, 176:161–234.

Marr, D. (1976) Early processing of visual information. *Phil. Trans. Roy. Soc. B*, 275:483–524.

Marr, D. (1982) *Vision: a Computational Investigation into the Human Representation and Processing of Visual Information*. San Francisco: Freeman.

Marr, D. & Poggio, T. (1977) From understanding computation to understanding neural circuitry. *Neuro. Res. Prog. Bull.*, 15:470–488.

Mayr, E. (1984) Species concepts and their applications. In E. Sober (ed.) *Conceptual Issues in Evolutionary Biology: An Anthology*. Cambridge, Mass.: MIT Press, pp. 531–541.

Richards, W. (1979) Natural Computation: Filling a Perceptual Void. In W.G. Vogt & M.M. Mickle (eds.) *Modelling and Simulation 10*, pp. 193–200.

Richards, W. & Bobick, A. (1988) Playing twenty questions with nature. In Z. Pylyshyn (ed.), *Computational Processes in Human Vision*. Norwood, N.J.: Ablex.

Riley, M.D. (1977) "Discrimination of bar texture with differing orientation a length distributions". B.S. dissertation, MIT, Dept. E.E. & C.S.

Stebbins, G.L. & Ayala, F.J. (1985) Evolution of Darwinism. *Sci. Amer.*, 253(1):72–82.

Ullman, S. (1979) *The Interpretation of Visual Motion*. Cambridge, Mass.: MIT Press.

Yilmaz, H. (1967) A theory of speech perception. *Bull. Math. Biophys.*, 29:793–824.

1

II

Image Interpretation:
Information at Contours

Image Interpretation: Information at Contours

1.0 The Goal

"Seeing" is the construction of meaningful symbolic descriptions from images. Object recognition is one such task, and one that is often taken as the primary goal of a visual system. Surprisingly, a significant obstacle in the path of understanding object recognition is that we lack a precise definition of what constitutes an object. Without such a definition, how can we possibly know where we are headed? Furthermore, any computational theory of object recognition becomes impossible, for what is to be computed?

To illustrate the difficulty, consider the following: Are the wrinkles on our skin objects? Or the bark or roots of a tree? Is a caravan of cars an object, or a line of pedestrians waiting for the bus? Yet despite such questionable cases we all have a strong intuitive sense of what is and what is not an object. Our strategy seems to be one of defining certain categories of "things", such as animal or automobile, tree or flower, whose members we accept as objects just as we agree upon what phrases constitute a language. But how, then, do we define a category and its membership? The proposal we will adopt here is that category membership depends critically upon the nature of a member's parts and their (geometric) relations to one another. For example, the category animal might be defined as "objects" having a torso, with head and limbs appropriately attached. In turn, each of these components can be defined in terms of other parts and their relations. Thus,

a head is an object with eyes, ears, nose, mouth, etc. in appropriate relation to one another. As we shall see more clearly in Chapter 12, category membership is very much like a language, where a common set of rules applies throughout a hierarchical structure of parts (or phrases) and sub-parts (or sub-phrases.)

Such a part-based representation for specifying object categories is an extremely powerful convention. Its roots are not simply cognitive. Rather, its power comes from the fact that our world is highly structured and patterned (Principle of Natural Modes). These patterns or structures include "optimal" solutions to problems of survival, given a particular

Figure 1 The left-hand panels show two por tions of the bird—one a texture, the other a "shape". Clearly the simple shape of an eye alone provides an important pointer to the class of object, namely "animal", whereas the texture patch alone offers few clues.

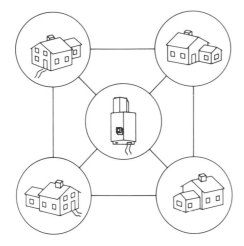

Figure 2 Five bird's eye views of a house and their relations to one another. (Some intermediate views have been omitted.) Note that all the general part structures of the house are revealed by any one of the four side views. Each node should be considered as one of Marr's 2 1/2 D sketches, with information about the 3D relations between parts.

environment and its pressures. Hence it makes sense to group together objects or things which look similar, for generally they occupy similar niches in the world. Seeing a particular type of part, therefore, can be highly predictive of the niche an object occcupies, and hence its class or category. For example, as illustrated in Figure 1, the very simple shape of an eye immediately implies the class "animal". Consequently, we expect that this "thing" will also have a head, eyes, mouth, etc. all in a certain relationship. Seeing the "beak" at an appropriate position further constrains the animal to "bird". The shape of a part clearly is one of the most important attributes for categorizing and hence identifying objects. Fortunately,

unlike "objects", a part can be rigorously defined. Or rather, as we shall see later, its boundaries can be specified precisely. So "parts" provide a computationally feasible strategy for describing object classes and their members.

Object descriptions which we will stress here are those based upon part-descriptions and their topological and geometrical relations. So, for example, a head will be described as an ovoid with a face on one side, with two ears on opposite sides adjacent to the face, and a neck on a side adjacent to both the face and ears. The face, in turn, would be described as having eyes, nose, and mouth in certain relations (see selection 12 for a more precise and formal description). Exact metrics are not important.

To give an example of the kind of representation we will use for object descriptions, imagine your house. Probably the first visual image that comes to mind is the side view most commonly seen - perhaps the one with the front or back door, whichever is used the most. Next may be the second most common view, or perhaps one adjacent to the first. My point is that what is recalled is a series of 2D views, not a 3D model. As first pointed out by Koenderink & van Doorn (1976) a natural way of representing a 3D shape is by a network where each node carries a different topological view of the structure, and the network shows the relations between the views. Figure 2 gives part of such a network for a simple house. Later, we show how the adjacency relations between the nodes and their parts can be used to build up a graph structure of the object which has a description similar to a natural language description. For the moment, however, our immediate objective will be to grasp some of the problems encountered in simply inferring 3D shape from the 2D view of one particular node.

2.0 Blocks World Example

To illustrate how we begin to assemble 2D image information into 3D shape descriptors, we use a simplified "blocks world" language, first introduced in the late 60's by D.A. Huffman of UCSC & SRI and M.B. Clowes of Sussex University. This world consists of untextured objects with planar surfaces, with no more than three planes intersecting to form a vertex (see Figure 3). Such a world is guaranteed to produce image contours that arise only from the edges of objects — an important constraint on our problem.

An edge is defined as the intersection of two half-planes. If this edge is then projected into the image, we create an image contour called a line segment. Our "givens" are the projections of such edges, namely the collection of line segments in the image. Our goal is to identify the 3D edges and vertices associated with these line segments. Such an identification is a first step in describing an object as a particular arrangement of planar surfaces.

For example, a cube has nine visible edges, which create nine line segments in the image. Around the outside of the cube, the edges are said to be occluding, because the visual ray just grazes the edge, but does not penetrate into the object. Similarly the three interior edges are said to be convex, or, alternatively concave if the vertex points away from the viewer. By considering all possible views of two intersecting half-planes, it is easy to show that these are the only possible types of edges (for our chosen domain), which we label as shown in Figure 4.

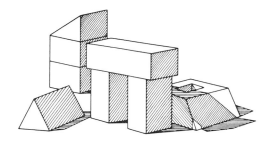

Figure 3 A sample of "Blocks-World" objects, extended to include cracks and shadow edges. (From Winston, 1975)

The visible portion of a cube can thus be described as six occluding edges enclosing three interior convex edges which come to a trihedral vertex. Our first task is to make this inference from the unlabeled line segments. Specifically, given a line segment in the image, infer which type of edge it is in the 3D blocks world. Later, we will assemble this information into an object description.

We approach this initial problem in four steps: First all possible types of projections of an edge into the basic line segments are determined. (We just did this.) Second, we enumerate all possible types of trihedral vertices formed by the intersection of three half-planes. There are seven of these. Thirdly, for each of the (seven) possible types of trihedral vertices, we enumerate all possible types of projections into the image, labeling the line segments for each projected vertex. Such a labeled vertex in the image we will call a junction. At this point we have exhaustively analyzed how edges and vertices map into the image. We must now explore the *inverse* mapping, namely from the 2D image back into the 3D world. So our final (fifth) step is to show that for each type of junction (of line segments)

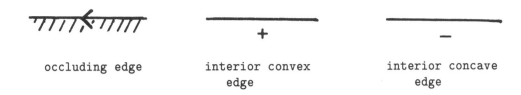

occluding edge	interior convex edge	interior concave edge

Figure 4 Line segments derived from the three possible edge types and their notation.

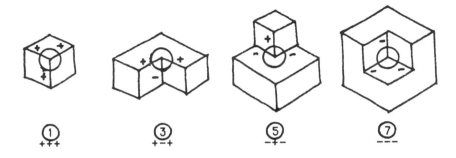

Figure 5 Four 3D vertices from which the Waltz set can be derived: 1, 3, 5 and 7 octants filled.

in the image there corresponds only one 3D vertex in the world.

To show there are only seven types of vertices, consider a large cube constructed from eight identical smaller cubes. Given the constraint that any vertex must be formed by three half-planes (not four), we can remove our small cubes one at a time to explore possible vertices. However, because when even-numbered octants are filled the 3D vertices are redundant, we obtain only the five basic configurations shown in Figure 5 (Huffman, 1971). For each of these configurations we can apply labels to the edges, for all topologically different viewpoints. The result is sixteen different labeled junctions (projected ver-

tices) as seen in the image (see Figure 6). We call these the "Waltz labels", for it was David Waltz at MIT who developed this approach to include blocks-world objects with shadows, cracks, and other types of edges. So Figure 6 gives the primitive Waltz set.

Waltz's approach was to use this set of "legal" junctions as a constraint imposed upon the labeling of any blocks-world figure. To start, the outer-most line segments of the figure are labeled with arrows, indicating that these lines arise from occluding edges. (Actually, Waltz began with an arbitrary junction, having first attached all possible legal labels to each junction, and then imposed the additional

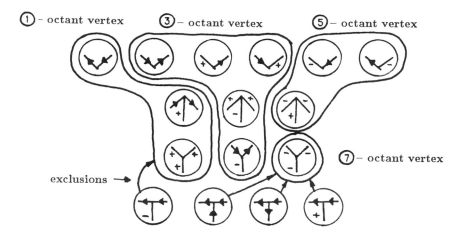

Figure 6 The partition of the Waltz set. T-junctions only partially constrain the interpretation. (From Goldstein, 1985).

constraint of consistent labeling along a line segment.) Having labeled the outside, one can then proceed inwards, assigning all possible legal labels to the interior line segments. For example, an exterior arrow junction will be forced to have its shaft labeled $+$, whereas an exterior fork will require that its shaft be labeled $-$, etc. These results are then propagated inward until all lines have labels. There are two outcomes to this procedure: either all line segments are labeled consistently or they are not. If not, then the drawing does not correspond to a real 3D blocks world object. Are we done?

Recalling the requirements presented in Chapter 1 for a complete theory of competence, we still have not shown two things. First, given a consistent line labeling for the drawing, can we prove that this labeling is unique? Can there ever be two or more sets of line labels for the same drawing? Secondly, are there drawings which can be consistently labeled, yet do not correspond to real blocks-world objects? If so, then we have potential tests

for comparing these false targets (illusions) with our own perceptions to see if the human visual system interprets line drawings using a similar, local procedure.

The second question is the easiest to answer, for we need just one example, which is given in Figure 8-12 (Figure 8 of Selection 12). The Penrose triangle is one of many illusory constructions which will give consistent labels. However, this is not necessarily damaging, for our impression of these figures, unlike that of the devil's pitchfork shown in Figure 12-9, is of a stable, realizable object. Our instant psychophysics test thus suggests that local labeling of junctions (vertices) is consistent with our own perceptual strategy for inferring object shape.

Returning now to the first question of the uniqueness of the labeling, for any blocks world drawing, is there only one solution? Is this solution unique in that no topologically different blocks world object will have the same arrangement of labels? Waltz addressed this question, but only experimentally. The first to show that the Waltz labels will be unique—that any blocks world object will have only one arrangement of labels—was Seth Goldstein in a 1985 term paper in Natural Computation. Goldstein noted that each junction type is affiliated with only one type of vertex (see Figure 6). Hence there is a one-to-one mapping between junctions and vertices. (Thus the constraint-propagation scheme used by Waltz is not necessary—the solution can be found directly from outside-in labeling.) Surprisingly, the same is true for the more complex Waltz set of labels that include shadows and cracks. Thus, given a labeled junction, there is only one possible vertex to which it corresponds. Why this should be the case is not clear to us (i.e. we have no formal proof of this fact other than by enumeration) and I have thus called this the "Goldstein problem".

3.0 Identifying the Origin of Contours

In our blocks problem, constraints imposed upon objects in the world allowed the perceiver to identify the origin of the line segments or contours in the image. For example, we knew that all image contours arose only from edges created by intersecting half-planes. Although a similar analysis can be made for curved, rather than planar surfaces (Huffman, 1971, Koenderink, 1987), the restriction that all surfaces be smooth and untextured is unrealistic. For natural images, there are four primary sources of image contours: the external occluding edge, a crease or fold, a shadow or illumination effect, and surface markings or texture. Although all four types of contours provide information about surface shape, their inference rules differ. For example,

the curvature of a smooth occluding edge gives one directly the sign of Gaussian curvature of the 3D shape that produced this edge (Koenderink & van Doorn, 1982). Whereas, for shading or texture, gradients must be analyzed, which are mute regarding the sign of 3D curvature. Thus the recovery of shape from natural images requires identifying which type of edge created the image contour. At present, this is an unsolved problem in that no complete theory of edge assignment to image contour has been proposed.

3.1 Occluding edge algorithms

Hence we proceed by illustrating three schemes that appear promising and have some biological support. The first is Witkin's, who examines a set of constraints that apply to three types of edges: occlusions, cast shadows, and local intensity perturbations. The scheme is based upon the expected behavior of ribbons of intensities that parallel an image contour. For example, if the intensities in two adjacent (plus one) ribbons are highly correlated, then the implication is that each ribbon arises from the same surface. But if one crosses an occluding contour, an entirely new material will be encountered, and hence the intensity pattern in the two ribbons should be quite different.

In the next selection, Mutch & Thompson consider the dynamic case where the occluding boundary is in motion. As an object moves, it will cover and uncover portions of the more distant surfaces, causing the appearance and disappearance of regions adjacent to itself. The constraints underlying this scheme are similar to those presented by Witkin, except now we must consider also the direction of object motion. If intensity correlations are made between two adjacent regions or ribbons, then we expect no change in the overall intensity pattern as long as the regions lie within the object itself. However, in the direction of motion, the advancing boundary of the object will replace the background (deletion), whereas the region trailing the object will change in favor of the background (accretion). The correlations between ribbons must anticipate this effect. Psychophysically, we are very sensitive to such changes as can be seen by moving one random-dot transparency over another (Julesz, 1971; MacKay, 1976). Mutch & Thompson provide some insight into this method. Note that the same procedure can also be recast into a very primitive stereo mechanism, although finding hidden images with relative motion is much easier than with the stereopsis provided by our two eyes.

Finally, a third method for identifying occluding boundaries is presented in the "CARTOON" selection. Again, the key insight first mentioned by Marr & Hildreth (1980) is that at occluding edges there is a change from one surface material to another. In theory, this change will be a step discontinuity in intensities which will appear at all spatial scales of resolution. (In fact, the range will depend upon the 3D surface structure and object size.) So the strategy is to look for a coincidence in image contours across a range of scales. However, because the bandpass filters used to extract the contours integrate information in the neighborhood of the edge, the marked location of an edge is distorted, and exact coincidence across scales is rarely possible. The cartoon scheme overcomes this problem simply by multiplying the sign bits of the convolved

image. At each scale, the processed image is also broken into a positive and negative part—just as the on and off receptive fields must do to a first approximation. These two "black" and "white" images, which are not merely complements of one another, are used later to extract a hierarchy of nested black and white blobs whose shape will be encoded. The type of bandpass filter chosen is not arbitrary. In order that these blobs be nested properly within one another, a filter equivalent to the second derivative of a gaussian is required (Koenderink, 1984; Witkin, 1983; Yuille & Poggio 1987.)

Unfortunately, none of these three methods for identifying occluding contours is fail-safe. This can be seen in part in the cartoon algorithm, if we examine the possible false targets and misses (Figure 7.) For example, highly-textured shadow edges will pass through both high and low spatial frequency channels, being confused with a "step edge". Also, simple cast external shadows[1] where the object lies much closer to the projecting surface than the viewer's eye, will appear as "step-like" in the image. If either of these types of shadows moves, then accretion and deletion will occur, suggesting an object movement (perhaps a beneficial illusion in some cases). Also, fractal-like surfaces with 3D texture such as leafy trees or hair, will generally not yield ideal step edges across a wide range of scales and hence may be missed by the algorithm. Without a true theory of occluding edges, we are not able to predict our competence.

---

[1]See problem 4-2 for the distinction between external and internal shadows and their images.

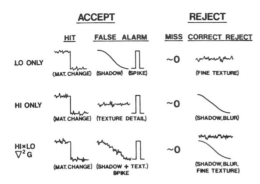

Figure 7 Table showing correct Rejections as well as some of the common False Edges accepted by the first stages of the CARTOON algorithm. The "ACCEPT" and "REJECT" columns correspond respectively to whether the incoming signal passes the CARTOON component shown in the left-most column. By logically combining the outputs from a lo- and hi-pass filter, the rejection rate improves (last column). To improve further the Hit Rates over False Alarms (third column), another stage must be included that incorporates the phase information provided by *POSitive* and *NEGative* masks.

3.2 Biological support

In spite of rather severe theoretical drawbacks, the three algorithms for finding occluding contours do receive some support from their similarity to biological mechanisms. For example, the edge-coincidence technique of "CARTOON" when applied to images yields outputs that closely resemble those of neurons in the visual pathway (e.g. Figures 3-9, 3-10). So it is not too surprising to learn that cortical neurons do indeed have behaviors that appear to address the occluding contour problem,

as presented in Selection 5 by von der Heydt, Peterhans & Baumgartner. But what perhaps is most striking indeed is that such powerful assertions about occluding edges may be made so early in visual processing (see also Gregory, 1972; Lawson & Gulick, 1967).

In particular, consider the edge created by phase-shifting part of a grating, as illustrated in Figure 5-1D or 5-3A. In the real world, such an edge might correspond to a fold or wrinkle on a striped T-shirt—a very complex surface! So if visual cortex is striving to infer occluding edges, then it is quite appropriate for a neuron to respond to this type of contour as well as a similar edge formed by two different materials. However, note that the image contours are quite different in each case, specifically one set is perpendicular to the other and is at a finer scale. (Note that CARTOON has to be modified to capture this property.) Constructing a neural model which responds to both types of edges and is to assert the presence of an "occluding edge" is non-trivial. (A simple network that will respond to both edges is given by Wilson & Richards, 1988. However, the output of the network can not make the assertion that an edge is occluding.) If indeed the same network also infers illusory Kaniza-type edges (Figure 5-1A,B), then it is clear that neural activities at neighborhoods must be compared in the network, and that these comparisons are not necessarily of colinear line elements, since a Kaniza illusion can be created that gives the impression of curved edges, even ones appearing in depth (Shipley, 1987).

The possibility suggested by von der Heydt et al. that assertions about occluding edges are made as early as area 18 is very exciting. Not only is this portion of visual cortex readily accessible in many primates, but also understanding its circuitry is within reach. And perhaps most encouraging for those who may be daunted by the difficulty in deciding which image contours arise from occlusions, nature's solution can not be that complex if the assertion is made so early in the visual pathway. The "trick" simply needs to be hit upon. Perhaps one promising, unexplored area is the direction Witkin took, looking at the relations between texture ribbons along a contour, and the shape (i.e. smoothness) of the contour itself.

3.3 Toward a theory

One obvious oversight of all the occluding edge algorithms is that the nature of the 3D surface itself is not incorporated into a description of its silhouette. To begin a theory of occluding contours, we must first describe our surface and how it is seen by the viewer, just as we did for the blocks-world example. In that case, the only image contours arose from edges. For more general textured surfaces, image contours are also created by illumination effects (shadows), textural changes, and markings on the surface, as well as discontinuities in the surface. As shown in Selection 15, these effects are multiplicative and can be described by the following very fundamental equation:

$$I(x, y, \lambda) = \rho \cdot E \cdot (N \cdot L) \cdot R \qquad (1)$$

where ρ is spectral reflectance of the surface pigment, E is the illumination strength, N is the surface normal vector, L is the illuminant direction, and R is the reflectance function describing the matte and specular properties of the surface. At the occluding edge, all three surface parameters change drastically (ρ, N, R).

However, for the moment consider only the behavior of the surface normal N. At the occluding boundary, our visual ray V just grazes the surface. Hence the image contour created by the discontinuity in N will correspond to a surface oriented perpendicular to our line of sight. (This was the line segment in the blocks world example.) More formally,

$$V \cdot N = 0 \ . \qquad (2a)$$

Similarly, at a shadow boundary, we have

$$N \cdot L = 0 \qquad (2b)$$

The above analysis assumes smooth surfaces, which will generate smooth silhouettes. However, what about rough or hairy 3D surfaces and their jagged or even "transparent" occluding edges? What relations are expected between the silhouette and the 3D surface structure? Obviously, if the surface texture expresses all and only the 3D roughness of the surface, then the silhouette should also. The panels of Figure 8 illustrate how the contour and texture constrain one's interpretation of the edge (and also the figure-ground relations.) For example, the middle panel with a fractal-like silhouette but no interior texture is seen as flat, as it should be, whereas if internal texture consistent with the edge texture is added, that side takes on volume and there is no question as to which side is figure and which is ground. Similarly, the smooth contour without texture assumes a 3D shape because a texture-free interior implies a smooth surface, again consistent with the edge texture. Clearly, understanding the nature of the fluctuations of the surface normal within a region of a surface is critical to asserting correctly the occluding contours.

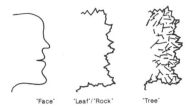

'Face'   'Leaf'/'Rock'   'Tree'

Figure 8 Effect of interior upon interpretation of an occluding edge. Left: textureless interior implies smooth edge, which is consistent. Middle: textureless interior implies smooth surface, but edge is fractal; region is seen as flat. Right: fractal interior implies fractal silhouette, which together produces a 3D impression.

Let us look again at equation (1), and attempt to recast it to accomodate rough, fractal-like 3D surfaces. If the surface is truly a fractal, then this property can be described by a parameter "h", which is a measure of roughness which takes on values between 0 and 1. A value of 0 indicates a completely smooth (differentiable) surface. In addition, the measuring unit used by the observer to describe the appearance of an edge must be included. I choose the unit visual angle, α, which corresponds to the particular spatial scale used by the observer. The addition of these parameters leads to a modification of (2) to

$$V(\alpha) \cdot N(p, q, h) = 0 \qquad (3a)$$

$$L(\beta) \cdot N(p, q, h) = 0 \qquad (3b)$$

to describe the relation between the surface normal on a silhouette and the line of sight (or illuminant direction). For a given choice of spatial scale which is equivalent to choosing a solid angle (α) for the visual ray, the surface parameter h dictates the accuracy with which the surface normal can be estimated. For very rough surfaces,

where h approaches 1 in a direction parallel to the contour, the estimate of the surface normal parameters p, q degenerates completely. As the surface roughness increases, we might also expect that the width of the contour will also increase. For a surface with a 3D fractal texture, one might hope that the expected spatial width of the occluding edge could be estimated from the fractal measure of surface "roughness" (See Selection 20).

4.0 Parts of 2D Shapes

Once occluding contours have been identified, strong inferences can be made about the shape of objects. This is obvious from the ease with which we can interpret cartoons and silhouettes. So given the silhouette of an object, how do we infer its correct 3D shape from the infinity of possible shapes which could have produced the silhouette? What rules and constraints apply? What is the nature of the representation we use to describe shapes? These are the primary issues addressed in the next few selections.

Recall that when we describe an object, we do so in terms of its parts and their relations to one another. Fortunately, although we cannot define precisely what constitutes an object, we can define what constitutes a part. Thus if our description of an object is in terms of its parts, then the description is potentially computable. As first recognized by Hoffman (1983), the "parts" of an object can be isolated by noting their intersections with one another. Such intersections produce concavities in the silhouette (Figure 6-3), which are recoverable from the image (see Selection 7). To illustrate the issues encountered in building a parts-based representation for

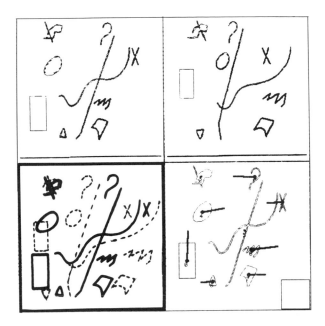

Figure 9 A sloppy stereogram, where images presented to each eye (upper two panels) include shapes that underwent distortions, changes in size and articulations. Matching by shape is robust to these distortions, just as matching to memory must be for recognition (although of course the tolerance for stereopsis is much less!)

shapes, let us consider the case of plane curves, such as those which arise when a silhouette is projected into the image plane. Our first problem is to decide how to represent this curve in our data base. Do we want a string of points with their x, y locations? Or perhaps a polar coordinate representation? One problem with both of these choices is that they do not make explicit the feature of the curve which allows us to describe its shape. What we need is a feature which supports and helps to build a part-based description. Because intersecting parts produce concavities in the image curve, a more desirable choice of feature primitive is curvature, or more explicitly, curvature extrema. This choice of curvature as the parameter to describe plane curves has some rather surprising

consequences. First, if the singularities of curvature are used to describe the parts of a shape, then there are only five different kinds of primitive parts for plane curves, which we call "codons" (see Figure 6-4). Any plane curves can be described (at an abstract level) by its sequence of codons. Second, this sequence or codon string is robust under projective distortions and changes in scale, for it is solely a description based on ordinal relations (metric information will add sparingly later). As mentioned previously, a representation for shape that stresses the topological properties and relations seems preferred for recognition over one which emphasizes metrical information.

To illustrate the power of the codon description for recognition, consider the two sloppy stereograms shown in Figure 9. Matching the shapes correctly in each figure corresponds to matching the current image (say left stereogram) with the ikon in memory (say right stereogram). Note that rather severe distortions or articulations of the "objects" may be made and still the codon scheme finds the correct partners. What is a bit surprising is that more complex shapes (having longer codon strings) are easier to match than simpler shapes (having shorter strings). This is because a few errors in the string, such as when part of one object becomes occluded, can be tolerated for long strings but not for short ones. Hence isolated, complex objects are often easier and more reliably "recognized" than simple objects—a message for those struggling with early vision correspondence problems.

In order to use the codon scheme for object recognition, curvature along the plane curve of the silhouette must be computed. There are several technical problems encountered here, even when the occluding boundary is well isolated. These are addressed in Selection 7. The most significant and still unsolved is the problem of parts occurring at several different scales. Is each hair or wrinkle on a hand a part? Or is it texture? As yet we have no answer. Generally, the current approach is to find first the biggest parts, subdivide the shape, then proceed with another iteration to find the sub-parts, etc. However, recent psychophysics challenges this coarse-to-fine approach (Wilson & Richards, 1987). Surprisingly, the human observer seems to extract curvature (and hence part boundaries) at the finest scale possible, and then presumably builds up

from these data to coarser scales. However, integrating fine-scale information is not equivalent to coarse-scale filtering, except in very special cases (see Problem 7-3). So our visual system must depend upon a constraint not yet fully identified when extracting a shape description.

Recently, it has also been shown that the extraction of curvature in human perception does not proceed with the exact same method outlined in Selection 7 (although, of course, the problems remain the same.) Instead, two different operators are used over different ranges of curvatures. For high curvatures, a local computation is made analogous to comparing the outputs of two receptive fields illustrated in Figures 5-2. This is roughly equivalent to the machine technique discussed, namely differentiating an edge or line locally. For low curvature below 5 deg^{-1}, however, an entirely different scheme is adopted. Here, our visual system tests for symmetry in the orientation of tangents located at displaced positions along the curve. This is equivalent to determining whether two tangents lie on the same circle (i.e. are co-circular) as proposed by Parent & Zucker, 1985. This second scheme thus involves comparisons over a neighborhood, just as is required for completing the illusory Kaniza edge, or for isolating the overlapping line drawings of the frontispiece illustration.[2] Furthermore, because the co-circularity scheme makes explicit the symmetry relations, it could also serve to initiate Blum's (1973) axial-based shape descriptions which terminate at curvature extrema (Leyton, 1987). Thus we see that the neural hardware required for computing curvature is the precursor to

---

[2]Note that the problem of linking overlapping lines can also occur in 3D, such as the crossed lines in the sloppy stereogram of Figure 9, suggesting that the co-circularity test might be applied profitably in 3D. (See also the 3D Kaniza contour illustrated by Shipley, 1987.)

mechanisms which will make even higher-level, more detailed computations about 2D shape properties.

5.0 Inferring 3D Shape

Here, in the next few selections, we address the problem of recovering the 3D shape of a surface from the occluding contour or surface markings. Two papers, the selection by Brady & Yuille and Stevens' contribution consider 3D sheets; the next two selections deal with 3D volumes. Because different constraints are required in each case, it is helpful to group them accordingly.

5.1 Inferring local surface orientation

Local surface orientation can be inferred both from the occluding boundary and from the interior surface markings. Brady & Yuille consider the first case, Stevens the second [although Brady & Yuille's extremum principle can also be applied to recover interior surface orientation (Witkin, 1981)—see also Problem 8-1].

Earlier we had presented equation (2) which stated that the surface normal must be perpendicular to the line of sight at smooth occluding boundaries. Hence the surface orientation is known. However, if this rule were to be applied to a leaf or a table-top, our inference would be incorrect (see also Figures 8-1). For planar surfaces, therefore, our rule must be different, and we must also have some method of ascertaining whether it is reasonable to invoke the rule. The rule Brady & Yuille propose is to minimize the area to perimeter-squared along segments of the image contour. This is equivalent to

fitting the curve with an ellipse and then back-projecting the ellipse into a circle to recover the surface normal (or, alternatively slant (σ) and tilt (τ).) As illustrated by their figures, there is some biological plausibility to this scheme (Sutherland, 1960.) However, the answer obtained is clearly quite different from that specified by equation (2). How do we know which is correct? One possible solution is to compare the surface orientation of a texture ribbon next to the image contour, using techniques described by Stevens or Witkin for example. However, a more direct test was illustrated previously in the middle panel of Figure 8. The absence of interior texture suggests a smooth surface, but the jagged fractal edge suggests a rough surface. These are conflicting implications which suggest one process created the edge, and another created the interior surface. A sheet with cut edges would be an example. The same argument applies to polygonal shapes with sharp corners but no visible sides, like a parallelogram or the angle in Figure 8-1.

Stevens' approach to recovering local surface orientation contrasts sharply with that of Brady & Yuille. The key idea or underlying constraint is that surface markings tend to follow lines of curvature of the surface. For example, the bark of a tree is ruptured along lines of curvature as the trunk grows, producing two dominating sets of cracks—one parallel to the axis of the trunk, the other perpendicular. As lines of curvature are necessarily orthogonal, we have a powerful constraint: construe intersecting surface markings as being perpendicular unless evidence is to the contrary. Stevens shows that this simple constraint can be applied profitably even if only one set of parallel markings are presented to the viewer, as in Fig-

Figure 10 Typical flexnosities of the visual contour. (The dotted parts indicate the object). (a) A convex arc. This happens only for a synclastic patch. (b) A concave arc. This happens only for an anticlastic patch. (c) An inflexion. This happens only for a monoclastic point. (d) An ending contour. This happens only when you look along an asymptotic ray. Note that the ending contour is always concave. (e) A T-junction. At a T-junction the visual ray grazes the surface a two distinct points. It coincides with a bitangent ray of the surfaces. (From Koenderink, 1987.)

ures 9-3. However, again caution must be exercised here, for the competence of the proposal is not fully understood. In particular, our assumption that the surface is locally cylindrical seems quite appropriate for singly curved surfaces with parallel rulings, but a more complex analysis is required for the more general doubly-curved surfaces which may tend to be given developable interpretations (Stevens, 1981).

5.2 Inferring the shape of 3D volumes

Most objects of interest in our world occupy space. The simplest class of these objects are those which are solid with completely smooth exteriors. This, of course, is an idealization for many objects such as trees occupy space but are fractured and transparent with fractal-like surfaces. However, as a starting point, we will first consider completely smooth, differentiable surfaces without texture or pattern. Surprisingly, there are only five configurations of image contours that are stable over small displacements of the viewer's position (Koenderink, 1987). These are illustrated in Figure 10. All are instances

of occluding boundaries where equation (2) applies. Each results from a catastrophe in the observed surface orientation, whereby a slight perturbation in the visual ray off the surface will lead to an arbitrary change in surface orientation. Along the silhouette of the object such a catastrophe is obvious. Not so obvious is the behavior of the visual ray at terminations of image contours, such as at the base of the pillar in Koenderink & van Doorn's example [also (d) in Figure 10]. In this latter case, one immediately knows that the corresponding 3D region is hyperbolic—or has negative Gaussian curvature. Another type of generic singularity is the "T" junction where one occluding boundary covers another. Finally, for our simplified world of smooth objects, there is only one more event to be noted, namely the inflections in the contours. As discussed in selections 10 and 11 it is now possible to recover the general topological shape of an object from its image contours. Given this topological description, we can build a representation similar to that illustrated in Figure 11. Here we show all possible topological views of a pear-shaped object. Of these, only three are stable—the remainder are seen only in passing through some special viewing positions. Following Koenderink's suggestion, each view has been placed at a node of a network. As we move around the object (or as the object is rotated), we must pass from one node to the next as indicated by the net. The network is thus a complete 2 1/2 D description of the object. Such a representation, abbreviated to include only the fewest most common views that include all the parts, seems to me to be favored by our visual system over a complete 3D model.[3] In the last selection "From Waltz to Winston", a form of this network called the 3D skeleton was used to build a bridge from vision to language.

Given the progress made with smooth 3D objects, how can one move toward describing irregular, fractal-like shapes? Recall first the key elements which led to an understanding of object-from-image reconstruction. In the case of Waltz, we began by enumerating all possible types of image features (junctions) and explored their origin in the blocks world. Exactly the same approach was used for generically smooth (non-planar) objects, but in this case we relied principally upon a proof by Whitney (1955) that only two basic types of image catastrophes could be expected, plus observations made by Koenderink regarding the relation between surface curvature and image contour curvature. These relations were derived from equation (2). To follow the same approach, we must now extend our surface definition to include a specification of its roughness and our ability to measure this roughness. This was the idea behind extending equation (2) to equation (3). It leads to a notion of inherent instabil-

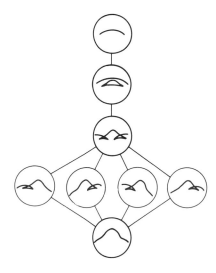

Figure 11 Views of the rim, where $V \cdot N = 0$, for the top of a pear-shaped object (a bump), ordered in a network that reveals the transitions from one view to the next (Koenderink, 1987). Only the solid nodes are generic. A suitable representation for the shape is the bottom node, which reveals all the parts of the shape.

ity in our perception of surface normal. Certain catastrophes which are not expected for generically smooth surfaces must now be expected, depending upon our resolving power and on the nature of the 3D volume. For example, when we look at a tree, it makes no sense to simply assign a surface normal to its silhouette. Rather, we should say this is my best estimate if forced to make such a commitment, but a better description is that the boundary of the tree has an orientation that fluctuates roughly between so-and-so, at least for the scale of resolution that I give to its surface. Similarly, a single visual ray directed to the tree may hit many parts of the tree as it penetrates,

---

[3]Recent experiments by Warrington & James (1986) provide excellent support for this view.

again, depending upon the angular size of the ray. The chance of encountering catastrophes other than those depicted by Whitney for generically smooth surfaces can increase drastically, depending upon how one defines contact between the visual ray and the surface. For example, a solid ray grazing a wrinkle or crack in the bark and another branch or leaf would be commonplace. We need a theory of the types of events appearing in the image for fractal-like objects.

6.0 A Language for Visual Perception

At the outset, one of our goals was the recognition of objects from their projections into the image plane. For the class of objects which are constructed from smooth, opaque volumes, all image contours will be occluding edges, and strong inferences about 3D shape can be made— just as was done by Waltz, Clowes & Huffman for the simple blocks world, and by Koenderink for smooth generic surfaces. Along the way, we finessed the issue of exactly what constitutes an object, other than defining objects as entities composed of "parts". In our last selection for this section, we return briefly to the problem of defining objects within a framework suitable for recognition and for semantic interpretation. Again, the key insight is that we view objects as a collection of parts and subparts.[3] Our immediate goal is then to create a formal language which defines a part and its relations to other parts. An important constraint imposed upon the language is that its structure and grammar should be appropriate for all lev-

Figure 12 A complete object description language must be capable of describing actions and intentions, as well as physical connections between parts. What constraints limit the formal attachments between actions and objects? (Illustration by Carl Fallberg, © MGM, Inc. 1967.)

els of abstraction of an object description. The proposed Object Description Language (ODL) satisfies these constraints, and bears a strong resemblance to certain formal natural language grammars (Kaplan & Bresnan, 1982.)

Recalling that topology is stressed over metrics, the different types of topological connections possible between parts serve as a critical ingredient of the language. Naturally, the number of different types of attachments will depend upon the shape of the most elemental parts. (Note that the shape of each part can be given

---

[3]Part is not defined rigorously, but it can be for volumes by specifying interior of surfaces and the logical inclusion of interiors of intersecting volumes—see Bennett & Hoffman, 1987.

a formal mathematical description—see Problem 12-1.) In this selection, where a blocks-world is chosen for illustration, only three different types of attachments are allowed (on equal, opposite, or adjacent faces.) As the language is developed, it becomes clear that a rank ordering must be given to each of these different attachments in order that an object description can be placed in canonical form to permit matching to memory during the recognition process. This is accomplished using an intermediate representation called the Connection Table (CT). A simple experiment (Problem 12-3) demonstrates that our own visual system has a preferred rank ordering of attachments when representing structures such as the arch shown in Figure 2 of Selection 12, which has three possible CT descriptions. As yet, the constraints governing the rank ordering of attachments are not understood.

In addition to the ODL and CT, a third level of representation is needed to move conveniently from images to object descriptions. This is the feature-based "3D Skeleton", which shows the relations between the image features—equivalent to a Waltz labeling in 3D. Note that this Skeleton itself need not be 3D, but rather should be viewed as a mapping between several 2 1/2 D views, which together reveal all the features of the object. Parts are found in the 3D skeleton by segmentation at concavities, and then the Connection Table is built. This procedure has been implemented by S. Truve for the simple blocks world domain.

In the more general case, the 3D Skeleton and hence also the ODL and CT must be extended to include actions between parts and objects. Several difficult problems are raised by including dynamics. Not the least is simply defining the beginning and end of an action, just as was done for "parts" (Engel & Rubin, 1986; Marr & Vaina, 1982; Rubin & Richards, 1985). Once this has been done, an Action Connection Table and an ODL could be written showing the relations between the parts of a movement, for any given object. But should the action be attached to a part, or vice versa? For example, when a leg kicks (a ball), should the action "kick" be attached to the part "leg", or does kick imply the presence of a leg, with the limb attached to the action "kick". Note that as before for the blocks world parts, the nature of the "object" greatly constrains the types of possible attachments, and clearly these constraints should drive the language specification.

Again, at the level of the Connection Table, actions between the parts of a single object can be incorporated by adding columns to the table. But what about actions between objects not connected, such as when a a bullet is fired at an attacking animal? These relations are easily visualized and described, but have essentially been ignored in computational vision. Yet such descriptions are an important goal of the visual process (Jackendoff, 1987).

Finally, will it be sufficient to build separate 3D skeletons for each object, simply indicating directions of part movements in a local 3D frame, or will a larger, more global 3D frame also be needed? If the latter, then this global frame may take on its own special character, somewhat reminiscent of the "where" versus "what" distinction made by Schneider (1969). These problems are exciting new directions for formal study, and have the advantage of being able to tap the wealth of experimental data already available (Held, 1965; Ingle & Schneider, 1970; Lynch, 1960; Stevens & Coupe, 1978;

Thorpe, 1962). By extending the ODL to include both function and also more global spatio-temporal relationships, we can move more closely toward an ability to reason about object behaviors, completing the bridge between Waltz (1972) and Winston (1984).

References

Arnold, V.I. (1986) *Catastrophe Theory.* Berlin: Springer-Verlag.

Bennett, B.M. & Hoffman, D.D. (1987) Shape decomposition for visual recognition: the role of transversality. In W. Richards & S. Ullman (eds.), *Image Understanding 1985-86*, Norwood, N.J.: Ablex, Chapt. 8.

Blum, H. (1973) Biological shape and visual science. *J. Theor. Biol.*, 38:205–287.

Clowes, M. (1971) On seeing things. *Artif. Intell.*, 2:79–116.

Engel, S.A. & Rubin, J.M. (1986) Detecting visual motion boundaries. *Proc. IEEE Workshop on Motion*, IEEE Computer Soc. Press, New York.

Goldstein, S. (1985) "Distilling a view-independent representation from a 2 1/2 D sketch". Term paper in Natural Computation, MIT.

Gregory, R.L. (1972) Cognitive contours. *Nature*, 238:51–52.

Held, R. (1965) Plasticity in sensory-motor systems. *Sci. Amer.* (November).

Hoffman, D.D. (1983) "Representing shapes for visual recognition". Ph.D. thesis, Dept. of Psychology, Massachusetts Institute of Technology.

Huffman, D. (1971) Impossible objects as nonsense sentences. In B. Meltzer & D. Michie (eds.), *Machine Intelligence 6*, Edinburgh: Edinburgh Univ. Press.

Ingle, D. & Schneider, G.E. (1970) Subcortical visual systems. *Brain Behav. & Evol.*, 3:1–352.

Jackendoff, R. (1987) On Beyond Zebra: the relation between linguistic and visual information. *Cognition*, 26:89–114.

Julesz, B. (1971) *Foundations of Cyclopean Perception.* Chicago: Univ. of Chicago Press.

Kaplan, R. & Bresnan, J. (1982) Lexical-functional grammar, a formal system for grammatical representation. In J. Bresnan (ed.) *The Mental Representations of Grammatical Relations.* Cambridge, Mass.: MIT Press, pp. 173–281.

Koenderink, J.J. (1987) An internal representation based on the toplogical properties of the apparent contour. In W. Richards & S. Ullman (eds.), *Image Understanding 1985-86.* Norwood, N.J.: Ablex, chapt. 9, pp. 257–285.

Koenderink, J.J. (1984) On the structure of images. *Biol. Cybernetics.*, 50:363–370.

Koenderink, J.J. & van Doorn, A.J. (1976) The singularities of the visual mapping. *Biol. Cybernetics*, 24:51–59.

Koenderink, J.J. & van Doorn, A. (1982) The shape of smooth objects and the way contours end. *Perception*, 11:129–137.

Lawson, R.B. & Gulick, W.L. (1967) Stereopsis and anomalous contour. *Vis. Res.*, 7:271–297.

Acknowledgment: John Rubin kindly helped to improve the flow and content of this introduction.

Leyton, M. (1987) Symmetry-curvature duality. *Comp. Vis., Graphics, & Image Proc.*, 38:327–341.

Leyton, M. (1987) A process-grammar for shape. *Artif. Intell.*, 34:213–247.

Lynch, K. (1960) *The Image of the City.* Cambridge, Mass.: MIT Press.

MacKay, D. (1976) Perceptual conflict between visual motion and change of location. *Vis. Res.*, 16:557–558.

Marr, D. & Hildreth, E. (1980) Theory of edge detection. *Proc. Roy. Soc. Lond. B*, 207:187–217.

Marr, D. & Vaina, L. (1982) Representation and recognition of the movement of shapes. *Proc. Roy. Soc. Lond. B*, 214:501–524.

Parent, P. & Zucker, S.W. (1985) Trace inference, curvature consitency and curve direction. Computer Vision & Robotics Lab. Report CIM-86-3, Montreal: McGill.

Rubin, J. & Richards, W.A. (1985) Boundaries of visual motion. MIT A.I. Lab. Memo 835.

Schneider, G.E. (1969) Two visual systems. *Science*, 163:895–902.

Shipley, T. (1987) Field processes in stereo vision. *Documenta Ophthal.*, 66:95–170.

Stevens, K.A. (1981) The visual interpretation of surface contours. *Artif. Intell.*, 17:4a7–73.

Stevens, A. & Coupe, P. (1978) Distortions in judged spatial relations. *Cog. Psych.*, 10:422–437.

Sutherland, N.S. (1960) Theories of shape discrimination in Octopus. *Nature*, 186: 840–844.

Thorpe, W.H. (1962) *Learning and Instinct In Animals.* Cambridge, Mass.: Harvard Univ. Press.

Waltz, D. (1972) "Generating semantic descriptions from drawings of scenes with shadows". Ph.D. dissertation, Department of Electrical Engineering, MIT, Cambridge, Mass.

Waltz, D. (1982) Artificial intelligence. *Sci. Amer.*, 247(4), October, pp. 118–133.

Warrington, E. & James. M. (1986) Visual object recognition in patients with right-hemisphere lesions: axes or features? *Perception*, 15:355–366.

Whitney, H. (1955) On singularities of mappings of Euclidean spaces. I. Mappings of the plane into the plane. *Ann. Math.*, 62:374–410.

Wilson, H.R. & Richards, W. (1987) Mechanisms of curvature discrimination. *Jrl. Opt. Soc. Am. A*, 4(13), Tech. Digest 22, p. 26.

Wilson, H.R. & Richards, W. (1988) Cuvature and separation discrimination at texture boundaries. *Invest. Ophthal. & Vis. Sci.*, 29 (ARVO), p. 408.

Winston, P.H. (1975) *The Psychology of Computer Vision.* New York: McGraw Hill.

Winston, P.H. (1984) *Artificial Intelligence.* Reading, Mass.: Addison-Wesley.

Witkin, A.P. (1981) Recovering surface shape and orientation from texture. *Artif. Intell.*, 17:17–45.

Witkin, A. (1983) Scale space filtering. *Proc. IJCAI*, Karlsruhe, pp. 1019–1021.

Yuille, A. & Poggio, T. (1987) Theorems for zero crossings. In W. Richards & S. Ullman, *Image Understanding 1985-86*, Norwood, N.J.: Ablex, chap. 6, pp. 147–174.

Intensity-Based Edge Classification

Andrew P. Witkin

Fairchild Laboratory
for Artificial Intelligence Research
Palo Alto, CA

1.0 Introduction

Edges in images arise from several very different kinds of scene event—occluding contours, discontinuities of surface orientation, material changes, cast shadows, etc. Each kind of edge contributes its own significant constraints to image interpretation (Barrow & Tenenbaum, 1981; Binford, 1981; Clowes, 1971; Huffman, 1971; Marr, 1977; Stevens, 1981; Waltz, 1972; Witkin, 1981) but these constraints cannot be exploited unless edge types can be distinguished from each other. Edge classification is therefore of considerable importance to image interpretation.

Edge classification in idealized line drawings has been treated in terms of junction constraints (Barrow & Tenenbaum, 1981; Binford, 1981 Clowes, 1971; Huffman, 1971; Marr, 1977; Stevens, 1981; Waltz, 1972; Witkin, 1981), but the perfect line drawings required to identify junctions have proved difficult to obtain from natural images. Horn (1977) has suggested that the intensity profiles across edges (peak vs. step, etc.) may provide distinguishing signatures for some edge types. However, this technique depends on quantitative photometry, and its effectiveness has never been demonstrated for complex imagery.

This paper describes a classification technique that, like line-junction methods, relies on structural rather than quantitative photometric properties of the image and scene, but unlike those methods, utilizes the raw image intensities in the neighborhood of the edge, without requiring elaborate analyses of edge structure. The method follows from basic properties of image edges—occluding contours and cast shadows in particular will be considered—and from basic properties of scene structure. Occluding contours are "seams" in the projective fabric, curves across which surface points that may be widely separated in space are juxtaposed in the image by the vagaries of projection. Cast shadows are curves across which the shadowed surface's image undergoes a systematic (ideally, linear) transformation. Given this characterization, two basic complementary properties of scenes suffice to distinguish cast shadows and occluding contours from each other and from arbitrary image curves: (1) the processes that shape, color, and illuminate natural surfaces act continuously almost everywhere, and (2) the properties of widely separated scene constituents are independent.

Given these properties, we conclude that intensities at nearby points on either side of an arbitrary curve in the image are likely to he highly correlated, due to the coherence of surface structure, intensities at nearby image points across an

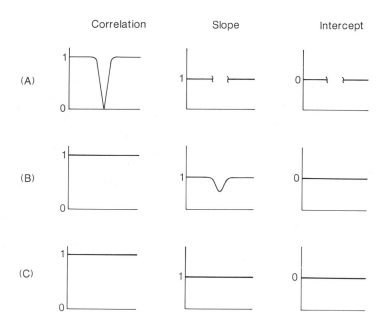

Figure 1 Idealized edge signatures. Each row of plots represents and idealized sequence of linear regressions across an edge. (a) Occluding contour: a sharp notch in correlation across the edge. The plots for the slope and intercept of the regression equation are broken to indicate that the regression equation is meaningless in the low-correlation area. (b) Cast shadow: sustained high correlation across the edge, with disturbance of one or both regression parameters. The nature of this disturbance depends on the sense of the edge (i.e., whether the shadow lies on the left or right), and on details of the imaging and digitizing process. In practice, nonlinearities perturb the correlation slightly. (c) No edge present: a sustained high correlation without disturbance in the regression parameters implies that the edge is not physically significant. An additional case, not illustrated, is that of low correlation throughout. This indicates low contrast or lack of surface structure, implying that no decision about edge type can be made.

occluding contour are likely to be uncorrelated, because they are actually the projections of distant, hence independent, surface points; and intensities across a cast shadow edge are likely to be highly correlated under a systematic (ideally, linear) transformation, arising form the interaction of the the continuous underlying surface structure with the illumination transition.

These observations are applied to image edges by constructing a family of parallel curves around the edge, and performing a sequence of linear regressions of the intensity values along each curve onto those along its neighbor. The following behavior is predicted for each of several edge types:

- A precipitous drop in correlation at the nominal edge location signifies an occluding contour.

2

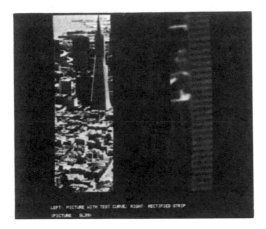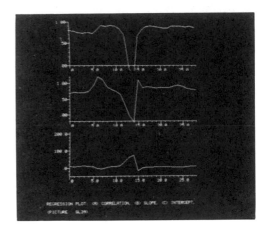

Figure 2 Example of an occluding edge. In the left panel is the original image, with the selected edge highlighted. The right half of the panel shows the rectified strip, whose midline corresponds to the edge. The right panel shows the plots for correlation, slope, and intercept. The overall high correlation, with a sharp plunge near the edge location, corresponds closely to the idealized form of Figure 1a. Remember that slope and intercept of the regression line are meaningless where the correlation is low.

- High correlation with an abrupt shift in the regression parameters signifies a shadow.

- Sustained high correlation with the additive and multiplicative regression parameters near zero and unity, respectively, implies that no significant edge is present.

- Low correlation throughout implies lack of coherent surface structure, and no edge type can be assigned.

These ideal structural "signatures" were shown to closely predict regression sequences obtained from images of natural edges.

2.0 Defining the Problem

Because edge types are defined in terms of the scene events they denote, any method for edge sorting must provide some basis for discriminating those events by their appearance in the image. We therefore begin by characterizing the distinctive properties of occluding contours and cast shadow edges, and defining the computational problem of identifying those edges.

Occluding contours: the projective mapping from image to scene tends to be continuous, because physical surfaces tend to be continuous. Almost everywhere in a typical image, therefore, nearby points in the image correspond to nearby points in the scene. This adjacency is preserved over any change in point of view or scene con-

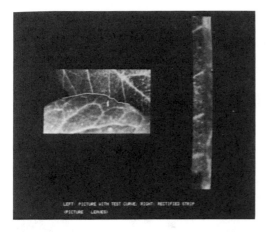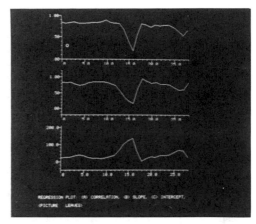

Figure 3 A low-contrast occluding edge. Although the edge contrast is low, the correlation across the edge dips to about .15, compared to about .85 in the surrounding region.

figuration, short of rendering the connected surfaces of which the scene is composed. This distinguishing property of occluding contours (which may be defined as discontinuities in the projective mapping) is their systematic *violation* of this rule: the apparent juxtaposition of two surfaces across an occluding edge represents no fixed property of either surface, but is subject to the vagaries of viewpoint and scene configuration. For example, if you position your finger to coincide with a particular feature on the wall or outside the window, a small change in the position of head or hand may drastically affect their apparent relation. Because the false appearance of proximity is the hallmark of occluding edges, the problem in identifying those edges may be cast as that of distinguishing in the image the actual proximity of nearby points on con-

nected surfaces from accidental proximity imposed by projection.

Cast shadows in outdoor scenes usually represent transitions from direct to scattered illumination caused by the interposition of an occluding body between the sun and the viewed surface. The problem in identifying cast shadows is to distinguish these transitions in incident illumination from changes in albedo, surface orientation, and so forth. This discrimination presents a problem because the effects of all these parameters are confounded in the image data—a change in image brightness may reflect a change in albedo or surface orientation, as well as incident illumination. Because the relation among illumination, reflectivity, orientation, and image irradiance is well known, the presence of shadows in an image could be readily detected if a constant reference pattern could be placed in the scene: when

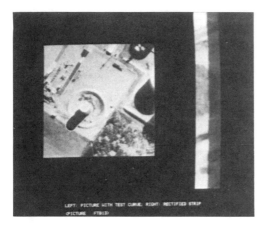
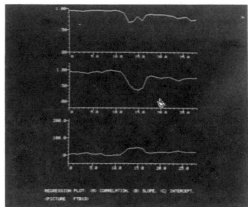

LEFT: PICTURE WITH TEST CURVE; RIGHT: RECTIFIED STRIP
(PICTURE FTB1D)

REGRESSION PLOT: (A) CORRELATION, (B) SLOPE, (C) INTERCEPT.
(PICTURE FTB1D)

Figure 4 A cast-shadow edge. The shadow transition appears primarily as a dip in the slope of the regression line (a dip rather than a bump because the left-to-right transition is from light to shadow.) The perturbation in the additive regression term, and the dip in correlation to about .75 are due primarily to nonlinearities in the film response.

the apparent brightness of a constant pattern varies with location, the change in brightness must, by elimination, be attributed to a change in illumination. Of course such active intervention is generally impractical. The problem may be viewed as that of achieving the effect of viewing a constant pattern across the shadow edge, without actually placing such a pattern in the scene. This could be achieved if some fixed relation were known to hold between the surface strips on each side of the shadow.

In short, occluding contours are curves across which points that may be distant in space are placed in apparent juxtaposition by projection, violating the continuity of the projective mapping that holds over most of the image. To identify occluding contours therefore requires that actual proximity be distinguished from apparent proximity imposed by projection. Cast shadows edges are contours across which the pattern of surface reflectance has been systematically transformed by an abrupt change in illumination. To identify cast shadow edges the effects of illumination must be distinguished from those of albedo and surface orientation, as if a constant reference pattern had been placed across the edge.

3.0 Continuity and Independence

The solution we have devised rests on two simple complementary principles: (1) Continuity: Surfaces, surface markings, and illumination are almost everywhere continuous. Therefore, the projective mapping is almost everywhere continuous, and image intensities at nearby points tend to be highly correlated. (2) Independence: The factors governing the structure of a scene—the shapes of objects, and their placement with respect to each other, to illuminants, and to the viewer—are so complex that properties of distinct or widely separated scene constituents may for most purposes be regarded as causally independent. [This independence principle is related to the principle of general position (Binford, 1981; Marr, 1977), which assumes isotropy for viewpoint and object position and orientation.]

One simple measure of continuity or coherence across an image curve (there are many others) is linear correlation between the image intensities a small distance on either side of the curve: a high positive correlation implies that the image strips on either side of the curve are closely related, a low correlation implies no (linear) relation. Given a high correlation, a regression equation can be computed to describe the linear transform relating the intensities across the curve. Several predictions about correlations and regressions across edges follow from the continuity and independence principles:

The continuity principle implies that high correlations should often be observed across arbitrarily selected curves in the image. However, a low correlation could just imply low contrast or fragmented surface structure.

The independence principle implies that high correlations should almost *never* be observed across occluding contours, because the points meeting along those curves are not the projections of nearby points in space.

The independence principle implies

that a cast shadow edge would not have any unusual properties, were the shadow body removed, because the light source and the shadowed and shadowing objects do not "conspire" to achieve special alignments. Therefore, apart form the effects of the shadow itself, a cast shadow edge should show the same correlational properties as an arbitrarily selected curve. Shadows in outdoor scenes are often transitions between two roughly constant levels of illumination—scattered and direct—and the effect of an illuminant change on image intensity may be very roughly idealized as linear. To the extent these idealizations hold, linear correlations across cast shadow edges are likely to be as high as those across arbitrary curves, but the illumination transition will appear as a perturbation of the regression equation (ideally, a multiplicative factor for linear digitization, an additive one for logarithmic digitization.)

Given a candidate edge in the image, these observations leave us with strong implication that a high correlation of intensities across the edge *excludes* the possibility that the edge is an occluding contour, and that a high correlation through a substantial linear transform signals a shadow. The latter implications are weaker because lack of correlation may just signify conditions, such as low contrast, that don't favor correlation. Our conclusions about occluding contours and shadows may be strengthened by examining a larger neighborhood around the edge. By embedding the given edge in a series of parallel curves, a sequence of regressions can be performed one onto the next. A low correlation throughout signals low contrast or lack of texture, and no conclusion can be drawn. However, a sharp notch in an otherwise high

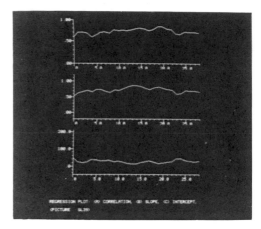

Figure 5 Regression where no physical edge is present. As expected, a fairly high correlation, with stable regression parameters, is maintained across the "edge".

correlation, where the regression sequence crosses the edge, argues against global low contrast or lack of texture, providing a stronger indicator that the edge is an occluding contour. Likewise, sustained high correlation with an abrupt perturbation in one or both regression parameters is good evidence for a shadow. Finally, sustained high correlation with no perturbation of the regression equation provides evidence that the edge is not physically significant.

4.0 Implementation and results

Our implementation assumes that an edge has been located by edge-finding techniques (see Chapter 2, for an example). Hand-traced edges and zero-crossings in a $\nabla^2 G$ convolution (Marr & Hildreth, 1979) were tried as inputs. A parallel family of curves was constructed around the edge as follows: at fixed intervals of arc length along the edge, a line normal to the edge was constructed. The set of points lying some fixed distance from the edge along each normal line then defines a "parallel" curve. A family of curves was constructed by varying that perpendicular distance. This construction amounts to warping a strip of the image, surrounding the edge, into a rectangular region, whose central column corresponds to the original edge. The vertical dimension of this "rectified strip" denotes arc length on the edge, and the horizontal dimension denotes perpendicular distance form the edge. The columns surrounding the central one correspond to parallel curves on either side of the edge. Intensity values for the rectified strip were obtained by bilinear interpolation of the intensities in the original image, to reduce quantization error.

Once the rectified strip was constructed, a sequence of linear regressions was performed between columns. To avoid spurious correlation imposed by the imaging and digitizing process, regressions were computed between the ith column and the $(i+2)$th. The outcome of this computation was a normalized correlation, an additive regression term, and a multiplicative regression term, each a function of column position. The midpoints of these plots represent the regression across the original edge. Points to either side of the plots' midpoints represent regressions between adjacent parallel curves on either side of the original edge.

The idealized edge type "signatures", as developed in the preceding section, are shown and explained in Figure 1 in terms of these regression sequence plots.

Actual image edges, together with rectified strips and regression plots, are shown and described Figures 2–5. (The edges in these cases were hand-traced.) Marked correspondence between the actual and idealized plots is evident to inspection. No attempt has yet been made to automate this comparison, although a variety of simple thresholding schemes might well prove empirically adequate to the classification task.

5.0 Conclusions

Two conclusions may be drawn from these results: first, the correlational properties of intensities in the neighborhood of an edge carry important information about the edge's physical significance, and second, the every basic principles of continuity and independence can provide strong an useful constraints on image interpretation.

Acknowledgment: This work was performed while the author was a member of the Artificial Intelligence Center at SRI, International. Support was provided in part by NASA contract NAS1–16282, NSF grant MCS–7901830, and DARPA contract DAAG–29–79–C–0218

References

Barrow, H.G. & Tenenbaum, J.M. (1981) Interpreting line drawings as three dimensional surfaces, *Artif. Intell.*, 17:75–116.

Binford, T.O. (1981) Inferring surfaces from images, *Artif. Intell.*, 17:205–244.

Clowes, M.B. (1971) On seeing things, *Artif. Intell.*, 2:79–112.

Horn, B.K.P. (1977) Understanding Image Intensities, *Artif. Intell.*, 21(11):201–231.

Huffman, D.A. (1971) Impossible objects as nonsense sentences. In *Machine Intelligence*, Edinburgh: Edinburgh University Press.

Marr, D.C. (1977) Analysis of occluding contour, *Proc. Roy. Soc. Lond.* 197:441–475.

Marr, D.C. & Hildreth, E. (1979) A theory of edge detection, MIT A.I. Lab. Memo 518.

Stevens, K.A. (1981) The visual interpretation of surface contours, *Artif. Intell.*, 17:47–74.

Waltz, D.L. (1972) Generating semantic descriptions from drawings of scenes with shadows, MIT A.I. Lab. Technical Report AI-TR-271.

Witkin, A.P. (1981) Recovering surface shape and orientation from texture, *Artif. Intell.*, 17:17–46.

Reprinted from: *Proceedings AAAI*, 1982.

Analysis of Accretion and Deletion at Boundaries in Dynamic Scenes

Kathleen M. Mutch*
William B. Thompson

University of Minnesota

1.0 Introduction

Locating object boundaries in images is an important but difficult problem. Intensity-based edge detection provides ambiguous or misleading boundary information in many situations, such as textured regions. Motion-based techniques can provide more reliable results in these cases. At object boundaries where occlusion occurs, surface regions will typically appear or disappear over time when motion is present. These regions of changing visibility may be used to indicate both object boundaries and the side of the boundary corresponding to the occluded surface.

At a typical object boundary, one surface will be blocking the view of another more distant surface. In the presence of motion, regions of the more distant surface will often either appear or disappear from view over time. Such regions are called areas of *accretion* or *deletion*, respectively. A similar situation arises in stereo vision, where a region of the more distant surface near an occlusion edge will be visible in one image of the pair but invisible in the other image. Thus, recognition of accretion/deletion regions is a means of locating object boundaries in image sequences. In addition, accretion and deletion regions will belong to the occluded surface, providing sufficient information to determine which of the two surfaces at a boundary

is being occluded. To recover the information available from such regions, it is necessary to determine both how regions of accretion and deletion in the imagery may be identified, and what characteristics of such regions permit identification of the occluded surface.

This paper describes a scheme to locate regions of accretion and deletion, and to identify occluding surfaces at a boundary using these regions. A technique which matches image features in two frames is used to determine feature displacement on the image plane. Areas in the image with a high percentage of features which are unmatchable in a previous or subsequent image are identified as accretion or deletion regions, respectively. These regions indicate the presence of an occlusion boundary. Since the accretion/deletion region belongs to the occluded surface, it will be displaced on the image plane in the same fashion as nearby areas of that surface. The occluded surface is then identified by determining which of the two surfaces adjacent to the accretion/deletion region displays a similar displacement on the image plane. This identification combines information about accretion and deletion with optical flow to produce a description of the occlusion boundary more complete than any existing technique based purely on flow alone.

2.0 Previous Work

Several research efforts in computational vision have utilized motion information to recover object boundaries. The basic idea behind most motion-based approaches is that image plane motion, or optical flow, across the object surface will be constant or slowly-varying, and discontinuities in flow will occur only at object edges. Previous approaches either search for discontinuities in the optical flow, or group together regions of similar flow. Nakayama & Loomis (1974) propose a local, center-surround operator for detecting object boundaries in flow fields. Clocksin (1980) shows that zero-crossings will occur at edge locations in the Laplacian of the magnitude of the optical flow field when an observer translates through an otherwise static environment. Thompson et. al. (1982, 1984) demonstrate that the Laplacian is useful as an edge detector in the more general case of unconstrained motion. After obtaining point velocities by template matching, Potter (1977) groups all points with the same velocity into single object regions. Similarly, Fennema & Thompson (1979) use the spatial and temporal gradients of intensity to obtain point velocities, and then consider all points with similar velocities to be part of the same object. Thompson (1980) develops a grouping scheme based upon both intensity and velocity information. Regions of both identical intensity and identical velocity are formed, followed by merging of adjacent regions based upon similarities, or at least lack of conflict, in intensity and velocity. With the exception of Clocksin's work (1980), these flow-based techniques are unable to provide any indication of the occluded surface at an edge.

Accretion and deletion are fundamental to motion analysis based on differencing (Jain, 1981; Jain et al., 1979). These techniques subtract one image from another and then use the presence of regions of significant difference to infer properties of object boundaries and motion. The approach is most effective when a reasonably homogeneous object is moving relative to a homogeneous background with different luminance. Covering and uncovering of the background leads to significant differences between frames, allowing boundaries to be located. Analysis of these difference regions over time can often be used to associate the difference region with adjacent, non-changing areas of the image sequence and thereby identify which side of the boundary is being occluded. This scheme is intensity-based, and suffers when intensity contrasts occur that are not related to object structure. A textured object which changes location on the image plane, for example, will produce many regions of intensity difference which are not accretion or deletion regions.

Only limited experimentation has been directed at the role of accretion and deletion in human perception. Kaplan (1969) showed that patterns of accretion and deletion in fields of moving random dots provide sufficient information for the judgment of relative depth by human subjects. In his stimuli, a single edge separated two regions of random dots, where each region moved coherently. The edge was implicit, being the line along which accretion and/or deletion occurred, and thus was not visible if all of the dots were stationary. Subjects consistently perceived the more distant surface to be the one which was undergoing accretion or deletion at a greater rate. This was true even when the implicit edge moved with a velocity different than the velocity of points on either surface. In these cases of inconsistent edge motion, there was more ambiguity in the perceptions of subjects, although the statistically significant perception was that the surface with a greater rate of accretion or deletion was more distant. This suggests that both edge velocity and accretion/deletion are important factors in the perception of depth at an edge, but that accretion/deletion information may be dominant.

3.0 Detecting Accretion/Deletion Regions

A motion-based scheme for identifying accretion and deletion regions is developed here. To recover motion on the image plane, corresponding structures in each frame of an image pair are located. The result of this is a *disparity vector field*, where each vector represents the change in image plane location of a structure. (Disparity is the discrete representation of optical flow arising from image sequences that are discretely sampled in time.) This correspondence is accomplished by *token matching*. A token is a distinctive region in the image, which is identified by some predefined local operator. A set of tokens is obtained for each image in the pair, and an organized search is performed to match tokens from the first image to corresponding tokens in the second image using the relaxation labeling technique described in Barnard & Thompson (1980). Possible matches between tokens in the two frames are evaluated based on two criteria: the similarity between properties of the tokens, and a surface smoothness measure that favors matches with disparities similar to neighboring tokens. An important

aspect of this particular matching technique is that it can determine that a token in one frame is *unmatchable* if no token in the other frame satisfies the appropriate matching criteria. By basing the analysis on the motion of tokens in the image, many of the intensity contrast problems of a differencing system are circumvented.

Regions of accretion and deletion are identified by analyzing unmatchable tokens in either image. A token may not be matchable either because the token detector failed to find the corresponding structure in the other image of the pair, or because the corresponding token is not visible in the other image. Regions with a high ratio of unmatchable tokens to total tokens are likely to be regions of accretion or deletion. This motion-based, token-matching approach is an implementation of Kaplan's model for detecting such regions (Kaplan, 1968). Kaplan argues that accretion and deletion are detected in the human visual system by isolating clusters of elements of optical texture, tracking them over time, and responding when they change in some way that is not topologically permissible. Token identification is equivalent to isolating elements of optical texture; token matching serves the purpose of tracking such elements over time; and analyzing unmatchable tokens is a response to some change which may be due to appearance or disappearance of a region.

4.0 Identifying Occluded Surfaces.

Not only can accretion/deletion patterns be used to locate boundaries, they provide information that allows the identification of the side of the boundary being occluded. Such information is beneficial when inter-

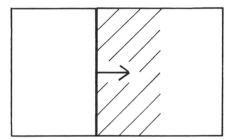 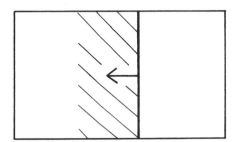

Figure 1 Location of an accretion/deletion region relative to the boundary indicates the direction of the occluded surface. In both cases shown above, the vertical line represents a boundary, and the shaded area represents an accretion or deletion region. The arrow points toward the occluded surface.

preting dynamic scenes. Several specific approaches are possible, though all are based on associating the accretion or deletion region with a surface on one side of the boundary. That surface is the one being occluded. One approach relies upon the relative location of the accretion/deletion region with respect to the precise position of the image of the boundary. This boundary is the actual point of occlusion, the accretion/deletion region being on the same side of the boundary as the occluded surface. Figure 1 illustrates this concept. The primary difficulty in this approach is identifying the boundary location relative to the accretion/deletion region. In particular, motion-based edge detection cannot locate the boundary precisely enough without first knowing which surface is occluded. The inadequacies of intensity-based edge detectors for this purpose are well known, particularly when applied to textured surfaces.

An alternative approach involves iden-

tifying the location of an accretion or deletion region relative to the location of such a region at a previous instant in time (Thompson & Barnard, 1981). New accretion regions will appear to the side of previous accretion regions opposite the remainder of the occluded surface. New deletion regions will occur on the same side of previous deletion regions as the occluded surface (see Figure 2). A disadvantage of this approach is the necessity to track and locate whole accretion/deletion regions over time.

The approach for identifying occluded surfaces from accretion/deletion regions which is developed in this paper requires the recognition of similarities between such regions and one of the two surfaces on either side of the boundary. Since the accretion/deletion region belongs to the occluded surface, it will share certain properties with that surface. The common property could be intensity or texture, although the problems inherent in most

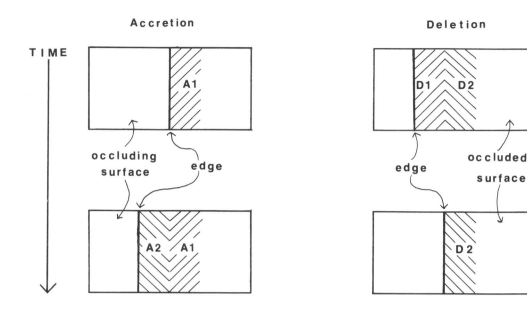

A1 - first accretion region
A2 - second accretion region
D1 - first deletion region
D2 - second deletion region

Figure 2 The location of new accretion/deletion regions relative to previous such regions indicates the direction of the occluded surface. The second accretion region appears to the opposite side the first accretion region as the occluded surface. The second deletion region occurs to the same side of the first deletion region as the occluded surface.

intensity-based analyses make these alternatives undesirable. Once again, motion-based properties may be more reliable. One such property is the disparity of tokens on the image plane. Disparity varies slowly over the surface of almost all rigid objects. Accretion or deletion tokens will thus exhibit disparities which are nearly identical to nearby token disparities on the same surface, while token disparities

on different surfaces will usually vary.

5.0 Implementation

The system which was developed to detect occluded surfaces from regions of accretion or deletion uses token matching to obtain disparity vector fields. Unmatched tokens in clusters of high density are classified as accretion or deletion tokens, depending on whether they have matches in subsequent or previous frame pairs. The disparity of accretion tokens after their appearance, or of deletion tokens prior to their disappearance, is obtained. Nearby tokens which are not accretion or deletion tokens and which have known disparities are identified and are used to identify the surface to which the accretion or deletion tokens belongs. Such tokens with similar disparities to an accretion or deletion point lie on the occluded surface.

Three frames in an image sequence are required. Disparity fields D1 and D2 are obtained for frames 1 and 2, and for frames 2 and 3, respectively. Accretion points are not visible in frame 1, but do appear in frames 2 and 3. Tokens first appearing in frame 2, and thus having no associated match in frame 1, are noted. If these tokens have a match in frame 3, and if they are in a region with a high ratio of such tokens to total tokens, they are considered to be points of accretion. The disparity of accretion points is provided by D2. For every accretion point, a search is made within a neighborhood about the point location in frame 2. Tokens which are matched in D2, but which are not marked as accretion points are found. All of these tokens which have disparities similar to the accretion point are considered as a cluster. A vector pointing towards the center of the cluster is assigned to each accretion point, and indicates the direction from that point to the occluded surface.

Deletion points are visible in frames 1 and 2, but not frame 3. Tokens which are indicated as unmatchable in frame 2 are noted. If these tokens have a match in frame 1 and if they are in a region with a high ratio of such tokens to total tokens, they are considered to be points of deletion. The disparity of deletion points is

provided by D1. For every deletion point, a search is made within a neighborhood about that point location in frame 1. Tokens which are matched in D1, but which are not marked as deletion points are found. All of these tokens which have disparities similar to the deletion point are considered as a cluster. As before, a vector in the direction of the center of the cluster is assigned to each deletion point and indicates the direction from that point to the occluded surface.

6.0 Limitations

This boundary detection technique requires a moderately dense token set, both to find accretion/deletion regions, and to determine image-plane displacements. This means that the two surfaces adjacent to the edge must be distinctly textured. In addition, there must be some component of optical flow perpendicular to the occlusion boundary, or neither accretion nor deletion will occur. In particular, motion exactly parallel to the boundary will produce no accretion or deletion regions (see Figure 3). Perspective viewing of translating objects in principle leads to difficulties similar to those associated with rotation in depth (see below), as the perspective effects can be locally described as a combination of rotation and scale change. Fortunately, the practical difficulties caused by perspective effects are minimal. When objects are translating in front of a background, the size of accretion/deletion regions due to translation is almost always much greater than accretion/deletion regions that appear due to effective rotation of the object.

Certain rotations lead to potentially confusing situations when analyzing occlu-

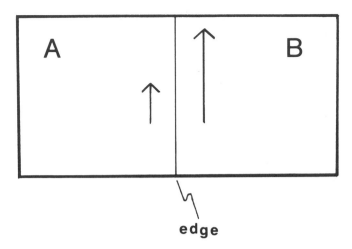

Figure 3 The optical flow of surfaces A and B is indicated by the vectors on those surfaces. Since neither surface exhibits any flow perpendicular to the edge, there will be no accretion or deletion regions.

sion boundaries. Figure 4a shows an overhead view of a cylinder rotating in depth. Figure 4c shows the accretion/deletion regions that arise if there is no relative motion between the cylinder and the background surface. The analysis above assigns the accretion and deletion regions to the cylinder. Thus, the cylinder, not the background surface, is indicated as the surface being dynamically occluded. This is the correct interpretation, as the rotation in depth causes the cylinder to occlude itself over time. However, while the dynamic occlusion is correctly recognized, no information is directly available about the relative depths to the surfaces on either side of the boundary. In fact, it is possible that the surrounding surface in the image is actually in front of the cylinder (Figure 4b), yet generates the same image sequence.

A different complication occurs if the rotating object is moving with respect to the background surface, the cross sec-

tion of the object is not circular, or the object is not rotating about its axis of symmetry. In all of these situations, accretion and/or deletion will be occurring on both sides of the actual boundary. The method given above is still valid and will identify both sides of the boundary as occluded surfaces. The problem again arises when trying to infer relative depth given an identification of the occluded surface. The determination of relative depth at a dynamic occlusion boundary when rotation is occurring is made possible by combining accretion/deletion analysis as described in this paper with an optical flow based approach (Thompson et. al, 1985). This second technique uses the relationship between the flow of a boundary and the surface flows on either side of the boundary to identifying occlud*ing* surfaces. Accretion/deletion analysis locates occlud*ed* surfaces. When taken together, both the occlusion of one surface by another and the self-occlusion resulting from

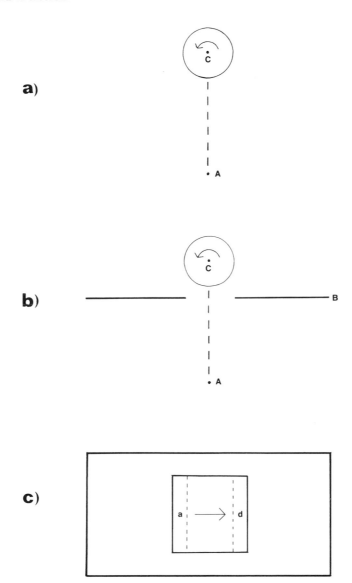

Figure 4 A. Overhead view of a cylinder rotating counter-clockwise about an axis at C, in front of a stationary background B. The viewer is at A, and the line of sight is along the dotted line. B. The rotating cylinder seen through an aperture in surface B which is now in front. C. When either A or B are viewed from point A, accretion regions (a) will occur along the left edge on the cylinder, deletion regions (d) along the right edge. While the cylinder is correctly identified as the occluded surface, there is insufficient information to determine the relative depth between the cylinder and the surface at B.

3

FRAME 1   FRAME 2   FRAME 3

Figure 5 Image sequence in which leopard is translating from left to right.

rotation in depth can be recognized and appropriately interpreted.

7.0 Example

The system implementation described above was applied twice to the image sequence shown in Figure 5, first processing the sequence in the order shown, then in reverse order. All images had a resolution of 128 x 128. There were approximately 1000 tokens identified in each image, and over 800 of these were matched in every image pair. As is usual with token matching systems, the density of tokens (and thus disparity vectors) varied across the image, being higher in areas of fine texture. An 11 x 11 square neighborhood, centered at an unmatched point, was used for computing the density of unmatched tokens. This size was chosen to be small enough so that most of the neighborhood fell within the accretion/deletion region, yet big enough to contain a reasonable number of tokens (usually 6 to 12). If 80% of the tokens in this neighborhood were unmatched in the same way as the point under consideration, then the point was labeled "accretion" or "deletion". This ratio was chosen to be selectively high, and yet to allow for some incorrect matches in the neighborhood, or some extension of the neighborhood out of the accretion/deletion region. A 31 x 31 window,

centered at the accretion/deletion point, was searched to find clusters of similar disparity vectors. This size was chosen to be large enough to include portions of both surfaces outside the accretion/deletion region, yet not so large as to extend beyond these surfaces. Disparity vectors were considered "similar" if they differed by no more than 2 pixels in each of the x and y components. The actual values of most of these parameters will, in general, depend upon factors such as the resolution of the images, the amount of texture, and the maximum expected disparity.

The results of processing in the forward direction are shown in Figure 6a. All of the square white points represent accretion or deletion frame 2 tokens, which were matched in the second (D2) or first (D1) disparity field. The line which emanates from each box projects toward the surface which the algorithm indicates is being occluded. The set of tokens to the right of the leopard are deletion points. Tokens near the left border of the image are accretion points, which appear as more of the leopard moves into the field of view. Vectors associated with these points indicate that the leopard is being occluded by the surrounding frame. Except for six noise points, all accretion and deletion tokens have an associated vector pointing in the correct direction. The noise points are not in the accretion

 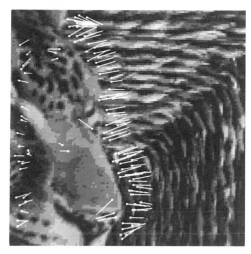

A   **B**

Figure 6 A. Results of occluded surface determination based upon accretion/deletion regions for the sequence of three frames in Figure 1. Square white boxes are locations of accretion or deletion points in frame 2. The line emanating from each box points in the direction of the occluded surface. B. Results of occluding surface determination when the sequence of three frames in Figure 5 is processed in the reverse order.

or deletion regions, but rather occur in or near untextured regions, or on the edge of the accretion/deletion regions. As a result, there are either no other tokens in the vicinity, or else a large number of unmatched tokens in the neighboring accretion/deletion region. These points are thus incorrectly identified as accretion or deletion points.

Figure 6b shows the results when the image sequence of Figure 5 is processed in the reverse order. The disparity field D1 is now the set of matches for frames 3 and 2, and D2 for frames 2 and 1. Tokens to the right of the leopard are now accretion points, and tokens near the left border of the image are deletion points. Once again, except for nine noise points, all vectors correctly point toward the occluded surface. The noise points are due to the same causes described in the previous paragraph.

References

Barnard, S.T. & Thompson, W.B. (1980) Disparity analysis of images. *IEEE Trans. Pattern Analysis and Machine Intelligence*, PAMI-2, pp. 333–340.

Clocksin, W.F. (1980) Perception of surface slant and edge labels from optical flow: a computational approach. *Perception*, 9:253 – 269.

Fennema, C.L. & Thompson, W.B. (1979) Velocity determination in scenes containing several moving objects. *Comput. Graphics Image Process.*, 9:301 – 315.

Jain, R. (1981) Extraction of motion information from peripheral processes. *IEEE Trans. Pattern Analysis and Machine Intelligence*, PAMI-3, No. 5, pp. 489 – 503.

Jain, R., Martin, W.N. & Aggarwal, J.K. (1979) Segmentation through the detection of changes due to motion. *Comput. Graphics Image Process.*, 11:13 – 34.

Kaplan, G.A. (1968) "Kinetic disruption of optical texture: The perception of depth at an edge". Ph.D. dissertation Cornell University, Ithaca, New York.

Kaplan, G.A. (1969) Kinetic disruption of optical texture: The perception of depth at an edge. *Perception & Psychophysics*, 6:193 – 198.

Nakayama, K. & Loomis, J.M. (1974) Optical velocity patterns, velocity sensitive neurons, and space perception: a hypothesis. *Perception*, 3:63 – 80.

Potter, J.L. (1977) Scene segmentation using motion information. *Comput. Graphics Image Process.*, 6:558 – 581.

Thompson, W.B. (1980) Combining motion and contrast for segmentation. *IEEE Trans. Pattern Analysis and Machine Intelligence*, PAMI-2, pp. 543 – 549.

Thompson, W.B. & Barnard, S.T. (1981) Low-level estimation and interpretation of visual motion. *Computer*, August.

Thompson, W.B., Mutch, K.M. & Berzins, V.A. (1982) Edge detection in optical flow fields. *Proc. Second National Conference on Artificial Intelligence*, August, 1982.

Thompson, W.B., Mutch, K.M. & Berzins, V.A. (1985) Dynamic occlusion analysis in optical flow fields. *IEEE Trans. Pattern Analysis & Mach. Intell.*, PAMI-7:374 – 383.

Reprinted from *IEEE Trans. Pattern Analysis and Machine Intelligence*, PAMI-7:133 – 138 (1985).

*The first author is now at the Department of Computer Science, Arizona State Universtiy, Temple, Arizona.

CARTOON: A Biologically Motivated Edge Detection Algorithm

W. Richards, H.K. Nishihara and B. Dawson

Massachusetts Institute of Technology

1.0 Introduction

One of the first tasks faced by any vision processor—whether it be biological or artificial—is to encode the image on its retina into a more economical and meaningful form. Because most of the information in the image is carried by the intensity changes (Attneave, 1954; Barlow, 1961), a large effort over the years has been devoted to creating and describing these changes (see reviews by Pratt, 1978; Rosenfeld & Kak, 1976). Although many researchers have recognized the need for a more symbolic description of the gray levels in an image, Marr (1976) was the first to state clearly the goals of these early stages and to address the problems raised by these goals. Following leads from neurophysiology, Marr (1976, 1982) argues for the construction of a "Primal Sketch"—a primitive but rich description of the image intensity changes which are given labels such as "sharp edge," "shaded edge," "line," "termination" or "blob". Although these symbolic descriptions hint at some external physical cause, they are in fact only image tokens from which the physical features of the scene are deduced (Marr & Nishihara, 1978). Such features include shadows or specularities, surface markings or texture, shapes, contours and the like. One such physical event of particular interest here is the location of surface discontinuities, or where one material abuts another, such as at occluding boundaries, or where grass meets pavement (Rubin & Richards, 1982). The intent of the algorithm is to make strong assertions about the locations of these events in particular.

2.0 The Problem

In an artificial world made of smooth, matte Lambertian surfaces, whenever two objects made of different materials overlap, there will usually be a step change in intensity in the image. In the natural world, this underlying step change is grossly corrupted by specularities, texture, and shading. Our task is to find the step changes in the presence of these confounding factors.

Figure 1 illustrates the problem in greater detail. The upper graph is an intensity profile taken through a vertical slice of an image (PYRAMID). In this profile, there are only seven changes in materials, as noted at the top of the figure. Nowhere is there an ideal "step edge." Furthermore, some intensity changes not associated with material changes are much greater than those arising from the edges of interest. (Compare the sky-to-pyramid transition with some of the texture profiles produced by hieroglyphic markings.)

4

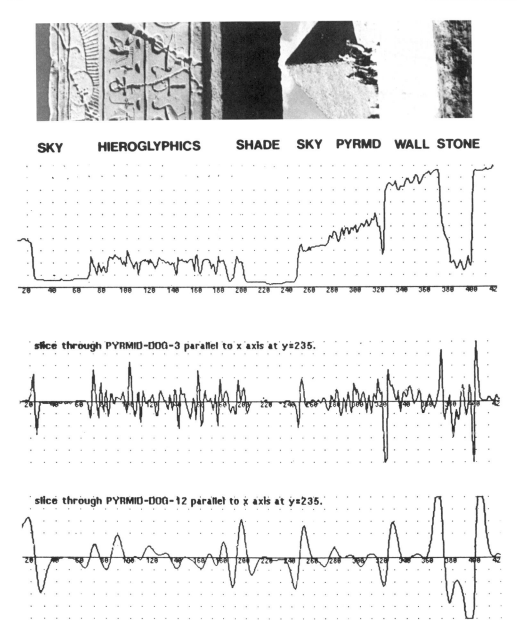

Figure 1 The first graph is the intensity profile of a slice of the image PYRAMID, shown in the top panel. The third and fourth panels show slices of the convolutions of the image, with each slice taken at the same positions as the intensity profile. The two image convolutions were made with a difference-of-Gaussians mask depicted in Figure 2, with mask widths of 3 and 12 pixels.

The complexity of the problem appears to be further increased by the fact that, for biological systems at least, the raw image intensities are not readily available for analysis. Instead, the first stage of processing in neuron-based visual systems is bandpass filtering by so-called "center surround" operators (Kuffler, 1953). Our available input representation is thus not the image profile itself, but rather several filtered versions of the image. Two such filtered versions of the pyramid image profile are shown in the lower panels of Figure 1. In spite of initial appearances of further complexity, this bandpass filtering step will be shown critical to finding the locations of material changes in an image.

Figure 2 gives a clearer picture of the data base from which we start. The lower two panels show the image WINNIE filtered using one of two bandpass filters, in this case the difference of two Gaussians, which closely matches the first stage neural filter used in biological systems (Enroth-Cugell & Robson, 1966; Richter & Ullman, 1982; Rodieck, 1965; Schade, 1956; Wilson & Bergen, 1979) This type of spatial operator or "mask" has the desirable property of preserving both the location and waveform of an intensity change, as seen at the scale of the filter (Marr & Hildreth, 1980; Marr & Poggio, 1979; Sakitt & Barlow, 1982). It has the further property of being ideally suited to detect intensity steps corrupted by noise (Jernigan & Wardell, 1981; Shanmugan et al., 1979)

Because a difference-of-Gaussians filter approximates a second derivative operator, the zeros in the filter's output (i.e. the convolution) correspond to maxima in the intensity change, which are located at the putative "edges" in the original image. In the above figure, these "edges"

or their second-derivative correlates occur at each black to white transition, which is where the sign of the convolution output changes from positive (white) to negative (black). Surprisingly, this representation which shows only the locations of the zero-crossings in the convolution at each scale is remarkably rich (Curtis & Oppenheim, 1987; Marr & Poggio, 1979; Marr et al., 1979; Nishihara, 1980; Rotem & Zeevi, 1986), and does indeed constitute a simple data base from which the locations of material changes can be deduced with reasonable certainty.

If all material changes produced a sharp step in intensity, then finding these edges from the outputs of the bandpass filters would be straightforward. Because the circular masks are bandpass filters, their convolution with a step intensity profile will be zero when the mask lies exactly centered on the ideal step. This will be true for all mask sizes, as long as the edge intensity profile is straight and longer than the entire extent of the mask (Marr, 1976). Thus, for an ideal step edge, the convolution profiles for all mask sizes will cross the zero axis at exactly the same position, just as it does at the right edge of Figure 1. Certainly such a coincidence in the locations of the zeros in the mask outputs is a rare event and should be noted as having special significance (Marr & Hildreth, 1980). However, for natural images where ideal step profiles are perturbed and corrupted, such exact coincidences are rare. How then can this coincidence idea be made more robust?

3.0 A Solution

To identify those image intensity contours that arise from material changes we adopt

4

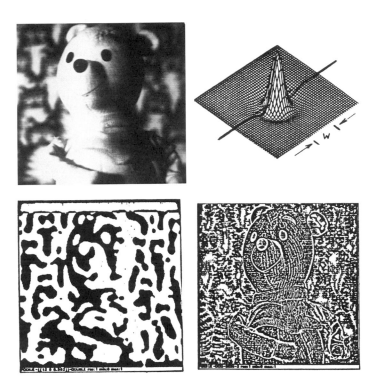

Figure 2 The original 512 x 512 image of *WINNIE* has been bandpass filtered using a difference-of-Gaussians mask of size W=16 (lower left) and W=3 (lower right). The mask profile is shown in the upper right panel, where W is defined as the width of the positive part of the mask. Only the sign bits of the convolutions have been displayed.

a "reject-accept" strategy suggested by Rubin & Richards (1982). Quite simply, we wish to "reject" clear instances of image profiles that cannot arise from a material change, leaving a much smaller number of candidate profiles for closer examination. Two image characteristics that arise from material changes will be used: the broad spectral power of the resulting step edge and the phase coherence of its Fourier components.

Figure 3 illustrates the approach in more detail. As previously noted, the basic

waveform underlying all material changes is the step edge. Regardless of the corruption of this ideal step, such as by shading or texture, the transform must contain power over a wide range of frequencies, S. The addition of texture or shading cannot eliminate this broad-based power of the underlying step, but only alter (broaden) the phase relationships ϕ among the different frequency components.

Now consider first the case of texture or a shadow alone (lower two panels). The shadow edge has power only at low fre-

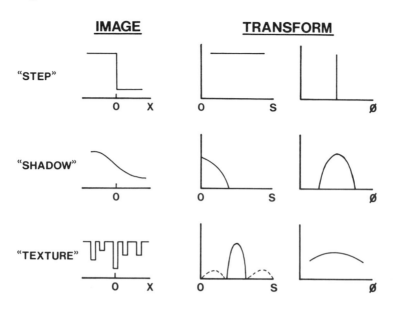

IMAGE | **TRANSFORM**

Figure 3 Image profiles of several types of "edges" and their one-dimensional Fourier transforms.

quencies, whereas texture has principally a high frequency spectrum. In general, neither of these intensity profiles alone will cover a broad spectrum. Thus an intensity profile whose power is confined to *only* one portion of the spectrum can be rejected as being caused by a material change.

On the other hand, since a material change produces an underlying step edge with a broad spectrum, any intensity profile that contains both high and low frequency components should be considered as a candidate material change. We thus wish to retain profiles that will survive simultaneous low and high-bandpass filtering, and reject profiles that pass only one or the other filter alone. Our CARTOON algorithm accomplishes this by taking the logical "AND" of the outputs of a low and high bandpass filter, as il-

lustrated schematically in Figure 4. The two-dimensional intensity profile is first convolved with two separate difference-of-Gaussians masks, yielding a low and high-bandpassed image. The positive sign bit of this filtered image is then assigned the value "1", otherwise the value will be zero. These binary outputs of the two filters are then multiplied at each point in the array, in effect testing for "coincidences." The resulting product identifies the candidate step edges; isolated "shadow" and "texture" edges are rejected. Not rejected will be approximately 25% of the pixels, because 50% of the pixels in each of the two convolved images will be set to "1" anyway, at least in the case where the filtered images are independent. To reduce these false acceptances, additional independent masks might be used. There are more powerful techniques however, which are presented in the next sections.[1]

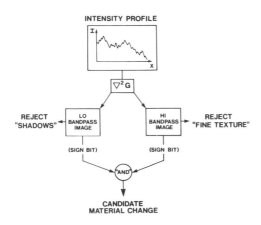

Figure 4 Schematic Flow Diagram of first stages of CARTOON algorithm.

3.1 Utility of "positive" and "negative" masks

One of the striking properties of all biological vision systems is that the early neural processing is performed by two complementary mask types (Hartline, 1938; Kuffler, 1953). The profile of one is simply the inverse of the other. Thus, the mask profile depicted in Figure 2 is designated as a *"POSitive"* mask, its complement, the *"NEGative"* mask will simply have the inverted stalactite profile. Of course, for neural systems whose digital signals must of necessity be positive numbers, it is obvious that both mask types are needed to represent the complete waveform of the convolution. However, there is a second, deeper reason for positive

and negative masks: their complementarity provides a modicum of additional (phase) information about the intensity profile that reduces the false alarm rate by allowing texture within shading to be rejected or "spikes" to be identified if so

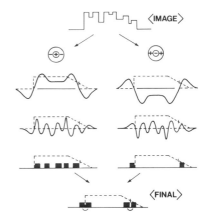

Figure 5 The hypothetical image intensity profile shown at the top center is crudely depicted in the subsequent figures as the dotted line. For appropriately tuned large masks the output of the convolution to this image profile will be either all positive (second row, left) or all negative (second row, right). The small mask convolutions, on the other hand, will have both positive and negative values because of the "texture." "ANDING" the outputs of the sign bits of the two masks will thus yield different patterns of coincidence (third row). By testing for neighboring coincidences in the *POSITIVE* and *NEGATIVE* CARTOON outputs, a truer separation of step edges is obtained (fourth row).

---

[1]Interestingly, our initial motivation for using the sign bits of the convolution was to preserve the locations of T-junctions, which are annihilated by noise if only zero-crossings are encoded (see Figure 2, lower right).

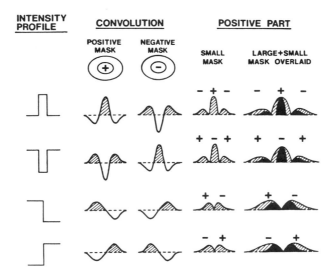

INTENSITY PROFILE | CONVOLUTION | POSITIVE PART

Figure 6 *"POSitive"* and *"NEGative"* masks provide some information about the phase of the Fourier components of an intensity profile. A negative "spike" or "step" can be discriminated from its positive inverse by the complemented position of the sign bits for each mask as shown in columns two and three. The "spike" and "step" waveforms can also be discriminated, in turn, by the union of the outputs of the POSitive (+) and NEGative (−) masks (column four). The effect of mask size on the step-spike discrimination is shown in the final column, which shows the result of "anding" the large and small mask outputs. Note that the combined (+) and (−) mask outputs are not immediately adjacent for spikes, whereas they abut for step edges.

desired. This use of phase coincidence is similar to that proposed by Marr & Hildreth (1980) although our scheme is quite different.

To see how a CARTOON based on both Positive and Negative masks can reduce the False Alarm rate, consider the intensity profile in Figure 5. (This profile is an idealized version of the wall-stone image profile shown on the right side of Figure 1.) If a suitable large Positive mask is passed over such a textured plateau, the output will be all-positive within the plateau region of the image, whereas the Negative mask output will be all-negative over the same region (Figure 5, second row).

Smaller positive and negative masks, on the other hand, will produce convolutions with both positive and negative values over the same region (Figure 5, third row). The CARTOON algorithm then takes these positive sign bits and multiplies them, to yield the pulses shown in the fourth row. Some high-frequency texture detail thus passes the "ANDING" of the two positive masks, leaving a false indication of several changes in material. On the other hand, "ANDING" the two negative masks (right column) rejects this fine texture detail, marking only the desired step edge (left) and the location of the shaded edge (right).

4

Unfortunately, because of the complementary nature of the positive and negative masks, the sign bits associated with step edges will lie on opposite sides of the zero-crossing as shown in Figure 5, row four (or Figure 6, bottom two rows). This seeming disadvantage is actually the additional phase information we seek, however. Since any true step edge (or material change) must produce adjacent sign bits for both mask types, this phase relation identifies the true step edge profile. Thus, the final stage of the CARTOON simply checks for *pairs* of adjacent sign bits obtained from using both *POSitive* and *NEGative* masks (Figure 5, last row). Our False Alarm rate has thus been significantly reduced for a textured shadow. [Either texture or color or both could be utilized to further eliminate this kind of false target if so desired—see Rubin & Richards (1982) for a suitable operator.]

The second type of false target is an intensity spike. The fourth column of Figure 6 shows the relation between the positive sign bits of the opposite sign masks. Clearly both the spike and the step edge produce adjacent sign bits from the two complementary masks. However, if the mask size is increased, each sign bit profile will be magnified along the horizontal axis as shown by comparing the crosshatched areas of the profiles shown in the two right-most columns of Figure 6. For the spike, this scaling will cause the locations where the two flanking sign bits abut the central mode to move outward as the mask size increases. This displacement of the abutting position will cause a gap between the resultant "positive" sign bits obtained after "ANDING" masks of two different sizes as shown by the filled portion of the cross-hatching. For the step edge, however, the position where

the sign bits abut will remain fixed at the two scales, and this location is preserved after the "ANDING" operation. The final coincidence check illustrated in the bottom row of Figure 5 will thus preserve the step edge but reject the "spike".

To summarize, the complete CARTOON uses four mask types—a coarse and a fine plus the positive and negative profiles for each. A "positive" cartoon is then created by "ANDING" the outputs of the two positive masks. Similarly, a "negative" cartoon is produced from the two negative masks. The sign bits of the positive and negative cartoons are then circularly smeared at each point by half of the fine mask width, and then multiplied using the logical "AND". The smearing allows the sign bits which are adjacent in both the positive and negative images to be retained. Texture detail and clutter will be rejected as illustrated in Figure 5. (A slightly greater rejection rate is possible if the "smearing" operation is applied only to an oriented segment and not to isolated points, but this requires more computation.) The result is the final CARTOON that delivers the location of true step edges (or material changes) with high reliability. Figure 7 shows the results of these operations on the image "Winnie".

4.0 Noise Reduction

Both biological and artificial vision systems suffer from two types of noise. One noise source is at the receptor level, and is due to quantum fluctuations in the input, or simply, to differences in the transfer functions between receptors. Because these noise sources are associated primarily with the transduction stage of

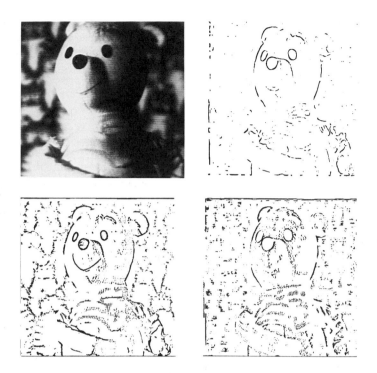

Figure 7 The lower two panels show the output of the first stages of the CARTOON algorithm using either positive (left) or negative (right) mask profiles applied to the original image of WINNIE (upper left). Note that different contours are passed by each operator. After smearing the positive and negative cartoons, the sign bits are multiplied to check for the coincidence of common contours, yielding the final cartoon shown in the upper right panel. (Mask sizes, $W = 3$, $W = 16$; 10% threshold by using an imbalanced mask.)

processing, they will be grouped together as transducer or external noise.

A second source of noise is internal to the system and arises from receptor instabilities (usually thermal) or to noisy components (i.e. neurons or computer hardware). For biological systems based on neurons, internal noise can be substantial (see Figure 10). However, if such noise is common to two channels, then it can be eliminated by subtracting the outputs of the two channels, thereby eliminating the common noise component. The fact that

biological filters for visual signals consist of two types, whereby one is merely the inverse of the other (i.e. "positive" and "negative" units), suggests that this scheme for reducing some internal noise is plausible. Referring to Figure 1, we see immediately that the positive and negative parts of the convolution of necessity will overlap nowhere. Thus, any signal common to both the positive and negative mask outputs must be internal noise, which can be eliminated by subtracting the positive outputs from each mask type

4

from the other before assigning the sign bit.

4.1 The thresholding method

For machine vision, the simplest thresholding technique is simply to set to zero all values of the filter that are less than 5% of the maximum output. This scheme is easy to implement, because the output range of the camera and the subsequent convolution is known. For biological systems, however, the voltage range of the receptors depends upon the light level, whereas the neural signal range is fixed. Thus, although 5% of the receptor output is a trivial analog signal at low light levels, when the incident intensity is raised 1000 fold or more, this small percent of the higher output would greatly exceed the input range for neural signals. In order that the thresholding be independent of the actual signal input, a possible scheme would be to bias the weights of the center and surround components of the filter such that a steady signal over the entire field actually caused a 5% inhibition. (Thus, the smaller Gaussian component would have only 95% of the volume of a larger Gaussian counterpart.) For our implementation, we mimicked this neural scheme because it has the further advantage of automatically producing a 5 to 10% threshold without the need to normalize for the intensity range.

5.0 Trying out "CARTOON"

5.1 "Winnie"

The result of applying the full CARTOON algorithm to the image "WINNIE" has already been shown in Figure 7. Note the significant noise reduction that follows the logical combination of the positive and negative cartoons.

5.2 Market

One of the most difficult images in our library posed to the CARTOON is the market scene shown in the upper left quadrant of Figure 8. The final cartoon (upper right) leaves only a complex splattering of sparse contours that, unlike the face of "WINNIE", are largely uninterpretable. Nevertheless, certain distinctive features of the original image are clearly highlighted in the cartoon, namely the melon in the lower center, the oblique edge of the crates, and the panels at the upper right. These seem to be the features that first attract the eye when the scene is first inspected.

The lower two panels show the earlier stage positive (left) and negative (right) cartoons. Note that the texture detail preserved in one image is often absent in its complement. (Compare the melons and the texture on the wall in both panels, or the lettering on the boxes.) In some cases, therefore, it may be advantageous to stop the cartoon at either the positive or negative stage—but which and how to determine when? Certainly scale factors play a significant role here, for if only the region of the melons, or only the shopper were inspected at increased resolution, the caricature would be clearer. Therefore CARTOON suffers from scale dependence and lack of spectral or textural information. However, it is a biologically motivated procedure that is generally quite successful at noting the

Figure 8 The cartoon of a market scene is shown in the upper right quadrant. The lower two panels are the positive (left) and negative (right) cartoons. Mask widths are 3 and 16 with a 10% imbalance. (Reprinted through the courtesy of American Airlines and George Olson.)

significant material changes present in the image at the scale of the masks used.

6.0 Relation to Neurophysiology

To see the biological relevance of CARTOON more clearly, we can compare its known behavior with that of neurons. Since the work of Hartline (1938), Kuffler (1953) and Hubel & Wiesel (1962), it has been known that biological vision systems compress image information presented on their retinae by first noting the location of in-

tensity changes, and then grouping these locations into oriented segments. The first stage of processing occurs in the retina itself using circular masks (or units) of the type shown in Figure 2. A subsequent (cortical) stage then combines the outputs of several such neural units aligned along various common orientations, presumably to make explicit information about the contours of the image. At this cortical level of processing, the neural response will be a rather abstracted version of the original image, as shown in Figure 10,

4

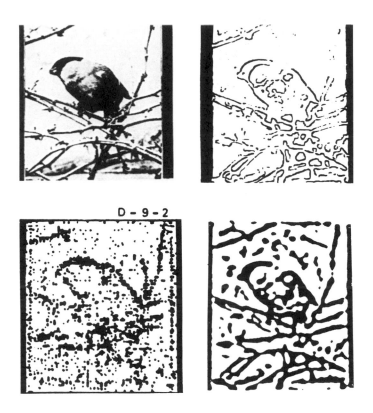

D - 9 - 2

Figure 9 Bullfinch on Twigs Original image, upper left. The positive (smeared) cartoon is shown at the lower right, to be compared with the cortical cell's response depicted at the lower left. The upper right panel is the final cartoon.

lower left. [This figure shows a plot obtained by Creutzfeld & Nothdurft (1978) of the activity of four cortical cells to various portions of the Bullfinch image shown in the upper left panel.]

For comparison, the negative (smeared) cartoon is shown at the lower right, while the upper right panel is the final cartoon. The cortical response and the cartoon images seem quite similar.

Presumably other models might be invoked to simulate such cortical data more directly than the CARTOON algorithm, which requires several intermediate steps. For example, the first stage of

the CARTOON is the filtering of the image with bandpass masks of at least two different scales. How does the output of these masks then compare with neuronal units at a comparable stage of processing?

Fortunately, Creutzfeldt & Nothdurft (1978) also obtained responses to the image Bullfinch, at an earlier way-station, the lateral geniculate, the neuronal properties of which resemble the circularly symmetric masks used in the CARTOON. Figure 10 makes the comparison between the behavior of these neural "masks" (left) and the output of the cartoon filters (right). Once again, the initial resemblance be-

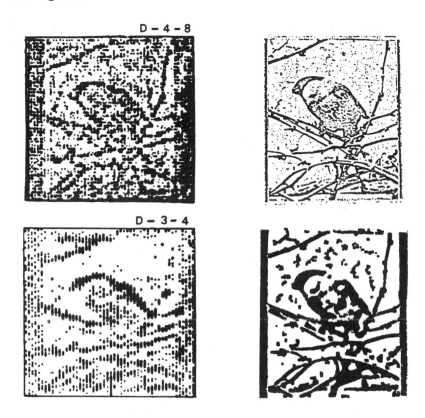

Figure 10 The left panels are geniculate cell responses obtained from the Bullfinch Image. The right panels are the mask outputs that generated the CARTOON of Figure 9. Scale effects are illustrated by comparing the two rows. TOP: Positive mask (or cell), $W = 3$. BOTTOM: Positive mask (or cell), $W = 16$.

tween the biological and artificial vision systems responses is striking.

For all the panels shown in Figure 10, there is considerable noise and clutter which does not appear in the original image. Yet by the time these images have been brought together in the cortex, the debris and clutter has been eliminated (Figure 9). The CARTOON algorithm accomplishes this noise reduction without any arbitrary thresholding, but simply by corroboration of data points at the various locations in the filtered image. It is tempting to speculate that the neural processing proceeds along similar lines, probably adding the additional constraint that any near-coincidence of mask outputs must satisfy a smooth contour condition that would require orientation encoding (Marr & Hildreth, 1980). If so, then the orientation constraint should be imposed only by the higher-frequency masks. The cortical organization recently reported by Hubel & Livingstone (1981) is attractively compatible with such a modified CARTOON algorithm.

7.0 Beyond the "CARTOON"

The CARTOON algorithm is simply a procedure for making strong assertions about the most probable locations of points on occluding contours, where one material changes to another. It does not make these contours explicit, but is only a precursor to actually identifying these contours. Marr (1976, 1982) makes this distinction quite clear when examining how zero crossing positions can be joined to form zero crossing segments—the precursors of the contour representation. Similar strategies must be invoked to take the CARTOON into a representation of occluding edges (or material changes).

Once these contour segments have been made explicit, then there is the further task of linking these isolated contours. One important lesson demonstrated by the CARTOON algorithm is that, although occluding contours of necessity must be closed, they will rarely appear closed in a filtered image. Certainly color, texture, and grouping strategies based upon the 3D properties of objects and surfaces are needed to determine which image contours properly belong together. These are challenging issues beyond early vision.

Acknowledgment. This report describes research done at the Department of Psychology and the Artificial Intelligence Laboratory of the Massachusetts Institute of Technology. Support for this work is provided in part by the Advanced Research Projects Agency of the Department of Defense under Office of Naval Research contract N00010-80-C-0505 and in part by NSF and AFOSR under a combined grant for studies in Natural Computation, grant 79-23110-MCS. The helpful comments of many members of the Vision Group, especially Ellen Hildreth, were greatly appreciated. A portion of this work was begun with Elmar Noeth in the summer of 1980, particularly the effects of imbalanced masks.

References

Attneave, F. (1954) Informational aspects of visual perception, *Psychol. Rev.* 61:183 – 193.

Barlow, H.B. (1961) Three points about lateral inhibition. In W.A. Rosenblith (ed.), *Sensory Communication*, Cambridge, Mass.: MIT Press, 217 – 234; 782 – 786.

Creutzfeldt, O.D. & Nothdurft, H.C. (1978) Representation of complex visual stimuli in the brain, *Natur wis sen schaf ten*, 65:307 – 318.

Curtis, S.R. & Oppenheim, A.V. (1987) Reconstruction of multi-dimensional signals from zero crossings. *J. Opt. Soc. Am. A*, 4:221 – 231.

Enroth-Cugell, C. & Robson, J.G. (1966) The contrast sensitivity of retinal ganglion cells in the cat, *J. Physiol.*, 187:517 – 552.

Hartline, H.K. (1938) The response characteristics of single optic nerve fibers of the vertebrate eye to illumination of the retina, *Amer. J. Physiol.*, 121:400 – 415.

Hubel, D.H. & Wiesel, T.N. (1962) Receptive fields, binocular interaction and functional architecture in the cat's visual cortex, *J. Physiol. Lond.*, 160:106 – 154.

Hubel, D.H. & Livingstone, M.S. (1981) Regions of poor orientation tuning coincide with patches of cytochrome oxidase staining in monkey striate cortex, *Soc. of Neurosci. Abstr.*, 7:357.

Jernigan, M.E. & Wardell, R.W. (1981) Does the eye contain optimal edge detection mechanisms? *IEEE Trans. Systems, Main & Cyber.*, SMC-11:441–444.

Kuffler, S.W. (1953) Discharge patterns and functional organization of mammalian retina, *J. Neurophysiol.*, 16:37–68.

Marr, D. (1976) Early processing of visual information, *Phil. Trans. R. Soc. Lond. B.*, 275:483–524.

Marr, D. (1982) *Vision: A Computational Investigation into the Human Representation and Processing of Visual Information*, San Francisco: Freeman.

Marr, D. & Hildreth, E. (1980) A theory of edge detection. *Proc. R. Soc. Lond.*, 207:187–217.

Marr, D. & Nishihara, H.K. (1978) Visual information processing: Artificial intelligence and the sensorium of light, *Tech. Rev.*, 81:1–23.

Marr, D. & Poggio, T. (1979) A computational theory of human stereo vision, *Proc. Roy. Soc. Lond. B.*, 204:301–328.

Marr, D., Poggio, T. & Ullman, S. (1979) Bandpass channels, zero crossings, and early visual information processing, *J. Opt. Soc. Am.*, 69:914–916.

Nishihara, H.K. (1980) Reconstruction of DOG filtered images from gradients at zero-crossings. In (ed.) P.H. Winston, *Proceedings of an Image Understanding workshop.*

Pratt, W. (1978) *Digital Image Processing*, New York: J. Wiley.

Richter, J. & Ullman, S. (1982) A model for the temporal organization of X and Y-type ganglion cells in the primate retina, *Biol. Cybern.*, 43:127–145.

Rodieck, R.W. (1965) Quantitative analysis of cat retinal ganglion cell response to visual stimuli, *Vis. Res.*, 5:583–601.

Rosenfeld, A. & Kak, A. (1976) *Digital Picture Processing.* New York: Academic Press.

Rotem, D. & Zeevi, Y.Y. (1986) Image reconstruction from zero-crossings. *IEEE Trans. Acoust. Speech Signal Process*, ASSP-34:1269–1277.

Rubin, J.M. & Richards, W.A. (1982) Color vision and image intensities: When are changes material? *Biol. Cyber.*, 45:215–226; also MIT A.I. Lab. Memo 631.

Sakitt, B. & Barlow, H.B. (1982) A model for the economical encoding of the visual image in the cerebral cortex, *Biol. Cybern.*, 43:97–108.

Schade, O.H. (1956) Optical and photoelectric analog of the eye, *J. Opt. Soc. Am.*, 46:721–739.

Shanmugan, K.S., Dickey, F.M. & Green, J.A. (1979) An optimal frequency domain filter for edge detections in digital pictures, *IEEE Trans. on Pattern Analysis and Machine Intelligence*, PAMI-1:37–49.

Wilson, H.R. & Bergen, J.R. (1979) A four mechanism model for spatial vision, *Vis. Res.*, 19:19–32.

Adapted from MIT A.I. Lab. Memo 668 (1982).

Illusory Contours and Cortical Neuron Responses

R. von der Heydt
E. Peterhans
G. Baumgartner

Department of Neurology
University Hospital Zurich
8091 Zurich, Switzerland

A basic task in visual perception is to segregate the visual input into objects. Given a flat retinal image of a three-dimensional world, this is not trivial. An object boundary may be defined by a physical discontinuity in the image due to a difference in color or luminance between object and background, although any change in illumination, or a movement of the object or the observer, can change these conditions. Nevertheless, the contours of objects appear to be invariant. Contours may also be seen in the absence of discontinuity in the stimulus (Schumann, 1900) (for example, Figure 1, A, B, and D). These illusions[1] show that perceived contours are the result of an image analysis performed in the brain. The nature of this process is not known, and different theories have been proposed (Gregory, 1972; Kanizsa, 1979). We have examined the activity of cells in the visual cortex of monkeys during presentation of conventional stimuli producing contours by luminance gradients and of stimuli producing illusory contours. In area 18 we found responses that paralleled some of the perceptual phenomena. These responses could not be easily predicted from the known receptive-field properties of cells in the visual cortex.

Rhesus monkeys *(Macaca mulatta)* were trained to perform a visual fixation task. To receive a reward they had to pull a lever when a fixation target appeared and to release it upon detecting a 90° turn of the target, which occurred after an unpredictable delay. The target consisted of two parallel short lines whose orientation could be resolved only in foveal vision. It appeared in the center of a display at a viewing distance of 40 cm; the other stimuli were also presented on that display. For recording, the animal's head was fixed by means of a bolt implanted in the skull. Otherwise the animal was free to take a comfortable position in a boxlike primate chair. Single units were recorded with microelectrodes inserted through the intact dura throughout an experimental session.

Figures 2 and 3 shows three examples of neurons recorded in area 18. Neuron 1 responded to the lower right edge of a light bar (Figure 2A). Its responses indicated precisely where, and in which orientation, a light-dark boundary appeared in the

---

[1] Illusory contours are known also as "Scheinkanten", as "quasi perceptive", "anomalous", "subjective", and "cognitive" contours, or "contours without gradients". See Kanizsa (1979) for a discussion of the terminology.

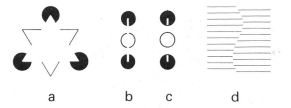

Figure 1 Illusory contours. Such contours are perceived in A, B, and D, at sites where the stimulus is homogeneous. Small alterations in the stimulus can have dramatic effects on the appearance of these contours (C).[3]

visual field: the response field measured 0.9° by 0.4° visual angle and was located 1.8° below the fixation point; only orientations between 46° and 101° produced a response.[2] We then tested a stimulus in which a strip of 1.3°, covering the cell's response field, was blanked out, thus reducing the bar to a pair of notches (Figure 2B). If one looks at such a stimulus with the notches moving back and forth together, one has the illusion of a light bar moving in front of two dark bars. The cell responded to this stimulus as it had to the edge of the bar, though less strongly. The response occurred at the same position, and the optimal orientation also remained the same.

In general, illusory contours disappear when only part of the inducing configuration is viewed. When, for example, one of the disk sectors in Figure 1A is occluded, not only the corner of the tri-angle disappears, but also the adjacent flanks. The Gestalt psychologists stated that the whole is greater than the sum of its parts. We found a similar effect in the neuronal responses. Neither half of the stimulus of Figure 2B excited the unit (Figure 2, C and D; E shows the spontaneous activity), whereas both together did (Figure 2B). The exact width of the gap between the two halves was not critical for this effect. With 2° instead of 1.3°, the cell still responded, and 4.1, 0.8, and 0.7 spikes per cycle were obtained for the whole figure, the upper and lower halves, respectively. We have tested the influence of the gap width in several other cells; all gave gradually weaker responses when the gap was increased. The largest gap at which a response was still obtained was 4.4° in a cell whose center of response field was located 3° from the fixation point. It could be argued that these

---

[2]The range of orientations was obtained from the orientation tuning curve by determining the points where the regression lines fitted to the flanks of the curve crossed the level of spontaneous activity. The length of response field, L, was similarly determined from a response curve obtained by scanning the field with the appropriate edge of a bar, taking as L the distance between the bars in the two limiting positions. The correctness of this determination was confirmed by the fact that the stimuli in Figure 2, C and D, singly did not produce a response; because of the choice of the gap width (1.3°) they were outside the response field (L= 0.9°).

[3]Part A and D are reproduced from Figures 4.2 and 12.12 in Kanizsa (1979); parts B and C are Figures 1, C and D, in Smith & Over (1976).

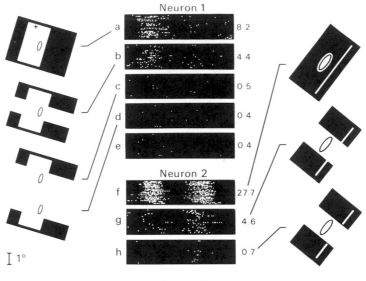

Figure 2 Responses of neurons in area 18 of the monkey visual cortex to edges, bars, and stimuli producing illusory contours. The stimuli (insets) were moved back and forth across the receptive fields (neuron 1, 1° at 1 Hz; neurons 2 and 3, 2° at 1 Hz). Each was presented 24 times; blocks of eight repetitions were alternated in pseudorandom order. For neurons 1 and 2, the response fields (the regions in the visual field where the neurons could be activated by a bar or edge) are represented by ellipses, and the fixation point is marked by crosses in A and F; the responses are represented by rows of dots; mean numbers of spikes per stimulus cycle are indicated on the right. Neuron 1, which responded to the lower right edge of the light bar (A), was activated also when only the illusory contour passed over its response field (B). Either half of the stimulus failed to evoke a response (C and D); (E) spontaneous activity. Neuron 2 responded to a narrow bar (F) and, less strongly, to the illusory bar stimulus (G). When the ends of the "bar" were intersected by thin ones, however, the response was nearly abolished (H). [To simplify the figure, stimuli have been reproduced in reversed contrast; the parts shown in black were actually lighter than the background (about 2.5 versus 1 foot lambert). To avoid confusion, the text has been made consistent with the figure.]

responses were due to stray light falling into the response field and moving along with the notches and that the light coming from only half the figure might just not reach the cell's threshold. However, we have observed the same nonadditivity in the stimulus-response relationship at a sixfold stimulus intensity. Again, neither half of the stimulus alone produced a response. This result argues against a simple threshold explanation.

Small changes in configuration can have dramatic effects on the appearance of illusory contours. An example is the closing lines in Figure 1C. A similar effect could be observed in the neuronal responses, as demonstrated by neuron 2. It responded well to a narrow bar (Figure 2F) and also gave a regular response to the illusory bar stimulus bridging a gap of 2° (Figure 2G). When the notches were closed by line segments 5 minutes of arc wide, the response was almost abolished (Figure 2H). Nearly all cells that responded to the illusory bar stimulus showed this reduction; in some cells, lines as narrow as 2 minutes of arc had an effect. Again, the gap width was not critical; as long as the cell responded, closure reduced the response.

The responses so far seem to indicate the ability of the cortex to extrapolate lines to connect parts of the stimulus which might belong to the same object. The abutting gratings of Figure 1D show an illusory contour which is not an extrapolation of the stimulus since it runs more-or-less perpendicular to the inducing lines. We have tested a contour that was straight and perpendicular to the lines. It could be moved back and forth along the lines, leaving the stimulus margin stationary. Responses were recorded for various orientations. Neuron 3, for example, responded to the illusory-contour stimulus better than to any of the conventional stimuli (Figure 3A). Furthermore, the peak responses were obtained at virtually

the same orientation for contour and bar. The curve of the illusory contour bends upward at both ends, indicating a second peak 90° from the optimum. This can be interpreted as a response to the inducing lines. Other cells showed only the peak related to the contour and thus were not activated by the gratings at all. When the cells also responded to the illusory bar stimulus, the optimal orientations were similar for both types of illusory contour.

To see the contour, a minimum number of lines are required; no contour is visible at the end of just one line, but it is usually perceived with four or more line ends. There was a similar threshold for the neuronal response (Figure 3B). The density of lines, on the other hand, was not critical. Keeping the overall size of the stimulus constant, the responses were equal for line spacings of 12, 24, and 48 minutes of arc, and slightly less for 72 minutes of arc, but still stronger than the response to the bar.

There was a marked difference between striate and prestriate cortex.[4] Of 70 cells tested in area 17, none showed responses related to the contour between abutting gratings,[5] whereas about one-third (21 of 68) of the cells in area 18 did. Also, the results obtained with the other type of illusory contour (Figure 2, B and G) were negative in area 17 (11 cells) but positive in 13 of 38 cells in area 18. (With this type of stimulus, the demonstration of the effect of closure (Figure 2, G and H) was taken as a criterion.)

---

[4]Most of the cells assigned to area 18 were recorded in the posterior bank of the lunate sulcus. The cortical area was judged also from physiological criteria such as the presence of the typical activity of layer IVc in area 17 (Poggio et al., 1977) and the topography of receptive fields; it has been confirmed histologically for part of the data. A few cells recorded near the 17-18 border were not counted.

[5]The orientation tuning curves obtained with the illusory contour stimulus in area 17 typically showed a single peak corresponding to the orientation of the grating lines.

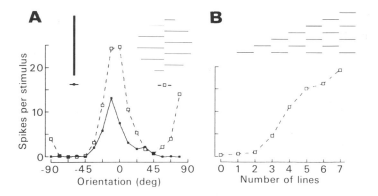

Figure 3 (A) Response of another neuron in area 18. An edge created by two abutting gratings (see inset), elicited a strong response. A. The orientation tuning curves show corresponding peaks for bar and illusory contours. B. When the lines inducing the contour were reduced in number to less than three, the response disappeared; compare the lines above the curve (the actual stimuli were centered over the response field). The lines were 1 minute of arc wide and spaced 48 minutes apart. Each symbol represents the mean of 8 (A) or 16 (B) responses.

We were not able to relate responsiveness to illusory contour stimuli to the conventional classification of cells into simple or complex, end-stopped (hypercomplex) or not end-stopped (Hubel & Wiesel, 1968). With bars and edges, monotonic length-summation curves were usually obtained, but end-inhibition was also observed.

Responses of cells in area 18 that required appropriately positioned and oriented luminance gradients when conventional stimuli were used could often be evoked also by the corresponding illusory contour stimuli. In this area, one would be able to infer location and orientation of the various types of contours from the responses of single cells. In area 17, this would be possible only for edge or line type contours produced by luminance or color differences. Responses in area 18 showed several other parallels to perception, such as the relation between the responses to

a figure and to its parts and the dramatic effect of small elements added to the figure.

Gregory (1972) formulated an antithesis between physiological and cognitive explanations of illusory contour effects. According to his cognitive approach, the contours are perceived because an illusory object is "postulated" as a perceptual hypothesis to account for the sensory data. The explanation suggested by the present experiment is physiological, but it differs from the one stated in Gregory's antithesis (and criticized by him) that "feature detector cells of the striate cortex are activated by the disk sectors [of the Kanizsa triangle]... to give the appearance of continuous lines, though only their ends are given by stimulation" (Gregory, 1972, p. 51). Our results do not support this idea. With stimulus configurations like those of B or G in Figure 2, cells in area 17 did not respond, some of them not even when the gap was narrowed so that the ends of the bar entered the response field. The responses in area 18 on the other hand cannot be interpreted simply as suboptimal excitation due to partial stimulation of the response field, since they can be evoked by stimuli well outside that field and are affected by small changes in configuration that are negligible in terms of luminous flux. Also the responses to stimuli with lines perpendicular to the cell's preferred orientation reveal an unexpected new receptive field property. The way widely separated picture elements contribute to a response resembles the function of logical gates. The important elements in our stimuli seem to be corners on opposite sides of the response field (Figure 2, B and G) and line ends arranged in a row (Figure 3, A and B). Line ends and corners are in fact emphasized in certain signals of area 17 (Hubel & Wiesel, 1968), and a number of such signals might converge on neurons of area 18. Corners and line ends play a role in the formation of contours because these picture elements are frequently produced by interposition of objects, that is, when an object partially occludes others. Thus, several such elements aligned in a row are likely to mark an object boundary.

References

Gregory, R.L. (1972) Cognitive contours. *Nature (London)*, 238:51–52.

Hubel, D.H. & Wiesel, T.N. (1968) Receptive fields and functional architecture of monkey striate cortex. *J. Physiol. (London)*, 195:215–243.

Kanizsa, G. (1979) *Organization in Vision. Essays on Gestalt Perception.* New York: Praeger.

Poggio, G.F., Doty, R.W. Jr. & Talbot, W.H. (1977) Foveal striate cortex of behaving monkey: single-neuron responses to square-wave gratings during fixation of gaze. *J. Neurophysiol.*, 40:1369–1391.

Schumann, F. (1900) Beiträge zur Analyse der Gesichtswahrnehmungen. *Z. Psychol.*, 23:1–32.

Smith, A.T. & Over, R. (1976) Color-selective tilt aftereffects with subjective contours. *Percept. Psychophys.*, 20:305–308.

Reprinted from *Science*, 224:1260–1262 (1984).

Representing Smooth Plane Curves for Recognition: Implications for Figure-Ground Reversal

D.D. Hoffman*
W.A. Richards

Massachusetts Institute of Technology

1.0 Introduction

A vision system sometimes must compute its initial descriptions of a shape without benefit of context. Yet these descriptions should highly constrain the set of possible matches with memory if they are to be useful for recognition. For example, though one cannot reasonably predict the contents of Figure 1 prior to seeing it, the shapes are readily recognized. This simple demonstration implies the existence of context-independent rules that provide shape descriptions which can be used to initiate the recognition process. Such rules for smooth plane curves are the subject here.

To be useful for triggering the recognition process the initial rules should be computable on images, should yield descriptions which are invariant under translations, rotations[1] and uniform scaling and should provide a first index into a table of shapes in memory. Although a plane curve $\gamma(s) = [x(s), y(s)]$ can be specified in many different ways, a description based

upon its curvature $\kappa(s)$ is attractive. Such a representation satisfies two of the invariance conditions, namely translation and rotation independence (Do Carmo, 1976). For any rotation θ and translation (u, v), $\gamma(s)$ is uniquely given by

$$\gamma(s) = \left[\int \cos\theta(s)ds + u, \right.$$
$$\left. \int \sin\phi(s)ds + v \right],$$

where

$$\phi(s) = \int \kappa(s)ds + \theta$$

However, because curvature is scale dependent, a means for representing $\kappa(s)$ into units which can be described qualitatively. A reasonable approach is to exploit singular points of orders 1 and 0, i.e. maxima, minima and zeros of curvature (Attneave, 1954; Duda & Hart, 1973), since the property of being a singular point is invariant under rotations, translations and uniform scaling.

---

[1] More precisely, the early descriptions should decouple the position, rotation and overall scaling of a shape from the shape itself. This allows the position, rotation, scaling and shape to be made explicit separately, and allows their effects on the recognition process to be disentangled. Thus the goal of rotational invariance for shape descriptions, for example, in no way implies that the rotation of a shape cannot effect its interpretation (Rock, 1974).

Figure 1 Some shapes recognizable without benefit of context.

2.0 Maxima, Minima and Curve "Orientation"

Which points are maxima of curvature depends on the orientation of the curve. Though in general curvature is an unsigned quantity, in the case of plane curves it is possible to assign a sign to the curvature consistently once one of the two possible orientations for the curve is chosen. The orientation is usually specified in figures by an arrow on the curve pointing in the direction in which the curve is to be traversed. By a change in orientation of a plane curve the sign of the curvature changes everywhere along the curve. In particular maxima become minima and vice versa. The convention adopted here is that figure is to the left and ground to the right as the curve is traversed in an orientation. Thus knowing which side is figure determines the choice of orientation on a curve or, conversely, choosing an orientation determines which side is figure by convention. Minima are then typically associated with concavities of the figure, maxima with convexities (see Figure 2). It is possible however for minima to have positive curvature, as in the case of convex closed curves, or maxima to have negative

curvature, as when the orientation of the convex closed curve is reversed.

3.0 Segmentation

Maxima, minima and zeros of curvature are all candidate points for partitioning a curve into units in a manner invariant under rotations, translations and uniform scaling. To choose among them we require that the units should reflect natural parts of shapes (Marr, 1977, 1982). Fortunately, when 3D parts are joined to create complex objects concavities will generally be created in the silhouette. Segmentation of the image at concavities therefore immediately encodes in a straightforward manner an important property of the natural world that is not captured by maximas or zeroes of curvature. This is our *general position* argument for segmentation at minima of curvature.[2]

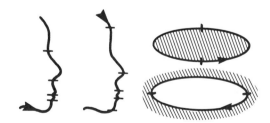

Figure 2 Minima of curvature (indicated by slashes). Extrema of negative curvaure corresponds to part boundaries. Arrows indicate curve orientation.

---

[2]When general position is violated special rules may be needed to partition and describe the resulting image contour (Marr, 1977). This will not be considered here.

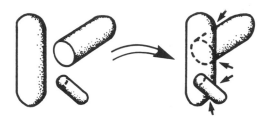

Figure 3 Joining parts generally produces concavities in the resulting silhouette.

4.0 Description of Parts: Contour Codons

Minima of curvature are used to break a curve into segments, whereas maxima and zeros are used to describe the shape of each segment. There are five basic types of segments, which we call "contour codons". Furthermore, only certain codon joins (pairwise connections) are allowable.

First, all curve segments contain zero, one or two points of zero curvature. This assumes that when $\kappa(s) = 0$, $\kappa'(s) \neq 0$. Segments with no zeros are called type 0 codons, those with two zeros are called type 2 codons. If a segment has exactly one zero, the zero may be encountered either before (type 1^-) or after (type 1^+) the maximum point of the segment when traversing the curve in the chosen orientation.

The type 0 codons may be further subdivided into 0^+, 0^- and (∞) to yield six basic codon types. Consider Figure 2 once again. Note that as the ellipse is traversed in different directions, the extrema of curvature change signs as expected. In the lower ellipse, the extrema have negative curvature, and hence the boundary is 0^-, whereas in the upper ellipse the ex-

trema are positive of type 0^+. Note that the 0^- codon constitutes a part boundary, whereas the type 0^+ codon must appear only as a shape descriptor. Finally, the type ∞ codon simply is the degenerate case of a straight line that has an infinity of zeros.

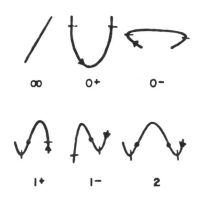

Figure 4 Contour codons (as defined in section 4). Zeros of curvature are indicated by dots on the curves, minima by slashes. The straight line (∞) is a degenerate case included for completeness, although it is not treated in the text.

If desired, codons can be further described by noting the positions of the maximum and any zeros of curvature within the segment, normalized by the total arc length of the segment. This should be done qualitatively at first and then more quantitatively as is necessary. For example, label the first minimum encountered in traversing a segment the "tail" of the segment, and the other minimum label the "head". Then the position of the maximum can be given crudely as much closer to the head, much closer to the tail, or approximately in the middle. This gives the "skew" of the curve. Zeros can similarly be described as closer to the maximum point, closer to the head/tail, or approximately in the middle between the maximum and the head or tail.

Figure 5 Curve segments with identical singularities but different shapes.

As shown in Figure 5, two segments can have identically placed maxima and zeros, identical curvatures at the maxima and minima, and yet appear quite different. The difference is the behavior of the curvature between the singular points. This behavior can be described in an appropriately invariant manner by the integral of curvature between each of the singular points:

$$\int_a^b \kappa(s)ds = \theta(b) - \theta(a),$$

where $\theta(s)$ is the angle of the tangent at $\gamma(s)$ given by $\theta(s) = \tan^{-1}(y'(s)/x'(s))$. A representation which notes the integral of curvature between the singular points will give different descriptions for curves A and B in Figure 5.

There are restrictions on how codons may be joined at minima. Define a *codon join* by the operation aob, $a, b \in [0^-, 0^+, 1^-, 1^+, 2]$ indicating that the head of a is smoothly connected to the tail of b. Note that in general $aob \neq boa$ and hence the codon sequence is critical. Not all conceivable codon joins are possible (Figure 6).

The fact that not all conceivable codon joins are allowable suggests that

the codon representation may be amenable to error-correction techniques. Consider, for example, the codon string $\ldots c_{j-1}c_j$ $c_{j+1}\ldots$ If all codon joins were allowable then c_j could take any one of the five values $[0^-, 0^+, 1^+ 1^- 2]$ regardless of the values of c_{j-1} and c_{j+1}. Thus the value of c_j would be independent of its context. Using Figure 6, however, one can show that in actuality the context of a codon restricts its range of possible values to two on average. One can also show that in one-half of the contexts c_j is actually uniquely determined.

	0^-	0^+	1^-	1^+	2
0^-	$+$	$-$	$+$	$-$	$+$
0^+	$-$	$+$	$-$	$+$	$-$
1^-	$-$	$+$	$-$	$+$	$-$
1^+	$+$	$-$	$+$	$-$	$+$
2	$+$	$-$	$+$	$-$	$+$

Figure 6 Table of allowable codon joins. Rows and columns are labeled by codon type, with the intended codon join sequence at each table entry being (row type, column type). Legal joins are indicated by $+$, others by a $-$.

5.0 Relation to Perception

The representation of plane curves for recognition proposed here can explain the

well known observation that a curve can
look very different depending on which
side is perceived as figure and which as
ground (Attneave, 1971). (See Figure 7a).
The explanation is that a curve looks different because its representations under
the two possible orientations are completely different. Since the positions of
the minima of curvature are not invariant
under a change in orientation (direction of
traversal) of a curve, the parts of a curve
as specified in its representation can be
quite different for the two orientations (see
Figure 7b). If one chose to define parts by
zeros of curvature (Hollerbach, 1975), or
by minima *and* maxima (Attneave, 1954;
Brady, 1982; Duda & Hart, 1973), the
parts would not differ under a change in
orientation of a curve.

face-goblet illusion (Rubin, 1958). If the
locations of minima are indicated by occlusions, then the perception of the curve
is biased toward one of its two orientations
and either the face or goblet impression
becomes more apparent (Figure 8). However, when this figure is viewed at a
distance so the added lines are not visible, then the classical instability returns.
Neither highlighting the zeros nor highlighting the maxima has comparable effect
because they do not correspond to natural
points for segmentation.

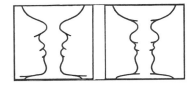

Figure 8 Rubin's face-goblet illusion
segmented at minima to reduce the
instability.

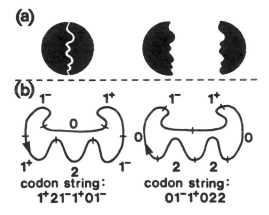

Figure 7 (a) Figure-ground reversal
makes bounding curve appear different.
(b) Different codon string descriptions
are assigned to the same curve in its
two orientations.

The perceptual significance of minima can also be demonstrated by a simple modification of Rubin's ambiguous

6.0 Lock-Key and Mirror Reversal Transforms

The codon representation is designed to
decouple the shape of a contour from
its disposition in space and its overall
size. Consequently the shape description is
invariant under rotation, translation and
uniform scaling of the contour. However,
as demonstrated in Figure 7b, the shape
of a contour is not invariant when the
direction of traversal along the contour
is reversed. It is not difficult to convince
oneself also that the shape description
is not invariant under a mirror reversal
of the contour. The question naturally
arises, are there simple rules that define

| SIGN OF CURVATURE AT | | NUMBER OF | CODON | BINARY |
START MINIMA	END MINIMA	INFLECTIONS	TYPE	CODE
−	−	0	0^-	$\phi\phi$
+	+	0	0^+	$\phi\phi$
−	+	1	1^-	1ϕ
+	−	1	1^+	$\phi1$
−	−	2	2	$1\,1$

Table 1 Mapping between Codon Types and a binary code. A "1" indicates an inflection. (One extra bit per string may be required to differentiate the 0^+ and 0^- codons when the binary representation is used.)

how the codon string of a contour is transformed when the contour undergoes a mirror reversal or a reversal in direction of traversal (change in orientation)?

In the case of a mirror reversal the rule is quite simple. The mirror transform of a codon string is obtained by reversing the direction in which the string is read (right to left rather than left to right) and reversing the sign attached to each type 1 codon. Thus the mirror transform of $< 1^+21^-1^+01^- >$ is $< 1^+01^-1^+21^- >$. This rule can also be used to find symmetries within a single contour. If, for example, one half of a codon string is found to be the mirror transform of the remainder of the string, a necessary condition for the curve to be symmetric has been found. Note that this applies to skew symmetry as long as zeros of curvature are not made to appear or disappear by the skew.

When the sense of traversal of a curve is reversed the codon string transformation rule, called the lock-key transform, is unique but apparently not simple. It is perhaps most easily specified as a map

from pairs of concatenated codons to codon singletons. The codon doublets which map to each codon singleton are $[(00, 01^+, 1^-0, 1^-1^+) \mapsto 0], [(01^-, 02) \mapsto 1^-], [(1^+0, 20) \mapsto 1^+]$ and $[(1^+1^-, 1^+2, 21^-, 22) \mapsto 2]$. This lock-key mapping can be used, for example, to transform each of the codon strings of Figure 7b into the other.

7.0 Summary

An approach to the representation of plane curves for recognition has been sketched. It is suggested that minima of curvature can be used to break a curve into parts. This approach explains why a curve can appear quite different when figure and ground are reversed. Extensions of the approach to piecewise-smooth curves and surfaces are presented in Hoffman & Richards (1984).

Acknowledgments: We thank J. Rubin, J. Schuehammer, S. True, K. Stevens and A. Bobick for comments of previous drafts.

6

Appendix

As shown in Section 4.0 and Figure 6, sequences of codons for smooth plane curves is highly constrained. If a smooth plane curve is closed, for example, there are 5^3, or 125 unconstrained sequences of five codons, but of these only 6 outlines are possible (Richards & Hoffman, 1985). Such constraints upon smooth codon joins permit a binary representation for smooth codon strings that are known not to include the ∞ codon. Five basic codon types would normally require at last three bits for a binary coding. However the redundancy in the representation allows only 13 codon pairs, or less than 2 bits per codon. Utilizing the constraint that between every minima there is at least one maxima (provided the positive minima of 0^+ are noted), we need only encode the position and number of inflections in relation to the maxima. (This was the basis for the codon definitions.) If "1" represents an inflection and "ϕ" represents no inflection, then the mapping rule is shown in Table 1. Thus, the "face" profile in Figure 2 can be represented by the binary string $111\phi\phi1111\phi$. This form of the codon representation has obvious advantages for computational efficiency and is also useful for encoding mirror-symmetry or figure-ground reversals (Hoffman & Richards, 1982).

References

Attneave, F. (1971) Multistability in perception. *Sci. Am.*, 225(6):63–71.

Attneave, F. (1954) Some informational aspects of visual perception. *Psychol. Rev.*, 61:183–193.

Brady, M. (1982) Parts description and acquisition using vision. *Proceedings of the Society of Photo-optical and Instrumentation Engineers.*

Do Carmo, M. (1976) *Differential Geometry of Curves and Surfaces.* New Jersey: Prentice-Hall.

Duda, R. & Hart, P. (1973) *Pattern classification and scene analysis.* New York: Wiley, pp. 337–341.

Hoffman, D. & Richards, W. (1982) Representing plane curves for visual recognition. MIT A.I. Lab. Memo 630.

Hoffman, D.D. & Richards, W. (1984) Parts of recognition. *Cognition*, 18:65–96.

Hollerbach, J. (1975) Hierarchical Shape Description of Objects by Selection and Modification of Prototypes. MIT A.I. Lab. Technical Report 346, pp. 47–51.

Marr, D. (1982) *Vision: A Computational Investigation into the Human Representation and Processing of Visual Information.* San Francisco: Freeman.

Marr, D. (1977) Analysis of occluding contour. *Proc. R. Soc. Lond. B*, 197:441–475.

Richards, W. & Hoffman, D. (1985) Codon constraints on closed 2D shapes. *Computer Vision, Graphics, and Image Processing*, 31:265–281.

Rock, I. (1974) The perception of disoriented figures. *Sci. Am.*, 230:78–85.

Rubin, E. (1958) Figure and ground. In D.C. Beardslee & M. Wertheimer (eds.), *Readings in Perception.* New York: D. Van Nostrand.

Reprinted and updated from *Proc. AAAI*, 1982, pp. 5–8.

*The first author is now at the Department of Computer Science, University of California, Irvine.

Encoding Contour Shape by Curvature Extrema

Whitman Richards
Benjamin Dawson
Douglas Whittington

Massachusetts Institute of Technology

1.0 Introduction

Line drawings and silhouettes testify to the power of the shape of a contour as a means for object recognition. As demonstrated by Attneave (1954) and more recently by Biederman (1985), much of this information about shape is carried by the curvature extrema—a result quantified by Resnikoff (1985). One reason why curvature extrema are critical to recognition is that they divide the outline into its parts (Hoffman & Richards, 1982), and from these parts and their relations to one another we can deduce what the object is. As discussed by Hoffman (Hoffman, 1983; Hoffman & Richards, 1984), a representation for objects based upon its parts is particularly powerful and useful because the possible configural properties of an object are decoupled from a description of the object itself. Furthermore, a parts-based representation for objects permits object identification even when the object is partly occluded, because the recognition process can still be driven using the visible parts. To find the "parts" of an outline, however, requires finding the concavities or extrema of curvature in an image curve. Here we first present a representation of shape based on extrema of curvature and then show how these extrema may be extracted from a silhouette.

2.0 The Representation

To build a part-based representation for shape recognition, we must define what we mean by a "part". Unfortunately, there is no a priori shape that encompasses all types of parts. However, there is a property of boundaries that is true of almost all parts. The insight comes when we consider what happens when two spatially separated objects are joined to create a new object, as illustrated in Figure 3 of the previous chapter, or in Figure 1 where the wings intersect the body of the aircraft. Along the contour where the two surfaces are interpenetrated to form the new object, a concave discontinuity in the tangent plane will be formed. This property of intersecting surfaces derives from the transversality principle (Guillemin & Pollack, 1974)—except for very special intersections a concave contour will always be created when two surfaces intersect. Thus, the part boundary defined by the concave contour will be preserved if the disposition of the part is altered such as when one moves a finger or leg. It is this regularity which underlies our definition of what should constitute a "part".

7

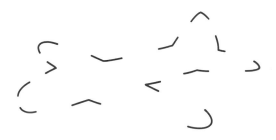

Figure 1 Curvature extrema carry significant information about shape.

Definition: A "part" is a region of a surface bounded by a contour of concave discontinuity of the tangent plane.

More generally, the above definition can be extended to smooth surfaces if the part boundary is defined in terms of extrema of (negative) curvature, of which the concave discontinuity is a special case (Bennett & Hoffman, 1987). Clearly such extrema of curvature will generally be preserved upon projection into the image. Hence the rule for partitioning the outlines of objects as seen in the 2D image follows trivially:

Partitioning Rule: To segment an image curve into its parts, divide the curve at concave cusps (or, more generally, at the extrema of negative curvature).

Thus, in Figure 2, the plane curves are divided into parts by noting the extrema of negative curvature. To find these extrema, we first specify which side of the curve should be taken as the "object". In the left-most illustration, which appears

as a face, the object is to the left of the curve. We adopt the convention that the "object" is always to the left of the direction of traversal of the plane curve. Negative curvature is then defined when the tangent direction rotates clockwise; positive curvature is when the tangent direction rotates counterclockwise as the curve is traversed. The extrema of negative curvature thus occur at points where the tangent to the curve rotates at the greatest rate in the clockwise direction. Obviously, if the curve is now traversed in the opposite direction, then the extrema of positive and negative curvature are exchanged. The parts of the "face" of Figure 2 now become transformed to the parts of a "vase"—an illusion noted as early as 1819 by Turton (1819). Our task is to show how these curvature extrema may be extracted from an image contour.

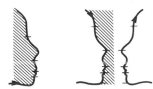

Figure 2 Partitioning plane curves into its parts. Extrema of negative curvature is indicated by slashes. Arrows indicate direction of traversal of curve. "Figure" is taken to be to the left of the direction of traversal.

3.0 Codons: Primitive Part Descriptors

As discussed in the previous chapter, there are three singularities of curvature: the extrema of positive curvature, the extrema of negative curvature, which define our part boundaries, and the zeros of curvature. There are five different relations between these curvature singularities, each of which defines a primitive part descriptor called a "codon". These five codon types are shown in Figure 3 and provide the basis for a representation that will describe the abstract shape of any smooth plane curve (Hoffman & Richards, 1982, 1984). The representation will appear as a sequence of digits, such as $21^-1^+21^-$ which describes the "face" profile of Figure 2. It is this string which we wish to compute to represent the shape of an image contour.

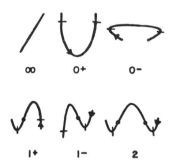

Figure 3 The primitive codon types. Zeros of curvature are indicated by dots, minima by slashes. The straight line (∞) is degenerated case included for completeness, although it is not treated in the text.

4.0 Two Obstacles: Noise and Scale

Before presenting our algorithm for computing a codon representation for an image curve, there are two ever-pervasive problems that must be addressed. One is signal noise and pixel sampling artifacts which distort the true shape of the curve, and the second is the problem of identifying the proper scale at which curvature should be computed.

4.1 Sampling noise

Any camera or retina has resolution limits in space, time, and contrast. Additional noise may also be introduced during the signal processing, especially in neural systems. Of immediate concern here is sampling and contrast noise in the image array, for subsequent digital processing introduces negligible errors. The sampling noise arises from the pixel resolution of the 512^2 array, plus the contrast limits imposed by the 8-bit gray scale. The result is that the digitized version of any curve will be a string of pixels that are linked along one of four orientations—horizontal, vertical and the 45° and 135° diagonals. From this linked list, we recover first a tangent direction and then a local curvature using a method to be described below. The method entails smoothing the digitized string, which of necessity introduces some error. This error is greater than that predicted simply from sampling theory, because the image location of the "edge" of a region or of the exact position of any contour depends upon the contrast difference across the edge. When the figure and its background have the same gray scale value, the edge is obviously displaced. For a 4-bit gray scale image, these displacements will occur for every sixteenth pixel, on the average, assuming a roughly uniform figure on a white-noise background. In practice, the errors are greater because the distribution of gray scales is not white-noise, but closer to log-Gaussian (Richards, 1982). We assume that errors of this kind introduce fluctuations in the calculated tangent angle

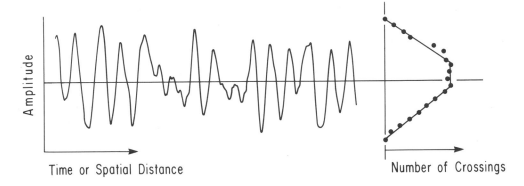

Figure 4 A sample of band-passed noise and the resulting distribution of signal level-crossings versus amplitude (right) [adapted from Bracewell (1978)].

that have roughly a binomial distribution about the correct value.

To compute curvature, we first compute the tangent to the curve and then perform numerical differentiation of the tangent angles. This operation amounts to low-pass filtering a noisy curve. However, because the bandwidth of the filter is known in advance, we can make strong predictions about the nature of the power spectrum of the output, given that we know the character of the noise in the spectral region. For example, if the noise is white in this region, then the power spectrum will be that of the filter. This behavior of the power spectrum allows us to identify when the fluctuations in the tangent direction are simply random, as compared with changes that reflect the image structure of interest.

Figure 4 illustrates the scheme. A noise sample has been band-pass filtered. The values of the signal fluctuate about a mean value (near-zero), but are confined to a range set by the filter. The greatest number of level-crossings of the filtered signal will occur about the mean, for these changes have the highest probability of

occurrence. The fewest number of level-crossings will occur at the extremes of the range. These probabilities are set (for white noise) simply by the shape of the filter (Bracewell, 1978). Thus, if we count the number of level-crossings at any signal level, we obtain a curve (right) that reflects the filter shape. A simple test for noise, which we shall use, is to compare such a plot of the distribution of level crossings with the known filter shape.

4.2 Natural scale

When we inspect Figure 5, we see a "pear" shape underlying all the patterns. In one case the basic underlying shape has a uniform "sinusoidal" texture, whereas in another it has a "spiny" texture like a pineapple. Yet in spite of this surface structure, the underlying pear shape is still apparent. Part boundaries must therefore be specified at a scale. How do we find this scale? Will this choice be a subjective one, or will it indeed reflect the actual structure of the object?

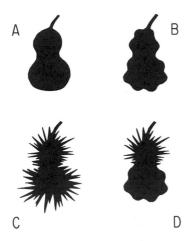

Figure 5 Pears with different surface textures.

In his discussion of the fractal geometry of nature, Mandelbrot (1982) illustrates how the length of one's measuring stick (i.e. filter) can affect the observed structure or "dimension" of an object. Thus, a ball of yarn seen at a coarse scale may appear simply as a smooth sphere. But upon closer inspection at a finer scale, the cylindrical character of the yarn becomes apparent, then at a still finer scale one might see the fibers that make up the yarn, etc. Each of these processes may have different structural dimensions. For example, the process that wraps the yarn into a ball acts in three dimensions, whereas the building of the yarn itself from fibers is essentially a two-dimensional process. The observed structural dimension of a natural process thus has an objective basis, because over the range of scales at which a particular process acts, the dimension of that process will be constant. Some evidence for this is apparent in Richardson's data on coastline lengths [page 33 of Mandelbrot (1982)]. Like Witkin (1983, 1984) and Hoffman (1983), we argue that one important task of the

observer is to discover the natural scale of the different processes that make up an object, or its silhouette. The parts of an object, such as the lobes of the pear in Figure 5, must be differentiated from the textural properties—the ripples or "hair". To discover the scales for the parts and surface texture of a silhouette, we propose a constraint upon the structure of natural objects that allows us to use the "noise testing" technique of the previous section to identify the proper natural scale for part boundaries and curvature extrema.

Structural Hypothesis (Marr):
The spatial structure of an object (outline) is generated by a number of different processes, each operating at a different scale.

This hypothesis, which we credit to Marr (1980, 1982) because of his early applications of this constraint, has the implication that if we filter an image using different size filters, then over one range of scales the filter output will be determined primarily by one process, whereas over another (non-overlapping) range, a second process will determine the filter output. Thus, we expect that the form of the output from the filters over one range of scales will be different from that over another. Furthermore, over that range scale where only one process is in effect, the filter outputs should be very similar. For example, if we note the pattern of zero-crossings in the filtered signal versus signal position, then this pattern should remain the same. (This is Witkin's (1984) scale-space representation.) However, when we move from one process to another, then there will be a confusion of two structures—one dying out whereas the other coming in—that should reflect more noise than structure.

Our scheme, like Witkin's, is to note these regions of scale space where the filtered signal retains its structure across a range of scales.

To assist us in noting these regions, we can take advantage of the fact that if the distribution of level crossings of a filtered signal looks like our (known) filter shape, then we are filtering noise. Thus, unlike Witkin, who proceeded to segment an image curve into regions regardless of the obtained distribution of the zero-crossings, we require evidence that the distribution of these zero-crossings is not due to noise. Our scheme seems more appropriate for an image region that should reflect one process at each scale over the entire image contour, whereas Witkin's scheme is more appropriate if no parsing of the 2D image has taken place, for then the overall signal can reflect many different structures as we move from one object to another in the scene.

Referring to Figure 6, we present the result of filtering at several scales the "smooth" and rippled versions of the outline of a pear shape. Using a method to be described in detail later, tangents are calculated at each position of the silhouette, and then the curve of tangent angle versus arc length is filtered to obtain curvature versus arc length. Because calculating curvature is a second-derivative operation, we have in effect band-pass filtered the silhouette at a particular scale. The relative scales of the operator are given on the ordinate. Distances along the abscissa indicate the edge list position (i.e. the relative position on the silhouettes). Now our expectation is that if there is no structure in the silhouette, then a distribution of level crossings versus signal strength (i.e curvature) should fall off in proportion to the shape of our filter, which is approximately triangular, just as it did in Figure 4. However, if structure is present in the shape of the silhouette, then this structure should also be reflected in the filtered output as a fixed number of level-crossings regardless of the signal strength (i.e. the magnitude of curvature). Both of these points are illustrated in Figure 6.

At the bottom of the figure two level-crossing histograms appear as insets, one for each silhouette. These are based on the curvature scale-plot using the operator with the smallest width (1/8). Note that both histograms are similar, because the maximum curvature power for each silhouette is roughly the same and is due to the stem. From these histograms, we know the range of curvatures expected for a white noise input. We take as our "noise band" 50% of this range. This is indicated by the vertical solid bars in the middle of the figure. Curvature extrema lying outside this band are marked as "significant", as indicated by the filled portions of two of the curves in Figure 6.

Once the significant extrema are marked, then they can be tracked across the scale-space, just as Witkin did for zero-crossings of the convolved intensity profile (Witkin, 1984). Here we find at the coarsest scale for Figure 6A the two major part boundaries defined by the extrema of negative curvature through which we have drawn vertical lines. For the smooth pear, there are no other extrema of significance that span several scales except one positive one that appears at all scales. This extremum corresponds to the stem of the pear.

In Figure 6B, the pattern is similar, with two major part boundaries and the dominant positive extremum of the stem also showing at all scales. In addition, however, we now see at the intermediate

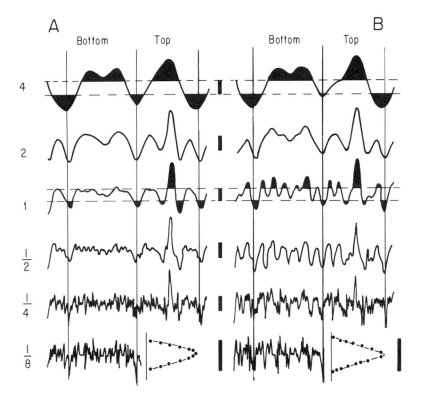

Figure 6 Curvature-space and level-crossing plots for the smooth pear (A) and rippled pear (B) shown in Figure 5. The numbers along the ordinate show the relative widths of the curvature operator; positions on the abscissa correspond to positions on the silhouette. All edge lists are normalized to the same length. The two major part boundaries are indicated by the three vertical lines through the significant extrema of negative curvature. The vertical bars between the two graphs indicate the region within which extrema are not marked, unless a "plateau" appears in the level-crossing histogram. These bars correspond to 50% of the range of the filter-width indicated by the level-crossing histograms shown as insets at the bottom. These graphs show only the first pass at the "part" decomposition.

and fine scales the appearance of more extrema of curvature due to the rippled surface texture. Although these ripples are not fully captured by the noise-band cut-off rule, they will be found by two adjunct procedures. First, we also mark as significant extrema those that create plateaus in the level-crossing histogram, for such

plateaus will lie outside the triangular-shape due to the filter, and hence can not be "noise". The ripples at level 1/2 in Figure 6B would get marked by this latter rule. Second, a more powerful procedure for discovering the texture ripples will be described later, and entails isolating the "parts" at the coarse scale and then repeating the curvature analysis for each part. In effect this procedure will raise the amplitude of the ripples to a level well above the noise.

We can now define more formally what is meant by the significant structure of an image contour:

> **"Significant" Structure** (Witkin) is reflected by the presence of curvature extrema across a range of scales that lie outside the level-crossing distribution expected from noise. The relative "significance" of the structure can be measured in terms of the range of scales spanned.

By this definition, the most "significant" extremum in both scale plots of Figure 6 is that due to the stem; the next are the two major part boundaries that divide the pear into its top and bottom. This result agrees with our own visual impressions of these two silhouettes (see Figure 5).

4.3 The scale set

At present we have only examined our silhouettes at the finest scale of resolution available. Clearly we have the option of varying the scale of the 2D filtering or "blurring" of the original silhouette. Indeed, to recover the full global structure of an object, it may be necessary to apply coarse 2D filtering of the image, despite Figure 6 to the contrary. For example, the two major parts of the spiny pear can not be recovered simply by applying a wider and wider 1D curvature operator to a high-resolution tangent list.

To describe the entire structure of an image region from its silhouette thus requires a set of 2D silhouettes obtained using a range of 2D filters, with the 1D curvature operator applied to each set of silhouettes. We define such a 1D x 2D scale space as a "scale set". Unfortunately, such a three-dimensional representation is extremely unwieldy. It can be simplified in one of two ways, however. First, at any 2D scale of image filtering, only one curvature operator could be chosen, and the "parts" at that 2D scale defined by this simple result. Alternately, only one 2D scale of image filtering could be used, such as the finest, and curvature could be examined over a range of scales, as in Figure 6. Fleck (1985) presents arguments for examining most of the scale set. For the moment, however, we prefer not to use the entire scale set representation to decompose a silhouette into its "parts", but rather continue to examine only the highest resolution outline available. (Occasionally, we also inspect the edge list of one coarse 2D filtered image as a check on our fine-scale decomposition.) There are two reasons for our reluctance to deal with the more complete "scale-set" representation. First, the three-dimensional nature of this representation greatly increases the complexity of the analysis, and secondly, preliminary psychophysical experiments suggest that the human observer uses only the finest 2D scale space when decomposing a silhouette into "parts". This is not to deny, however, that a hierarchical representation based upon the size of regions or "blobs" is constructed. Indeed, our machine parsing of the image proceeds with the construction of a "blob" hierarchy. The codon shape descriptors are applied within this hierarchy. This distinction will be clarified further in the description of the algorithm that follows.

5.0 The Algorithm

To compute the codon representation for the shape of an image curve, we proceed in six steps:

i) Filtering of the image by a set of 2D filters.

ii) Extraction of a blob hierarchy from the set of filtered images.

iii) Calculation of the tangents to the blob contours.

iv) Calculation of a set of curvature scale space plots for each contour.

v) Assignment of curvature extrema to a set of curvature scale plots.

vi) The assignment of part boundaries and shape descriptors.

We will elaborate each stage in the sections below.

Mask for Gaussian Reduce

1	4	6	4	1
4	16	24	16	4
6	24	36	24	6
4	16	24	16	4
1	4	6	4	1

Figure 7 Gaussian pyramid of "Snoopy" created using the mask shown.

5.1 2D image filtering

Although biological systems perform early 2D image filtering using a single difference-of-Gaussian operator (or near equivalents) (Marr, 1982; Marr & Hildreth, 1980), we

proceed in two steps using the Gaussian pyramid scheme of Burt and Adelson (Burt & Adelson, 1983; Burt, 1982) followed by the application of a Laplacian operator. Practically, we find little difference between the optimal biological filter and the pyramid scheme, which is computationally more efficient. We begin by applying the Gaussian mask shown in Figure 7 to a 256^2 video image, skipping every other row and column of the input image. This simultaneously low-pass filters the image (the mask is roughly a Gaussian) and reduces the image in size by a factor of two in each dimension. The "reduced" image thus generated is itself reduced again, and so forth until the image size is 16 by 16 (upper right hand corner of Figure 7). The sequence of filtered images can be thought of as a pyramid with the largest (original) image on the bottom and the successively smaller ones stacked above it. Thus each successive level up in the pyramid represents an additional stage of low-pass filtering. Clearly the reduction in image size provides a similar reduction in computational load.

Each filtered image in the pyramid is then convolved with an unbalanced Laplacian operator to isolate "dark" or "light" blobs. An unbalanced Laplacian is a Laplacian operator with a strong DC (baseband) term. The result of this is that the DC selectively shifts light or dark areas (depending upon the mask) and the Laplacian component sharpens the edges of the blobs. Figure 8 shows a "slice" outline of the masks used and the actual convolution kernel values below for each level of the pyramid. The net effect is similar to convolving the original image with a set of $\nabla^2 G$ or difference-of-Gaussian operators or Gabor filters of different sizes, and has some biological plausibility (Richards

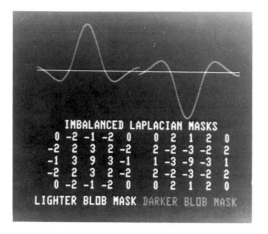

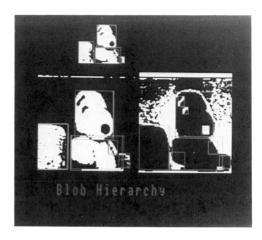

Figure 8 Slice outline of un-balanced mask values showing convolution kernel.

Figure 9 Two levels of blob hierarchy constructed from binary pyramids.

et al., 1982). The theoretical advantage of these filters over others is that the nesting of the blobs within the hierarchy will be well behaved (Babaud et al., 1983; Koenderink, 1984; Yuille & Poggio, 1985). (For the same reason our curvature operator is the derivative of a Gaussian, which guarantees that the extrema will not cross as one moves through the scale space.)

Next we form a binary image by thresholding. This is mostly a matter of computational convenience. We use a simple threshold (35% signal pixels over the image). The blob finder could be improved by using an "average" grey level computed from the higher levels of the pyramid to set the threshold in a local fashion at a lower level. For example, if there are smaller objects embedded in a larger object, the larger object will set the "average" background for the smaller objects which appear at lower levels of the pyramid. Figure 9 shows two levels of blobs constructed from the binary pyramids. In the left panel, white signals lighter blobs, and in the right panel, white signals darker

blobs. A single 5 by 5 mask and no adaptive thresholding was used for all the images.

5.2 The blob hierarchy

We now start to generate a symbolic representation for the image. In human and animal vision, we must first find "where" an object is before we can say "what" it is. Similarly, we build a hierarchical tree structure containing the location and size of each blob, and the sub-blobs in the black and white pyramids below it.

Starting at the highest (coarsest) level we find the light and dark blobs by linear search. Some image processing systems have a histogram/feature processor which allows a list of blobs to be quickly generated. When a blob is found, its location, area, and maximum horizontal and vertical dimensions are recorded in a linked list tree structure. Then the next level down in both the black and white blob pyramid is searched for sub-blobs. The search area is confined to a box twice the size of the maximum horizontal and vertical dimensions, centered on the superior blob. Again, this is not optimal, but is quite efficient. Sub-blobs may have child sub-blobs, etc.

Blobs below a certain minimum size are considered noise and discarded. In this fashion, each pyramid level is roughly band-passed filtered for blobs. Sub-blobs slightly larger than a superior blob are allowed, to give increasing edge detail as one descends the hierarchy. The resulting data structure is similar to a quad-tree representation, but built in reverse from a normal quad-tree generation. We intend to prune this hierarchy by deleting similar size blobs that appear at the same location across scales, keeping only the one with the longest edge list per area. Further details appear elsewhere (Dawson & Treese, 1985).

5.3 Finding edges and tangents

With all the blobs located, an edge list is generated by starting at the top of the blob, and encoding the edge in a counter-clockwise fashion. Our algorithm (Dawson & Treese, 1984) is an adaptation of a standard edge crawl (Ballard & Brown, 1982; Duda & Hart, 1973), using 8-way connectivity. Between a pixel and the previous pixel in the edge list there is a "tangent"— one of eight directions. To find the next pixel in the sequence we project a vector normal to this simple tangent vector (90 degrees clockwise rotation) and then sweep this vector counter-clockwise until it finds the next pixel. In this fashion we "hunt" between object and background and generate the edge list. The implementation is simplified by using only the eight possible vectors in an 8-connected

area around the pixel. The edge lists are then attached to appropriate spots in the blob hierarchy, which serves as our representation for 2D scale.

Given the edge list, we now need to calculate the tangents to the blob outline for each point on the list. A standard set of edge masks could be used here (Ballard & Brown, 1982; Duda & Hart, 1973; Pratt, 1978; Rosenfeld & Kak, 1982). However, since we are dealing with "blobs", it is more computationally efficient to compute the principal normal. While the tangent points along the edge of the blob, the principal normal points towards the inside of the blob, perpendicular to the tangent. Intuitively, the scheme works as follows: consider an edge point and the points immediately surrounding it. Each surrounding point that is part of the blob (signal), can be thought to pull on rubber bands attached to an imaginary vector emanating from the edge point. The sum of these pulls will tend to point the vector towards the center of the blob, and hence the vector will approximate the principal normal.

Computationally, we use the masks shown in Table 2, and similar but larger masks. The area around the edge points are convolved with these masks, and the sums from the x mask and y masks are accumulated separately. For the binary case, it is obvious that these masks are identical to standard horizontal and vertical edge masks, but here they are used differently. With a 3 by 3 convolution, there are 24 possible orientations for the principal normal. Each point on the edge list is assigned one of these orientations. The tangent can be found by rotating the principal normal clockwise 90 degrees.

7

X COMPONENT MASK			Y COMPONENT MASK		
−1	0	1	1	1	1
−1	0	1	0	0	0
−1	0	1	−1	−1	−1

Table 2 Principal Normal Masks.

5.4 Computing curvature

The digital nature of the blob edges and tangents makes the direct calculation of curvature impossible. Smoothing is needed not only to reduce digital "noise", but also to set the scale of the curvature extrema. Here we choose the first derivative of the Gaussian as our convolution operator, which is applied to the tangent histogram. The space constant of the operator is set to a variable fraction of the length of the edge list, to create a set of curvature scale-space plots, as shown in Figure 6 Our choice of operator insures that the alignment of the resulting curvature extrema will be well behaved across scales (Babaud et al., 1983; Koenderink, 1984; Yuille & Poggio, 1985). In Figure 10, we show the curvature computed at two scales for the binary blob that corresponds to Snoopy's head. (The tangent histogram for this blob is shown at the lower left.)

5.5 Assignment of curvature extrema

The codon description requires searching extrema in the computed curvature. To find reliable extrema of curvature we apply our "noise" analysis using the scheme based on the distribution of level crossings.

As illustrated in Figure 7, we calculate the extent of the "noisy" region by using the data obtained with the finest curvature operator. Because the curvature scale-space plots are normalized in amplitude, the same threshold can be applied to all plots—at least for uniformly textured silhouettes. The level-crossings are counted over one cycle of the list in steps corresponding to 1/20th the maximum (normalized) curvature. Plateaus in the distribution of these level crossings that range over 4 levels and lie outside the filter are counted "significant". The curvature extrema that contribute to these plateaus are then marked for each 1D scale of the curvature operator used. The most negative curvature extremum at the coarsest scale is also noted, for the codon string will be computed from this point, which represents one of the major part boundaries. The lower right panel of Figure 11 shows the result for two scales of the curvature convolution applied to Snoopy's head.

5.6 Interpreting the marked curvature-space

The potential part boundaries—i.e. extrema of negative curvature—have now been identified for each curvature plot, and these marked positions on the edge list

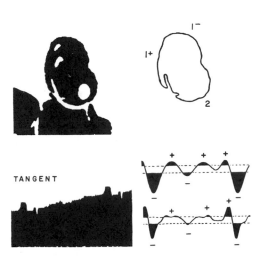

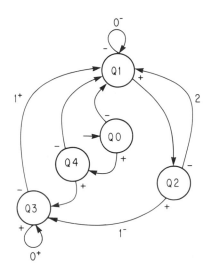

Figure 10 Codon labeling for Snoopy's head, shown here at one scale of the binary pyramid. Lower left: tangent angle versus position along the contour. Lower right: coarsest scale of the curvature space, showing marked curvature extrema. Upper right: resultant codon labeling.

Figure 11 Hoffman's finite state machine, which computes codon descriptions from a sequence of curvature extrema (Hoffman, 1983).

must now be linked across the 1D scales. Within the 1D curvature scale space, the problem is similar to that implemented by Witkin (1984) for his zero-crossing analysis, or Brady and Asada (Asada & Brady, 1984; Brady & Asada, 1984) for their analysis of smooth local symmetries. Rather than tracking zero-crossings (which requires taking one more derivative of curvature), we prefer simply to check for coincidence in the marked extrema by logical "AND" operators (Richards et al., 1982). As can be seen by inspecting Figure 6 and 10, the extrema align nicely as long as the surface texture is uniform. However, a problem arises when the parts of a silhouette have different surface textures, such as the fourth pear in Figure 5 with the spiny head and rippled bottom.

Now the edge lists for each part have quite different lengths, and technically different scale curvature masks must be applied separately to each part of the edge list. As mentioned previously, we propose to handle this problem by an iterative procedure. The parts found at the coarsest scale 1D filters are to be split apart, each with their own separate edge lists, from which a new set of curvature scale-space plots are created. These sub-parts are then decomposed again, if necessary until only noise remains in the edge list. This iterative procedure will automatically produce an explicit hierarchical "tree-structure" for the "parts-based" representation.

At present, however, we simply deliver a sequence of positive and negative curvature extrema for each curve within the curvature scale-space. We then use Hoffman's (1983) finite state machine shown in Figure 11 to transform this list of extrema into the desired codon string. The upper right panel of Figure 10 shows the coarse-scale description of Snoopy's head. This description (together with a finer scale textural description if present) is then entered into the blob hierarchy.

6.0 Conclusions

Although our own visual system readily finds part boundaries and easily can describe the surface texture of these parts, such computations by machine are not trivial. As with most vision problems, the key issues involve setting non-arbitrary criteria for choosing an appropriate scale for the "parts" and, given the scale, deciding when a curvature extremum that defines a part boundary is significant or not. Here, we propose defining significant extrema of curvature as those which lie outside the curvature fluctuations expected given our (known) tangent filter and a white-noise input. Significant extrema are those present over at least two octaves of the curvature scale space.

We wish to emphasize that our analysis of the scale-space differs from others in an important way: "Parts" found at the coarse scale of the initial edge list are used as the basis for segmenting the entire list into sublists which are then examined independently for curvature extrema which define sub-parts (or texture). This iterative procedure can be continued and will capture the different structural processes which occur separately at different scales. The output is then a hierarchical decomposition of the shape of the silhouette

in terms of the major parts and their sub-parts, etc.

One intriguing issue raised by our implementation is whether the curvature extrema of a silhouette need be computed using a range of both 1D curvature operators as well as a range of 2D image filters. Preliminary results suggest that the human observer uses only the most detailed available image of the silhouette. If such a powerful vision system as ours indeed does not explore curvature over a range of 2D scales, then it would be important to know under what conditions the shape information contained in the 1D curvature scale space will be essentially complete if only the finest-scale 2D image filter is used to specify the shape. Clearly if the recognition of most natural objects is not severely impaired, a parts-based shape description built only from the finest scale tangent list would have great computational advantages.

Acknowledgments The authors thank William Gilson and George Treese of M.I.T. for their help, and Eric Saund for comments. This work was supported by NSF and AFOSR under a combined grant for studies in Natural Computation, grant 79-23110-MCS, and by the AFOSR under an Image Understanding contract F49620-83-C-0135.

References

Asada, H. & Brady, M. (1984) The curvature primal sketch. MIT A.I. Lab. Memo 758.

Attneave, F. (1954) Some informational aspects of visual perception. *Psychol. Rev.*, 61:183–193.

Babaud, J., Witkin, A. & Duda, R. (1983) Uniqueness of the Gaussian kernel for scale-space filtering. Fairchild Tech. Rep. 645, FLAIR 22 Fairchild Artificial Intelligence Laboratory, Palo Alto, CA.

Ballard, D.H. & Brown, C.M. (1982) *Computer Vision.* Englewood Cliffs, NJ: Prentice-Hall.

Bennett, B. & Hoffman, D.(1987) Shape decompositions for visual recognition: The role of transversality. In W. Richards & S. Ullman (eds.), *Image Understanding 1985-86*, Norwood, N.J.: Ablex.

Biederman, I. (1985) Human image understanding: recent research and a theory, *Comp. Vis., Graphics and Image Proc.*, 32:29 – 73.

Bracewell, R.N. (1978) *The Fourier Transform and Its Applications.* New York: McGraw Hill.

Brady, M. & Asada, H. (1984) Smooth local symmetries and their implementation. *Int. Jrl. Robotics*, 3:36 – 61.

Burt, P.J. (1982) The pyramid as a structure for efficient computation. Image Processing Laboratory technical paper IPL-TR-038, Rensselaer Polytechnic Institute, Troy, N.Y.

Burt, P.J. & Adelson, E.H. (1983) The Laplacian Pyramid as a compact image code. *IEEE Trans. on Communications. Vol COM-31, No. 4.*, 532-540.

Dawson, B.M. & Treese, G. (1984) Computing curvature from images. *SPIE*, 504:175 – 182.

Dawson, B.M. & Treese, G. (1985) Locating objects in a complex image. *SPIE*, 534:185 – 192.

Duda, R.O. & Hart, P.E. (1973) *Pattern Classification and Scene Analysis.* New York: Wiley-Interscience.

Fleck, M.M. (1985) Local rotational symmetries. MIT A.I. Lab. Memo 852.

Guillemin, V. & Pollack, A. (1974) *Differential Topology.* Englewood Cliffs, N.J.: Prentice Hall.

Hoffman, D.D. (1983) "Representing shapes for visual recognition". Ph.D. dissertation, Massachusetts Institute of Technology, Department of Psychology.

Hoffman, D.D. & Richards, W. (1982) Representing smooth plane curves for recognition: implications for figure-ground reversal. *Proc. Nat. Conf. on Art. Intell. AAAI*, pp. 5 – 8.

Hoffman, D.D. & Richards, W. (1984) Parts of Recognition, *Cognition*, 18:65 – 96.

Koenderink, J.J. (1984) The structure of images. *Biol. Cybern*, 50:363 – 370.

Mandelbrot, B.B. (1982) *The Fractal Geometry of Nature.* San Francisco: W.H. Freeman.

Marr, D.C. (1982) *Vision: A Computational Investigation into the Human Representation and Processing of Visual Information.* San Francisco: W.H. Freeman.

Marr, D. & Hildreth, E. (1980) Theory of edge detection. *Proc. R. Soc. Lond.*, 207:187 – 217.

Pratt, W.K. (1978) *Digital Image Processing.* New York: John Wiley & Sons.

Resnikoff, H. (1985) *The Illusion of Reality: Topics in Information Science.* New York: Springer-Verlag.

Richards, W. (1982) Lightness scale from image intensity distributions. *Applied Optics*, 21:2569 – 2582.

Richards, W.A., Nishihara, H.K. & Dawson, B.M. (1982) CARTOON: a biologically motivated edge detection algorithm. MIT A.I. Lab. Memo 668.

Rosenfeld, A. & Kak, A.C. (1982) *Digital Picture Processing*. New York: Academic Press.

Turton, W. (1819) *A Conchological Dictionary of the British Islands* (frontispiece), printed for John Booth, London. [This reference was kindly pointed out to us by D.D. Hoffman and J.F.W. McOmie.]

Witkin, A.P. (1983) Scale space filtering. *Proc. 7th Int. Joint Conf. Artif. Intell.*, Karlsruhe, pp. 1019–1021.

Witkin, A.P. (1984) Scale space filtering: a new approach to multiscale description. In S. Ullman & W. Richards (eds.), *Image Understanding 1984*, Norwood, NJ: Ablex.

Yuille, A.L. & Poggio, T. (1985) Fingerprint theorems for zero-crossings. *Jrl. Opt. Soc. Am. A*, 2:683–692.

Reprinted with minor editorial changes from *J. Opt. Soc. Am. A*, 3:1483–1491 (1986).

Inferring 3D Orientation from 2D Contour (An Extremum Principle)

Michael Brady*
Alan Yuille

Massachusetts Institute of Technology

1.0 Introduction

An important goal of early vision is the computation of a representation of the visible surfaces in an image, in particular the determination of the orientation of those surfaces as defined by their local surface normals (Brady, 1982; Marr, 1982). Many processes contribute to achieving this goal, stereopsis and structure-from-motion being the most studied in image understanding. In this paper we consider the computation of shape-from-contour. Figure 1 shows a number of shapes that are typically perceived as images of surfaces which are oriented out of the picture plane. The method we propose is based on a preference for symmetric, or at least compact, surfaces. Note that the contour does not need to be closed in order to be interpreted as oriented out of the image plane. Also, in general, contours are interpreted as curved three-dimensional surfaces.

We develop an extremum principle for determining three-dimensional surface orientation from a two-dimensional contour. Initially, we work out the extremum principle for the case when the contour is closed and the interpreted surface is planar. Later, we discuss how to extend our approach to open contours and how to interpret contours as curved surfaces.

The extremum principle maximizes a familiar measure of the compactness or symmetry of an oriented surface, namely the ratio of the area to the square of the perimeter. It is shown that this measure is at the heart of the maximum likelihood approach to shape-from-contour developed by Witkin (1981) and Davis et al. (1982). The maximum likelihood approach has had some success interpreting irregularly shaped objects. However, the method is ineffective when the distribution of image tangents is not random, as is the case, for example, when the image is a regular shape, such as an ellipse or a parallelogram. Our extremum principle interprets regular figures correctly. We show that the maximum likelihood method approximates the extremum principle for irregular figures.

Kanade (1981, p. 424) has suggested a method for determining the three-dimensional orientation of skew-symmetric figures, under the "heuristic assumption" that such figures are interpreted as oriented real symmetries. We prove that our extremum principle necessarily interprets skew symmetries as oriented real symmetries, thus dispensing with the need for any heuristic assumption to that effect. Kanade shows that there is one-parameter

8

family of possible orientations of a skew-symmetric figure, forming a hyperbola in gradient space. He suggests that the minimum slant member of the one-parameter family is perceived. In the special case of a real symmetry, Kanade's suggestion implies that symmetric shapes are perceived as lying in the image plane, that is having zero slant. It is clear from the ellipse in Figure 1 that this is not correct. Our method interprets real symmetries correctly.

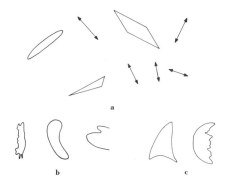

Figure 1 1a. Two-dimensional contours that are often interpreted as planes that are oriented with respect to the image plane. The commonly judged slant is shown next to each shape. 1b. Some unfamiliar shapes that are also interpreted as planes that are oriented with respect to the image plane. 1c. Some shapes that are interpreted as curved three-dimensional surfaces.

First, we review the maximum likelihood method. In Section 3, we discuss several previous extremum principles and justify our choice of the compactness measure. In Section 4, we derive the mathematics necessary to extreme the compactness measure, and relate the ex-

tremum principle to the maximum likelihood method. In Section 5, we investigate Kanade's work on skew symmetry. One approach to extending the extremum principle to interpret curved surfaces, such as that shown in Figure 1c, is sketched in Section 6.

This paper is an abbreviated version of (Brady & Yuille, 1983), which should be referred to for the details of derivations. In that paper we also discuss the psychophysical literature on slant estimation and Ikeuchi's work on shape from texture.

2.0 The Sampling Approach

Witkin (1981) has treated the determination of shape-from-contour as a problem of signal detection. Subsequently, Davis et al. (1982) utilized Witkin's approach to propose two efficient algorithms for computing the orientation of a planar surface from an image contour. Witkin's approach uses a *geometric model* of (orthographic) projection and a *statistical model* of (a) the distribution of surfaces in space (statistics of the universe) and (b) of the distribution of tangents to the image contour. We utilize the geometric model, but dispense with the second part of the statistical model in favor of an extremum principle.

First, the geometric model. Suppose that a curve is drawn in the plane (σ, τ) and denote by β the angle that the tangent makes at a typical point on the curve. Let α be the tangent angle in the image plane at the point corresponding to β. Then α and β are related by $\tan(\alpha - \tau) = \tan\beta / \cos\sigma$.

We now turn to the statistical model, which consists of two assumptions called *isotropy* and *independence*. Isotropy reasonably supposes that all surface orientations are equally likely to occur in nature and that tangents to surface curves are equally likely in all directions. More succinctly, it is assumed that the quantities (σ, τ) are randomly distributed, and that their joint probability density function ("density") $D(\sigma, \tau)$ is given by (Davis et al., 1982).

$$D(\sigma, \tau) = \frac{1}{\pi} \sin \sigma$$

the independence assumption requires that the image tangents

$$\{\alpha_t : 1 \leq i \leq n\}$$

are statistically independent. That is, it is assumed that the tangent directions at different points on the image curve are independent. This is only true if the contour is highly irregularly shaped, or if the number of samples is small. In any case, the assumption of independence is an inherent weakness of the sampling approach [see for example Witkin (1981) p. 36].

It is easy to show that the conditional density $D(\alpha|\sigma, tau)$ of an individual image tangent angle α projected from a plane (σ, τ) is given by (Witkin, 1981):

$$D(\alpha|\sigma, \tau) = \frac{1}{\pi} \frac{\cos \sigma}{\cos^2(a - \tau) + \cos^2 \sigma \sin^2(\alpha - r)} \quad (2.1)$$

Denote the sample $\alpha_1, \alpha_2 \ldots, \alpha_n$ by A (the sample is independent by assumption). It has conditional density

$$D(A|\sigma, \tau) = \prod_{i=1}^{n} D(\alpha_i|\sigma, \tau) \quad (2.2)$$

By Bayes' formula we obtain

$$D(\sigma, \tau|A) = \frac{D(A|\sigma, \tau)D(\sigma, \tau)}{\int \int D(A|\sigma, \tau)D(\sigma, \tau)d\sigma \, d\tau} \quad (2.3)$$

Observe that the numerator is independent of σ and τ. The sampling approach takes a random sample A and defines the most likely orientation of the plane (σ, τ) to be that which extremizes $D(\sigma, \tau|A)$. Witkin (1981) quantizes σ and τ, and describes an algorithm to find the maximizing (σ_i, τ_k). Davis et al. (1982) develop a more efficient algorithm that first estimates σ and τ and then uses those estimates in a Newton iterative process. They provide evidence that their method is more accurate than Witkin's. Curiously, however, they state (Davis et al., 1982, p. 24) that "the iterative algorithm was not used (in the experiments they report) because the initial estimates (whose computation is trivial) are very accurate and the iterative scheme often failed to converge to the solution".

3.0 Extremum Principles

There are several plausible measures of a curve that might be extremized in order to compute shape-from-contour. Contrary to what appears to be a popular belief, given an ellipse in the image plane, $\oint \kappa^2 ds$ not extremized in the plane that transforms the ellipse into a circle (Brady & Yuille, 1983, Appendix B). Since ellipses are normally perceived as slanted circles, we reject the square curvature as a suitable measure.

Another possible measure is proposed by Barrow & Tenenbaum (1981, p. 89). Assuming planarity, the torsion along the curve is zero, and their measure reduces to

$$\oint \left(\frac{d\kappa}{ds}\right)^2 ds.$$

The first strong objection to this measure is that it involves high-order derivatives of the curve. This means it is overly dependent on small scale behavior. Consider, for example, a curve which is circular except for a small kink. The circular part of the curve will contribute a tiny proportion to the integral even when the plane containing the curve is rotated. The kink, on the other hand, will contribute an arbitrarily large proportion and so will dominate the integral no matter how small it is compared with the rest of the curve. This is clearly undesirable. For example, it suggests that the measure will be highly sensitive to noise in the position and orientation of the points forming the contour.

A second objection to the measure proposed by Barrow & Tenenbaum is that it is minimized by, and hence has an intrinsic preference for, straight lines, for which $d\kappa/ds$ zero. This means that the measure has a bias towards planes that correspond to the (non-general) side-on viewing position. These planes are perpendicular to the image plane and have slant $\pi/2$.

We base our choice of measure on the following observations:

1. Contours that are the projection of curves in planes with large slant are most effective for eliciting a three-dimensional interpretation.

2. A curve is foreshortened by projection by the cosine of the slant angle in the tilt direction, and not at all in the orthogonal direction.

We conclude that three-dimensional interpretations are most readily elicited for shapes that are highly elongated in one direction. Another way to express this idea is that the image contour has large aspect ratio or is radially asymmetric. The measure we suggest will pick out the plane orientation for which the curve is most compact or most radially symmetric. Specifically, our measure is

$$M = \frac{(\text{Area})}{(\text{Perimeter})^2} \qquad (3.1)$$

This is a scale invariant number characterizing the curve. For all possible curves it is maximized by the most symmetric one, a circle. This gives the measure an upper bound of $1/4\pi$. Its lower bound is clearly zero and it is achieved for a straight line. It follows that our measure has a built-in prejudice against side-on views for which the slant is $\pi/2$.

In general, given a contour, our extremum principle will choose the orientation in which the deprojected contour maximizes M. For example an ellipse is interpreted as a slanted circle. The tilt angle is given by the major axis of the ellipse. It is also straightforward to show that a parallelogram corresponds to a rotated square. Brady & Yuille (1983, Appendix B) show how several simple shapes are interpreted by the measure. In particular, an ellipse is interpreted as a slanted circle, a parallelogram as a slanted square, and a triangle as a slanted equilateral triangle. In Section 5 we extend the parallelogram result to the more general case of skewed symmetry.

We note that the quantity M is commonly used in pattern recognition and industrial vision systems (Ballard & Brown, 1982; Duda & Hart, 1973) as a feature that measures the compactness of an object. [There is also evidence suggesting use of this measure in biological vision (Sutherland, 1960).] Furthermore, we can show that the measure M defined in Equation (3.1) is at the heart of the geometric model in the maximum likelihood approach.

From Section 2, we see that the maximum likelihood approach maximizes the product of a number of terms of form

$$f(a) = \frac{\cos \alpha}{\cos^2(\alpha - r) + \cos^2 \sigma \sin^2(\sigma - r)} \quad (3.2)$$

Differentiating the geometric model with respect to the arc length s_I along the image curve and s_R along the rotated curve respectively we obtain

$$\frac{\kappa_I ds_I}{\kappa_R ds_R} = \frac{1}{f(\alpha)} \quad (3.3)$$

where κ_I and κ_R are the curvature at corresponding points of the image contour and its deprojection in the rotated plane respectively. In fact, $\kappa_I = d\alpha/d\sigma_I$ and $\kappa_R = d\beta/ds_R$. There is no σ or τ dependence in the numerator of Equation (3.3). We can write each term $\kappa\, ds$ as $ds\, ds/\rho\, ds$ where ρ is the radius of curvature. Now observe that $\rho\, ds/ds\, ds$ is just a local computation of area divided by perimeter squared! Hence maximizing each (α) in the maximum likelihood approach is equivalent to locally maximizing area over perimeter squared. In section (4) we will examine this connection more rigorously.

4.0 Extremizing the Measure

We now write down the measure for a curve with arbitrary orientation and then extremize with respect to the orientation. Let the unit normals to the image plane and the rotated plane be k and n respectively. The slant σ of the rotated plane is given by the scalar product $cos\sigma = k \cdot n$.

Let Γ_R and Γ_I be the contour in the rotated and image planes. A vector r in the image plane satisfies $r \cdot k = 0$, and is the projection of a vector v in the rotated plane that satisfies $v \cdot n = 0$. Now Γ_R and Γ_I have (vector) areas A_R and A_I which are related by

$$\|A_R = \frac{\|A_I\|}{\cos \sigma}$$

We find

$$P_R = \oint_{\Gamma_R} \left[(dr)^2 + \frac{(n \cdot dr)^2}{(n \cdot k)^2} \right]^{\frac{1}{2}}$$

In general there is no simple relationship between the perimeters analogous to that holding between the areas. Nevertheless, we have $A_R/P_R^2 = A_I/P_R^2 \cos\sigma$. Thus, our extremum principle is equivalent to extremizing $\cos^{1/2} \sigma P_R$ which we write as

$$I = \oint_{\Gamma_R} \left[(n \cdot k) dr^2 + \frac{(n \cdot dr)^2}{(n \cdot k)} \right]^{\frac{1}{2}}$$

We extremize this with respect to the orientation n of the rotated plane, maintaining the constraint that n is a unit vector by a Lagrange multiplier $A/4$. After algebraic manipulation (Brady & Yuille 1983), this reduces to

$$2 \oint \left[\cos^2 \sigma + (n \cdot t)^{\frac{1}{2}} \right]^{-\frac{1}{2}} (t \cdot n) dr =$$

$$- k/(k/n) \oint \left[\cos^2 \sigma + (n \cdot t)^2 \right]^{\frac{1}{2}} dr$$

where $t = dr/\|dr\|$ is the unit tangent to the image contour. Let the unit vectors in the x and y directions in the image plane be i and j and let k be the normal to the image plane. The tangent vector t and the normal n can be written:

$$t = \cos \sigma\, i + \sin \sigma\, j$$

$$n = \sin \sigma \cos \tau i + \sin \sigma \sin \tau j + \cos \sigma\, k$$

where α is the tangent angle in the image. We now form the scalar products of Equation above with i and j to obtain eventually

$$\frac{\partial}{\partial \sigma} \left(\frac{1}{\cos^{\frac{1}{2}} \sigma} \oint (\cos^2 \sigma + \right.$$

$$\left. \sin^2 \sigma \cos^2(\alpha - r))^{\frac{1}{2}} dr \right) = 0 \quad (4.1)$$

$$\frac{\partial}{\partial \tau}\left(\frac{1}{\cos^{\frac{1}{2}}\sigma}\oint(\cos^2\sigma+\right.$$

$$\left.\sin^2\sigma\cos^2(\alpha-r))^{\frac{1}{2}}dr\right)=0 \quad (4.2)$$

to emphasize that they correspond to extremizing with respect to σ and τ.

To conclude this Section, we show that these equations are similar, though not identical, to those obtained by the maximum likelihood method in the limit as the number of sample tangents tends to infinity. To see this we recall that this method involves extremizing $D(A|\sigma, \tau)$ with respect to σ and τ. Since the denominator is independent of σ and τ, this amounts to extremizing $D(A|\sigma, \tau)D(\sigma, \tau)$. This is the same as extremizing

$$\log D(A|\sigma, \tau)D(\sigma, \tau).$$

We find

$$E = n\log\cos\sigma + \log\sin\sigma-$$

$$\sum_{i=1}^{n}\log(\cos^2(\alpha_i-r)+\cos^2\sigma\sin^2(\alpha_i-r))$$

where we have ignored factors of π which will vanish on differentiation. Dividing E by n and taking the limit as n tends to infinity gives:

$$F = \log\cos\sigma\oint dr-$$

$$\oint\log(\cos^2\sigma(\alpha-\tau)+\cos^2\sigma\sin^2(\alpha-r))dr.$$

Using the identity:

$$\cos^2(\alpha-r)+\cos^2\sigma\sin^2(\alpha-r)=$$

$$\cos^2\sigma+\sin^2\sigma\cos^2(\alpha-r)$$

gives

$$F = \log\cos\sigma\oint dr-$$

$$\oint\log(\cos^2\sigma+\sin^2\sigma\cos^2(\alpha-r))dr$$

This formula is similar to Eqs. 4.1 and 4.2. Thus we expect the Extremum Method to give similar results to the Sampling Method when the contour is sufficiently irregular.

5.0 Skew Symmetry

We now consider a more general class of shapes for which the maximum likelihood approach is not effective. Kanade (1981, sec. 6.2) has introduced *skewed symmetries*, which are two-dimensional linear (affine) transformations of real symmetries. There is a bijective correspondence between skew symmetries and images of symmetric shapes that lie in planes oriented to the image plane. Kanade proposes the heuristic assumption that a skew symmetry is interpreted as an oriented real symmetry, and he considers the problem of computing the slant and tilt of the oriented plane.

Denote the angles between the x-axes of the image and the images of the symmetry axis and an axis orthogonal to it (the skewed transverse axis) by α and β respectively. The orthogonality of the symmetry and transverse axes enable one constraint on the orientation of the plane to be derived. Kanade uses gradient space (p, q) [see Brady (1982) for references] to represent surface orientations. He shows (Kanade 1981, p. 425) that the heuristic assumption is equivalent to requiring the gradient (p, q) of the oriented plane to lie on the hyperbola

$$p_1^2\cos^2\frac{(\alpha-\beta)}{2}-q_1^2\sin^2\frac{(\alpha-\beta)}{2}=$$

$$-\cos(\alpha-\beta) \quad (5.1)$$

where

$$p_1 = p\cos\left(\frac{\alpha+\beta}{2}\right) + q\sin\left(\frac{\alpha+\beta}{2}\right)$$
$$q_1 = -p\sin\left(\frac{\alpha+\beta}{2}\right) + q\cos\left(\frac{\alpha+\beta}{2}\right)$$
$$(5.2)$$

Kanade (1981, p. 426) further proposes that the vertices of the hyperbola, which corresponds to the least slanted orientation, are chosen within this one-parameter family. This proposal is in accordance with a heuristic observation of Stevens (1980). In the special case that the skew symmetry is a real symmetry, that is in the case that $\alpha - \beta = \pm\pi/2$, the hyperbola reduces to a pair of orthogonal lines passing through the origin. In such cases the slant is zero. In other words, Kanade's proposal predicts that real symmetries are inevitably interpreted as lying in the image plane, and hence having zero slant. Inspection of Figure 1 shows that this is not the case. A (symmetric) ellipse is typically perceived as a slanted circle, particularly if the major and minor axes do not line up with the horizontal and vertical.

Although Kanade's minimum slant proposal does not seem to be correct there is evidence [for example (Stevens 1980)] for Kanade's assumption that skew symmetries are interpreted as real symmetries. We can show that the assumption can in fact be *deduced* from our Extremum Principle (Brady & Yuille 1983, Section 5). As a corollary we can determine the slant and tilt of any given skewed-symmetric figure (Brady & Yuille 1983, Appendix C); only in special cases does it correspond to the minimum slant member of Kanade's one-parameter family.

6.0 Interpreting Image Contours as Curved Surfaces

Figure 1c shows a number of contours that are interpreted as curved surfaces. In this section we discuss one method for extending our extremum principle to this general case. The key observation, as it was for Witkin (1981), is that our method can be applied locally. To do this, we assume that the surface is locally planar. At the surface boundary, corresponding to the deprojection of the image contour, the binormal coincides with the surface normal. The idea is to compute a local estimate of the surface normal by the extremum principle described in previous sections and then to use an algorithm, such as that developed by Terzopoulos (1983) to interpolate the surface orientation in the interior of the surface. Details of one implementation can be found in (Brady & Yuille 1983).

Acknowledgments: The authors thank Ruzena Bajcsy, Chris Brown, John Canny, Eric Grimson, Ellen Hildreth, Tommy Poggio, Demetri Terzopoulos, and Andy Witkin for their comments.

References

Ballard, D.H., & Brown C.M. (1982) *Computer vision.* Englewood Cliffs, NJ: Prentice-Hall.

Barrow, H.G. & Tenenbaum, J.M., (1981) Interpreting line drawings as three dimensional surfaces. *Artif. Intell.*, 17:75–117.

Brady, M. (1982) Computational approaches in image understanding. *Computer Surveys*, 14:3–71.

Brady, M. & Yuille, A. (1983) An extremum principle for shape from contour. MIT A.I. Lab. Memo 711.

Davis, L.S., Janos, L. & Dunn, S. (1982) Efficient recovery of shape from texture. Computer Vision Laboratory, University of Maryland, TR-1133.

Duda, R.O. & Hart, P.E. (1973) *Pattern Classification and Scene Analysis.* New York: Wiley.

Kanade, T. (1981). Recovery of three-dimensional shape of an object from a single view. *Artif. Intell.*, 17:409–460.

Marr, D., (1982). *Vision: A Computational Investigation into the Human Representation and Processing of Visual Information.* San Francisco: Freeman.

Stevens, K.A. (1980). Surface perception from local analysis of texture. MIT A.I. Lab. Technical Report TR512.

Sutherland, N.S. (1960) Theories of shape discrimination in Octopus. *Nature,* 186:840–844.

Terzopolous, D. (1983) Multilevel reconstruction of visual surfaces. *Comp. Graphics and Image Proc.*, 24:52–96.

Witkin, A.P. (1981). Recovering surface shape and orientation from texture. *Artif. Intell.*, 17:17–47.

Reprinted from: IJCAI 1983 Proceedings, Karlsruhe.

*The first author is now at Oxford University, Department of Engineering Science.

The Line of Curvature Constraint and the Interpretation of 3D Shape from Parallel Surface Contours

Kent A. Stevens

University of Oregon
Eugene, OR

1.0 Introduction

The parallel curves in Figure 1 are interpreted in 3D as lying across an undulating surface. (Ideally one should examine these figures monocularly, perpendicular to the line of sight, with an occluding mask that reduces the evidence that they are merely drawn on the printed page, and for several seconds to allow the 3D shape to develop fully.) Our perception of surface shape in this figure is so immediate and effortless that we must be reminded that the image could correspond to any of an infinite set of possible configurations, including the literally correct 2D interpretation as lines of ink on the flat printed page (which is surprisingly difficult for us to hold). The fact that we choose a definite 3D interpretation (subjects make precise judgment of local surface orientation and different observers make similar judgments) suggests that the visual system strongly constrains the 3D interpretation.

Observe that the undulating curves in figure 1 appear to be lines of curvature on a cylinder [a developable surface having parallel rulings—see, e.g. Hilbert & Cohn-Vossen (1952)]. That is, the curves appear geodesic, planar, and oriented perpendicular to the ridges and troughs of the surface. The same interpretation can be had with even simpler configurations, such as in Figure 2, where the curved contour (line of curvature) appears to intersect the straight line (ruling) at a right angle. Note again that the curved contour appears geodesic and planar, regardless whether seen as a physical edge (e.g. of a sheet of paper) or as a line across the surface. It turns out that considerable constraint on the 3D interpretation is afforded by assuming that the curves are lines of curvature seen in general position, particularly for the case of parallel curves in an image.

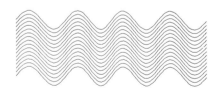

Figure 1 A set of parallel sinusoids appears as a ribbon in 3D. Why?

A theory of the underlying constraints is given in (Stevens, 1981a), which can account for these qualitative observations. We will review the theory and report quantitative support provided by an implementation that embodies these constraints. The implementation predicts 3D shape that corresponds rather closely to the subjective impression of shape seen in these images. While the implementation is not meant as a perceptual model but only a means for examining the 3D shape predicted by the constraints, it does have relevance to computer vision as a method for estimating local surface orientation from certain image configurations.

Prior to discussing the theory and examining the implementation it will be useful to comment on certain points that one might raise on first examination of these figures.

1. A shading effect is apparent in Figure 1 (especially noticeable when blurred). Shading likely enhances the apparent surface impression, but it cannot be the sole cause of the three-dimensionality, since we perceive 3D shape where shading is negligible [see Figures 2, 4, and the surfaces suggested by dotted lines and subjective contours in (Stevens, 1982, Figure 2)].

2. When these figures reverse in depth, the perceived surface may change its appearance radically. For example, Figure 1 rotated 90 deg will reverse readily, and with each reversal the troughs become ridges and vice versa (rotating the figure defeats our tendency to assume that distance increases towards the top of an image). The global changes in surface shape may be attributed, however, to local ambiguity in the *direction* of tilt: the apparent tilt reverses by 180 deg while the slant remains constant. [Slant is the angle, 0-90 deg, between the line of sight and the surface normal; tilt is the direction, 0-360 deg, of the gradient of distance from the viewer to the surface, and also the direction of the projected surface nor-

mal (Stevens, 1979, 1983a; Marr, 1982)]. Tilt direction cannot be expected to be determined in these orthographic projections. It is presumably disambiguated by subsequent visual processes, as part of the problem of deriving a consistent depth interpretation from local surface orientation information. It is well know that image orientation is important to this process, as rotating Figure 1 demonstrates.

3. The surface contours discussed here are distinct from contours of foreshortened surface texture [e.g. Kender (1980); Witkin (1981)]. Consider, e.g., the mottled pattern of sunlight and shadows cast on the ground below a tree, which project to foreshortened texture contours in an image. Provided the surface texture is isotropic, the image texture projected from a slanted surface is anisotropic, and the direction and magnitude of the anisotropy [measured, e.g., in terms of contour curvature as a function of tangent direction (Witkin, 1981)] indicates the tilt and slant of the surface in each locality (Brady & Yuille, 1983). In addition to isotropy, the physical curves must lie flush on a surface that is approximately planar in each vicinity, otherwise the contour curvature in the image texture would be confounded by surface curvature (Stevens, 1981b). So on the one hand, texture contours are apparently interpreted as asymptotic: all of their curvature lies in the tangent plane. On the other hand, surface contours are apparently interpreted as geodesic: all of their curvature lies normal to the tangent plane. (In other words, all of the curvature of a surface contour is attributed to surface curvature, while none of the curvature of a texture contour is.)

4. Parallelism between contours in the image may be regarded as a potential triggering criterion for this analysis, analogous to bilateral symmetry between contours potentially triggering their interpretation as silhouette (or occluding) contours of smooth generalized cones (Marr, 1977). Note that for the contours we study the corresponding 3D curves may or may not correspond to physical surface edges (examine the contours in Figures 1 and 2). When seen as a physical edge, the surface orientation varies across the contour discontinuously, i.e., the edge, is sharp, in contrast to the contours along the silhouette of smooth objects.

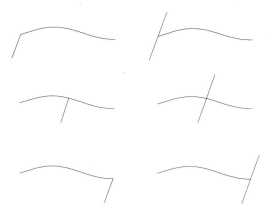

Figure 2 Three dimensional impressions can be elicited from only two intersecting contours.

5. It is useful to consider three distinct categories of contour: texture contours (Witkin, 1981), occluding contours (Marr, 1977), and surface contours (Stevens 1981a). Each category of contour poses a different computational problem and each is expected to be solved by substantially independent perceptual processes. But since the three categories are often present simultaneously in a natural image there is need for integrating the surface shape information contributed by each process, presumably within the 2 1/2-D Sketch (Marr, 1978). The implementation that we shall discuss does not address the integration issue; it is meant only as an empirical demonstration of the plausibility of the constraints.

2.0 Geometric Constraints on the Interpretation of Surface Contours

The definiteness of our perception of surface shape from these contours suggests that we effectively constrain the infinite range of possible 3D surfaces down to a unique perceived surface (and its reflection, as discussed in point 2 above) by applying certain specific geometric constraints. The important question is precisely what are the constraints.

There are many possible starting points for pondering this question. One is to characterize the problem as one of smooth surface interpolation, where perhaps a computation starts with a plane parallel to the image that is continuously deformed in 3D until it becomes the solution surface when certain criteria are satisfied, such as minimizing quadratic variation. Consideration of the details of the computation of this sort, however, does not directly provide insight into the constraints that allow the solution. I refer here to the distinction between a theory of competence (an explanation of what is accomplished) and a description of the algorithms that implement it (how is it accomplished) that Marr & Poggio (1977) discuss. We therefore defer discussion of the computation and consider the constraints themselves.

Surface contours, such as those in Figure 1, are assumed to be the projection of physical contours that lie across a continuous surface. If we assume general position of viewpoint we may conclude that parallel contours in an image correspond to parallel physical contours on the underlying surface. Parallelism weakly constrains how the surface may lie between the contours, particularly assuming the surface is opaque. Stronger constraint comes from assuming that the placement of the contours is generic, that their location on the surface does not conspire with the underlying surface geometry to mislead the viewer. This general position argument implies that the underlying surface is a cylinder, since cylinders are the only surfaces on which parallel contours may lie, in general. The third assumption, that the contours are lines of curvature, implies that they are also planar and geodesic, as consequences of being lines of curvature on cylinders. These constraints allow the estimation of local surface orientation in the following way.

2.1 Parallel correspondence

The lines in Figure 1, by this hypothesis, are treated as lines of curvature across a cylinder. Moreover, the rulings that run perpendicular to these lines can be reconstructed by a straightforward geometric construction on the image, giving us the image of an orthogonal net lying across the surface. Since the rulings on a cylinder are parallel straight lines that project as parallel to the troughs and ridges in the figure and intersect successive curves at a constant angle, to reconstruct their projection it is sufficient to identify, for each point p on a contour, the point p'

on the adjacent contour whose tangent is parallel to the tangent at p. The line pp' is the image of the ruling through p. Note that the constructed lines will themselves be parallel. Two such constructions are shown in Figure 3a. This process may be regarded as establishing a parallel correspondence (Stevens, 1981a) between adjacent contours. Note that contour parallelism detected by these means might serve to trigger the surface contour interpretation (see 4, above).

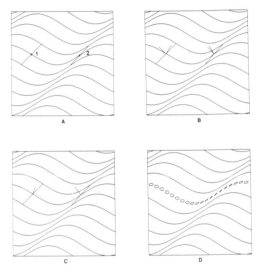

Figure 3 Construction of surface orientation assuming visible contours are lines of curvature. Calculated ellipses in D correspond to circles on the surface.

2.2 The perpendicular between lines of curvature and rulings

The lines of least and greatest curvature on a surface are mutually perpendicular, hence the intersections in Figure 3a are foreshortened images of right angles (examine the intersections in Figures 2 and 4 as well). The perpendicularity places constraint on the range of possible surface orientations in these figures; both the slant and tilt are increasingly restricted as the right angle is increasingly foreshortened towards 180 deg in the image (Stevens, 1981a). The restriction on tilt can be determined by a simple construction in the image plane. At a point on a given image curve construct the perpendicular to the tangent and likewise the perpendicular to the ruling passing through that point, giving an angle less than 90 deg (Figure 3b); the surface normal is then restricted so as to project within this range. Note that in Figure 3b the surface orientation is least constrained at point 1 (tilt = 96.4 ± 38.6°) and most constrained at point 2 (tilt = 128.5 ± 6.5°).

Where the range of tilts is strongly constrained (and hence the slant is as well) the bisector is a good unbiased estimator of the tilt. For example at point 2 in Figure 3c the bisector results in a tilt estimate of 128.5 deg, which implies a slant of 83.5 deg at that point. This estimate at point 2 allows surface orientation to be solved elsewhere along the contour where the orientation is less constrained. Since the lines of curvature on a cylinder are both geodesic and planar, the surface normal is constrained to rotate in the osculating plane, and once it is know at one point on the curve, it rotates in a predictable manner along the curve [see Stevens (1981a, expressions 4 and 5)]. Thus, based on the solution at point 2, these expressions predict tilt = 69.8 deg and slant = 47.4 deg at point 1. The surface normals at points 1 and 2 are depicted in Figure 3c by directed line segments.

Figure 3d shows how the surface orientation may be solved by the same method at any point along the contour. Surface orientation is indicated in this figure by superimposing ellipses that correspond to circles lying on the "perceived" surface.

Some final points should be made regarding tilt estimation by the bisector: (i) the estimate is increasingly accurate as the right angle is increasingly foreshortened towards 180 deg, (ii) it is an unbiased estimator, (iii) the bisector chosen as the tilt estimate corresponds to the the least surface slant at that point (Stevens, 1979), and (iv) while this method is applicable because lines of curvature form an orthogonal net across a surface, it is not central to the overall theory of constraint on the interpretation of parallel surface contours.

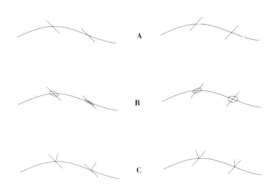

Figure 4 Two methods for indicating surface orientation.

3.0 Surface Orientation Predicted by the Theory

In Figure 4a two simple figures are presented, each suggesting in 3D a curve intersected at right angles by short line segments.

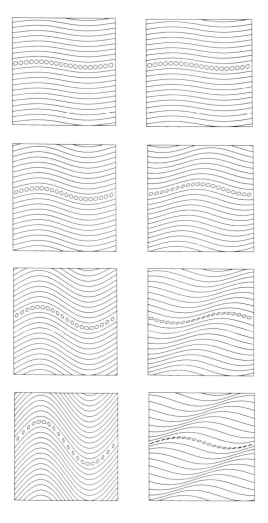

Figure 5 Ellipses show calculated surface orientations for a variety of sinusoidal images.

The predicted surface orientation was computed at the intersection points and indicated by foreshortened circles in Figure 4b and by surface normals in Figure 4c. The surface normal display in Figure 4c is a sensitive probe of apparent tilt [particularly using tachistoscopic techniques (Stevens, 1983b)]. However indicating surface orientation by ellipses has two advantages over depicting surface normals. The first is the greater sensitivity that we have judging slant from the shape of an ellipse than from the projected length of a surface normal. (Observe that the differences in *slant* at the two intersections is much more apparent in Figure 4b than in Figure 4c.) The second advantage of using ellipses is that when the surface reverses in depth the ellipses reverse with it, while with normals, the reversal causes the line to appear to protrude behind the surface.

The implementation has been applied to a variety of contour configurations that suggest cylindrical surfaces, such as Figures 5 and 6. Note that the surface orientation predicted by the theory corresponds rather closely with the apparent surface orientation in these figures.

4.0 Discussion

The implementation supports the hypothesis that our visual interpretation of parallel surface contours is constrained by assuming that the image curves are projections of line of curvature, and by assuming that both the viewpoint and the contour placement are representative. The cylindricality of the surface, the fact that the rulings can be reconstructed by determining parallel correspondence, and the fact that the rulings are perpendicular to the lines of curvature combine to constrain the surface shape. The constraint is of two sorts. First the perpendicularity property restricts the surface orientation, secondly the geometry of cylinders allows one to compute the surface orientation at any point along a line of curvature as long as it is known at one point.

The performance of the implementation also lends some support to the bisector method for estimating surface orientation at the point of greatest constraint due to perpendicularity. The use of the bisector, while not critical to the overall theory, seems consistent with our perception of local surface orientation in these figures.

is locally cylindrical. The doubly-curved surface in Figure 7 seems amenable to such an interpretation.

Finally, to return to questions of algorithm, I suggest that the line of curvature constraint, cylindricality in the case of parallel contours, and the restrictions caused by the orthogonality of the lines of greatest and least curvature are used primarily to estimate local surface orientation. This local information is then integrated with other information contributed from shading, texture and so forth, in order to derive an at least locally consistent description of the scene. It is premature to propose a specific algorithm until we know how this integration proceeds.

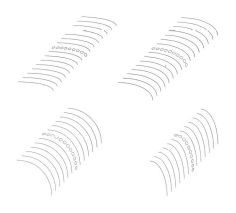

Figure 6 Calculated orientations for some cylindrical surfaces.

Figure 7 A doubly-curved surface.

The theoretical emphasis thus far has been on the simplest configurations of surface contours, namely, those that suggest singly-curved surfaces. In (Stevens, 1981a) it is proposed that more complicated configurations of roughly parallel contours, which suggest doubly-curved surfaces, are analyzed locally by detection of local parallelism among the contours, and exploitation of the constraints that arise by assuming (falsely) that the surface

Acknowledgments: The late David Marr made important contributions to this work. I also thank Whitman Richards, Shimon Ullman, Donald Hoffman and Eric Grimson for helpful discussions. This work was conducted at the Artificial Intelligence Laboratory of the Massachusetts Institute of Technology, and was supported in part by the Advanced Research Projects Agency under ONR contract N00014-80-C-0505 and in part by the AFOSR and

9

NSF grant 23110MCS.

References

Brady, M. & Yuille, A. (1983) An extremum principle for shape from contour. IJCAI 1983 Proceedings, Karlsruhe.

Hilbert, D. & Cohn-Vossen, S. (1952) *Geometry and the Imagination*. New York: Chelsea.

Kender, J.R. (1980) "Shape from texture". Ph.D. dissertation, Computer Science Department, Carnegie-Mellon University.

Marr, D. (1977) Analysis of occluding contour. *Proc. Roy. Soc. Lond. B.*, 197:441 – 475.

Marr, D. (1978) Representing visual information. *Lectures on Mathematics in Life Sciences*, 10:101 – 180.

Marr, D.C. (1982) *Vision: A Computational Investigation into the Human Representation and Processing of Visual Information*. San Francsico: W.H. Freeman.

Marr, D. & Poggio, T. (1977) From understanding computation to understanding neural circuitry. *Neurosci. Res. Prog. Bull.*, 15:470 – 488.

Stevens, K.A. (1979) Representing and analyzing surface orientation. In P.H. Winston & R.H. Brown (eds.), *Artificial Intelligence: an MIT perspective*, Cambridge, Mass.: MIT Press.

Stevens, K.A. (1981a) The visual interpretation of surface contours. *Artif. Intell.*, 17:47 – 73.

Stevens, K.A. (1981b) The information content of texture gradients. *Biol. Cyber.*, 42:95 – 105.

Stevens, K.A. (1982) Implementation of a theory for inferring surface shape from contours. MIT A.I. Lab. Memo 676.

Stevens, K.A. (1983a) Slant-Tilt: the visual encoding of surface orientation. *Biol. Cyber.*, 46:183 – 195.

Stevens, K.A. (1983b) Surface tilt (the direction of slant): a neglected psychophysical variable. *Perception and Psychophysics*, 33:241 – 250.

Witkin, A.P. (1981) Recovering surface shape and orientation from texture. *Artif. Intell.*, 17:17 – 45.

Reprinted from *Proc. 8th Annual Int. Joint Conf. on Artif. Intell.*, 1057 – 1061 (1983).

The Shape of Smooth Objects and the Way Contours End

Jan J. Koenderink & Andrea J. van Doorn

Rijksuniversiteit Utrecht, The Netherlands

1.0 Shape of Smooth Objects in Mathematics, Perception, and the Theories of Academic Art

Geometrically a smooth object can be defined as a connected, bounded portion of space, such that the boundary possesses a unique tangent plane everywhere. More generally, an object may be smooth except for a finite number of points (e.g. the apex of the right circular cone, the corners of a cube) or curves (e.g. the edges of a cube). If we take a sufficiently small surface patch (so that it is 'of one shape'), then what are its possible shapes? Quite different answers are provided by mathematics (differential geometry) and theories of academic art—and the later no doubt voices convictions gained by visual perception.

In mathematics the basic dichotomy is between isoclastic and anticlastic curved patches (also called elliptic and hyperbolic patches), as shown in Figure 1 (Hilbert & Cohn-Vossen, 1932). The importance of this basic division was clearly outlined by Gauss in his classic paper *Disquisitiones generales circa superficies curvas* (1827) although the elementary facts were already known at that time (e.g. Meusnier's law). In the case of an elliptic patch the object lies completely on one side of the tangent plane, whereas in the case of a hyperbolic patch the surface cuts the tangent plane. Thus elliptic patches 'enclose' space: the outside of an egg is everywhere an elliptic surface ('ovoid'), but so is the *inside* of an eggshell. Both the inside and the outside are positively curved (elliptic), although one speaks of a convex patch in the former case and of a concave patch in the latter case. Thus, elliptic patches bound either material (convex) or pockets of air (concave). On the other hand the hyperbolic patch cannot enclose anything: as shown in Figure 1, it is a saddle-shaped surface. (There exist no smooth objects that are completely enclosed in a hyperbolic 'skin': there *must* be elliptic patches, or else the surface contains creases.)

In general, the surface of a smooth object can be divided into elliptic and hyperbolic areas. The dividing curves are called parabolic lines. (On such a line the surface is of a cylindrical nature.) The parabolic lines are generically a family of nested, closed curves, which outline the elliptic patches or 'object-like' (in the sense of space-enclosing) parts: bulges of material and pockets of air.

In both theory and practice of plastic art the basic dichotomy is not that of elliptic versus hyperbolic, but of convex versus concave (both elliptic!) whereas the hyperbolic patch is scarcely noticed. We present some examples from both theory and practice.

Perhaps the earliest well articulated text on European academic art theory that treats the subject in depth was writ-

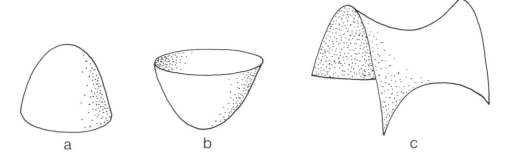

Figure 1 (a) A convex, elliptic patch; (b) a concave, elliptic patch—a bowl-like shape; (c) a hyperbolic patch—or saddle shape.

ten by Leon Battista Alberti (1435). His summing up of the possible forms that a surface patch can assume reads as follows:

"We have now to treat of other qualities which rest like a skin over all the surface of the plane. These are divided into three sorts. Some planes are flat, others are hollowed out, and others are swollen outward and are spherical. To these a fourth may be added which is composed of any two of the above. The flat plane is that which a straight ruler will touch in every part if drawn over it. The surface of the water is very similar to this. The spherical plane is similar to the exterior of a sphere. We say the sphere is a round body, continuous in every pat; any part on the extremity of this body is equidistant from its center. The hollowed plane is within and under the uttermost extremities of the spherical plane as in the interior of an eggshell. The compound plane is in one part flat and in another hollowed or spherical like those of the interior of reeds or on the exterior of columns."

Remarkably, the possibility of the hyperbolic patch is not included. This list has been repeated through the centuries up to our time. For instance, in the important book of Kurt Badt (1963) on plastic art we read (our translation):

"There are three basic possibilities: plane, convex, and concave curvatures. Of these three only the convex is—as a sign and expression of the visibly surging vital force—fundamentally plastic."

Thus, little has changed a century and a half after Gauss's paper!

Experimental psychologists seem to be better acquainted with the theory of art than with mathematics. For instance, Arnheim (1956) in a paragraph on plastic form discusses convex patches but completely neglects the hyperbolic case, whilst Gibson (1979) discusses under 'surface geometry' the space-enclosing properties of convex and concave patches, and also does not mention other possibilities.

In the practice of plastic art we encounter the same phenomenon. Delacroix (quoted in Rawson, 1969) once remarked that you can spot a piece of genuine classic sculpture among pieces of renaissance art by the fact that the ancients grasped form 'par des mileux'. He must have meant the quatrocento, because from the early sixteenth century onward European artists have done the same thing (see Figure 2): they treated form as a conglomerate of

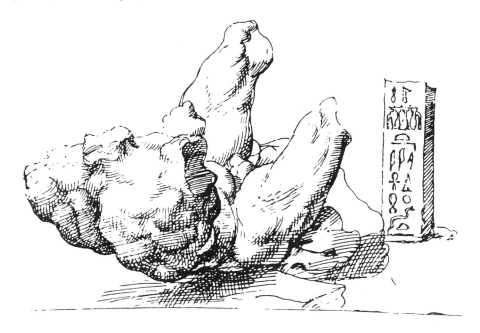

Figure 2 An example of a conglomerate of ovoids. Maarten van Heemskerk: Torso.

ovoid shapes. In its crudest form this leads to the treatment of a human body as a 'bag of melons' [cf. Cellini's (1728) famous derogatory description in his *Vita* of a piece by Bandinelli]. In drawing, the torso acquires a knotty appearance. The draftsman indicates the ovoids by strongly curved lines (Rawson, 1969), mostly in pairs with the concave sides facing each other, and the object is depicted by a concatenation of a great many of such pairs indicating bulges next to bulges and inside bulges, etc. In fact only the elliptic patches are indicated. The sculptor does the same: bulges border on bulges in such a way that the hyperbolic part in between dwindles to a V-shaped furrow, as in Figure 3. Thus art theory and practice go hand in hand (Badt, 1963).

In naturalistic art it does not matter how you deform the hyperbolic parts as long as the elliptic patches are suffi-

ciently articulated. Thus the elliptic parts have a 'figure'-like (thing-like), the hyperbolic parts a 'ground'-like (no-thing-like), character. The hyperbolic patches are perceptually only regions of transition—the 'glue' that keeps things together but is of itself of little interest.

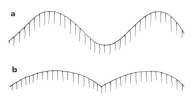

Figure 3 Schematic sections through an undulating surface (a) and its common expression in plastic art (b).

Perhaps the mathematician Felix Klein had the same idea when he sought the key

10

for aesthetics in plastic art in the pattern of parabolic lines. We cannot be sure because Klein published no material on this subject. But from a secondary source (Hilbert & Cohn-Vossen, 1932) we know that he had the parabolic lines drawn on a bust of the Apollo of Belvedere for this reason (Figure 4). (This bust survived the wars: we succeeded in tracing it to the Institute of Mathematics of the Göttingen University.) The result is not particularly enlightening and it seems that Klein gave up this idea. It is our aim to show here that the role of the parabolic lines in the perception and depiction of solid shape is nevertheless of key importance.

2.0 The Contours of the Projection of Objects

It is not possible to see the entire surface of an opaque smooth object simultaneously: parts of the surface are necessarily occluded by the object itself. The curve on the object that divides potentially visible from nonvisible parts is called the *rim* in this paper. By 'potential visibility' we mean visibility except for 'contingencies' like occlusion by a second body or distant parts of the same body. It helps to think of the body as made of 'tinted air'. Then you can see through its volume and 'contingencies' do not count any more. The rim is then the locus of points where the visual direction grazes the surface of the body. The rim consists of a family of smooth loops on the surface. The border of the object's projection in the visual field is called its *contour*. Like the rim, the contour is a closed curve (possibly a nested collection of loops). However, the contour is not necessarily smooth everywhere. Remember that the contour is in the visual field (the space of all visual

directions) whereas the rim is on the object. In practice only part of the contour is visible (except when the body is made of tinted air), because of interposition. In a drawing, the body is demarcated by its *outline*. Thus rim, contour and outline are different concepts in the context of this paper and should not be confused. The contour is the visible projection of the rim. The outline is a subjective expression of the visible part of the contour and what the draftsman knows and feels about the object. If the draftsman aims at 'photographic veridicality' we would expect a similarity between outline and the visible part of the contour.

Figure 4 Bust of Apollo.

In the case of an ovoid—an object bounded by an elliptic surface only—the contour is a single, smooth, closed curve. In such cases the visible contour has no end. In the general case the visible part of the contour *can* end. It can be shown (see Appendix) by mathematical means that visible contours always end

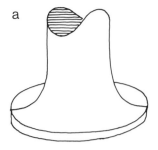 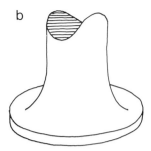

Figure 5 Wrong (a) and right (b) depiction of the contours of a pillar base.

in a simple, lawful manner. The visible contour must be concave at its end points, and the corresponding part of the rim must lie inside a hyperbolic patch. This simple natural law seems to be essentially unknown. Even in texts that aim at a didactic exposition of types of contours the fact is not only not noticed, but there are even illustrations with contours that end in an impossible way (Kennedy, 1974).

Most draftsmen seem also reluctant to concede this natural law: in fact most contours in drawing end in a *convex* way. In cases where a convex ending would show up strangely the artist often devises devious ways to avoid the ending contour. The base of the cylindrical (not fluted) pillar (Figure 5) is a nice case in point: the artist can avoid the ending contour by taking the contour to the edge of the base. This oddity is quite common.[1]

3.0 What Do People Draw?

We have already offered the hypothesis that vision grasps a shape as a conglomerate (or hierarchical structure) of pot-like space enclosures, much like a bunch of grapes. This was exemplified by

the case of the 'ovoid-method' in drawing and sculpture. How could one define such ovoids geometrically? Here a simple method presents itself.

Clearly the ovoid is an isolated elliptical patch. On the body it is demarcated by a closed parabolic line. In the visual field the ovoid is demarcated by the projections of the visible portion of this parabolic line and the visible portion of the rim where the rim traverses the elliptic patch. Thus the contour is *not* necessarily present, nor is the projection of the parabolic line (see Figure 7). If both are simultaneously present, then the contour and the projection of the parabolic line join smoothly, without a 'corner'. Thus the boundary of the elliptic patch in the visual field is a closed, smooth loop that consists of the projection of the parabolic line, the contour, or both. Presumably the draftsman indicates as much of this loop as is needed to suggest the ovoid.

Thus in naive drawings the female breast viewed *en face* is often completely encircled (thus stressing its 'thing-like' nature), whereas a photograph would often show no contour at all; in the case where there is no contour the draftsman indicates the projection of the parabolic

---

[1]A good example is provided by Dürer's woodcut from the series *Seventeen Cuts from the Life of the Virgin*, 1505 (cat. no. Bartsch 88).

Figure 6 Picasso: *Nu couché* 1920.

line. In three-quarter view part of the contour and part of the projection of the parabolic line are drawn.

The importance of the parabolic line for visual perception and depiction is also clear from yet another consideration. At the parabolic line one of the principal curvatures of the surface changes from convex to concave. As a result, the angle of a fixed direction (e.g. the principal direction of light) with the tangent plane reaches an extreme value at the parabolic line (see Figure 8). Thus it is understandable, and it can be proved mathematically (Koenderink & van Doorn, 1980), that the extrema of the illumination, the highlights and shadows, cling to the parabolic lines.

Consequently the art of shadowing (chiaroscuro) also necessarily stresses the parabolic lines. The drawing of parabolic lines may even be regarded as a rudimentary way of shadowing: some study reveals that the draftsman tends to draw

the parabolic line on the shadow side, and leave it out on the light side.

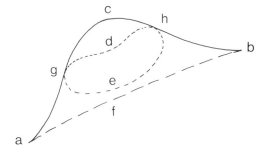

Figure 7 Typical example of an elliptic bulge in three-quarter view: $a\,c\,b$, visible part of contour; $a\,f\,b$, invisible part of contour; $g\,e\,h$, visible part of projection of parabolic line; $g\,d\,h$, invisible part of projection of parabolic line. The 'ovoid' would be bounded in projection by the loop $g\,c\,h\,e$.

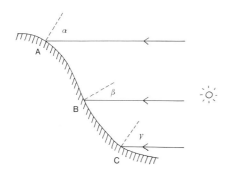

Figure 8 In a section of the object, B is at a parabolic line. The angle of a fixed direction (e.g. of sunlight) with the normal direction to the surface reaches an extreme value at B: $\alpha > \beta$ and $\gamma > \beta$.

He merely sought in the wrong direction, probably expecting to find some infallible rule for the placement of these curves as a recipe for beauty. Such a rule—like the Golden Section—would fall outside the realm of science. But a strong case can be made for the hypothesis that vision grasps shape as a hierarchical structure of elliptic patches, and this hierarchy is identical with that of the family of nested parabolic loops.[2]

It is a sobering thought that in the scientific study of shape perception the same ignorance of the basic geometrical facts is common: here the stimulus is very much defined in terms of the response.

4.0 Discussion

Felix Klein was certainly right when he suspected the importance of the parabolic lines for our visual appreciation of shape.

References

Alberti, L.B. (1435) *Della Pittura*. English translation by J.R. Spencer *On Paint-*

---

[2] A referee pointed out to us that we should draw no conclusions about how people *see* things from how they *draw* things. We believe this to be a subjective standpoint. Since the point is debatable, we add here a few lines to make our standpoint.

Both draftsmen and sculptors in many European and Asiatic stylistic periods build their shapes from 'ovoids' (in academic practice), that is elliptically bounded pot-like volumes. This is seen most directly from the exclusion of certain facts of nature from artistic artifacts, such as the concavely ending contour in drawing and the direct juxtaposition by way of V-shaped furrows of bulges in sculpture. The fact that academic theory neglects hyperbolic shape and that all talk about 'positive' and 'negative' shapes is only about convex and concave *elliptic* patches, corroborates academic practice.

The referee's standpoint is common, perhaps originating with Michelangelo who is reported to have said that he drew with his head (*col cervello*) instead of with his hands (*con la mano*). By way of writers on art (like Zuccaro, Bellori) the problem attracted philosophers and it became known as the problem of 'Raphael without hands' (Lessing). We believe that the philosopher of art Conrad Fiedler (1887) definitively demolished this fiction. The interested reader should consult his lucid writings, as we can only state the argument in too few lines here. Suppose someone manifests himself to you through generally incoherent utterances. You would certainly consider his discursive thinking to be defective. Now suppose someone is only able to offer you incoherent drawings: we would say that his visual thinking deficient! (Remember that you cannot put your visual experience into words!)

ing. London: Routledge & Kegan Paul (1956).

Arnheim, R. (1956) *Art and Visual Perception*. London: Faber & Faber.

Badt, K. (1963) Wesen der Plastik. In *Raumphantasien und Raumillusionen*. Köln: M. DuMont Schauberg.

Cellini, B. (1728) *La Vita*. First edition. Naples: Antonio Cocchi. There have been many subsequent editions in most European languages.

Fiedler, C. (1887) *Der Ursrung der künstlerischen Tätigkeit.* reprinted in 1977 *Schriften über Kunst* (with an introduction by H. Eckstein). Köln: DuMont Buchverlag.

Gauss, C.F. (1827) *Disquisitiones generales circa superficies curvas*. Translated into English *General Investigation of Curved Surfaces*. New York: Raven Press (1965).

Gibson, J.J. (1979) *The Ecological Approach to Visual Perception*. Boston: Houghton Mifflin.

Hilbert, D. & Cohn-Vossen, S. (1932) *Anschauliche Geometrie*. Berlin: Springer.

Kennedy, J.M. (1974) Icons and information. In *Media and Symbols: The Forms of Expression, Communication, and Education*, Seventy-third Yearbook of the National Society for the Study of Education. Chicago, Ill.: The University of Chicago Press, chap. 9, pp. 211–240.

Koenderink, J.J. & van Doorn, A.J. (1980) Photometric invariants related to solid shape. *Optica Acta*, 27:981–996.

Rawson, P. (1969) *Drawing*. London: Oxford University Press.

Appendix: The Ending Contour

For initiates of the catastrophe theory or differential geometry a very general and elegant proof (without formulae!) consisting of only a few sentences would suffice.[3] Such knowledge is not assumed here and a 'pedestrian' proof is offered. This cannot be done without some formulae. Figure A1 illustrates the steps.

Consider Cartesian coordinates (x, y, z). Let the points $(x, y, F(x, y))$ describe the points of the surface, such that the 'material' is at points $z \leq F(x, y)$ and 'air' at points $z > F(x, y)$. Let the origin be a point of the surface, and let the $x - y$ plane be a tangent plane at this point. The eye is thought to view the object from a large distance (effectively from infinity), say from $x = +\infty$, $y = z = 0$. It is always possible to choose the axes such that this situation applies.

In the neighborhood of the origin $F(x, y)$ is approximated by its Taylor series. Terms up to the third order have to be retained for the description of an ending contour. No generality is lost by neglecting higher-order terms. Thus, set

$$F(x, y) =$$
$$\frac{1}{2}(ax^2 + 2bxy + cy^2) +$$
$$\frac{1}{6}(ex^3 + 3fx^2y + 3gxy^2 + hy^3) \ .$$

The condition for the rim is

---

[3]The projection of the surface of the body in the visual field has as generic singularities only folds and cusps. The folds are the smooth part of the contour, the cusps belong to points where one looks in an asymptotic direction. Thus only one of the branches is visible and it is concave.

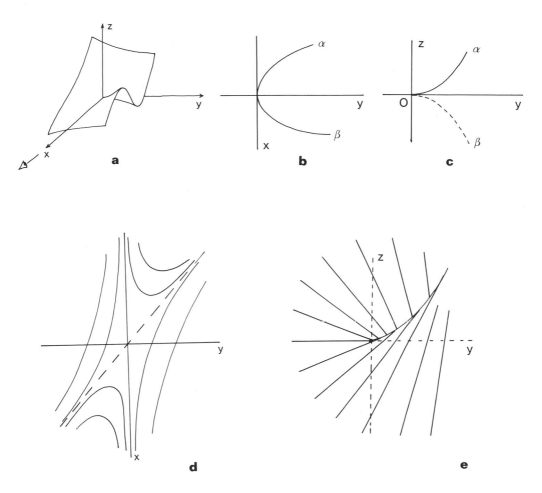

Figure A1 Geometrical properties of a three dimensional object.

(a) General impression of the object in case of an ending contour. In this example the surface is: $F(x,y) = xy + y^2 - \frac{1}{3}x^3$.

(b) The rim projected on the ground plane. The rim is, of course, a space curve. In this example the rim is $y = x^2$.

(c) Projection of the rim on the $y - z$ plane is similar to the contour in the (two-dimensional) visual field. The branch $O\alpha$ is visible, the branch $O\beta$ not. In this example the contour is: $z = \pm\frac{2}{3}y^{3/2}$.

(d) Equal height, $F(x,y) = k$, curves in the $x - y$ plane. The x-axis is an asymptote. In this example we have $y(x + y) = \epsilon$.

(e) Curves of equal distance to the eye projected on the $y - z$ plane (visual field). these curves touch the contour. In general the contour is the envelope of the equidistant curves. In this example the equation of the equidistance lines is $z = x_0 y - \frac{1}{3}x_0^3$.

10

$$\frac{\partial F}{\partial x} =$$

$$ax + by + \frac{1}{2}(ex^2 + 2fxy + gy^2)$$

$$= 0 \, .$$

This is a parabola. If we stipulate that the contour must end at the origin, and must be visible for $y > 0$ only, then this parabola must be of the form

$$y - kx^2 = 0 \quad (k = \text{a positive constant}).$$

This yields the following conditions for the coefficients:

$$a = f = g = 0; \quad e/b < 0 \, .$$

Elimination of x yields the contour, that is the projection of the rim in the $y - z$ plane:

$$z = \pm A y^{3/2}$$

$$\text{where } A = \frac{2}{3}b\left[-\frac{2b}{e}\right]^{\frac{1}{2}}$$

(higher-order terms are irrelevant).

This is a semicubic parabola with a cusp at the origin. Only one of the branches (plus sign) is visible. Thus the contour ends concavely. The level lines of $F(x, y)$ are $F(x, y) = \epsilon$, or

$$bxy + \frac{1}{2}cy^2 +$$

higher order terms $= \epsilon$.

Near the origin the higher-order terms may be neglected, and we obtain

$$y\left(bx + \frac{1}{2}cy\right) = \epsilon,$$

a pair of hyperbolae with asymptotes $y = 0$ and $bx + \frac{1}{2}cy = 0$. Thus we reach the following conclusions:

(i) the patch is hyperbolic for the surface lies on both sides of the tangent plane $z = 0$;

(ii) at the ending contour one looks directly in the direction of the asymptote $y = 0$.

We may think of the asymptotes as 'drawn on the surface'; they are fixed whenever the shape is given. The contour must end whenever the rim (a curve that depends on the viewing position) touches such an 'asymptotic line'.

The sketches in Figure A1 clarify the geometry of the ending contour.

Reprinted from *Perception*, 11:129 – 137 (1982).

Inferring 3D Shapes from 2D Silhouettes

Whitman Richards

Massachusetts Institute of Technology
Cambridge, MA

Jan J. Koenderink

Rijksuniversiteit Utrecht, The Netherlands

D.D. Hoffman

University of California, Irvine
Irvine, CA

1.0 Introduction

Our aim is to understand how unique 3D interpretations can be made from 2D silhouettes. For example, the outline P3 of Figure 1 looks like a "dumbbell", whereas T3 of Figure 2 looks like a "croissant", or T4 looks like a "pear". Yet each of these silhouettes could have arisen from an infinity of 3D objects, considering that we are given no information about the bumps and dents on either the back or front side of the surface. Why, therefore, do we tend to pick only one or two 3D shapes? Clearly some very powerful constraints must be imposed upon our interpretations. One of these, to be elaborated below, is that we do not propose protrusions or indentations of a surface without evidence for such. However, this rule by itself is not sufficient to drive unique interpretations of these silhouettes. To this end, we identify some intrinsic properties of smooth surfaces that are implicitly understood when 3D shape interpretations are made.

Before embarking upon our analysis of inferring 3D shape from 2D silhouettes, we first introduce a method for enumer-ating all possible silhouettes. Without such an enumeration scheme, our selection of outlines might be rather ad hoc and arbitrary. We choose a representation of plane curves that is based upon curvature. In this way we can capture the general form of all types of invaginations and protrusions, but not at the expense of carrying scale and metrical information. For our purposes, our choice of using extrema or singularities of curvature has perceptual relevance, because these extrema make explicit the "parts" of an outline. Arguments for our choice are presented elsewhere, including in the companion article (Beusmans et al., 1987; Hoffman & Richards, 1984, 1982). The most primitive "parts" of a 2D shape are called codons, which have been described earlier in selections 7 and 8. The codon set provides a complete basis for describing any wiggly curve, like a silhouette, and hence can be used to enumerated a class of silhouettes. The representation has the further advantage of making explicit certain features of an outline that permit 3D interpretations, such as the Gaussian curvature.

2.0 Silhouettes from Codons

Our procedure for enumerating all possible silhouettes is simply to build closed codon strings of increasing length. Without constraint, we can expect 5^N possible sequences of length N. However, silhouettes are closed outlines that are not self-intersecting. If we also impose the constraint that the silhouette be smooth (i.e. without cusps), then the number of possible sequences is reduced to roughly $3 \cdot 2^{N-2}$. For example, of the 3125 combinations of codon strings of length 5, only 25 will satisfy the smooth silhouette constraint (Richards & Hoffman, 1984; Hamscher, 1986; Leyton, 1986). Allowing a single cusp raises the number to 457.

Codon Triples (6)

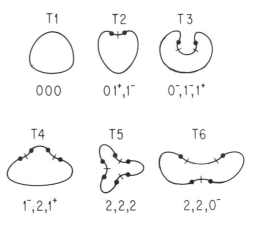

Figure 2 Legal smooth, closed codon triples. The tick marks indicate the extrema of negative curvature, which are generally the part boundaries, whereas the dots show the inflections.

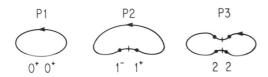

Figure 1 Legal smooth, closed codon pairs. Figure is indicated by cross hatching. Part boundaries are noted by the slashes.

In order to keep our silhouettes manageable, therefore, we consider only smooth silhouettes of codon length 4 or less. All these possibilities are shown in Figures 1, 2 and 3. Their construction is discussed elsewhere (Leyton, 1986; Richards & Hoffman, 1984). These figures thus present the data we wish to analyze. Although this set appears limited, it will be seen that our techniques are readily generalizable.

3.0 The "Canonical" View

We begin by examining the simple outlines of Figure 1, the "ellipse", "peanut" and "dumbbell", for the analysis of these simple silhouettes provides us with the tools needed to interpret the more complex shapes of Figures 2 and 3. The simplest of these three outlines is the ellipse, which we naturally interpret as the silhouette of an ellipsoid or "egg". But why? If the outline is a special view of an object, such as the "end-on" view of the dumbbell or peanut, we could be fooled. Our interpretation thus assumes that our view is such that none of the bumps or dents of the object are occluded or invisible. To capture this notion we propose our first interpretation rule:

Codon Quads (12)

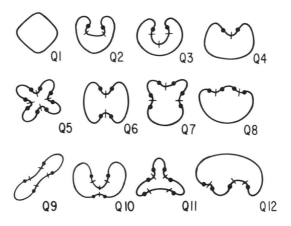

Figure 3 Legal smooth, closed codon quadruples. The tick marks indicate the extrema of negative curvature. The dots show inflections through which the flexional loci must pass.

R1: Do not propose undulations of the 3D surface without evidence for such.   (1)

The above rule is an extension of the "general position" restriction, which requires that the view of an object is not a special one and is stable under perturbation. For our purposes the restriction states that a slight shift in viewpoint should not change the topology of the viewed structure, such as suddenly revealing a bump or dent in the surface that was previously hidden by occlusion. We define such views of a surface as being "generic". Our interpretation rule thus implicitly assumes that the observer's view is generic. It also implies that all the undulations of the surface needed to infer a plausible 3D shape are visible. The view of the silhouette is thus assumed to be a special generic view, namely one which might be called "prototypic". As more information is added about the 3D surface, it might

be expected that the inferred shape will evolve in a graceful manner. This captures the notion expressed by Marr in his principle of least commitment (Marr, 1976). Thus, in the case of the ellipse outline of Figure 1, the most plausible 3D interpretation according to the rule is an ellipsoid.

4.0 Gaussian Curvature

The ellipse is a very special outline, because it has no undulations and hence its sign of curvature everywhere is the same, namely positive. The peanut and dumbbell are more complex, however, with bumps and dents. Clearly we need a means of describing undulations on 3D surfaces in order that we can enumerate all possible 3D interpretations of the 2D outlines. We choose for this purpose an intrinsic property of 3D surfaces, namely the Gaussian curvature.

n	f_n	g_n
0	1	1
2	1	1
4	3	2
6	15	5
8	105	14
10	945	42
12	10,395	132
14	135,135	429
16	2,027,025	1,410

Table 1 The total number of non-generic (f_n) and generic (g_n) pairings of n flexional (parabolic) points lying on a silhouette , $f_n = n!/(n/2)!2^{n/2}$ and $g_n = \binom{n}{n/2}/(n/2+1)$ (from Beusmans et al., 1987).

At any point on a smooth (non-planar) surface, there is a direction where the surface curves the most and another direction where the surface curves the least. These two directions are the directions of principal curvature and they are always perpendicular (Hilbert & Cohn-Vossen, 1952). The Gaussian curvature is simply the product of these two curvatures. Of interest to us is the sign of Gaussian curvature, which permits a qualitative description of the topology of a surface. When the direction of both principal curvatures is identical, such as on an ellipse, the Gaussian curvature is positive; when the principal curvatures are in opposite directions, such as on a saddle, the Gaussian curvature is negative. If one of the principal curvatures is zero, such as on a cylinder, then the Gaussian curvature will be zero also. Any point on a surface will thus have either positive, negative, or zero Gaussian curvature, depending upon whether it is locally elliptical, hyperbolic

(saddle), or cylindrical. A 3D dumbbell may now be defined as a single hyperbolic region of negative Gaussian curvature (the neck) joining two protrusions of positive Gaussian curvature (the two ovoids). A 3D peanut is a hyperbolic region (saddle) lying within an ellipsoid of positive Gaussian curvature.

In addition to providing the basis for a taxonomy of 3D shapes, Gaussian curvature has another distinct advantage for our purposes. Consider a point on the 3D surface that projects into the 2D silhouette. Then the following is true:

> **C1:** The sign of the Gaussian curvature of points on the 3D surface that project into the silhouette is the same as the sign of curvature of those projections.   (2)

This theorem by Koenderink & van Doorn (1976) thus assures us that the Gaussian curvature of the 3D shape is positive at points on the surface that project into regions of positive curvature on the silhouette. Thus, both the peanut and dumbbell outlines of Figure 1 require that the corresponding 3D shapes have hyperbolic (saddle) regions of negative Gaussian curvature within a region (or two) of positive Gaussian curvature.

At this point, one might be misled to the false conclusion that our problem is essentially solved. But consider again the simple dumbbell P_3, which has four inflection points indicated by dots. By Theorem (2) these points lie on lines of zero curvature, which separate regions of positive and negative Gaussian curvature. Because we can join the dots in three different ways, there are at last three different interpretations of this simple silhouette. Similarly, there will be 15 possible 3D interpretations of the "rabbit-head" silhouette Q7 if the embedding of regions of positive and negative Gaussian curvature is unconstrained. And for the Jack shape Q5, which has 8 inflections, there are 105 possibilities, as shown in Table 1. Yet in each case we see these 2D shapes in only one or two ways as three dimensional objects. Clearly the constraints and rules we invoke must be quite powerful. In the next section, we introduce one more important mathematical constraint, and subsequently add another interpretation rule to further constrain the 3D possibilities.

5.0 Types of Surface Undulations

Consider a surface of hills and valleys, with perhaps also a depression that might collect water after a rainfall. The hill, being a "bump" on the surface will have positive Gaussian curvature (such as your interpretation of T4). But so will its inverted shape that creates the "dent" or depression, for the product of two negative principal curvatures will be positive. The positive sign of Gaussian curvature thus does not tell us whether the surface is convex or concave.[1] Similarly, there will be two kinds of regions of negative (hyperbolic) Gaussian curvature, which we will call "saddles" and "humps" (these latter regions may also be called "furrows" and "ridges"). A saddle (or furrow) is a region of negative Gaussian curvature within an elliptical region, whereas a hump (ridge) is an elliptical region within a hyperbolic one. Shapes T2 and Q8 tend to be given the two interpretations. We thus have four types of surface undulations: bumps and dents, and saddles and humps. Together,

they form a complete qualitative description of any smooth surface (Cayley, 1859; Koenderink & van Doorn, 1981, 1980; Maxwell, 1870).

We next need a simple scheme for representing the relations between the four types of surface undulations. For this we choose the Gaussian sphere. Our intent is to project the silhouette onto the Gaussian sphere and to use this projection, together with the topology of the silhouette, to constrain the possibilities of 3D shapes.

The Gaussian sphere is simply a parallel mapping of all the surface normals into the unit sphere, with the tail of each normal placed at the center (Hilbert & Cohn-Vossen (1952). Each point on the surface of this sphere thus corresponds to a particular orientation [see Horn (1984), for an extended discussion]. In the case of a convex object with positive Gaussian curvature everywhere, no two points on the surface will have the same projection onto the sphere. However, for objects with concavities, the same point on the Gaussian sphere may represent two or more points on the object's surface.

Consider now the mapping of a silhouette, such as that of the "peanut" onto the Gaussian sphere. Assume for the moment parallel projection. Then each visual ray which gives rise to the silhouette must strike the surface in such a way to be perpendicular to the surface normal at the point of contact. All surface normals on the surface contours which gives rise to the silhouette must therefore lie in the frontal plane, parallel to the image plane. This plane when mapped into the Gaussian sphere will pass through the origin of the sphere. Hence the locus of any silhouette seen under parallel projection will be

---

[1]Little has proposed a notation that removes this ambiguity. We will simply use the words "bump" or "dent". See Little (1985).

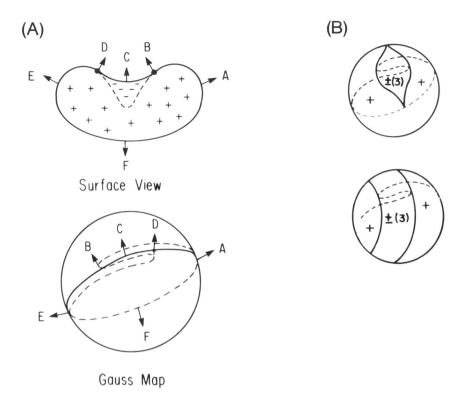

(A)

Surface View

Gauss Map

(B)

$\pm(3)$

$\pm(3)$

Figure 4 The outline of a 3D shape seen under parallel projection maps onto a great circle on the Gaussian sphere. A "peanut" –shaped outline with two inflections will have two folds on the Gauss map, as shown by the dashed line. The extremities of these folds must lie on flexional lines of zero Gaussian curvature as suggested in the 3D rendition of the silhouette (top left). The two insets at right show the only two possible ways of closing the two flexional loci that intersect the folds on the great circle (Whitney, 1955). The (lower) example with two loops is not appropriate for the silhouette of the peanut, which has only two inflections. Thus, the upper inset correctly describes the Gauss map of the peanut. We indicate the triple covering of the Gauss map within the flexional lines by the $\pm(3)$ notation.

a great circle on the Gaussian sphere (see Figure 4).

Let us now trace the surface normals A-E of the silhouette of the peanut onto the appropriate great circle of the Gaussian sphere. Starting at A, we move through the vertical to position B, which is one of the two inflections. Passing through

this point to the second inflection at D requires that we traverse a position on the silhouette with a vertical normal (C). The surface normal at the bottom of the well at C thus has the same direction as the normal to the two "bumps" at the top of the peanut. Thus this point C on the Gaussian sphere actually corresponds to three points on the object's surface. In Figure 4, the dashed contours on the Gaussian spheres is the locus of the silhouette of the peanut. The ends of the two "folds" on these lines are the inflection points (dots) on the silhouette (B and D) where the direction of rotation of the surface normals change as one moves along the contour. Of necessity, the end of any such fold is a point of zero Gaussian curvature where the outline (or surface) goes from a region of positive to negative Gaussian curvature. Between the folds the Gauss map is said to be "triply covered" in this case because each point on the sphere corresponds to three points on the surface.

For the class of generic surfaces we are considering, it is not possible to have an isolated point of zero Gaussian curvature. Rather, all points of zero Gaussian curvature must lie on closed lines (Koenderink & van Doorn, 1981). We call these lines the flexional lines of a surface, for they are the boundaries between regions of positive and negative Gaussian curvature and produce an inflection on the surface (or silhouette). [Flexional lines are also called parabolic lines in some texts.] Koenderink & van Doorn (1980, 1981) have proven the following important property of flexional lines:

> **C2**: For generic surfaces, the flexional (parabolic) lines are (3) closed and non-intersecting.

Thus we now know that on the Gaussian sphere, the flexional lines must also be closed.

Returning to our peanut example in Figure 4, this means that the ends of the two folds on the Gauss sphere must lie on closed curves. As shown by Whitney (1955) and others (Banchoff et al., 1982; Koenderink & van Doorn, 1980), there are only two ways we can close flexional curves on the Gauss map: either we can join the ends in a smooth loop, or we can create a cusp. If the flexional curve is closed with a cusp on the Gauss map, then this specifies a wrinkle on the surface (i.e. a saddle or hump), and there must be a cusp on the opposite side of the great circle locus of the silhouette (dashed lines). This case is illustrated in the top right of Figure 4. (We call this a "pleat".) If the flexional curves are closed by simple loops, then we now are left only with the possibility of joining the folds on the Gauss map with two loops (lower right) (Whitney, 1955). But two loops on the Gauss map indicate four folds because each loop will cross the great circle of the silhouette twice. Hence the remaining possibility of two loops is also excluded because four folds on the Gauss map require four inflections on the silhouette and the peanut has only two. The "peanut" silhouette thus must correspond to an ovoid of positive Gaussian curvature with a single "saddle (furrow)" of negative Gaussian curvature, which is the 3D peanut.[2]

---

[2]Of course, other interpretations of the "peanut" outline are still possible, given our interpretation rule and constraints, namely a planar shaped "pond" or a "potato chip". Why do we tend to infer the 3D object over these two other possibilities? Perhaps one explanation is that neither of the two alternatives are truly general position views of three-dimensional surfaces. For example, the "outline" of the potato chip or of a planar region has little to do with the actual shape of the surface. This is not the case for opaque 3D objects, however. Hence given a 2D outline from which one is to infer 3D shape, only opaque, volumetric 3D shapes have powerful enough constraints on their projections to allow a unique inference.

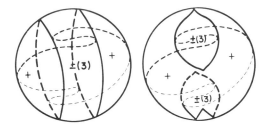

Figure 5 The "dumbbell" outline has two pairs of folds when mapped onto the Gaussian sphere (dashed lines). Closed non-intersecting flexional lines can thus be created in three ways: either by "fusing" the folds on each side of the sphere, creating two pleats with four cusps (right), by creating two "loops" and no cusps (left), or by fusing the cusps on one side of the great circle, leaving a gap in the fused contours to create one big pleat with two cusps. The "fusing" versions are like an ellipsoid with one or two separate furrows, whereas the "loop" version is the true dumbbell. Again, as in Figure 4, the $\pm(3)$ regions are triply covered.

Notice that a "dent" in an ellipsoid is not included in our interpretations of the peanut-shaped outline. If a "dent" is to appear on a smooth silhouette, then its hyperbolic "lip" must be visible. But this would require two visible flexional lines on the silhouette—an impossibility. Hence the following constraint appears for interpreting smooth silhouettes:

> **C3**: A region of negative curvature on a silhouette always is interpreted as a saddle (or "neck") in 3D, never as a dent. (4)

Inspection of the shapes illustrated in Figures 1, 2 and 3 shows that this is the

case. Note that this constraint follows directly from R1 and C1.

6.0 The "Dumbbell" (or "Pear")

The analysis of the dumbbell silhouette now follows quite simply. Its Gauss map is shown in Figure 5. There are two pairs of folds, each pair corresponding to the upper and lower views of the bar of the dumbbell. The flexional lines through the extremities of these folds may be closed in two ways, as illustrated: either we can fuse the pairs as we did previously with the peanut to create an "egg" with either one or two indentations, or we can form two rings, or "loops" to create a 3D dumbbell. These are the only two possibilities, given our interpretation rule (1) that no undulations of the surface should be proposed without evidence for such. But of these two possibilities, which do we pick? Again, we invoke a natural extension to our interpretation rule. To see two saddles, the 3D object must be oriented more carefully with respect to the viewer than in the case of the dumbbell. For example, if the saddles were on the front and back faces of the shape, then the silhouette could be an ellipse. The dumbbell shape is thus a more general position interpretation, and should be preferred. A corollary to our interpretation rule is thus:

> **R2**: Pick the most general position 3D interpretation, namely that 3D shape which preserves the signs of the curvature of the silhouette over the widest range of viewpoints. (4)

This corollary to our interpretation rule now excludes the egg with one or two saddles, for such an interpretation requires that the egg be viewed in a somewhat restricted manner. Thus the preferred 3D interpretation for the dumbbell outline should be the "dumbbell".

7.0 Loops and Pleats

A strategy for enumerating the 3D shapes now emerges. When the silhouette is mapped onto the Gaussian sphere, the inflections of the silhouette map into folds on the Gauss map. These points on the folds occur in pairs and delimit a region of either positive or negative Gaussian curvature. (The silhouette gives us the sign of curvature of the region.) We have two ways of joining the flexional loci that intersect the extremity of these folds: either by forming "loops" or "pleats" that create cusps on the Gauss map. The "loop" choice will correspond either to a "bump" or "dent" on the surface or to a "neck" or "knuckle" in the 3D shape, the latter cases requiring an inflection to appear at (roughly) opposite sides of the parts of the silhouette. The second, "pleat" scheme corresponds either to a hump (ridge) or saddle (furrow) on one side of the 3D shape. Whether the region between the flexional loci on the Gauss map is a hump, saddle, etc., is given by the sign of curvature of the silhouette (3). In total, our "parts" of a surface will be either a "bump", "hump", "knuckle", or their complements, the "dent", "saddle" or a "neck".[3]

If we have only two inflections as in the peanut, then there is only one possibility. This is the pair of cusps or pleat on the Gauss map (i.e. furrow in the 3D shape) because the loops would create two more inflections on the silhouette which are not seen and hence are inferred not to be present. Referring to Figure 2 and 3, the same argument applies to the codon triples T2 and T3 ("croissant") or the three quadruples Q2 ("bib"), Q3 and Q4 ("apron").

If we have four inflections positioned in the silhouette as in shapes T4, T6 or Q6, Q9, Q10, we still only have the "loop" and "pleat" possibilities to consider as we did before with the dumbbell. The preferred choice is two "loops" on the Gauss map, rather than two pleats, because the first solution yields a surface of revolution whose canonical silhouette will always be the same. The argument is identical to that given previously for the "dumbbell", although in this case shape T4 would be a "pear" with the indentations corresponding to a neck.

Figure 6 summarizes the interpretations given to the silhouettes. Rather than showing all silhouettes, only the major classes are illustrated. For example, the dumbbell shapes T6 and Q7, Q9, Q10 are topologically identical to P3, so only P3 is shown. Likewise, T2, T3, Q2, Q3, Q4 are similar to the simple peanut P2. The remaining outlines to be interpreted thus fall in the class T4, T5, Q7, Q8 and Q12.

Shape T4 is now trivial. The Gauss mapping of the flexional loci are the same as the dumbbell. Hence the preferred interpretation will be a "pear" as indicated. For similar reasons, the "jack" silhouette T5 should also be interpreted as having three "fingers", as illustrated. But Q7 can

---

[3] We can continue this taxonomy of 3D parts further to define "knobs", "caps", "cavities", "tongues", "grooves", etc., by placing restrictions on the relations between the normals at the folds, such as was done for the "neck" and "knuckle". Such a scheme is an extension of that proposed by Maxwell (1870), but is beyond the scope of this paper.

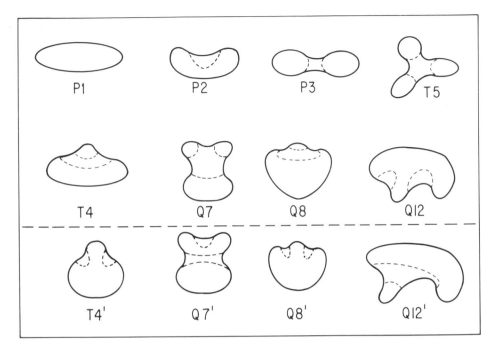

Figure 6 Different classes of the outlines to be interpreted. Dotted lines are the preferred flexional (parabolic) loci.

be similarly interpreted as a body with two limbs, for its Gauss mapping is similar to that of T5. Hence we are left with only two remaining silhouettes, Q8 and Q12.

Our present constraints are not powerful enough to find a preferred interpretation for shape Q8. Unlike shapes Q6 and T4, which also have four inflections, there is no symmetry axis about which the silhouette Q8 can be rotated to produce the same 3D outline. Thus, the two indentations of Q8 can not correspond to a "neck" in a surface of revolution. Instead, because all four inflections are on one side of the outline, we will have a region on the Gauss map that will be five-times covered (rather than the triple covering characteristic of the "neck" in Figure 5.) Reviewing possible pairings once more,

and excluding dents by constraint (4), we have on the Gauss map the following three possibilities as illustrated in Figure 7.

a) two adjacent pleated contours (two saddles)

b) a single pleat (a saddle)

c) a pleat enclosed by a pleat (a hump in a saddle)

Unfortunately, our present interpretation rules do not force a unique choice between the three alternatives illustrated in Figure 7. Although there may be a preference for 7C (hump in a saddle), our general position rule (4) is not sufficiently formulated to exclude 7A and B. Underlying our choice of 7C seems to be the notion that the probability of two saddles being

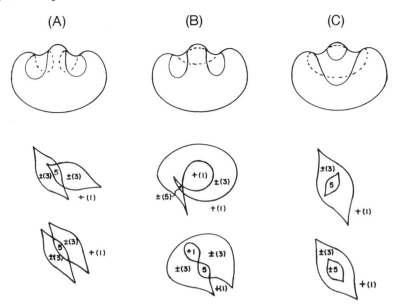

Figure 7 Three possible interpretations of the silhouette Q8. The flexional (parabolic) lines on the surface are illustrated in the top row. Beneath each of these possibilities are sketched the shape of the flexional loci on the Gauss map. The numbers in parenthesis indicate the coverings. The first case is two furrows (A), the second is a single furrow (B), and the third is a ridge in a furrow (C).

aligned with the viewer as in 7A and B is less likely than if one single saddle is so aligned as in 7C. A similar argument applies to shape Q12.

8.0 Discussion

8.1 Effect of constraints

Our four interpretation rules and constraints have allowed us to assign one preferred 3D interpretation to each of the silhouettes shown in Figures 1, 2 and 3. These silhouettes are all the possibilities for smooth codon strings of length four or less. Without constraints, these are 625 different sequences of four codons, or 625 possible 2D outlines that are generically

different (i.e. have different sequences of the extrema of curvature). Closure and smoothness reduce this number to the twelve outlines shown in Figure 3. In a similar manner, we can ask, given a single outline in Figure 3, how many different 3D shapes are possible? Clearly there is a very large number, which increases as smaller and smaller undulations are tolerated.

If we now introduce the simple mathematical constraint that the flexional loci can not intersect on the surface (3), the possibilities are markedly reduced, but still substantial for example, for eight inflection points. Koenderink's rule reduces the number of pairings that must be considered from 105 to 14, as shown in Table 1. However, when our viewing constraint is added, together with the stipulation that "loops" are given preference over "pleats", provided (4) is not violated, then our preferred interpretations become almost unique, at least for the 2D outlines examined. Two simple interpretation rules, therefore, plus two mathematical theorems, provide very powerful constraints on the interpretation of silhouettes.

8.2 Instant psychophysics

Of course the 2D outlines of Figure 6 do not always give a unique interpretation. Our constraining rules are not rigid. For example, the "spade" outline Q8 by our rules should be seen as a hump in a shallow saddle (Figure 7). However, it is easy to imagine Q8 as a convex blob with two saddles, which correspond to two pleats on the Gauss map, although this is not our constrained solution. The outlines given in the lower panel of Figure 7 illustrate such less preferred interpretations. Similarly, outlines T5 and Q7 have alternate 3D interpretations of a saddle in the base of a necked shape. Instead of all loops, the alternate choice would then be two loops and a pleat on the Gauss map. Because these are viable alternatives, we conclude that our preference rules are tentative and seek verification from shading. Also it is clear that at some level, the metrics of the outline, its orientation, and the familiarity of the shape come into play in our judgment. At present, we are only proposing interpretation rules given no information other than the general topology of the Gauss map.

9.0 Conclusion

We invoke four simple constraints for interpreting smooth 2D outlines as 3D shapes. Three are simply mathematical properties of smooth surfaces, namely (i) that the sign of curvature of the silhouette reflects the sign of Gaussian curvature, (ii) that the flexional loci are closed and non-intersecting, and (iii) that these loci form either loops or pleats on the Gauss map. The (iv) fourth constraint is an interpretation rule that undulations not seen in the 2D outline are not present in 3D. This rule is an extension of the notion of general position. A corollary to this interpretation rule is that "necks" on the surface, which correspond to "loops" on the Gauss map, are preferred over saddles which in turn are preferred over dents.

Acknowledgment: This work was supported by a NATO grant for international collaboration, and by the AFOSR under an Image Understanding contract $F49620-83-C-0135$. Comments by Michael Leyton and Jim Little were greatly appreciated. William Gilson provided technical help in the preparation of the manuscript.

References

Banchoff, T., Gaffney, T. & McCrory, C. (1982) *Cusps of Gauss Mappings.* Boston, Mass.: Pitman.

Beusmans, J.M.H., Hoffman, D.D. & Bennett, B.M. (1987) A description of solid shape and its inference from occluding contours. *Jr. Opt. Soc. Amer.*, in press.

Cayley, A. (1859) On contour and slope lines. *Lond. Edinburgh, and Dublin Phil. Mag. and J. Sci.*, 18(120): Oct., Ser. 4, 264–268.

Hamscher, W. (1986) Codon constraints on 2D cusps. Personal communication.

Hilbert, D. & Cohn-Vossen, S. (1952) *Geometry and the Imagination*. Trans. P. Nemeny. New York: Chelsea Publishing Co.

Hoffman, D. & Richards, W. (1982) Representing smooth plane curves for recognition: Implications for figure-ground reversal. *Proc. National Conference on Artificial Intelligence, August 18-20, 1982, Carnegie-Mellon University – University of Pittsburgh.*

Hoffman, D. & Richards, W. (1984) Parts of recognition. MIT A.I. Lab. Memo 732 and *Cognition*, 18:65 – 96.

Horn, B.K.P. (1984) Extended Gaussian images. *Proc. IEEE*, 72(12):1671 – 1686.

Koenderink, J.J. (1987) An internal representation for solid shape based on the topological properties of the apparent contour. In W. Richards & S. Ullman, *Image Understanding 1985-86*, Norwood, N.J.: Ablex.

Koenderink, J.J. & van Doorn, A.J. (1976) The singularities of the visual mapping. *Biol. Cybernetics*, 24:51 – 59.

Koenderink, J.J. & van Doorn, A.J. (1980) Photometric invariants related to solid shape, *Optica Acta*, 27:981 – 996.

Koenderink, J.J. & van Doorn, A.J. (1981) A description of the structure of visual images in terms of an ordered hierarchy of light and dark blobs. *Second Int. Visual Psychophysics and Medical Imaging Conference, IEEE Cat. No. 81CH 1676 – 6.*

Leyton, M. (1986) A process grammar for shape. Referenced in "Symmetry-curvature duality", *Computer Vision, Graphics and Image Processing*, in press 1986.

Little, J.J. (1985) Recovering shape and determining attitude from extended Gaussian images. University of British Columbia Department of Computer Science Technical Report, TN85 – 2.

Marr, D. (1976) Early processing of visual information. *Phil. Trans. Roy. Soc. Lond. B*, 275:483 – 524.

Maxwell, J.C. (1870) On hills and dales. *Lond. Edinburgh, and Dublin Phil. Mag. and J. Sci.* 40(269):Dec., Ser. 4, 421 – 427.

Richards, W. & Hoffman, D. (1984) Codon constraints on closed 2D shapes. MIT A.I. Lab. Memo 769. Also *Computer Vision, Graphics, and Image Processing*, 31:265 – 281 (1985).

Whitney, H. (1955) On singularities of mappings of Euclidian spaces. I. Mappings of the plane into the plane. *Ann. Math.*, 62:374 – 410.

Reprinted from *Jrl. Opt. Soc. Amer.* 1987.

11

From Waltz to Winston via the Connection Table

Staffan Truvé

Chalmers University of Technology S-412 96 Sweden

Whitman Richards

Massachusetts Institute of Technology

1.0 Introduction

What kind of representations are useful for moving from image-based descriptions to more abstract semantic descriptions that resemble natural languages? Here, we propose that a part-based representation form the bridge between a feature based description which is roughly analogous to Marr's 2 1/2 D sketch, and a model-based description which carries the seeds for semantic interpretation.

A parts-based representation seems to us the natural way of creating an object description (Biederman, 1986; Hoffman & Richards, 1984). Thus, an animal is often described as a body with a head, legs and tail, each in a certain relation to one another, and where each of these parts may be further specified. The representation is of necessity hierarchical and is reminiscent of Minsky's frames (Minsky, 1975). Such object descriptions lend themselves readily to natural language translations.

As illustrated in Figure 1, we suggest three major levels of description: 1) An Object Description Language, which is the base representation used for semantic interpretation; 2) a Connection Table, which describes the (syntactic) relations between the parts of an object, and 3) a 3D-skeleton, describing the relations between "features" as found in an image,

which can be considered to be the lexical level of representation. In the blocks-world case, which we use or illustrative purposes, this 3D-skeleton is a Junction (and/or Face) Network which describes the relations between the faces of the object. We first present brief descriptions of the Object Description Language and the 3D-skeleton. The utility of the Connection Table then becomes obvious.

2.0 Definitions

We start by giving the definitions of some terms that will be used frequently. An **Object** is considered to be a solid, opaque, physical entity, such as one defined by the union of a set of intersecting convex solids (Barr, 1984; Pentland, 1985). A **Part** is an object used to build a more complex object. A **Primitive Part** is an object not built from any sub-parts, and hence is completely convex, such as a cylinder, cone or ellipsoid. A **3D-Skeleton** is a complete description of an object in terms of some primitive features. In the blocks-world, such features would be labeled vertices and faces. Note that this description is 3D and hence inferences about hidden features are included in the skeleton. A **Connection Table** describes the way in which parts are put together to form an object. A **Primitive Connection**

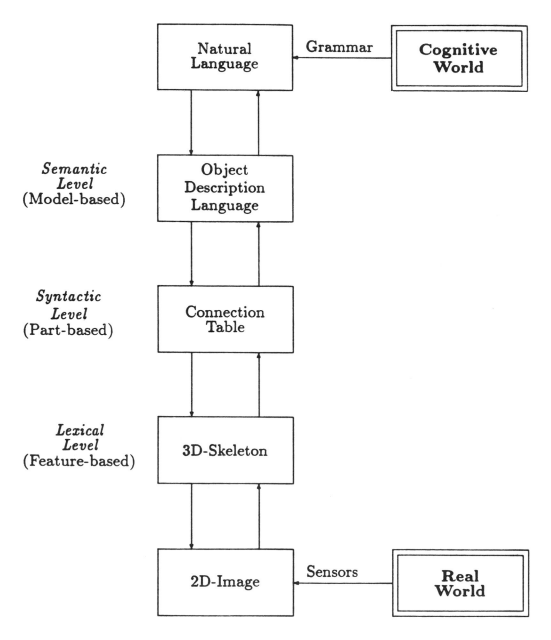

Figure 1 A general outline of the different levels of representation being suggested. The middle three boxes represent the major topic of this paper.

```
Object ≡ MODULE
          Faces : Type
          Parameters : Type
          Equal : Faces → {Faces}
          Opposite : Faces → {Faces}
          Adjacent : Faces → {Faces}
      END
```

```
cone ≡ OBJECT-TYPE
          DEFINING
              Faces = {1,2};
              Parameters = {height,radius};
              Equal = {<1,{1}>,<2,{2}>};
              Opposite = {};
              Adjacent = {<1,{2}>,<2,{1}>}
      END
```

Figure 2 The module signature specification of a primitive part (left), and an instance of it, the specification of a cone (right).

Table is a connection table containing only primitive parts, which are described by an arrangement of features common to the 3D-skeleton. A **Canonical Connection Table** is a unique canonical form of a connection table. The **Object Description Language** is a language where block structure and grammar is common to all kinds of parts and relations. A **Description**, finally, defines a class of objects. It can be thought of as a predicate (or a function $Object \rightarrow Bool$), which given an object yields TRUE/FALSE as result, depending on if the object belongs to the class specified by the predicate or not. A description can be expressed as a connection table or using the description language.

3.0 An Object Description Language [ODL]

One useful purpose of a high-level description language is to give us a convenient, yet formal method of describing and communicating efficiently the way we consider objects to be created by the connection of different parts. Thus, the language description should be parts-based. Our desire to allow stepwise refinement of descriptions implies that our language should have a hierarchical structure, right down to the level of the most primitive convex parts. Like most previous languages, therefore, (Brooks, 1981; Connell & Brady, 1985; Winston et al., 1983) the structure and grammar should be appropriate for all levels of abstraction of an object description. In this respect, our ODL language will resemble the feature (or functional) structures of certain formal models of natural language grammar (Bresnan, 1985).

A second major constraint imposed upon our language and intermediate representation is that local, topological properties are stressed rather than metric properties. Thus, relations between the parts of an object are made explicit (Koenderink, 1987; Koenderink & van Doorn, 1977; Ullman, 1984), and indeed the complexity of these relations will serve later as a measure of the "importance" of a particular part, rather than its size or shape, or partic-

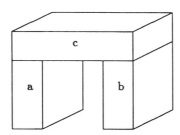

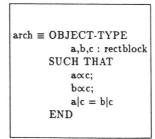

Figure 3 A simple arch (left) and the language description of it (right).

ular deformation. Although this decision may first appear somewhat arbitrary, the intuition is that (at least for recognition), a person's head or face which has many parts (e.g. ears, eyes, nose, mouth, etc.) should be given more "weight" than the size of his torso.

This section presents the ingredients of one such language by giving a few examples. A more formal description is given in Truvé (1987).

3.1 Primitive parts

When two parts are joined transversally, a concavity is created where their surfaces intersect (Bennett & Hoffman, 1986; Hoffman & Richards, 1984). A concavity thus indicates a boundary between two parts. Because a primitive part is defined as having no sub-parts, such a part has no concavities.[1] Cones, rectangular blocks, cylinders, etc., are possible primitive parts. Such parts are defined by specifying the face types and the relations between the faces, which are features provided by the 3D-skeleton (an example follows). Clearly, the possible relations between the faces of a part will depend upon the types of primitive parts included in the domain. This in turn will affect the kinds of attachments possible for a part. Hence, the relations between faces specified at the primitive part level impose a stringent constraint upon the language at all levels.

Here, we wish to illustrate our approach using a "blocks-world". In such a world where the primitive parts are rectangular blocks, there are only three basic relations we need consider: two faces are either equal, opposite, or adjacent. By equal we mean that two faces have the same relations to all other faces. (Later we define a complex part where a face may be considered equal—i.e. having the same attachments—not only to itself but to other faces.) Note that each face has four adjacent faces, but only one that is opposite. For a world built from polyhedra with more than six faces, more complicated relational primitives might be desired. However, our simple blocks world is sufficient to illustrate the general structure of our language.

More formally, then, primitive parts can be thought of as specified by *modules*. We can define their *signature* (using a notation similar to that in (Nordström & Petersson, 1985) in the way shown in Figure 2. One instance of such a specification, that for a *cone*, is also shown.

---

[1]An exception occurs when deformations of parts are allowed, such as bending (see Barr, 1984).

We see that our specification of a *cone* corresponds quite closely to a description in English: *A cone is a part with 2 faces that are adjacent to one another. There are no opposite faces (thus distinguishing a cone from a hemisphere). The cone's dimensions are specified by its height and radius.*

The Appendix contains more examples of primitive part definitions.

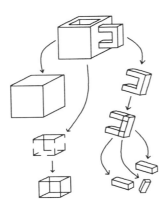

Figure 4 The object *mug* and a possible decomposition of it. (Alternatively, the body of the mug can be broken into five rectangular blocks. We will address ambiguities like this subsequently.)

3.2 Describing attachment

Having specified the primitive parts in terms of features available in the 3D-skeleton (faces, in the blocks-world case), we can now describe *how* these parts are put together, i.e. which faces are glued to each other (Ansaldi et al., 1985). This description is divided into two sections, one in which we specify only which faces are attached to each other (we call this describing the *connections*) and another in which we describe where on a face a part is glued (this is what we will call *positions*). Here, for brevity, we deal only with the *connection* of parts. Again, we stress that the major constraint imposed upon our language requires that attachments between parts is specified using the same relations that define the primitive parts.

3.2.1 Connections

To describe which face is attached to which, we use a basic attachment operator, $\propto$.

In the *arch* example, we begin by declaring an arch to consist of three primitive parts, a, b and c, all of which are rectangular blocks (defined as primitive parts in the Appendix). We then go on to give clauses that constrain the way in which these parts can be put together to form an arch; The *attachment operator*, written $\propto$, tells us that a is attached to c, and that b is also attached to c. The "|"-operator returns a set of attachment-faces. For example, the expression $a \mid c$ returns a set, the elements of which are the faces of c to which a is attached. Therefore, the equality between the two "|"-expressions tells us that a and b are attached to the same side of c.

The attachment operator ($\propto$) is the only language primitive available for saying that two parts are glued to each other. To state that two objects may *not* be attached to each other, we include a clause of the form NOT($a \propto b$). To describe which faces they are glued to, we have three basic operators in the language, one for equal sides ($=$), one for opposite sides ($\rightleftharpoons$) and one for adjacent sides ($\bowtie$). We see now the importance of defining the basic relations on the primitive parts—they

```
mug ≡ OBJECT-TYPE
          base,H1,H2,H3 : rectblock;
          hole : negrectblock
     SUCH THAT
          H1∝H3;
          H2∝H3;
          H1∝base;
          H2∝base;
          hole∝base;
          H1|H3 = H2|H3;
          H1|base = H2|base;
          H3|H1 ⇌ base|H1;
          H3|H2 ⇌ base|H2;
          hole|base ⋈ H1|base
     END
```

```
newmug ≡ OBJECT-TYPE
          handle : named-arch;
          base : rectblock;
          hole : negrectblock;
     SUCH THAT
          handle∝base;
          hole∝base;
          hole|base ⋈ handle|base;
          base|handle = handle.ends
     END
```

Figure 5 Two *mug*-descriptions in terms of parts. The right description capitalizes on the block structure of the language, using a predefined object *named-arch*.

are needed to allow us to use the primitive parts when building more complex objects.

As another example, consider the *mug* in Figure 4. A simple description is that it has three parts—a body, a handle, and a hole. The handle in turn can be decomposed into three rectangular blocks, and the hole can be seen as a "negative rectangular block". [2] A complete language description of the *mug* is given in Figure 5.

3.3 Complex parts: adding block structure to ODL

The language presented so far allows us to define objects using only primitive parts. By adding *block structure* to the language we allow the use of complex objects as parts. In addition, libraries of frequently used subparts can be introduced, and symmetries described in a more straightforward way. This corresponds to the use of abstract data types in high-level programming languages. To introduce block structure we add three rules about how objects can be defined: 1) The type of a part in a declaration can now be a type definition in itself. 2) We allow object type definitions in the declaration section of an object type definition. 3) We also allow nested object type definitions.

Because we now define and use complex parts, we must be able to refer to certain faces in such a part. This is achieved by *naming* faces in an object. We can also define relations (such as equality and adjacency) between named faces. An example, defining an arch with named faces, is shown in Figure 6. Here, the face

---

[2]Introducing primitive parts that represent "negative" blocks might not be the best method of representing holes in objects. This paper, however, does not deal with this problem, and will assume that negative primitive parts can be defined rigorously and identified in the 3D-skeleton.

```
named-arch ≡ OBJECT-TYPE
                a,b,c : rectblock
             SUCH THAT
                a∝c;
                b∝c;
                NOT(a∝b);
                a|c = b|c;
             NAMING
                end1 ⇌ c|a;
                end2 ⇌ c|b;
                ends ← end1 ∪ end2;
                top ⇌ a|c
             DEFINING
                Faces = ends ∪ top;
                Equal = {<x,ends> | x ∈ ends} ∪ {<x,top> | x ∈ top};
                Opposite = {<x,ends> | x ∈ top} ∪ {<x,top> | x ∈ ends};
                Adjacent = {}
             END
```

Figure 6 An arch with some named faces.

names *end1, end2* and *top* are defined, and the two ends are then given a joint name, *ends.*

To illustrate the use of complex parts (with named faces) we give a new definition of a mug, where we let the *handle* be a *named-arch* (see Figure 5, right). Note the dot-notation used to refer to a named set of faces of the arch. A description like this can of course be "flattened", i.e. transformed into the corresponding definition with only primitive parts. The right description can thus be "flattened" resulting in the left one. Different descriptions of an object, using parts of varying complexity, can be seen to form a *lattice* like that shown in Figure 7. This lattice will be used later to look for equality of two different object descriptions.

3.4 Summary

The basic operators of the object description language are summed up in Table 1. They allow us to describe attachments, and relations between different face attachments. A more formal specification of the syntax and of the types and semantics of the operators is given in Truvé (1987).

3.5 Why the ODL is not enough

Again, the main advantage of the ODL is that it gives us a convenient and formal method of describing how objects are created by the connection of different parts. Unfortunately, there are many different ways of describing an object in ODL. Figure 8 shows one example of this by giving two different descriptions of

Operator	Symbol	Typewriter Symbol
Object type declaration	≡	==
Attachment	∝	@
Faces of attachment	|	|
Equal faces	=	=
Opposite faces	⇌	<=>
Adjacent faces	⋈	><

Table 1 The basic operators in the description language.

the same object. Note that all relations between an object's parts need not be explicitly stated in order to fully describe it. This is because some relations can be deduced from the primitive part definitions. Another drawback of the language representation is that it is difficult to compute a canonical form for a description given in it.[3] Our suggested solution to these problems is to transform the language descriptions to another representation, called Connection Tables. These tables capture *all* relations between an object's parts, including those not explicitly stated (cf. Figure 8), and are more easily transformed to a canonical form.

4.0 The 3D-skeleton

A 3D-skeleton is our base feature representation, derived from a 2D-image. It makes explicit the 3D relations between vertices and faces, for example. To com-

plete the skeleton *world knowledge* must be introduced, for instance about how a blocks-world results in an image with lines and junctions, and how these can be used to find the faces of different blocks. There is however no need for any *model knowledge*, i.e. knowledge about which kind of objects and parts could be present in the picture. Building a 3D-skeleton is thus a pure bottom-up task. Note that different sets of primitive parts will need different algorithms for building 3D-skeletons from an image, and that these skeletons might contain different kinds of features. Our current implementation deals only with a blocks-world, but shows the feasibility of building these skeletons. Indeed, this representation is the target for most early vision programs (Binford, 1982; Brady et al., 1985; Cernushi-Frias & Cooper, 1984; Mackworth, 1977; Nevatia & Binford, 1977).

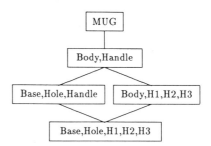

Figure 7 A lattice formed by two different descriptions of a mug.

The skeleton itself poses two difficult problems. First, its construction is obviously non-trivial, for 3D inferences are made from 2D data (Binford, 1981; Draper, 1981; Kanade, 1981). Second, however, and more germane to our pro-

---

[3]One possible way of computing canonical language descriptions is actually given in Truvé, 1987. The method is based on the aforementioned idea of deducing relations from primitive part definitions, and generating *complete* language descriptions.

```
┌─────────────────────────────────┐   ┌─────────────────────────────────┐
│  thing-1 ≡ OBJECT-TYPE          │   │  thing-2 ≡ OBJECT-TYPE          │
│         a,b,c,d,e:rectblock     │   │         a,b,c,d,e:rectblock     │
│       SUCH THAT                 │   │       SUCH THAT                 │
│          c∝a;                   │   │          c∝a;                   │
│          b∝a;                   │   │          b∝a;                   │
│          d∝c;                   │   │          d∝c;                   │
│          e∝a;                   │   │          e∝a;                   │
│          c|a = b|a;             │   │          c|a = b|a;             │
│          d|c ⇌ a|c;             │   │          d|c ⇌ a|c;             │
│          e|a ⇌ c|a              │   │          e|a ⇌ b|a              │
│       END                       │   │       END                       │
└─────────────────────────────────┘   └─────────────────────────────────┘
```

Figure 8 Two different language descriptions (compare the last clause in the two definitions), both corresponding to the object and the connection tables presented in Figure 9.

posal, is that there is no unique way to decompose a complex object into primitive parts. To analyze an image, we must introduce *model knowledge*, telling us what possible objects and parts might occur in a picture. Utilizing this, we can decide on preferred interpretations of images.

We thus need a procedure for taking two sets of primitive parts and their relations (one suggested by the skeleton and one provided by the model), and testing whether the two more complex assemblies (or objects) are equivalent. For example, an *arch* can be decomposed by planar cuts at its two concavities into four different collections of three rectangular blocks. When any of these triplets are connected, they do however result in the same complex object. Thus we need a way of describing how a 3D-skeleton can be analyzed in terms of different sets of primitive parts connected to each other. This task can not be performed in the description language (ODL), because we have no simple way of testing whether two different descriptions in the ODL specify

the same class of objects. We thus need a representation that can map onto the description language, but where descriptions can be put into some canonical form. This new representation, which is intermediate between the ODL and the 3D-skeleton, we call a Connection Table.

5.0 Connection Tables [CT]

In our presentation of the ODL and the 3D-skeleton we have concluded that an additional, intermediate representation is needed to give complete, canonical descriptions of relations between an object's parts. We now proceed to suggest one such representation, the Connection Tables [CT]. After the formal definition we show how to compute the canonical form of a CT, and then discuss the correspondence between the ODL, the 3D-skeleton and the Connection Table.

We define Connection Tables in the following way:

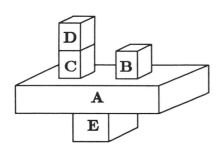

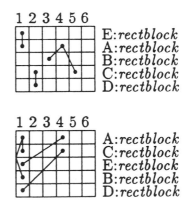

Figure 9 An object (left) and two possible connection tables describing it (right). Note that each face of the primitive parts has a label corresponding to the face label given in the part's specification, so that faces 1 and 4, 2 and 5 and 3 and 6 are opposite to each other, respectively. The lower connection table is in canonical form.

Definition 1 *A* CONNECTION TABLE *for an object with n parts is an array with n rows. Each row has m slots, where m is the number of defined faces of the part corresponding to that row. Each slot in the Connection Table contains a set of pointers, one to each of the slots representing a face to which the slot's face is connected.*

The CTs should be viewed as a graph-representation of the way in which parts are connected to form an object. It differs from the 3D-skeleton in that it is part-based and not feature-based, and from the ODL in that the precise arrangement of connections between parts is made explicit "graphically" rather than semantically. Figure 9 shows two examples of connection tables.

5.1 Canonical connection tables

The definition of a connection table given above does not give a unique form, since there is still ambiguity with respect to faces (for example, all faces of a cube are "equal", so there are many rotations of the cube corresponding to the same connections). In order that two CTs be tested for equality, we need to transform them to a canonical form. We first describe how to get the *canonical rotation* of each part, and then turn to the question of generating a *canonical connection table*.

Definition 2 *The weight function $\mathcal{W}$ of a part is defined as*

$$\prod_{i=1}^{n} P_i^{c_{ij}}$$

where n is the number of faces defined for that part, P_i the $(i+1)$st prime number, and c_{ij} is the number of connections de-

---

[4]Note that all rotations of a part are not allowable, because adjacency and other relations must be preserved. For example, the two circular faces of a cylinder are interchangeable with each other, but not with the lateral surface.

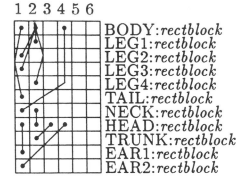

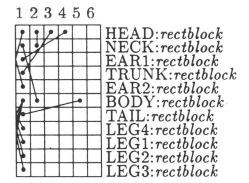

Figure 10 Two connection tables for the heffalump, the right one in canonical form. The ears and the trunk have equal weights in this coarse description, and are thus indistinguishable.

fined for slot i by a particular rotation j of the part.[4]

Definition 3 *The* Canonical Rotation *of a part is defined to be a rotation that minimizes the weight function* $\mathcal{W}$.

Note that each value of the weight function corresponds to exactly one rotation of the part, since each natural number has a unique prime factorization and thus corresponds to exactly one distribution of connections over the different faces. Thus, no two rotations have the same weight function, so there exists one rotation with a unique minimum value for $\mathcal{W}$. The effect of this particular weight function is to order the parts in terms of the number and the complexity of their connections. We have chosen this function over one based on size, for example, because our measure stresses the topological significance (see the Heffalump-example below). We feel recognition, for example, can proceed faster with this scheme, but, of course, this remains an open issue.

As an example, the weight function for a rectangular block is $\mathcal{W} = 2^{c_1} \cdot 3^{c_2} \cdot 5^{c_3} \cdot 7^{c_4} \cdot 9^{c_5} \cdot 13^{c_6}$, where c_i is the number of connections to the ith face of the block. For a cube with a single connection (such as part **E** in Figure 9), the weight function is trivially minimized by assigning the connection to face 1. Minimizing $\mathcal{W}$ for a cube with two connections on opposite faces (such as **C** in the same figure) means assigning the two connections to faces 1 and 4 (cf. Figure 9, bottom right). At present, our weight function gives priority to attachments on equal faces over adjacent, over opposite. This order is not critical, since our weight function will always have a unique minimum value (and a corresponding rotation of the part).

Once we have all parts canonically rotated[5], each part will have an assigned weight. This weight could be the minimum value of $\mathcal{W}$ (as in our current implementation), or the value of some other suitable weight function. The following al-

---

[5]This can for example be done by generating all possible rotations, and selecting the one with the lowest weight function value.

gorithm will generate the canonical form of an entire connection table (the function *maxweight* returns a set containing all the parts with the highest weight function value, given a set of parts):

Algorithm 1 *Getting the Canonical Form of a Connection Table.*

Input: A connection table C with all the parts rotated canonically.

Output: The Canonical Form C' of the connection table C.

```
LET R = a set of all rows (parts) in C
LET C' = empty connection table
DO BEGIN
        IF R = ∅ THEN RETURN
        LET M = maxweight(R)
        put M at bottom of C'  (* CTs grow downwards *)
        LET R' = R \ M  (* \ means set minus *)
        LET T = all parts in R' connected to parts in M
        LET R'' = R' \ T
        call algorithm recursively with T
        call algorithm recursively with R''
END.
```

5.2 An example: the heffalump

To show the difference between a canonical and a non-canonical connection table, we show a simple model of a *heffalump* (Milne, 1926) in Figure 10. This "mythological" creature has a body, four legs, a tail, a neck, a head, two ears, and a trunk. The canonical form of its connection table is constructed by first finding the "heaviest" part, in this case the head, and adding it to the CT. The algorithm is then called with a set containing all parts directly connected to the head. The heaviest of these is the neck, and all the other (ears and trunk) have equal weight. The heaviest part not directly connected to the head is

the body, so that follows next, and so on. Note how *equivalent parts*, i.e. parts with the same weight function value which are connected to the same part, stay together in the canonical CT.[6]

5.3 Connection table lattice

When creating a connection table, we could work at different levels of detail. For instance, a *man* might be described as having a torso, a head and (preferably) two arms and two legs. Alternatively, the description could be refined to include different parts of the arms, hands, and fingers. Such different descriptions form

---

[6]Equivalent parts might however be of different *types* (such as legs and tail). We could compensate for this by adding more information, such as the size or color of objects. This would allow us to distinguish parts with identical weights.

a lattice, where at the top level we just have a complex object with none of its sub-parts even mentioned, and at the bottom the same object is described with all its different sub-parts, all decomposed into nothing but primitive parts. We obviously wish the CTs in the lattice to be in canonical form, since we intend to use the lattice for recognition (see below).

6.0 Description Language and Connection Tables

We have now shown how a description given in our language can be flattened to yield a description containing only primitive parts, and how doing this step-wise gives us a language description lattice. We have also shown how a connection table description computed from a 3D-skeleton can be given with different levels of exact-

ness, also resulting in a description lattice. Not surprisingly, because both lattices are "part-based" and make explicit the same kinds of relations, there is a strong correspondence between language descriptions and connection tables.

To make this relation explicit, we give an algorithm (2) for constructing a connection table from a language description; going the other way is trivial (Truvé, 1987). Notice that using these algorithms and the previously defined way of calculating the canonical form of a CT, we could actually compute the canonical form of a language description. [7]

Algorithm 2 *Constraint Reasoner for transforming an Object Language Description into a Connection Table.*

Input: An Object Language Description of an object.
Output: The corresponding Connection Table.

```
BEGIN
      SORT all clauses in order ⇌, = , ⋈
      CREATE  an empty CT, called O
      LET C = {O}
      FOR ALL clauses DO BEGIN
          (* Assume clauses are of form a | c op b | c *)
          LET c1 = {previous connection between a and c,
                    0 if no connection exists}
          LET c2 = {previous connection between b and c,
                    0 if no connection exists }
          IF c1 ≠ 0 AND c2 ≠ 0
          THEN FOR each CT in C IF connections and operator agree
                          THEN go on
                          ELSE LET
                          C = C\{CT not agreeing
                                with operator}
```

---

[7]For this to be true, the resulting language canonicalizer must be *idempodent*, i.e. such that $\mathcal{F}(a) = b \rightarrow \mathcal{F}^+(a) = b$.

```
            ELSE IF c1 ≠ 0
                THEN LET C = C ∪ {all possible new CTs given
                                       connections and operator}
                ELSE IF c2 ≠ 0
                    THEN LET C = C ∪ {all possible new CTs given
                                           connections and operator}
                    ELSE LET C = C ∪ {all possible new CTs given
                                           operator}
        END.
    END.
```

This algorithm (2) generates all possible connection tables (i.e. all possible rotations) that agree with all the clauses. It is vastly inefficient, but several speed-up tricks can be used, since we are only interested in generating *one* connection table agreeing with the description (this could then be canonicalized).[8]

We have thus given one possible solution to the problems of matching multiple descriptions of the same object (cf. Section 4).

7.0 Validity of the Language and the Lattice

When introducing a language it is important to give not only its syntax and semantics, but to discuss why it looks the way it does, and what its limitations are. In the previous sections, we showed how the primitives of the language are given by our way of defining primitive parts, and how the relations between these parts (as expressed in the language) correspond to relations between parts in the "real world". Thus the relational constraints imposed by the structural specification of the 3D-skeleton serve as a common thread, bridging all levels of abstraction, and are also imposed on the two higher levels of representation. However, in addition to these constraints on relational operators for the ODL, the CTs, and the skeleton, each representation has further constraints of its own. At lower levels, we have the demand for Waltz labeling consistency (Waltz, 1975). The connection tables can be used for some validity checks, such as the "simple parts constraint", which tells us that given two primitive, completely convex parts there is at most one 3D plane such that the two parts have faces connected to each other in that plane. At the highest level, we are constrained by what can be expressed in the language. Each level thus has its own "net" to catch errors in object specifications. The "Devils Pitchfork" and the "Penrose Triangle" are two interesting examples. The first is impossible to describe in ODL, whereas the other can be described without any difficulty, and is in fact even representable as a connection table or a 3D-skeleton (see Figure 11).

---

[8]Our current implementation of the constraint reasoner actually uses a better algorithm, in which we do not generate *all* possible connection tables. It is still not optimal in terms of the number of CTs generated, however, since a simple backtracking algorithm would produce exactly *one* solution.

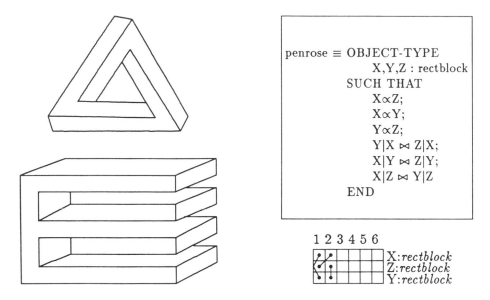

Figure 11 Two interesting objects, the Devils Pitchfork and the Penrose Triangle (left). Language description of triangle and its connection table (right).

In English, the Pitchfork is also difficult to describe (try!), but the Triangle can (albeit with some difficulty) be described in terms of its three parts. Furthermore, it is impossible to give a consistent Waltz labeling for the Pitchfork, whereas this can be done for the Triangle. Given this domain (i.e. a blocks-world without a notion of deformations), the Penrose Triangle is thus valid at all three major levels of representation, because of constraint propagation from the 3D-skeleton to the ODL. The Pitchfork is, on the other hand, invalid at all levels of representation, albeit for different reasons at the different levels.

8.0 Recognition and Learning

Once a connection table has been generated from an image, one important goal is to recognize the object represented by that table. In the simple case, where we have a single non-occluded object, analyzed as a 3D-skeleton, this only involves searching for a Connection Table defined in the current model that is equal to the CT generated from the image. This is trivial, since we assume all connection tables to be available in their canonical form. To further facilitate this search, extra information such as size, color and texture of parts and faces might prove valuable.

In a system for general recognition we can not allow ourselves the luxury of assuming such ideal conditions as suggested above. The image will contain several objects, and we will have to deal with problems of occlusion, which result in incomplete 3D-skeletons. This means that looking for simple equality between connection tables is no longer enough for recognition. Instead, what is needed is a way of searching the description lattices of our model for a "best fit" (Brooks, 1981; Grimson & Lozano-Perez, 1984). Although this area obviously needs extensive study, we would like to point out that our weight function, which measures the topological significance of a part (rather than size, for example), appears to us quite useful for facilitating search.

8.1 Learning an object description

In building a library of object models, learning and the ability to reason about the representations within the system becomes critical. Indeed, the similarity between our ODL and previous languages in not fortuitous. Capitalizing on Winston's and others' work (Brooks, 1981; Winograd, 1971; Winston, 1975; Winston et al., 1983), we argue that learning by analogy and constraint transfer can be thought of as taking place at the object description language level, where rather abstract object descriptions can be easily manipulated.

In our system, given pictures of objects, we wish to describe them in the language, and then to find a generalized description for all of them. When generalizing two different object descriptions in the ODL, different types (e.g. *rectblocks* and *cylinders*) will then be replaced by a *supertype*, such as α*type*. This new type will inherit properties from the first two types. For example, both rectangular blocks and cylinders have faces that are opposite to each other, and this is probably one of the properties we should expect from α*type* as well. In a similar way, negative examples can tell us what properties α*type* should *not* have. In this study, our aim has not been to address the learning issue, but rather to show that

our language can serve as a substrate for learning and other similar cognitive tasks.

8.2 Relation to natural language

Not surprisingly, the object descriptions in our ODL resemble the feature structures of several formal models of natural language grammar, such as Lexical Functional Grammar (Bresnan, 1982/85) or Functional Unification Grammar (Kaspar & Rounds, 1985). In such grammars, only certain "attachments" or relations between objects and actions are licensed, and these licenses are carried in the lexicon. In our terminology, for example, ARM is licensed to be attached to a TORSO at one end and a HAND at the other. Similarly, rather than relating objects by other objects, we could elect to relate two objects by an *ACTION*. Thus HAND and BALL might be related by the action GRASP. This relation could be specified in an "action" (or verb) module for GRASP, or within the object module for HAND (in which case the action verb would take one less argument). Currently, most formal natural language grammars choose the verb to specify these relations. Three types of "attachments" are distinguished: the benefactor (subject), the beneficiary (object) and the benefit (sentential complement). Thus for the sentence "John kicked the ball to Mary", "John" is the benefactor, "Mary" is the beneficiary and "ball" is the benefit. In this case, the action KICK would have LEG as the allowable benefactor, thereby licensing the relation "John kicks" because John has legs. Similarly, the module CAR could be licensed (via WHEELS, etc.) to "start, stop, translate, etc.", but not to WALK or FLY because these latter actions accept as benefactors only LEGS or WINGS, which are not proper parts for CAR. Alternately just as KICK or WALK accept only LEGS, the action SLIDE might accept any OBJECT for its benefactor, but only a SMOOTH SURFACE for its beneficiary. Clearly this system of assigning attachments capitalizes on world regularities, just as we did. However, whether such licensing relations belong in the OBJECT module or ACTION module or both is not yet clear. But in any case such extensions to our ODL would allow it to become a proper subset of certain formalisms for natural language grammars, thereby offering a tentative bridge between vision and natural language.

9.0 Conclusions

We have presented one approach to the problem of transforming image-based descriptions of objects into language-based, and vice versa. This approach depends on three major levels of representation: At the top level, a hierarchical, parts based Object Description Language allows us to describe both primitive parts (i.e. convex objects not describable in terms of parts), and more complex objects (created by the connection of parts) within the same framework. This high-level representation lends itself to the kind of semantic reasoning necessary in tasks such as learning. At the bottom level, we have introduced the 3D-Skeleton, which is a complete description of 3D features computable in a bottom-up manner from a 2D image. Representations of this kind are the target of most early vision systems. To bridge these two high- and low-level representations we introduce the Connection Tables. They provide us with a conve-

nient way of describing the decomposition of 3D-Skeletons into parts, and also show a strong correspondence with descriptions in the language. An algorithm for computing a connection table from a language description is presented, showing the feasibility of such transformations. The connection tables are useful in recognition, since they can be transformed into a canonical form allowing for fast test of equality between two connection tables. An algorithm for computing the canonical form is presented, and the uniqueness of this form is discussed.

Language descriptions are shown to form a lattice (with parts of varying complexity), with a bottom element corresponding to a description in terms of nothing but primitive parts. Connection tables derived from 3D-skeletons based on images of varying detail also form a lattice. We have shown that there is a strong correspondence between these two lattices.

The main contribution of our work is that the representations suggested are not *ad hoc*, but have strong formal underpinnings. The notion of parts and the topological relations between these parts are the constraints which play key roles. The three major levels of representation are motivated, and have been shown to capture different properties of a description. The canonical form of the connection tables seems to us particularly useful.

Acknowledgments: We would like to thank Peter Dybjer and Kent Petersson for their many comments on earlier drafts of this paper, and Seth Goldstein for his work on creating a 3D-skeleton from an image, and Donna Lardiere for her comments.

Staffan Truvé is supported by grants from the Swedish Fulbright Commission, The Royal Swedish Academy of Science, The Marcus Wallenberg Foundation, and Chalmers University of Technology and University of Göteborg, and Whitman Richards is supported by grants from AFOSR F49620 – 83 – 6 – 0135, ONR N14 – 84 – K – 0650 and NFS 8312240 – IST.

References

Ansaldi, S., De Floriani, L. & Falcidieno, B. (1985) Geometric modeling of solid objects by using a face adjacency graph representation. *SIGGRAPH*, 19:3.

Barr, A.H. (1984) Global and local deformations of solid primitives. *Computer Graphics*, 18:21 – 30.

Bennett, B.M. & Hoffman, D.D. (1986) Shape decompositions for visual recognition: the role of transversality. In W. Richards & S. Ullman (eds.), *Image Understanding 1985-86*, Norwood N.J.: Ablex.

Biederman, I. (1986) Human image understanding: recent research and theory. In A. Rosenfeld (ed.), *Human and Machine Vision II*, Orlando, Fla.: Academic Press.

Binford, T.O. (1981) Inferring surfaces from images. *Art. Intell.*, 17:205 – 244.

Binford, T.O. (1982) Survey of model-based image analysis systems. *The International Journal of Robotics Research*, 1(1):18 – 64.

Brady, M., Ponce, J., Yuille, A. & Asada, H. (1985) Describing surfaces. MIT A.I. Lab. Memo 822.

Bresnan, J. (1982/85) *The Mental Representation of Grammatical Relations.* Cambridge, Mass.: MIT Press, 1982/85.

Brooks, R.A. (1981) Symbolic reasoning among 3D models and 2D shapes. *Artif. Intell.*, 17:285-348.

Cernushi-Frias, B. & Cooper, D.B. (1984) 3-D space location and orientation parameter estimation of lambertian spheres and cylinders from a single 2-D image by fitting lines and ellipses to thresholded data. *IEEE Transactions on Pattern Analysis and Machine Intelligence*, PAMI-6, No. 4.

Connell, J.H. & Brady, M. (1985) Generating and generalizing models of visual objects. MIT A.I. Lab. Memo 823.

Draper, S.W. (1981) The use of gradient and dual space in line-drawing interpretation. *Artif. Intell.*, 17:461 – 508.

Grimson, W.E. & Lozano-Perez, T. (1984) Model-based recognition and localization from sparse range or tactile data. *Int. Journ. Robotics Res.*, 3.

Hoffman, D.D. & Richards, W. (1984) Parts of recognition. *Cognition*, 18: 65 – 96.

Kanade, T. (1981) Recovery of 3D shape from an object from a single view. *Artif. Intell.*, 17:409 – 460.

Kaspar, R.T. & Rounds, W.C. (1985) A logical semantics for feature structures. *Amer. Jrl. Computational Linguistics*, 11:257 – 266. *Proc. 23rd Annual Meeting, ACL.*

Koenderink, J.J. (1987) An internal representation for solid shape based on the topological properties of the opponent contour. In W. Richards & S. Ullman (eds.), *Image Understanding 1985-86*, Norwood, N.J.: Ablex.

12

Koenderink, J.J. & van Doorn (1977) How an ambulant observer can construct a model of the environment free from the geometrical structure of the visual flow. In G. Hauske & E. Butenandt (eds.), *Kybernetic*, Munich: Oldenburg.

Mackworth, A.K. (1977) How to see a simple world: an exegesis of some computer programs for scene analysis, *Machine Intelligence*, 8; Edinburgh: Edinburgh University Press.

Marr, D. (1982) *Vision: A Computational Investigation into the Human Representation and Processing of Visual Information*. San Francisco, Calif.: Freeman.

Milne, A.A. (1926) *Winnie-the-Pooh*, New York: E.P. Dutton.

Minsky, M. (1975) A framework for representing knowledge. In P.H. Winston, *The Psychology of Computer Vision*. New York:McGraw -Hill.

Nevatia, R. & Binford, T.O. (1977) Description and recognition of curved objects. *Artif. Intell.*, 8:77–98.

Nordström, B. & Petersson, K. (1985) *The Semantics of Module Specification in Martin-Löf's Type Theory*. Programming Methodology Group, University of Göteborg and Chalmers University of Technology.

Pentland, A.P. (1985) Perceptual organization and the representation of natural form. SRI Technical Note 357.

Truvé, S. (1987) Towards a specification language for physical objects. Available from: Programming Methodology Group, Dept. Computer Science, Chalmers University of Technology, Göteborg, Sweden.

Ullman, S. (1984) Visual routines. *Cognition*, 18:97–159.

Waltz, D.L. (1975) Understanding line drawings of scenes with shadows. In P.H. Winston, *The Psychology of Computer Vision*. New York: McGraw-Hill.

Winograd, T. (1971) Procedures as representation for data in a computer program for understanding natural language. MIT A.I. Lab. Memo 84.

Winston, P.W. (1975) Learning structural descriptions from examples. In P.H. Winston, *The Psychology of Computer Vision*. New York: McGraw-Hill, 1975.

Winston, P.W., Binford, T.O., Katz, B. & Lowry, M. (1983) Learning physical descriptions from functional definitions, examples and precedents. MIT A.I. Lab. Memo 679.

Reprinted from the Proceedings ICCV'87, excepting Appendices A and C.

Appendix: Some Primitive Part Definitions

We give here the definitions of some primitive parts. The definitions are not in any way the only "right" ones (one could for example specify the surface of a sphere as being opposite to itself), but are included for reference.

```
rectblock ≡ OBJECT-TYPE
        DEFINING
            Faces = {1,2,3,4,5,6};
            Parameters = {height,width,length};
            Equal = { <1,{1}>,<2,{2}>,<3,{3}>,
                        <4,{4}>,<5,{5}>,<6,{6}>};
            Opposite = { < 1,{4}>,<2,{5}>,<3,{6}>,
                            <4,{1}>,<5,{2}>,<6,{3}>};
            Adjacent = { <1,{2,3,5,6}>,<2,{1,3,4,6}>,<3,{1,2,4,5}>,
                            <4,{2,3,5,6}>,<5,{1,3,4,6}>,<6,{1,2,4,5}>}
        END
```

```
cylinder ≡ OBJECT-TYPE
        DEFINING
            Faces = {1,2,3};
            Parameters = {height,radius};
            Equal = {<1,{1}>,<2,{2}>,<3,{3}>};
            Opposite = {<1,{2}>,<2,{1}>};
            Adjacent = {<1,{3}>,<2,{3}>,<3,{1,2}>}
        END
```

```
cone ≡ OBJECT-TYPE
    DEFINING
        Faces = {1,2};
        Parameters = {height,radius};
        Equal = {<1,{1}>,<2,{2}>};
        Opposite = {};
        Adjacent = {<1,{2}>,<2,{1}>}
    END
```

```
sphere ≡ OBJECT-TYPE
    DEFINING
        Faces = {1};
        Parameters = {radius};
        Equal = {<1,{1}>};
        Opposite = {};
        Adjacent = {}
    END
```

12

III

Image Interpretation: Property Tags:
Color, 3D Texture, Flow Fields

Image Interpretation: Property Tags: Color, 3D Texture, Flow Fields

1.0 The Goal

In the previous selections which comprised Chapter 2, our primary goal was the recovery of 3D shape from image contours, such as a silhouette. Here we are concerned with the "stuff" that makes up these shapes. Given an isolated blob or region in the image, what is the material in the world which created this observed pattern of image intensities? Is it wood or water, rock or rug, or simply a piece of metal or plastic? As illustrated in Figure 2 such distinctions can often be made fairly reliably even from static images and without the shape information provided by an object's silhouette. How is this accomplished?

The approach we take is called Graphics Psychophysics. Just as the interpretation of image contours for shape required first an understanding of how the edges of surfaces are generated and projected into the image, here we begin by first trying to understand how a particular property of a surface leads to its own distinguished pattern of image intensities. The texture of a leafy tree clearly differs from that of water, and hence the images of these textures look different. But how are we to make this difference explicit so it can be understood? The solution we adopt is to use a computer program to create a picture of a tree, or water, etc. Writing such a program requires an explicit model that captures the essential processes that create the material under study. By twiddling the parameters of the model, those relevant to vision can be determined. Computer graphics allows us the luxury of creating such a picture. The psychophysics part of the approach is then simply to observe how realistic the picture appears. All but one of the panels in Figure 2 were created this way. Examples of other synthetic scenes can be found in the annual proceedings of SIGGRAPH or in the ACM Transactions on Graphics (e.g. Fournier & Reeves, 1987). The state of this art is now so advanced that very realistic scenes can be generated, such as Lucas Films' short film segment entitled Wally & André.

Figure 1 shows the strategy. A realistic picture (or patch of material) is created on the computer screen, using an explicit physical model of the world. If the scene looks realistic, then all the relevant parameters have been identified. Furthermore, we now know the origin or cause of each image intensity element $I(x, y, \lambda, t)$ on the retina of our eye, for we have specified this function explicitly in our program. Hence the mapping from the world to the image plane is known. Given this knowledge, our problem is then to invert the mapping to recover the material type— or equivalently the values of the relevant physical parameters which make up our model. This is the hard part, because any given image intensity element confounds all these parameters. This confounding will be clarified in the first selection by Land & McCann. The problem now becomes one of discovering constraints and conditions that untangle the effects of each physical parameter. Once this has been done, the material type can be identified.

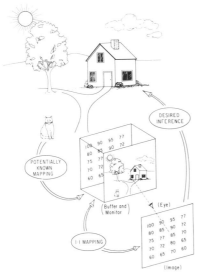

Figure 1 Graphics Psychophysics.

To accomplish the inference process from images to materials, it will be seen that most often no single arbitrary patch of the image will be sufficient (in spite of the impression given by Figure 2!). This should not be a surprise, however, because twice before we have encountered this problem in trying to recover shape from contour. The first instance was the reliable identification of occluding contours, which required knowledge obtained from texture ribbons adjacent to the contour. The second instance was the recovery of the 3D shape from the silhouette, where knowledge from different parts of the contour had to be pieced together. In the recovery of material properties, we also must collect information from several different and special spatial locations. These may include a region of

maximum intensity, an occluding contour, terminators (a shadow line), ending contours, or hyperbolic regions, which are generally shadowed. Often surface shape and material type are intimately coupled. So the recovery of material type, just like the recovery of shape, requires an integration of information obtained both from selected contours and from special image patches.

2.0 Spectral Reflectance or Albedo (ρ)

One of the early examples of the first step in the Graphics Psychophysics approach was some simple experiments by Maxwell in 1855. Following proposals by Thomas Young and others, Maxwell proved experimentally that any colored light could be matched by the proper combination of three spectral sources. There was no need to change the spectral location of these three sources when matching the different colored lights. Just their amplitudes change. This demonstration showed that the human visual system took only three spectral samples of the scene, rather than ten or twenty or more as in a physical spectrophotometer. The tri-variant character of human color vision is a limitation which permitted practical color photography and TV communication. If all spectral bands were to be transmitted, the excessive bandwidth required would be crippling. So the fact that the graphics screen requires only three guns—red, green, and blue—to simulate all the spectral colors we see in the world, is a small, but important first step in our understanding of the recovery of spectral reflectance. The next step is to show, given the outputs of our three guns, namely their red, green and blue intensities, how we can correctly infer the spectral composition of the surface.

The first computational attack on this problem appeared in 1971 in a classic paper by Land & McCann. In this paper was not only a theory of inferring spectral reflectance, but also an algorithm and implementation, thus becoming one of the first clear examples of a computational study of a perceptual problem. (Another was Horn's 1970 treatment of shape-from-shading.) What makes the recovery of spectral reflectance difficult is that even in their simplified Mondrian world, each image intensity measurement $I(x,y)$ confounds two parameters, the reflectance or albedo (ρ) and the illumination E:

$$I(x,y) = \rho(x,y)\,E(x,y) \qquad (1)$$

The problem is to untangle the effects of E in order to recover ρ.

Land & McCann's solution to this problem is quite elegant. Three constraints are invoked. First, reflectance (albedo) values must lie between 0 and 1. Second, $E(x,y)$ will not change at an edge, because reflectance edges and illumination effects are independent processes. Consequently if we measure the two image intensities on each side of an edge, then their ratio must equal the reflectance ratio:

$$I_i/I_j = \rho_i/\rho_j \qquad (2)$$

where i and j are abutting patches of the Mondrian. Finally, the third constraint is that at least one patch in the display has reflectance equal to one. The reflectances for the Mondrian can now be determined by applying equation (2) recursively, subject to the constraint that $\rho_i \leq 1.0$ for all i.

Two algorithms for computing reflectance are given in the article. More recently, additional methods have been proposed which are more robust and which relate more closely to biological mechanisms (Land, 1986). However, the basic principles and constraints remain the same. But so do some unforeseen problems, which became most obvious when algorithms were implemented. First, intensity measurements at an edge consume some spatial extent, and hence an error term must be included in equation (2). Second, real-world images are textured and may arise from curved, non-planar surfaces. Finally, most surfaces have a specular component, which violates the restriction that reflectance values do not exceed 1.0. Not withstanding these difficulties, the insights provided by Land's very simple and elegant proposal set the framework for future computational studies of color vision.

In Selection 14, we make a second attempt to disentangle the effects of illumination and reflectance. In contrast to Land, who started by simplifying the world, Rubin & Richards simplify the goal and retain the complexities of a natural world.[1] Thus, rather than attempting to recover spectral reflectance, $\rho(\lambda)$, they ask under what conditions can we assert simply that ρ has changed? The edge between two different materials, for example, will be the most common instance of a change in albedo. To solve the problem, they begin with a much more general version of equation (1) that includes surface orientation effects, specular reflectance, intensity gradients and ambient illumination. In spite of this more complex formulation (see Equation 3), the key observation is

---

[1] The underlying philosophy is that simplicity in the desired inference is preferred over the creation of an artificially simple world.

Figure 2 Some fractal textures. Which are synthetic?

that the (matte) spectral reflectance component of the image-intensity equation— i.e. the component which characterizes the surface pigment type—retains its general shape across wavelength when projected into the observed image intensities. Neither highlights nor shadows, nor changes in surface orientation will effect the general form of the observed albedo function over wavelength. Therefore if two patches of the image have two differently shaped spectral intensity functions, then these two patches must correspond to different materials. (Note that if they have the same spectral shape, this does not mean that they necessarily correspond to the same material!). Just as Witkin noted for material edges, namely that the intensity profiles of ribbons lying on each side of the edge will be different, here the same is also true for the spectral reflectance function. However, unlike Witkin, we have two well-specified conditions that can arise *only* if a change in material has produced the image contour. These two conditions are (1) when the two spectral reflectance functions cross (cross-point condition) and (2) when they have oppositely signed slopes of intensity versus wavelength (opposite slope-sign condition.) Perhaps of interest to neurophysiologists is that the receptive field which would detect the cross-point or opposite slope-sign condition superficially resembles a "double-opponent" cell (Daw, 1968; Livingstone & Hubel, 1984; Michael, 1978). But of course, we have two different and independent material-charge conditions, so therefore we must expect two different types of "double-opponent" units. Figure 3 shows how these units differ in the way logical and arithmetic operations are combined. If the scheme proposed here is correct, then we predict that these units play different roles in color processing. One (the crosspoint version) provides normalization data for discounting the illuminant, while the other (the opposite slope sign version) sets up the color space, which is to represent materials by pigment types (e.g. chlorophyll, xanthophyll, flavanoids, etc.).

Recently, several other computational approaches have appeared which also draw upon spectral information to infer material properties, as well as illumination effects. These studies differ from the previous two by attempting to find the spectral composition of the illuminant directly, rather than making an assumption about the distribution of reflectances as do Land & McCann (1971), Rubin & Richards (1984) and Richards (1982). For example, Lee (1986) notes that many highlight effects involve a weighted, linear sum of the illuminant and the matte reflectance of a flat surface patch. Consequently in color space any mixture of these two components will lie along a straight line. The intersection of several of these lines calculated for different patches will therefore indicate the spectral composition of the illuminant, which can then be used to correct the observed spectral intensitites. (Thus, this scheme could replace the cross-point distribution assumption made in Selection 14.) Shafer (1985) and

Gershon et al. (1987) propose a slightly more complicated version of this same method. If the highlight appears on a curved surface, then the observed intensities originating from the matte reflectance will vary depending upon the geometry of the surface and the viewer position. However, again, each of these observed variations will be linear in color space. So now the observed pattern of intensities arising from a highlight plus matte reflectance will be along two lines—one attributed to the highlight and the other to the matte reflectance. This combination will lead to an "elbow" locus in color space, where one arm of each elbow—the one characteristic of the highlight—should point toward the illuminant color.

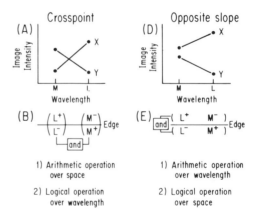

Figure 3 Construction of cross-point and opposite slope sign operators, using logical and arithmetic operators. Note that double-opponent cells would be useful for opposite slope sign, but not for the crosspoint. (From Rubin & Richards, 1984.)

Finally, Maloney & Wandell (1986) have presented still another method that attempts to recover both the spectral re-

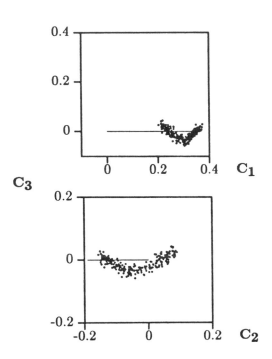

Figure 4 If highlights (mirror) and matte components add linearly and are independent, then variations in the geometry of the surface will distribute the highlight and matte intensities along two separate, but intersecting lines in a color space. Two projections are shown above. (Highlight on mandrill nose from Gershon et al., 1987.)

flectance function of the material, as well as the illuminant composition. The "trick" in their approach is to assume knowledge of a special set of spectral functions, from which the material reflectance and illumination can be constructed. Then an equation-counting method is used to determine the minimum number of samples required (see also Yuille, 1984; Sasaki et al., 1984). This type of scheme may be more appropriate for machine vision than

for biological vision unless modified along the lines suggested by Brill (1978, 1986).

Although several limited implementations of these new computational approaches to color vision have appeared, it is not yet clear how successful these proposals will be in general. Not only may the constraints be invalid or too weak, but also none of the algorithms, including our two selections, have built-in procedures that allow the observer to know when not to make an assertion. Hence our theory of inference of spectral reflectance is not complete. Furthermore, work is also required to understand surfaces with mixtures of pigment types, such as a quilt of yellow and green, red and brown, etc. Such mixtures when seen at a coarse scale will yield one interpretation, but under fine scale viewing demand another (see Problem 14-5). Understanding the effects of scale becomes particularly important if one wishes to use a material-based color-space for scene segmentation, along the lines proposed by Tominaga (1985).

3.0 The Reflectance Function, R

Spectral reflectance, or more properly albedo, $\rho(\lambda)$, is probably the simplest, and certainly the most colorful surface parameter in the image-intensity equation. But in addition, we must also consider R—the reflectance function itself.

$$I = \rho(\lambda) \cdot E(\lambda) \cdot (N \cdot L) \cdot R \qquad (3).$$

Equation (3) summarizes again our basic relation between surface parameters, illumination, and image intensities. In the selection by Blinn, this equation is elaborated in more detail, with special emphasis upon the reflectance parameter,

R. Here, the matte versus specular aspects of the surface are collected, as well as textural effects. Following Torrance & Sparrow (1967), Blinn considers the textural component of the surface at the optical level, so the micro-texture itself is not visible [although see Blinn (1978) for a treatment of visible textural effects]. Recently we have proposed an elaboration of this scheme that makes the surface roughness an explicit *visual* parameter in the representation of material type, just as we did in Chapter 1. The basic idea is that facets on the surface may appear over a range of scales, some visible, some not, depending upon the viewing distance. What is needed is a parameter that captures this surface property. One natural choice is a fractal measure. The new representation includes the parameter $\bar{h}$, which is the Hausdorff dimension less 1, and hence ranges from 0 (the roughest surface) to 1 (smoothest surface). As illustrated in Figure 5, the space of R then becomes three-dimensional with axes ρ (albedo), $\bar{h}$ (roughness), and η (specular component). Each takes on values between 0 and 1. For example, whenever ρ, $\bar{h}$ or η is zero, then the surface will appear black, for then (1) either the albedo ρ is 0, or (2) the surface is so rough that no light can escape to the viewer (a black body!), or (3) the surface is a perfect mirror with index of refraction $n = 0$, where light can not be reflected to the viewer except under very special conditions (such as retro-reflect materials).

Thus, in our formulation for the reflectance function, all the matte properties of the surface are captured by the albedo parameter, ρ. All the specular properties thus appear in the reflectance function, R, whose two major parameters are η

(index of refraction) and $\bar{h}$, which describe the surface roughness.[2] The recovery of the surface material would require estimating these parameters from image intensities—a very difficult task because of the complexity of the full image intensity equation as presented by Blinn. Perhaps the only hope of recovering these reflectance function parameters is to seek conditions where the image-intensity relation becomes quite simple, either by choosing particular locations on a surface (occluding edge, bright spot, hyperbolic region, etc.), or by considering materials which have very special surface properties. Selection 16 is an example of the latter approach. Water is a mirror-like

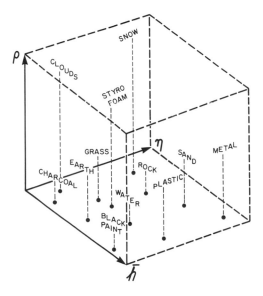

Figure 5 Representation for reflectance. Axes are: albedo, ρ; Hansdorf dimension less 1, $\bar{h}$, and a measure of the index of refraction, η, scaled to be between 0 and 1.

[2] As an alternative to the fractal measure, see Lewis, 1987.

surface with no matte component. Hence
the image-intensity equation is greatly
simplified; the only relevant parameter is
the index-of-refraction, n, because only
Fresnel reflection applies to this surface.

To demonstrate that our simplification of the image-intensity equation is
justified, computer graphics is used to
generate a picture of water based on the
Fresnel model (see Figure 2). This psychophysical experiment revealed that two
other conditions had to be met: first,
hemispheric rather than point-source illumination is required, and second, the 3D
surface-shape must be roughly sinusoidal
to create the proper texture pattern (see
also Fournier & Reeves, 1986). Selection
16 thus tells us which physical variables are
significant in the mapping of the surface
water into the observed image intensities.
We are now left with the much more difficult task of showing how, given these
image intensities, one can make the inference "water". At present, our solution is
to translate the problem into a geometrical one. It can be shown that for the usual
imaging conditions for a water surface, the
resultant pattern in the image will always
have elongated elliptical-like shapes, but
with the ends cusped rather than rounded
(something like a filled-out type 2 codon.)
The shape is thus reminiscent of how a
cartoonist would draw water waves. Figure 6 illustrates the form of these features,
and their organization. Thus, although we
feel the distinguishing image feature for
water is understood, still missing is a complete treatment of the inference process
which also specifies the range of possible false targets. It is also important to
note that the reflectance parameter, n,
could not be recovered independently of
the surface structure. Solving the image-
intensity equation (3), therefore, seems to

require a simultaneous analysis of shape
(Horn, 1970).

Figure 6 Water waves characterized
by type 2 codons.

4.0 Flow Fields

Water is but one of many surfaces that
create an organized pattern of identical
elements on our retina. Figure 7 is another
(wood). Sometimes these elements are not
stationary, but move either in swirls or
simply translate as water waves do. In
either case, this flow field provides a rich
source of information about the surface.
The dynamic case is particularly valuable,
for from the motion of the surface elements
we can deduce whether the surface is
rigid or rubbery, fluid or viscous, and
often whether the surface is undergoing
deformation or distortion. How then can
a flow field be measured and how should
it be represented?

We begin with the simple case of a rigid contour in motion, with the objective of determining the direction of motion of the contour. Our surface is thus rigid and is scarred with crevices, cracks, etc., which create texture markings. In the beginning of Selection 17, Hildreth points out that given a single (linear) segment of an image contour, its direction of motion is ambiguous. This is the aperture problem. If the motion is simply a translation, then two such segments are needed to determine the correct direction. However still more information is required if rotation and dilation are allowed (See Problem 17-1.) Hildreth proposes a smoothness constraint which allows her to use optimization techniques to find a solution. Unfortunately, such an approach does not allow us to understand fully the competence of the proposal. (In this regard, see an analysis by Waxman & Wohn, 1986.) However, Hildreth's method has the appeal of being easily implemented in simple, local, parallel networks so common in biological systems, and her comparisons with psychophysical observations are very supportive. More recently, Heeger (1987) has shown how a biological network could implement these calculations. Because the method can be set-up locally to run on zero-crossing contours, it is also possible to estimate the discontinuities in the flow field, thereby isolating objects in motion. However, I have placed Hildreth's contribution in this Chapter rather than earlier with Mutch & Thompson, because the recovery of a flow field provides an important source of information about how a surface is deforming and hence whether it is rubbery or rigid.

Recently, other approaches to recovering surface deformations have appeared. For example, Koenderink & van Doorn (1986) present a treatment of globally non-rigid shapes composed of locally rigid polygons. An overview of additional work can be obtained from ICCV '87.

5.0 Patterns and Processes

A flow field need not be just a pattern of velocity vectors such as those delivered by Hildreth. A flow field can also be created from stationary line elements of dots as illustrated in Figure 8. Obviously such a description provides important information about the processes that formed the surface, and hence often tells us what that material is. The unique pattern of wood grain illustrated in Figure 7 is an obvious example. So how can we proceed to analyze and represent this kind of information? Kass & Witkin address this problem. They show how line elements

Figure 7 Wood (rendered by D. Honig, 1985).

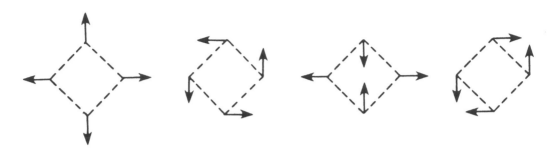

Figure 9 Basic elements of a flow field (dilation, rotation, stretch and shear).

(virtual or real) may be aggregated into an explicit flow field representation—one powerful enough to "fill-in" the knot hole in wood grain. To be complete to first

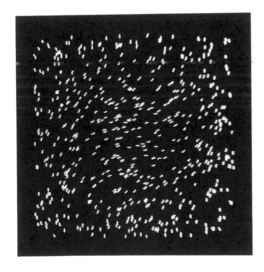

Figure 8 Marroquin flow field of dots.

order, such a description must make explicit the four local components of all flow fields—the rotation, dilation, stretch and shear (See Figure 9). Whether the human

visual system is capable of recovering all these components is still unclear (Glass & Perez, 1973; Marroquin, 1968; Richards & Lieberman, 1982; Regan & Beverley, 1985) and more psychophysics is badly needed in this area. A complete theory of the recovery of flow field components is also sadly lacking, even though this problem has been attacked many times over the past fifteen years. A strong hint from psychophysics comes from the experiments of Stevens (1978), who showed that neighborhoods of eight points seem sufficient to recover at least the rotation and dilation components of the flow field (see Problem 18-2).

From a more theoretical point of view, a paper by Koenderink & van Doorn (1976) is particularly impressive. Although this paper is principally concerned with the optical flow field generated by ego-motion, one observation is particularly crucial for understanding how we can recognize the surface flow patterns that characterize a material and its processes of formation: all the four local components of a flow field can be recovered from measurements of changes in orientation of line elements at a point. Thus, similar computations underline both the recovery of flow and of curvature. Later, we shall see that the recovery of surface slant using steropsis can utilize a similar operator, suggesting that our visual system should be exquisitely sensitive to changes in orientation, for this parameter can serve many modules.

Once a flow pattern has been described locally, we then have the problem of creating a more global description. For example, is it symmetric? If so, about which axes, etc.? We have many choices (e.g. Gorenstein, 1985; Hoffman & Dodwell, 1985; Leyton, 1986). Perhaps the simplest global descriptors are those which apply to crystalline structures. Here the theory of groups apply, and the allowable tesselations (in any dimension) are well known (Grünbaum & Shephard, 1986; Hilbert & Cohn-Vossen, 1952; Zucker, 1976). For example, in a plane, we naturally think first of rectangular tesselations (or their deformations), and then hexagonal, or triangular tesselations. These are also expected projections of regular, crystalline-like shapes, which are often common in biology (Thompson, 1968). Such patterns are of interest to the visual scientist because they obviously reveal information about the processes that created the structure.

These observed tesselations constrain not only the texture of a surface, but also its occluding boundary if the surface is "rough". Is their any evidence that our visual system encodes such information? Perhaps the most intriguing demonstration comes from ophthalmic migraines, which reveal an illusory honey-comb pattern of flickering lines triggered by a spontaneous wave of activity in the visual cortex (Airy, 1870; Lashley, 1941; Richards, 1971). Within this outer fortifi-

cation pattern often appear tesselations, which include not only hexagons, but also triangular and parallel grids. Certainly then our cortex has the organizational capacity to encode the basic 2D regular tesselations (see Figure 10).

Figure 10 Tesselations observed in visual migraines (from Lashley, 1941).

6.0 3D Texture

For many non-crystalline surfaces, the texture pattern is formed from elements oriented haphazardly in 3D, such as trees or shrubs, or the hair of an animal. Furthermore, these elements themselves may be in motion, such as when the wind blows across long grass. These are 3D textures.

Figure 11 is one simple (artificial) example. Other, more compelling, examples appear in Selection 19. It is here that stereopsis exerts its real power, for, unlike the object separation, where material boundaries are usually obvious even to the

Figure 11 An artificial 3D texture—"grass". Six geometrical properties are controlled by six different variables. One variable controls stereo parallax. The others determine size, shape, position and orientation of the triangle in its unmarked cell. Note that the "roughness" of the surface is observed well before the curved shape of the underlying surface on which the bases of the triangles lie (adapted from Pickett, 1968).

single eye, the 3D textural structure of a tree or grass is not readily susceptible to monocular analysis. (Julsez's random-dot or Kaufman's (1965) letter stereograms are well-known laboratory analogs.) How then can the two eyes act in concert to recover the surface structure? This problem is not the one commonly addressed in most computational studies of stereopsis, which have stressed surface shape and object separation over surface structure and texture. But trees and shrubs—a rather common surface in a natural world—have a rich and complex 3D fractal-like structure (Honda, 1971; Smith, 1984). Such structures violate most theories of stereopsis which generally assume smooth surfaces. Furthermore, the nature of the surface elements—the blade of grass, the size of the trunk or twig often set important constraints upon the 3D shape of the surface (McMahon, 1975). Such constraints are important for the realistic rendering of trees and plants, and hence

might also be usefully incorporated into a stereoscopic theory which attempts to recover these types of structures.

In Selection 19 Ninio moves in this direction by considering the effects of the organization of the surface feature upon the perception of surface orientation (see also Mayhew & Frisby, 1981). One of his surprising findings is that randomly distributed line elements provide more robust stereopsis than patterns which reveal the underlying shape. Why? Perhaps one reason is that when a flow field is obvious, then we have not one but two problems to solve at once. These are (1) the flow field of the pattern on the surface, as well as (2) the shape of the surface. In other words, the pattern of surface markings and the surface shape are confounded in the visible flow field. For Ninio's random surface markings, however, all the visible organization is due to the surface shape.

The second half of Selection 19 is also a bit unusual, considering most treatments of the geometry of stereopsis. First, here are some tools which may prove useful for a representation of shape based on collections of 2D views, as favored in Chapter 1. Second, and perhaps more relevant to this chapter, are the proofs of minimal requirements for stereopsis given points as features and the demonstration of how a limited number of correspondences can be used to discover more correspondences. Similar proofs would be desirable for more complex features, such as oriented lines and angles for example. Ninio's observations are key building blocks for a theory of recovering 3D shape from stereo texture using simple feature elements. The reader is referred to other papers by Ninio that take these ideas further, and attempt to translate them into feature maps that are biologically relevant.

If we are to leave the artificial world of smooth objects, and also proceed to extend our matching features to oriented lines, such as blades of grass, then the roughness of the surface is a parameter that should be recovered simultaneously with its shape, for these two variables are tightly coupled. Hence we turn naturally once again to fractals.

In the past few years, we have seen a tremendous growth in fractals as a basis for rendering surfaces and shapes which look quite realistic and natural (Mandelbrot, 1975; SIGGRAPH, 1985, 1986). Pentland's contribution shows that we have the ability to estimate the fractal dimension by judging surface roughness, and that the fractal dimension is recoverable from the image. These results gave plausibility to our ρ, n, h representation for surface material type. However, they also suggest how monocular information about surface roughness and 3D stereo information might come together. Clearly, for a fractal surface, the stereoscopic solution should be consistent with the roughness estimate obtained from the monocular (2D) image texture. This comparison requires stereo processing over a range of scales, with the fine scales playing at least and possibly a more important role than the coarse scales. If indeed the two modules—texture and stereo—agree in their estimates of surface "roughness", then we have the further benefit of being able to recover the correct surface shape independent of fixation distance (see Problem 20-4). How then should stereopsis and texture be brought together in a single representation? What is the feature appropriate for this representation: lines, points, or the "roughness" of image patches? What is the relation between this sort of representation and material categories in the world? Is there another kind of Hering's "texture space" which maps readily into hair, feathers, grass, waves, clouds, etc., just as the color-space described in Selection 14 maps into natural pigment categories? These are exciting questions for future study.

References

Airy, H. (1870) On a distinct form of transient hemiopsia. *Phil. Trans. Roy. Soc. Lond.*, 160:247 – 264.

Blinn, J.F. (1978) Simulation of wrinkled surfaces. SIGGRAPH 78 (ACM – Special Interest Group in Graphics), pp. 286 – 292.

Brill, M.H. (1978) A device performing illuminant-invariant assessment of chromatic relations. *Jrl. Theor. Biol.*, 71:473 – 478.

Brill, M.H. (1986) Decomposition of Cohen's matrix R into simpler color invariants. *Amer. Jrl. Psychol.*, 98:625–634.

Daw, N.W. (1968) Color coded gangleon cells in the goldfish retina: extension of their receptive field properties by means of new stimuli. *J. Physiol.*, 197:1669–1680.

Fournier, A. & Reeves, W.T. (1986) A simple model of ocean waves. *SIGGRAPH '86*, 20:75–84.

Fournier, A. & Reeves, W.T. (1987) Special issue on the modelling of natural phenomena. *ACM Trans. Graph.*, 6:165–166.

Gershon, R., Jepson, A.D. & Tsotsos, J. (1987) Highlight identification using chromatic information. *Proc. 1st Int. Conf. on Comp. Vision*, IEEE 777, 161–170.

Glass, L. & Perez, R. (1973) Perception of random dot interference patterns. *Nature*, 246:360–362.

Gorenstein, D. (1985) The enormous theorem. *Sci. Amer.*, 253(6):104–115.

Grünbaum, B. & Shephard, G.C. (1986) *Tilings and Patterns.* New York: W.H. Freeman.

Heeger, D.J. (1987) A model for the extraction of image flow. *Jrl. Opt. Soc. Amer. A.* 4:1455–1471.

Hilbert, D. & Cohn-Vossen, S. (1952) *Geometry and the Imagination.* New York: Chelsea.

Hoffman, W.C. & Dodwell, P.C. (1985) Geometric psychology generates the visual Gestalt. *Can. J. Psychol.*, 39:491–528.

Honda, H. (1971) Description of the form of trees by the parameters of the tree-like body. *J. Theor. Biol.*, 31:331–338.

Honig, D.A. & Richards, W.A. (1985) Why does wood look like wood? *J. Opt. Soc. Amer. A*, 2(13):P29.

Horn, B.K.P. (1970) Shape from shading: a method for obtaining the shape of a smooth opaque object from one view. Tech. Report MAC-TR-79, Project MAC, MIT. Also see P.H. Winston (ed.), *Psychology of Computer Vision*, New York: McGraw Hill, 1975, pp. 115-155.

ICCV '87 (1987) Proceedings First International Conference on Computer Vision. IEEE Computer Society Order Number 777, P.O. Box 80452, Worldway Postal Center, Los Angeles, Calif. 90080.

Julesz, B. (1971) *Foundations of Cyclopean Vision.* Chicago: Chicago University Press.

Kaufman, L. (1965) Some new stereoscopic phenomena and their implications for theories of stereopsis. *Amer. Jrl. Psychol.*, 78:1–20.

Klinker, G.J., Shafer, S.A. & Kanade, T. (1987) Using a color reflection model to separate highlights from object color. *Proc. 1st Int. Conf. Comp. Vision*, IEEE 777, 145–150.

Koenderink, J.J. & van Doorn, A.J. (1976) Local structure of movement parallax of the plane. *Jrl. Opt. Soc. Amer.*, 66:717–723.

Koenderink, J.J. & van Doorn, A.J. (1986) Depth and shape from differential perspective in the presence of bending deformations. *Jrl. Opt. Soc. Am. A*, 3:242–249.

Land, E.H. (1986) Recent advances in retinex theory. *Vision Res.*, 26:7–21.

Land, E.H. (1986) An alternative technique for the computation of the designator in the retinex theory of color vision. *Proc. Natl. Acad. Sci.*, 83:3078–3080.

Land, E.H. & McCann, J.J. (1971) Lightness and retinex theory. *Jrl. Opt. Soc. Am.*, 61:1–11.

Lashley, K. (1941) Patterns of cerebral integration indicated by the scotomas of migraine. *Arch. Neurol. Psychiat., Chicago*, 46:331–339.

Lee, H.-C. (1986) Method for computing the scene illuminant chromaticity from specular highlights. *Jrl. Opt. Soc. Am. A*, 3:1694–1699.

Lewis, J.P. (1987) Generalized stochastic subdivision. *ACM Trans. on Graphics*, 6:167–190.

Leyton, M. (1986) A theory of information structure. II. A theory of perceptual organization. *J. Math. Psychol.*, 30:257–305.

Livingstone, M.S. & Hubel, D.H. (1984) Anatomy and physiology of a color system in the primate visual cortex. *J. Neurosci.*, 4:309–356.

McMahon, T.A. (1975) The mechanical design of trees. *Sci. Amer.*, 233(1):93–102.

Maloney, L.T. & Wandell, B.A. (1986) Color constancy: a method for recovering surface spectral reflectance. *Jrl. Opt. Soc. Am. A*, 3:29–33.

Mandelbrot, B.B. (1975) *The Fractal Geometry of Nature*. San Francisco: Freeman.

Marroquin, J.L. (1968) "Human visual perception of structure". S.M. dissertation, Massachusetts Institute of Technology, Dept. Electrical Engineering. (See also Marr, D., *Vision*, 1982, p. 50.)

Maxwell, J.C. (1855) Experiments on colours, as perceived by the eye, with remarks on colour-blindness. *Trans. Roy. Soc. Edinb.*, 21:275.

Mayhew, J.E.W. & Frisby, J.P. (1981) Psychophysical and computational studies towards a theory of human steropsis. *Artif. Intell.*, 17:349–386.

Michael, C.R. (1978) Color-sensitive complex cells in minkey striate cortex. *J. Neurophysiol.*, 41:1250–1266.

Pickett, R.M. (1968) Perceiving visual texture: a literature survey. AMRL-TR-68-12 Aerospace Medical Res. Lab., Wright-Patterson AFB, Ohio.

Richards, W. (1971) The fortification illusions of migraine. *Sci. Amer.*, 224 (May).

Richards, W.A. (1982) Lightness scale from image intensity distributions. *Appl. Optics*, 21:2569–2582.

Richards, W. & Lieberman, H.R. (1982) Velocity blindness during shearing motion. *Vision Res.*, 22:97–100.

Regan, D. & Beverley, K.I. (1985) Visual responses to vorticity and the neural analysis of optic flow. *Jrl. Opt. Soc. Amer. A*, 2:280–283.

Rubin, J.M. & Richards, W.A. (1984) Color vision: representing material categories. MIT A.I. Lab. Memo 764.

Sasaki, K., Kawata, S. & Minami, S. (1984) Estimation of component spectral curves from unknown mixture specra. *Appl. Optics*, 23:1955–1959.

Shafer, S.A. (1985) Using color to separate reflection components. *COLOR Research and Application*, Vol. 10, No. 4, 210–218. Univ. Rochester TR 136, 1984, Computer Science Dept.

SIGGRAPH 85 (1985, etc.) Proceedings of Annual Conference. Published by ACM, 11 West 42nd St., New York, N.Y. 10036.

Smith, A.R. (1984) Plants, fractals, and formal languages. *Computer Graphics*, 18:1–10 (SIGGRAPH'84).

Stevens, K.A. (1978) Computation of locally parallel structure. *Biol. Cybernetics*, 29:19 – 28.

Thompson, D'Arcy W. (1968) *On Growth and Form.* Cambridge: The University Press.

Tominaga, S. (1985) Expansion of color images using three perceptual attributes. BPRA 3rd Internation Conference, St. Andrews, Scotland. Also see *Jr. Opt. Soc. Amer. A*, 4:P20 (1987).

Torrance, K.E. & Sparrow, E.M. (1967) Theory for off-specular reflection from roughened surfaces. *Jrl. Opt. Soc. Am.*, 57:1105 – 1114.

Waxman, A.M. & Wohn, K. (1986) Contour evolution, neighborhood deformation and image flow: textured features in motion. In W. Richards & S. Ullman (eds.), *Image Understanding 1985-86*, Norwood, N.J.: Ablex, chapt. 4, pp. 72 – 98.

Yuille, A. (1984) A method for computing spectral reflectance. MIT A.I. Lab. Memo 752.

Zucker, S. (1976) On the structure of texture. *Perception*, 5:419 – 436.

Lightness and Retinex Theory

Edwin H. Land & John J. McCann

Polaroid Corporation

Most of us assume that, subject to a variety of compensatory factors, we see in terms of the amount of the light coming from objects to our eye; we think that in a particular scene there is more light coming from white objects than from black objects; we think there is more long-wave light (so-called red light) coming from red objects than from blue objects.

Yet, when we measure the amounts of light in the world around us, or when we create artificial worlds in the laboratory, we find that there is no predictable relationship between flux at various wavelengths and the color sensations associated with objects. Accordingly, we believe that the eye must have evolved a system which, though using light as the communication medium with the world, has become as nearly independent of energy as is biophysically possible. In short, color sensations must be dependent on some as yet undefined characteristic of the field of view, a characteristic that can be communicated to us by the light with which we see, even though the amount and composition of the light are everywhere variable and unpredictable; the eye must have evolved around such a permanent characteristic of the field of view. This paper describes our search for that characteristic.

A major visual phenomenon is that objects with low reflectance look dark, objects with high reflectance look light, objects with reflectance higher in the long-wave portion of the spectrum than in the short-wave look reddish, objects with reflectance higher in the short-wave portion than in the long-wave look bluish, and so on. It is with reflectance that sensation of color is strongly correlated when we view the world around us (Chevreul, 1839; Mach, 1865).[1] Yet ascertaining reflectance in any of the familiar ways requires an operational step which the eye cannot take. For example, the eye cannot insert a comparison standard next to the object which it is regarding.

Furthermore, what reaches the eye from each point is clearly the product of the reflectance and the illumination. The illumination from the sun is modulated by clouds, atmosphere, water, mountains, trees, houses, etc. As every photographer

---

[1] Although sensations of lightness show a strong correlation with reflectances in most real-life situations, there are many important departures from this strong correlation. The color-contrast experiments of Chevreul (1839) and Mach bands (1865) are examples of such departures. In addition, in complex images, there are small but systematic changes of lightness when the overall level of illumination changes (Bartleson & Breneman, 1967; Jameson & Hurvich, 1961). And, of course, any general theory must, as well, explain the simple situators in which surround comprises the entire environment (Hess & Pretori, 1884; Stevens & Galanter, 1957; Wallach, 1948).

knows, the sun and sky produce every conceivable combination of sunlight and skylight. Even less uniform illumination is provided by artificial light because the distance from the light source drastically affects the illumination falling on any point.

We are then left with the circular logical problem that, because the light coming to our eye is the product of the reflectance and illuminance, our eye could not determine reflectance unless the illuminance is uniform and the eye could not determine illuminance unless the reflectance is uniform. In general, across the field of view, neither reflectance nor illuminance is known; and neither is uniform.

Independence of Color Sensation from Flux-Wavelength Distributions

To demonstrate the extent to which color sensation is independent of flux-wavelength distribution, we will describe a simple quantitative laboratory experiment. An extended array of rectangular, colored papers is arranged to look like the paintings of the artist Mondrian (Daw, 1962).[2] To reduce the role of specular reflectance, the papers are not only matte, but are also selected to have a minimum reflectance as high as or higher than 10% for any part of the visual spectrum. The Mondrian-like pattern is illuminated by three illuminating projectors with sharp-cut bandpass filters (Land, 1964), one passing long waves, one middle-length waves, and one short waves (Figure 1). The flux from each of the three projectors is changed

by a separate variable transformer. The filters are selected on two bases: first, to minimize the diversity of color sensations from the array of colored papers when only one projector is turned on; second, while satisfying the first condition, to transmit as wide a band of wavelengths, and as much light as possible.

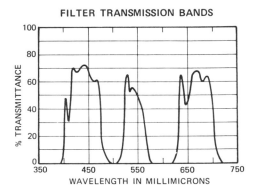

Figure 1 Spectral transmittance of bandpass interference filters.

With all three illuminating projectors turned on, the variable transformers are set so that the whole array of variegated papers is deeply colored, and so that, at the same time, the whites are good whites. This is not a critical setting. Then, using one projector at a time, and hence only one waveband at a time, we measure with a telescopic photometer the luminance at the eye from any particular area, say a white rectangle. Thus, we obtain from a white rectangle three numbers that are proportional to the three luminances at the particular location of the eye. (The

---

[2] We avoided the use of a pattern of squares because previous experience had taught us the hazard of the superposition of afterimages as the eye moves (Daw, 1962). Our completed display uses rectangles in an array the format of which reminded us of a painting by Piet Mondrian in the Tate Gallery in London. Thus we call our display the Mondrian.

subsequent procedures constitute a null experiment. The radiance-vs-luminance function, the particular units of measure, luminance function, the particular units of measure, the wavelength sensitivity, and the linearity of the meter are not significant in the experiment.)

In one example, the readings from a white area were 6 long-wave units, 35 middle-wave units, and 60 short-wave units. We turned the photometer to another area, such as a dark brown. We then separately adjusted the transformers to settings such that the three luminances at the eye were 6, 35, 60. Thus the luminances from the new area were identical to the three luminances previously reaching the eye from the first rectangle. The color sensation from the new area remained essentially unchanged (dark brown) despite the fact that the wavelength-luminance composition, for that area had changed from whatever it might have been to 6, 35, 60. We then pointed the photometer towards a series of different areas: bright yellow, blue, gray, lime green, and red. The illumination of each area was readjusted, in turn, so that the three luminances coming to the observer's eye were 6, 35, 60. After each of the new illuminations was adjusted so that the photometer read 6, 35, 60 for the long, middle, and short wavelengths, each area appeared essentially unchanged. Thus, the observers reported that the color sensations from the series were yellow, blue, gray, green, and red. When the variable transformers were changed in this way to produce the standard set of three luminances for any square, then all the other areas nevertheless continued to generate their original color sensation (although in a few areas there were some slight changes). Dramatically, the retention of

the color sensations was related to the reflectances of the papers—not to the product of reflectance times illumination, although this product appears to be the only information reaching the eye.

Therefore, the color sensations in the display have a completely arbitrary relation to the composition of light in terms of wavelength and luminance of any one point. The luminance-vs-wavelength distribution of each object in the world around us cannot tell us whether an object is white, gray, or black; the ratio of fluxes at various wavelengths cannot determine whether a point on an object is reddish, greenish, bluish, or grayish. The mystery then is how we can all agree with such precision about blacks, whites, grays, reds, greens, browns yellows, when there is no obvious physical quantity with which to describe how we know at all the color of the objects we are seeing.

It might occur to the reader that such a large change of relative luminance, a change such as we produce by altering the output of the long-wave projector relative to other projectors, is countered by a compensatory adaptation in the eye. If, in the previous experiments, changes of adaptation compensated for the changes of flux coming to the eye, then deliberately causing changes of adaptation should have a significant effect on the color appearance of objects. To produce an extremely large difference between the state of adaptation to long waves and the state of adaptation to middle and short waves, we asked observers to wear deep-red, dark-adaptation goggles, described by Hecht (Hecht & Hsia, 1945), for 1/2 h. to allow maximum regeneration of middle- and sort-wave visual pigments. In order to insure an ample domain for adaptation, the level of illumination of the display was maintained at a sufficiently high level. (The white areas had luminances for the middle- and short-wave bands between 100 and 1000 times higher than the threshold for cone response after 30 min in the dark.) When the observers removed the goggles, they reported at the first instant, as well as later, that the colors of the paper squares in the Mondrian were essentially unchanged. The experiment was repeated with the deep-red, dark-adaptation filter over only one eye. At the end of the adaptation period, the observers, using the binocular-comparison technique, reported slight shifts of the color sensations but none so large as to change the color names. (Indeed, in our theory a change of photochemical adaptation is unimportant, for the same reasons that a change of the flux of one of the illuminants is unimportant. Similarly, reasonable variations of the naive concentrations of visual pigments are not important from time to time, or from individual to individual.)

In another set of adaptation-related experiments the 6, 35, 60 Mondrian experiments were repeated with the observers seeing the Mondrian for less that 1/100s. The experimental procedure was exactly the same as in the first 6, 35, 60 Mondrian experiments, with the exception that the observers looked at the Mondrian through a photographic shutter. The projectors were set so that the long-middle-, and short-wave luminances from a white area were 6, 35, 60 and the observers reported that the area appeared white. The projectors were then set so that other areas had luminances of 6, 35, 60 and the observers reported that these areas, as before, produced sensations of brown, yellow, blue, gray, green, and red.

These experiments are significant because they show that the visual system uses a processing mechanism that is not merely independent, but instantaneously independent of the wavelength-luminance composition of the light coming to the eye. These mechanisms are not controlled by processes that are time dependent, such as the changes of the visual pigments that are due to differences of duration or intensities of adapting illumination.

If a particular rectangle is moved to various positions in the Mondrian, where it is surrounded by new sets of colored rectangles, the color sensation does not change significantly. The color sensation depends only on the long-, middle-, and short-wave reflectances of the rectangle and not on the properties of the neighboring rectangles. This independence of the neighboring rectangles holds for all flux settings of the illuminating projectors.

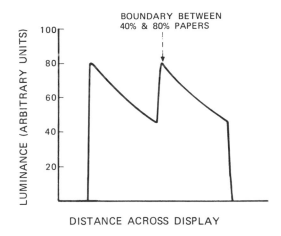

Figure 2 Luminance vs position for two-squares-and-a-happening experiment.

Because all these experiments, which show that any given wavelength-luminance combination, within limits as wide as the reflectance variations of these papers, can produce any color sensation, and because of many other kinds of laboratory experiments (Land, 1959a,b,c, 1962; McCann & Benton, 1969), we came to the conclusion that a color sensation involves the interaction of at last three (or four) retinal-cortical systems. Each retinal system starts with a set of receptors peaking, respectively, within the long-, middle-, or sort-wave portion of the visible spectrum. Each system forms a separate image of the world; the images are not mixed but are compared. Each system must discover independently, in site of the variation and unknowability of the illumination, the reflectances for the band of wavelengths to which that system responds.

We invented a name, retinex, for each of these systems. A retinex employs as much of the structure and function of the retina and cortex as is necessary for producing an image in terms of a correlates of reflectance for a band of wavelengths, an image as nearly independent of flux as is biologically possible.

It is convenient to refer to the differences in this image as steps of lightness (Committee on Colorimetry, 1953; Evans, 1948; Land, 1959, 1962; LeGrand, 1968; McCann & Benton, 1969), the whites being called light, and the blacks being called dark. Unfortunately, as Evans (1948) points out, dark is also used to describe the quite different family of experiences associated with change of illumination. Nevertheless, following him, we shall call the steps in the scale from black to white, steps of lightness. In our theory, it is an image in terms of lightness, which is produced by each retinex for the portion of the spectrum to which its pigment responds.

Figure 3 Picture of two-squares-and-a-happening experiment. Place a pencil over the boundary between the two gray areas.

The color sensation for any area is determined by the three lightnesses that are arrived at independently by the three retinexes. Because the lightnesses of an area are here defined as the biologic correlates of three reflectances, it follows within this conceptual framework that the color sensation is not dependent on illumination or flux, but on reflectance. Our original problem is converted into a new one: How does each retinex generate for each area the appropriate lightness, the biological correlate of reflectance that is independent of illuminance?

The scheme that we are about to describe for answering this question is one of a number of approaches that we have been investigating. All these schemes are designed to solve the same problem, namely: For one retinex, given the flux from each point in an entire scene, and assuming that nothing is known about the pattern of illumination and nothing is known about the reflectances, how can the biologic system generate a set of values that we experience as lightness? The particular scheme we will describe is the first that we have found to satisfy our criteria.

Edges

The experiment that we call two squares and a happening provides striking evidence of edges as the source of lightness information. A piece of paper that reflects 80% of the light that falls on it is placed to the right of a piece of paper that reflects 40% of the light. A fluorescent tube is mounted in front and to the left of the papers. The tube is carefully positioned so that twice as much light falls on the center of the 40% paper as falls on the center of the 80% paper. The light, being a line source, produces an approximately linear gradient across the papers, and the reflected luminances at each corresponding point of the two papers are equal. The graph of luminance vs position on the display is shown in Figure 2. The 40% paper on the left looks darker than the 80% paper on the right. Figure 3 is a photograph of the experiment.

What increases our interest is that when a long narrow object, a happening, obstructs the boundary between the left and right areas, the two areas are then perceived as having the same lightness. Long narrow strips of colored papers in parallel, or three-dimensional objects such as a pencil or a piece of yarn, make the two areas change from looking uniform and different to looking uniform and indistinguishable; yet, the only alteration of the display is the obscuration of the edge. We can see this by placing a pencil on the boundary between the areas in Figure 3.

The experiment was important in the development of our ideas of how the vi-

sual system could generate lightnesses. The fact that obscuring the edge information could change the appearance of these areas meant that the edges are a very important source of information. It suggested that the change of luminance at the junction between areas both constituted an edge and also led to the visual difference between the whole two areas. The word edge suggests a sharp, in-focus boundary. Experiments, however, show that the sharpness or focus of the boundary is not at all critical. For example, Figure 3 can be viewed through optometric lenses to change the boundaries from being sharp and in focus to a variety of fuzzy out-of-focus stages. Areas with boundaries quite out of focus look essentially the same as when they are in sharp focus.

What mechanism can we imagine that would discover edges and characterize adjacent areas in a way consistent with our experiences with the happening, a mechanism that will also discover the reflectances in the Mondrian even when it is in nonuniform illumination?

Let us imagine two light detectors placed to measure the luminance from two different places on a piece of paper. If the illumination is nonuniform, then the luminances at these two positions will, of course, be different. When the two detectors are placed closer and closer together, the luminances approach the same value and the ratio of the outputs approaches unity. This will be true of almost any two adjacent points. However, if the two detectors bridge the boundary between two areas of differing reflectance, then the ratio of the outputs of these detectors will approach the ratio of the reflectances. Thus, the simple procedure of taking the ratio between two adjacent points can both detect an edge and eliminate the effect of nonuniform illumination. Processing the entire image in terms of the ratios of luminances at closely adjacent points generates dimensionless numbers that are independent of illumination. As the distance between detectors is decreased, each number approaches a limit equal to the ratio of the reflectances, the reflectances themselves having not yet been ascertained.

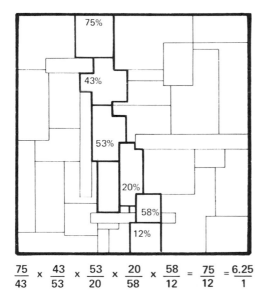

$$\frac{75}{43} \times \frac{43}{53} \times \frac{53}{20} \times \frac{20}{58} \times \frac{58}{12} = \frac{75}{12} = \frac{6.25}{1}$$

Figure 4 Reflectance along one path between the top and bottom of a black-and-white Mondrian. The numbers at the bottom indicate the ratios of reflectance at adjacent edges along the path.

Entire Field of View

Given a procedure for determining the ratio of reflectances between adjacent areas,

the next problem is to obtain the ratio of reflectances between any two widely separated areas in an entire scene. We solve the problem in the following way: Find the ratio of luminances at the edge between a first and a second area, and multiply this by the ratio of luminances at the edge between the second and a third area. This product of sequential ratios approaches the ratio of reflectances between the first and third areas, regardless of the distribution of illumination. Similarly, we can obtain the ratio of reflectances of any two areas in an image, however remote they are from each other, by multiplying the ratios at all the boundaries between the starting area and the remote area. We can also establish the ratio of the reflectance of any area on the path to the reflectance of the first area by tapping off the sequential product at that area.

Consider a Mondrian similar to the colored one in complexity and randomness, but consisting of black, gray, and white papers. The reflectance of each area along one path between the top and the bottom are shown in Figure 4. If we apply the sequential-multiplication technique to these reflectances, we can determine the ratio of the top reflectance to the bottom reflectance, as shown in Figure 4. Note that the number we get by sequential multiplication, 75/12, equals the number we would get if the bottom area were contiguous to the top area and we took the ratio of their luminances. We are now coming close to the solution of the problem that we defined at the beginning of our discussion. How can the eye ascertain the reflectance of an area without, in effect, placing a comparison standard next to the area? The sequential product can be used as a substitute for the placement of two areas adjacent to each other, thus defining a photometric operation conceptually feasible for the eye.

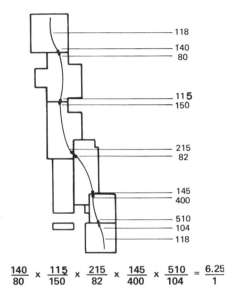

$$\frac{140}{80} \times \frac{115}{150} \times \frac{215}{82} \times \frac{145}{400} \times \frac{510}{104} = \frac{6.25}{1}$$

Figure 5 Luminances of Mondrian (illuminated from below) at particular points along the path from top to bottom. The numbers at the bottom indicate the ratios of luminances at adjacent edges along the path.

We placed a fluorescent tube to illuminate the Mondrian from below so that more light fell on the bottom of the display than on the top. we adjusted the position of the light so that exactly the same luminance was coming to the eye from a high-reflectance area at the top of the display and a low-reflectance area near the bottom. If the luminance determined the lightness of an area, the low-reflectance area and the high-reflectance area should look essentially alike; in fact, they do not. Although the luminances of the two areas are equal, the high-reflectance area at the top looks dramatically lighter than the low-reflectance area at the bottom.[3] Clearly, the visual processes that determine the lightness of an area are not governed by the luminance of that area.

Figure 5 shows the luminances along a path from the top of the Mondrian to the bottom. Note that the luminance at the center of the top area is the same as the luminance at the center of the bottom area. Considering the top area alone, note that the luminance (in arbitrary units) increases from 118 at its center to 140 at its lower edge. The ratio between the bottom edge of the first area and the top edge of the second area is 140 to 80. The luminance of the second area increases from 80 to 115 from upper edge to lowers edge. the ratio of the second area to the third is 115 to 150. As we continue down the path, we obtain the ratios shown at the bottom of Figure 5. The product of all the ratios along the path from the high-reflectance area at the top to the low-reflectance area at the bottom is 6.25. This number is equal to the ratio of reflectances of the top and bottom areas. Thus, without determining

---

[3]This figure was actually was made as a transparency so that the photograph would be the best possible reproduction of the original experiment. The range of luminances of the original display was about 500 to 1. The reproduction must have a range of transmittances that approaches that range of luminances of any areas by non-linearities of the film response. It is very difficult to obtain both these properties in reflection prints, whereas the greater intrinsic dynamic range of a transparency allowed us to satisfy both conditions. In addition, the optical densities of each area across the horizontal midline of this figure was made are the same as those in Figure 4. See original article for copies of these transparencies.

the reflectances and without determining the illumination, however it varies, we have determined a number exactly equal to the ratio of reflectances of these two areas. Yet the two areas have the same luminance as each other and are remote from each other by the whole width of the display. Furthermore, this procedure of sequential multiplication of edge ratios can generate values equivalent to relative reflectance for all areas along the path.

Consistency of Sequential Products on Different Paths

Let a number of different paths start from a given area and wander back and forth over the display, all to arrive finally at a distant area, which we wish to evaluate with respect to the starting area. If we compute the sequential products along each of these paths, we obtain the ratio of reflectances of the remote area to the starting area for each path. In this case the starting and remote areas for all the paths are the same, therefore the terminal sequential products are identical.

If, instead of having all the paths start from a single area, the paths start from different areas, wander over the display, and all terminate in a single remote area, then once again the sequential products give the ratios of reflectances of the starting areas to the single terminating area. However, because all the starting areas had different reflectances, the sequential products at the single distant area will be different from each other. Our ultimate purpose is to describe any area by relating its reflectance to a single, standard, high reflectance somewhere in the Mondrian or to several equally high reflectances. Therefore, we require at this stage of our

analysis that all the paths start from areas having the same reflectance. If the value of the starting reflectance is 100% (by some standard), then the sequential product for any area in the display will be numerically equal to the reflectance of the area (related to the same standard). Therefore, we approach the problem of locating a standard area by seeking the area of highest reflectance. A variety of operations can be used.

One that seems simple, but is not, is to scan the entire scene to find the area or areas with the highest reflectance. This technique requires two separate operations: finding the highest reflectance and then computing the sequential products. Now finding the highest reflectance would require taking all the sequential products, comparing the results, selecting the highest value, and then starting all over again to determine the reflectance relative to the area that had this highest value. This second step requires that the information about the areas of highest reflectance be sent back to the receptors, from wherever the operation of comparing the selecting takes place, and a subsequent procedure such that every path starts with an area thus identified as having the highest reflectance. Although this technique is mathematically valid we feel that it is not readily transposed into biological mechanisms.

We therefore sought a technique that can automatically establish the highest reflectance without a separate first scanning step. We adopted the convention that the initial ratio is the ratio of the signal of the second receptor to that of the first (followed by the third to the second, etc.). Then, regardless of the true reflectance of an area, our technique supposes that the first receptor in any path is reporting from an area that reflects 100% of the light. Because of the deliberately adopted fiction that the starting area reflects 100%, irrespective of its real reflectance, the sequential product becomes greater than 1.0 whenever the path reaches an area whose reflectance is higher than that of the starting area. Attainment of a sequential product greater than 1.0 indicates that the sequence should be started afresh and that this new, higher reflectance should be next supposed to be 100%. Note the very important condition that the sequence is not started afresh by a single ratio that is greater than 1.0, but only when the sequential product for the whole chain to that point becomes greater than 1.0. This distinction is at the heart of the technique for finding the highest reflectance in the path. As the path proceeds, the sequential product always starts over at unity when the path encounters an area with a reflectance higher than the highest previously encountered. We will discuss later the role of sequential products tapped off before the final reset to unity at the highest reflectance on a path.

A Physical Model

Imagine a long fibrous path, like a wire of some kind, on which pairs of photoreceptors are mounted close together. These pairs do not know where the edges fall. They take the ratio at adjacent points along the wire. Most of the ratios will approach 1/1, indicating no change. In the immediately following discussion, let us assume that any ratio that approaches 1.0 is exactly equal to 1.0. Later we will discuss how this can be acceptable. When a pair of photoreceptors happens to straddle an edge, they indicate a larger or smaller ratio. If the pattern is lit from its bottom and even if there is 10 times as much light falling on the bottom as on the top, the close spacing of the photoreceptors insures us that, at any given point, the difference of illumination will be small. Every bridge pair of photocells will read the ratio of adjacent points as 1.0 until an edge intervenes. The bridge pairs of photocells, not knowing anything about edges, sometimes generate ratios equal to 1.0 and at other times larger or smaller ratios.

Figure 6 is a specific example of how the machine operates. The pattern consists of a series of papers that reflect 60, 20, 40, 100, 60, 80, and 30% of the light falling on them. Let us assume, for the moment, that the illumination is uniform, so that we can assign one value per area rather than many different luminances. If we set the uniform illuminance equal to 100 in arbitrary units, the luminance will be equal to the percent reflectance of the papers. This facilitates comparison of the output of the machine with the reflectance of the display.

The members of the first pair of detectors read 60 and 20; as a bridge, they read the ratio as 20/60 or 0.33. This means that the machine, having assigned to the first area a lightness equivalent to 100% reflectance, reads at the second area 33%. These values do not correspond with the actual reflectances but are proportionately correct. The next pair lies within the boundaries of an area and has a ratio of 20/20 or 1.0. Thus, multiplying by 1.0 transmits the edge-ratio signal across an area. We shall see later the benefits of treating the system logarithmically; then, for pairs of receptors between boundaries the log of 1.0, namely 0, is added to the log sequential product. The next reading on the path is 40/60, which when multiplied by 20/60 equals 40/60 or 0.67, corresponding to a proportionately correct, but absolutely incorrect, reflectance of 67%.

The operation of the next pair of receptors shows how the system automatically finds the highest reflectance and restarts there. The edge ratio from this pair is 100/40. We have already had fractions from edge ratios that are larger and smaller than 1.0. However, in this case, 100/40 times the continued product 40/60 equals 100/60 and this is the first sequential product that has a value greater than 1.0. The policy that we have established is that any value greater than 1.0 will be reset to equal 1.0. For all fresh starts, the assigned value is 100%; thus the output with the sequential product 100/60 will also be 100%. Once again, throughout the rest of the string of receptors, the sequential product will establish the reflectances relative to the r^flectance of the area at which the sequential product was reset to 100%. But this 100% is either a real 100% reflectance or, being the highest value on this whole path, is a permanent substitute for the real 100% on this path. There will be no further fresh starts, and the reflectances are from that point on as close as they are going to be to real reflectance.

What do we do with the areas between the start and the first maximum reflectance? If we think about the properties of along path that closes on itself, it becomes clear that the highest reflectance on the chain will finally dominate the chain, if we assume that the image is stationary long enough for the system to reach a steady state.

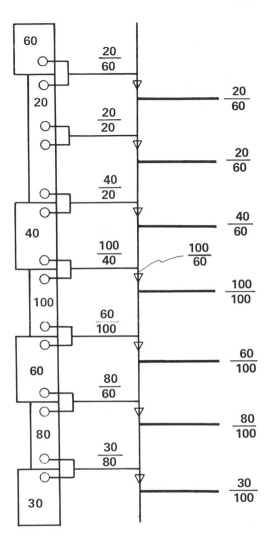

Figure 6 Specific example of how the machine operates. The numbers at the left are the luminances of various areas in a display. Pairs of receptors that straddle the boundaries between adjacent areas generate the ratios of reflectances shown in the center column of figures. These ratios are multiplied to form sequential products that are reset if larger than 1.0 and read off the fiber, to form the output of the system.

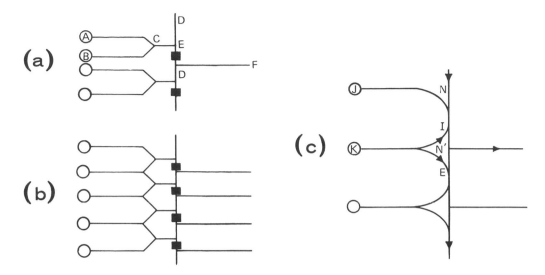

Figure 7 A variety of equivalent sequential-products models. In (a), two opposed logarithmic receptors (A,B) first sum with each other (C) and then sum with the continued product (D at E). This total quantity is both the readout of the system (F) and the new continued product (D$'$) that is combined with the next receptor pair output. In (b), each photocell is the leading photocell for one bridge pair and the trailing photocell for the next bridge pair. In (c), a third variation is perhaps more biologically oriented. The receptor K transmits its signal to its synapses I and E. Synapse I is an inhibitory synapse and adds to the sum of J and the sequential product N. The new sequential product is formed at L and is tapped off the chain between the two synapses I and E. Synapse E is excitatory and combines with this new sequential product N$'$ for the computation of the next sequential product.

If the paths do not circle back on themselves and if there were only one area of maximum lightness in the scene, then the output of lightness values would still be highly accurate if the number of paths were sufficiently large. Let us examine the properties of two paths going in opposite directions. If we consider the example in Figure 6, the first path would have percentage outputs of 100, 33, 67, 100, 60, 80, and 30. A path in the opposite direction would have 60, 20, 40, 100, 75, 100, and 100. Thus averaging only two paths gives the values 80, 27, 53, 100, 68, 90, and 65 compared to the actual reflectances 60, 20, 40, 100, 60, 80, and 30. The average of the two paths is more accurate than either of the separate paths.

For convenience, these schematic examples have used uniform illumination and luminance numerically equal to reflectances. Because the members of each bridge are close to each other, the readings of the bridge pairs on a pathway will not change significantly as the illumination is made nonuniform. The machine will continue to read approximate reflectances and will be independent of luminance: It is this competence that is the essential purpose of the machine.

Figure 8 Photograph of retinex machine reproducing the white, gray, and black wheel. The spotlight on the far left illuminates the wheel on the back wall and the camera on the center left forms an inverted image of it. The photocell pairs in the camera send the ratios of luminances to the electronics on the right which computes the sequential product and transmits it to the display below. The machine gives the same outputs regardless of the position of the spotlight.

If we were to build an electronic model, we would probably make some changes for practical reasons. The most obvious change would be to use logarithmic receptors so that any multiplication could be performed by the summation of positive and negative voltages or excitatory and inhibitory responses. Figure 7(a) shows a simplified conception of the scheme. Two opposed logarithmic receptors (A, B) first sum with each other (C) and then sum with the continued product (D at E). When the logarithm

of the sequential product is greater than 0, then the path restarts and the logarithm of the sequential product is reset to 0. This operation is indicated in the diagram by the black square below E. This total quantity is both the readout of the system (F) and the logarithm of the continued product (D′) that is combined with the output of the next receptor pair. Furthermore, a logarithmic system has properties that assist in implementing the scheme of resetting the chain where the advent of a new high yields a sequential ratio greater than unity. Because the logarithm of 1.0 is 0, we use an electrical system that is negative only and that will reset any positive potential to 0 voltage, thus limiting the sequential product.

Figure 8 shows a photograph of the retinex machine. It consists of a camera, with photocells in the film plane, electronics for computing the sequential product, and a unit to display the sequential products. The white, gray, black wheel mounted on the back wall is illuminated by the spotlight on the left. The inverted image of the wheel can be seen in the ground glass of the camera on the left. Bridge pairs of photocells are arranged on the ground glass so that each pair straddles an edge in this image. The pairs of photocells are silhouetted on the ground glass. The output of the photocells is processed by the electronics to produce a sequential product for each area in the wheel. The wires going from the electronics to the display in the foreground transmit the sequential product to the lamps mounted in boxes behind the ground-glass panel. The lightnesses of these boxes, when the machine is operating, are the correlates of the original reflectances. No matter how drastically the illumination is changed on the orig-

13

inal papers in the wheel, the lightnesses in the final display will be independent of the changes of illumination and hence independent of luminance. Figure 9 shows a schematic diagram of the machine.[4]

Approaches to a Neural System

Although, in the machine, the locations of the edges are known, in the actual retinal image, the locations of the edges are of course unknown, yet it is important that a pair of receptors detect every edge. If any edge is not detected, all the subsequent readings along the path would be incorrect. If a great many pairs of receptors are closely packed, then the probability of missing an edge is small. Closest packing occurs in a system in which a single receptor is in the leading side of one bridge pair and the trailing side of the next bridge [Figure 7(b)].

If we are considering a small number of widely spaced receptor pairs, it is sufficient to say that for each bridge the ratio of energies within an area of uniform reflectance approached 1.0; thus we eliminate the effect of uneven illumination. If, however, pursuing the purpose of capturing every edge, we consider very large numbers of tightly packed receptors, we must be concerned with the fact that across the expanse of an area of uniform reflectance, even though the ratios individually approach 1.0, the small deviation from each 1.0 for each pair leads to the accumulation of a substantial deviation from 1.0 on the exit side of the area.

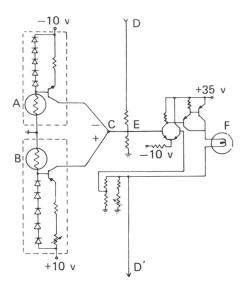

Figure 9 Schematic diagram for one receptor pair of the electronic embodiment of the system. The output of the photocell A is logarithmically amplified and opposed to the logarithmically amplified output of the photocell B. The opposed signals are summed at C and then summed with the continued product D at E. In the machine, as contrasted with the scheme in Figure 7(a), the signal is amplified to drive bulb F and to isolate the continued product output D′ which is passed on to the next receptor pair. The bulb F in the schematic diagram is in the display panel. Because the bulbs were chosen so that, under the particular condition of their use, they have an antilogarithmic response, there is no separate antilog amplifier. The flux from the bulb corresponds with the lightness value computed by the sequential product up to that point on the chain.

---

[4] We are deeply indebted to L. Feranni and S. Kagan for developing the electronic representation of the system for finding the sequential product. The work on this display helped us to clarify our analysis.

However, we suggest that in the physiologic model the very small systematic differences from 1.0 are lost at the synaptic thresholds, thus making feasible the continuum of contiguous cells in a chain of bridges. Such a chain cannot miss an edge and will not react to substantial but gradual changes of illumination across the field. Such a chain will also be completely indifferent to change of illumination as a function of time.

The schemes in Figures 7(a) and (b) lead to a third important system (c). This is a biological system which derives the sequential product by means of excitatory and inhibitory synapses. In this biological system, the electrical concept of resetting is replaced by the hypothesis that an inhibitory signal greater than the signal coming down the chain will block it entirely rather than making it negative (Ratliff, 1965). In this third scheme, a signal travels along the chain, being increased or decreased by successive receptors until it meets an inhibitory signal that is larger than the signal from the sequential product. At this point the old sequential product is blocked and the receptor K transmits its signal to its synapses I and E. Synapse I is an inhibitory synapse and operates on the signal from the sum J plus the sequential product N. This operation forms a new sequential product N′ after I and is read out from the chain between the two synapses I and E. Synapse E is excitatory and combines its contribution with this new sequential product N′, and so on.

In all the diagrams in Figure 7, each receptor has been a member of only a single path. Just as a single receptor can be a member of two or more bridges on the same path, a single receptor can also be a member of many bridges on a number of different paths. The readout that corresponds to the reflectance of a point in an object can be the average of the sequential products read out for a number of different paths that pass through that point. The receptor can serve many paths, and the readout can average the sequential products of many paths at one point, without destroying the individuality and independence of each path.

By designing computer programs based on the lightness model we have described here, and by designing programs that relate computer to observers(McCann et al., 1970), we have been able to arrive at a correlation between predicted lightnesses and observations.

Sequential Products and the Colored Mondrian

We have shown how a single retinex determines the lightnesses on the black, white, and gray Mondrian. The essence of retinex theory is that each retinex is served by one set of cones, that there are three retinexes and three sets of cones, and that each set of cones contains a pigment with an absorption curve different from that of the other two. All the cones with the same spectral sensitivity cooperate to generate the sequential product for their portion of the spectrum and for their retinex. In building the theory of the sequential product, we used the black, white, and gray Mondrian rather than the colored Mondrian, we must take into account the facts that the three pigments in the three sets of cones have broad absorption curves, and that each colored area implies a variation of reflectance over the bandwidth of each set of cones. Because the three pigments in the three sets of cones have broad absorption curves (Brown & Wald,

1964; Dartnall, 1953; Marks et al., 1964) (Figure 10) the signal fed into the neural pathway by a cone in one of these sets will depend on the integral of the spectral product of the absorbance of the pigment times the irradiance times the reflectance of the paper in the colored Mondrian. For these colored papers, the sequential ratio across an edge between rectangles will equal the ratio of the integrals, rather than the ratio of the luminances. (For the black, white, and gray papers, the sequential product obtained from a ratio of integrals is equal to that obtained from the ratio of the luminances.) It is important to emphasize that the integrals that form the sequential ratios for a given retinex use in the integrand the absorbance of the pigment for that retinex. The substitution of the ratio of integrals for the ratio of reflectances does not change the first important characteristic of the sequential product, namely, invariance with change of the over-all illumination of the whole Mondrian.

However, the variation of reflectance of a colored paper across the response band of one pigment is a weighting factor for a change of relative irradiance with wavelength for the flux from that paper. Therefore, for each retinex, the lightness scale for each of the colored papers in the Mondrian may shift a little with large changes of the wavelength composition of the illumination used by that retinex.

The experiment described at the beginning of this paper showed that changes of illuminance as great as the ratio of the reflectances do not change the color names of the papers. There were, however, some small changes and we can now understand these. If we compare the curves of the sharp-cut bandpass filters (Figures 1 and 10) with the curves for the absorbance

of the visual pigments, we see that each pigment, although absorbing principally from the light designed to illuminate it, also absorbs some light from the other filters. Therefore, for any one retinex, the values of the integrals at the junctions of the rectangles will vary somewhat with changes of the relative illumination from the three projectors. Consequently, there will be a small change of relative lightness of a given area on the three retinexes, a change small enough to be apparent on only a few of the colored rectangles.

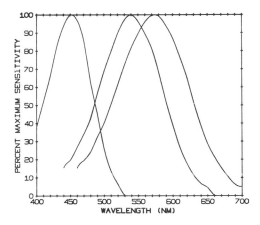

Figure 10 Absorption curves of visual pigments. These curves we calculated using the Dartnall nomogram (Dartnall, 1953) and the maximum wavelengths 570, 535, and 445.

The integral, over the absorption band of a pigment, of the product of absorbance times irradiance times reflectance, corresponds with the familiar integral in colorimetry, but is used here in an entirely different way. Here, the integrals are related to each other only for one retinex (by the sequential product); the three integrals for the three pigments for the flux coming from a point on a colored paper are not compared. Whereas the function of colorimetry is to classify reflectances into categories with similar visual properties, the function of retinex theory is to tell how the eye can ascertain reflectance in a field in which the illumination is unknowable and the reflectance is unknown.

Acknowledgments: We wish to thank Julius J. Scarpetti for extensive experimentation in reproducing the Mondrian experiments and for the production of the transparency inserts. We are grateful to J.L. Benton and S.H. Perry for their assistance, comments, and criticism in all phases of this work, and to P. Dubois for his thoughtful discussions. In addition, we wish to thank M.A. Watson for her assistance with many drafts of this paper.

References

Bartleson, C.J. & Breneman, E.J. (1967) *J. Opt. Soc. Am.*, 5:953.

Brown, P.K. & Wald, G. (1964) *Science*, 144:45.

Chevreul, M.E. (1839) *De la Loi du Contraste Simultane des Couleurs.* Paris: Pitois-Levraul.

Committee on Colorimetry, Optical Society of America, (1953) *The Science of Color.* Crowell, NY, p. 52 (available from Optical Society, Washington, D.C.).

Dartnall, H.J.A. (1953) *Bull. Brit. Med. Council*, 9:24.

Daw, N. (1962) *Nature*, 196:1143.

Evans, R.M. (1948) *An Introduction to Color.* New York: Wiley, p. 119.

Hecht, S. & Hsia, Y. (1945) *J. Opt. Soc. Am.*, 35:261.

Hess, C. & Pretori, H. (1884) *Arch. Ophthalmol.*, 40:1.

Jameson, D. & Hurvich, L.M. (1961) *Science*, 133:174.

Land, E.H. (1964) *Am. Scientist*, 52:247.

Land, E.H. (1962) *Proc. Roy. Soc. (London)*, 39:1.

Land, E.H. (1959) *Proc. Natl. Acad. Sci. U.S.*, 45:115.

Land, E.H. (1959) *Proc. Natl. Acad. Sci. U.S.*, 45:636.

Land, E.H. (1959) *Sci. Am.*, 201(May).

LeGrand, Y. (1968) *Light, Colour and Vision.* 2nd ed. London: Chapman and Hall, p. 225.

Mach, E. (1865) *Sitzber. Math. Naturw. Kl. Kais. Akad. Wiss. Wien*, 52/2: 303.

Marks, W.B., Dobelle, W.H. & MacNichol, E.F. (1964) *Science*, 143:1181.

McCann, J.J. & Benton, J. (1969) *J. Opt. Soc. Am.*, 59:103

McCann, J.J., Land E.H. & Tatnall, S.M. (1970) *Am. J. Optom. Arch. Acad. Optom.*, 47:845.

Ratliff, F. (1965) *Mach Bands: Quantitative Studies on Neural Networks in the Retina.* San Francisco: Holden-Day, p. 110.

Stevens, S.S. & Galanter, E.H. (1957) *J. Exptl. Psychol.*, 54:377.

Wallach, H. (1948) *J. Exptl. Psychol.*, 38:310.

Reproduced from *Jrl. Opt. Soc. Am.*, 61:1–11 (1971).

For more recent work, see Land (1986) *Vision Res.*, 26:7–21.

Color Vision: Representing Material Categories

John M. Rubin & W.A. Richards

Massachusetts Institute of Technology

1.0 Introduction

The human visual system performs a remarkable feat. The pattern of light that
reaches the eye from a scene is the result
of a complex interaction among several
factors: the quality of the illuminant, the
geometry of the scene, and the properties of the materials composing the visible
surfaces. Yet somehow these confounded
factors are mostly separated in our perception. We see particular spatial arrangements of objects. These objects appear
bounded by surfaces having properties—
color and texture—roughly invariant over
a range of conditions of geometry and illumination. To compute invariant descriptions of the material properties of surfaces
is an important goal of any visual system.
Such material descriptors are useful for
object recognition and visual search.

It's commonplace to assume color vision has something to do with capturing
the albedoes of surface materials.[1] But
exactly what aspect of the albedo function would serve a visual system best?
Consider the grandiose goal of recovering
a material's albedo as a continuous function of wavelength. Not only is this goal
impractical; it is counter to the aim of
finding invariant descriptors. With such
an over-zealous representation, unimportant variations in a surface would prevent
its being recognized as a single region, a
patch of one kind of stuff. The perception
of the world would be shattered with spectral acuity too fine; one literally wouldn't
be able to see the forest for the trees.

Here we seek a representation of material reflectance in which trivial surface
variations can be overlooked in order to
appreciate important similarities.[2] At the
same time, the representation must allow some discrimination among different
materials. Below we develop such a categorical color space, based on a theoretical
solution to the problem of identifying material changes. A trichromatic system, it
will be shown, yields a two-dimensional
color space in which the axes will turn out
to represent boundaries between different materials. The four quadrants of the
two-dimensional space represent material
categories.

2.0 Spectral Information at Edges

When two image regions arise from different materials in the scene, the transition
from one material to another will usually

---

[1] The albedo of a material is a function of wavelength $\rho(\lambda)$, with range $(0, 1)$, that indicates
what fraction of photons (emitted by some light source) at each wavelength will be reflected.
[2] We are not suggesting any spectral information be thrown away. We are merely exploring a
single problem. Other problems may require detailed spectral information.

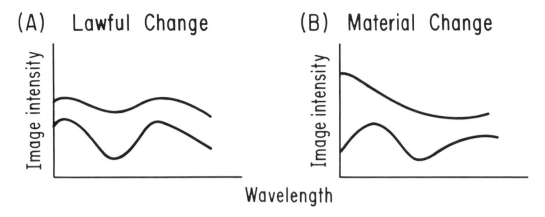

Figure 1 Graphs of image intensity versus wavelength. Each curve represents the image intensity measurable from one image region. A) Two graphs of same shape: a likely lawful change. B) Two graphs of different shape: a candidate for material change.

bring about an edge in the image. Thus we restrict our search for material changes to edges. How can we decide whether an edge is due to a material change?

An edge in the image will usually arise from a single event or state of affairs in the three-dimensional scene (Marr, 1982). The most common edge types are shadows, highlights, surface orientation discontinuities, and pigment density changes.[3] Alternatively, an edge may be due to a material change, a discontinuity between two different kinds of stuff.[4] How can a material change edge be distinguished from other types of edges? Rubin & Richards (1982) attempted to answer this question. Edges which arise from shadows, orientation changes and highlights are *lawful* in the sense that there are equations that describe how image in-

tensities will change across these edges. By contrast, material changes are completely unpredictable; they are arbitrary changes, and as such, can only be inferred by ruling out, at a given edge, the possibility of any of the above lawful changes.

To infer material changes, we now face the awkward prospect of having to reject, one by one, each of the lawful changes. A method of rejecting all of those edges *en masse* would be desirable. Fortunately, there is a simple ordinal rule common to all the edges formed by lawful processes: if the intensity at one wavelength decreases across a lawful edge (shadows, highlights, and so on) then the intensity must also decrease at all other wavelengths taken across the same edge (Rubin & Richards, 1982). When this condition is violated, we say there is a "spectral crosspoint" across

---

[3]Surface orientation change and shadow can coincide at an edge, but this exception is unimportant to the arguments that follow. See Rubin & Richards, 1982, footnote 16.

[4]We consider materials to consist of some spectrally neutral embedding material (e.g., cellulose) impregnated with a single pigment (e.g., chlorophyll). A material change is a change in pigment type, or a change in both pigment and embedding material.

14

the edge. Spectral crosspoints imply material changes; a spectral crosspoint is illustrated in Figure 2a. The spectral crosspoint is not the only means of discovering material changes, however. We will show that a second and independent condition holds for each of the lawful processes— namely the preservation of ordinality of image intensity across wavelength. A violation of this condition implies a material change.

3.0 The Opposite Slope Sign Inference

3.1 The lawful processes

Figure 1a shows two image intensity graphs of the same shape. Intuitively, the two graphs, of similar shape, arise from measurements taken on either side of a "lawful" edge type. Figure 1b shows two graphs of different shape. None of the lawful edge types could have produced such a distortion, and intuitively it seems that a material change edge is the best explanation. We now must make explicit what we mean by "same shape" and then show that this definition of spectral shape remains invariant across edges created by shadows, changes in surface orientation, highlights or variations in pigment density—namely the lawful conditions we wish to reject as material changes.

> **Definition:** Two curves of intensity versus wavelength have the *same shape* if the ordinal relations of image intensity across wavelength are preserved.

More formally, if $I_X(\lambda)$ and $I_Y(\lambda)$ are image intensities as functions of wave-

length measured on both sides, X and Y, of an edge, then $I_X(\lambda)$ and $I_Y(\lambda)$ have identical ordinality if, for all λ_1 and λ_2, $I_X(\lambda_1) < I_X(\lambda_2)$ iff $I_Y(\lambda_1) < I_Y(\lambda_2)$. Note that two image intensity functions of identical ordinality will have local extrema at the same values of wavelength.

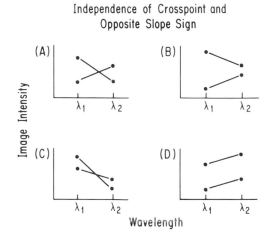

Figure 2 Graphs of image intensity (ordinate) versus wavelength (abscissa). Two wavelength samples, λ_1 and λ_2, are shown. An image region yields two samples of intensity, one for each wavelength, and is represented by the line segment connecting the two sample values. a) & c) Two examples of the spectral crosspoint (Rubin & Richards, 1982). a) & b) Two examples of the opposite slope sign condition. This is the minimal configuration that shows different ordinalities. Note that the crosspoint and opposite slope sign condition are completely independent, since they can occur together (a), or each can occur alone (b and c), or neither can occur (d).

Given this ordinal definition of "same shape", Appendix 1 shows that the ordinality relationship is preserved across all edges arising from the lawful edge types, provided that the following two conditions hold:

Gray world condition: The average of all the different albedos in the scene will be a spectrally flat "gray", so that the diffuse reflected light will have the same spectral character as the direct light.

Spectral normalization: The spectral samples of image intensity have been normalized with respect to the spectral content of the illuminant.

Spectral normalization is a transformation of spectral sample values to what they would have been under white illumination. White light has the same photon flux at all wavelengths. The need for spectral normalization will be eliminated below.

3.2 The opposite slope sign operator

We now can proceed to test for "same shape" using the ordinality relation. If ordinality is violated across an edge, then we infer the edge does not arise from one of the "lawful" processes and hence must represent a material change (provided also, of course, that our grey world condition is not violated).[5]

What is the simplest way to seek violations of ordinality? A pair of spectral samples suffices. Let the image intensities on both sides of an edge be measured at wavelengths λ_1 and λ_2. If image intensity at λ_1 is greater than that at λ_2 on one side of the edge, then the ordinality condition requires the same relationship hold on the other side. So if the two sides of the edge do not have greater intensity in the same spectral sample, ordinality is violated; the edge cannot be lawful. (Details are given in Appendix 1.) This condition is called the *opposite slope sign condition*.[6] Examples are shown in Fig. 2a and 2b. The "slope" of the opposite slope sign condition is the slope of the graph of intensity versus wavelength; it is the derivative of the spectral image intensity function, $dI/d\lambda$.

More formally, given two regions X and Y across an edge and intensity samples I taken at two wavelengths λ_1 and λ_2, we have the following test for a material change:

Opposite Slope Sign Condition:

$$(I_{X,\lambda_1} - I_{X,\lambda_2})(I_{Y,\lambda_1} - I_{Y,\lambda_2}) < 0 \quad (1)$$

---

[5] It is possible when the grey world assumption is wrong, material changes will be inferred from images. This is not entirely bad news; if human perception also goes awry when the grey world assumption is violated, then our theory will gain support as an account of biological visual systems.

[6] The opposite slope sign condition is described here as existing statically, across an edge. It is a spatial comparison of spectral information. A comparison of spectral information in time is equivalent. Such a *temporal opposite slope sign condition* would work as follows: An eye could sweep across an edge, and the spectral information before and after the movement could be compared. Similarly, there is a temporal equivalent of the crosspoint. Consequences of these isomorphic computations in the temporal domain will not be explored here.

where $I_{X,\lambda_1} = I_X(\lambda_1)$. Condition (1) may be contrasted with the previously derived crosspoint condition (Rubin & Richards, 1982):

Spectral Crosspoint Condition:

$$(I_{X,\lambda_1} - I_{Y,\lambda_1})\,(I_{X,\lambda_2} - I_{Y,\lambda_2}) < 0 \quad (2)$$

Note that the spectral crosspoint and the opposite slope sign conditions are completely independent. Figure 2a shows the two occurring together. Each condition can arise alone, as shown in Figure 2b and 2c. Finally neither condition is necessary, as shown in Figure 2d.

The two conditions are related by a kind of symmetry. The spectral crosspoint must make two comparisons across an edge (one for each wavelength), and combine them logically (both comparisons must work out in the correct way). The opposite slope sign condition must make two comparisons, one within each image region, and then combine them logically across the edge. These operations require a structure similar to that of the double-opponent cells found by Daw (1972) and Michael (1978) in goldfish and primates.

To summarize: the spectral crosspoint—our original means of finding material changes—has been augmented by a second and independent material change condition: opposite slope sign. The opposite slope sign condition is the key theoretical result on which we will base our spectral representation of material types. We choose opposite slope sign rather than the crosspoint, because the opposite slope sign condition tells us something about each of the two regions that produce it. Namely, one region has positive spectral slope, the other negative. By contrast, the spectral crosspoint cannot be decomposed into assertions about the two regions that

produce it. In a crosspoint, spatial and spectral information are hopelessly intertwined. We do not cast aside the crosspoint, though; it is essential for spectral normalization.

4.0 Spectral Normalization

For the opposite slope sign test to find material edges successfully, it is necessary for the measured spectral intensities to be normalized with respect to illuminant color. That is, these samples must be transformed to what they would have been under a white (spectrally flat) illuminant. Without this correction, the spectral skew of an illuminant may not only reduce the number of observed opposite slope sign pairs, but more seriously, may transform pairs having the same slope sign (under white light) into opposite slope sign pairs.

By contrast, the spectral crosspoint condition is insensitive to the spectral content of the illuminant, as can be seen by inspecting panels A and C of Figure 2. (See Rubin & Richards, 1982, for a more formal treatment.) We capitalize on this property of the crosspoint to devise a theory of spectral normalization.

Consider now a scene composed of a large number of randomly selected materials. For each image region (simple closed curves defined by edges), take two samples of intensity I_{λ_1} and I_{λ_2} at wavelengths λ_1 and λ_2. Each region will be associated with a spectral slope sign, which is just the sign of the difference $I_{\lambda_1} - I_{\lambda_2}$. If the illuminant were white, we would expect to have roughly equal numbers of regions of positive spectral slope and regions of negative spectral slope. This expectation is based on two assumptions. The first is that there is a random collection of materials in the scene. The second is that materials in the world are such that a random collection of them will be divided equally between positive and negative spectral slope.

As suggested above, normalization requires a collection of image regions that arises from a random set of materials. What about using *all* image regions? The set of all image regions is not likely to represent a random collection of materials, because many materials will recur in several image regions. For example, if a cast shadow cuts across a single piece of material, that material will be twice represented, once for each side of the shadow edge. A second example arises with pigment density changes. In a forest scene, all leaves are composed of the same material (chlorophyll embedded in a cellulose base). A sensible normalization scheme would not take each leaf as a distinct patch of material; minor variations in pigment density from leaf to leaf ought to be ignored.

It seems clear, then, that not all image regions should participate in normalization. Instead we should use a subset of image regions that represents a random collection of materials. Suppose we considered only pairs of regions that have a spectral crosspoint on the edge between them. Then we would be guaranteed that each pair of regions would correspond to distinct materials, randomly chosen. The pairs of different material regions found

with the crosspoint will be the subset of image regions that will be used for normalization.

Our normalization scheme works as follows. Recall that we expect the regions found by the crosspoint to represent a random collection of materials. So we expect roughly the same number of regions having positive spectral slope as negative. For the subset of image regions defined by the crosspoint, tally the number having positive spectral slope and the number having negative slope. If the numbers are approximately equal, our expectation has been met; we can infer that the illuminant is white (spectrally flat).[7] Suppose to the contrary that the number of regions of positive spectral slope exceeds the number of negative-slope regions. Then we can infer that the illuminant is more intense at long wavelengths than at short. (Positive spectral slope means greater intensity in the longer wavelength sample.) Now simply multiply all long wavelength samples by some number less than one. For a large number of samples, the multiplicative constant of normalization can be calculated from the mean value of the spectral slopes of all regions participating in crosspoints. The desired result is an equal number of positive and negative spectral slopes. Further details of the algorithm are given in Appendix 2.

This crosspoint normalization scheme has some useful properties. Each image region used has the same potency in nor-

---

[7]Note there must be some crosspoints for normalization to proceed. If there are no crosspoints, there are no regions to consider. So although it is technically true that there are equal numbers of positive–slope regions and negative-slope regions (namely, zero), we do not want to infer the illuminant is white for two reasons. First, we have no information about any image region, and thus it seems imprudent to guess blindly that the light is white. Second, we have evidence that the scene consists of a single material since it has no crosspoints. Normalization would bring about material change assertions via the opposite slope sign condition, in contradiction to the evidence of uniformity from the crosspoint.

malization, regardless of the size of the region. That is, each pair of image regions (found with the crosspoint) maps to a pair of data points, one for each region. This is good for two reasons. First, the scheme is independent of image region areas. This is desirable since we would not want visual systems to treat an image of a large blue thing and a small red thing differently from an image of a small blue thing and a large red thing. Second, the scheme is independent of the length of an edge separating two regions; each crosspoint edge contributes two points regardless of its length.

It is worth comparing our crosspoint normalization with Land's latest normalization theory. Land's (1983) scheme involves comparing the image intensity of a target region with that of a few hundred *random* locations in the image. In such a theory, the larger an image region, the more random locations it will contain. Land's theory therefore depends on the areas of image regions; ours does not. Our theory makes different predictions from Land's: we expect no effect on normalization from the sizes of image regions, or from the lengths of image edge segments.

5.0 Choosing a Representation

Assume now that the image has been normalized using the spectral crosspoint condition, as described in section 4. We next select a representation of spectral information based on that rule. In particular, *we seek a simple, convenient spectral representation of materials that is invariant under shadow, highlight, surface orientation change, and pigment density change.*

For any region in the image, intensity can be measured at a long wavelength and at a second, shorter wavelength. Call these two measurements of image intensity L and S, respectively, for each image region. Suppose we'd like to represent the spectral character of a region with a single number, namely some mapping of the pair (L, S). Furthermore, we would like the mapping (L, S) to be invariant under the lawful changes. The recognition of material differences would be easy in such a representation. A single material in its different guises—fully lit, shadowed, having different densities of pigmentation, with different surface orientations—would map ideally to a single point. If there were such a mapping, then whenever two image regions mapped to distinct points, we would know they corresponded to distinct materials.

The lawful edge types are unfortunately so diverse that there is no function giving us the desired mapping. No single, nontrivial, continuous function of (L, S) will be invariant under multiplicative (shadow), exponential (pigment density), and additive (highlight) changes. Material change, then, cannot be reduced to the problem of distinguishing two points in the range of some function.

The problem isn't hopeless, however, for there is a continuous function invariant under *some* of the lawful changes, namely the multiplicative ones (shadow and surface orientation change). Consider again the two image intensity samples S and L. The quotient L/S will have the identical value on both sides of a surface orientation change or a shadow edge. The simple quotient is not unique in remaining constant across an orientation edge. We will choose among three simple functions having this property:

$$\frac{L}{S} \quad \frac{L}{L+S} \quad \frac{L-S}{L+S} \qquad (3)$$

How can we select among these candidates? The function $\frac{L}{S}$ takes image regions into the unbounded interval $(0, \infty)$, while the other two functions take image intensities into closed intervals. ($L/L+S$ maps intensities into $[0, 1]$; $(L-S)/(L+S)$ maps into $[-1, 1]$.) The function L/S will be rejected, since any reasonable computational system will be better off using quantities that fall within a closed interval, rather than those that could be arbitrarily large. To choose between the two remaining candidate functions we consider the ease of discovering material changes in these two maps. In particular, how does the opposite slope sign condition appear in each of the candidate mappings?

Given two image regions X and Y, let F denote the function $L/L+S$, so that $F(X)$ and $F(Y)$ are the values of the function F of regions X and Y, respectively. Then for F, the opposite slope sign condition is expressed by $[sign(F(X) - 1/2) \neq sign(F(Y) - 1/2)]$. (The reason for this expression is that the function F takes on the value $1/2$ whenever $L = S$.)

Let G denote the function $L - S/L + S$, a common measure of contrast. This is a simple function that facilitates the computation of material change. The sign of G is the sign of the spectral slope of an image region. That is, $[sign(G(X)) \neq sign(G(Y))]$ emerges as the opposite slope (material change) condition.

We prefer the function G to the F for our representation. Whereas to determine material change with G requires only a sign check, with F, the system must maintain the constant $1/2$ and perform

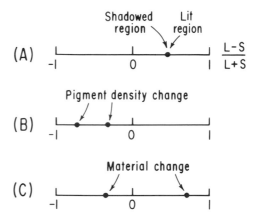

How Edges Map into the Spectral Representation

Figure 3 How various processes appear in the spectral representation implied by the mapping $L - S/L + S$, the range of which is [-1,1]. a) Two image regions differing only in surface orientation or shadow map to a single point. b) Two regions differing as matte and highlighted, or as two different degrees of pigmentation density, map to the same half of the range, i.e., they map to points having same-sign coordinates. c) Only two different materials can map to points straddling the zero, i.e., to points of different-sign coordinates.

two subtractions. The particular choice of F or G, though, seems not to be critical for the goals we have in mind.

Figure 3 shows the interval $[-1, 1]$, the range of the function G. Two image regions corresponding to lit and shadowed versions of the same material, or two different surface orientations, will, by design of G, be mapped to the same point. This is shown in Figure 3a. Two image regions of different pigment density have

14

the same slope sign; hence, in the G map, the corresponding pair of points cannot straddle the zero. The same holds for a pair of points corresponding to a highlight and a neighboring matte region. The latter two edge types are shown in the G mapping in Figure 3b. If two image regions are mapped to points straddling the zero (Figure 3c), they arise from different materials.

To summarize, we sought a function of spectral information invariant over the lawful changes. That goal being impossible, we chose $L - S/L + S$ for two reasons. First, it is invariant across shadows and surface orientation changes. Second, finding material changes with the opposite slope sign condition is easy. The range of the function can be divided into two parts, $(-1, 0)$ and $(0, 1)$. Materials with albedoes of positive spectral slope sign will map into the positive half of the range, and negative-sloping albedoes to the negative part of the range.[8]

Finally, it's worth reiterating why we built our spectral representation around the opposite slope sign condition, and not the spectral crosspoint. Spectral slope sign is an invariant property of a material's albedo function. [9] The opposite slope sign condition can be decomposed into separate meaningful statements about properties

of two image regions: The slope sign of one region is positive, and that of the other, negative. We know something about each region. The crosspoint, by contrast, hopelessly confounds spatial and spectral information. Higher goals of color vision involve describing the properties of individual image regions, and cannot be reached by the crosspoint alone.

6.0 Trichromacy: Finding More Material Changes

Suppose we add a third spectral sample, call it M, to our original S and L samples. Adding a third spectral sample will allow the detection of new kinds of material changes.[10] However, more importantly, the number of basic material categories will be increased from two to six.

In the two–wavelength–sample material representation, an image region is encoded essentially by the rank order of the spectral samples, or equivalently by the sign of the slope of the line segment connecting the samples. Thus, given two wavelength measurements, there are two types of material—negative slope and positive slope. With three wavelength samples, an image region is associated with three slope signs—a slope between each pair of samples (SM, ML, SL).

---

[8]Many continuous maps share the same invariance. We selected our map on the basis of *algorithmic* considerations. The particular choice is independent of the *theory* of finding material change edges.

[9]Since a material is defined as a kind of stuff, a single material can have different albedoes as pigment density changes. What stays constant over these changes in density of pigment is spectral slope sign.

[10]The additional number of material changes detected with each new spectral sample will drop sharply after the third sample. The reason is that the albedoes of natural objects (in the visible range) are typically slow-changing functions of wavelength (Krinov, 1971; Snodderly, 1979). Cohen (1964) showed that three carefully chosen functions of wavelength captured over 99% of the albedo functions of Munsell chips.

Trichromatic Representations

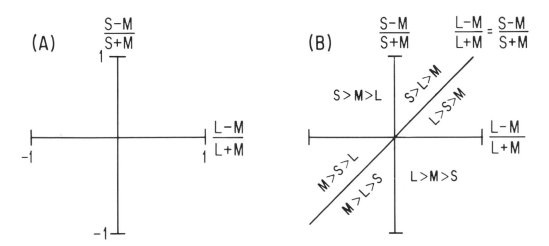

Figure 4 Steps in the construction of the trichromatic material representation. a) Two axes comparing L and M, and S and M samples, are joined orthogonally. Each quadrant is a material category. Points in different quadrants correspond to distinct materials. Points within one quadrant may belong to the same material; they are considered equivalent in this representation. b) The line of unit slope in the figure above represents the comparison between S and L samples. Adding the unit slope line divides the color space into six regions or "hextants." Points in different hextants arise from different materials. Note the hextants do not have equal areas.

There are six possible rank orderings of the measurements ($3! = 6$), and thus six possible basic material types. Any two regions that produce distinct rank orderings of the wavelength samples will bring about one or more opposite slope signs. Any two such regions must therefore be distinct materials.

As a first step in constructing the trichromatic material representation, we combine slope information from two of the three pairs of samples. Arbitrarily, we begin with SM and LM, combining the information in a two-dimensional space as shown in Fig. 4a. Image regions are mapped to points in the square $[-1, 1]$

X $[-1, 1]$, and a pair of points separated by an axis (or both axes) correspond to two regions of different material, just as did a pair of points straddling the zero in Figure 3c. Any pair of points in a single quadrant may arise from a single material. This is the sense in which quadrants represent material categories. Without yet considering comparisons between S and L samples, we already have a categorical representation in Figure 4a, in which in each quadrant corresponds to a material category.

Let's now examine the third pairing of samples, S and L. What condition holding between a pair of points in the

14

preliminary representation of Figure 4a corresponds to the opposite slope sign condition between S and L? It is easily shown that if a pair of points straddles the line of unit slope, the points arise from materials with opposite (S and L) slopes.[11] Furthermore, not just the sign, but the continuous value $(L - S)/(L + S)$ of the L to S comparison is contained implicitly in the representation defined by ordered pairs $(S - M/S + M, L - M/L + M)$ that Figure 4a illustrates. [12]

The unit slope line in the SM–LM space therefore has special significance, and is added to the representation as a third material change axis in Figure 4b. A pair of points lying across any of the three axes will correspond to distinct materials. Thus, each of the six sectors of Figure 4b corresponds to a material type, or equivalently, to a rank ordering of the three samples. The particular rank ordering associated with each "hextant" is shown in Figure 4b. Note the hextants of Figure 4b do not have equal areas. The original pair of axes can be joined in a skew fashion to allocate more or less area to the different material categories.

To summarize, image intensities are measured at S, M and L, normalized according to the crosspoint normalization of section 4, and mapped to $(L - M/L + M, S - M/S + M)$ in a rectangular coordinate system, initially creating four basic material types. A further subdivision into six types can arise by using the line of unit slope as a third axis, dividing the region $[-1, 1]^2$ into six regions, each corresponding to a different material type. Points

in different hextants arise from different materials, whereas points common to one hextant may arise from lawful edge events occurring on a single material.

7.0 Relation to Psychophysics: The Unique Primaries

Our spectral representation of material types is so far only an abstract model of biological color vision. In our theory, certain terms are left undefined. For example, neither the "spectral samples" of the theory, nor the psychological correlate of "materials" are specified. How then can we assess its relevance? One simple linking assumption will guide the interpretation of our theory: of the traditional psychological color variables, hue, saturation, and lightness, it is hue that encodes material type. (Saturation and lightness likely encode other material properties.)

One hundred years ago, Ewald Hering (1878, 1920, 1964) offered a simple model for categorical color perception, based upon the notion of "opponent processes." He observed that "redness and greenness, or yellowness and blueness are never simultaneously evident in any color, but rather appear to be mutually exclusive." *Reddish* and *greenish* are mutually exclusive hue categories, and if hue is encoding material properties, then the two categories will partition materials. See Figure 5a. Similarly, *bluish* and *yellowish* will partition materials. See Figure 5b. These two sets of mutually exclusive hue pairs divide the color space into four re-

---

[11] The line of unit slope is given by $S - M/S + M = L - M/L + M$. This is equivalent to $(S - M)(L + M) = (S + M)(L - M)$, or $S = L$. Points above this unit slope line correspond to $L > S$, points below to $S > L$.

[12] Given the values $(S - M/S + M, L - M/L + M)$, we can compute the value of $L - S/L + S$. Let $Q = S - M/S + M$ and $R = L - M/L + M$. Then $L - S/L + S = Q - R/QR - 1$.

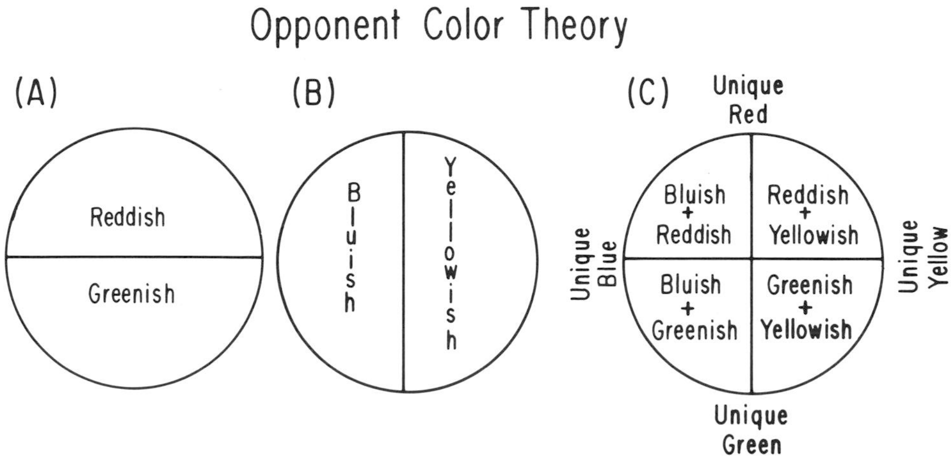

Opponent Color Theory

Figure 5 Hering's notion of opponent color processes. a) All colors are either reddish or greenish, but never both. b) All colors are either bluish or yellowish, but never both. c) The two pairs of mutually exclusive colors divide the color circle into four quadrants, similar to the trichromatic representation that we develop in Figure 6a.

gions, as in Figure 5c, just as did our trichromatic color space (Figure 4a).

Our claim that Hering's color quadrants correspond to our material categories is predictive: we expect that shadows, surface orientation changes, and pigment density changes would only rarely cause perceived hue to change from *reddish* to *greenish* (or vice versa), or from *yellowish* to *bluish* (or vice versa). (However, as noted in Appendix I, highlights could be troublesome.)

The fact that there are four hue categories supports the idea that trichromatic human vision uses two opposite slope sign checks, as in Figure 4a, but not the third, as shown in Figure 4b. (Goethe [1808], however, proposed a theory of color perception based on six hue categories, which might correspond to the use of all three opposite slope sign checks.) Evidence from infants (Bornstein et al., 1976) supports Hering's theory of four hue categories

as independent of language and culture. Pigeons also have categorical color perception (Wright & Cumming, 1971), suggesting the computational scheme that we propose here is fundamental to color vision across species.

Hering's notion of opponent color processes implies four special hues. They are indicated in Figure 5c. These hues, which Hering called the unique psychological primaries, are the boundaries that separate color categories. Primary red is that hue among the reddish hues that separates the yellowish from the bluish; primary blue is that hue among the bluish that splits the reddish from the greenish; and so on. These primary colors are unstable in the sense that any deviation from them involves a change of color categories. Hering's psychological primaries correspond to the axes of our trichromatic representation (Figure 4a).

Of course, one might argue that the

particular location of the primaries in the spectrum is set by the creatures' photopigments, which in turn optimize material discriminations in the habitat (Levine & MacNichol, 1982; McFarland & Munz, 1975; Snodderly, 1979). However, the psychological material boundaries can also be changed by weighted combinations of the existing photopigments. One sort of combination of two spectral samples S and L is a rotation; that is, new coordinates $(S\cos\theta - L\sin\theta, S\sin\theta + L\cos\theta)$ can be created for some angle of rotation θ. The original and rotated coordinate systems will not always agree about whether two image regions satisfy the opposite slope sign condition. That is, the two spectral coordinate systems differing only by a rotation will make different material distinctions. An angle θ can therefore be selected to maximize the number of material changes detected.

In sum, our spectral representation of material categories is a two-dimensional space in which each quadrant represents a material type, and the axes represent the boundaries between categories. Image regions that map to different quadrants necessarily arise from distinct materials; image regions that map to the same quadrant may arise from a single material. Supposing that hue encodes material type, Hering's observation about human color vision makes sense: hues are divided into four fundamental "material" categories by the mutually exclusive red-green and blue-yellow pairs.

8.0 Summary

Our theory of color vision presents two types of operators—the spectral crosspoint for normalization and the opposite slope sign—which suffice in most cases to normalize for the illuminant and to categorize the albedoes in the scene. Our scheme should differentiate between the common natural pigments (chlorophylls, xanthophylls and flavanoids, for example), but not between the density variations of any one of these pigments. The theory does not address this latter problem—namely how we interpret the fine changes in the grain of a piece of teakwood. A quantitative color vision system, of greater complexity than the qualitative computations described here, is needed for such fine discriminations. However, categorical color vision does allow coarse but rapid and reliable judgments about materials.

Appendix 1: Lawful Processes

This appendix shows that image edges that arise from 1) change in surface orientation, 2) pigment density variations, 3) shadows and 4) highlights all preserve the ordinal relations of image intensities across that edge, and hence cannot cause the opposite slope sign condition.

A1.1 Surface Orientation Change

Let X and Y be regions on either side of an edge due solely to a surface orientation discontinuity. Then the image intensities (as functions of wavelength) $I_X(\lambda)$ and $I_Y(\lambda)$, measured in X and Y, respectively, are related multiplicatively. That is, $I_X(\lambda) = \alpha I_Y(\lambda)$ for some constant α (Rubin & Richards, 1982; Horn & Sjoberg, 1979). Two functions differing only by a multiplicative constant have identical ordinality.

A1.2 Pigment Density Variation

Suppose X and Y are two regions on a planar piece of a single material that differ only in pigment density. Then if the albedo (as a function of wavelength) of region X is $\rho(\lambda)$, the albedo of Y can be approximated [13] by $\rho^b(\lambda)$, where b is a constant related to pigment density (Rubin & Richards, 1982; Wyszecki & Stiles, 1967).

The light measured from regions X and Y is the product of the albedoes of X and Y with the radiant intensity of the illuminant. Since X and Y are assumed coplanar (recall that pigment density change is stipulated as the *sole* cause of the edge), and the illumination is the same for both, then any difference between measured intensities from the two regions will be due to a difference in albedo functions. But the albedo functions are related by an exponential constant, and two functions so related have identical ordinality. Therefore, image intensities across a pigment density change will have identical ordinality. [Examples of this relation for natural pigments can be seen in Krinov (1971), Francis & Clydesdale (1975) or Snodderly (1979).]

A1.3 Shadow

Illumination generally consists of two components. *Direct* light comes from a source, which is usually localized. *Diffuse* light is source light that has been reflected off other surfaces (Goral et al., 1984), and is roughly global. Now consider an edge separating a lit region from a shaded one.

Both lit and shaded regions reflect diffuse illumination toward the viewer. The lit region, in addition, reflects a direct source. If $I_{lit}(\lambda)$ and $I_{shad}(\lambda)$ are image intensities (as functions of wavelength λ) from lit and shaded regions, respectively, then:

$$I_{shad}(\lambda) = E_{diffuse}(\lambda)\rho(\lambda)$$
$$I_{lit}(\lambda) = [E_{diffuse}(\lambda) + E_{direct}(\lambda)]\rho(\lambda)$$
$$(4)$$

where $E_{diffuse}(\lambda)$ and $E_{direct}(\lambda)$ are the diffuse and direct components of illumination, and $\rho(\lambda)$ characterizes the albedo of the material.

By inspection of equations (4), it is clear that ordinality can be violated in the case of shadow. That is, a false target is possible. The visual world, fortunately, offers certain regularities. There is usually some close relation between diffuse and direct illumination. This is not surprising, since diffuse light results from diverse, random reflections of the direct light from a variety of materials in the scene. An assumption will be made that this is usually the case: a visual system can presume that diffuse light has the same spectral character as the direct light. That is, $E_{diffuse}(\lambda) = kE_{direct}(\lambda)$, for some constant k. This we call the "grey world" assumption (see Section 3.1), because it is implied by the statement that all the albedoes of a scene will average to grey. Anecdotal data support the grey world assumption. Hailman (1979) measured spectral irradiance functions in a pine woods in a sunny area and in nearby shade. The functions are strikingly similar in shape, and are shown in Figure 6.

---

[13]This exponential relation presumes that the embedding material is spectrally neutral. If the embedding layer reflects different wavelengths unequally, then change in pigment density has a more complex description. In particular, pigment density changes can mimic material changes.

Invoking the grey world assumption, equations (4) become:

$$I_{shad}(\lambda) = kE_{direct}(\lambda)\rho(\lambda)$$
$$I_{lit}(\lambda) = (1 + k)E_{direct}(\lambda)\rho(\lambda) \quad (5)$$

Note that the lit and shaded regions now give rise to multiplicatively related image intensity functions. Ordinality will therefore be preserved.

Shadow and Wavelength

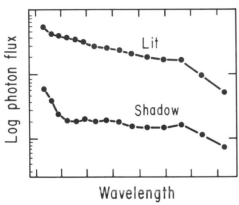

Figure 6 Measurements of the spectral irradiance functions of direct sunlight and nearby shade in a Florida pine woods, adapted from Hailman (1979), Figure 7a. On the ordinate is the logarithm of photon flux. The abscissa shows wavelength.

A1.4 Highlights

The analysis of highlights is slightly more complex. The following equations (Rubin & Richards, 1982; equations 14a) express the image intensities to be found in a highlight and neighboring matte region:

$$I_{matte}(\lambda) = (E_{diffuse}(\lambda) + E_{direct}(\lambda))\rho(\lambda)$$
$$I_{highlight}(\lambda) = \delta E_{direct}(\lambda) + (1 - \delta)$$
$$[E_{diffuse}(\lambda) + E_{direct}(\lambda)]\rho(\lambda)$$
$$(6)$$

where $I_{matte}(\lambda)$ and $I_{highlight}(\lambda)$ are the images intensities (as functions of wavelength) in matte and highlighted regions, and $\delta \in (0, 1)$ is a constant that indicates to what extent the surface is mirrorlike ($\delta = 1$ describes a perfect mirror). (See Richards et al., 1982, for a more extended treatment.) The equations express the fact that both highlighted and matte regions reflect both direct and diffuse light. In addition, the highlight, acting as a partial mirror, reflects the direct light.

Applying the grey world assumption, equations (6) become:

$$I_{matte}(\lambda) = (1 + k)E_{direct}(\lambda)\rho(\lambda)$$
$$I_{highlight}(\lambda) = \delta E_{direct}(\lambda) + \quad (7)$$
$$(1 - \delta)(1 + k)E_{direct}(\lambda)\rho(\lambda)$$

which reduces to

$$I_{matte}(\lambda) = (1 + k)E_{direct}(\lambda)\rho(\lambda)$$
$$I_{highlight}(\lambda) = E_{direct}(\lambda)[\delta + \quad (8)$$
$$(1 - \delta)(1 + k)\rho(\lambda)]$$

By inspecting equations (8), it can be seen that highlights can produce a spurious violation in ordinality. Assume now that the image has been normalized with respect to the color of the illuminant. Normalization is any scheme that allows recovery of the spectral character of the illuminant. (Such a computation is presented in section 4.) Normalization is equivalent to a transformation of the image intensities to what they would have been had the illuminant been white; it allows us to set $E_{direct}(\lambda) = \beta$, where β is some constant.

Both equations (8) can now be rewritten substituting β for $E_{direct}(\lambda)$, yielding

$$I_{matte}(\lambda) = \beta(1 + k)\rho(\lambda)$$
$$I_{highlight}(\lambda) = \beta[\delta + (1 - \delta)(1 + k)\rho(\lambda)]$$
$$(9)$$

With the two assumptions of grey world and spectral normalization, highlights will not produce violations in ordinality. This can be seen in equations (9), where the image intensity function of the highlighted region is simply related to the image intensity function of the neighboring matte region. The intensity in the matte region is multiplied by a constant $(1 - \delta)$, and then a constant function $(I(\lambda) = \delta\beta)$ is added. These two operations preserve ordinality; hence no opposite slopes will arise given our assumptions.

Appendix 2: Algorithm for Spectral Normalization and Material Categorization

Given a full-color image of a scene lit by an unknown illuminant, and a way of finding edges and regions, regions can be assigned to one of a small number of material categories using the following algorithm. The first step is to correct for colored illumination; the second is to categorize.

A2.1 In the Beginning

The original full–color image can be viewed through three spectral filters, yielding three distinct maps of image intensity, say R, G, and B. See Figure 7a. These three maps of image intensity we call "spectral images." The number of filters, or their spectral characteristics, should not be important. All that matters is that the filters yield independent measurements.

A2.2 Spectral Normalization

First, apply an edge operator to the image to produce a closed set of edges.[14] Next, edge segments must be made explicit. See Figure 7b. This involves understanding vertices. For example, a T-vertex terminates the edge that is the leg, but not the edge that's the crossbar. Identifying edge segments is important because we will iterate through a list of them.

For each edge segment, two narrow strips must be defined, one on each side. Call the strips X and Y. (Understanding vertices is important because the strips must be free of edges.) See Figure 7c

Average the intensity values of each of the spectral images R, G, and B in both the X and Y strips. The output of this step is six values R_X, R_Y, G_X, G_Y, B_X, and B_Y.

For each edge segment, check for two types of crosspoint, RG, and BG.[15] (The conditions are $(R_X - R_Y)(G_X - G_Y) < 0$ and $(G_X - G_Y)(B_X - B_Y) < 0$, respectively.) Note the possibility of a third crosspoint involving the R and B samples.

---

[14]If algorithm for edge detection does not produce closed edges, then regions must somehow be identified using edge fragments.

[15]The R and G samples can yield crosspoints, and independently, so can the B and G samples. The G sample could just as easily be taken as the photopic luminosity function.

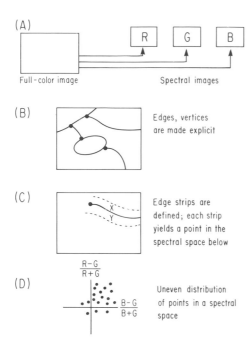

(A) Full-color image   Spectral images

(B) Edges, vertices are made explicit

(C) Edge strips are defined; each strip yields a point in the spectral space below

(D) Uneven distribution of points in a spectral space

Figure 7 a) The full-color image is run through three spectral filters R, G, and B. b) Edge segments have been found and made explicit. This image shows five edge segments. Vertices have been found, and are here marked with large black dots. c) On either side of one of the edges, narrow strips X and Y are defined. No edge segments should be in the strips. Intensity averages will be taken in the three spectral images in both of the strips, yielding six measurements. This is done for each edge segment in the image. d) Measurements taken from strips about each edge map to points in a spectral space defined by axes as labeled. Normalization consists of multiplying R and B values by factors such that equal numbers of points will be found in each quadrant.

Suppose an image has n crosspoint edge segments. For each crosspoint, record spectral information about the two abut-ting strips. In particular, store two color contrast values per region:

$$\frac{R_i - G_i}{R_i + G_i}, \frac{B_i - G_i}{B_i + G_i}, \; i = 1, \ldots, 2n \quad (10)$$

where i is an index ranging over the $2n$ edge strips defined around n crosspoints. This particular form of ratio is useful because its value must lie in the closed interval $[-1, 1]$. The spectral information recorded can be considered as $2n$ points in a two-dimensional spectral space (with axes of $R - G/R + G$ and $B - G/B + G$) shown in Figure 10d. (See also Figure 4a.)

Let $\mathcal{U}$ be the number of points in the upper half-plane of the spectral space (Figure 7d), and $\mathcal{L}$ be the number of points in the left half-plane. Under a white illuminant, we'd expect a random assortment of materials to yield $\mathcal{U} \approx \mathcal{L} \approx n$; that is, points should be roughly equally distributed among the quadrants of the spectral space.

If the $2n$ points are not divided equally among the quadrants of the spectral space, we must seek normalization constants α and β that satisfy the following criterion:

$$MEDIAN \left[\frac{\alpha R_i - G_i}{\alpha R_i + G_i} \right]_{i=1,\ldots,2n} = \\ MEDIAN \left[\frac{\beta B_i - G_i}{\beta B_i + G_i} \right]_{i=1,\ldots,2n} = 0 \quad (11)$$

For a large enough number of image regions, we can take

$$\alpha = \frac{1 - \overline{C}_{RG}}{1 + \overline{C}_{RG}} \; \beta = \frac{1 - \overline{C}_{BG}}{1 + \overline{C}_{BG}} \quad (12)$$

where $\overline{C}_{RG}$ and $\overline{C}_{BG}$ are means of the sets of measurements (12):

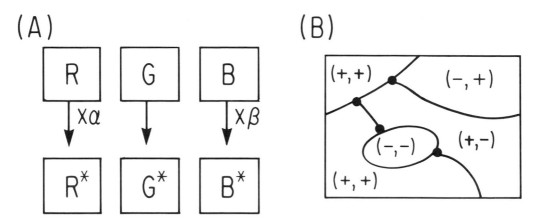

Figure 8 a) The three spectral images R, G, and B are normalized using the multiplicative constants produced by the procedure shown in Figure 11. The normalized spectral intensity maps are R^*, G^*, and B^*. b) The regions of the image sketched in Figure 7b labeled with material categories. Each region is assigned one of four possible ordinal doublets.

$$\overline{C}_{RG} = \frac{1}{2n} \sum_{i=1}^{2n} \frac{R_i - G_i}{R_i + G_i}$$

$$\overline{C}_{BG} = \frac{1}{2n} \sum_{i=1}^{2n} \frac{B_i - G_i}{B_i + G_i}$$
(13)

The values of α and β in (12) will provide a correct normalization (i.e. normalization criterion (13) will hold) given some simple statistical conditions. [16]

The correctness of the normalization constants α and β can easily be checked by verifying that criterion (13) holds. If not, the values of α and β can be adjusted incrementally in an iterative procedure.

Once correct values of the normalization constants are returned by the algorithm, the three spectral images R, G and B can be transformed into a set of normalized spectral images. All values in

the R image are multiplied by α, yielding R^*. (The asterisk superscript denotes normalized intensity.) Similarly, $B^* = \beta B$. Spectral image G is unchanged: $G = G^*$. See Figure 8a.

A2.3 Spectral Categories

Suppose that when closed edge segments were found that image regions were made explicit. For each region i, measure the average values of the normalized spectral images, yielding the triplet (R_i^*, G_i^*, B_i^*). A triplet of numbers yields one obvious pair of ordinal relations:

$$(R_i^*, G_i^*, B_i^*) \mapsto (sign_{RG}, sign_{BG})_i \quad (12)$$

where $sign_{RG}$ is "+" if $G_i^* > R_i^*$, and "−" otherwise.

Each region can therefore be assigned to one of four material categories: $(+,+)$,

---

[16]There must be at least 12 independent crosspoint edges, and the mean and median of the set of measurements $R_i - G_i / R_i + G_i$ must approach the same value as $i \mapsto \infty$, and similarly for the set of measurements $B_i - G_i / B_i + G_i$. (See Siegel, 1956.)

$(-, +)$, $(-, +)$, $(+, -)$. This is shown in Figure 8b. Two regions that are in different categories are composed of distinct materials.

Note that a third ordinal relation is sometimes independent, the $R^* - B^*$ comparison. If this relation is included, six spectral categories obtain.

Finally, note that while the algorithm described here is categorical, continuous information has not been lost; it is still available for more refined purposes. For each region i, the continuous-valued coordinates

$$\left[\frac{R_i - G_i}{R_i + G_i}, \frac{B_i - G_i}{B_i + G_i}\right] \tag{13}$$

should be useful.

Acknowledgment: The research was done at the Department of Psychology and the Artificial Intelligence Laboratory of the Massachusetts Institute of Technology, and was supported by NSF and AFOSR under a combined grant for studies in Natural Computation, grant $79 - 23110 -$ MCS, and by the AFOSR under an Image Understanding contract $F49620 - 83 - C - 0135$. John Rubin was supported by an NSF Graduate Fellowship, and by a predoctoral fellowship from the M.I.T. Center for Cognitive Science. The authors would like to thank T. Poggio, Nancy Kanwisher, Andrew Knapp, and the members of the Natural Computation group for their comments, and Bill Gilson for a meticulous reading of the manuscript.

References

Bornstein, M.H., Kessen, W. & Weiskopf, S. (1976) Color vision and hue categorization in young human infants. *J. Exp. Psych: Human Perception and Performance*, 2:115 – 129.

Cohen, J. (1964) Dependency of the spectral reflectance curves of the Munsell chips. *Psychon. Sci.*, 1:369 – 370.

Daw, N.W. (1972) Color-coded cells in goldfish, cat and rhesus monkey. *Invest. Ophthal.*, 11:411 – 417.

Francis, F.J. & Clydesdale, F.M. (1975) *Food Colorimetry: Theory and Applications*. Westport, CT: AVI Publishing Co.

Goethe, J.B. von (1808) *Zur Farbenlehre, Didaktischer Teil*, 1808. See R. Matthaei (ed.), *Goethe's Color Theory*, 1970. New York: Van Nostrand Reinhold Co.

Goral, C.M., Torrance, K.E., Greenberg, D.P. & Battaille, B. (1984) Modelling the interaction of light between diffuse surfaces. *Computer Graphics*, 18(3):213 – 222.

Hailman, J.P. (1979) Environmental light and conspicuous colors. In *The Behavioral Significance of Color*, (ed.) E.H. Burtt, Jr., Chap. 7, pp. 289 – 357, New York: Garland Press.

Hering, E. (1878) *Zur Lehre vom Lichtsimm*. Wien: Carl Gerald's Sohn.

Hering, E. (1920) *Grundzuge der Lehre vom Lichtsimm*. Berlin: Julius Springer.

Hering, E. (1964) *Outline of a Theory of the Light Sense*. L.M. Hurvich and D. Jameson, translators. Cambridge, MA: Harvard University Press.

Horn, B.K.P. & Sjoberg R.W. (1979) Calculating the reflectance map. *Applied Optics*, 18:1770–1779.

Krinov, E.L. (1971) Spectral reflectance properties of natural formations. National Research Council of Canada, Technical Translation 439.

Land, E.H. (1983) Recent advances in retinex theory and some implications for cortical computations: color vision and the natural image. *Proc. National Acad. Sci. USA*, 80:5163–5169.

Levine, J.S. & MacNichol, E.F., Jr. (1982) Color vision in fishes. *Sci. Am.*, 246 (2):140–149.

Marr, D. (1982) *Vision: A Computational Investigation into the Human Representation and Processing of Visual Information*. San Francisco: W.H. Freeman & Co.

McFarland, W.N. & Munz, F.W. (1975) Part III: The evolution of photopic visual pigments in fishes. *Vis. Res.*, 15:1071–1080.

Michael, C.R. (1978) Color vision mechanisms in monkey striate cortex: simple cells with dual color-receptive fields. *J. Neurophys.*, 41:1233–1249.

Richards, W.A., Rubin, J.M. & Hoffman, D.D. (1982) Equation counting and the interpretation of sensing data. *Perception*, 11:557–576.

Rubin, J.M. & Richards, W.A. (1982) Color vision and image intensities: when are changes material? *Biol. Cybern.*, 45, 215–226.

Rubin, J.M. & Richards, W.A. (1984) Color vision: representing material categories. MIT A.I. Lab. Memo 764.

Siegel, S., (1956) *Nonparametric Statistics*. New York: McGraw Hill.

Snodderly, D.M. (1979) Visual discriminations encountered in food foraging by a neotropical primate: implications for the evolution of color vision. In *The Behavioral Significance of Color*, (ed.) E.H. Burtt, Jr., chap. 6, pp. 238–285, New York: Garland Press.

Wright, A.A. & Cumming, W.W. (1971) Color-naming functions for the pigeon. *Journal of the Exp. Anal. of Beh.*, 15:7–17.

Wyszecki, G. & Stiles, W.S. (1967) *Color Science: Concepts and Methods, Quantitative Data and Formulas*. New York: Wiley.

This selection is an abridged version of MIT A.I. Lab. Memo 764 (1984).

14

Models of Light Reflection
for Computer Synthesized Pictures

James F. Blinn

University of Utah
Salt Lake City, UT

Introduction

In producing computer generated pictures of three dimensional objects, two types of calculation must be performed. The first, and most popularly discussed, is the hidden surface problem: determining the objects visible on the screen and the surface normal vectors to these objects at the visible points. The second is the intensity calculation: given the surface normal vector and the position of the light sources, what is the proper intensity for the corresponding spot on the picture. Typically, very simple models are used which simulate ideal diffuse reflectors. Such reflectors will obey Lambert's law, which states that the surface will diffuse incident light equally in all directions. Differences in intensity are then caused by the different amounts of incident light per unit area intercepted by portions of the surface at various angles to the light source. This will be proportional to the cosine of the angle between the normal to the surface, $\mathbf{N}$, and the vector to the light source, $\mathbf{L}$. This cosine is evaluated by computing the dot product of the two vectors after normalizing them to a length of 1. If this dot product is negative it indicates that the viewer is on the opposite side of the surface from the light source. The intensity should then be set to zero.

In addition, some constant value is usually added to the intensity to simulate the effects of ambient light on the surface. This assumes that a small amount of light falls on the surface uniformly from all directions in addition to the main point light source. The integral of this ambient light from all directions yields a constant value for any normal direction. The net function is:

$$I_{\text{diff}} = \max\left(0, \mathbf{N}{\cdot}\mathbf{L}\right)$$
$$I = aI_{\text{amb}} + dI_{\text{diff}}$$

where

I = perceived intensity

a = proportion of ambient reflection

d = proportion of diffuse reflection

$\mathbf{N}$ = normal vector to surface

$\mathbf{L}$ = light direction vector

this model is simple to compute and quite adequate for many applications.

Simple Highlight Models

A more realistic lighting model was introduced by Phong (1975) as part of a technique for improving the appearance of images of curved surfaces. The function makes use of the fact that, for any real surface, more light is reflected in a direction making an equal angle of incidence with reflectance. The additional light reflected in this direction is referred to as the specular component. If the surface was a perfect mirror light would only reach the eye if the surface normal, **N**, pointed halfway between the source direction, **L**, and the viewer direction, **V**. We will name this direction of maximum highlights **H**, where

$$\mathbf{H} = \frac{\mathbf{L} + \mathbf{V}}{\text{length}(\mathbf{L} + \mathbf{V})}$$

For less perfect mirrors, the specular component falls off slowly as the surface normal direction moves away from the specular direction. The cosine of the angle between **H** and **N** is used as a measure of the distance a particular surface is away from the maximum specular direction. The degree of sharpness of the highlights is adjusted by taking this cosine to some power, typically 50 or 60. The net Phong shading function is then:

$$I_{\text{diff}} = \max(0, \mathbf{N}{\cdot}\mathbf{L})$$
$$I_{\text{spec}} = (\mathbf{N}{\cdot}\mathbf{H})^{C_1}$$

$$I = aI_{\text{amb}} + dI_{\text{diff}} + sI_{\text{spec}}$$

where

$$I = \text{perceived intensity}$$
$$s = \text{proportion of specular reflection}$$
$$I_{\text{spec}} = \text{amount of specular reflection}$$
$$c_1 = \text{measure of shininess of surface}$$
$$\text{other values as defined previously}$$

In addition, when simulating colored surfaces, there is a different intensity value for each R, G, B primary. These should be calculated by scaling only the diffuse and ambient components by the color of the object. The highlights then appear desaturated or white.

Torrance-Sparrow Model

The reflection of light from real surfaces has been the subject of much theoretical and experimental work by physicists (Middleton & Mungall, 1952; Torrance & Sparrow, 1966) and illumination engineers (Gilpin, 1910). The experimental results generally match the Phong shading function but some differences do arise. The main one is the fact that the height of the specular bump, represented by the parameter s above, varies with the direction of the light source. Also the direction of peak specular reflection is not always exactly along **H**. In 1967 Torrance & Sparrow derived a theoretical model to explain these effects. The match between their theoretically predicted functions and experimentally measured data is quite impressive. In this section we derive the Torrance-Sparrow highlight function in terms of the vectors **N**, **L**, **H** and **V**, all of which are assumed to be normalized.

The surface being simulated is assumed to be composed of a collection of mirror-like micro facets. These are oriented in random directions all over the surface. The specular component of the reflected light is assumed to come from reflection from those facets oriented in the direction of **H**. The diffuse component comes from multiple reflections between facets and from internal scattering. The specular reflection is then a combination of four factors:

$$I_{\text{spec}} = \frac{D\,G\,F}{(\mathbf{N}{\cdot}\mathbf{V})}$$

D is the distribution function of the directions of the micro facets on the surface. G is the amount by which the facets shadow and mask each other. F is the Fresnel

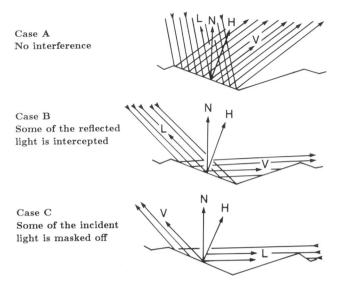

Case A
No interference

Case B
Some of the reflected
light is intercepted

Case C
Some of the incident
light is masked off

Figure 1 Three possibilities for reflection off a rough surface.

reflection law. Each of these factors will now be examined in turn.

The light reflected specularly in any given direction can come only from the facets oriented to reflect the light in that direction. That is, the facets whose local normal vectors point in the direction of **H**. The first term in the specular reflectance function is the evaluation of the distribution of the number of facets pointing in that direction. The distribution used by Torrance & Sparrow was a simple Gaussian:

$$D_2 = e^{-(\alpha c_2)^2}$$

D_2 is the proportionate number of facets oriented at an angle α from the average normal to the surface. The factor c_2 is the standard deviation for the distribution and is a property of the surface being modeled. Large values yield dull surfaces and small values yield shiny surfaces. We are interested in the number of facets

pointing in the direction of **H** so the angle α here is $\cos^{-1}(N \cdot H)$.

Since the intensity is proportional to the number of facets pointing in the **H** direction, we must take into account that the observer will see more of the surface area when the surface is slanted. The increase in area is inversely proportional to the cosine of the angle of slant. The slant angle is the angle between the average surface normal, **N**, and the eye, **V**. This explains the division by $(N \cdot V)$.

Counteracting this effect is the fact that some of the facets shadow each other. The degree to which this shadowing occurs is called the "geometrical attenuation factor", G. It is a value from 0 to 1 representing the proportionate amount of light remaining after the masking or shadowing has taken place. Calculation of G assumes that the micro facets exist in the form of V shaped grooves with the sides at equal but opposite angles to the average surface normal. We are interested only in grooves where one of the sides points in the specular direction **H**. For differing positions of the light source and viewer position we can have one of three cases illustrated in Figure 1.

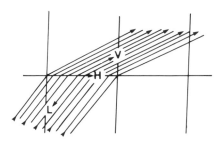

Figure 2 Top view of reflection from a micro-facet.

Note that the vectors **L** and **V** do not necessarily lie in the plane of the figure (i.e. the plane containing **N** and **H**). We can see this by considering a top view as in Figure 2.

The value of G for case A of Figure 1 is 1.0, signifying no attenuation.

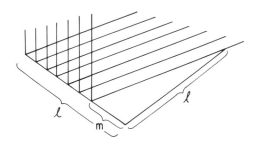

Figure 3 Light which escapes is $1 - (m/l)$.

To compute G for case B we need to compute the ratio $1 - (m/l)$ which

is the proportionate amount of the facet contributing to the reflected light. See Figure 3.

We can reduce the problem to two dimensions if we project **V** onto the plane containing **N** and **H** (the plane of the diagram). Calling this projection $\mathbf{V_p}$ and labeling relevant angles we have Figure 4. Applying the law of sines we have

$$m/l = \sin f / \sin b$$

Then we note that

$$\sin b = \cos e$$
$$\cos b = \sin e$$

Since the angle of the triangle must sum to 2π we have

$$\sin f = \sin(b + c)$$
$$= \sin b \cos c + \cos b \sin c$$

Due to the symmetry of the groove and the complementarity of d and a

$$c = 2d$$
$$\cos c = 1 - 2\sin^2 d = 1 - 2\cos^2 a$$
$$\sin c = 2\cos d \sin d = 2\sin a \cos a$$

Plugging these into the expression for $\sin f$

$$\sin f = \cos e(1 - 2\cos^2 a) + 2\sin e \cos a$$
$$\sin a$$
$$= \cos e - 2\cos a(\cos e \cos a - \sin e$$
$$\sin a)$$
$$= \cos e - 2\cos a \cos(e + a)$$
$$= (\mathbf{H \cdot V}_p) - 2(\mathbf{N \cdot H})(\mathbf{N \cdot V}_p)$$

Since $\mathbf{V}_p$ is the projection of **V** onto the **N**, **H** plane then $\mathbf{N \cdot V}_p = \mathbf{N \cdot V}$ and $\mathbf{H \cdot V}_p = \mathbf{H \cdot V}$ so that

$$G_b = 1 - \frac{m}{l} =$$
$$2(\mathbf{N \cdot H})(\mathbf{N \cdot V})/(\mathbf{V \cdot H})$$

Examining the diagram for G_c we see that it is the same as that for G_b but with the roles of **L** and **V** exchanged. Thus

$$G_c = 2(\mathbf{N \cdot H})(\mathbf{N \cdot L})/(\mathbf{H \cdot L})$$
$$= 2(\mathbf{N \cdot H})(\mathbf{N \cdot L})/(\mathbf{V \cdot H})$$

For a particular situation, the effective value of G will be the minimum of G_a, G_b and G_c.

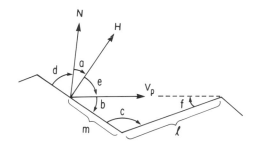

Figure 4 Measurement of m/l.

The final factor in the specular reflection is the Fresnel reflection. This gives the fraction of the light incident on a facet which is actually reflected as opposed to being absorbed. This is a function of the angle of incidence on the micro facet and the index of refraction on the substance. It is given by

$$F = \frac{1}{2}\left[\frac{\sin^2(\phi-\theta)}{\sin^2(\phi+\theta)} + \frac{\tan^2(\phi-\theta)}{\tan^2(\phi+\theta)}\right]$$

where $\sin\phi = \sin\phi/n$

ϕ = angle of incidence

n = index of refraction

In our case, the angle of incidence is $\phi = \cos^{-1}(\mathbf{L \cdot H}) = \cos^{-1}(\mathbf{V \cdot H})$. The interesting thing about this function is that it has a substantially different form for metallic vs. nonmetallic substances. For metals, corresponding to large values

of n, $F(\phi, n)$ is nearly constant at 1. For non-metals, corresponding to small values of n, it has a more exponential appearance, starting out near zero for $\phi = 0$ and going to 1 at $\phi = \pi/2$.

Facet Distribution Functions

One thing in the above model can be improved upon. This is the facet distribution function. This function takes an angle, α, and a measure of the shininess of the surface and computes the proportionate area of facets pointing in that direction. The angle α is the angle between **H** and **N**; we can evaluate its cosine as $(\mathbf{N \cdot H})$.

The Phong model effectively uses the distribution function of the cosine raised to a power.

$$D_1 = \cos^{c_1}\alpha$$

The Torrance-Sparrow model uses the standard Gaussian distribution already mentioned.

$$D_2 = e^{-(\alpha c_2)^2}$$

A third function has been proposed by Trowbridge & Reitz (1975). They showed that a very general class of surface properties could be generated by modelling the microfacets as ellipsoids of revolution. This leads to the distribution function

$$D_3 = \left[\frac{c_3^2}{\cos^2\alpha(c_3^2-1)+1}\right]^2$$

Where c_3 is the eccentricity of the ellipsoids and is 0 for very shiny surfaces and 1 for very diffuse surfaces.

Each of these functions has a peak value of 1 at $\alpha = 0$ (for facets pointing along the average surface normal) and falls off as α increases or decreases. The rate of fall off is controlled by the values

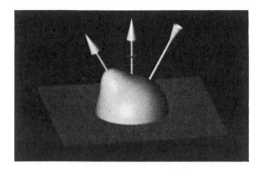

Phong Model   Torrance-Sparrow Model

Figure 5 Comparison of Phong and Torrance-Sparrow reflection distributions for incident light at 30° from normal.

c_1, c_2 and c_3. In comparing the functions it is necessary to specify this rate in a uniform unit. A convenient such unit is the angle at which the distribution falls to one half. In terms of this angle, β, the three coefficients are:

$$c_1 = -\frac{ln\ 2}{ln\ \cos\beta}$$

$$c_2 = \frac{\sqrt{ln\ 2}}{\beta}$$

$$c_3 = \left[\frac{\cos^2\beta - 1}{\cos^2\beta - \sqrt{2}}\right]^{\frac{1}{2}}$$

If these three functions are plotted with values of β it can be seen that they are very similar in shape. However, since there is some experimental as well as theoretical justification for D_3 and since it is the easiest to compute, it is the one we shall choose.

Computational Considerations

There are several observations which can be made to speed up the computation of the highlight function.

If β does not change within a frame the function D_3 can be calculated using the intermediate values (calculated once per frame):

$$k_1 = 1/(c_3^2 - 1)$$

$$k_2 = k_1 + 1$$

whereupon

$$D_3 = \left[\frac{k_2}{\cos^2\alpha + k_1}\right]^2$$

A simplification which is often made is to assume that the light source is at infinity. Thus the vector $\mathbf{L}$ is a constant for each point of the picture. We may also model the eye as being far away from the object so that $\mathbf{V} = (0\ 0\ -1)$. This allows the calculation of the direction of $\mathbf{H}$ to be done once per change in light direction.

It is possible to avoid a potential division by zero when computing G by combining it with the term $1/(\mathbf{N}\cdot\mathbf{V})$ and finding the minimum of Ga, Gb and Gc before doing the divisions:

15

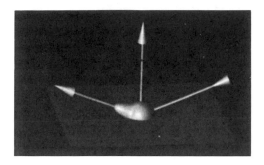

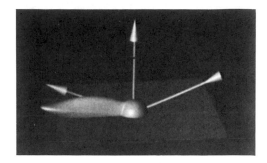

Phong Model   Torrance-Sparrow Model

Figure 6 Comparison of Phong and Torrance-Sparrow reflection distributions for incident light at 70° from normal.

if $(\mathbf{N}{\cdot}\mathbf{V}) < (\mathbf{N}{\cdot}\mathbf{L})$ then
  if $2(\mathbf{N}{\cdot}\mathbf{V})(\mathbf{N}{\cdot}\mathbf{H}) < (\mathbf{V}{\cdot}\mathbf{H})$ then $G :=$ $2(\mathbf{N}{\cdot}\mathbf{H})/(\mathbf{V}{\cdot}\mathbf{H})$
    else $G := 1/(\mathbf{N}{\cdot}\mathbf{V})$

else

  if $2(\mathbf{N}{\cdot}\mathbf{L})(\mathbf{N}{\cdot}\mathbf{H}) < (\mathbf{V}{\cdot}\mathbf{H})$ then $G :=$ $2(\mathbf{N}{\cdot}\mathbf{H})(\mathbf{N}{\cdot}\mathbf{L})/(\mathbf{V}{\cdot}\mathbf{H})(\mathbf{N}{\cdot}\mathbf{V})$
    else $G := 1/(\mathbf{N}{\cdot}\mathbf{V})$

The Fresnel reflection is a function only of the index of refraction and the dot product $(\mathbf{V}{\cdot}\mathbf{H})$. If $\mathbf{V}$ is assumed constant at $(0\ 0\ -1)$ then this calculation needs to be made only once per change in light source direction. In addition, by some trigonometric identities it can be shown that the Fresnel formula can be calculated by:

$$F = \frac{1}{2}\frac{(g-c)^2}{(g+c)^2}\left[1 + \frac{(c(g+c)-1)^2}{(c(g-c)+1)^2}\right]$$

where $c = (\mathbf{V}{\cdot}\mathbf{H})$

$$g = \sqrt{n^2 + c^2 - 1}$$

Note that at normal incidence, F is a

simple function of n, namely $[(n-1)/(n+1)]^2$.

Comparison with Phong Shading

Now that we have derived this highlight function we should compare it with the Phong function to see where and by how much they differ. Figure 5 shows a plot of the amount of light reflected from a surface as a result of an incident ray at 30 degrees from the surface normal. The distance of the surface in a particular direction from the center represents the amount of light reflected in that direction. The incoming ray is from the right. A vector pointing to the left at the specular direction is shown for reference. The hemispherical portion of the function is the diffuse reflection; equal amounts in each direction. The bump is the specular reflection. For this angle of incidence the functions are almost identical. Figure 6 shows the same function for an incident ray at 70 degrees. Note that the specular bump is much larger for the Torrance Sparrow function and not in quite the same direction. This indicates that the new function will be materially different only for shallow angles of incident light and that the specular reflection will be much higher there. This may be verified by the simple experiment of holding a matte sheet of paper edge on to a light and noting that it looks quite shiney.

Figure 7 shows images of an object made using the two highlight functions with both an edge-on lighting direction and a front-on direction. Figure 7a simulates an aluminum metallic surface using the experimentally measured parameters:

$$s = .4$$
$$d = .6$$
$$n = 200$$
$$c_3 = .35$$

Figure 7b simulates a Magnesium Oxide ceramic (a standard diffuse reflector) using the experimental parameters:

$$s = .667$$
$$d = .333$$
$$n = 1.8$$
$$c_3 = .35$$

Note that the ceramic looks quite diffuse for light hitting it almost perpendicularly and very specular (even more so than the aluminum) for light hitting it almost tangentially.

Varying Surface Shininess

In Blinn & Newell (1976) and Catmull (1975) a technique for mapping texture patterns onto bicubic surfaces was described. The object was defined as a biparametric surface and the parameter

values were used as input to a texture function which scaled the diffuse component of the reflection. This form of mapping is good for simulating patterns painted on the surface but attempts to simulate bumpy surfaces were disappointing. This effect can, however, be better approximated by using the same texture mapping approach applied to the local surface roughness c_3.

If c_3 is going to change from place to place on the surface we must worry about normalization of the D_3 function. In its original derivation in Trowbridge & Reitz (1975) D_3 differed from that shown here by a factor of c_3^2. This additional factor was included here as a normalizing constant to make $D_3(0) = 1$. Since, now, c_3 is varying across the surface, we wish to use a constant normalizing factor based on its minimum value over the surface. The texture modulated distribution function should then be:

$$c_3 = c_{\min} + (1 - c_{\min})\, t(u, v)$$

$$D_4 = \left[\frac{c_{\min} c_3}{\cos^2 \alpha (c_3^2 - 1) + 1} \right]^2$$

where $t(u, v)$ = texture value.

Figure 8 shows some images made with various texturing functions.

Conclusions

The Torrance-Sparrow reflection model differs from the Phong model in the inclusion of the G, F and $1/(\mathbf{N} \cdot \mathbf{V})$ terms. This has a noticeable effect primarily for non-metallic and edge lit objects. The use of the D_3 micro facet distribution function provides a better match to experimental data and is, happily, easier to compute than D_1 or D_2. This savings effectively offsets the extra computation time for

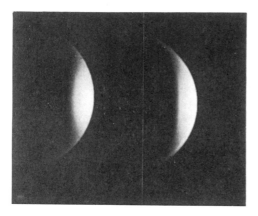
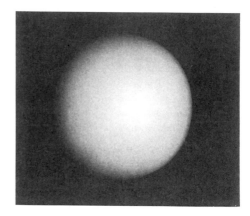

Phong   Torrance-Sparrow   Both Models Essentially Same
          Edge Lit   Front Lit

(a)

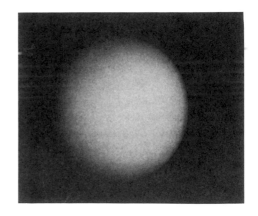

Phong   Torrance-Sparrow   Both Models Essentially Same
          Edge Lit   Front Lit

(b)

Figure 7 (a) Simulation of aluminum surface. (b) Simulation of Magnesium Oxide Surface.

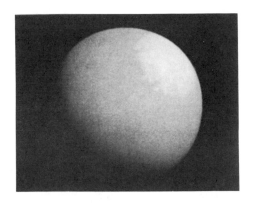 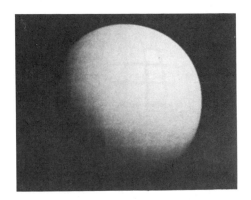

Figure 8 Surface shininess varying as a function of two different texture patterns.

G and F yielding a highlight generation function having a high degree of realism for no increase in computation time.

References

Blinn, J.F. & Newell, M.E. (1976) Texture and reflection in computer generated images. *Comm. ACM 19*, 10: 542–547.

Catmull, E.A. (1975) Computer display of curved surfaces. *Proc. Conf. on Computr. Graphics*, May 1975 (IEEE Cat. No. 75CH0981–1C), 11–17.

Gilpin, F.H. (1910) Effect of the variation of the incident angle on the coefficient of diffused reflection. *Trans. Illum. Engl. Soc.*, 5:854–873.

Middleton, W.E.K. & Mungall, A.G. (1952) The luminous directional reflectance of snow. *J. Opt. Soc. Am.*, 42:572–579.

Phong, B.-T. (1975) Illumination for computer generated images. *Comm ACM 18*, 6:311–317.

Torrance, K.E. & Sparrow, E.M. (1966) Polarization, directional distribution, and off-specular peak phenomena in light reflected from roughened surfaces. *J. Opt. Soc. Am.*, 56:916–925.

Torrance, K.E. & Sparrow, E.M. (1967) Theory for off-specular reflection from roughened surfaces. *J. Opt. Soc. Am.*, 57:1105–1114.

Trowbridge, T.S. & Reitz, K.P. (1975) Average irregularity representation of a roughened surface for ray reflection. *J. Opt. Soc. Am.*, 65:531–536.

This article first appeared in *Computer Graphics*, 11(2):192–198 (1977).

15

Inferring "Water" from Images

T.J. Kung
W.A. Richards

Massachusetts Institute of Technology

1.0 Introduction

Water waves are recognizable from a black and white photo. What is the image information that allows us to make this inference? In order to answer this question, we use computer graphics to simulate water. Once a perceptually deceiving simulation of water is obtained, then the study of the inference process can proceed. This report presents a model for generating near-natural images of water waves.

Computer generated water waves have been created previously for flight simulators. However, these images did not look very realistic, probably because very simple models were used. For instance, Max (1981) presented a ray-tracing procedure in which ocean waves and islands are rendered. Although he was able to render good reflection images off waves, the ocean waves do not look like real waves. Ogden (1985) generated a real-time animation sequence of water by using the Burt Pyramid (1983), but again her model was not based on the physics of water. Furthermore, because the method essentially generated fractals in the image plane, there was no real description of the 3D surface. Here, our objective is to create a 3D surface of water undergoing wave motion, and to be able to view this surface from any arbitrary angle. Complicated effects like

the reflection of an object off the water surface are not considered in this paper.

We divide the problem into three parts: (1) reflection, (2) surface shape, and (3) dynamics. In interpreting images, basically we are trying to infer the surface properties and shape from the image intensities. As a first step in understanding this inference process, we must understand what properties make water characteristically different from other surfaces. If we knew these properties and how to describe them mathematically we should be able to create a realistic image. Among the surface properties, we are only interested in the optically related properties, i.e. the reflectance function. A dynamic view yields a considerably stronger impression, therefore a brief discussion of wave dynamics is included also.

2.0 Reflectance Function

Because water is a transparent material, the intensity and color of the visible light emerging from the sea depends on

(i) *The illumination.* The elevation of the sun and the sky and cloud cover determine the quantity and spectrum of downwelling incident light.

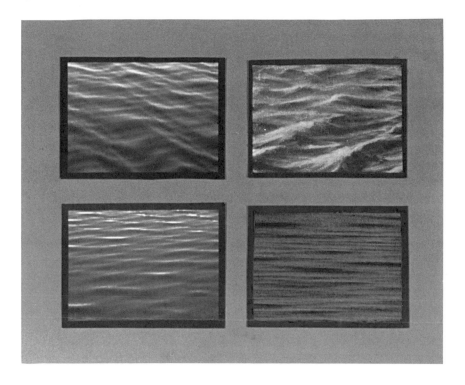

Figure 1 Synthetic water images are shown in the two left-hand panels. The upper right panel is an artist's rendition. A photographic image of water is shown in the lower right. Most people prefer one of the synthetic images, demonstrating that our model is capturing the psychophysically relevant information.

(ii) *The optical properties of the sea-water itself.* The light which penetrates into the sea is spectrally modified by absorption inside the medium before being partly backscattered toward the atmosphere. These absorption and backscattering processes have their origin in the water molecules, and also in all the other substances present in the sea as dissolved or particulate matter.

People can recognize water waves from a black and white photo, therefore the most important thing in perceiving water waves is the relative intensity of

emerging light from different places of the water surface, not the details of spectrum and quantity. This fact makes it possible to simplify the reflectance function without considering the functional dependency on the wavelength of lights.

Cook & Torrance (1982) proposed a reflectance model for computer graphics as follows:

$$I = R_{amb}E_{amb} +$$
$$\sum E_{dir}(\mathbf{NL})(dR_{mat} + sR_{spec}) \quad (1)$$

where E is the intensity of light source, $\mathbf{N}$ is surface normal unit vector, and $\mathbf{L}$ is the light direction of a point light source. The point light sources are linearly

16

combined with the ambient light source. Each point light source is further divided into a specular component and matte component. The d and s in equation (1) are the fractions of reflectance that are matte and specular. The specular component is given by:

$$R_{spec} = \frac{F}{\pi} \frac{DG}{(\mathbf{N} \cdot \mathbf{L})(\mathbf{L} \cdot \mathbf{V})} \qquad (2)$$

where F is a Fresnel term which describes how light is reflected from each smooth microfacet. It is a function of incidence angle and wave length. The geometrical attenuation factor G accounts for the shadowing and masking of one facet by another. The facet slope distribution function D represents the fraction of the facets that are in the direction $\mathbf{H}$ (Figure 2).

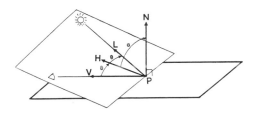

Figure 2 The geometry of reflection.

In rendering water, we use Cook & Torrance's model with some modifications. As discussed before, water backscatters part of the incident light. Although the backscattered light is a function of the incident light spectrum, optical properties of the water itself, and the elevation of viewing position, we assume these conditions are fixed in a limited area and within a short period of time. Therefore the backscattered light is a constant and is uniform over the water surface.

Figure 3 shows the value of Fresnel

term for various indexes of refraction n. The Fresnel term is significant only when the incident angle is greater than 70 degrees. For water the index of refraction equals 1.32. Based on this property, we make two simplifications. First, we neglect the matte term because a water surface only reflects light in very limited directions. Second, we neglect the point light source-sun. By doing so we eliminate the special cases when it is dawn and when it is dusk, and also scintillation effects which are easy to mimic.

The ambient light source (sky) is considered as a hemi-sphere light source. No matter where the viewing position is, it is always possible to see some lights from somewhere in the dome directly reflected off the water to the eyes. When the viewing angle is less than 70 degrees, so is the incident angle, and the reflected light is much less than when the viewing angle is greater than 70 degrees. In other words, the intensity of reflected light from the water surface is a function solely of the angle between the viewing direction and the surface normal of the facet.

As a conclusion of above discussion, our reflectance model for water waves is

$$I_{total} = I_{bs} + I_{amb} \int_{dome} \frac{FDG}{(\mathbf{N} \cdot \mathbf{L})(\mathbf{L} \cdot \mathbf{V})} d\omega \qquad (3)$$

where I_{bs} is the backscattered light intensity and is a constant. The integration term is for the ambient light source. Since this term is a function of the angle between $\mathbf{N}$ and $\mathbf{V}$ only, we calculate these values numerically for different angles and store them in a table. In rendering the images, we then just find the value of this integration term from that table. In order to simplify the integral work, the Gaussian model is used for the facet slope

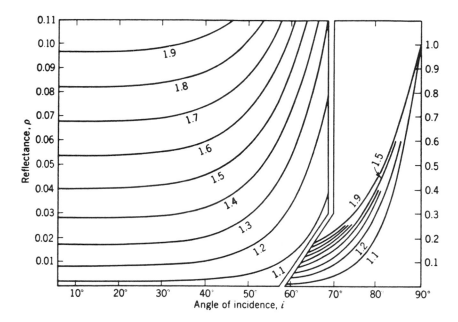

Figure 3 Fresnel reflectance as function of incident angle. The parameter on the curves is the index of refraction, n. Note the change in scale for the right portion of the graph.

distribution function D

$$D = \exp\left(-(\alpha/m)^2\right) \qquad (4)$$

where α is the angle between $\mathbf{N}$ and $\mathbf{H}$ (Figure 2). 0.8 is used for m. With this value D is small when α is greater than 20 degrees and then the integration can be neglected. In other words, the integrated region can be reduced from a hemi-sphere to a cone of 20 degree radius. The expression for G is

$$G = \min\left[1, \frac{2(\mathbf{N}\cdot\mathbf{H})(\mathbf{N}\cdot\mathbf{V})}{(\mathbf{V}\cdot\mathbf{H})}, \right.$$
$$\left. \frac{2(\mathbf{N}\cdot\mathbf{H})(\mathbf{N}\cdot\mathbf{L})}{(\mathbf{V}\cdot\mathbf{H})}\right]. \qquad (5)$$

The cone is further divided into three areas based on which term in Eq. (5) is important. The full expression of F used

in the integration term is

$$F = \frac{1}{2}\frac{(g-c)^2}{(g+c)^2}\left[1 + \frac{[c(g+c)-1]^2}{[c(g+c)+1]^2}\right] \qquad (6)$$

where

$$c = \mathbf{V}\cdot\mathbf{H}$$
$$g^2 = n^2 + c^2 - 1.$$

For water, n is 1.32. The ratio of I_{bs}/I_{amb} was set to $1/3$ in our simulation.

3.0 Surface Shape

Traditionally, sinusoidal functions are used to model ocean waves (Bigelow & Edmondson, 1952; Gross, 1972). There is a strong theoretical basis to assume that the ocean surface is formed by sums of

Component Number	1	2	3	4	5
Mean wave-length 1	25	30	37.5	10.7	16.7
Amplitude A	0.3	0.4	0.4	0.15	0.25
Modulation Rate r	0.1	0.1	0.1	0.1	0.1
Angle (dgr) β	110	90	65	120	60

Table 1 Static wave parameters.

long crested sinusoids:

$$w(x,y) = \sum \left[C + B * \cos \right.$$

$$\left. \left(\frac{2\pi}{\lambda_x}x + \frac{2\pi}{\lambda_y}y + \phi \right) \right] \quad (7)$$

Since this model requires the sum of a large number of wave forms to obtain a realistic picture, it is not practical for image generation. Schachter (1980) proposed a narrow-band noise model to overcome this problem. In this model, it is assumed that envelopes and phase shifts are slowly varying:

$$w(x) = a(x) * \cos(\mu x + \phi(x)) \quad (8)$$

Although this model has the advantage of being able to simulate different textures, the results show that the water generated by this model does not have the shape randomness that real water does.

We propose another model which is a summation of squared of sine waves with slowly varying wave length:

$$w(x,y) = \sum \left[A * \left(1 + \sin \right. \right.$$

$$\left. \left. \left(\frac{2\pi}{\lambda(x,y)}(x\cos\beta + y\sin\beta) + \phi \right) \right) \right]^2 \quad (9)$$

Here we assume waves traveling in the x, y plane and β is the angle between x-axis and the traveling wave direction. The ideal wave form is sinusoidal but a lot of factors can distort waves from their ideal forms, for instance winds, nonlinearity, and nonuniform water depth for shallow water waves (Bascom, 1980). Normal wave crests tend to go steep before collapse. Consequently, the distorted wave form is steep at the crest and flat at trough. We found it takes less computation to get the distorted wave form by using a function which has its shape close to the distorted wave form such as the sine squares than by using Fourier series (summation of sinusoidal waves).

Because of nonlinear effects, wave trains are always modulated when traveling in a field. Instead of assuming slowly varying amplitude and phase shift as Schachter does, we assume slowly varying wave length. The amplitude is assumed to be a constant because the variation is too small to be noticed in short distances. Nonlinear instability theory tells us that instability causes steep gravity waves to evolve into the three-dimensional spilling breaking waves. This three dimensional wave form is the normal wave form we see in an open sea. To simulate the three dimensional wave patterns, it is necessary to have at least three components in equation (9). It was found that to generate a nice looking water wave image, each component should travel in a direction about 20 to 30 degrees apart from the other. The image looks even better with one more minor component on each side of the three major ones (with amplitude and wavelength about one third of the average values of the major components).[1] In Table 1 these directions are specified by parameter β which is the angle measured counterclockwise from the horizontal axis (x-axis). After testing several functions, we decided to use the following function for the slowing varying wave length

$$\lambda(x,y) = \frac{\ell}{1 + r\sin(px + py)} \qquad (10)$$

where l is the mean wave length and r is the normalized deviation of wavenumber, and p is the parameter which shows how slowly the wavelength varies. In our simulation p was fixed at 0.1. The actual values of the other parameters are listed in Table 1. The unit for wave length and amplitude is the pixel.

4.0 Wave Dynamics

The wave dynamics are solved from Navier-Stokes equation (Currie, 1975). With the assumptions that the Coriolis force are negligible, water is inviscid and incompressible, density is constant, and water

motion is irrotational, the Navier-Stokes equation can be reduced to

$$\nabla^2\psi = 0 \qquad (11)$$

where ψ is the velocity potential. There are two boundary conditions at the air-water interface. The kinematic boundary condition says that particles at free surfaces remain on the free surface and the dynamic boundary condition says that the forces balance at free surface. One more boundary condition says that the vertical component of fluid velocity is zero on the ocean floor or bottom.

The surface tension can not be neglected from the dynamic boundary condition when the wave length is less than 7 cm. These kind of waves are just the ripples on top of the larger gravity waves. By gravity wave, we mean that the gravity force is the only restoring force for a wave system.

For a gravity wave, if the wave length λ satisfies

$$h > 0.28\lambda \qquad (12)$$

where h is the ocean depth, then this wave is called a short wave or deep water wave. In this case, a wave travels with velocity

$$C = \frac{1}{2}\sqrt{g\lambda/2\pi} \qquad (13)$$

Because this velocity depends on wave length, longer waves travel faster than shorter waves and the wave system is dispersive. On the other hand, if the wave length satisfies

$$h < 0.07\lambda \qquad (14)$$

This wave is called a long-wave or shallow water wave. In this case, the waves travel with the same speed

---

[1]Texture psychophysics has shown that only 5 or 6 components are required to mimic very complex sums of sinusoids (Richards, 1979).

16

Component Number	1	2	3	4	5
Mean wavelength l	25	30	37.5	10.7	16.7
Deep water $(h > 0.28\lambda)$	0.9ϕ	1.0ϕ	1.1ϕ	0.58ϕ	0.74ϕ
Shallow water $(h < 0.07\lambda)$	1.0ϕ	1.0ϕ	1.0ϕ	1.0ϕ	1.0ϕ

Table 2 Phase shift ϕ between frames used to generate dynamic water waves.

$$C = \sqrt{gh} \qquad (15)$$

Therefore waves are nondispersive in shallow water.

In order to have an idea about how these two modes of waves look, we simulated traveling waves in both cases based on our static model described before. We generated 40 static pictures, being the maximum allowed by our computer memory. Each picture was phase shifted from the previous one. For deep water waves this phase shift was proportional to the square root of wavelength and for shallow water waves it was independent of wavelength. The exact values of phase shift we used are listed in Table 2. We cycled these pictures sequentially and video taped the whole procedure. It turned out that the deep water mode looks better than shallow water mode. This result is consistent with our daily life experience. Except for shore waves and turbulent streams, we hardly see a pond, river, or sea with water depth less than a quarter of the average wave length.

5.0 Conclusions

A procedure for generating near-natural water-wave images by a computer has been presented. Three factors play the dominant role in our perception of static water images. The first is the Fresnel term in the reflectance function. The second is hemispheric illumination. Although a point light source, such as the sun, was not included in our simulation, this is obviously the key factor for the speckle and scintillation effects of water (Longuet-Higgins, 1960). The shape and composition of the wave-itself was also found to be important. For dynamic water-waves, it is necessary to include non-linear terms that mimic the behavior of deep water wave systems.

References

Bascom, W. (1980) *Waves and Beaches.* New York: Anchor Press/Doubleday.

Bigelow, H.B. & Edmondson, W.T. (1952) Wind waves at sea, breaks and surf. U.S. Navy Hydrographic Office, H.O. Pub. No. 202.

Burt, P.J. & Adelson, E.H. (1983) The Laplacian pyramid as a compact image code. *IEEE Trans. Commun.,* COM-31:532 – 540.

Cook, R.L. & Torrance, K.E. (1982) A reflectance model for computer graphics. *ACM Trans. on Graphics,* 1:7 – 24.

Currie, I.G. (1975) *Fundamental Mechanics of Fluids*. New York: McGraw-Hill.

Daugman, J.G. (1988) Complete discrete 2D Gabor transforms by neural networks for image analyses and comparison. *IEEE Trans. on Acoustics, Speech & Singnal Processing*, ASSP-36, No. 7, July.

Gross, M.G. (1972) *Oceanography*. New York: Prentice-Hall.

Koenderink, J.J. & van Doorn, A. (1982) The shape of smooth objects and the way contours end. *Perception*, 11:129–137.

Kung, T.J. & Richards, W.A. (1985) Rendering water. *Jrl. Opt. Soc. Am.*, 2(13):P29.

Lighthill, M.J. (1978) *Waves in Fluid*. Cambridge, England: Cambridge University Press.

Longuet-Higgins, M.S. (1960) Reflection and refraction at a random moving surface. *J. Opt. Soc. Am.*, 50:851–856.

Max, N.L. (1981) Vectorized procedural models for natural terrain: waves and islands in the sunset. *Computer Graphics*, 15(3):317–324.

Morel, A. (1980) In-water and remote measurements of ocean color. *Boundary-Layer Meteorology*, 18:177–201.

Ogden, J.M. (1985) Generation of fractals using the Burt Pyramid. *Optics News*, 11(9):100.

Richards, W. (1979) Quantifying sensory channels: Generalizing colorimetry to orientation and texture, touch, and tones. *Sensory Processes*, 3:207–229.

Schachter, B. (1980) Long crested wave models. *Computer Graphics and Image Processing*, 12:187–201.

Schachter, B. (1983) *Computer Image Generation*. New York:Wiley.

Van Dyke, M. (1982) *An Album of Fluid Motion*. The Parabolic Press, California.

Appendix

In the main body of this paper we used computer graphics to determine which physical properties were significant factors in creating images that looked like water. Ignoring dynamics, these were i) Fresnel reflectance, ii) hemispheric illumination, and iii) a wave packet composed of (non-linear) sinusoids of low amplitude. Here we proceed with the second step of our graphics approach to image understanding, namely identifying an image feature characteristic of "water" or other fluids in motion.

The top half of Figure 4 shows a cross-section of a water wave viewed from an angle of about 20°. The visual ray is tangent to the wave at R, which is a point on the "rim" of the surface (Koenderink & van Doorn, 1982). The locus of all such rim points will be a great circle on the Gauss map. If we now place the viewer direction normal to the page (bull's-eye), then the rim will be the outline of the Gaussian sphere, as illustrated in the lower half of the same figure.

Consider now the isoluminance contour of 5% reflectance on the wave surface. For a Fresnel reflectance function, this corresponds to a 60° viewing angle. We wish to determine the general shape of this contour, and hence of the dark region it encloses. Referring to the Gauss map, the region of 60° Fresnel reflection will be described simply by a circle centered about the bull's-eye, assuming hemispheric illumination without wavelet occlusions.

16

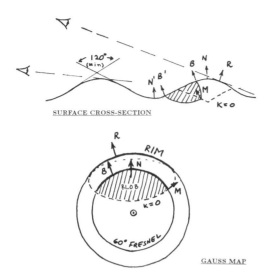

SURFACE CROSS-SECTION

GAUSS MAP

Figure 4 The top panel shows a cross-section through a surface formed by two orthogonal sinusoids of equal wavelength and amplitude. The cutting plane contains the line of sight and two vertical surface normals, and hence is a special view. The cross-hatched region will appear as a darker "blob", defined by an isoluminance contour corresponding to an emittance angle of 60°. In the lower panel, the surface normals are mapped on the Gaussian sphere, with the viewer direction normal to the plane of the page. The line of zero Gaussian curvature is shown as dashed ($\kappa = 0$).

To determine which part of the 60° Fresnel circle is visible, consider the locus on the sinusoidal surface which has zero Gaussian curvature ($\kappa = 0$). For our surface waveform of crossed sinusoids, this locus can be shown to be a distorted square (or rectangle) on the Gauss map, with the square centered about N. The region contained by both the Fresnel circle and the $\kappa = 0$ square thus represents the surface orientations of the dark "blob".

On the Gauss map, this shape will have cusps at the extremal views. (Obviously the exact choice of cut-off for the angle of incidence is not critical.)

If the "blob" region on the Gaussian sphere is now mapped back onto the surface, we obtain two dark regions abutting at the locus $\kappa = 0$. We wish to show that the extremal ends of this region, namely where the surface normal has orientation M, will be seen as "cusped". (A cusp on the Gauss map in itself is not a sufficient condition for a cusp on the surface.) One approach is to solve analytically for the isoluminance contour and show that the first derivatives are discontinuous here. Alternatively, we note that as we move toward M along the blob contour, for there not to be a cusp at M, the isoluminance contour must be perpendicular to the parabolic line $\kappa = 0$, because M is an extremal point of the contour. But generally this will not be the case, because the behavior of the isoluminance contour and the $\kappa = 0$ contour are controlled by independent processes, and hence generally will intersect transversally as they do on the Gauss map. The extremal end-points of the dark "blobs" of water should thus be cusped. (Close inspection of photos of water confirm this prediction.)

In the above, our analysis assumed a special viewing position and a special waveform. First, it should be obvious that the cusped property of the blob will remain unchanged if the wavelength of either one of the sine waves is increased (except in the limit as the wavelength becomes infinite). Similarly, we expect no effect of small non-linearities of wave shape. However, it is clear that viewing angle can alter the geometry of the blob drastically, for example when the surface normal N approximates the viewer direction, such as when we look almost directly down at water. In this case the tangent to $\kappa = 0$ at M may lie in the plane of the view vector, causing the cusp angle to reach $\pi/2$, thereby eliminating the discontinuity at M. The cusped feature for water is thus guaranteed only for shallow ($< 30°$) viewing angles.[2]

One final point can be made about the shape of these dark "blobs" characteristic of water. Once the amplitude of a wave is such that its bitangents intersect at less than 120° (see Figure 4), then the wave will crest. Because the wave silhouette (rim) sets bounds on the shape of the blob, it too must be elongated sufficiently in order not to violate this constraint. Our characteristic image feature for water will thus be a very elongated, horizontal elliptical-like blob having cusped end-points at its extremal viewing positions. It is of interest to note that Ogden (1985) created an illusion of a water surface by convolving with image noise a mask consisting of two such blobs of opposite sign (simply by splitting an ellipse). Similarly, properly chosen packets of Gabor filters can also generate "water-like" textures by (thresholded) convolution with noise (Daugman, 1988). Both of these masks create image patterns with dark, elongated, cusped blobs.[3]

---

[2]Note that for very shallow view angles the lower portion of the dark blob of one wave will be occluded by the bright ridge of the next nearer wave, also resulting in cusped ends, or even in an extra pair of cusps, depending upon the view angle.

[3]For a more complete treatment, see final report ONR contract No. N00014-84-K-0650, "Inferences from Images". This work was first reported at the annual meeting of the Optical Society (Kung & Richards, 1985).

16

Computing the Velocity Field Along Image Contours

Ellen C. Hildreth

M.I.T. Artificial Intelligence Laboratory

Cambridge, MA

1.0 Introduction

The organization of movement in the changing retinal image provides a valuable source of information for analyzing the objects and environment in terms of textured surfaces in motion. A description of this movement is not provided to our visual system directly, however; it must be inferred from the pattern of changing intensity that reaches the eye. Motion in the image may be described by a two-dimensional vector field $\mathbf{V}(x, y, t)$ that specifies the direction and magnitude of velocity at points with image coordinates (x, y) at time t. The measurement of visual motion may then be formulated as the computation of the local velocity field $\mathbf{V}(x, y, t)$ from the changing retinal image intensities $I(x, y, t)$. Unfortunately, the movement of elements in the image is not determined uniquely by the pattern of changing intensities. Thus, the true velocity field is not determined uniquely from the initial local motion measurements. Two factors contribute to this ambiguity of motion. The first is the loss of information due to the projection of the three-dimensional world onto a two-dimensional image; multiple surfaces, undergoing different motions in space, may project to the same two-dimensional image. The second factor is the loss of information due to the projection into a pattern of changing intensity. The image that a surface projects onto the eye may not be sufficient to determine its movement in space. As an extreme example, a matte white sphere, rotating about a central axis, cannot be determined as such, on the basis of its projected image.

Figure 1 presents two simple examples that illustrate the ambiguity of the velocity field. In Figure 1a, the solid and dotted lines represent the image of a moving circle, at different instants of time. In the first frame (solid line), the circle lies parallel to the image plane, while in the second frame (dotted line), the circle is slanted in depth. One velocity field that is consistent with the two frames is derived from pure rotation of the circle about the central vertical axis, as shown to the left in Figure 1a. (The arrows represent a sample of the local velocity vectors along the circle.) There could also be a component of rotation in the plane of the circle, about its center, as shown to the right in Figure 1a. In addition, this changing image might represent the projection of a different three-dimensional curve that is deforming over time, giving rise to yet another projected velocity field. This ambiguity is not peculiar to symmetric figures such as circles; it is a fundamental problem that is always present. In Figure 1b, the curve C_1 rotates, translates and deforms over time, to yield the curve

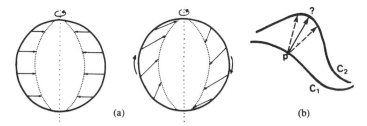

Figure 1 Ambiguity of the velocity field. (a) The arrows represent two possible velocity fields that are consistent with the changing image. (b) The curve c_1 rotates, translates and deforms over time to yield the curve C_2. The velocity of the point p is ambiguous.

C_2. The motion of points from C_1 to C_2 is again ambiguous (consider, for example, different possible velocities for the point p). In general, there are infinitely many two-dimensional velocity fields that are consistent with the changing image.

To compute motion uniquely, an additional constraint is therefore required, in the form of basic assumptions about the physical world that generally hold true. The main focus of this paper is the derivation of a particular constraint, the *smoothness constraint*, that allows the computation of a unique two-dimensional velocity field from the changing image of three-dimensional surfaces undergoing general motion in space.

2.0 The Initial Motion Measurements

In order to detect movement in a changing image, there must be a variation of intensity over space and time; the combination of the two variations can be used to measure the direction and magnitude of velocity. The explicit comparison of spatial and temporal derivatives of intensity forms the basis of a class of motion measurement schemes referred to as *gradient*

schemes (Fennema & Thompson, 1979; Horn & Schunck, 1981; Marr & Ullman, 1981). Other examples of motion detection mechanisms that utilize spatial and temporal intensity changes include those suggested by Hassenstein & Reichardt (1956) and Barlow & Levick (1965).

In principle, motion measurements may be obtained wherever there is a variation of intensity over space and time. Marr & Ullman (1981) proposed, however, that initial motion measurements in the human system are made only at the locations of significant intensity changes. To detect these intensity changes, Marr & Hildreth (1980) proposed that a powerful operator for the initial filtering of an image is the Laplacian of a Gaussian, $\nabla^2 G$ (approximated in shape by the difference of two Gaussian functions). The elements in the output of an image convolved with $\nabla^2 G$, which correspond to the locations of intensity changes, are the zero-crossings (Marr & Poggio, 1979). Figure 2 shows an image that has been convolved with a $\nabla^2 G$ operator, and the resulting zero-crossing contours. Marr & Ullman (1981) proposed that initial motion measurements take place at the locations of these zero-crossings, using a mechanism that com-

17

(a) 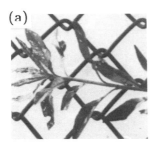 (b) 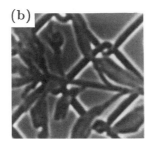 (c)

Figure 2 Initial Processing of an Image. (a) The original image, containing 320×320 picture elements. (b) The convolution of the image with a $\nabla^2 G$ operator. (c) The resulting zero-crossing contours.

bines spatial and temporal gradients of the filtered image [a second mechanism was proposed by Poggio (1983)].

From a computational standpoint, restricting the measurement of motion to the location of significant intensity changes, which give rise to zero-crossings in the filtered image, has two advantages over schemes that base the initial measurements of motion on variations in the original image intensities, wherever the image intensity gradient is nonzero. First, motion measurements are more reliable where the intensity gradient is steeper. The zero-crossings of $\nabla^2 G * I$ (where $*$ denotes the convolution operation) correspond to points in the image at which the intensity gradient is locally maximum, yielding the most reliable local velocity measurements. Second, the zero-crossings are tied more closely to physical features; if they move, it is more likely to be the consequence of movement of an underlying physical surface. There are confounding factors, such as changing illumination, that cause intensity to change locally. A scheme that infers motion directly from changing intensity is clearly susceptible to inferring motion incorrectly from changes caused by these confounding

factors. While the zero-crossing contours may also be influenced by factors such as changing illumination, their positions are generally more stable.

In two dimensions, the initial measurements face the aperture problem, shown in Figure 3a. For the case of contours, local motion measurements provide only the component of motion in the direction perpendicular to the orientation of the contour (Adelson & Movshon, 1982; Fennema & Thompson, 1979; Horn & Schunck, 1981; Marr & Ullman, 1981; Wallach, 1976). The component of velocity along the contour remains undetected. More formally, the two-dimensional velocity field along a contour may be described by the vector function $\mathbf{V}(s)$, where s denotes arclength. $\mathbf{V}(s)$ can be decomposed into components tangent and perpendicular to the contour, as illustrated in Figure 3a. $\mathbf{u}^\top(s)$ and $\mathbf{u}^\perp(s)$ are unit vectors in the directions tangent and perpendicular to the curve, and $v^\top(s)$ and $v^\perp(s)$ denote the two components:

$$\mathbf{V}(s) = v^\top(s)\mathbf{u}^\top(s) + v^\perp(s)\mathbf{u}^\perp(s)$$

The component $v^\perp(s)$, and direction vectors $\mathbf{u}^\top(s)$ and $\mathbf{u}^\perp(s)$, are given directly by the initial measurements from the

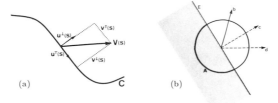

Figure 3 (a) The aperture problem. An operation that views the moving edge through the local aperture A can compute only the component of motion C in the direction perpendicular to the edge. The true motion of the edge is ambiguous. (b) Decomposition of velocity. The local velocity $\mathbf{V}(s)$ is decomposed into components perpendicular and tangent to the curve. $\mathbf{u}^{\perp}(s)$ and $\mathbf{u}^{\top}(s)$ are unit direction vectors, and $v^{\perp}(s)$ and $v^{\top}(s)$ are the two velocity components.

changing image. The component $v^{\top}(s)$ is not, and must be recovered, to compute $\mathbf{V}(s)$. Intuitively, the set of measurements given by $v^{\perp}(s)$ over an extended contour should provide considerable constraint on the motion of the contour. Additional constraint is still required, however, to

determine this motion uniquely. Thus the computation of $\mathbf{V}(s)$ requires the integration of the constraints provided by $v^{\perp}(s)$ along the contour, together with additional constraints necessary to compute $\mathbf{V}(s)$ uniquely.

3.0 Additional Assumptions for Motion Measurement

Much of the previous work in motion analysis assumes pure translation of objects in the image plane. Most gradient schemes, for example, assume that velocity is constant over an area of the image (Fennema & Thompson 1979; Marr & Ullman 1981). For gradient schemes, the constraint on velocity imposed by a single measurement of $v^{\perp}(s)$ can be illustrated graphically in *velocity space*, in which the x and y axes represent the x and y components of velocity, which we denote by $\mathbf{V}_x$ and $\mathbf{V}_y$, shown in Figure 4. When mapped to velocity space, the velocity vector at a point on the contour must terminate along the line l perpendicular to the vector $v^{\perp}(s)\mathbf{u}^{\perp}(s)$; examples are shown by the dotted arrows. For the

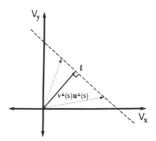

Figure 4 Velocity Constraints in Velocity Space. The x and y axes represent the x and y components of velocity, $\mathbf{V}_x$ and $\mathbf{V}_y$. $v^{\perp}(s)$ is the perpendicular component of velocity, and $\mathbf{u}^{\perp}(s)$ is the unit perpendicular direction vector, at a point p on the image curve. The velocity vector at p must project to the line l; examples are shown with dotted lines.

case of uniform translation, the lines of constraint formed by the measurement of $v^\perp(s)$ along a contour intersect at a single point in velocity space. Some schemes for motion measurement make explicit use of this intersection point (Adelson & Movshon, 1982; Fennema & Thompson, 1979; Thompson & Barnard, 1981). Marr & Ullman (1981) proposed a zero-crossing based scheme, in which each local motion measurement restricts the true direction of velocity of a patch to lie within a 180° range of directions to one side of the zero-crossing contour. A set of measurements taken at different orientations along the contour further restrict the allowable velocity directions, until a single direction is obtained, which is consistent with all the local measurements.

Motion measurement schemes based on the cross-correlation of intensity, used both in computer vision (Leese et al., 1970; Lillestrand, 1972; Smith & Phillips, 1972; Wolferts, 1974) and in modelling biological vision systems (Anstis, 1970, 1980; Bell & Lappin, 1973; Lappin & Bell, 1976; Pantle & Picciano, 1976; Petersik et al., 1978; Reichardt, 1961), also rely on pure translation. In addition, several correspondence schemes assume local translation of features in the image (for example, Potter, 1975, 1977; Lawton, 1983).

Some motion measurement schemes allow objects to undergo rigid rotation and translation in the image plane (for example, Davis et al., 1982; Nagel, 1982; Ullman & Hildreth, 1983). For the case of contours moving rigidly in the image, if the direction of velocity is known at two points on the contour, then the direction of velocity may be obtained everywhere, using a simple geometric construction (Ullman & Hildreth, 1983). If, in addition, $v^\perp(s)$ is

known along the contour, the full velocity field $\mathbf{V}(s)$ may be computed.

Methods for motion measurement that assume rigid motion in the image plane may be useful for the initial detection and rough measurement of motion, the analysis of motion during smooth pursuit eye movements, or the recovery of observer motion from optical flow (Bruss & Horn, 1983; Lawton, 1983; Longuet-Higgins & Prazdny, 1981; Prazdny, 1980). Analysis of the projected motion of arbitrary surfaces undergoing rigid and non-rigid motion in space requires a more general assumption, however.

4.0 The Smoothness Constraint

In this section we derive a more general constraint on the velocity field, that allows the computation of the projected motion of three-dimensional surfaces that move freely in space, and deform over time. We rely on the physical assumption that the real world consists predominantly of solid objects, whose textured surfaces can be considered smooth compared with their distance from the viewer. Such a surface in motion usually generates a smoothly varying velocity field. Thus, intuitively, we seek a velocity field that is consistent with the motion measurements derived from the changing image, and which varies smoothly. Unfortunately, there is an infinity of velocity fields that satisfy these two properties. Horn & Schunck (1981), in their work on the optical flow computation, suggest that a single solution may be obtained by finding the velocity field that varies as little as possible. We show how this constraint may be formulated in a way that guarantees a velocity field so-

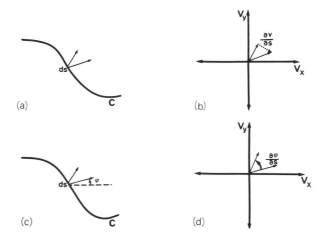

Figure 5 Measuring Variation in Velocity. (a) The velocity vectors $\mathbf{V}(s)$ are displayed at two nearby points on the image curve C. (b) The velocity vectors drawn in velocity space, where $\partial\mathbf{V}/\partial s$ is indicated by the dotted arrow. (c) The direction of velocity for points on the contour is represented by the angle φ. (d) The velocity vectors of (c) are drawn in velocity space, where $\partial\varphi/\partial s$ is shown.

lution that is mathematically unique and physically plausible.

4.1 Measuring variation in velocity

To find the velocity field that varies the least, some means of measuring the variation in velocity along a contour is required. This can be accomplished in many ways. For example, we could measure the change in direction of velocity as we trace along the contour. Total variation in velocity could then be defined as the total change in direction over the entire contour. A second possibility is to measure the change in magnitude of velocity along the contour. Third, the change in the full velocity vector could be measured, incorporating both the direction and magnitude of velocity. Other measures are also possible. The goal of the computation is to find a velocity field that is consistent with the

changing image, and minimizes one of these measures of variation in velocity.

We can describe a measure of variation more formally by defining a mathematical functional, Θ, which maps the space of all possible vector fields (along the contour), $\mathbf{V}_c$, into the real numbers: $\Theta : \mathbf{V}_c \mapsto \Re$. This functional should be such that the smaller the variation in the velocity field, the smaller the real number assigned to it. Two candidate velocity fields may then be compared, by comparing their corresponding real numbers. This formulation allows the development of an explicit method for computing the velocity field of least variation.

We can now derive a set of possible functionals, based on the measures of variation that we previously mentioned informally: (1) variation in the full velocity vector, $\mathbf{V}(s)$, (2) variation in the direction of velocity, and (3) variation in the magnitude of velocity, all with respect

17

to the contour.

1. Variation in $\mathbf{V}(s)$

The local variation of $\mathbf{V}(s)$ with respect to the contour is given by $\partial\mathbf{V}/\partial s$. A scalar measure may be obtained by taking its magnitude: $|\partial\mathbf{V}/\partial s|$. In Figure 5a, two nearby velocity vectors along the image contour C are shown. The vectors are translated to a common origin in velocity space in Figure 5b, where the vector $\partial\mathbf{V}/\partial s$ is shown as a dotted arrow. A measure of the total variation in the velocity field over an entire contour may be derived by integrating this local measure, suggesting a functional such as:

$$\Theta(\mathbf{V}) = \int \left|\frac{\partial\mathbf{V}}{\partial s}\right| ds$$

Variations on this functional may also be considered, involving higher order derivatives, or higher powers, such as:

$$\Theta(\mathbf{V}) = \int \left|\frac{\partial^2\mathbf{V}}{\partial s^2}\right| ds$$

or

$$\Theta(\mathbf{V}) = \int \left|\frac{\partial\mathbf{V}}{\partial s}\right|^2 ds$$

2. Variation in Direction

Let the direction of velocity be described by the angle φ, measured in the counter-clockwise direction from the horizontal, as shown in Figure 5c. In Figure 5d, the local change in direction for two nearby velocity vectors along the image contour, given by $\partial\varphi/\partial s$, is shown in velocity space. Total variation in direction along the contour may again be obtained by integrating this

local measure, leading to functionals such as the following:

$$\Theta(\mathbf{V}) = \int \left|\frac{\partial\varphi}{\partial s}\right| ds$$

or variations involving higher order derivatives, or higher powers.

3. Variation in Magnitude

Finally, the total change in magnitude of velocity alone could be measured, using functionals such as:

$$\Theta(\mathbf{V}) = \int \frac{\partial|\mathbf{V}|}{\partial s} ds$$

Again, we could also consider variations on this measure.

The functional that is used to measure variation may also incorporate a measure of the velocity field itself, rather than strictly utilizing changes in the velocity field along the contour, by incorporating a term which is a function of $|\mathbf{V}|$. This might be useful if we sought a velocity field that also exhibits the least total motion. In addition, the functional could become arbitrarily complex in its combination of $|\partial\mathbf{V}/\partial s|$, $|\partial\varphi/\partial s|$, $\partial|\mathbf{V}|/\partial s$, or higher order derivatives.

Given that there are many possible measures of variation, what criteria can be used to choose a single measure? First, from a mathematical point of view, there should exist a unique velocity field that minimizes the particular measure of variation; this requirement imposes a set of mathematical constraints on the functional. Second, the velocity field computation should yield solutions that are physically plausible. Third, if we suggest that such a constraint underlies the motion computation in the human visual system, the minimization of this measure of variation should yield a velocity field that is consistent with human motion perception. These three criteria are important for any additional assumption that is proposed for the motion measurement computation.

4.2 Mathematical uniqueness of the velocity field

An examination of these measures of variation from a mathematical viewpoint suggests that a measure incorporating the change in the full velocity vector is necessary for the velocity field computation. The use of functionals that incorporate only a measure of direction or magnitude of velocity, for example, does not in general lead to a unique velocity field solution (Hildreth, 1983). It can be shown, however, that given a simple condition on the constraints that are derived from the image, there exists a unique velocity field that satisfies these constraints, and minimizes the particular measure of variation given by: $\int |\partial \mathbf{V}/\partial s|^2 ds$. To obtain this result, we take advantage of the analysis used by Grimson (1981) for evaluating possible functionals for performing surface interpolation from sparse stereo data. The basic mathematical question is, what conditions on the form of the functional, and the structure of the space of velocity fields, are needed to guarantee the existence of a unique solution? These conditions are captured by the following theorem from functional analysis [see also (Rudin, 1973)]:

Theorem: Suppose there exists a complete semi-norm Θ on a space of functions H, and that Θ satisfies the parallelogram law.[1] *Then, every non-empty closed convex set*

$E \subset H$ contains a unique element v of minimal norm, up to an element of the null space. Thus, the family of minimal functions is

$$\{v + s \mid s \in S\}$$

where

$$S = \{v - w \mid w \in E\} \cap \mathcal{N}$$

and $\mathcal{N}$ is the null space of the functional

$$\mathcal{N} = \{u \mid \Theta(u) = 0\}.$$

Hildreth (1984) has shown that the functional $\Theta = \{\int |\partial \mathbf{V}/\partial s|^2 ds\}^{1/2}$ is a complete semi-norm that satisfies the parallelogram law. Second, it was shown that the space of possible velocity fields that satisfy the constraints derived from the changing image, is convex. It then follows from the above theorem that this space contains a unique element of minimal norm, up to possibly an element of the null space. The smoothness measure is non-negative, so that minimizing $\{\int |\partial \mathbf{V}/\partial s|^2 ds\}^{1/2}$ is equivalent to minimizing $\int |\partial \mathbf{V}/\partial s|^2 ds$.

The null space in this case is the set of constant velocity fields, because the condition that $\int |\partial \mathbf{V}/\partial s|^2 ds = 0$ implies that $|\partial \mathbf{V}/\partial s| = 0$ everywhere, which implies that $\mathbf{V}(s)$ is constant. Suppose there is a point $(x(s_i), y(s_i))$ on the contour, where $v^\perp(s_i)$ is known. This measurement constrains the velocity $\mathbf{V}(s_i)$ to lie along the line L_1 parallel to the tangent of the contour at this point, as shown in Figure 6a. Suppose there is a velocity field that is consistent with $v^\perp(s_j)$. A uniform translation component can then be added only along the direction of L_1, in order to obtain another velocity field that is still consistent with this local measure. If a second measurement $v^\perp(s_j)$ is known at a point $(x(s_j), y(s_j))$, for which

---

[1]See Glossary for definitions of semi-norm and parallelogram law.

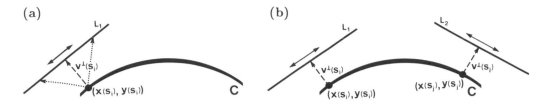

Figure 6 Uniqueness of the Velocity Field. (a) The constraint imposed by a single measurement of $v^\perp(s)$ on the contour C. Only a uniform translation along the line L_1 can be added to the velocity field. (b) The constraint imposed by two measurements of $v^\perp(s)$ on C.

the direction of the tangent is different (see Figure 6b), then a uniform translation component can be added only along this second direction, in order to obtain a velocity field that is still consistent with $v^\perp(s_j)$. A uniform translation cannot be added to the entire velocity field, which is consistent with both local measurements. Thus, we conclude the following: If $v^\perp(s)$ is known everywhere along the contour, and there exists at least two points at which the local orientation of the contour is different, then there exists a unique velocity field that satisfies the known velocity constraints and minimizes $\int |\partial \mathbf{V}/\partial s|^2 ds$.

An extended straight line does not yield measurements at two different orientations, but in all other cases, there is sufficient information along a contour to guarantee a unique velocity field solution. The smoothness constraint can be used to compute a projected two-dimensional velocity field for any three-dimensional surface, whether rigid or nonrigid, undergoing general motion in space. While it is not yet clear whether this general formulation of the smoothness constraint, or the particular measure $\int |\partial \mathbf{V}/\partial s|^2 ds$, is the most appropriate for the motion computation, it is important that this measure

satisfies certain essential mathematical requirements, that the other measures do not. It is essential that the computation underlying the measurement of motion be mathematically well-founded.

4.3 Physical plausibility of the velocity field solution

The second criterion for evaluating a particular measure of variation in velocity is the physical plausibility of the resulting solution. One question that can be asked is, under what conditions will the velocity field that minimizes $\int |\partial \mathbf{V}/\partial s|^2 ds$ be the correct physical velocity field? If we assume orthographic projection of the scene onto the image, there are at least two classes of motion for which this is true. The first consists of arbitrary rigid objects undergoing pure translation. In this case, $\partial \mathbf{V}/\partial s = 0$ everywhere along contours in the image, and hence $\int |\partial \mathbf{V}/\partial s|^2 ds = 0$. Since zero is the smallest value that the measure can obtain, it follows that if there exists a valid solution that is consistent with pure translation, then this solution minimizes $\int |\partial \mathbf{V}/\partial s|^2 ds$. Consequently, motion measurement schemes that rely on pure translation (such as Adelson & Movshon, 1982; Fennema & Thompson,

1979; Marr & Ullman, 1981) address a special case of this more general method.

The second class of motions includes rigid polyhedra, undergoing general motion in space. In Hildreth (1984) I have shown that a rigid three-dimensional object, consisting of straight lines intersecting in space, projects onto the image plane, using orthographic projection, in such a way that line intersections are preserved (that is, two lines intersect in the image if and only if their generators intersect in space). Further, suppose that this object undergoes a general displacement in space. Then the two-dimensional velocity field that satisfies $v^{\perp}(s)$ measured along lines in the image, and minimizes $\int |\partial \mathbf{V}/\partial s|^2 ds$, is the correct projected two-dimensional velocity field.

Recently, Yuille (1983) derived a general condition under which the velocity field that minimizes $\int |\partial \mathbf{V}/\partial s|^2 ds$ is the correct velocity field. Let $\mathbf{V}'(s)$ denote the true projected two-dimensional velocity field for a curve in motion, and let $\mathbf{T}(s)$ denote the tangent vector along the curve. If the following relationship holds at every point on the curve:

$$\mathbf{T}\frac{\partial^2 \mathbf{V}'}{\partial s^2} = 0$$

then the velocity field $\mathbf{V}(s)$ that satisfies the constraints imposed by $v^{\perp}(s)$ and minimizes $\int |\partial \mathbf{V}/\partial s|^2 ds$ is the true velocity field $\mathbf{V}'(s)$. The two classes of motion mentioned above correspond to cases for which $\partial^2 \mathbf{V}'/\partial s^2 = 0$ along the curve, so that this general condition holds trivially.

For the class of smooth curves, moving arbitrarily in space, the velocity field of least variation is, in general, not the physically correct one. Empirical studies suggest, however, that it is often qualitatively similar (Hildreth, 1983). Where

the two velocity fields differ significantly, it appears that the smoothest velocity field may be more consistent with human motion perception (see Hildreth, 1984).

A possible constraint on the velocity field, that is not considered explicitly, is the rigidity of the underlying surface. The computation of a *smoothest* velocity field does not necessarily seek a solution that corresponds to rigid motion, in either two or three dimensions. This may at first seem physically implausible. When a three-dimensional curve rotates in space, however, its two-dimensional projection may undergo significant distortion in the image. Without knowing the three-dimensional structure of the curve, it is very difficult, if not impossible, to find a two-dimensional velocity field that corresponds to a single rigid motion in three dimensions. It is also the case that some of the motion that we encounter arises from surfaces that are nonrigid. If the analysis of motion is a two-stage process, with the measurement of two-dimensional motion preceding the derivation of three-dimensional structure from motion, a constraint such as smoothness may be the most restrictive type of constraint that may be used, which yields a unique solution, and still allows the analysis of general motion.

5.0 An Algorithm and an Illustrative Example

The velocity field computation has been formulated as an optimization problem. We seek a solution that satisfies the constraints imposed by $v^{\perp}(s)$, and minimizes the measure of variation given by: $\int |\partial \mathbf{V}/\partial s|^2 ds$. The computation may also be described as seeking a solution for which neighboring velocity vectors are as

(a)   (b)

Figure 7 A natural image sequence. (a) and (b) Two natural images, containing 256
x 256 picture elements, taken in sequence from an airplane.

similar as possible. To further test the
adequacy of this approach, it is necessary
to specify an algorithm, and examine its
results for a number of motion sequences.
An important aspect of this formulation is
that it lends itself naturally to algorithms
that are biologically feasible, in that they
involve simple, local, parallel operations
(Grimson, 1981; Marr, 1982; Ullman,
1979b). To implement the computation,
we chose a standard iterative algorithm
from mathematical programming, known
as the *conjugate gradient algorithm* (Luenberger, 1973). This particular algorithm
is certainly not appropriate as a model for
human vision. Our aim is to test the basic
idea of computing the velocity field of least
variation. If the results of the algorithm
support the feasibility of this idea, from
a physical and perceptual viewpoint, we
can then explore alternative algorithms
to implement the theory, that are more
appropriate for the human system.

A detailed account of the application
of the conjugate gradient algorithm to the
velocity field computation is given in the
Appendix. Because the image is discrete,
an image contour consists of a set of n discrete points. The input to the algorithm
is the set of n perpendicular components
of velocity along the contour. The output
of the algorithm is the set of x and y components of velocity at the n points. The
algorithm computes the velocity components that minimize a discrete correlate
to the continuous functional, subject to
the constraint imposed by $v^{\perp}(s)$.

As our single illustrative example,
we present the results of the algorithm
for the sequence of aerial photographs
shown in Figure 7. (A more complete set
of examples appears in Hildreth, 1984.)
The images contain 256×256 picture elements. The two images were convolved
with a $\nabla^2 G$ operator whose central diame-
ter was 12 picture elements. The resulting
zero-crossings, for the two images, are
shown in Figures 8a and 8b. The contours
cover a large extent of the image in this
case; this is a consequence of the small
size of the image, and large displacements,
which required a large initial $\nabla^2 G$ oper-

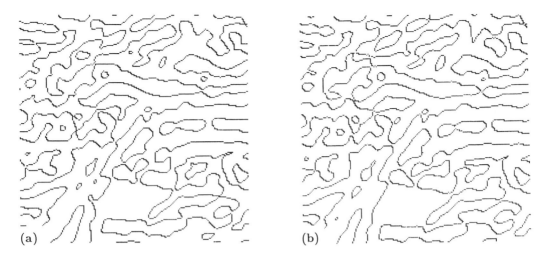

Figure 8 Initial zero-crossing descriptions, derived from the images in Figure 7.

ator. If the image were analyzed with higher spatial and temporal resolution, the two-dimensional velocity field could also be obtained with higher resolution. In Figure 9, the two zero-crossing descriptions are shown superimposed, in order to illustrate the relative displacements between the two images. The zero-crossings from the first image are shown in white, those from the second are black, and the background is grey. Points at which zero-crossings occurred in both images are shown in white. Qualitatively, it can be seen that displacement increases in magnitude as we move from the top to the bottom of the image. In addition, the displacements vary in direction over the image, having a larger horizontal component toward the top of the image, and a larger vertical component toward the bottom.

The initial perpendicular components of velocity $\mathbf{V}^{\perp}(s)$ were computed along the zero-crossing contours in the first filtered image by comparing the local gradient at the zero-crossings with the time derivative, obtained by subtracting the two filtered images. The conjugate gradient algorithm was then run over each contour separately, to obtain the velocity field along the zero-crossing contours of the first image. In Figure 9b, the zero-crossings are shown in black, with the resulting velocity vectors in white. The vectors shown represent a sampling of the velocity field along the contours. Very small contours, and some of the contours that occurred at the image boundary, were not included in this analysis. The length of the vectors in this display is equal to their displacement in the image. Qualitatively, the magnitude of the displacement vectors increases from the top to the bottom of the image, and their directions also vary in a way that reflects the displacement of the zero-crossing contours in Figure 9a. Figure 9c shows a sampling of the final velocity field, superimposed on one of the original images. The results compare well with the actual displacements between the two frames.

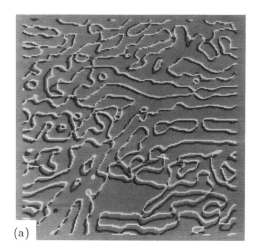 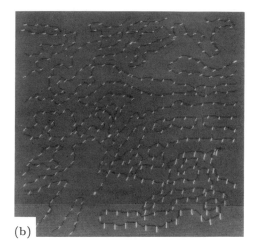

(a)   (b)

Figure 9 (a) Superimposed zero-crossings. The zero-crossings of Figure 8(a) are shown in white; those of Figure 8(b) are superimposed in black. (b) The computed velocity field. The zero-crossing contours are shown in black, and a sampling of the computed velocity field is shown in white.

6.0 Summary and Conclusions

We have presented a computational study of the measurement of visual motion. The problem was formulated as the computation of an instantaneous two-dimensional velocity field from the changing retinal image. A theory for the derivation of the velocity field was proposed, with three main components. First, initial measurements of motion in the image take place at the location of significant intensity changes, which give rise to zero-crossings in the output of the convolution of the image with a $\nabla^2 G$ operator, as suggested by Marr & Ullman (1981). These initial measurements provide only the component of velocity in the direction perpendicular to the local orientation of the contours. Second, these initial measurements are integrated along contours to compute the two-dimensional velocity field. A fundamental problem for this integration stage

is that the velocity field is not determined uniquely from information available in the changing image. The third component of the theory is then the formulation of the additional constraint of smoothness of the velocity field, based on the physical assumption that distant surfaces can be considered smooth, which allows the computation of a unique velocity field. A theoretical analysis of the conditions under which this computation yields the correct velocity field suggests that the solution is physically plausible. Empirical studies show that in situations for which the true and smoothest velocity fields differ, the smoothest velocity field may be more consistent with human motion perception. It also appears that this formulation of the motion measurement problem may be biologically feasible, in that it leads naturally to algorithms that involve simple, local, parallel operations.

Figure 10 The computed velocity field. At evenly spaced points in the image, the computed velocity vectors are shown in black, superimposed on the original image, reduced in contrast.

Acknowledgments: I thank Shimon Ullman for valuable supervision of this work, which was done at the Artificial Intelligence Laboratory of the Massachusetts Institute of Technology. Support for this research was provided by the Air Force Office of Scientific Research under contract F49620-83-C-0135.

References

Adelson, E.H. & Movshon, J.A. (1982) Phenomenal coherence of moving visual patterns. *Nature, Lond.*, 300:523 – 525.

Anstis, S.M. (1970) Phi movement as a subtraction process. *Vision Res.*, 10:1411 – 1430.

Anstis, S.M. (1980) The perception of apparent motion. *Phil. Trans. R. Soc. Lond. B.*, 290:153 – 168.

Anstis, S.M. & Rogers, B.J. (1975) Illusory reversal of visual depth and movement during changes of contrast. *Vision Res.*, 15:957 – 961.

Barlow, H.B. & Levick, R.W. (1965) The mechanism of directional selectivity in the rabbit's retina. *J. Physiol., Lond.*, 173:477 – 504.

Bell, H.H. & Lappin, J.S. (1973) Sufficient conditions for the discrimination of motion. *Percept. Psychophys.*, 14:45 – 50.

Bruss, A. & Horn, B.K.P. (1983) Passive navigation. *Comp. Vision Graph. Image Processing*, 21:3 – 20.

Clocksin, W.F. (1980) Perception of surface slant and edge labels from optical flow: a computational approach. *Perception*, 9:253 – 269.

Davis, L., Wu, Z. & Sun, H. (1982) Contour-based motion estimation. In *Proceedings: Image Understanding Workshop (Palo Alto, California)*, pp. 124-131. Arlington, Virginia: Science Applications.

Fennema, C.L. & Thompson, W.B. (1979) Velocity determination in scenes containing several moving objects. *Comp. Graph. Image Processing*, 9:301 – 315.

Grimson, W.E.L. (1981) *From Images to Surfaces. A Computational Study of the Human Early Visual System.* Cambridge, MA: MIT Press.

Hassenstein, B. & Reichardt, W. (1956) Systemtheoretische analyse der zeit-, reihenfolgen- und vorzeichenauswertung bei der bewgungs-perzeption der russelkafers. *Chlorophanus. Z. Naturf.*, IIb:513 – 524.

Hildreth, E.C. (1983) "The measurement of visual motion". Ph.D. dissertation, Department of Electrical Engineering and Computer Science, Massachusetts Institute of Technology.

Hildreth, E.C. (1984) The computation of the velocity field. *Proc. R. Soc. B.*, 22:189 – 220.

Horn, B.K.P. & Schunck, B.G. (1981) Determining optical flow. *Artif. Intell.*, 17:185 – 203.

Lappin, J.S. & Bell, H.H. (1976) The detection of coherence in moving random dot patterns. *Vision Res.*, 16:161 – 168.

Lawton, D.T. (1983) Processing translational motion sequences. *Comp. Vision Graph. Image Processing*, 22:116 – 144.

Leese, J.A., Novak, C.S. & Taylor, V.R. (1970) The determination of cloud pattern motion from geosynchronous satellite image data. *Pattern Recognition*, 2:279 – 292.

Lillestrand, R.L. (1972) Techniques for change detection. *IEEE Trans. Computers*, c-21:654 – 659.

Longuet-Higgins, H.C. (1981) A computer algorithm for reconstructing a scene from two projections. *Nature*, 293:133 – 135.

Longuet-Higgins, H.C. & Prazdny, K. (1981) The interpretation of moving retinal images. *Proc. R. Soc. Lond. B.*, 208:385 – 397.

Luenberger, D.G. (1973) *Introduction to Linear and Nonlinear Programming.* Reading, MA: Addison-Wesley.

Marr, D. (1982) *Vision: A Computational Investigation into the Human Representation and Processing of Visual Information.* San Francisco: W. H. Freeman.

Marr, D. & Hildreth, E.C. (1980) Theory of edge detection. *Proc. R. Soc. Lond. B.*, 207:187 – 217.

Marr, D. & Poggio, T. (1979) A computational theory of human stereo vision. *Proc. R. Soc. Lond. B.*, 204:301 – 328

Marr, D. & Ullman, S. (1981) Directional selectivity and its use in early visual processing. *Proc. R. Soc. Lond. B.*, 211:151–180.

Nagel, H.-H. (1982) On change detection and displacement vector estimation in image sequences. *Pattern Recognition Letters*, 1:55–59.

Pantle, A.J. & Picciano, L. (1976) A multistable display: evidence for two separate motion systems in human vision. *Science*, 193:500–502.

Petersik, J.T. (1980) The effect of spatial and temporal factors on the perception of stroboscopic rotation stimulations. *Perception*, 9:271–283.

Petersik, J.T., Hicks, K.I. & Pantle, A.J. (1978) Apparent movement of successively generated subjective patterns. *Perception*, 7:371–383.

Poggio, T. (1983) Visual algorithms. In O.J. Braddick & A.C. Sleigh (eds.), *Physical and Biological Processing of Images*, Berlin: Springer-Verlag.

Potter, J.L. (1975) Velocity as a cue to segmentation. *IEEE Trans. Systems, Man, Cybernetics*, SMC-5:390–394.

Potter, J.L. (1977) Scene segmentation using motion information. *Comp. Graph. Image Processing*, 6:558–581.

Prazdny, K. (1980) Egomotion and relative depth map from optical flow. *Biol. Cybernetics*, 36:87–102.

Reichardt, W. (1961) Autocorrelation, a principle for the evaluation of sensory information by the central nervous system. In W.A. Rosenblith (ed.), *Sensory Communication*, Cambridge, MA: MIT Press.

Rudin, W. (1973) *Functional Analysis.* New York: McGraw-Hill.

Smith, E.A. & Phillips, D.R. (1972) Automated cloud tracking using precisely aligned digital ATS pictures. *IEEE Trans. Computers*, C-21:715–729.

Thompson, W.B. & Barnard, S.T. (1981) Lower-level estimation and interpretation of visual motion. *IEEE Computer*, August, 20-28.

Ullman, S. 1979a *The Interpretation of Visual Motion.* Cambridge, MA: MIT Press.

Ullman, S. (1979b) Relaxation and constrained optimization by local processes. *Comp. Graph. Image Processing*, 9:115–125.

Ullman, S. (1980) The interpretation of three-dimensional structure from motion. *Proc. R. Soc. Lond. B*, 203:405–426.

Ullman, S. (1981) Analysis of visual motion by biological and computer systems. *IEEE Computer*, August, 57-69.

Ullman, S. (1983a) Computational studies in the interpretation of structure and motion: summary and extension. MIT A.I. Lab. Memo 706.

Ullman, S. (1983b) Maximizing rigidity: the incremental recovery of 3-D structure from rigid and rubbery motion. MIT A.I. Lab. Memo 721.

Ullman, S. & Hildreth, E.C. (1983) The measurement of visual motion. In O.J. Braddick & A.C. Sleigh (ed.), *Physical and Biological Processing of Images*, Berlin: Springer-Verlag.

Wallach, H. (1976) On perceived identity: 1. The direction of motion of straight lines. In H. Wallach (ed.), *On Perception*, New York: Quadrangle.

Wallach, H. & O'Connell, D.N. (1953) The kinetic depth effect. *J. Exp. Psychol.*, 45:205–217.

Wolferts, K. (1974) Special problems in interactive image processing for traffic analysis. *Proc. Second International Joint Conf. Pattern Recognition*, 1-2.

Yuille, A.L. (1983) The smoothest velocity field and token matching. MIT A.I. Lab. Memo 724.

Zeeman, W.P.C. & Roelofs, C.O. (1953) Some aspects of apparent motion. *Acta. Psychol.*, 9:159–181.

Appendix

The velocity field computation is formulated as an optimization problem. We seek a solution which satisfies the constraints derived from the image, and minimizes the measure of a discrete correlate to $\int |\partial \mathbf{V}/\partial s|^2 ds$ over the image curve. Here we present an algorithm based on the smoothness constraint.

To develop the algorithm, we utilize techniques from mathematical programming (Luenberger, 1973). First, we express our functional in terms of the x and y components of velocity, $\mathbf{V}_x$ and $\mathbf{V}_y$. The continuous functional becomes:

$$\Theta = \int \left[\left(\frac{\partial \mathbf{V}_x}{\partial x} \right)^2 + \left(\frac{\partial \mathbf{V}_y}{\partial s} \right)^2 \right] ds$$

The general mathematical programming problem can be stated as:

minimize $\theta = f(x)$
subject to $h_i(x) = 0$ $i = 1, \ldots, m$
             $g_j(x) \geq 0$ $j = 1, \ldots, r$
             $x \in S$

where x is an n-dimension vector of unknowns, $x = (x_1, x_2 \ldots, x_n)$. The objective function f, and constraints h_i, $i = 1, \ldots, m$ and g_j, $j = 1, \ldots, r$ are real-valued functions of the variables x_1, x_2, $\ldots, x_n$. The set S is a subset of the n-dimensional space.

In our case, we let:

$$x = \{V_{x1}, V_{x2}, \ldots, V_{xn},$$
$$V_{y1}, V_{y2}, \ldots, V_{yn}\}$$

That is, x consists of the n x-components and n y-components of velocity, for n points along a contour. For now, we assume that the points are evenly spaced along the contour, but the computation can easily be extended to allow points that are not evenly spaced. For the case of a closed contour, we choose the following discrete formulation of the function f:

$$f_c(x) = \sum_{i=2}^{n} \left[(\mathbf{V}_{xi} - \mathbf{V}_{xi-1})^2 \right.$$
$$+ (\mathbf{V}_{yi} - \mathbf{V}_{yi-1})^2 \right]$$
$$+ [(\mathbf{V}_{x1} - \mathbf{V}_{xn})^2 + (\mathbf{V}_{y1} - \mathbf{V}_{yn})^2]$$

For the case of an open contour, a different expression for the derivative at the endpoints is used to compute $f(x)$.

With regard to the constraints we have derived from the image, we can either force the velocity field to satisfy the constraints exactly, or satisfy them approximately. In the first case, these constraints are of the form:

$$\mathbf{V} \cdot \mathbf{u}^\perp - v^\perp = 0$$

The constraint states explicitly that the normal component of velocity for the computed velocity field should be equivalent to the measured normal component. Letting $\mathbf{V} = (\mathbf{V}_x, \mathbf{V}_y)$ and $\mathbf{u}^\perp = (u_x^\perp, u_y^\perp)$, the constraints are simple linear constraints:

$$\mathbf{V}_{xi} u_{x1}^\perp + \mathbf{V}_{xi} u_{y1}^\perp - v_i^\perp = 0$$

At this point, we can either set up the computation as a constrained or unconstrained optimization. In the constrained case, we specify the above linear constraints explicitly. To obtain an unconstrained problem, we first use the constraints to express the y-components of velocity in terms of the x-components:

$$\mathbf{V}_{yi} = \frac{v_i^\perp - \mathbf{V}_{xi} u_{xi}^\perp}{u_{yi}^\perp}$$

We can now substitute these expressions for the y-components into $f(x)$ and let $x = \{\mathbf{V}_{x1}, \mathbf{V}_{x2}, \ldots, \mathbf{V}_{xn}\}$. There is no further constraint on the x-components of velocity.

In general, there will be error in the measurements of $v^\perp$. From a practical standpoint, it may be advantageous to require that the velocity field only approximately satisfy the image constraints. This can be accomplished by requiring that the difference between $\mathbf{V} \cdot \mathbf{u}^\perp$ and the measured $v^\perp$ be small. The continuous functional can be extended as follows:

$$\Theta = \int \left[\left(\frac{\partial \mathbf{V}_x}{\partial s} \right)^2 + \left(\frac{\partial \mathbf{V}_y}{\partial s} \right)^2 \right] ds +$$

$$\beta \int \left[\mathbf{V} \cdot \mathbf{u}^\perp - u^\perp \right]^2 ds$$

β is a weighting factor, which expresses our confidence in the measured velocity constraints. The second term describes the least squares difference between the computed and measured normal components of velocity. The above functional leads to the following objective function:

$$f_u(x) = f_c(x) +$$

$$\beta \sum_{i=1}^{n} \left[\mathbf{V}_{xi} u_{xi}^\perp + \mathbf{V}_{yi} u_{yi}^\perp - v_i^\perp \right]^2$$

The space S is the entire n-dimension space. Expressed in this way, the problem is an unconstrained optimization. In general, there may be points where $\mathbf{V}$, or the direction of velocity alone, is known. This additional constraint would transform the problem back into a constrained optimization.

For the example presented, we set up the velocity field computation as an unconstrained optimization, in which the image constraints are only approximately satisfied. The conjugate gradient algorithm is used to obtain the solution. This is an iterative algorithm which utilizes the gradient of the objective function to choose an optimal path to follow along the solution surface to the final solution (see Luenberger, 1973, for details of the algorithm). Our initial velocity field is given by the normal velocity vectors $u^\perp \mathbf{u}^\perp$ along the curve. After a number of iterations, the algorithm converges to a unique solution.

Reprinted slightly abridged from *Artif. Intell.*, 23:309–354 (1984).

Analyzing Oriented Patterns

Michael Kass & Andrew Witkin

Schlumberger Palo Alto Research
Palo Alto, CA

1.0 Introduction

A central focus in computational vision has been the decomposition of the original intensity image into intrinsic images (Horn, 1977; Barrow & Tenenbaum, 1978; Marr, 1982), representing such properties as depth, reflectance, and illuminance. These intrinsic properties are believed to be more meaningful than image intensity because they describe basic independent constituents of the image formation process. Thus, for example, in separating shape from illumination, we can recognize an invariance of shape regardless of changing illumination.

The advantages of decomposing what we see into its more-or-less independent parts extends beyond the image formation process to the shapes and patterns on which that process operates. For instance, decomposing a bent rod into a straight rod and a bending transformation reveals the similarity between a bent rod and one that hasn't been bent, or some other solid that's been bent the same way (Barr, 1984).

Just as we need to know a good deal about the image-forming process to decompose an image into intrinsic images, we need to know about the processes that generate patterns to decompose them into their intrinsic parts. But while there is only one image-forming process, a stag-gering variety of processes shape and color the world around us. Our only hope of dealing with this complexity is to begin with some basic pattern classes that recur in nature, and understand how to decompose and describe them.

One such class are oriented patterns, notably those produced by propagation, accretion, or deformation. To understand an oriented pattern we must be able to say (1) what is propagating, accreting, or deforming, and (2) which way and how much. More precisely, we must estimate everywhere the direction and magnitude of anisotropy (which we will call the flow field,) and describe the residual pattern, independent of that field. Why this decomposition leads to simpler, more regular descriptions is best illustrated by example:

- A typical oriented pattern created by propagation is the streaked trail left by a paint brush dipped in variegated paint. The flow field describes the trajectory of the brush, the residual pattern depending only on the distribution of paint on the brush.

- Accretion typically results in laminar structures, such as wood grain. Here, the flow field gives isochrones (the moving accretion boundary,) and the residual pattern describes the change in color or brightness of the accreting material over time.

- If an isotropic body is deformed, the

flow field principally describes the bending and stretching it has undergone, while the residual pattern describes the undeformed body.

In all these cases, separate descriptions of the flow field and the residual pattern are appropriate because they describe different processes. The path of propagation for many physical processes is controlled by very different mechanisms than control the coloration of the trail left behind. Similarly, the mechanisms which control the shape of an accretion boundary are frequently unrelated to the processes controlling the color of the accreted material. Finally, the forces which deform a piece of material are often completely unrelated to the process which created the piece of material in the first place. By separately describing these processes, we can create descriptions of the whole which are often simpler than is possible without the separation because each of the pieces may have different regularities.

Orientation selective mechanisms have been extensively studied by physiologists since Hubel & Wiesel's (1968) discovery of orientation selective cells in mammalian visual cortex [see Schiller et al. (1976) for a comprehensive example]. There has also been considerable interest among psychologists in the perception of oriented patterns, particularly dot patterns (Glass, 1969). Only recently have the computational issues involved received attention. Stevens (1978) examined the grouping of tokens in Glass patterns based on orientation. While successful with Glass patterns, his methods were never extended to work on natural imagery. Zucker (1983) investigated the estimation of orientation by combining the outputs of linear operators. Zucker's estimation method for what he calls "Type II" patterns, while differing in many respects, is quite close in spirit to our own.

Little progress has been made in using local orientation estimates to interpret patterns, perhaps because reliable estimates have proved difficult to obtain. The key difference between our work and earlier efforts lies in our use of the flow field to build a natural coordinate system for analyzing the pattern.

The remainder of the paper covers the computation of the flow field by local estimation of orientation, the construction of a coordinate system using the flow field, and some examples of analysis and description using flow coordinates.

In Section 2 we develop an estimator for the local flow direction, that direction in which intensity tends to vary most slowly due to an underlying anisotropic process. The estimator, based on the direction of least spatial variance in the output of an oriented filter, is computed as follows: After initial filtering, the intensity gradient is measured at each point in the image. The gradient angle, θ, is then doubled (by treating the gradient vectors as complex numbers and squaring them) to map directions differing by π into a single direction. The transformed vectors are then summed over a weighted neighborhood around the point of interest. The angle of the summed vector is halved, undoing the previous transformation. This gives an estimate for the direction of *greatest* variance, which is then rotated by $\pi/2$ to yield the flow direction.

In section 3, we describe the construction and use of coordinate systems based on the result of local estimation. Integral curves in the flow field are computed numerically, by following the estimated vectors from point to point. A coordinate system is constructed in which the integral curves are parameter lines. Transforming the image into these "flow coordinates" straightens the pattern, removing the effects of changing orientation. We present several examples of analysis and description of the flow field and the straightened pattern.

2.0 Flow Computation

For intensity patterns created by anisotropic processes such as propagation, accretion, or deformation, variation in the flow direction is much slower than variation in the perpendicular direction. Anisotropy in such patterns will be evident in the local power spectrum. The high frequency energy will tend to cluster along the line in the Fourier domain perpendicular to the flow orientation.

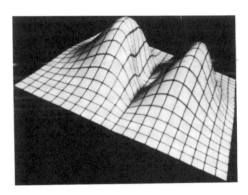

Figure 1 The power spectrum of the filter in equation 1 for $\sigma_2 = 2\sigma_1$.

A simple way to detect this clustering is to sum the energy in an appropriate region of the power spectrum and examine how the sum is affected by rotations. This can be done by examining the energy in the output of an appropriate orientation-selective linear filter. The orientation at

which the energy is maximal can be expected to be perpendicular to the flow orientation.

Selection of the filter involves a number of tradeoffs. Very low spatial frequencies are affected more strongly by illumination effects than surface coloration, so they are inappropriate for measuring textural anisotropy. Very high spatial frequencies are sensitive to noise and aliasing effects so they too are inappropriate. Hence some type of roughly bandpass filtering is required. The orientation specificity of the filter is also quite important. If the filter is too orientation-specific then a large spatial neighborhood will be required in order to make a reliable measurement of the energy. Conversely, if the filter responds over a wide range of orientations then it will be difficult to localize the orientation very accurately. Thus there is a trade-off between angular- and spatial-resolution.

One reasonable choice for the frequency response of the filter is

$$F(r, \theta) = \left[e^{r^2 \sigma_1^2} - e^{r^2 \sigma_2^2} \right] 2\pi i r \cos(\theta). \quad (1)$$

The filter is bandpass determined by σ_1 and σ_2. In our experience, ratios of the sigmas in the range of 2.0 to 10.0 work well. The orientation specificity or *tuning curve* is provided by the cosine dependence of the filter on θ. This appears to strike a reasonable balance between angular- and spatial-resolutions for the range of patterns we have examined. The filter's power spectrum is shown in Figure 1.

The cosine orientation tuning-curve of the filter has some unusually good properties for computing the filter output at different orientations. The impulse response $S(x, y)$ of the filter is

$$S(x, y) = \frac{\partial}{\partial x} H(x, y)$$

where

$$H(x,y) = \left[\sigma_1^{-2} e^{r^2/\sigma_1^2} - \sigma_2^{-2} e^{r^2/\sigma_2^2}\right]$$

is an isotropic filter. Let $C = H * I$ and let $R_\theta[S]$ denote a counter-clockwise rotation of S by an angle θ. Then the convolution $R_\theta[S] * I$ is just the directional derivative of $H * I$ in the θ direction. The directional derivative can easily be written in terms of the gradient so we have

$$R_\theta[S] * I = (\cos\theta, \sin\theta) \cdot \nabla H * I. \quad (2)$$

Thus a single convolution suffices for all orientations.

Since the filter S severely attenuates very low frequencies $R_\theta[S] * I$ can be safely regarded as zero-mean. Thus the variance in its output can be estimated by the expression

$$V(\theta) = W * \left(R_\theta[S] * I\right)^2$$

where $W(x,y)$ is a local weighting function with unit integral. We use Gaussian weighting functions $W(x,y)$ because approximate Gaussian convolutions can be computed efficiently (Burt, 1980).

Using the gradient formulation of the filter output in equation 2, we can write the variance $V(\theta)$ as

$$V(\theta) = W * \left[\cos(\theta)C_x + \sin(\theta)C_y\right]^2. \quad (3)$$

A. Interpretation of Filter Output

There remains the issue of interpreting $V(\theta)$. Assume that there is only one axis of anisotropy. Then $V(\theta)$ will have two extrema π apart corresponding to that axis. Let $V_2(\theta) = V(\theta/2)$. Then $V_2(\theta)$ will have a single extremum in the interval $0 < \theta < 2\pi$. A computationally inexpensive way of estimating the position of this extremum is to consider V_2

as a distribution and compute its mean. Since θ is periodic, V_2 should be considered as a distribution on the unit circle. Hence its mean is the vector integral $(\alpha, \beta) = \int_0^{2\pi} V_2(\theta)(\cos\theta, \sin\theta)d\theta$. The angle $\tan^{-1}(\beta/\alpha)$ is an estimate of the angle of the peak in V_2 and hence twice the angle of the peak in V. Thus the angle θ of the *greatest* variance can be written

$$\phi = \tan^{-1}(\beta/\alpha)$$
$$= \tan^{-1}\left(\frac{\int_0^{2\pi} V_2(\theta)\sin(\theta)d\theta}{\int_0^{2\pi} V_2(\theta)\cos(\theta)d\theta}\right)/2 \quad (4)$$
$$= \tan^{-1}\left(\frac{\int_0^{\pi} V(\theta)\sin(2\theta)d\theta}{\int_0^{\pi} V(\theta)\cos(2\theta)d\theta}\right)/2$$

These integrals have been evaluated (Kass & Witkin, 1985) and show that the angle of anisotropy ϕ can be written

$$\phi = \tan^{-1}\left(\frac{W * 2C_x C_y}{W * (C_x^2 - C_y^2)}\right)/2 \quad (5)$$

which directly yields a simple algorithm for computing ϕ.

B. Combining Gradient Orientations

Notice that the right hand side of equation 5 can be regarded as the orientation of a locally weighted sum of the vectors of the form $J(x,y) = (C_x^2 - C_y^2, 2C_x C_y)$. These vectors are related in a simple way to the gradient vectors $G(x,y) = (C_x, C_y)$. The magnitude of $J(x,y)$ is just the square of the magnitude of $G(x,y)$ and the angle between $J(x,y)$ and the x-axis is twice the angle between $G(x,y)$ and the x-axis. This follows easily from the observation that $(C_x + C_y i)^2 = C_x^2 - C_y^2 + 2C_x C_y i$.

One might be tempted to believe that smoothing the gradient vectors $G(x,y)$ would be nearly as good a measure of

18

 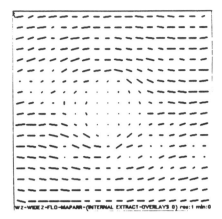

Figure 2 An image of wood grain and its flow-field. Estimated flow directions are given by the black needles. The length of the needle encodes coherence. Notice that coherence is low within the knot at the center.

anisotropy as smoothing the rotated squared gradient vectors $J(x, y)$. This is emphatically not the case. Consider an intensity ridge such as $I(x, y) = \exp(-x^2)$. The gradient vectors on the left half-plane all point to the right and the gradient vectors on the right half-plane all point to the left. Adding them together results in cancellation. By contrast, if they are first rotated to form the J vectors, they reinforce. The types of oriented patterns we are concerned with often have nearly symmetric distributions of gradient directions around the axis of anisotropy. In such patterns, if the gradients are added together directly, the cancellation is so severe that the result often has little relation to the direction of anisotropy. Thus the difference between rotating the gradient vectors or leaving them be is often the difference between being able or unable to detect the anisotropy. Note also that smoothing the image first and then computing the gradients is exactly the same as computing the gradients and then smoothing. It will not avoid the difficulties of cancellation.

2.4 Coherence

In addition to finding the direction of anisotropy, it is important to determine how strong an anisotropy there is. If the orientation of the local J vectors are nearly uniformly distributed between 0 and 2π, then the orientation ϕ of slight anisotropy is not very meaningful. Conversely, if all the J vectors are pointing the same way then the indication of anisotropy is quite strong and ϕ is very meaningful. A simple way of measuring the strength of the peak in the distribution of J vectors is to look at the ratio $\chi(x, y) = |W * J|/W * |J|$ which we will call the *coherence* of the flow pattern. If the J vectors are close to uniformly distributed, then the ratio will be nearly zero. If the J vectors all point the same way, the ratio will be one. In between, the ratio will increase as the peak gets narrower.

2.5 Summary

The computation of the flow direction and

local coherence can be summarized as follows. First the image $I(x,y)$ is convolved with the isotropic portion $H(x,y)$ of the filter response. The result $C(x,y)$ is then differentiated (by finite differences) to form $C_x(x,y)$ and $C_y(x,y)$. The resulting vectors $(C_x(x,y), C_y(x,y))$ are rotated by computing $J_1(x,y) = 2C_x(x,y)C_y(x,y)$ and $J_2(x,y) = C_x^2(x,y) - C_y^2(x,y)$. The gradient magnitude $J_3(x,y) = [C_x^2(x,y) + C_y^2(x,y)]^{1/2}$ also has to be computed in order to measure the coherence. The next step is to convolve $J_1(x,y)$, $J_2(x,y)$, and $J_3(x,y)$ with the weighting function $W(x,y)$ to obtain $J_1^*(x,y), J_2^*(x,y)$, and $J_3^*(x,y)$. The angle $\phi(x,y)$ of anisotropy and the coherence $\chi(x,y)$ can then be computed from the formulas

$$\phi(x,y) \approx \tan^{-1}\left(J_1^*(x,y)/J_2^*(x,y)\right)2$$

and

$$\chi(x,y) = \left(J_1^*(x,y)^2 + J_2^*(x,y)^2\right)^{1/2}/J_3^*(x,y).$$

An example of this computation applied to a picture of a piece of wood is shown in Figure 2. the flow direction $\phi(x,y) + \pi/2$ is displayed by the orientation of small needles superimposed on the image. The lengths of the needles is proportional to the coherence $\chi(x,y)$. Note that the pattern is strongly oriented except near the knot in the middle.

2.6 Relation to prior work

The flow computation just described bears an interesting relation to an early proposal of David Marr that information about local distributions of oriented edge elements be included in the *primal sketch* (Marr, 1976). If this proposal is combined with his later work with Hildreth on edge detection (Marr & Hildreth, 1980) it results

in a special case of the above computation. Marr & Hildreth define edges as zero-crossings in the Laplacian of the Gaussian smoothed image. The natural combination of Marr's proposal with this definition of edge elements calls for examining the local density of zero crossings as a function of orientation. For stationary zero-mean Gaussian processes the square of the oriented zero-crossing density is approximately $V(\theta)$. Thus in the special case where the point spread function of the filter is $S = (\partial/\partial x)\nabla^2 \exp(-(x^2 + y^2)/2\sigma^2)$ our computation can be viewed as computing the direction of minimal edge density in the Marr-Hildreth theory.

Zucker's work on flow (Zucker 1983) is also related to a special case of the above computation. For biological reasons, he prefers to use oriented second derivatives of Gaussians as the initial filters. These have $F(r,\theta) = r^2 \exp(-r^2/2)\cos^2(\theta)$. Instead of looking at the variance of the filter outputs as the orientation is changed, he combines the outputs in a biologically motivated relaxation process. Although quite different in detail, the computation described here has much in common with his technique.

3.0 Flow Coordinates

The orientation field is an abstraction, perceptually and physically distinct from the anisotropic pattern that defines it. We can, for example, get the same spiral field from a pattern composed of bands, irregular streaks, dot pairs, *etc.* In addition to measuring the orientation field, it is quite useful to be able to produce a description of the underlying pattern independent of the changing direction of anisotropy. Such a description would make it possible to

18

recognize, for example, that two very different orientation fields are defined by the same kind of bands or streaks.

Figure 3 A flow coordinate grid obtained for the image of Figure 2.

A powerful way to remove the effects of changing orientation is to literally "straighten" the image, subjecting it to a deformation that maps the flow lines into straight, parallel lines in a canonical (e.g. horizontal) orientation. Performing this deformation is equivalent to viewing the image in a coordinate system (u, v), with $u = u(x, y)$ and $v = v(x, y)$ that everywhere satisfies

$$\nabla u \cdot (\sin \phi, -\cos \phi) = 0. \qquad (6)$$

Equation 6 does not determine a unique coordinate system. An additional constraint may be imposed by choosing lines of constant v orthogonal to those of constant u, i.e.

$$\nabla v \cdot (\cos \phi, \sin \phi) = 0 \qquad (7)$$

which has the desirable effect of avoiding the introduction of spurious shear in the deformation.

Even with Equation 7, an additional constraint is needed, because we are free to specify arbitrary scaling functions for the u and v axis. In the spirit of Equation 7, we want to choose these functions to avoid the introduction of spurious stretch or dilation. Although difficult to do globally (one might minimize total stretch,) we will usually want to construct a fairly local coordinate frame around some point of interest. For this purpose, it suffices to take that point as the origin, scaling the axes $u = 0$ and $v = 0$ to preserve arc-length along them.

Intuitively, the flow field describes the way the pattern is bent, and viewing the image in these *flow coordinates* straightens the pattern out. Figure 3 shows the flow coordinate grid for the wood-grain image from Figure 2. The grid lines were computed by taking steps of fixed length in the direction $(\cos(\phi), \sin(\phi))$ or $(-\sin(\phi), \cos(\phi))$ for lines across and along the direction of flow respectively, using bilinear interpolation on the orientation field. Since ϕ is always computed between 0 and π, we must assume that there are no spurious discontinuities in direction to track smoothly.

For many purposes it is unnecessary to compute the deformed image explicitly, but doing so vividly illustrates the flow coordinates' ability to simplify the pattern. Figure 4 shows the deformation from image coordinates to flow coordinates in several stages. Indeed, the grain lines straighten and the knot shrinks and vanishes. The deformed images were anti-aliased using texture-map techniques (Williams, 1983). The deformed image shows, to a reasonable approximation, what the grain would have looked like had it not been subjected to the deforming influence of the knot.

Thus far, we have separated the image into a flow field, and a pattern derived by

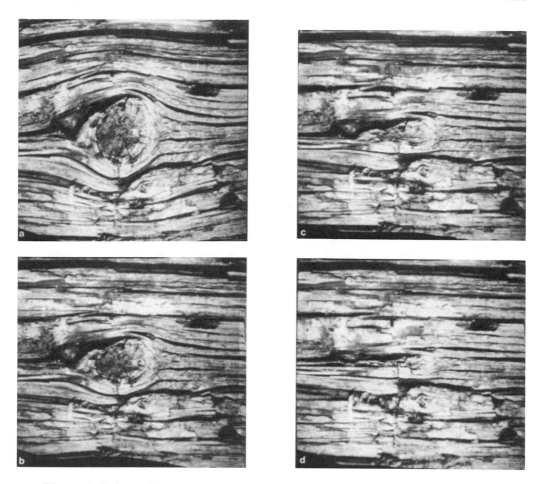

Figure 4 Deformation, in stages, from image coordinates to flow coordinates. Upper left: The original image; Lower left, upper right: two intermediate stages, in which the grain's curvature has diminished, and the knot compressed. Lower right: the image as seen in flow coordinates: the grain lines are straight and the knot has vanished, showing approximately what the grain would have looked like had it not been deformed by the intrusion of the knot.

viewing the image in flow coordinates. We argued earlier that the advantage of this decomposition, like the decomposition of an image into intrinsic images, is that the components are liable to be simpler and more closely tied to independent parts of the pattern-generating process than is the original image. To exploit the

decomposition, we need ways of analyzing, describing, and comparing both the flow field and the straightened pattern. These are difficult problems. In this section, we present several examples illustrating the utility of the decomposition.

18

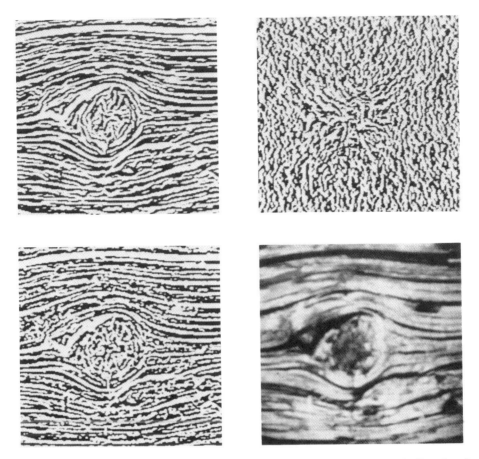

Figure 5 Using flow coordinates for edge detection. Upper left: 2nd directional derivative across the flow direction. Upper right: 2nd directional derivative along the flow direction. The first of these highlights the oriented structure, the second suppresses it. Lower left: the sum of the directional derivatives is the Laplacian.

A. Coordinate Frame for Edge Detection

Oriented measurements have been widely used in edge detection. For example Marr & Poggio (1979) employed directional second derivative operators, whose zero-crossings were taken to denote rapid intensity changes. Due to the difficulty in selecting an orientation, Marr & Hildreth (1980) later abandoned this scheme, in favor of zero-crossings of the Laplacian, a non-directional operator.

The flow field provides two meaningful directions—along and across the direction of flow—in which to look for edges within an oriented pattern. Zero-crossings in the second directional derivative in the direction of ϕ (against the grain) should highlight edges that contribute to defining the flow field, while zero-crossings in the second derivative perpendicular to ϕ

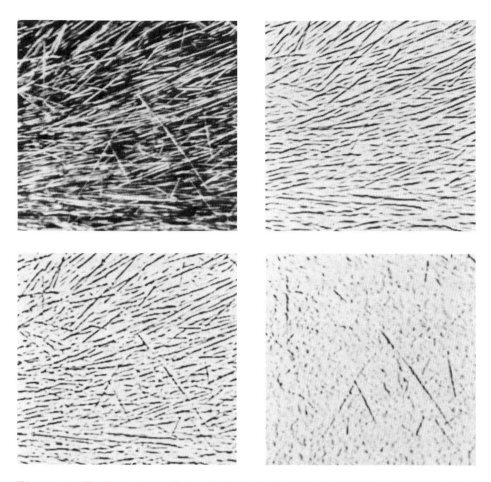

Figure 6 "Finding the needle in the haystack." In this straws pattern, directional derivatives across the flow direction show elements aligned with the pattern (upper right). Those along the flow direction show anomalous elements (lower right). The Laplacian (lower left) shows both.

(with the grain) should highlight anomalous elements or terminations. The sum of these two derivatives is the Laplacian.

The two directional derivatives of the wood grain image are shown, with the Laplacian, in Figure 5. Indeed, the derivative against the grain captures all the elements comprising the grain pattern, while the derivative with the grain does not appear meaningful. The Laplacian

confuses these very different signals by adding them together.

The derivative along the grain can also be meaningful, where anomalous elements are present. In addition to being perceptually salient, such anomalies are often physically significant, with origins such as cracks, intrusions, or occlusions, that are distinct from those of the main pattern. In man-made structures,

18

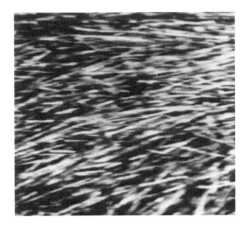 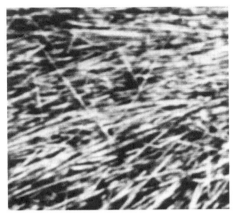

Figure 7 Left: the straw picture from Figure 6. Right: the anomalous elements have been removed by directional median filtering in the flow direction. (Following a suggestion by Richard Szeliski.)

anamolies are often important because they indicate some variety of flaw.

Figure 6 shows a pattern of aligned elements (straw) with some anomalous elements. The directional second derivatives along and across the flow direction are shown, together with their sum (which is just the Laplacian.) Differentiating along the grain highlights anomalous elements, attenuating the rest (thus finding the "needles" in the haystack.) Differentiating across the grain suppresses the anomalies. The Laplacian shows both.

A related demonstration is shown in Figure 7, in which the anomalous elements have actually been removed by directional median filtering in the flow direction.

B. Singularities

We have shown several ways in which viewing an oriented pattern in flow coordinates facilitates analysis and description of the pattern. Describing and analyzing the flow field itself is the other side of

the coin. The topology of a flow field, as of any vector field, is determined by the structure of its singularities, those points at which the field vanishes. Identifying and describing singularities is therefore basic to describing the flow field. The singularities provide the framework around which metric properties, such as curvature, may be described. Singularities are also perceptually salient (see Figure 8).

A robust basis for identifying singularities is the index or winding number (Spivak, 1979.) Suppose we follow a circuit along a close curve on a vector field. As we traverse the circuit, the vector rotates continuously, returning to its original orientation when the circuit is completed. The index or winding number of the curve is the number of revolutions made by the vector in traversing the curve. The index of a point is the index of a small circle as we shrink it around the point:

Figure 8 A spiral Glass pattern and its flow lines. The pattern is perceptually dominated by the singularity at the center. Since the flow field vanishes at a singularity, the flow lines obtained by integrating the flow field tend to become ill behaved as they approach one.

5.0 Conclusion

$$\text{ind}(x, y) = \lim_{\epsilon \mapsto 0} \frac{1}{2\pi} \int_0^{2\pi} \frac{\partial}{\partial \theta} \phi$$
$$(x + \epsilon \cos \theta, \, y + \epsilon \sin \theta) d\theta$$
$$= \lim_{\epsilon \mapsto 0} \frac{1}{2\pi} \int_0^{2\pi} (-\sin \theta, \, \cos \theta)$$
$$\cdot \nabla \phi (x + \epsilon \cos \theta, \, y + \epsilon \sin \theta) d\theta.$$

To compute the winding number numerically, we divide the flow field into suitably small rectangles, summing the rotation of ϕ around each rectangle. As in computing the flow lines, we assume that ϕ has no spurious discontinuities. Where the result is non-zero, the rectangle surrounds a singularity. Figure 9 shows an example of the detection of singularities using winding number, for a fingerprint. We are currently working on classifying the singularities, and using them to describe the topology of the flow field.

We addressed the problem of analyzing oriented patterns by decomposing them into a flow field, describing the direction of anisotropy, and describing the pattern independent of changing flow direction.

A specific computation for estimating the flow direction was proposed. The computation can be viewed as a) finding the direction of maximal variance in the output of a linear filter, b) combining gradient directions locally, or c) finding the direction of maximal edge density.

The flow field was then used to form a coordinate system in which to view the pattern. Two orthogonal families of curves—along and across the direction of flow—from the coordinate system's parameter lines. Viewing the pattern in these flow coordinates amounts to deforming the pattern so that the flow lines become parallel straight lines. This deformation produces a pattern that is simpler, more regular, and therefore more amenable to

 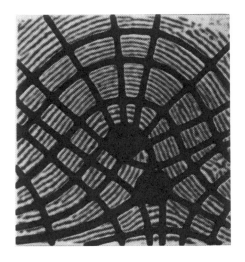

Figure 9 A fingerprint and its flow coordinate grid. The two black circles represent the major singularities, which were detected by measuring the flow field's winding number.

analysis and description than the original one.

References

Barr, A. (1984) Global and local deformation of solid primitives. *Comp. Graph.*, 18:21–30.

Barrow, H. & Tenenbaum, J.M. (1978) Recovering intrinsic scene characteristics from images. In *Computer Vision Systems*, Hanson & Riseman (Eds.), New York: Academic Press.

Brodatz, P. (1966) *Textures.* New York: Dover.

Burt, P. (1980) Fast, hierarchical correlations with Gaussian-like kernels. Dept. Computer Science TR 860, University of Maryland.

Glass, L. (1969) Moire effect from random dots. *Nature*, 243:578–580.

Horn, B.K.P. (1977) Understanding image intensities. *Artif. Intell.*, 8:201–231.

Hubel, D.H. & Wiesel, T.N. (1968) Receptive fields and functional architecture of monkey striate cortex. *J. Physiol., Lond.*, 195:215–243.

Kass, M. & Witkin, A. (1985) Analyzing oriented patterns. Schlumberger AI Tech. Report 42, January.

Marr, D. (1976) Early processing of visual information. *Proc. Royal Soc. B*, 275:484–519.

Marr, D.C. (1982) *Vision: A Computational Investigation into the Human Representation and Processing of Visual Information.* San Francisco: W.H. Freeman

Marr, D. & Hildreth, E. (1980) Theory of edge detection. *Proc. Roy. Soc. B*, 207:187–217.

Marr, D. & Poggio, T. (1979) A computational theory of human stereo vision. *Proc. Roy. Soc.*, 204:301–328.

Papoulis, A. (1965) *Probability, Random Variables and Stochastic Processes.* New York: McGraw-Hill.

Rice, S.O. (1945) Mathematical analysis of random noise. *Bell Sys. Tech. J.*, 24:46 – 156.

Schiller, P.H., Finlay, B.L. & Volman, S.F. (1976) Quantitative studies of single-cell properties in monkey striate cortex. II. Orientation specificity and ocular dominance. *J. Neurophysiology*, 39:1320 – 1333.

Spivak, M. (1979) *Differential Geometry.* Berkeley, Calif.: Publish or Perish.

Stevens, K. (1978) Computation of locally parallel structure. *Biological Cybernetics*, 29:29 – 26.

Williams, L. (1983) Pyramdial Parametrics. *Computer Graphics,* 17(3).

Zucker, S. (1983) Computational and psychophysical experiments in grouping. In Beck, Hope, Rosenfeld (eds.), *Human and Machine Vision,* New York: Academic Press, 1983.

Reprinted from Schlumberger AI Tech. Report 42, January 1985. (Also appeared in Proc. Int. Joint Conference for Artif. Intell., August 1985.)

18

3D Texture: Stereo Psychophysics and Geometry

Jacques Ninio*

Institut Jacques Monod
Paris, France

1.0 Introduction

The random-dot stereogram technique has emerged as one of the major tools in the study of the mechanisms of binocular vision (see Anstis et al., 1978; Georgeson, 1979; Julesz, 1971, 1978). I present here a new variant of Julesz's random-dot stereogram: random-curve stereograms. The initial motivation for this work was to construct stereograms which could be used to probe the brain's knowledge of three-dimensional geometry along the lines of work reported earlier (Ninio, 1977, 1979).

Many theoretical discussions of binocular vision implicitly assume the visual axes to be nearly parallel and neglect the fact that stereopsis can be obtained with convergent visual axes, making angles of 20° or even 40° with each other. This can be seen in the lack of concern for vertical disparities (however, see Longuet-Higgins, 1982). Under parallel viewing, the corresponding image-points on the two retinas lie on a horizontal line; but as the angle of convergence increases the effect of vertical disparity becomes more important. The stereograms presented here should be viewed with visual axes converging at an angle of 24°. [Editor's note: the size of the original panels was 4.7 × 4.7cm.] Furthermore, they are constructed as point projections in such a way that the geometry of the projection system matches

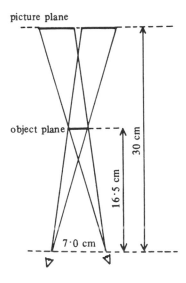

Figure 1 The projection system used for the construction of the stereograms shown in Figures 2 to 6, with the exception of 3b. Note that the pair of projections is made to be viewed by convergent squinting. The advantage is to allow the geometry of the viewing apparatus to match exactly the geometry of the projection system. In Figure 3b the inner cones correspond to eyes 4 cm apart and the outer cones of eyes 14 cm apart. Furthermore, the separation of the two images was changed in this case, and made equal to the separation obtained for a 7 cm interpupillary distance.

rather well the geometry of the observer's visual apparatus (Figure 1).

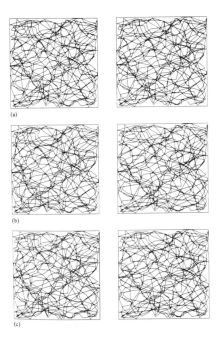

Figure 2 Three different surfaces generated by the same random walk: (a) is made of five planar sections and contains a lozenge-shaped cliff along a diagonal, (b) contains four hemi-spherical globes as in an egg-box, (c) contains a half-torus (usually described as a volcano or a baking pan).

2.0 Methods of Producing Random-curve Stereograms

The method consists of generating a "random walk" in space, with the constraint that the walking point remains bound to the surface one wishes to represent. Then one draws two projections of the curve linking successive points of the random

walk. Because of the random character of the curve, the shape of the surface on which it lies can only be guessed under monocular viewing.

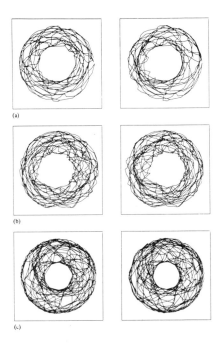

Figure 3 (a) Surface of revolution with a sinusoidal cross-section; (b) two cones, one inside the other, drawn with special rules (see caption to Figure 1); (c) full torus. As for all stereo panels, the original size was 4.7cm × 4.7cm.

In the main variant, a flat random walk is generated inside a square. Let a_n and b_n be the coordinates of the running point at step n. A reproducible random-number generator provides a random increment to each coordinate to produce step $n+1$. The shape of the surface comes in through the introduction of a third coordinate $c_n = f(a_n, b_n)$. The two projections of the running point are then computed, and the pen of a Benson drawing machine joins the successive points of the projected random walk to make a continuous curve (Figure 2). Approximately eight hundred points were used to generate these stereograms..

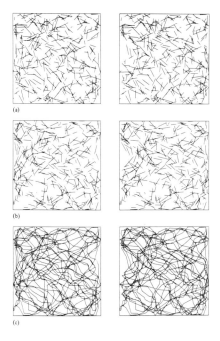

(a)

(b)

(c)

Figure 4 A horizontal cylindrical surface (hill or bath) represented with random needles in (a) and (b). The needles were obtained by representing in an interrupted manner the random curve of (c).

In a second variant, we start again with a flat random walk inside a square. The sheet containing the square is then folded, to form various shapes, e.g. a torus, a cone, or a cylinder (Figure 3).

In a third variant the curves are drawn discontinuously. For instance, point n is joined to point $n + 1$ only if n is odd (Figure 4a), or only if n is even (Figure 4b). In this case, the stereogram resembles the random-needle or random-line stereograms of Julesz & Frisby (1975). However, the methods of generation and hence the applications are quite different.

In a fourth variant, the basic random walk is different. We generate a unit vector, the tip of which moves at random on the surface of a unit sphere (Figure 5a). The coordinates of the tip a_n, b_n, c_n are then used as parameters to define the cartesian coordinates x_n, y_n, z_n of a point moving on the surface one wishes to represent. Figures 5b and c illustrate this technique for two other surfaces.

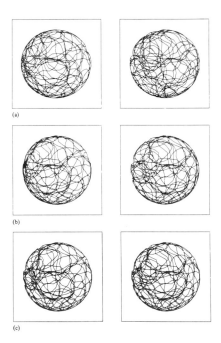

(a)

(b)

(c)

Figure 5 (a) Full sphere; (b) conical bucket; (c) globule on a flat disk.

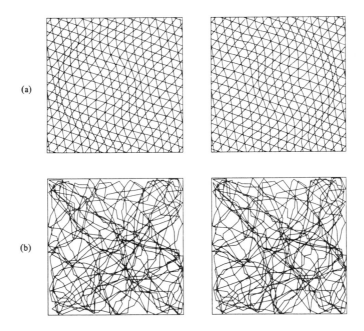

(a)

(b)

Figure 6 The half-torus of Figure 2c is represented with (a) oblique lines and (b) again with a random curve.

3.0 Discussion

3.1 Nature of the input

All the random stereograms produced by Julesz involve a large number of matching picture elements (dots, needles, squares, triangles). Here it can be seen that continuous random curves are also acceptable inputs for stereopsis. Some theoreticians will probably suggest that the curve is first decomposed into a large number of elements which are then subjected to point by point matching. Stereograms like those in Figure 4 may be used to compare the efficiency of stereopsis with continuous or discontinuous stimuli. Note that each display produces a strong sensation of a smooth surface in depth.

In Figure 6a, a surface is portrayed by a set of lines which form regular textures.

Below in Figure 6b, the same surface is represented with a random curve. The regular textures make the shape apparent monocularly. However, the random-curve stereogram gives a better depth-sensation.

3.2 Importance of the projection system

Apart from minor effects which have not yet been investigated, the surface perceived by the observer corresponds well to the mathematical surface defined by the programmer. This is true when the stereograms are viewed by convergent squinting, i.e. when the geometry of the visual apparatus agrees with the geometry used for generating the projections (Figure 1). However, when the stereograms are viewed with a stereoscope, distorted surfaces with

19

exaggerated depth are seen. Thus, the conical surfaces of Figures 3b and 5b look almost cylindrical when viewed with a stereoscope.

3.3 Accuracy of reconstruction

Many observers viewing random-curve stereograms have the feeling that some sections of the curve cross the perceived surface rather than lie exactly upon it. This is a justifiable interpretation, as points on the surface are connected by straight lines. Where the surface is quite curved and the line in that region long enough it will indeed be seen as crossing the surface.

3.4 One or many interpretative systems?

The stereogram in Figure 3b represents two conical surfaces, one inside the other. Actually, the two cones belong to two different projection systems. The outer is a steep cone with rays making a 30° angle with the cone's axis and it was projected as though the eyes were only 4 cm apart. The inner cone is more open with rays at 60° from the axis. It was projected as though the eyes were 14 cm apart. Despite this, there is no conflict. It would appear that the brain uses a uniform interpretative system which makes the inner cone steeper and the outer one wider.

3.5 One depth or many

Some observers (including myself) fail to interpret stereogram 5a as representing a full sphere and to a lesser extent stereogram 3c as representing a full torus. These are the only surfaces in this article that have a back and a front, i.e. two depths per cyclopean direction. Part of this effect may be due to the large disparities exhibited in these figures. (See Ninio & Mizraji, 1985, for more recent work on this subject.)

Acknowledgment

I am indebted to Jean Pierre Dumas for his patient collaboration as an observer, and many useful suggestions[1].

References

Anstis, S.M., Howard, I.P. & Rogers, B. (1978) A Craik-O'Brien-Cornsweet illusion for visual depth. *Vision Research*, 18:213–217 (Appendix: A cheap way to make random-dot stereograms).

Georgeson, M.A. (1979) Random-dot stereograms of real objects: observations on stereo faces and moulds. *Perception*, 8:585–588.

Julesz, B. (1971) *Foundations of Cyclopean Perception*. Chicago, IL: University of Chicago Press.

Julesz, B. (1978) Global stereopsis: co-operative phenomena in stereoscopic depth perception. In R. Held, H.W. Leibowitz & H.L. Teuber (eds.), *Handbook of Sensory Physiology*, vol. VII *Perception*, Berlin: Springer-Verlag, pp. 215–256.

Julesz, B. & Frisby, J.P. (1975) Some new subjective contours in random-line stereograms. *Perception*, 4:145–150.

Longuet-Higgins, H.C. (1982) The role of the vertical dimension in stereoscopic vision. *Perception*, 11:377–386.

Ninio, J. (1977) The geometry of the correspondence between two retinal projections. *Perception*, 6:627–643.

Ninio, J. (1979) An algorithm that generates a large number of geometric visual illusions. *Jrl. Theoretical Biol-ogy*, 79:167–201.

Ninio, J. & Mizraji, E. (1985) Errors in the stereoscopic separation of surfaces represented with regular textures. *Perception*, 14:315–328.

Reprinted with some editorial inclusions from *Perception*, 10:403–410 (1981).

Appendix

The Geometry of the Correspondence between Two Retinal Projections (abridged)

1.0 Introduction

Descriptive geometry, a branch of applied geometry, teaches how the properties of a figure may be deduced from its projections on two different planes. The main methods of descriptive geometry were devised by Gaspard Monge around 1790. For a history of the subject, see Taton (1951). Descriptive geometry involves orthogonal projections on two planes which are perpendicular to each other, as in Figure 1. The technique is extensively used in architectural and engineering drawing. The deductions that give the reconstruction of a curve in three-dimensional space from its two orthogonal projections are straightforward and there is no need to proceed by trial-and-error searching for disparities between various parts of projections.

The orthogonal projections that are used in descriptive geometry may be taken as a particular case of perspective representations. The branch of geometry that deals at the most fundamental level with the relationship between a figure and its projections is called projective geometry. Its main foundations were set by Girard Desargues around 1640. Desargues formulated the mathematical concept of point at infinity. His work permitted the treatment in a rigorous manner of all the perspective problems that were more or less empirically solved by the Renaissance painters. A good understanding of projective geometry enables one to make the appropriate transpositions between the properties of orthogonal projections—which can be intuitively understood by most people—and the general-perspective representations, which are less obvious. I shall resort to such transpositions from problems in binocular stereopsis to problems in descriptive geometry.

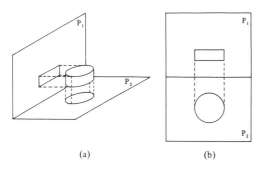

(a)   (b)

Figure 1 Descriptive geometry. Objects in space may be represented by their orthogonal projections on two perpendicular planes, P_1 and P_2. Thus, the disk shown in (a) may be represented by a circle and a rectangle as in (b). Some of the main principles of descriptive geometry can be transposed without difficulty to other systems of projections, such as the idealized retinal projections that are discussed in this article. In particular, the ambiguity problems are almost exactly the same, whatever the system of projections.

1.1 Conventions

We make here the simplification that the eye is as black box with a pinhole (Ω) at the front, the back of the box, the retina, being a plane P. A point M of the external world has a representation M_l on the left retina and M_r on the right one. The geometric operation leading to these representations is a projection on the plane P through the point Ω. Hence, M_l is the intersection of the straight line $M\Omega_l$ with the plane P_l (Figure 2).

It is crucial to make the distinction between two kinds of elements: geometric elements (points, lines) and their physical counterparts. The objects and their traces on the retinas will be qualified as

real. The image of a small luminous spot on the retina will be assimilated to a real point. Whenever the qualifier real is omitted, it implies that we are talking of abstract geometric elements. For instance, the retina contains an infinity of points and lines, but the number of real points (physical signals of the presence of an external object) may be small or nil.

Two points M_l and M_r on the two retinas that *may* correspond to a same external point will be said to be *conjugate*. Two real points M_l and M_r which *do* correspond to a same external real point will be qualified as *synonymous*.

2.0 The Ambiguity Problem

Discussions of the ambiguity problem in stereopsis are usually based upon representations similar to Figure 3a [see for instance Julesz & Johnson (1968); Marr & Poggio (1976)]. Suppose the two real points A and B give the projections A_l, B_l and A_r, B_r. Reconstructing the optical pathways through the centers of projections Ω_l and Ω_r, one obtains the two points U and V in addition to the source points A and B. Thus, it has been argued (Kaufman, 1974, chapter 8) that, if binocular stereopsis did involve such reconstructions, the ghost images U and V would be perceived in addition to A and B. On the other hand, starting with the same premises (the representation of Figure 3a), Julesz & Johnson (1968) successfully constructed "stereograms portraying ambiguously perceivable surfaces". Thus, there are no ghost images but—in the absence of depth clues—the brain alternates between two hypotheses about the source of the stimuli: (A and B) or (U and V).

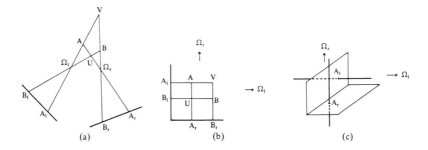

Figure 3 The ambiguity problem with points. (a) Traditional representation of the ambiguity problem. The projections of A and B may as well correspond to the "ghosts" U and V. (b) An analog, in terms of orthogonal projections, of the preceding drawing. (c) Why the sketches (a) and (b) are misleading. In general, a pair of points of the two projection planes cannot even define a single point in space.

Actually, the representation of Figure 3a or Figure 3b is misleading. It lacks generality. The fundamental peculiarity

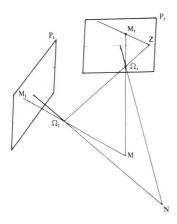

Figure 2 An idealized representation of the geometry of the visual system. Let Z be the projection of Ω_l on plane P_r and let M_r be the projection of M. All the points in space which project as M_l on P_l belong to the line $M\Omega_l$. Hence their projection on P_r belongs to the line that goes through M_r and Z.

in it is that the centers of projections Ω_l and Ω_r are in a same plane with the

projections of A and B. In general, three points define a plane, and if a fourth point is chosen at random, its chances of being in the plane of the three others will be negligible.

Consider the more general representation of Figure 3c. The lines $A_l\Omega_l$ and $A_r\Omega_r$ simply do not meet in three-dimensional space. Thus a pair of projections A_l and A_r will not generally give back a source point, contrary to the peculiar situation of Figure 3a. If two eyes are presented separately with two sets of uncorrelated random distributions of points, rivalry would be predicted, rather than a multiplicity of ghost images. Actually, the two uncorrelated patterns that were studied by Ramachandran et al. (1973) did not produce rivalry. Fusion was observed, each point of the left pattern being combined with its "nearest neighbor" of the right pattern. These, and other more classical experiments demonstrating the fusion of nonexactly matching patterns [for instance tilted or stretched stereograms (Julesz, 1971)] suggest that the actual strategy for binocular stereopsis is flexible. It takes into account the possibility of errors in the determination of the instantaneous position of the two eyes, and the possible imperfections of the optical system.

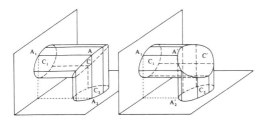

Figure 4 The ambiguity problem with curves. The curve C on the left has the two orthogonal projections C_1 and C_2. The point A of curve C projects as A_1 and A_2. Reciprocally, if we start with A_1 on curve C_1, it may either correspond to A_2 on curve C_2, or correspond to A'_2 on the same curve. Whereas the couple A_1, A_2 gives back the point A, the couple A_1, A'_2 corresponds to A' (shown on the right). The plane containing A, A', A_1, A_2, A'_2 is a cross-section of the type shown in Figure 3b. If we let A_1 move around curve C_1 and impose the condition that its conjugate (A_2 or A'_2) should move continuously on curve C_2 (and not jump from one side to the other) then the corresponding point in space A or A' will describe one of the two curves C or C'. Thus, despite the fact that every point of the projection C_1 may have two conjugates on C_2, the number of global solutions is limited. In addition to the initial source-curve C, we have here only one ghost-curve C'. These considerations are transposable without difficulty to the idealized system of retinal projections. The drawing was made according to the rules of cavalier perspective.

The preceding considerations apply to the problem of fusing patterns made of points. The problem of matching lines is somewhat different. Let C_1 and C_2 be the two projections of a space curve C. We can construct the cone of summit Ω_1 and the base C_1 (the "visual pyramid") and the similar cone (Ω_2, C_2). Their intersection gives back the initial curve plus in some cases a finite number of ghost curves. Little is needed to remove the ambiguity. The knowledge of a single point-to-point correspondence on the two projections, and the reasonable hypothesis that the projections correspond to a well-behaving continuous curve, suffice to remove the ambiguity (Figure 4).

The lines that are dealt with by the perceptual apparatus are not always the projections of real lines in space. They may correspond to apparent *contours*. A sphere determines on the two retinas two apparent contours—circles. When the sphere moves, the motions of the circles are strongly correlated, and thus it would be reasonable to assign them to a same object. However, it is important in that case not to interpret the two circles as projections of a same space curve. Thus, a algorithm that would transform the primary visual input into a "primal sketch" (Marr, 1976) should distinguish carefully between edges and contours if it is to precede binocular fusion.

3.0 Unicity Properties

Let us take an arbitrary point M_l on the left retina. Where on the right retina can we locate its conjugate M_r? Any point M of the line $M_l\Omega_l$ has M_l for projection on the left retina (Figure 2).

In particular, consider two real points M_1 and M on the line $M_l\Omega_l$. They project as M_l on the left retina, and project as two different points on the right retina. This peculiar configuration gives rise to

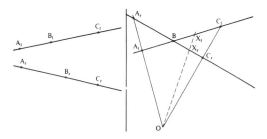

Figure 5 Anharmonic ratio. A_l, B_l, C_l on one side, A_r, B_r, C_r on the other, are assumed to be the retinal projections of three aligned points in space. From there, the complete point-to-point correspondences between the points of the line A_l, B_l, C_l and the points of the line A_r, B_r, C_r can be established, owing to the invariance of the anharmonic ratio. A geometric construction may be used to that effect. Move one of the lines in order to bring one point over its conjugate (here, B_l and B_r have been superimposed). Maintaining the orientations of the lines is not a necessity. Join A_rA_l and C_rC_l which intersect at point O. Any line that goes through O intersects the lines A_lC_l and A_rC_r on a pair of conjugate points. Consider for instance the line OX_l. Then we have a system of four lines which intersect at point O: OA_l, OB, OX_l, and OC_l. Any fifth line which intersects these four will generate four points, the anharmonic ratio of which is independent of the choice of the fifth line, thus: $(A_l, B, X_l, C_l) = (A_r, B, X_r, C_r)$ and X_r is the conjugate of X_l.

Panum's limiting case.

A straight line projects as a straight line. Thus, the locus of all the points M_r that may be the projections on the right retina of a point M belonging to the line $M_l\Omega_l$ is a straight line. We may call it the "scanning line" conjugate to M_l. Any point M_r of that scanning line is conjugate to M_l—i.e. the couple (M_l, M_r) may correspond to a same real point M in space. The scanning lines have a remarkable property: they all meet at a certain point Z. Consider that M is moving on line $M_l\Omega_l$: when it coincides with Ω_l, its projection M_r on the right retina is at the intersection of the line $\Omega_l\Omega_r$ with the plane P_r. This point which, by the way it has been generated, does not depend upon the initial choice of M_l, is the point Z.

In Julesz' AUTOMAP I (Julesz, 1963) the scanning lines are "horizontal". The conjugate on the right image of a point M_l of the left image is assumed to be somewhere on the same horizontal level as M_l. The random-dot stereograms are generally constructed in accordance with this rule. When the two eyes are looking at infinity, with the two retinal planes confounded, it is true that the conjugate of M_l must be at the same level as M_l. In that case, the line $\Omega_l\Omega_r$ is parallel to the planes P_l and P_r. Its intersection Z with plane P_r is set at infinity. All scanning lines have in common the point at infinity Z, thus they are parallel (and parallel to the "horizontal" line $\Omega_l\Omega_r$).

In general, however, there is no reason why the conjugate of a point should be on the level of that point. The family of horizontal lines that intervene in Julesz' geometry must be replaced by the family of intersecting scanning lines that was defined above.

4.0 Projective Properties

Let A, B, C, D be four points on a straight line. Their anharmonic ratio, defined as:

$$(A, B, C, D) = \frac{AC}{AD} \cdot \frac{BD}{BC} , \qquad (1)$$

is conserved upon projection on a plane. If four straight lines of a plane are concurrent, and are intersected by a fifth one at points A, B, C, D, the anharmonic ratio (A, B, C, D) is completely independent of the choice of the fifth line, and depends only upon the initial four lines.

If four points A, B, C, D of a line L project on the two retinas, one has, projecting through Ω_l:

$$(A_l, B_l, C_l, D_l) = (A, B, C, D) . \qquad (2)$$

Similarly, projecting through Ω_r, one has:

$$(A_r, B_r, C_r, D_r) = (A, B, C, D) ; \qquad (3)$$

thus

$$(A_l, B_l, C_l, D_l) = (A_r, B_r, C_r, D_r) . \qquad (4)$$

Suppose one has succeeded in establishing that three couples of points: A_l and A_r, B_l and B_r, C_l and C_r are conjugate, A_l being aligned with B_l and C_l on the left retina, and A_r, B_r, C_r being aligned on the right retina. Then, the entire correspondence between points of the two lines can be established unequivocally. Any point X_l belonging to the line $A_l B_l$ has one conjugate X_r on line $A_r B_r$ which is unequivocally determined by the relationship $(A_l, B_l, C_l, X_l) = (A_r, B_r, C, X_r)$. The position of X_t can be also obtained through a geometric construction

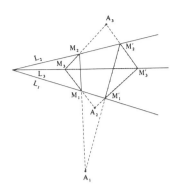

Figure 6 Desargue's theorem. Consider the concurrent lines L_1, L_2, L_3 and take arbitrarily M_1 and M_1' on L_1, M_2 and M_2' on L_2, and M_3 and M_3' on L_3. Construct as indicated, the intersections A_1, A_2, A_3. The theorem states that these three points are aligned. Consider now that L_1, L_2 and L_3 are the projections on one retina of three lines in space which are concurrent or parallel, but do not lie in a same plane. Suppose that the correspondence between the three lines L_1, L_2, and L_3 and their counterpart on the other retina has been established. Suppose we repeat the construction given above, on the second retina, starting with the conjugates of M_1, M_1', M_2, M_2', M_3, M_3'. We shall obtain three aligned intersections which are themselves conjugate to A_1, A_2, A_3. Since three points are sufficient to determine the conjugation relationships along a line, we have obtained in this way the information relative to the conjugation relationships along the projections of a certain new line in space, that was generated from the projections of Desargue's frame. By moving M_1, M_1' ... and their conjugates along the projections of Desargue's frame, and generating in this manner A_1, A_2, A_3 and their conjugates, the whole space can be explored, and all the conjugation relationships between points of the two retinas can be obtained.

(Figure 5) which is remarkably simple. This is the first important idea on how a limited number of correspondences may be used to discover more correspondences.

Consider two lines L and L' which do not belong to a same plane, and suppose that the point-to-point conjugation relationships between their projections have been established. One can try to make use of this knowledge to explore the conjugation relationships further. Take points M on L and M' on L' and construct the line MM'. The conjugation relationships are already established for the projections of the two points, M and M'. Then one only needs to find a third couple of conjugate projections relative to line MM' in order to be able to establish the entire correspondence between the two projections of MM'. By moving point M on line L and point M' on line L', the entire space can be explored. The problem is that, for every new line MM', one has to find a "third point".

The third point may be obtained automatically if one starts from a slightly more complex situation, owing to a famous theorem by Desargues.

Let us take three straight lines in space, L_1, L_2, and L_3, which are concurrent or parallel, but do not lie on a same plane, and let us give to that configuration the name of Desargue's frame. If the conjugation relationships are known along the two projections of Desargue's frame, then one can deduce all the conjugation relationships on the retinal planes. Desargue's frame plays in projective geometry a role similar to Descarte's reference frame in analytical geometry. Using a relatively simple geometric construction one may generate from Desargue's frame a family of lines which permit one to explore the whole space. The construction gives, for each line, the (conjugate) projections of three of its points (Figure 6).

Since a Desargue's frame is made of three lines, and since three points are needed to establish the conjugation relationships along the projections of a line, it follows that a complete knowledge of the potential correspondences between the two retinal projections can be obtained automatically as soon as *seven* point-to-point correspondences have been established: one for the summit of the Desargue's frame and two additional points on each of the three intersecting lines.

References

Julesz, B. (1963) Towards the automation of binocular depth perception (AUTOMAP-1). *Proceedings of the IFIPS Congress*, Munich, 1962, C.M. Popplewell (ed.), Amsterdam: North-Holland, pp. 439 – 443.

Julesz, B. (1971) *Foundations of Cyclopean Perception.* Chicago, IL: University of Chicago Press.

Julesz, B. & Johnson, S.C. (1968) Stereograms portraying ambiguously perceivable surfaces. *Proceedings of the National Academy of Sciences USA*, 61:437 – 441.

Kaufman, I. (1974) *Sight and Mind. An Introduction to Visual Perception.* New York: Oxford University Press.

Marr, D. (1976) Early processing of visual information. *Phil. Trans. R. Soc. Lond. B.*, 275:483 – 524.

Marr, D. & Poggio, T. (1976) Cooperative computation of stereo disparity. *Science*, 194:283 – 287.

Ramachandran, V.S. & Braddick, O. (1973) Orientation-specific learning in stereopsis. *Perception*, 2:371–376.

Taton, R. (1951) *L'Oeuvre Scientifique de Monge*. Paris: Presses Universitaires de France.

Adapted from *Perception*, 6:627–643 (1977).

*Author's full address is: Institut Jacques Monod, Tour 43, 2 Place Jussieu, 75251 Paris Codex 05, France.

Fractal-based Description of Surfaces

Alex P. Pentland

The Media Laboratory
Massachusetts Institute of Technology

1.0 Introduction

The world that surrounds us, except for man-made environments, is typically formed of complex, rough, and jumbled surfaces. Mountains, clouds and trees are examples. How can such common natural shapes and crenulated surfaces be represented, and how can their description be computed from image data? To solve these problems, we first need a good 3D model for these surfaces. Then we can examine the projection of these surfaces onto the image and describe the relation between image and surface.

A marked limitation of almost all previous models for reconstructing surfaces from images is the assumption that the surface is smooth (Ikeuchi & Horn, 1981; Witkin, 1981). Here, I propose using a fractal measure to describe just how smooth or rough a surface is, and show how this measure may be computed from image information.

Fractals are a novel class of naturally-arising functions, discovered primarily by Benoit Mandelbrot (1977, 1982). Mandelbrot and others (Fournier et al., 1982; Richardson, 1961) have shown that fractals are found widely in nature and that a number of basic physical processes, such as the aggregation of galaxies and clouds, or erosion and turbulent flow, produce fractal surfaces. Because fractals look

natural to human beings, much recent computer graphics research has focused on using fractal processes to simulate natural shapes and textures (see Figure 1), including mountains, clouds, water, plants, trees, and primitive animals (Carpenter, 1980; Kawaguchi, 1982; Norton, 1982). Additionally, we have recently conducted a survey of natural imagery (Pentland, 1984) and found that a fractal model of imaged 3-D surfaces furnishes an accurate description of both textured and shaded image regions, thus providing validation of this physics-derived model for both image texture and shading.

2.0 Fractals and the Fractal Model

Perhaps the most familiar examples of naturally occurring fractals are coastlines. When we examine a coastline (as in Figure 1), we see a familiar scalloped curve formed by innumerable bays and peninsulas. If we then examine a finer-scale map of the same region, we shall again see the same type of curve. It turns out that this characteristic scalloping is present at *all* scales of examination, i.e. the statistics of the curve are invariant with respect to transformations of scale. This fact causes problems when we attempt to measure the length of the coastline, because it turns out that the length we are measuring depends not only on the coastline but also

Figure 1 Fractal-based models of natural shapes (see Mandelbrot, 1982).

on the length of the measurement tool itself! This is because, whatever the size measuring tool selected, all of the curve length attributable to features smaller than the size of the measuring tool will be missed. Mandelbrot pointed out that, if we generalize the notion of dimension to include *fractional* dimensions (from which we get the word "fractal"), we can obtain a consistent measurement of the coastline's length.

2.1 The definition

A fractal is defined as a set for which the Hausdorff-Besicovich dimension is strictly larger than the topological dimension. Topological dimension corresponds to the standard, intuitive Euclidian definition of "dimension." Hausdorff-Besicovich dimension D, also referred to as the *fractal dimension*, may be illustrated (and

roughly defined) by the examples (1) of measuring the length of an island's coastline, and (2) measuring the area of the island.

To measure the length of the coastline we might select a measuring stick of length λ and determine that n such measuring sticks could be placed end to end along the coastline. The length of the coastline is then intuitively $n\lambda$. If we were measuring the area of the island, we could use a square of area λ^2 to derive an area of $m\lambda^2$, where m is the number of squares it takes to cover the island. If we actually did this, we would find that both of these measurements vary with λ, the length of the measuring instrument—an undesirable result.

In these two examples the length λ is raised to a particular power: the power of one to measure length, the power of two to measure area. These are two examples of the general rule of raising λ to a power

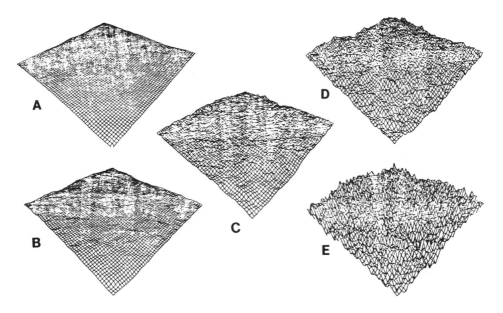

Figure 2 Surfaces of increasing fractal dimension. The fractal dimension corresponds closely to our intuitive notion of roughness.

that is the *dimension* of the object being measured. In the case of the island, raising λ to the topological dimension does not yield consistent results. If, however, we were to use the power 1.2 instead of 1.0 to measure the length, and 2.1 instead of 2.0 to measure the area, we would find that the measured length and area remained constant regardless of the size of the measuring instrument chosen.[1] The positive real number D that yields such a consistent measurement is the *fractal dimension*. D is always greater than or equal to the topological dimension.

The most important lesson the work of Mandelbrot and others teaches us is the following:

Standard notions of length and area do not produce consistent measurements for many *natural shapes: the basic metric properties of these shapes vary as a function of the fractal dimension. Fractal dimension, therefore, is a* necessary *part of any consistent description of such shapes.*

This result, which could almost be stated as a theorem, demonstrates the *fundamental* importance of knowing the fractal dimension of a surface. It implies that *any* description of a natural shape that does not include the fractal dimension cannot be relied upon to be correct at more than one scale of examination.

2.2 Instant psychophysics (Part I)

The fractal dimension of a surface corresponds roughly to our intuitive notion of jaggedness (see Figure 2). Thus, if when

---

[1]This example is discussed at greater length in Mandelbrot's book, *Fractals: Form, Chance and Dimension*. The empirical data are from Richardson, 1961.

we were to generate a series of scenes with the same 3-D relief but increasing fractal dimension D, we would obtain the following sequence: first, (a) a flat plane ($D \approx 2$), then (b) a rolling countryside ($D \approx 2.1$), (c) a worn, old mountain range ($D \approx 2.3$), (d) a young, rugged mountain range ($D \approx 2.5$), and finally (e) a stalagmite-covered plane ($D \approx 2.8$).

When subjects are shown sets of 1-D curves and 2-D surfaces similar to Figure 2 with varying fractal dimension but constant range, and asked to estimate roughness on a scale of one (smoothest) to ten (roughest), the mean of the subject's estimates of roughness had a nearly perfect 0.98 correlation ($p < 0.001$) with the curve's fractal dimension. In other words, fractal dimension is an excellent measure of perceptual roughness.

3.0 Fractals And The Imaging Process

Before we can use a fractal model of natural surfaces to help us understand images we must determine how the imaging process maps a fractal surface shape into an image intensity surface.

The first step is to define our terms carefully. Real images and surfaces can not, of course, be true mathematical fractals, because the latter are defined to exist at *all* scales. Physical surfaces, in contrast, have an overall size that places an upper limit on the range of applicable scales. A lower limit is set by the size of the surfaces' constituent particles. Fractals, in common with all mathematical abstractions, can only approximate physical objects over a range of physical parameters.

Because it is unreasonable to expect a physical surface to be fractal over *all*

scales, the only physically reasonable definition of a "fractal surface" is a surface that may be accurately approximated by a single fractal function over a *range* of scales. We shall say, therefore, that a surface is *fractal* if the fractal dimension is stable over a wide range of scales, the implication being that it can be accurately approximated over that range of scales by a single fractal function.

3.1 Fractal Brownian functions

Virtually all the fractals encountered in physical models have two properties: (1) each segment is statistically similar to all others; (2) they are statistically invariant over wide transformations of scale. Motion of a particle undergoing Brownian motion is the cannonical example of this type of fractal. The discussion that follows will be devoted exclusively to fractal Brownian functions, a generalization of Brownian motion.

A random function $z = B(x)$ is a fractal Brownian function if for all x and Δx then

$$Pr \left(\frac{B(x + \Delta x) - B(x)}{\|\Delta x\|^{H}} < z \right) = F(z) \quad (1)$$

where $F(z)$ is a cumulative distribution function, and the variable H is the *fractal scaling parameter*, which describes how the variance of the signal changes with scale. Another way of characterizing this function is by its Fourier power spectrum, for Equation (1) implies that the power spectrum $P_B(f)$ (where f is frequency) of $B(x)$ will be proportional to f^{-2H-1}. Note that both x and $B(x)$ can be interpreted as vector quantities, thus providing an extension to two or more topological dimensions.

If the topological dimension of $B(x)$ is T, the fractal dimension D of the graph described by $B(x)$ is:

$$D = T + 1 - H \qquad (2)$$

If $H = 1/2$ and $F(y)$ comes from a zero-mean Gaussian with unit variance, then $B(x)$ is the classical Brownian function. It should be noted that very highly patterned surfaces can be Brownian fractals; all that is required is that they scale appropriately.

Real surfaces, of course, cannot be exactly modeled by such infinite mathematical functions; in fact, they typically do not behave in a fractal manner over more than a limited range of scales. Thus we must define carefully define what we mean by a "fractal surface:"

DEFINITION: *A fractal Brownian surface* is a continuous function that obeys the statistical description given by Equation (1), with x as a two-dimensional vector at all scales (i.e. values of Δx) between some smallest (Δx_{min}) and largest (Δx_{max}) scales.

In a survey of a variety of natural images (Pentland, 1984) we found that images of the majority of homogeneous natural surfaces are well described as being spatially isotropic fractals over scale ranges of at least 1 : 8 (i.e. $\Delta x_{max}/\Delta x_{min} > 8$). This finding has since been confirmed by several other researchers. Note that "isotropic" in this sense means only that the fractal scaling parameter H is isotropic. it does *not* mean that the surface is not "stretched;" e.g., tree bark can be a perfectly good isotropic fracal surface.

3.3 The fractal model and imaging

With these definitions in hand, we can now address the problem of how homogeneous patches of a 3-D fractal surfaces appear in the 2-D image. We will then let $z = B(x,y)$ be a two-dimensional fractal Brownian surface, and let

$$\vec{L} = (\cos \tau \sin \sigma, \sin \tau \sin \sigma, \cos \sigma)$$

be the unit vector in the mean illuminant direction, where τ is the *tilt* of the illuminant (the angle the image plane component of the illuminant vector makes with the x-axis) and σ is its *slant* (the angle the illuminant vector makes with the z-axis). We will assume that the surface is Lambertian, illuminated by (possibly many) distant light sources, and not self-shadowing. In this case then the normalized image intensity $I(x,y)$ will be

$$I(x,y) = \frac{p \cos \tau \sin \sigma + q \sin \tau \sin \sigma + \cos \sigma}{(p^2 + q^2 + 1)^{1/2}}$$
$$(3)$$

where

$$p = \frac{\partial}{\partial x} B(x,y)$$

$$q = \frac{\partial}{\partial y} B(x,y)$$

If we then take the Taylor series expansion of Equation (3) about $p, q = 0$ through the quadratic terms [2], we obtain

$$I(x,y) \approx \cos \sigma + p \cos \tau \sin \sigma +$$
$$q \sin \tau \sin \sigma - \frac{\cos \sigma}{2}(p^2 + q^2) \quad (4)$$

This expression gives an excellent approximation if $p, q \ll 1$. We note that for real surfaces, such as mountains, the maximum surface slope rarely is more than $15°$, i.e. typically $p^2 + q^2 < 0.1$. Under these

---

[2]Note: in this discussion we will take $\Delta x_{min} > 0$ and Δx_{max} large.

conditions the linear terms of Equation (4) will dominate the power spectrum except when the average illuminant is within $\pm 6°$ of the viewer's position, i.e. when $\sin \sigma < 0.1$.

The complex Fourier spectrum F_B (f, θ) of $B(x, y)$ is

$$F_B(f, \theta) = f^{-\beta/2} e^{i\phi_{f,\theta}}$$

where $\beta = 2H + 1$, ϕ is a random variable uniformly distributed on $(0, 2\pi)$, and $\phi_{f,\theta}$ is the random value "drawn" at position (f, θ) in the Fourier plane.

Now since p and q are partial derivatives of B, their transforms F_p and F_q are related to F_B in an elementary fashion. We can write

$$F_p(f, \theta) = 2\pi \cos \theta f^{1-\beta/2} e^{i(\phi_{f,\theta} + \pi/2)}$$

$$F_q(f, \theta) = 2\pi \sin \theta f^{1-\beta/2} e^{i(\phi_{f,\theta} + \pi/2)}$$

There are now two cases to consider: oblique illumination, and illumination from the viewer's position.

Case 1: When p, q are small and the illuminant is not behind the viewer (e.g., $\sin \sigma > 0.1$) then we may neglect the quadratic terms of Equation (4) and consider

$$I_1(x, y) = \cos \sigma + p \cos \tau \sin \sigma + q \sin \tau \sin \sigma$$

In this case, the Fourier transform of the image I_1 is (ignoring the DC term):

$$F_{I_1}(f, \theta) = 2\pi \sin \sigma f^{1-\beta/2} e^{i(\phi_{f,\theta} + \pi/2)}$$
$$[\cos \theta \cos \tau + \sin \theta \sin \tau]$$

and the power spectrum P is

$$P_{I_1}(f, \theta) = 4\pi^2 \sin^2 \sigma f^{2-\beta}$$
$$[\cos \theta \cos \tau + \sin \theta \sin \tau]^2$$

This spectrum depends, as expected, upon the illuminant direction. As with the

fractal surface itself, however, the spectral falloff is isotropic: the log of the power spectrum of the image has slope $2 - \beta$ with respect to log frequency at almost all orientations (excepting a set of measure zero where $\theta = \tau \pm \pi/2$).

Case 2: When the mean illuminant vector is almost parallel to the viewing direction (i.e. $\sin \sigma \approx 0$) the quadratic terms of Equation (4) can dominate and the image of a fractional Brownian surface will look like

$$I_2(x, y) = \cos \sigma (1 - (p^2 + q^2)/2)$$

To within a constant factor, and ignoring DC, the power spectrum $\vec{F}_{I_2}$ of this image will be the Fourier transform of the autocorrelation function $R_{p^2+q^2}$ of $p^2 + q^2$. We note that

$$P_p * P_p \approx P_p \qquad P_{pq} * P_{pq} \approx P_{pq}$$

$$P_q * P_q \approx P_q$$

and thus

$$\log P_{I_2} \quad \alpha \quad \log P_R \quad \alpha \quad 2 - \beta$$

The conclusion, therefore, is that when the mean illumination is at the viewer's position the image will have a power spectrum falloff approximately proportional to $f^{2-\beta}$, i.e. the same relationship between surface fractal scaling parameter and image fractal scaling parameter that we found with oblique illumination.

Thus we have proved the following:

Fractal Imaging Theorem: A 3-D fractal Brownian surface with power spectrum proportional to $f^{-\beta}$ has an image with power spectrum proportional to $f^{2-\beta}$, assuming Lambertian surface reflectance and constant illumination and albedo.

Thus the fractal dimension of the 3-D surface dictates the fractal dimension of the image intensity surface—and *vice versa*. This relationship turns out to be an excellect psychophysical predictor of peoples' perception of 3-D surface roughness, and simulation of the imaging process with a variety of imaging geometries and reflectance functions indicates that this result will hold quite generally: The "roughness" of the surface seems to dictate the "roughness" of the image.

This proof, then, gives us a method for inferring a basic property of the 3-D surface—its fractal dimension—by examining the image data. That the fractal dimension is required to obtain a scale-invariant description of the surface's metric properties is an indication of its usefulness. That the fractal dimension has also been shown to correspond closely to our intuitive notion of roughness shows the fundmental importance of the measurement: We can now discover from the image data whether the surface is rough or smooth, isotropic or aniotropic. We can know, in effect, from what kind of cloth the surface was cut.

3.4 Instant psychophysics (Part II)

Fifteen naive subjects (mostly language researchers) were shown digitized images of eight natural textured surfaces drawn from Brodatz's collection of texture images (Brodatz, 1966). They were asked "if you were to draw your finger horizontally along the surface pictured here, how rough or smooth would the surface feel?," i.e., they were asked to estimate the 3-D roughness/smoothness of the viewed surfaces. This procedure was then repeated for the vertical direction, yielding a total of sixteen roughness estimates for each subject. A scale of one (smoothest) to ten (roughest) was used to indicate 3-D roughness/smoothness.

The fractal dimension of the 2-D image was then computed along the horizontal and vertical directions, as described in the following section, and the viewed surface's 3-D fractal dimension was estimated by the use of the Fractal Imaging theorem. The mean of the subject's estimates of 3-D roughness had an excellent 0.91 correlation ($p < 0.001$) with roughnesses predicted by use of the image's 2-D fractal dimension and the Fractal Imaging theorem, i.e., the 3-D fractal dimension predicted by use of the measured 2-D image's fractal dimension accounted for 83% of the variance in the subject's estimates of 3-D roughness. This result, therefore, supports the general validity of the Fractal Imaging theorem.

4.0 Properties of Fractal Brownian Functions

Fractal functions must be stable over common transformations if they are to be useful as a descriptive tool. It is easy to show that the dimension of a mathematical fractal surface is invariant with respect to linear transformations of the data and to transformations of scale: These transformations do not affect the exponent of the power spectrum's decrease as a function of frequency, and it is the exponent that defines the fractal dimension. Stability of fractal dimension estimates is also to be expected because the fractal dimension of the image is directly related to the fractal dimension of the viewed surface, a property of 3-D natural surfaces that is typically stable over a few octaves of scale. In actual practice our estimates of fractal dimension have inded proven to be robust with respect to these common transforms.

The fact that the fractal description is stable with respect to scale is a critically important property. After all, even though we move about in the world (and examine surfaces both foveally and peripherally) we want to compute a stable, viewer-independent representation of the world. If our information about the world is not stable with respect to scale, we can have no hope of doing this

Fractal functions must be stable over common transformations if they are to be useful as a descriptive tool. The following propositions prove that the fractal dimension of a surface is invariant with respect to linear transformations of the data and to transformation of scale. Estimates of fractal dimension, therefore, may be expected to remain stable over smooth, monotonic transformations of the image data and over changes of scale.

5.0 Contours And The Imaging Process

We have described a method whereby the fractal dimension of the surface can be inferred for homogeneous, uniformly lit surfaces. Even if the surface is not homogeneous or uniformly illuminated, however, we can still hope to infer the fractal dimension of the surface from imaged surface contours and bounding contours.

Contour shape is often primarily a function of surface shape; this is especially true for contours that lie mostly within a plane intersecting the surface. Common examples of such approximately-planar contours are bounding contours and contours that are "drawn" on the surface, e.g., cast shadows. The imaged projection

of such planar contours is simply a linear transform of the 3-D contour; recalling that linear transforms do not alter the fractal dimension of a function, we see that the fractal dimension of these imaged contours is the same as that of the 3-D contour.

Thus we may use the fractal dimension of imaged contours to directly infer that of the 3-D surface (the surfaces' dimension is simply one plus the contours' dimension). Consequently, the estimate of fractal dimension obtained from contours can be used to corroborate the one derived from image intensities.

6.0 Applicability of the Fractal Model

To determine whether it is valid to apply the fractal model to some particular surface and its image data we need to verify both the homogeneity and the fractal nature of the imaged surface. Verifying the homegeneity of the surface is outside of the scope of this paper; we will simply note that it appears that homogeneity can be determined by use of color information. To verify the fractalness of the image we first rewrite Equation (1) to obtain the following description of the manner in which the second-order statistics of the image change with scale:

$$E\left(|\Delta I_{\Delta x}|\right)\|\Delta x\|^{-H} = E\left(|\Delta I_{\Delta x=1}|\right) \quad (5)$$

where $E\left(|\Delta I_{\Delta x}|\right)$ is the expected value of the change in intensity over distance Δx. Equation (5) is an hypothesized relation among the image intensities; a hypothesis that we may test statistically. If we find that Equation (5) is true of the image intensity surface within a homogeneous region, then the Fractal Imaging theorem

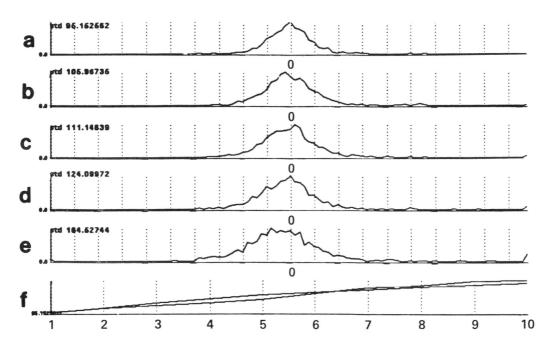

Figure 3 Results of testing for "fractalness" in a typical texture patch. Each distribution corresponds to the intensity differences at different pixel distances (see Equation 5).

tells us that the viewed surface must be a 3-D fractal Brownian surface, and thus that the the fractal model is appropriate. It is an important characteristic of the fractal model that we can know when (and when *not*) to use the model.

6.1 Evaluating the model

To evaluate the suitability of the fractal model for natural surfaces, the homogeneous regions from each of six images of natural scenes were densely sampled. In addition, detailed images of twelve textured surfaces (see Brodatz, 1966) were digitized and examined. The intensity values within each of these regions were

then approximated by a fractal Brownian function and the approximation error observed.

Figure 3 shows the results for a typical textured patch. The graphs (a) to (e) show the distribution of intensity differences (i.e. the second-order difference statistics) at one, two, three, five and ten pixel distances; the distributions are approximately Gaussian. Figure 3 (f) shows a plot of the standard deviation of these distributions as a function of scale (i.e. $E(|\Delta I_{\Delta x}|)$ as a function of Δx in pixels). Overlaid on this graph is a least-squares fit of a fractal rule. As can be seen, the fit is quite good—implying that the intensity surface in this region is actually a fractal

Brownian function, at least over the 10 : 1 range of scales measured.

For the majority of the textures examined (77%), the fit was as good or better than the example shown. In 15% of the cases the region was constant except for random, zero-mean perturbations; consequently, the fractal function correctly approximates the image data, although the estimated fractal dimension is equal to the topological dimension. The fit was poor in only 8% of the regions examined. In some of these cases it appeared that the image digitization had become saturated, and thus the poor fit may have been artifactual.

The fact that the vast majority of the regions examined were quite well approximated by a fractal Brownian function indicates that the fractal model will often provide a useful description of natural surfaces and their images. In those cases for which the fractal description is appropriate, the only statistical structure that remains unaccounted for by the fractal Brownian function is zero-mean unit-variance Gaussian noise—indicating that the fractal description effectively exhausts all of the second-order difference information within the image.

6.2 The relationship between fractals and regular patterns

Fractal Brownian functions do *not*, of course, describe regular or large-scale spatial structures such as are seen in the image of a brick wall or a tiled floor. Such structures must be accounted for by other means. It is important to realize, however, that while fractal Brownian surfaces are required to have particular second-order statistics, this does *not* mean that they cannot be regularly patterned.

To understand this, consider that the probability of a random number generator producing the string "1010..." is exactly the same as the probability of any other particular string with half 1's, half 0's. Both strings have the same statistics, and thus the same probability of occurrence, although one is regularly patterned and the other isn't. Similarly, a surface such as a brick wall can be a perfectly good Brownian fractal: the overall distribution of second-order statistics is correct; it simply contains position-dependent patterns.

The fact that fractal Brownian functions can exhibit regularities allows us to smoothly pass from random, chaotic surfaces to regular, patterned ones within the same conceptual framework. Regular surfaces, for instance, can be generated by adding constraints (patterning) to the random-number generator used in conjunction with computer graphics techniques for recursively generating fractal Brownian functions (Fournier et al., 1982).

6.3 Detection of edge points

It is an important characteristic of the fractal model that we can determine its appropriateness for particular image data, because this allows us to know when, and when *not*, to use the model. If we discover an image region that does not fit the fractal model, the Fractal Imaging Theorem allows us to infer that we are not viewing a homogeneous fractal surface.

Boundaries between homogeneous regions are one example of a physical configuration that does not fit well into the fractal model. Thus, when we examine points that lie on the boundary between two image regions we find that the fit between the fractal model and the image data is normally poor. The fact that boundaries seem to be the most common event giving rise to a nonfractal intensity surface provides a method of detecting image points that are likely to be edges.

One simple way to find such points is examination of the computed fractal dimension. It turns out that when we compute the fractal dimension of a region covering a boundary between two homogeneous areas, by using the region's Fourier power spectrum, we normally calculate a fractal dimension that is less than the topological dimension. As this is a physical impossibility, the implication is that the assumptions of the fractal model are inappropriate for that specific image data. When we observe a measured fractal dimension that is less than the topological dimension, therefore, we can reasonably expect that we have found a texture edge. Examples of this will be shown in the following sections.

7.0 Inferring Surface Properties

Fractal functions appear to provide a good description of natural surface textures and their images; thus, it is natural to use the fractal model for texture segmentation, classification and shape-from-texture. The first four headings of this section describe the research that has been performed in this area, and indicate likely directions for further research.

Fractal functions with $H \approx 0$ can be used to model smooth surfaces and their reflectance properties. For the first time, therefore, we can offer a single model encompassing both image shading and texture, with shading as a limiting case in the spectrum of texture granularity.

The fractal model thus allows us to make a reasonable and rigorous definition of the categories "texture" and "shading," thus enabling us to discover similarities and differences between them. The final heading of this section briefly discusses this result.

7.1 Some examples of texture segmentation

The Fractal Imaging Theorem tells us that, within a homogeneous region, the fractal dimension in the image is dependent upon that of the 3-D surface, thus giving us a technique for inferring a 3-D property of the viewed surface that closely corresponds to people's concept of roughness/smoothness. This suggests that measurement of the fractal dimension in the image will be useful in segmenting natural imagery.

In the following examples, the fractal dimension was measured using a least-squares regression of the Fourier power spectrum response over an 8×8 block of pixels. That is, since the power spectrum $P(f)$ is proportional to f^{-2H-1}, we may use a linear regression on the log of the observed power spectrum as a function of f (e.g. a regression using $\log(P(f)) = -(2H+1)\log(f) + k$ for various values of f) to determine the power H and thus the linearly-related fractal dimension.

Orientational information was not incorporated into measurement of the local fractal dimension—i.e. differences in dimension among various image directions at a point were collapsed into one average measurement. Repeating this process for each block of pixels produces a "fractal dimension image" which was then histogramed. This histogram of the fractal dimension was then broken at the "val-

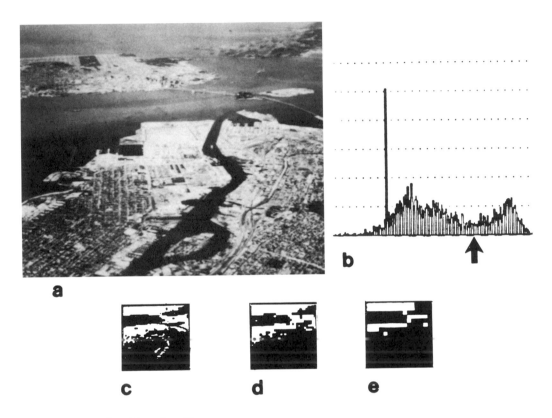

Figure 4 San Francisco Bay.

leys" between the modes of the histogram, and the image segmented into pixel neighborhoods belonging to one mode or another.

Figure 4(a) is an aerial view of San Francisco Bay. Figure 4(b) shows a histogram of the fractal dimensions computed over the whole image. Figure 4(c) shows the segmentation obtained by thresholding at the breakpoint indicated by the arrow under (b); each pixel in (c) corresponds to an 8 × 8 block of pixels in the original image. As can be seen, a good segmentation into water and land was achieved—one that cannot be obtained by thresholding on image intensity. The values to the left of the large spike in (b) have a computed fractal dimension which is less than the topological dimension; these points all occur along the water-land boundary and partially delineate that boundary.

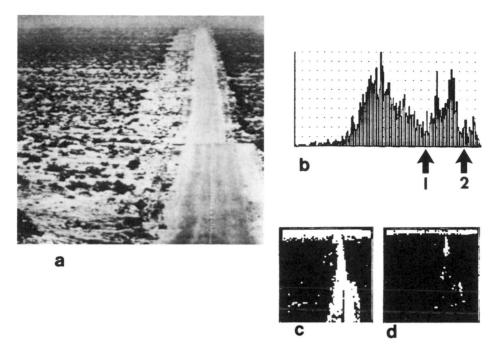

Figure 5 A desert scene.

This image was then averaged down, from 512 × 512 pixels into 256 × 256 and 128 × 128 pixel images, and the fractal dimension recomputed for each of the reduced images. Figures 4(d) and (e) illustrate the segmentations that result from using the *same* cut point as employed in the original full-resolution segmentation, demonstrating stability across wide (4 : 1) variations in scale.

A second example is the desert scene shown in Figure 5(a). This scene was segmented into three classes, based on the histogram shown in (b); the segmentations are shown in (c) (road and sky versus desert) and (d) (road and desert versus sky). As can be seen, there is a good segmentation into desert, road and sky.

Several other images have been segmented in this manner. In each case a good segmentation was achieved. The computed fractal dimension, and thus the segmentation, was found to be stable over at least 4 : 1 variations in scale; most were stable over a range of 8 : 1. Stability of the fractal description is to be expected, because the fractal dimension of the image is directly related to the fractal dimension of the viewed surface, which is a property of natural surfaces that has been shown to be invariant with respect to transformations of scale.

The fact that the fractal description of texture is stable with respect to scale is a critically important property. After all, consider: *how can we hope to compute a stable, viewer-independent representation of the world if our information about the world is not stable with respect to scale?* This example of texture property

20

measurement reiterates what we observed earlier, i.e. the fact that the fractal dimension of the surface is *necessary* to any consistent description of a natural surface.

7.2 Relationship to texture models

The fact that the fractal dimension of the image data can be measured by using either co-occurrence statistics in conjunction with Equation (1), or by means of the Fourier power spectrum, suggests one interesting aspect of the fractal model: it highlights a formal link between correlation and co-occurrence texture measures (Deguchi & Morishita, 1978; Haraleck et al., 1973; Laws, 1980; Pratt et al., 1978; Rosenfeld & Troy, 1970) and Fourier techniques (Bajcsy & Lieberman, 1976; Maurer, 1974). The mathematical results Mandelbrot derives for fractal Brownian functions show that the way interpixel differences change with distance determines the rate at which the Fourier power spectrum falls off as frequency is increased, and vice versa.

Thus, it appears that the fractal model offers potential for unifying and simplifying the co-occurrence and Fourier texture descriptions. If we believe that natural surface textures and their images are fractal (as seems to be indicated by the previous results), then the fractal dimension is the most relevant parameter in differentiating among textures. In this case we would expect both the Fourier and co-occurrence techniques to provide reasonable texture segmentations, as both yield sufficient information to determine the fractal dimension. The advantage of the fractal model would be that it captures a simple physical relationship underlying the texture structure—a relationship lost with either of the other two characterizations of texture.

7.3 Shading and texture

One of the most serious problems in determining local surface orientation N is that current shape-from-shading operators are limited to smooth surfaces (Ikeuchi & Horn, 1981), while shape-from-texture techniques have been developed only for the case of surface markings on smooth surfaces (Bajcsy & Lieberman, 1976; Witkin, 1981). They cannot, therefore, be reliably applied to the rough, natural surfaces described by the fractal surface model. Moreover, we cannot even discriminate "shaded" surfaces from "textured" ones, so that we cannot know what technique to apply in any case.

Fractal functions with $H \approx 0$ are planar except for random variations described by the function $F(z)$ in Equation (1). If the variance of $F(z)$ is small people judge these surfaces to be "smooth"; thus, the fractal model with small values of H is appropriate for modeling smooth, shaded regions of the image. If the surface has significant local fluctuations, i.e. if $F(z)$ is large, the surface is seen as being smooth but textured, in the sense that markings or some other 2-D effect is modifing the appearance of the underlying smooth surface. In contrast, fractals with $H > 0$ are not perceived as smooth, but rather as being rough or three-dimensionally textured.

The fractal model can therefore encompass shading, 2-D texture, and 3-D texture, with shading as a limiting case in the spectrum of 3-D texture granularity. The fractal model thus allows us to make a reasonable, rigorous and perceptually plausible definition of the categories "textured" *versus* "shaded," "rough" *versus* "smooth," in terms that can be measured by using the image data.

The ability to differentiate between "smooth" and "rough" surfaces is critical to the performance of current shape-from-shading and shape-from-texture techniques (Ikeuchi & Horn, 1981; Kender, 1979; Pentland, 1983, 1984; Witkin, 1981). For surfaces that, from a perceptual standpoint, are smooth ($H \approx 0$) and not 2-D textured ($\text{Var}(F(z))$ small), it seems appropriate to apply shading techniques. Indeed, it is *only* in these cases that measurement noise can be reduced (by averaging) to the levels required by shape-from-shading techniques without simultaneously destroying evidence of surface shape.

For surfaces that have 2-D texture it is more appropriate to apply available texture measures. Thus, use of the fractal surface model to infer qualitative 3-D shape (namely, smoothness/roughness), has the potential of significantly improving the utility of many other machine vision methods.

8.0 Computing a Description

Current methods for representing the three-dimensional world suffer from a certain awkwardness and inflexibility that makes them difficult to envisage as the basis for human-performance-level capabilities. They have encountered problems in dealing with partial knowledge or uncertain information, and they become implausibly complex when confronted with the problem of representing a crumpled newspaper, a clump of leaves or a puffy cloud. Furthermore, they seem ill-suited to solving the problem of representing a *class* of objects, or determining that a particular object is a member of that class.

What is wrong with conventional shape representations? One major problem is that they make too much information explicit. Experiments in human perception (Norman, 1976) lead one to believe that our representation of a crumpled newspaper (for instance) is not accurate enough to recover every z value; rather, it seems that we remember the general "crumpledness" and a few of the major features, such as the general outline. The rest of the newspaper's detailed structure is ignored; it is unimportant, *random*.

From the point of view of constructing a representation, the only important constraints on shape are the crumpledness and general outline. What we would like to do is somehow capture the notion of *constrained chance*, that is, the intuition that "a crumpled newspaper has x, y and z structural regularities and the rest is just variable detail," thus allowing us to avoid dealing with inconsequential (random) variations and to reason instead only about the structural regularities.

8.1 The process of computing a description

How shall we go about computing such a "constrained chance" description?[3] Let us consider the problem formally and see

---

[3]The term "representation" will be used to refer to the scheme for representing shapes, while the term "description" will be reserved for specific instances. Thus, one can compute a description of some object; it will be a member of the class of shapes that can be accounted for within the representation.

where that leads us. The process of computing a shape description (given some sensory data) seems best characterized as attempting to confirm or deny such hypotheses as "shape **X** is consistent with these sense data." Computation of a shape description, therefore, seems to be a problem in induction (Gregory, 1972).

If, naively, we try to use an inductive method, we start with the set of all possible shape hypotheses; we then attempt to winnow the set down to a small number of hypotheses that are confirmed by the sensory data. The "set of all shape hypotheses," however, is much too large to work with. Consequently, we must take a slightly different tack.

Using the Notion of Constrained Chance

Rather than attempting to enumerate "all shape hypotheses" explicitly, let us instead construct a *shape generator* that uses a random number generator to produce a surface shape description (I shall shortly describe how to do this). If we were to run this shape generator for an infinite period, it would eventually produce instances of every shape within a large class of shapes. If the generator were so constructed that the class of shapes produced was exactly the set of "all hypotheses" about shape, then the program for the shape generator, together with a the program for the random number generator, would comprise a description of the set of all shape hypotheses.

The shape generator illustrates how the notion of constrained chance may be used to obtain a compact description of an infinite set of shapes. By changing the constraints that determine how the output of the random number generator is translated into shape, we can change the set of shapes described; specifically, we can introduce constraints that rule out some classes of shape and thus restrict the set of shapes that are described. The ability to progressively restrict the set of shapes described allows us to use the constrained-chance shape generator as the basis for induction, rather than being forced to use the explicitly enumerated set of all shape hypotheses.

The process of computing a "constrained chance description" is straightforward. We use image data to infer (using knowledge of the physics of image formation) constraints on the shape, and then introduce those constraints into the shape generator. The end result will be a programlike description that is capable of producing all the shapes that are consistent with the image data; i.e. we shall have a description of the shapes confirmed by the image data. This, then, is the type of description we wanted: a description of shape that contains the important structural regularities that can be inferred from the image (e.g., crumpledness, outline), but one that leaves everything else as variable, random.

Some People are Already Doing This

Something very much like this constrained-chance representation is already being widely utilized in the computer graphics community. Natural-looking shapes are produced by a simple fractal program that recursively subdivides the region to be filled, introducing random jaggedness of appropriate magnitude at each step (Carpenter, 1980; Norton, 1982). The jaggedness is determined by specifying the fractal dimension. The shapes that can be produced in this manner range from planar surfaces to mountainlike shapes, depending on the fractal dimension. Current graphics technology often employs fractal shape generators in a more constrained mode; often the overall, general shape or the boundary conditions are specified beforehand. Thus, a scene is often constructed by first specifying initial constraints on the general shape, and then using a fractal shape generator to fill in the surface with appropriately jagged (or smooth) details. The description employed in such graphics systems, therefore, is exactly a constrained-chance description: important details are specified, and everything else is left unspecified except in a qualitative manner.

This type of description bears a close relationship to surface interpolation methods. Typically, such schemes fit a smooth surface that satisfies whatever boundary conditions are available. The initial boundary conditions, together with the interpolation function, constitute a precise description of the surface shape. Such schemes are limited to smooth surfaces, however, and therefore are incapable of dealing with most natural shapes. In contrast, a fractal-based representation allows either rough or smooth surfaces to be fit to the initial boundary conditions, depending upon the fractal dimension. This method of description, therefore, is quite capable of describing most natural surfaces—and that is why the graphics community is turning to the use of fractal-based descriptions for natural surfaces.

In order to make use of this type of description it is necessary to be able to specify the surface shape in a *qualitative* manner, i.e. how rugged is the topography? This specification of qualitative shape can be accomplished by fixing the fractal dimension. The fact that we have recently developed a method of inferring the fractal dimension of the 3-D surface directly from the image data means that we are now able, for the first time, to actually compute a fractal or constrained-chance description of a real scene from its image.

Not only terrestrial topography has been modeled by use of a constrained-chance representation, but also clouds, ponds, riverbeds, snowflakes, ocean surf and stars, just to name a few examples (Carpenter, 1980; Mandelbrot, 1982; Norton, 1982). Researchers have also used constrained-chance generators to produce plant shapes (Mandelbrot, 1977, 1982; Yawaguchi, 1982). A very natural-looking tree can be produced by recursively applying a random number generator and simple constraints on branching geometry. In each case a random number generator plus a surprisingly small number of constraints can be used to produce very good models of apparently complex natural phenomena. Thus, there is hope for extending this approach well beyond the domain of land topography.

8.2 An example of computing a description

Figure 6 illustrates an actual example of computing such a description. Figure 6(a) is an image of a real mountain. Let us suppose that we wished to use the image data to construct a three-dimensional model of the rightmost peak (arrow), perhaps for the purpose of predicting whether or not we could climb it. I will take the standard fractal technology used in the computer graphics community as the unconstrained "primal" shape generator, as it provides an apparently accurate model of a wide range of natural surfaces.

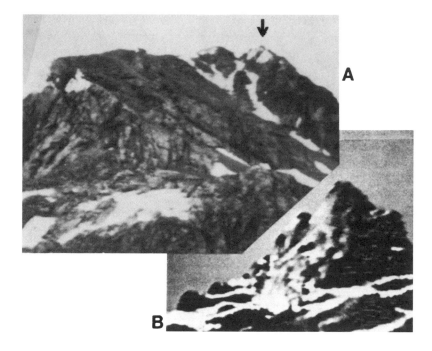

Figure 6 An example of computing a constrained-chance description.

All that is necessary to construct a description of this mountain peak is to extract shape constraints from the image and insert them into the primal shape generator. The fractal dimension of the 3-D surface is the principal parameter (constraint) required by our fractal shape generator; roughly speaking, it determines the ruggedness of the surface. The fractal dimension of the 3-D surface in the region near the rightmost peak was inferred from the fractal dimension of the image intensity surface in that area by use of the empirically-derived relationship between surface and image. Constraint on the general outline of this peak was derived from the estimated z-values of distinguished points (those with high curvature) along the boundary between sky and mountain. These two constraints, together with the

shape generator, *are* a 3-D representation of this peak; the question is: how good a representation? A view of a 3-D model derived from this representation is shown in Figure 6(b). It appears that these simple constraints are sufficient for computing a good perceptually adequate description.

9.0 Summary

Fractal functions seem to provide a good model of natural surface shapes. Many basic physical processes produce fractal surfaces. Fractal surfaces also *look* like natural surfaces, and so have come into widespread uses in the computer graphics community. Furthermore, we have conducted a survey of natural imagery and found that a fractal model of imaged 3-D surfaces furnishes an accurate description of both textured and shaded image regions. The fractal dimension of the surface is highly correlated with its perceived roughness, and can easily be computed from image data.

Fractal functions are also useful for addressing the related problems of representing complex natural shapes such as mountains, clouds, ocean surf, trees, etc. A constrained-chance fractal model seems particularly useful for representing these shapes.

Acknowledgement: The research reported herein was supported by National Science Foundation Grant No. DCR-83-12766, the Defense Advanced Research Projects Agency under Contract No. MDA 903-83-C-0027 (monitored by the U.S. Army Engineer Topographic Laboratory) and a grant from the Systems Development Foundation.

References

Bajcsy, R. & Lieberman, L. (1974) Computer description of real outdoor scenes. *Proceedings of 2d International Joint Conference on Pattern Recognition*, Copenhagen, August, pp. 174–179.

Bajcsy, R. & Lieberman, L. (1976) Texture gradient as a depth cue. *Computer Graphics and Image Processing*, 5:52–67.

Brodatz, P. (1966) *Textures: A Photographic Album for Artists and Designers*, New York: Dover.

Carpenter, L.C. (1980) "Vol Libre," Computer Generated Movie.

Deguchi, K. & Morishita, I. (1978) Texture characterization and texture-based image partitioning using two-dimensional linear estimation techniques. *IEEE Transactions on Computers*, C-27:739–745.

Fournier, A., Fussel, D. & Carpenter, L. (1982) Computer rendering of stochastic models. *Communications of the ACM*, 25(6):371–384.

Gregory, R.L. (1972) *Eye and Brain: The Psychology of Seeing.* New York: McGraw-Hill.

Haralick, R.M., Shanmugam, K. & Dinstein, J. (1973) Textural features for image classification. *IEEE Transactions on Systems, Man and Cybernetics*, SMC-3, pp. 610–621.

Ikeuchi, K. & Horn, B.K.P.H. (1981) Numerical shape from shading and occluding boundaries. *Artif. Intell.*, 17:141–184.

Kawaguchi, Y. (1982) A morphological study of the form of nature. *Computer Graphics*, 16:223–232.

Kender, J.R. (1979) Shape from texture: an aggregation transform that maps a class of textures into surface orientation. *Proc. Sixth Int. Joint Conf. Artificial Intell.*, Tokyo, Japan.

Laws, K. (1980) Textured image segmentation. Report 940, USC Image Processing Institute, Los Angeles, California.

Mandelbrot, B.B. (1977) Fractals: form, chance and dimension. San Francisco: W. H. Freeman and Co.,, California.

Mandelbrot, B.B. (1982) *The Fractal Geometry of Nature.* Freeman: San Francisco.

Maurer, H. (1974) Texture analysis with fourier series. *Proceedings of the 9th International Symposium on Remote Sensing of the Environment*, Ann Arbor, Michigan, April, pp 1411–1420.

20

Norman, D.A. (1976) *Memory and Attention*. New York: Wiley.

Norton, A. (1982) Generation and display of geometric fractals in 3-D. *Computer Graphics*, 16:61:67.

Pentland, A.P. (1983) Local computation of shape. SRI Artificial Intelligence Center Technical Memo 272.

Pentland, A.P. (1984) Fractal-based description of natural scenes. *IEEE Transactions on Pattern Analysis and Machine Intelligence*, PAMI-6, pp. 661–675.

Pentland, A.P. (1984) Shading into texture. *Proc. American Association for Artificial Intelligence 1984*, pp. 269-273, Austin TX.

Pratt, W.K., Faugeras, O.D. & Gagalowicz, A. (1978) Visual discrimination of stochastic texture. *IEEE Transactions on Systems, Man and Cybernetics*, SMC-8:460–473.

Richardson, L.F. (1961) The problem of contiguity: an appendix of statistics of deadly quarrels. *General Systems Yearbook*, vol. 6, pp. 139–187.

Rosenfeld, A. & Troy, E.B. (1970) Visual texture analysis. *IEEE Conference on Feature Extraction and Analysis*, Argonne, Ill. October, pp. 115–124.

Witkin, A.P. (1981) Recovering surface shape and orientation from texture. *Artif. Intell.*, 17:17–47.

Adapted from *Proc. IEEE Conf. on Computer Vision and Pattern Recognition*, Arlington, VA (1983).

IV

Sound Interpretation

Sound Interpretation

1.0 Introduction

How can we possibly interpret the myriad of sounds about us? If we examined the sound-pressure waveform (by looking at the output of a microphone, for example), we would see a complex, almost chaotic function of time. Embedded within this single-valued function are the various sounds, such as the passing car, a typewriter in action, the air-conditioner, or a conversation we overhear. Yet in spite of the complex mixing of these sounds, we easily decompose the acoustic signal into its meaningful components.

Most attempts at solving this problem have taken speech perception as their paradigm. Here, we will continue to be concerned primarily with object recognition. Speech, like writing and reading is a specialized skill of advanced animals, and understanding speech need not be the best route to understanding how we interpret the pattern of natural sounds that comprise most of the acoustic spectrum about us. In addition, we favor beginning our explorations into sound peception by choosing more modest goals. Our more limited goal, then, is: given a stream of intensities arriving at the ear, how can we separate and describe the sources of the sounds which produced this stream? In a very simple case, we might even seek to answer "Is the sound source Animal, Vegetable, or Mineral?" (Richards, 1982).

In contrast to vision, where our basic sensory data base can easily be visualized as a 2D picture projected onto our retinae, the acoustic scene is much harder to grasp intuitively, for we are primarily visual animals. (The ratio between fibers in the primary visual and auditory pathways is about 30 to 1.) We begin these next selections, therefore, with a comparison between the visual and auditory systems, and the data they deal with. Searle notes several important differences. First, for each eye the visual data base is a two dimensional spatial array, with the output of each element in the array (receptor or nerve) being modulated in time by a fluctuating pattern of intensities. The auditory input at the ear, on the other hand, has only one input element modulated in time (namely the tympanic membrane), and hence has zero spatial dimensions (see Figure 1). From here, the sound pressure waves are transduced in stages, eventually producing a wave motion of the basilar membrane, which in effect results in a short-term Fourier decomposition of the input signal. Position along the basilar membrane thus corresponds to temporal frequency, and hence neurons responding to the motion of this membrane are sensitive to different frequencies depending upon their location. The signal carried by the auditory nerve is thus a scale-space decomposition, except the dimensions are temporal frequency (Hz) and time rather than spatial frequency and space as in vision.

A second difference between the auditory and visual modalities is the wavelength of the signals. It is extremely difficult to grasp the fact that the acoustic

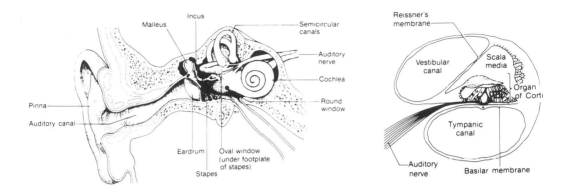

Figure 1 Gross anatomy of the human ear (left) and a cross-section through the cochlea (right). After travelling through the auditory canal, the acoustic signal impinges on the eardrum, whose vibrations are mechanically amplified by three bones in the middle ear, with the last of these (the stapes) driving the cochlear fluid, which fills the cochlear canals (right). Displacements of this fluid in the vestibular canal are relieved in the tympanic canal, causing motion of the basilar membrane, which constitutes part of the partition between the two canals. Hair cells lying on this membrane are then activated, producing an electrical response that is transmitted down the auditory nerve (from Goldstein, 1980).

wavelengths we hear range over two orders of magnitude from a few centimeters to meters, rather than over a very narrow, millimicron range as in vision. Hence acoustic signals are not simply reflected as light is, but interact viciously with visible objects and surrounding surface textures. Reflections of the sound waves off such objects may distort and contaminate the incoming wave—such as echos do, confounding the source signal much more drastically than in vision where the spectral content of the illuminant is essentially the only object-independent contaminant. A major problem in sound interpretation, then, is to discover source properties that are preserved under a variety of acoustic enviroments.

2.0 Levels of Representations

In vision, Marr & Nishihara (1978) proposed three different kinds of data structures, or levels of representation: 1) the Primal Sketch, 2) The 2 1/2 D Sketch and 3) The 3D Model. These have natural analogs in audition. The Primal Sketch is an intensity-based representation that serves to recast the incoming signals in a new form more convenient for future processing. Appropriate tokens might be onset or offsets or the strength of the signal and its temporal derivatives, the frequencies contained in the signal, and their derivatives, and also the intensity differences or delays between the signals arriving at the two ears. All of these are physiologically plausible (Evans, 1968;

Source	Power	Oscillator	Resonator	Coupler
Trumpet	lungs	lips	tube	horn
Violin	bow	string	post	body
Voice	lungs	glottis	tract	mouth
Piano	hammer	string	sound board	body/board
Drum	stick	membrane	body cavity	body sides
Gong	mallet	plate	plate	plate
Rain	gravity	drop fracture	ground	ground
Applause	hands	palm	concert hall	walls
Brook	gravity	turbulent fall	bank	bank

Table 1 Components of some familiar sound sources.

Knudsen & Konishi, 1978). A richer Primal Sketch might also include Formant tracking or temporal patterns. At the next level of representation, the 2 1/2 D Sketch, assertions are made about "visible" surface properties. In audition these might include such things as the direction of a sound source, the type of sound source (bell, cylindrical resonator, drum, whistle, impact, etc.), the material struck (metal, wood, glass, etc.),or the motion of the source. Finally, we have a 3D Model representation for the source that is object and action based: Is the source a bird or flute? What size? And what is its behavior? In these Selections, as in vision, there is a tight coupling between the 2 1/2 D and 3D Model representations. Indeed, because most sound sources are spatially isotropic, we shall see that the need for a 3D "volumetric" model is debatable.

3.0 The Acoustic Primal Sketch

Our raw primal sketch will be the short-term Fourier transform described by Searle in Selection 21. As in vision, the (temporal) filters in this scale-space are logarithmically related, thus allowing a balance between good frequency resolution and good temporal discrimination (see Figure 21-2). The result is a landscape of ridges and valleys, which reflect the structure of the acoustic signal (see Figure 21-1). Within this energy landscape several sound sources may be embedded. One powerful scheme for separating these sources is to obtain two separate "views" of the signals. Lyons shows how the binaural processing of the mixed signals obtained from two sources may be analysed to yield separated sound streams (Figure 22-2,3). Here, the proposed cross-correlation technique integrates directional cues based on signal phase, envelope modulation, onset time, and loudness—a battery of raw primal sketch features. A discussion of the origin and relative sensitivity of these features when used for binaural localization is given elsewhere (Altes, 1978; Searle et al., 1976).

Lyons' approach to sound source separation may be likened to the random-dot stereograms of Julesz (1971). In both cases, the separation technique uses no explicit monaural (or monocular) information about the sources. In vision, such information would be candidate occluding edges, object color, texture, or motion. In audition, the analogs might be onset or offset time (the former is used by Lyons, but not as an explicit token), tonal quality such as vibrato, harmonic structure, and frequency change. To utilize these features explicitly, additional primal sketch processing must take place, along the lines suggested by Riley in Selection 23. However, rather than choosing such acoustic features arbitrarily, one should first explore how sounds are produced. What physical processes are responsible for the acoustic signals we hear, and how do these processes differ from one another? The better the sound source is characterized, the easier the binaural localization task.

4.0 2 1/2 D Representations

Selection 24 by Sundberg discusses the four major components of all sound sources, using the human voice as an example. These components are: 1) a power source, P; 2) an oscillator, O; 3) a resonator R; and 4) a coupler, C. Table 1 gives examples of these components, stressing musical instruments whose physics have been studied extensively. We propose the "PORC" decomposition as a general model

for understanding the acoustic behavior of sound sources. Thus, the sound level, A, reaching the ear can be viewed as

$$A(f, t) = k \sum_{i}^{n} g_i(P, O, R, C) \qquad (1)$$

where each g_i is some function of time, frequency, and amplitude depending upon the source character (see Figure 24-2), and where k is an (unknown) environmental parameter representing the echos, reflections, reverberations, absorptions, etc. of the transmitting medium and surroundings. Obviously, this equation is as horrendous as the image-intensity equation required for vision understanding. Yet somehow our auditory system knows how to "solve" this equation—at least in certain instances—because we are able to separate the g_i's and to discount the confounding effects of the medium, k.

Although binaural listening can aid in solving equation (1) by isolating certain mixed sources, it is also clear that the single ear is quite adequate for deciphering most acoustic environments. (The cocktail party problem is special, because the sources are very similar.) In the natural world, most sources are quite different— i.e. their physical causes are different— and often they appear singly with quite distinctive onset and offsets, especially the narrow-band sounds produced by animals. In these cases, one might seek source signatures which involve constraints between the "PORC" model components. For example, small animals of necessity can produce only high-frequency sounds from their small vocal tracts, and the total power of these sounds will be less than that, say, of an elephant. Furthermore, we expect certain harmonics from the "open cylinder" vocal resonators of the mam-

MODE   FREQUENCY

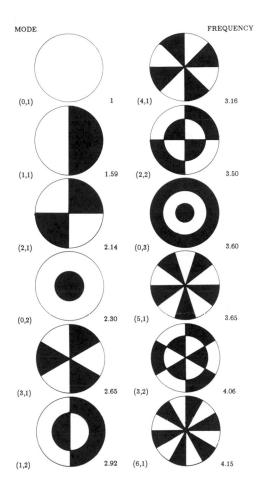

(0,1)   1   (4,1)   3.16

(1,1)   1.59   (2,2)   3.50

(2,1)   2.14   (0,3)   3.60

(0,2)   2.30   (5,1)   3.65

(3,1)   2.65   (3,2)   4.06

(1,2)   2.92   (6,1)   4.15

Figure 3 Some of the radial and circular modes of vibration for an ideal membrane, which include the modes of a steel plate, drum or bell. Note that the sequence is not harmonic. (Adapted from Rossing, 1982.)

mals, which are characteristically different from the resonances of enclosed cavities. In particular, the harmonics of a cylinder open at one end only, as discussed by Sundberg, will increase in proportion to $(2n+1)/4$. However, a cylinder with both ends either open or closed will have har-

monics at intervals proportional to $n/2$. One might expect, therefore, that a harmonic analysis of the resonant properties (R) of the source would be critical to sound interpretation (Eggen & Houtsma, 1986). This may be so for certain simple bird-like or animal sources. However, unfortunately in the more general case a decomposition of a sound into its overtones becomes very complicated. For example, even the simple rectangular resonator can have a variety of closely spaced modes, which are specified by

$$f_i = \frac{c}{2}(p^2/l^2 + q^2/w^2 + r^2/h^2)^{\frac{1}{2}} \quad (2)$$

where c is the velocity of sound, l, w, h are respectively the length width and height of the box and p, q, r are indexed from 0. A struck bell will have harmonics at almost every third octave (see Figure 3). Even the simple drum has a complex spectrum, which can be altered depending upon where it is struck (Figure 4). These complexities can be experienced easily by tapping a metal rod. If the rod is hit in the middle and held at one end, the result is a dull "thud" because the transverse vibrations are quickly damped. To generate the typical "ring" the rod must be held near the middle, allowing the transverse vibrations to continue without damping. [Incidently, the tone of the metal ring is dictated primarily by the sinusoidal vibrations of the metal, not by Equation (2)]. Thus, an analysis based solely on the harmonic content of the sound may yield little insight into the nature of the source. Instead, it appears more promising to study the relationships between the "PORC" components, such as those illustrated in Table 1. The very nature of the human vocal apparatus, which couples the power supply, vocal chords, and vocal tract, results in a modulation of the resonant speech modes—a vibrato—which when added to a pure tone immediately gives the sound a "human" quality (MacAdams, 1984). On the other hand, metal can not generate its own sound—it must be struck by an external object, and hence its tonal quality must better approximate an ideal ring. Rain fall, on the other hand, has no resonances but is simply a pattern of impacts whose individual frequency spectra depend principally upon drop size and velocity (see Problem 26-2). Sounds such as these merit study to determine constraints which force a unique interpretation.

In Selections 25 and 26 we present two other approaches to sound identification. Neither of these solves explicitly for a unique sound source, but rather shows how two attributes of sound sources can be recovered to aid in identification. The first shows how assertions of material type can be made (or rejected) when it is known that the power source is external to the object. The second illustrates the utility of examining the temporal pattern of sound activity.

Most sounds are generated by physical objects. In Selection 25 we ask whether it is possible to tell what material the sound source is made of. Is it glass, metal, or wood? For sounds elicited by a single crisp blow to an object, these distinctions are made easily. The blow to a piece of wood sounds quite different from the tapping of crystal glass. The recognition process proposed in Selection 25 is to compare the "ring" of the material with the decay of the "ring". Thus, for anelastic materials, the mechanical model of Zener shows that the decay should be proportional to the "Q", or bandwidth of the resonant mode, just as for the analogous

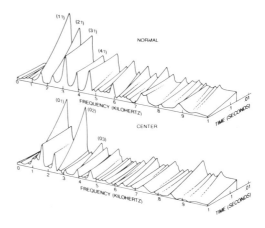

Figure 4 Two spectral diagrams for a kettledrum struck in different positions. Note how the amplitudes and decay rates of the overtones differ. The normal spectrum emphasizes the related (1,1), (2,1), (3,1) and (4,1) modes and conveys a definite pitch with a "ring". The center stroke emphasizes the unharmonic modes (0,1), (0,2) and (0,3), which decay rapidly as a "thump" (from Rossing, 1982).

electrical circuit. If these two measures lie along the constraint curve of Figure 25-4, then a specific material assertion is justified. If not, then probably other factors have entered into the sound production process, such as external clamping at an anti-node. Note that critical to the inference process is that the two parameters, Q and t, must be predictive of one another, for they are measures of the same physical parameter of the material, namely its internal friction. Any single measure alone would be insufficient, for we could never be sure if that single measured value was one free of damping or deformation, for example. Points which lie along the constraint curve of Figure 25-4 thus provide reliable measures of internal friction, which we are using as the material's signature.

A second approach to identifying sound sources or properties is to look at the temporal pattern of the sound. The breaking versus the bouncing of a glass bottle is the example treated by Warren & Verbrugge in Selection 26. Surprisingly, little has been done in this area, considering both the richness of the information available in temporal patterns, and the ease of generating these patterns. The action of a pair of scissors; the crunching of a piece of paper; footfalls; a typewriter; the biting of an apple—there are a myriad of sounds that can be analyzed in terms of the sound pattern, first breaking the sound into its "distinctive parts" and then exploring the relations between these parts just as we proposed in visual obect recognition.

4.0 3D Model Representations

In vision, the 3D Model representation is an object-centered description independent of viewing geometry. Earlier, we argued in favor of a set of 2 1/2 D views which captured the basic topology of the object. What is the auditory analog? If a sound is not directional, but rather radiates isotropically, then the viewing geometry is not critical—any view will result in the same percept. Hence if the 2 1/2 D representation of the sound is typical of that for a bird, why not let that data structure also be part of the 3D model? Essentially this is what we argued for in the construction of our 3D visual representation, preferring a collection of 2 1/2 D views which captured the basic topology of the object. Similarly, we can view our auditory model as consisting of

a hierarchy of "parts" of sub-sounds, such as the slicing and "click" of a pair of scissors, the starting of a car or fan, or even the special sequence of a bird call. To recognize these parts often requires an acute sense of temporal pattern and rhythm. Hence we end this chapter with a selection by Longuet-Higgins who gives an elegant analysis of temporal pattern information, partly from the viewpoint of language. What kind of conceptual structure might be required to represent temporal patterns? The perception of melodies—the rhythmic and tonal relations between individual tokens—is an excellent test. First, how can the underlying meter of a sound train be recovered in the presence of variations in onset time of the notes? Secondly, how does the "grammar" of the representation affect the interpretation of a note? Using the structural domain of music, Longuet-Higgins' treatment reflects directly upon the interpretation of speech sounds—of intonations which imply consequences or actions—and reveals how subtleties in temporal patterning can be recovered and used given a proper understanding of the contraints within the domain (see also Steedman, 1984). In a conceptual sense, is the bark of a dog one expressing anger or joy; or is a gait pattern typical of walking or running? Because music can express these differences, an understanding of this medium of communication is very appropriate.

5.0 A Plea

In sum, the interpretation of natural sounds is an almost virgin territory for computational studies. The physics is

Acknowledgment: Discussions with Campbell Searle were most helpful in organizing and preparing this introduction.

well understood, for acoustics is a mature science. Furthermore, given current computer technology, artificial sounds can be generated easily. What is missing is the interest in understanding the origins of the natural sounds we experience daily, and in their automatic recognition by machine. Why are some sounds so similar (as simulated hoof-beats of the Lone Ranger) although their physical origins are so different? This is important "Instant Psychophysics". Can we generate a taxonomy of sound classes based upon physical origins? What parameters must then be recovered in order to identify and separate these classes? What constraints apply within a class? This is an exciting field ripe for study.

References

Altes, R.A. (1978) Angle estimation and binaural processing in animal echolocation. *Jrl. Acoust. Soc. Amer.*, 63:155–174.

Eggen, J.H. & Houtsma, A.J.M. (1986) The pitch perception of bell sounds. Institute for Perception Research Annual Progress Report No. 21, Eindhoven, The Netherlands.

Evans, E.F. (1968) Cortical representation. In A.V.S. de Renck & J. Knight (eds.), *Hearing Mechanisms in Vertebrates*, London: J. & A. Churchill Ltd., pp. 272–287.

Goldstein, E.B. (1980) *Sensation and Perception.* Belmont, Calif.: Wadsworth.

Julesz, B. (1971) *Foundations of Cyclopean Perception.* Chicago, Ill.: University of Chicago Press.

Knudsen, E.I. & Konishi, M. (1978) Space and frequency are represented separately in auditory midbrain of the owl. *Jrl. Neurophysiol.*, 870–884.

MacAdams, S. (1984) "Spectral fusion, spectral parsing and the formation of auditory images". Ph.D. dissertation, Speech and Hearing Sciences, Stanford University.

Marr, D. & Nishihara, H.K. (1978) Visual information processing: artificial and the sensorium of sight. *Tech. Rev.*, 81, No. 1, 23 pages.

Richards, W. (1982) How to play twenty questions with nature and win. MIT A.I. Lab. Memo 660. See also Richards, W. & Bobick, A., in Z. Pylyshyn (ed.) *Computational Processes in Human Vision*, Norwood, N.J.: Ablex, (1988).

Rossing, T.D. (1982) The physics of kettledrums. *Sci. Amer.*, 247(5), November, 172.

Searle, C.L. & Braida, L.D., Davis, M.F. & Colburn, H.S. (1976) Model for auditory localization. *Jrl. Acoust. Soc. Am.*, 60:1164–1175.

Steedman, M.J. (1984) A generative grammar for jazz chord sequences. *Music Perception*, 2:52–77.

Representing Acoustic Information

C.L. Searle

Massachusetts Institute of Technology
Cambridge, MA

1.0 Introduction

Acoustic signals impinging upon the ear undergo a series of transformations aimed at making important information explicit. Here we discuss three such transformations. The first entails the transduction of acoustic signals to neural signals. The second is a scale-space representation, corresponding roughly to the first stage of a primal sketch. The third, which is quite speculative, draws upon analogies to color vision to set up a high-level representation for speech and complex sound patterns.

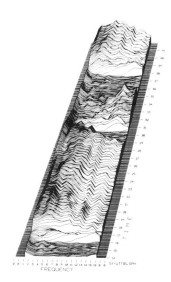

Figure 1 Running spectrum plot for the italicized portion of "*The watch*dog gave a warning growl". Abscissa: log frequency; ordinate: time.

2.0 Transduction: Biological Constraints

Several quite different experimental paradigms, auditory masking (Patterson, 1976), critical bands (summarized in Tobias, 1970), basilar membrane motion (Evans & Wilson, 1973; Johnstone & Boyle, 1967; Rhode, 1971), and tuning curves of primary auditory nerve fibers (Kiang & Moxon, 1974; Kiang et al., 1965), suggest that to first order, the peripheral auditory system performs a frequency analysis on the incoming sound with frequency resolution of about 100 Hz. A corresponding set of psychophysical measurements indicate that the temporal resolution of the auditory system is about two milliseconds (see, for example, Viemeister, 1979).

To model these results, we have constructed a "front end" acoustic analyzer consisting of a bank of 1/3 octave filters, covering from 125 Hz to 63 kHz, followed by envelope detectors. To obtain the roughly constant bandwidth below 400 Hz, we have added together the detector outputs of the 125 and 160 Hz channels, and also the 200 and 250 Hz channels. The detector time constants were chosen to produce fast rise time consistent with low ripple, hence we chose detector time constants commensurate with the filter rise times. Because filters with broader bandwidths have faster rise times, in our system the overall rise times of the filter-detector units have been made inversely

21

proportional to frequency. For example, the 1 kHz channel has an overall rise time of 6 milliseconds, the 2 kHz channel, 3 milliseconds, and so forth. The detectors are connected to a 16-channel multiplex switch, which samples the output of each channel every 1.6 milliseconds. (This rate is appropriate for the high-frequency channels, but over-samples the low channels.) The multiplexed output is then passed through a logarithmic amplifier to match the logarithmic nature of perceived loudness in the ear, and stored in computer memory (see Dockendorff, 1978).

Both the temporal and the spectral aspects of the sound can be visualized by plotting the data obtained with this filter system as a succession of spectra, that is, as log amplitude versus log frequency, with time as the parameter. An example of such a "running spectrum" for conversational speech is shown in Figure 1, which has been plotted in perspective to emphasize the three-dimensional character of this representation. The plot corresponds to the underlined portion of the sentence "The watchdog gave a warning growl". The time markers on the right represent blocks of 16 spectra, hence give a time scale of roughly 25 msec per division. The sharp changes in character between the voiced sounds, the unvoiced sound (Blocks 31 to 34), and the silent periods are clearly evident. Note, for example, the abrupt attack of the /d/ at time 37.5, where the spectrum changes from that of background noise to the burst spectrum of the /d/ in one time sample (i.e. 1.6 milliseconds).

We have used the filter-bank representation described above as the basis for automatic discrimination of stop consonants and fricatives in initial position. For details, see Raymond, 1977; Searle

et al., 1979; Kimberley & Searle (1979), Note 1. A few samples of music have also been examined (Searle, 1979/80).

3.0 An Early Primal Sketch

Let us now look at the sound analysis problem for a much broader point of view: What are the basic functions that the sensory systems must accomplish? First, some form of transduction must occur. The incoming sound, light, odor, etc., must be converted to electrical or chemical form for neural processing. At the same time, the incoming signal must be demodulated, detected, or otherwise slowed down to a rate compatible with the neural firing rate. Third, the neural system should systematically concentrate the important information in the incoming signal, and discard the irrelevant material. Finally, there must be some decision process to identify or categorize the stimulus. This latter process, involving context, memory, and a host of other higher-level mental processes, is beyond the scope of the present discussion. The transduction process, although equally important, will likewise not be considered here. Thus we will focus on how the incoming signal is slowed down to neural rate, and how the information might be systematically concentrated.

Initial Analysis

As previously noted, the ear divides up the incoming sound into roughly 1/3 octave frequency bands, and transmits to the brain either the rectified narrow-band signals, at low frequencies, or the average energy in the narrow-band signals, at high frequencies. Although the overall data rate is not reduced in this process, the data rate in each channel is now down by at least an order of magnitude (in our case a factor of 16) from the incoming rate. Let us examine in a more formal way how this representation is derived from the incoming signal.

One way of describing mathematically the filtering process in the ear (or eye) is the short-term Fourier Transform:

$$F(f_0, t) = \int_{-\infty}^{t} v(\tau) h(t - \tau) \cos 2\pi f_0 \tau d\tau$$

$$= -i \int_{-\infty}^{t} v(\tau) h(t - \tau)$$

$$\sin 2\pi f_0 \tau d\tau \qquad (1)$$

In words, we multiply the incoming signal by a weighting function, and sum these products; that is, we form a *weighted average* of the incoming signal. In the eye, this transform is calculated as above (except read "x" or "y" for "t"), by adding together the weighted outputs of a group of receptor cells on the back of the retina. The weighting function is the so-called Mexican Hat function, or difference of Gaussians, or $\nabla^2 G$ function. In the ear, an equivalent calculation is done by passing the signal through the cochlea, which in these terms amounts to a bank of filters with center frequency f_0, and shape and bandwidth determined by $h(t)$. The detected outputs from the filters can be represented as the *magnitude* of $F(f_0, t)$ (Flanagan, 1972). Note that $|F(f_0, t)|$ is a function of two variables, that is, amplitude as a function of both frequency and time, consistent with the plot in Figure 1.

From this point of view, there is really only one fundamental design parameter to be chosen for either the auditory or visual filter-bank, that is, h. This one

parameter determines both the temporal response (rise time) and the bandwidth of the auditory filter, (or correspondingly, the spatial resolution and the spatial-frequency resolution in the visual filter). This result is not a peculiarity of the particular method of signal processing we have chosen. There is a fundamental relationship between bandwidth and rise time imposed on all physical systems by the Heisenberg Uncertainty Principle, regardless of whether the signal processing is done by real filters, Fast Fourier Transforms, Linear Predictive Coding, neural summing, or any other method. In the present context, this relation is that the product of bandwidth and rise time cannot be less than 0.7, that is

$$\Delta t \cdot \Delta f \geq 0.7 \qquad (2)$$

Equation 2 implies that it is not possible to have both good temporal resolution and good frequency resolution in the same filter. If we wish, for example, to observe temporal details on the scale of 1 millisecond, then we cannot have frequency resolution better than 700 Hz. Gabor (1946) observed that this constraint can best be illustrated in terms of a time-frequency plot such as our running spectrum plot of Figure 1. If we consider the original speech or music signal to have a bandwidth of 10 kHz, then we cannot measure temporal details on a time scale smaller than about .1 millisecond. This is shown schematically in Figure 2a, where we have divided up the time-frequency space into narrow rectangles 10 kHz long and .1 millisecond wide. Equation 2 states that we can only measure one value of the incoming signal for each rectangle: We cannot, for example, learn anything more about the signal by trying to make measurements every 1/100 millisecond instead of every 1/10 millisecond. Of course, Equation 2 indicates that we are free to change the shape of the rectangle. For example, we might analyze one minute of a Beethoven symphony as a single unit, in which case Δt would be 60 seconds and the corresponding frequency resolution would be roughly 1/100 Hz, as suggested in Figure 2b. Now the frequency resolution is obviously excellent (even excessive), but the temporal structure of the music has been completely suppressed by the one-minute averaging time.

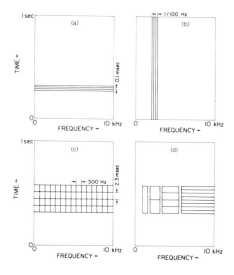

Figure 2 Various ways of dividing up the time-frequency plane corresponding to different filter bandwidths in the analysis system.

The diagrams in Figure 2a and 2b represent two extremes in the design of an auditory analyzer. Both are clearly unsatisfactory, the first because it has poor frequency resolution, and the second because it has poor temporal resolution. There are obviously an infinite number of intermediate designs which meet the constraint

of Equation 2. The sound spectrograph, for example, has been designed with 300 Hz bandwidth, and hence at best 2-3 millisecond temporal resolution, as suggested by Figure 2c. Again a compromise, with not quite adequate frequency resolution, and not quite adequate temporal resolution. The ear, however, has evolved a more imaginative design strategy: It is possible to obtain excellent frequency resolution and excellent temporal resolution, as long as we do not try to do both in one filter. Hence we use narrow bandwidth filters, perhaps 100 Hz wide, below 400 Hz to obtain excellent frequency resolution in this range, and increasingly wider bandwidth filters above 400 Hz to obtain good temporal resolution in that region. This design is shown in Figure 2d. For many sound patterns and especially for speech, this makes excellent sense. Good low-frequency spectral resolution is ideal for measuring vowel formants, and good high-frequency temporal resolution allows us to perceive sharp transients as in stop consonant bursts or percussive instrument attacks, without suffering unduly from the lack of spectral detail: we do not need the fine spectral detail on an /s/ sound—it is just random noise.

4.0 A Higher-level Representation

Thus far we have achieved a clever repackaging of the incoming sound wave which has preserved spectral (formant) shapes at low frequencies, and temporal attack profiles at high frequencies, while lowering the data-rate per channel to a value compatible with the neural system. But the overall data rate, summed across all channels, is roughly the same as that in the original sound wave. (This is true of all such systems, and specifically of all the analysis strategies shown in Figure 2.) How, then can we bring about a true reduction in the enormous amount of data cascading into the auditory system? What we would like to do is not just arbitrarily throw away data, but somehow reorganize the data so that the relevant information can be separated from the irrelevant, and then discard the irrelevant data. Such magic separation is of course not always possible. One scheme we find attractive is that proposed some years ago by Yilmaz (1967, 1968). Yilmaz suggested that vowel perception should in some way resemble color perception. Specifically he theorized that there should be a three-dimensional vowel space, with loudness, "hue", and "saturation", and three "primary" vowels from which all vowels should

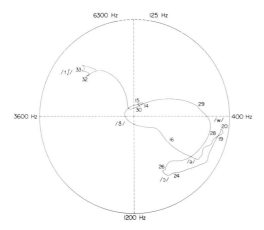

Figure 3 Yilmaz's "vowel circle" plot for the italicized portion of "*The watchdog gave a warning growl.*"

be constructed. Vowels could be displayed in two dimensions as a "vowel circle" similar to the color triangle, by deflecting the

X and Y axes of an oscilloscope with sine-weighted and cosine-weighted averages of the spectrum:

$$X = \sum_{n=1}^{N} S(n) \sin \frac{2\pi n}{N} \qquad (3)$$

$$Y = \sum_{n=1}^{N} S(n) \cos \frac{2\pi n}{N} \qquad (4)$$

where $S(n)$ is the log spectral magnitude from the critical-band filter, and N is the total number of filters. (Contemporary Vocoder literature would call these components the "fundamental frequency" Fourier sine and cosine components in mel-based cepstral analysis of the speech.)

By representing speech in this way, Yilmaz is implicitly stating that vowels and vowel-like sounds can be represented by substantially fewer parameters than were used to represent the original spectrum. He is suggesting that the brain does not have to pay attention to all the nuances of spectral shape shown in Figure 1, for example, in order to understand the speech. All we need are some broad averages, specifically the weighted averages calculated in Equations 3 and 4. Note that these equations are special cases of the Fourier transform given in Equation 1, in that here the weighted average is calculated on a log magnitude spectrum rather than a time signal. Also, only the "fundamental" sine and cosine terms are calculated. Yilmaz suggests that the remaining terms ($\sin 2x$, $\cos 2x$, $\sin 3x$, etc.) can be neglected.

The original Yilmaz papers offer very little experimental or theoretical justification for any of these claims, but subsequent work (Note 2, Note 3) would indicate that the concept is worthy of serious examination. To this end we have analyzed some representative speech spectra using Yilmaz's "color" method. Figure 3 shows the effect of transforming the data in Figure 1 in accordance with Equations 3 and 4, and forming the Yilmaz "vowel circle" plot, in direct analogy to the normal color triangle plot of color vision. To give some insight about this diagram, we have labeled around the circle the locations corresponding to various pure-tone inputs ("saturated sounds"), analogous to the location of the saturated colors on the color triangle.

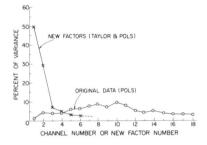

Figure 4 Plot of percent of variance in various components of the original filter-bank representation, and the new representation arising from principal components analysis [from Pols, 1977, and Taylor & Pols (1978), Note 4].

The succession of spectra in Figure 1 are converted to a succession of points in the new space, which describe a *trajectory*. The numbers shown beside the trajectory are the same time markers shown in Figure 1. Numbers close together in Figure 3 (i.e. 24, 26) correspond to almost steady-state sound, whereas when the numbers are far apart, (i.e. 15, 16, or 29, 30) the spectral shape is chang-

ing rapidly, corresponding to a transition between phonemes, or a stop-consonant burst. This can best be understood by viewing Figures 1 and 3 together. The trajectory starts at the neutral point ("White"), 14, 15, then a brief frication for the /ð/, 16, then a transition to the /ə/ at 17, flowing directly into /w/ at 19 and 20, and /ɔ/ at 24, 25, and 26. The silent period preceding the /ch/ forces a long transition back to the neutral point, 28, 29, 30 then an attack of the /ch/ 31, followed by the steady state /ch/, 32 and 33. Note the wide separation of the steady-state sounds /w/,/ɔ/ and /ch/ even for this very crude analysis. It should also be clear that phonemes characterized by rapid spectral change, such as stop consonants, will appear in this plot as trajectories rather than clusters.

Further support for this "color" analogue to representing speech sounds appears in the work of Cote (1981), Pols (1977), Schouten & Pols (1979a, b), and unpublished work of Taylor & Pols (1978, Note 4). Pols used a 17-channel filter bank modeled after the auditory system to analyze conversational speech. He generated log-magnitude spectra for a minute of speech (one spectrum every 10 milliseconds, or 6000 spectra) for each of 10 speakers (two languages, English and Dutch). For data reduction, he did not simply assume sine and cosine basis vectors (Equations 3 and 4) as did Yilmaz. Instead, he applied *principal components analysis*[†] to his 17-point spectra to derive a new picture of the data in which the maximum amount of the variance has been forced into the first component, the

[†]Principal components analysis is similar to factor analysis except that factor analysis uses sums and products of the *input* variables to account for the variance in the output data whereas principal components analysis uses linear combinations of the *output* variables to account for the output variance.

maximum remaining variance into the second component, etc. The results of this analysis are surprising and important on several quite independent counts. First, the transform is very effective in forcing the information into a few components, as shown by the variance plot in Figure 4. This plot shows that in Pols's running spectrum data, the variance is more or less uniformly distributed throughout the filter channels, with no one channel accounting for more than 11% of the variance. After the principal components transformation, 50% of the variance is in the first component, 29% in the second, and the other 21% in decreasing amounts in the remaining 15 components.

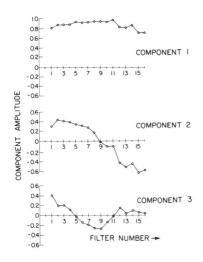

Figure 5 The first three basis vectors generated by principal components analysis for the sentence "The watchdog gave a warning growl".

The second important result of the Pols-Taylor analysis is that the transform is quite speaker independent, and language independent for English and Dutch.

Third, the basis vectors have a very simple structure to them: They strongly resemble a half cosine series. This resemblance is even stronger if the analysis is done in terms of spectral differences (the difference between two successive spectra 10 msec apart) rather than on the original spectral magnitude (Note 5). Using the same approach as in the Yilmaz discussion above, we have followed the methods of Pols and Taylor, and applied principal components analysis to our Watchdog sentence, Figure 1. Figure 5 shows the first three of the basic vectors resulting from our analysis. As in other studies, (Pols, 1977; Zahohan & Rothenberg, 1981) these turn out to be roughly a half-cosine series.

In Figure 6 we show the representation which results if we use a half-cosine series as basis vectors to transform the "watch dog" data of Figure 1. By comparing with Figure 1, we note that we have packed the speech data into substantially fewer channels than the original representation, as expected from the variance plot in Figure 4.

Let us now discuss these three results in more detail. First, we consider the efficient packing of the data, as indicated by the variance lot in Figure 4. Although the principal components analysis may be analyzing to some small extent the properties of the filter bank and detectors, it is mainly revealing properties of the sound (speech) wave. The results clearly show that the 16 or 17 narrow-band channels of speech in the original analysis are not independent. We see that speech has perhaps five degrees of freedom, rather than 17, a fact that is well-known to those studying speech production. Figure 6 shows that this same effect in another way: The spectral information now appears to be heavily concentrated in the first few components of the new space, and the "higher" components seem to be only weakly correlated with the speech.

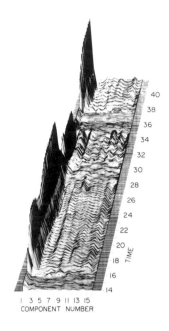

Figure 6 New representation of "The watchdog" derived using half-cosine basis vectors.

It is important, however, to keep these results in proper perspective. We have certainly managed to concentrate the variance into the few components in the new space, but this does not necessarily mean that we have concentrated in like manner the perceptually relevant information. Pols clearly understood this important distinction. For this reason he built a speech synthesizer to reconstruct speech from transformed data, such as Figure 6, with some of the "higher" channels "filtered out", that is, set to zero. He then examined in a few cases the perceptual effects of such filtering. As might

be expected, the perceptual experiment did not indicate as dense a packing of the information as the variance figure might suggest but, nonetheless, substantial data reduction was indicated. Further support for this notion has appeared more recently (Remez et al., 1984). These perceptual experiments are of key importance to the whole process of representation and data compression of speech, and hence must form a central part of any research program in this area.

5.0 Conclusion

What begins to emerge from these rather diverse research efforts is a possible fundamental representation for acoustic signals, in which at least two linear transformations are required, with an intervening nonlinear operation. Specifically, the evidence suggests that an initial spectral analysis is made, describable either in terms of a set of critical-band filters, or, correspondingly, a short-term Fourier Transform with varying window-width to match the critical-band data. The resulting signals are then processed in a nonlinear manner to produce log-magnitude versus log-frequency spectra. These spectra are then subjected to a second linear transform, possibly similar to the Discrete Cosine Transform, to reduce the data to a minimum number of perceptually important channels or dimensions. Related work on speaker recognition by Atal (1972) indicates that substantially higher recognition scores result when a discriminant analysis program operates on such carefully reduced data rather than on the original data set.

This three-step process of data reduction is obviously effective for vowels and other relatively steady-state sounds, as can be seen from Figure 3. But certain sounds, such as clicks, snaps, or stop consonants, are represented in this process not as clusters in the space but as trajectories through the space as a function of time. Hence, one possible direction for future research is to find a way to incorporate a temporal dimension into the space, so that by coordinate rotation, trajectories can be made to appear as clusters rather than lines.

Acknowledgments: Various parts of this work were supported by the National Research Council, the Medical Research Council, the Defense and Civil Institute of Environmental Medicine through the Department of Supply and Services (Canada) and the Vinton Hayes fund at M.I.T. The author gratefully acknowledges the help of M.M. Taylor, B.J. Frost, W. Richards, H. Secker-Walker, and T.E. Schwalm.

Notes

1. Kimberly, B.P. & Searle, C.L. (1979) Automatic discrimination of locative consonants based on human audition. Presented at the IEEE International Conference on Acoustics, Speech and Signal Processing, April, 1979.
2. Yilmaz, H., Ferber, L., Park, W., Kellett, H. & Koprucu, E. (1974) Perception continuous speech recognition. *TR 74 180, Rome Air Development Center.*
3. Ferber, L., Yilmaz, H., Kellett, H., Park, W. & Koprucu, E. (1975) Speech perception. *TR-75 265, Rome Air Development Center.*
4. Taylor, M.M. & Pols, L.C.W. (1978) Unpublished data, personal communication.
5. Taylor, M.M. (1981) Design considerations for a talker adaptive continuous speech recognition system. Unpublished memorandum, Defense and Civil Institute of Environmental Medicine, Toronto.

References

Ahmed, N., Natarajan, T. & Rao, K.R (1974) Discrete cosine transform. *IEEE Transactions on Computers*, C-25:90 – 93.

Atal, B.S. (1972) Automatic speaker recognition based on pitch contours. *Jrl. Acoust. Soc. Am.*, 52:1687 – 1697.

Cote, A.J. (1961) *A Relative Portrait of Some Vowel Sounds.* Johns Hopkins University.

Dockendorff, D.D. (1978) "Application of a Computer-Controlled Model of the Ear to Multiband Amplitude Compression". Unpublished M.Sc. dissertation, Queen's University, Kingston, Ontario.

Evans, E.F. & Wilson, J.P. (1973) Frequency selectivity in the cochlea. In *Basic Mechanisms in Hearing*, A.R. Moller (ed.), New York: Academic Press, pp. 519 – 554.

Flanagan, J.L. (1972) *Speech Analysis, Synthesis and Perception.* New York: Springer.

Gabor, D. (1946) Theory of communication. *Jrl. Institute of Electrical Engineers*, 93:429 – 441.

Johnstone, B.M. & Boyle, A.J.F. (1967) Basilar membrane vibration examined with the Mossbauer Effect. *Science*, 158:389.

Kiang, N.Y.S. & Moxon, E.C. (1974) Tails of tuning curves of auditory-nerve fibers. *Jrl. Acoust. Soc. Am.*, 55:620–630.

Kiang, N.Y.S., Watanabe, T.E.C. & Clark, L.F. (1965) *Discharge Patterns of Single Nerve Fibers in a Cat's Auditory Nerve.* Cambridge, MA: MIT Press.

Patterson, R.D. (1976) Auditory filter shapes derived with noise stimuli. *Jrl. Acoust. Soc. Am.*, 59:640–654.

Pols, L.C.W. (1977) *Spectral Analysis and Identification of Dutch Vowels in Monosyllabic Words.* Institute for Perception, TNO.

Raymond, S.G. (1977) "Phoneme Recognition Based on Feature Extraction from a Model of the Auditory System". Unpublished M.Sc. dissertation, Queen's University, Kingston, Ontario.

Remez, R.E., Rubin, P.E., Pisoni, D.B. & Carrell, T.D. (1984) Speech perception without traditional speech cues. *Science*, 212:947–950.

Rhode, W.S. (1971) Observations of the basilar membrane in squirrel monkeys using the Mossbauer Technique. *Jrl. Acoust. Soc. Am.*, 49:1218–1231.

Richards, W. (1979) Quantifying sensory channels: Generalizing colorimetry to orientation and texture, touch and tones. *Sensory Processes*, 3:207–229.

Schouten, M.E.H. & Pols, L.C.W. (1979a) CV- and VC- transitions: A special study of coarticulation. Part I. *Journal of Phonetics*, 7:1–23 (a).

Schouten, M.E.H. & Pols, L.C.W. (1979b) CV- and VC-transitions: A spectral study of coarticulation. Part II. *Journal of Phonetics*, 7:205–224 (b).

Searle, C.L. Jacobson, J.Z. & Rayment, S.G. (1979) Stop consonant discrimination based on human audition. *Jrl. Acoust. Soc. Am.*, 65:799–809.

Searle, C.L. (1979/80) Analysis of music from an auditory perspective. *Humanities Association Review, 1979/80*, 30:93–103.

Tobias, J.V. (1970) *Foundations of Modern Auditory Theory*, Vol. 1. New York: Academic Press.

Viemeister, N.F. (1979) Temporal modulation transfer functions based upon modulation thresholds. *Jrl. Acoust. Soc. Am.*, 66: 1364–1380.

Yilmaz, A. (1967) A theory of speech perception. *Bulletin of Mathematical Biophysics*, 29:793–824.

Yilmaz, H. (1968) A theory of speech perception, II. *Bulletin of Mathematical Biophysics*, 30:455–479.

Zahohan, S.A. & Rothenberg, M. (1981) Principal components analysis for low redundancy encoding of speech spectra. *Jrl. Acoust. Soc. Am.*, 69:832–845.

Zelinski, R. & Noll, P. (1977) Adaptive transform coding of speech signals. *IEEE Transactions on Acoustics Speech and Signal Processing*, 25:299–309.

Reprinted with minor changes from *The Canadian Jrl. Psychol.*, 36:402–419 (1982).

A Computational Model
of Binaural Localization and Separation

Richard F. Lyon

Schlumberger Palo Alto Research
Palo Alto, CA

1.0 Introduction

Binaural processing and other schemes for enhancement of speech in interference have not been very successful to date. Many researchers have shown that humans have a significant binaural listening advantage for intelligibility of speech in the presence of strong interference from reverberation or from sound sources in different directions, such as in the well known cocktail party effect. But monaural processed signals derived from binaural recordings have failed to show a significant increase in intelligibility, relative to monaural listening to one of the channels of the original unprocessed binaural recordings (Bloom & Cain, 1982). That is, there are as yet no signal processing techniques that can duplicate any reasonable fraction of the human's binaural signal separation abilities. Such techniques would be particularly interesting for their application to speech recognition by machine in noisy environments.

The approach of carefully modeling the important functions of human hearing, according to physiological and psychoacoustic clues, provides an important opening into a class of promising techniques. A previous paper (Lyon, 1982) discussed computational models for the "front-end" processing done in the cochlea. These models are time-domain algorithms whose outputs represent the signals that the nervous system gets from the ears. This paper discusses a computational model that represents one of the first important operations that the nervous system performs with the signals from the two ears, namely to separate them into signals from different sources or different directions.

The binaural models, or algorithms, are a natural outgrowth of the time-domain cochlear modeling approach; no similar algorithms could have been developed if the front-end processing had been a more conventional technique that characterized sounds simply by their short-time power spectra (i.e. without fine time structure, or phase).

Many of the ideas used in this paper have been discussed in the speech and hearing literature for many years, in the form of theories and descriptive models; particularly good surveys may be found in Tobias, (1972) and Colburn & Durlach (1978), and older important papers in Schubert (1979). Our main contribution here is to show that the descriptive models can be turned into useful algorithms, or computational models. The algorithms are described here in enough detail to allow others to experiment with them; the remaining details are expressed not by formulas or any mathematical rigor,

22

but by their ever changing implementation in LISP code.

2.0 Review of the Cochlear Model Algorithms

The model of the cochlea (Lyon, 1982) is basically a bandpass filterbank with channels corresponding to places on the basilar membrane. Each bandpass filtered version of the original signal is half-wave rectified, modeling the detection nonlinearity of the hair cells, then amplitude-compressed via a multi-loop coupled automatic gain control mechanism that models lateral inhibition, neural adaptation, fatigue, etc. The filters are designed as a direct physical analog to the cochlear transmission line, resulting in an efficient implementation of asymmetric transfer functions with very sharp high-side cutoffs (greater than 120 dB/octave). The bandwidths and the place-to-frequency mapping are motivated by critical bands and the Mel frequency scale. For low-frequency channels, the bandwidths are 100 Hz; high-frequency channels are constant-Q, with bandwidth equal to one tenth of center frequency. There is a graceful transition region around 1 kHz. Channel center frequencies are spaced in proportion to the local bandwidth, resulting in a frequency scale that is approximately linear below 1kHz and logarithmic above 1kHz; 84 channels cover 50 Hz to 10 kHz.

A picture of the cochlear model output, called a cochleagram, resembles spectrogram with a distorted frequency scale and improved time resolution; signal phase, or fine time structure, is preserved. In the time-frequency plane of the cochleagram, sounds tend to be localized into regions of high energy, which results in locally high signal-to-noise ratios when noise is present. Impulsive signals are localized in the time dimension, while narrow-band signals (tones) are localized in the frequency dimension. Voiced speech sounds are localized in both dimensions, as pitch pulses excite formant resonances. Classical "place", "volley", and "telephone" theories of hearing all describe limited aspects of the behavior of this more complete model.

An interesting property of this model is that it inherently preserves the fine time structure of a signal in a very redundant high rate multi-channel output (unlike most popular front ends, which strive to reduce the data rate needed to describe a sound). Rather than filter out components faster than a reasonable voice pitch (e.g. 400 Hz), the model maintains at least a bandwidth consistent with known timing properties of the auditory nervous system.

The binaural processing described here appears to be the most demanding application for fine time structure. Models of pitch perception based on autocorrelations of the channel outputs also demand access to the signal's fine time structure. Collectively, these and other techniques will allow versatile signal separation based on frequency content, time of occurrence, direction, pitch, and higher-level cues.

3.0 Binaural Processing Algorithm Overview

For the binaural processing algorithms, the details of the front-end filter transfer functions are probably not important, as long as they are somewhere near the correct bandwidths. What is important is that the filter outputs be half-wave rectified and maintained at high sample rate, so that they carry a realistic combination of envelope and phase information; a modest amount of smoothing may be used, as discussed in Section 6, but nothing so severe as used in typical envelope detection schemes. The 20 kHz sample rate of the original signal is maintained throughout the time-domain algorithms, eventually resulting in a 20 kHz cochleagram output, from which direct resynthesis is possible. The binaural processing is described in three stages below; further details are found in Section 6.

Stage 1: Computing Left-Right Cross-correlations

The outputs of corresponding frequency channels from the two ears are first combined by cross-correlation; cross-correlation coefficients are computed, for each value of relative left-right delay, by lowpass filtering the product of the left and right signals. The maximum delay parameter used is 0.65 msec (13 samples), which approximates the expected maximum interaural delay (or inter-microphone delay, which depends on the recording setup). Since each channel is delayed relative to the other, and since the zero-offset case is included, these parameters give rise to 27 correlation coefficients of interest. The filters that smooth the instantaneous correlation product are leaky integrators (one-pole lowpass filters) with time constants of only about 1 msec; thus the running approximation to the cross-correlation function still has considerable time-domain detail.

The output of the correlation processing described above can be printed s a "correlagram"—a picture that shows one time sample of the left-right correlation, parameterized along its two axes by interaural time-delay and by cochlear place,

or frequency channel. For a diotic sound (same signal in both ears), the correlagram is a simple symmetrical pattern with a fuzzy vertical stripe in the center and "sidelobes" characteristic of the filter resonances. Figure 1 shows the cochleagram and correlagram of a diotic square pulse of 1 msec duration. Notice the interesting interactions of time-domain and spectral information; spectral nulls at multiples of 1 kHz appear following the trailing edge of the pulse, but are not resolved well near the high end.

As a sound moves laterally, this pattern simply shifts left and right. In all cases, the darkness of the pattern carries spectral (formant) information, while its shape carries information about left-right timing relations, or direction of sound arrival.

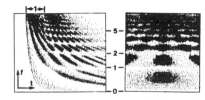

Figure 1 Cochleagram (left) and correlagram (right) of 1 msec diotic pulse. Abscissa: time (left) or time delay (right). Ordinate: cochlear place (roughly frequency).

Stage 2: Directional Interpretation of Correlation Data

Peaks in the short-time cross-correlation functions are simply interpreted as direction (only lateral directions are considered, not full spatial localization). At each time sample (every 0.05 msec) the delay parameter corresponding to the highest of the 27 correlation coefficients is interpreted as the *apparent direction* of the signal. Since this is done independently in every frequency channel and at every time sample, decisions reflect the apparent direction of many very local parts of the incoming sound mixture. Of course, the local apparent direction decisions often do not correspond to any real sound source, but are the result of mixtures of signals.

The cochlear model's separation of sounds enables the simple cross-correlation approach to perform reasonably well. The signal in any very small-time frequency region is most often dominated by the signal from a single source, so that the apparent direction will be close to a true source direction. With the preprocessing discussed in Section 6, the correlation peaks can integrate directional cues based on signal phase, envelope modulation, onset time, and loudness.

Stage 3: Separation into Distinct Sound Streams

Following the local directional interpretation, per-channel time-variable gains are applied to the input cochleagrams to produce output cochleagrams representing different sound streams. These gains change very quickly, typically reacting in under 0.5 msec to a change in correlation peak position caused by an onset from a different source. In the extreme case (locally high SNR), gains of zero and unity may be said to "gate" local sound fragments to the appropriate output stream. Thus, unlike techniques that compute a slowly changing optimal spectral modification of the signal, this model must be viewed as very much a time-domain technique, which takes advantage of both the fine time resolution and the frequency separating properties of the cochlea.

There are various possible schemes for adjusting the time-variable gains. The scheme implemented so far is specific to the problem of separating and dereverberating two sounds from slightly different directions. Eight time-varying gains map the two input cochleagrams into four output cochleagrams representing the left and right direct sound sources and the left and right reverberant energy, or echoes. Ideally, when the apparent direction of a sound fragment exactly matches a source direction or an extreme side, one of the eight gains is taken to be unity and the others are all zero (the unity gain is applied to the cochleagram from the ear on the same side as the sound). When the apparent sound direction is in one of the three regions between the ideal directions (e.g. between left echo and left sound), the sound fragment is arbitrarily assumed to be a mixture of the sounds from the two bracketing directions; accordingly, a pair of nonzero gains are picked by interpolating between the values (0, 1) and (1, 0); the other six gains remain zero.

When two of the gains are nonzero, one multiplies the left input and the other multiplies the right input. For example, when the direction is between the left echo and the left sound source, the left echo output is taken from the left ear cochleagram, and the left sound source output is taken from the right ear cochleagram; the heuristic motivation is that when a side echo is present, the sound source has less interference in the opposite ear.

4.0 A Preliminary Test of the Algorithms

The binaural algorithms are quite computationally intensive, and take a long time to evaluate, even on a dedicated processor running an efficient dialect of LISP (Zetalisp on a Symbolics LM-2). So far, one interesting 200 msec example has been run through the model several times, while exploring the effects of various algorithm modifications.

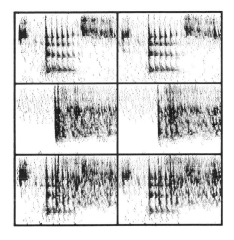

Figure 2 Cochleagrams of test signals. Top: left and right channels of speech sound. Middle: left and right channels of interfering *ping* sound, with reverberation. Bottom: left and right composite sounds, the inputs to the binaural separation test.

The binaural test signal was constructed by adding together two separately recorded binaural sounds, so the separate signals would be known. The speech signal, a fraction of the word /testing/, was recorded with microphones in the direct nonreverberant field, about 20 cm from the mouth, with path lengths differing by only about 1 cm (0.03 msec closer to the right "ear"). The interfering sound of a ping-pong ball being struck by a paddle was recorded about 3 m from the sound source in a very large reverberant room, with a path length difference equivalent to about 0.18 msec (closer to the left

"ear"). The speech-to-interference ratio changes from very good at the beginning to rather bad during the /s/ frication noise and reverberation at the end of /tes/. On playback of the sum, the word seems intelligible, even with monaural listening.

Figure 2 shows cochleagrams of the sounds: left and right channels of the original recordings, and left and right channels of the combined test stimulus. Notice that even in this time-reduced picture, there is enough time resolution to see the "ping" noise between pitch pulses of the vowel. Notice also that various echoes show up in only one signal of the left-right pair; the amplitude-sensitive modification discussed in Section 6 was included to handle such echoes.

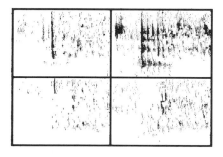

Figure 3 Separation results. Top: left and right separated sound streams. Bottom: left and right echoes, or reverberations.

Figure 3 shows cochleagrams of the outputs: four separated sound streams representing sounds from two presumed source directions and the left and right echoes. Notice that the separation is good where one signal or the other dominates, but is not as good when there is a mixture, or when there are a variety of directions as in the reverberation noise. It appears that the output representing the speech has been cleaned up, and that the ping sound has been separated from its own reverberation as well as from the speech; the test is encouraging, but performance conclusions can not yet be drawn.

5.0 Binaural Psychoacoustic and Explanatory Models

The binaural algorithms and their parameters are motivated by a wealth of experimental psychoacoustic data and by models that have been proposed to explain those data. Since each model typically explains only limited aspects of hearing, it is necessary to combine features and concepts from many models to arrive at a useful computational model of hearing. The 1948 neural net model of Jeffress has been very influential, and exemplifies the early work in this area; it is summarized in Jeffress et al. (1956):

> All of the monaural phenomena we have discussed can be understood through the use of a simple model—a narrow filter followed by an elementary detector. ... The spectacular phenomena of binaural interaction require a mechanism in addition to our monaural one. It must take the outputs of the detectors for the two ears and compare them for time difference. Such a device was proposed by Jeffress to explain localization of sound. It is about as simple as possible, is not altogether improbably physiologically, and satisfies the Huggins and Licklider principle of sloppy workmanship. The mechanism receives impulses from corresponding filter sections of the two ears and delays them progressively by small increments, either by means of fine nerve tissue with a slow conduction rate or by a series of synapses. The delay nets are in opposition, so that undelayed impulses from one side meet delayed impulses from the other. A time delay in the stimulus to one ear can therefore be matched by an equal delay in the neural channel from the other. A series of detectors, in the form of synapses requiring coincident impulses from both ears in order to respond, completes the mechanism. As is usual in such models, the device achieves precision statistically by the use of large numbers of elements.

Rather than use large numbers of coincidence elements working with statistically detected events, the present model uses a smaller number of detection elements, namely integrating multipliers, working with relatively precise numerical signal values. Since discrimination thresholds for interaural time-of-arrival differences have been reported in the range of 0.01 to 0.05 msec (but there is room for improvement). The detailed behavior of the model is of course different from that of the nervous system, but it should be a significantly useful behavior if we have succeeded in abstracting the important functional properties of the system.

Most psychoacoustic measurements and models concern binaural advantages in the form of direction difference limens and masking level differences, rather than the notions of enhancement and separation. Binaural masking level differences can be interpreted as potentially attainable improvement in SNR, or increase in interference tolerance for a given level of intelligibility, for a system that produces a single output from a binaural input (in dB, relative to using a monaural input). For detection of tones and clicks in various kinds of noise, comparisons of models and experiments are possible; binaural advantages of 10 to 16 dB are typical (Jeffress et al., 1956). Unfortunately, experimenters have not usually used speech in moderate levels of noise as the stimulus, partly because intelligibility is so tedious to measure. As a result, we do not have good estimates of how much enhancement is reasonable to hope for in a task like speech recognition; 6 dB is probably possible and useful.

The precedence effect and perceived fusing of sequential binaural click pairs (i.e. a left-right pair followed by another left-right pair with a possibly different interaural delay) give us clues to the integration and interpretation time constants that would be appropriate to use in the model (Wallach et al., 1949). A rather short integration time constant of 1 msec is consistent with the observation that click pairs have to be less than 1 msec apart in order for the fused directional percept to be a significant compromise between their individual directions. This short integration time constant is also consistent with optimal estimation of the direction of wideband events in uncorrelated noise, given a filterbank front-end with filter rise-times on the order of 1 msec.

For click pair separations greater than 1 msec, the model will judge the directions of the first and second pairs nearly independently. Perceptually, if the separation is not over about 10 msec, the result is a single directional percept determined by the first click pair; the second will not be heard separately, but will be suppressed, perhaps by some higher-level model.

6.0 Algorithm Modifications and Details

The algorithms described above are relatively simple, but the behavior that they are supposed to emulate is rather complicated; a few well-motivated modifications bring the algorithms more in line with the desired performance, with a modest increase in complexity.

For high-frequency stimuli, the directional percept is known to be dominated by envelope delay and loudness differences, and not by phase differences. Many researchers have postulated separate mechanisms for low and high frequencies, but in the present model a single mechanism suffices. By design, envelope structure (transient time difference) is already represented in the half-wave rectified outputs of the filters. To get a realistic reduction of phase detail, without suppressing envelope information, a first-order lowpass filter is added to each channel between the cochlear model and the binaural model; the corner frequency should be around 1.4 to kHz. This basically causes a blurring of the correlegrams, such that the many fine peaks at the high end blend together smoothly. Since the filterbank channels are quite wide at the high end, there is still plenty of fast envelope structure that will result in well-formed correlation peaks representing the direction of wideband sound sources. Narrowband high frequency tones will be left with no matchable time structure, and hence will not be easily localized, in agreement with experiment.

With a simple preprocessing of the inputs to the correlation operation, peaks in the cross-correlation function can be made to respond to intensity differences, too. It is only necessary to add to each input a delayed and amplitude-diminished version (e.g. 20%) of the corresponding contra-lateral input. The exact effect of this *ad hoc* modification is complicated, but in general it moves the correlation peak toward the side with the larger signal. If one signal is identically zero, the peak will move all the way to the delay value used in the pre-mixing. This will be one of the extreme positions if the delay used is 0.65 msec. Even with this modification, amplitude effects will usually be small compared to timing effects, as in hearing experiments that are done at reasonably high sensation levels (Mills, 1972).

A serious problem with the algorithms as described above is that the *correct* peak of the correlation function is often not the *highest-valued* peak. In particular, when a waveform being correlated is decaying in amplitude but is otherwise nearly periodic (with a period less than 0.65 msec), the peak at a time shift off by one period will exceed the correct peak (because the correlation coefficients that look at older time-shifted data get more signal energy when the signal amplitude is decreasing). The simple technique used to get around this problem is to multiply all correlation values by a "fudge-factor" before picking the peak; the factors used are 100% for straight ahead, decreasing linearly to 70% at the extreme sides. This gives a general bias toward the center, and retains some dependence on whether a signal is increasing or decreasing. Biases toward the center have been observed experimentally, and have been explained by an increased density of neural tissue servicing the region of equal delays (Jeffress, 1972); the fudge factor can be considered a crude model of this effect.

It has been observed by several experimenters that replacing a segment of signal by silence reduces intelligibility more than replacing the same segment by noise (Bloom, 1982). Thus, signal separation and noise suppression algorithms should be constrained to not go too far; separa-

tion gains should be constrained to be not less than 0.2 or so. This feature has not been incorporated in the algorithms tested so far, but will be when intelligibility tests are done.

Higher-level mechanisms are still needed to decide what the relevant source directions are, based on combining local evidence across channels and times. Combination across frequency channels can be done by simple addition of correlation functions, so that high-SNR wideband sounds will give rise to distinct and reliable peaks. Such peaks can be interpreted as genuine sound source directions, as needed in the separation stage. Other high-level heuristics are needed to decide when there is a new source, when a source moves, which source to pay attention to, etc.

7.0 Concluding Remarks

Compared to frequency-domain techniques, our techniques may seem relatively *ad hoc*; this is because they have much more of a physiological and speculative motivation than a mathematical motivation. For example, rather than pretend that the signals of interest are stationary within 30 msec analysis windows, we prefer to use the nonstationarity to advantage, to interpret several distinct events within a few msec of each other. The specific models tried so far serve to illustrate the possibilities, but leave plenty of room for improvement.

We hope that by the presentation of this work, more researchers will be convinced that good speech processing algorithms can be "discovered" by interpreting and implementing classical descriptive models of hearing. The resulting computational models will be much more amenable to objective evaluation than are descriptive models; such evaluations will contribute to a more effective synergy between hearing research and speech processing research.

References

Bloom, P.J. (1982) Perception of process speech and some implications for enhancement. *Proc. Inst. Acoust.*, spring meeting, University of Surrey.

Bloom, P.J. & Cain, G.D. (1982) Evaluation of two-input dereverberation techniques. *Proc. 1982 ICASSP*, Paris, 162–167.

Colburn, H.S. & Durlach, N.I. (1978) Models of binaural interaction. Chapter 11 in *Handbook of Perception*, vol. 4, E.C. Carterette & M.P. Friedman (Eds.), Academic Press.

Jeffress, L.A., Blodgett, H.C., Sandel, T.T. & Wood, C.L. III (1956) Masking of tonal signals. *J. Acoust. Soc. Am.*, 28:416–426. Reprinted in *Psychological Acoustics*, E.D. Schubert (ed.), Stroudsburg, PA: Dowden, Hutchinson & Ross, 1979.

Jeffress, L.A. (1972) Binaural signal detection: vector theory. In *Foundations of Modern Auditory Theory*, J.V. Tobias (ed.), Vol. II, New York: Academic Press.

Lyon, R.F. (1982) A computational model of filtering, detection, and compression in the cochlea. *Proc. 1982 ICASSP*, May, Paris, 1282–1285.

Mills, A.W. (1972) Auditory localization. In Tobias, J.V. (ed.) *Foundations of Modern Auditory Theory*, Vol. II, New York: Academic Press.

Schubert, E.D. (1979) ed., *Psychological Acoustics*. Stroudsburg, PA: Dowden, Hutchinson & Ross.

Tobias, J.V. (1972) *Foundations of Modern Auditory Theory*, Vol. II, New York: Academic Press.

Wallach, H., Newman, E.B. & Rosenzweig, M.R. (1949) The precedence effect in sound localization. *Am. J. Psychol.*, 62:315–336. Reprinted in *Psychological Acoustics*, E.D. Schubert (ed.), Stroudsburg, PA: Dowden, Hutchinson & Ross, 1979.

Reprinted from *Proc. ICASSP*, 83:1148–1151, Boston, 1983).

Schematizing Spectrograms for Speech Recognition

Michael D. Riley

Bell Laboratories
Murray Hill, NJ

1.0 Introduction

This paper addresses the initial processing of a sound wave for the recognition of wide vocabulary, continuous speech. Speech recognition is addressed in this general scope to discourage the use of inherently limited techniques that may work fairly well under very restricted conditions (e.g. isolated digit recognition of high quality speech) but which can not be modified to work well in less constrained circumstances. Instead, one is led to seek more robust processing that can effectively deal with the great variability found in large vocabulary, continuous speech. In fact, insights gained into this broader problem may even be crucial for high quality performance in more restricted applications.

To achieve such unrestricted, high performance speech recognition, it is argued that a representation is needed that is defined in terms of the speech signal's physical origin—time-varying "resonances", voice onsets, articulatory closures, and so forth. To obtain this representation, a priori representation should be available that richly describes significant temporal and spectral features of the speech signal without undue commitment to their particular origin. This latter step roughly consists of a reliable schematization of the prominent features, such as local spectral energy concentrations that are continuous in time, found in conventional spectrograms and related displays.

The approach of symbolic description preceding physical interpretation has been forcefully advanced by David Marr for visual information processing of natural images (Marr, 1982). His work has influenced the general methodology used here. Of course, the details of the appropriate processing for speech and for vision will be very different, since each domain has properties particular to it. But the more abstract principles of how to organize complex information processing tasks learned from studying visual processing may be applicable to speech processing.

This paper is divided into two parts. The first part consists of Section 2 through Section 5, and addresses some general representational issues for the initial speech processing. This part addresses: *"What descriptions should one produce from the speech signal?"*

The second part consists of Section 6 and Section 7, and presents some novel speech processing methods that find local spectral energy concentrations. The processing begins with smoothing and flattening convolutions in both the time and frequency dimensions of narrow-band spectrograms to select the appropriate temporal and spectral *scales*. Ridges in the resulting two-dimensional (time-frequency) surfaces correspond to local spectral energy concentrations. The tops of these ridges are found by the application of a two-dimensional differential operator at each point in the time-frequency plane. The operator consists of the inner product of the gradient vector and the unit vector in the direction of greatest downward curvature. Zero-crossings in this quantity (with some further restrictions) define spectro-temporal peak locations. This part of the paper addresses: *"How do you compute (some of) the descriptors for Part I?"*

2.0 The Acoustic-Phonetic Correlates of the Speech Signal

A speech sound arriving at our ears is due to the combination of several physical factors. These factors can be roughly categorized as:

1. Source characteristics: e.g. time of voicing onset and offset, frequency of fundamental as a function of time (when voiced).
2. Tract characteristics: e.g. frequency and band width of oral and nasal cavity formants ("resonances") and antiformants as a function of time, time of closures and releases.
3. Transmission characteristics: e.g. bandwidth of channel, frequency and bandwidth of channel resonances (when significant).

We shall call these attributes of the speech signal's physical origin, the *acoustic-phonetic correlates* or *factors* of the speech signal.

The traditional linear source-filter decomposition of the speech signal and the formant model for vowels (Fant, 1960) that we shall adopt here are, in fact, only first-order approximations of the true physical situation. Source-tract coupling, non-planar wave propagation, and rapid tract motions all occur to some extent and considerably complicate the precise physical description. Thus, calling a formant a resonance of the oral cavity is somewhat imprecise, since the term resonance is usually reserved for a pole of the transfer function of a linear time-invariant filter.

We shall not be too concerned with these difficult issues in this paper since, even though the above decomposition is inexact, it is close enough approximation of the actual physical origin of the speech signal for the conclusions that will be drawn below. Thus, we accept an approximate independence of source and tract, and define formants roughly as resonances of the vocal tract when "frozen" at a particular point in time. It remains a challenge for future work to provide a more rigorous, yet useful physical description.

3.0 Separating the Acoustic-Phonetic Correlates of the Speech Signal

Given the approximate validity and independence of the above acoustic-phonetic factors, a representation where these factors (or something like them) have been maximally separated would be a desirable intermediate step in speech recognition. Let us compare some general approaches for recovering the various source, tract, and transmission characteristics from the speech wave. We shall focus on finding the frequency (and perhaps bandwidth) of the characteristic "resonances" of the vocal tract as a function of time—so-called formant tracking.

3.1 Analysis-by-synthesis

One approach that is widely used in formant tracking begins by modeling short-time spectra as the product of several complex poles—one for each formant sought—and a usually fixed source and transmission channel spectrum. This leaves a small set of parameters, typically the frequency and sometimes the bandwidth of the poles, to be varied until the synthetic spectrum best fits the incoming spectrum as determined by a suitable spectral distance measure (e.g. RMS error). The resulting pole frequencies that minimize this measure are taken as the formant frequencies. This general approach is often called analysis-by-synthesis (Bell et al. 1961; Matthews et al., 1961; Olive, 1971), and includes the standard linear predictive coding (LPC) techniques (Atal & Hanauer, 1971; Markel & Grey, 1976) as a special case, since they can be viewed as fitting a fixed number of poles to sort-time spectra (e.g. see Rabiner & Schafer, 1978, p. 433).

Although these methods have had some success, it is doubtful that a recognizer based around them could ever approach human performance at recognizing unrestricted speech. In general, (short-time) spectral match with such models is an imperfect way to evaluate hypothesized formant locations, since real speech signals are far too variable to have their spectral envelopes very accurately specified by *solely* the true distribution of the formants and some simple source and transmission characteristic adjustment. Consider the following sources of spectral variation:

- Nasalization, which introduces both resonances and antiresonances in a variety of ways.
- Talking over the telephone, which bandlimits the speech signal to about 3 kHz.
- Talking in a noisy environment, which can greatly affect speech spectra, but for which humans show great immunity.
- Talking in a reverberant room, which can introduce many additional resonances without necessarily affecting intelligibility by humans (although it will give a characteristic quality to the speech).

Because of such factors, real spectra often deviate significantly from spectra synthesized from a prior models. Simple analysis-by-synthesis methods usually fail under these circumstances, delivering misplaced and spurious formant locations. The point is that the effects of all possible sources of variation in what arrives at the ear are just too diverse to be succinctly captured, a priori, by a parametric model of possible spectra, just as the effects of all possible obstacles that may partially obscure an object's image arriving at the eye are too diverse to be effectively anticipated by a parametric model of possible intensity arrays.

The fundamental difficulty with the analysis-by-synthesis approach is that no attempt is made to distinguish between phonetically relevant and irrelevant features of the incoming spectra, leaving deviations from the spectral model to be evaluated entirely by the distance measure. Many of these deviations are due to events that introduce orderly spectral and temporal features (e.g. the fixed resonances of a reverberant room) that could be interpreted, a posteriori, if only these features could be extracted and made available for interpretation. The distance measure for analysis-by-synthesis systems, however, is typically some simple metric such as RMS error, which is incapable of making this kind of distinction.

One could try devising a more complex distance measure that performs its comparison on a more abstract description of both the incoming and synthetic spectra. But then the synthesis of the spectra from the prior model would be unnecessary; only the more abstract description would have to be synthesized. This leads us away from what is usually called analysis-by-synthesis, and toward the next approach.

3.2 Feature analysis

A second approach, which has been found useful in visual information processing, is to begin by producing a representation that richly describes those features of the input data that (1) can be reliably detected in the data and (2) are useful for creating a later representation in which the different physical factors that generated that data are recovered (Marr, 1982). For visual information processing, the first representation would describe features such as intensity edges, bars, small blobs, and terminations in an image. These are then used to interpret that image in terms of physical factors such as surface orientation, surface discontinuities, surface reflectance, and illumination. The earlier representation is purely descriptive of the input data, since no specific commitment to the particular physical origin of the features represented is made at that stage. The simple but powerful idea of this first step is that

in making *explicit* a significant feature by giving it a name and associating properties with it, it is made available as a symbolic object that can be computationally manipulated. Until this is done, that feature rests only implicitly in the data. In information processing terms, this has been called the "principle of explicit naming".

To apply this general approach to speech processing one should begin by forming a representation that makes explicit a variety of spectral and temporal features that are robustly derivable from the speech signal and that provide a rich description useful for determining the acoustic-phonetic correlates of the speech signal. Interestingly, that is what one does, roughly speaking, to find formants in a spectrogram visually. One first attends to a variety of features in the spectrogram, such as the location of spectral energy concentrations and temporal discontinuities. One then interprets those features by using a variety of specific facts about speech, such as the expected piecewise continuity of formants across time.

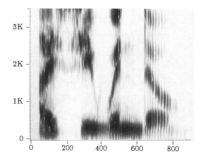

Figure 1 Wide-band spectrogram of the utterance "icy window". Note the merging of F1 and F2 at 400 msec.

For example, Figure 1 shows a wide-band (5 msec Hamming window) spectrogram of the utterance "icy window". In this example, each of the dark bands of concentrated spectral energy correspond for the most part to single, distinct, oral formants. Note that for a short time, however, the two lowest bands merge, which corresponds to the first and second formants coming close together at the /w/. One knows that the single dark band at this point corresponds to two formants, in part, by knowing that formants are piecewise continuous in time and by noticing that this band smoothly splits into two bands just before and just after it with no intervening temporal discontinuities that would suggest any abrupt change in vocal tract configuration.

This paper proposes that this kind of two step approach actually be used in the speech processing. The first step delivers a variety of reliable features of the speech signal—such as the location of spectral energy concentrations and temporal discontinuities. In a distinct second step, these features can be analyzed and reconciled with specific constraints about speech—such as the piecewise continuity of formants—over a time window large enough to give a near unique acoustic-phonetic interpretation in terms of formants, onsets, closures, etc. The interpretation step is by no means expected to be trivial, but it seems much more likely to succeed if it has available a large vocabulary of relevant features of the speech wave, than if, as in the previous approach, it has available only the raw speech wave and its short-time spectra.

4.0 Some General Constraints on Speech Signals

It has been argued above that a robust, wide vocabulary speech recognizer should begin by producing a rich description of the significant features in the speech signal without being forced at that step to relate those features to their particular acoustic-phonetic correlates. This can not be done, however, unless some general assumptions about the nature of speech signals are made. If speech signals were completely unconstrained, consisting of random pops, whistles, and broad-band noise with no underlying structure, one would be at a loss to describe them by anything other than a complete specification of their waveform. Fortunately, the sounds that arrive at or ears are seldom so chaotic. We can, in fact, identify at least two constraints that speech signals generally obey.

The first constraint is: the effects of the different acoustic-phonetic factors that produce a speech signal characteristically appear at different scales in the time and frequency domain. Saying these factors occur at different time scales means they have different characteristic durations, rates, and periods. For example, a burst onset occupies about a msec, while a significant continuous change (say 100 Hz) in formant frequency requires an order of magnitude more time. In other words, a burst onset occurs over a different time scale than formant motion.

These factors also appear at different scales in the frequency domain. For example, Figure 2 shows a narrow-band (50 msec Hamming window) spectrum of a portion of the vowel /i/. The fastest variations in the spectrum are found in the sharp peaks occurring at about 100 Hz intervals across the spectrum, and are due to the harmonic structure generated by the periodic vocal fold vibration. We shall call fast variations in a spectrum *fine scale* spectral structure. Somewhat

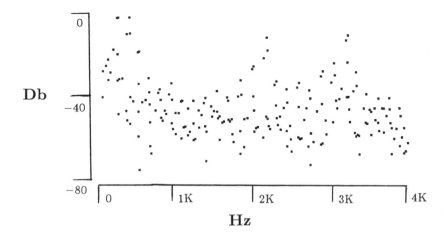

Figure 2 Short-time (50 msec Hamming window) spectrum in the steady-state portion of an /i/ vowel from a male speaker.

slower variations, superimposed on the spectral fine structure, are found in the local spectral energy concentrations of a few hundred Hz bandwidth, such as the the "bumps" at about 300, 2200, and 3100 Hz and are due to the oral formants. Such *intermediate scale* structure can also be due to nasal or transmission channel resonances and antiresonances. The slowest variations in the spectrum, often called the "spectral balance", are found in the overall tilt and gross distribution of energy across the spectrum. This *gross scale* spectral structure is determined by the shape of the source spectrum, the distribution of the formants (F-pattern), and the frequency characteristics of the channel. Thus, the different acoustic-phonetic factors making up a speech signal occur at different, although overlapping, ranges of scale in the frequency domain.

The second constraint is: the acoustic-phonetic factors that produce a speech signal usually vary continuously in time with only occasional discontinuities. Resonance frequencies do not abruptly change every

millisecond, but instead consist mostly of smooth motions in the frequency domain across time with discontinuities occurring only at certain events such as closures and releases. Likewise, pitch contours are piecewise continuous, and channel bandwidth is usually stable, with only occasional abrupt variation.

5.0 The Schematic Spectrogram

We shall now examine the implications of these constraints for the representation of temporal and spectral features of the speech signal. In this section, a broad outline of the kinds of important features that are expected to appear in speech signals and for which appropriate descriptors are needed is given. Following sections will be more specific on how to define descriptors for some of these features of the speech signal.

The first constraint indicates that features will emerge at different time and frequency scales, which suggests that there should be descriptors for this representation at a variety of such scales. Let us first discuss features at time scales of a few pitch periods or greater. Over this time range, there should be descriptors that capture the intermediate spectral structure, in particular, the location of spectral energy concentrations such as seen in the wide-band spectrogram in Figure 1. These descriptors can be used to help infer formant structure. There should also be descriptors that capture gross spectral balance information and changes in it; these descriptors can be used to help infer formant distribution, and the overall shape of the source and transmission channel spectra.

At the scale of a pitch period, there needs to be descriptors that capture the spacing and shape of the glottal pulses or their harmonic structure. These can be used to infer excitation type and pitch.

Very brief, aperiodic events (e.g. bursts) introduce features that emerge on a time scale less than a pitch period, and require their own descriptors. Note these features may be somewhat indistinct in conventional spectrograms because of their short duration relative to the transform window duration and because of their aperiodic nature.

The second constraint indicates that continuity across time can be expected for many of the features described above, and thus many of the descriptors can be restricted to features that are continuous across time. Further, when discontinuities occasionally do occur, they may reflect important phonetic events themselves, such as voice onsets, articulatory closures, and releases. Thus, descriptors should exist for temporal discontinuities of various kinds such as broad-band temporal edges and terminations of local spectral energy con-

centrations.

Since many of the descriptors for this representation of temporal and spectral features of the speech signal make explicit those features seen in spectrograms, we shall call this representation the "schematic spectrogram". Now that a broad outline of the kinds of features that require descriptors for this representation has been given, let us turn to the question of what specific descriptors to define on some of these features.

6.0 Selecting the Time and Frequency Scales

In order to select specific time and frequency scales of the speech signal, we shall begin with a narrow-band spectrogram, as in Figure 3a. This is produced by every 5 msecs windowing the speech with a 50 msec Hamming window and then computing the Fourier transform (DFT) of the windowed speech. The 50 msec window will cause aperiodic events much less than 50 msec to be "smeared" and perhaps lost in the spectrogram, but features related to very abrupt temporal changes can be dealt with separately.

To select a particular time and frequency scale, we need to smooth out variations faster than desired, and "flatten" out variations slower than desired in both the time and frequency dimensions of the spectrogram. The smoothing can be performed by convolving cross-sections of the narrow-band spectrogram in each dimension with a Gaussian smoothing mask of appropriate width. The "flattening" can be performed by convolving cross-sections with a smoothing mask of appropriate width and subtracting the result from the original cross-sections.

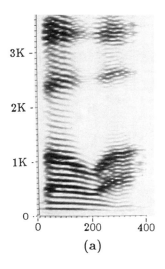
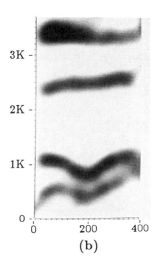

(a)   (b)

Figure 3 (a) Narrow-band spectrogram of the utterance "boa". (b) Convolved spectrogram designed to select intermediate scale spectral structure of (a).

For example, to select an intermediate frequency scale: (1) convolve spectral cross-sections of the narrow-band spectrogram with a Gaussian smoothing mask of 200 Hz half power bandwidth, smoothing out fast spectral variations, and (2) convolve spectral cross-sections of the narrow-band spectrogram with a Gaussian smoothing mask of 1000 Hz half power bandwidth and subtract these from the smooth cross-sections of (1), flattening out the slow spectral variations also. To further select a time scale of a few pitch periods or greater: (3) convolve time cross-sections of the result of (2) with a Gaussian smoothing mask of 30 msecs half power duration, smoothing out fast temporal variations. When these operations are applied sequentially to the narrow-band spectrogram shown in Figure 3a, their combined result is the smooth surface shown in Figure 3b.

Comparing Figure 3a and Figure 3b, we see that selecting a time scale of 30 msecs or greater and a frequency scale of 200 to 1000 Hz is fairly effective in separating the intermediate scale spectral energy concentrations from the many other kinds of variation seen in the raw narrow-band spectrogram.

Figure 4 gives a second example of this processing chosen to reveal intermediate spectral structure. The utterance is "may we" spoken by a female speaker. While the F2 location is somewhat indistinct in the narrow- and wide-band spectrograms in Figures 4a and 4b, it is brought forth quite nicely in the convolved spectrogram shown in Figure 4c. Here intermediate scale structure between 300 and 1000 Hz is displayed; somewhat more frequency smoothing is thus used for the higher pitched female speaker.

7.0 Detecting Spectral Energy Concentrations

Once temporal and spectral scales have

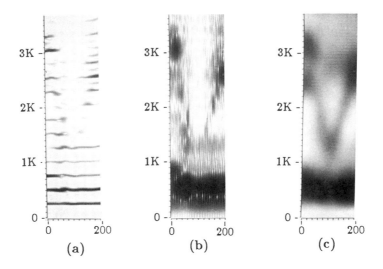

Figure 4 (a)Narrow-band and (b) wide-band spectrograms of the utterance "may we" from a female speaker. (c) intermediate scale convolved spectrogram of (a).

been selected, the features of interest that emerge at these scales need to be identified. This section addresses the detection of intermediate scale spectral energy concentrations like those seen in Figures 3b and 4b. These are of particular interest since they reflect the distribution of formants and channel resonances.

An obvious description of a local spectral energy concentration would include its center or peak frequency as a function of time. An apparently straight-forward way to find this would be to use the peaks (maxima) in spectral cross-sections of smoothed and flattened spectrograms as in Figure 3b. This particular method, however, has a serious difficulty as we shall soon see.

7.1 Detecting peaks in spectral cross-sections

Figure 5 shows the peaks in spectral (vertical) cross-sections in the convolved spec-

trogram in Figure 3b. Note that the computed peaks correspond fairly well to the

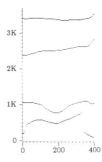

Figure 5 Peaks in spectral cross-section of the convolved spectrogram shown in Figure 3b. In this case, there is good correspondence between these computed peaks and the spectral energy concentrations.

tops of the surface ridges that we see. Figure 6a shows a narrow-band spectrogram of the utterance 'we owe eve", and Fig-

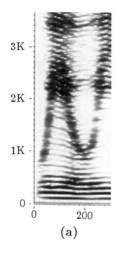 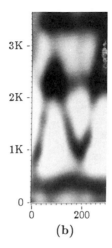

(a)   (b)

Figure 6 (a) Narrow-band spectrogram of the utterance "we owe eve". (b) Intermediate scale convolved spectrogram of (a).

ure 6b the corresponding smoothed and flattened spectrogram that selects an intermediate frequency scale of 200 to 1000 Hz and a time scale of 30 msecs or greater.

This convolved spectrogram appears to bring forth the formant structure, with two of the most prominent ridges corresponding to F1 and F2 (see Figure 6b). For this case, however, there is poor correspondence between the computed peaks in spectral cross-sections of the convolved spectrogram, shown in Figure 7a, and the tops of the surface ridges due to F2, shown in Figure 6b. Evidently, the peaks in spectral cross-sections will not always find the ridges of spectral energy concentration even when these ridges are quite apparent to the eye (as in Figure 6b).

The problem with using peaks in spectral cross-sections of these convolved spectrograms to identify the local spectral energy concentrations is that formants that rise or descend rapidly in frequency are "blurred" in the spectral cross-sections. As the formant rises more

rapidly, its peak in a spectral cross-section broadens due to the formant's increased frequency change over the duration of the analysis window. When the formant motion is rapid enough, the peak introduced by that formant becomes broad enough to be lost when added to the many other factors that shape the spectrum (e.g. effects of nearby formants, harmonic structure, irregularity in source spectrum envelope, etc.)

Evidently, rapidly rising or falling formants will be poorly tracked by peaks in spectral cross-sections due to this broadening effect. Since rapidly moving formants are very common in speech, it is clear that finding peaks in spectral cross-sections of these convolved spectrograms is a poor method for finding the peaks in spectral energy concentrations.

Further, any methods that try to find formants on a (short-time) spectrum-by-spectrum basis, such as the usual analysis-by-synthesis (including LPC) methods, will likewise have problems tracking fast

23

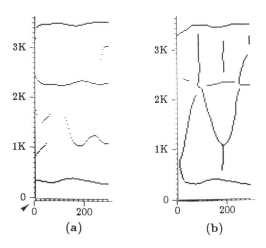

(a)   (b)

Figure 7 (a) Peaks in spectral cross-sections of the convolved spectrogram shown in Figure 6b. Because of rapid formant motion, there is poor correspondence between the computed peaks and the spectral energy concentration due to F2 seen in Figure 6. (b) Two-dimensional ridge tops of the convolved spectrogram shown in Figure 6b. Note that F2 is tracked well by this method.

moving formants because this "blurring" effect will be introduced by the analysis window. This adds another reason to why such methods are so prone to error.

7.2 Detecting peaks in two-dimensional ridges

How then can we find the peaks in the spectral energy concentrations that are so apparent in the convolved spectrogram in Figure 6b? The second general constraint on speech signals given above will help provide an answer. If the frequency of the spectral energy concentrations can be assumed to vary continuously in time almost everywhere, then the spectral energy concentrations should form continuous ridges in frequency and time in these convolved spectrograms. Consequently, the tops of these ridges considered two-dimensionally—not one-dimensionally in vertical (i.e. spectral) cross-sections as

was done above—can be used to define the peaks in the spectral energy concentrations.

This raises the question of how to define the top of a ridge on a smooth, two-dimensional surface. We begin with a mathematical definition or a ridge top. Then, an intuitive interpretation of this definition is given.

First, we need to introduce some notation. Let $f : R^2 \to R$ be a differentiable function, and let S denote the graph of f. Then S is a regular surface parameterized by $F(x,y) = (x, y, f(x,y))$. Let $\kappa 1(x,y) >= \kappa 2(x,y)$ denote the principal curvatures of S at $F(x,y)$, and let $E1(x,y)$ and $E2(x,y)$ denote the corresponding principal directions, assuming the usual orientation on S that assigns surface normals into the northern hemisphere. [For those unfamiliar with these terms from differential geometry, see e.g. Do Carmo (1976).]

Let $T(x,y)$ denote the tangent plane
of S at $F(x,y)$, and let $A : R^2 \rightarrow T(x,y)$
denote the differential $F'(x,y)$. Define the
direction of *greatest downward curvature*
as $gdc(x,y) = A^{-1}(E2)/|A(E2)|$. In other
words, $gdc(x,y)$ is a unit vector in the domain of F whose image under A is parallel
to the principal direction corresponding
to a lesser principal curvature. Define a
ridge top as a point (x,y) where the inner
product $< \mathrm{grad} f(x,y), gdc(x,y) >= 0$ and
$\kappa 2(x,y) < 0$.

To see why this is an intuitively reasonable definition of the top of a ridge, let
$g : R \rightarrow R^2$ be a parameterized differentiable curve with $g'(s) = gdc(g(s))$. In other
words, g traces out a curve in the domain
of F that is always tangent to the direction
of maximum downward curvature. Then
$d/ds[F(g(s))] = A(g'(s)) = A(gdc(g(s)))$ is
parallel to $E2(g(s))$, so $F \circ g$ traces out
a curve on the surface S that is always
tangent to the local direction of minimum
normal curvature.

If such a curve $F \circ g$ were to cross the
top of a ridge, we would expect the local
tangent $d/ds[F(g(s))]$ would be perpendicular to the top of the ridge. This follows
since the surface should curve downward
more sharply as one moves toward and
away from the ridge top than if one moves
along it.

Therefore, since the curve $F \circ g$ is
crossing perpendicular to the top of the
ridge, $F \circ g$ should go through a peak at the
ridge top. In other words, $d/ds[f(g(s))] = 0$
at the ridge top. By the chain rule, this
occurs precisely where $< \mathrm{grad} f, g'(s) >=<$
$\mathrm{grad} f, gdc(g(s)) >= 0$. If $\kappa 2 < 0$, this insures that the curve goes though a maxi-
mum. But this is just our above definition
of a ridge top.

Since $< \mathrm{grad}\ f, gdcF >$ may vanish
in between sample points in an imple-

mentation of this computation, one can
instead detect *zero-crossings* in this quantity between adjacent samples in the x–y
plane.

Figure 7b shows these computed two-
dimensional ridge tops for Figure 6b. In
this case, the computed ridge tops track
the tops of the prominent ridges quite
well. Experience so far with convolved
spectrograms of other utterances has also
shown good correspondence between the
ridges seen in displays of these surfaces and
the ridge tops computed by this method.

For instance, Figure 8a shows the
computed ridge tops for the utterance
"may we" used in Figure 4. For comparison, peaks in spectral cross-sections
(Figure 8b) and twelve order LPC pole
frequencies (Figure 8c) are also displayed.
Note that the higher pitched female speech
presents no particular problem for the two-
dimensional ridge top method, except requiring somewhat greater frequency
smoothing for the more widely spaced
harmonics.

If the spectra are not "flattened",
vertical ridges will result due to overall
amplitude variations across time. The
flattening removes DC and very slow variations in the spectra, eliminating this
influence of overall amplitude.

Note the vertical ridge at 180 msecs
and running from 500 to 1000 Hz in Figure 7. This ridge is not due to an overall
amplitude effect nor the peak frequency
region of a particular formant, but to the
change of direction of the formant F2. As
F2 approaches F1 in time, the spectral
valley between them rises in amplitude,
reaches a maximum at their closest approach, and then falls in amplitude, thus
creating a vertical ridge. This newly observed effect adds to the information these
ridges can deliver about formant struc-

23

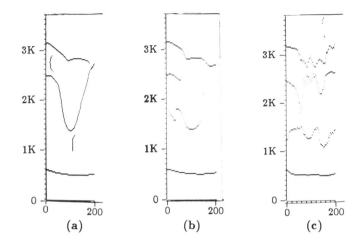

Figure 8 (a) Two-dimensional ridge tops and (b) peaks in spectral cross-sections of the convolved spectrogram shown in Figure 4b. (c) Pole distribution for twelve pole LPC analysis of utterance used in Figure 4.

ture, but also increases the complexity in interpreting them.

7.3 The aspect ratio problem

When such a two-dimensional approach is taken, some aspect ratio between time and frequency must be adopted, or the computations need to be defined so that they are stretch invariant. Since the notion of a two-dimensional ridge seems to be inherently dependent on aspect ratio (imagine a ridge produced by a hemisphere stretched alternately along the x and y axes) an appropriate aspect ratio must be chosen.

The following crude argument provides a preferred aspect ratio for these convolved spectrograms that is dependent on the scale of the spectral energy concentration sought. Suppose we have a time-dependent transfer function $H(t, f)$ with a single spectral peak of fixed bandwidth B. Suppose the time dependency of the spectral peak is described by $f = A(t)$,

and that the transfer function is described by $H(t, f) = P(f, B) * Q(t, f)$ where $Q(t, f) = \text{delta}(f - A(t)) + \text{delta}(f + A(t))$. Further, suppose that the excitation and the time variation of the transfer function are such that the time and frequency smoothed spectrogram $F(t, f) = H(t, f) * TS(t, C) * FS(f, D)$, where TS (t, C) is a time smoothing mask of duration C, and $FS(t, D)$ is a frequency smoothing ask a bandwidth D. In other words, the convolved spectrogram in this case can be described as a time and frequency smoothed version of the transfer function.

But then $F(t, f) = [P(f, B) * TS$ $(t, C) * FS(f, D)] * Q(t, f)$. Thus, if the aspect ratio is chosen so that the effective time and frequency width of $P(f, B) * TS$ $(T, C) * FS(f, D)$ are the same, then the cross-sectional width of the resulting two-dimensional ridge on the surface $F(t, f)$ will be maximally independent of the path $f = A(t)$. The desired aspect ratio r satisfies (frequency width) $B + D = r * C$ (time width), or $r = (B + D)/C$.

7.4 Alternative approaches to resolving rapidly moving formants

An alternative way to try to avoid the blurring effect of the analysis window and to succeed in tracking rapidly moving formants would be simply to use a shorter analysis window and less time smoothing. Then, one-dimensional analysis of each spectral cross-section might be adequate, and the two-dimensional approach taken above would be unnecessary. Unfortunately, using analysis windows shorter than a few pitch periods present some real difficulties.

If the analysis window is reduced, frequency resolution is lost. If a 5 msec Hamming window is used to create a wideband spectrogram, the effective resolution in the frequency domain is a few hundred Hz. Further, the frequency "smoothing" is phase dependent; sometimes nearby components reinforce, sometimes they cancel. This follows from the fact that the Fourier transform of the product of the Hamming window $h(t)$ placed at time T and the speech signal $x(t)$ is $H(w) * X(w) \exp(-iwt)$, where "$*$" denotes convolution. The magnitude spectrum thus contains artifactual structure due to a phase dependent window interaction.

If the analysis window is about the same duration as a pitch period, then the resulting spectrum will be very sensitive to the exact size and placement of the window, due to the interaction of the window and the pitch period. One could try pitch synchronous analysis in this case, i.e. try rectangular windowing of precisely each pitch period. Pitch synchronous analysis, however, requires

fairly precise determination of the boundaries of a pitch period early on in the processing. Further, such analysis would be inappropriate for speech with noise or mixed excitation (e.g. whispered speech, breathing voice). Since we are interested at this point in obtaining descriptions of the speech signal that are as robust and as general as possible, it would be best if the analysis used to obtain the intermediate scale spectral description did not have to depend so strongly on decisions about the exact details of the excitation.

This is why a longer analysis window, encompassing several pitch periods, and having a gradual onset and offset combined with some time smoothing of the result were used above. These steps reduce both phase dependent and excitation dependent interactions with the analysis window.

8.0 Discussion

The previous section explored methods for detecting and representing the local spectral energy concentrations that emerge at intermediate time and frequency scales like those seen in Figure 3b. Methods for representing spectral balance and its changes must also be devised, since whether a local spectral energy concentration corresponds to zero, one or two formants is reflected in the more gross scale spectral structure. How to appropriately capture this kind of information is under current investigation.

The way that spectral balance and other aspects of the proposed schematic spectrogram should be represented will depend, in part, on how this disparate information will be combined to produce the acoustic-phonetic interpretation in terms of formants, onsets, and so forth. The constraints about speech that are valid for this second step need to be formulated (e.g. the piecewise continuity of formants), and methods that exploit these constraints need to be developed. There is, in fact, much to be done before this approach can be used to produce, say, a high performance formant tracker.

Whether the kind of two step approach of symbolic description before physical interpretation presented here is appropriate for general purpose speech recognition will ultimately depend on how difficult a task speech recognition really is. If the acoustic-phonetic factors that make up a speech signal are often as conflated in that signal as suggested above, with the crucial information needed to recover any of them being intrinsically distributed among a variety of different kinds of features in speech signal, then the current approach would seem appropriate.

A distinct issue from the value of the general approach presented in Section 2 through Section 5 is how adequate the methods presented in Section 6 and Section 7 are for separating different time and frequency scales and for detecting local spectral energy concentrations. One possible way to improve upon the methods presented here would be to introduce the orientation selectivity of the analysis directly into the signal transform itself. In other words, construct a transform that expresses the speech signal in terms of sinusoids that increase or decrease linearly in time. If the appropriately sloped path along which to perform this trans-

form could be selected, say, for a rising formant, then considerably improved frequency resolution would result.

References

Atal, B. & Hanauer, S. (1971) Speech analysis and synthesis by linear prediction of the speech wave. *J. Acoust. Soc. Am.*, 50:637–655.

Bell, C. Fujisake, H., Heinz, J., Stevens, K. & House, A. (1961) Reduction of speech spectra by analysis-by-synthesis techniques. *J. Acoust. Soc. Am.*, 33:1725–1736.

Do Carmo, M. (1976) *Differential Geometry of Curves and Surfaces*. Englewood Cliffs, NJ: Prentice-Hall.

Fant, G. (1960) *Acoustic Theory of Speech Production*. Hague: Mouton.

Markel, J. & Gray, A. (1976) *Linear Prediction of Speech*. New York: Springer-Verlag.

Marr, D.C. (1982) *Vision: A Computational Investigation into the Human Representation and Processing of Visual Information*. San Francisco: W.H. Freeman.

Matthews, M., Miller, J. & David, E. (1961) Pitch synchronous analysis of voiced sounds. *J. Acoust. Soc. Am.*, 45:458–465.

Olive, J. (1971) Automatic formant tracking in a Newton-Raphson technique. *J. Acoust. Soc. Am.*, 50:661–670.

Rabiner, L. & Schafer, R. (1978) *Digital Processing of Speech Signals*. Englewood Cliffs, NJ: Prentice-Hall.

Reprinted from Bell Laboratories Tech. Memo, September 1983, File Case 38794–54.

Acoustics of the Singing Voice

Johan Sundberg

Royal Institute of Technology
Stockholm, Sweden

Clearly there is something quite unusual about the voice of a first-class opera singer. Quite apart from the music, the intrinsic quality of such a voice can have a forceful impact on the listener. Moreover, a well-trained singer produces sounds that can be heard distinctly in a large opera house even over a high level of sound from the orchestra, and can do so week after week, year after year. If a second-rate singer or a completely untrained one tried to be heard over an orchestra, the result would be a scream and the singer's voice would soon fail. Is it only training that makes the difference? Or is the instrument that produces an excellent singer's voice itself different from other people's?

Let us begin with a description of that instrument. The voice organ includes the lungs, the larynx, the pharynx, the nose and the mouth. The main voice function of the lungs is to produce an excess of air pressure, thereby generating an airstream. The air passes through the glottis, a space at the base of the larynx between the two vocal folds (which are often called the vocal cords but are actually elastic infoldings of the mucous membrane lining of the larynx). The front end of each vocal fold is attached to the the thyroid cartilage, or Adam's apple. The back end of each is attached to one of the two small arytenoid cartilages, which are mobile, moving to separate the folds

(for breathing), to bring them together and to stretch them. The vocal folds have a function apart from that of producing sound: they protect the lungs from any small objects entrained in the inspired airstream. Just above the vocal folds are the two "false" vocal folds, which are engaged when someone holds his breath with an overpressure of air in the lungs. The vocal folds are at the bottom of the tube-shaped larynx, which fits into the pharynx, the wider cavity that leads from the mouth to the esophagus. The roof of the pharynx is the velum, or soft palate, which in turn is the door to the nasal cavity. When the velum is in its raised position (which is to say during the sounding of all vowels except the nasalized ones), the passage to the nose is closed and air moves out through the mouth.

The larynx, the pharynx and the mouth together constitute the vocal tract, a resonant chamber something like the tube of a horn or the body of a violin. The shape of the tract is determined by the positions of the articulators: the lips, the jaw, the tongue and the larynx. Movements of the lips, jaw and tongue constrict or dilate the vocal tract at certain sites; protruding the lips or lowering the larynx increases the length of the tract.

Now consider the voice organ as a generator of voiced sounds. Functionally the organ has three major units: a power

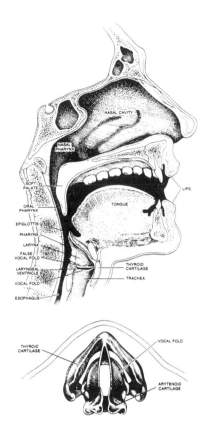

Figure 1 Voice organ is composed of the lungs and the larynx, pharynx, mouth and nose, shown in the longitudinal section (*top*). The larynx is a short tube at the base of which are twin infoldings of mucous membrane, the vocal folds. The larynx opens into the pharynx; the opening is protected during swallowing by the epiglottis. The larynx, pharynx and mouth (and in nasal sounds also the nose) constitute the vocal tract. It is a resonator whose shape, which determines vowel sounds, is modified by changes in the position of the articulators: the lips, the jaw, the tip and body of the tongue and the larynx. The vocal folds, seen from above in a transverse section (*bottom*), are opened for breathing and are closed for phonation by the pivoting arytenoid cartilages.

supply (the lungs), an oscillator (the vocal folds) and a resonator (the vocal tract). With the glottis closed and an airstream issuing from the lungs, the excess pressure below the glottis forces the vocal folds apart; the air passing between the folds generates a Bernoulli force that, along with the mechanical properties of the folds, almost immediately closes the glottis. The pressure differential builds up again, forcing the vocal folds apart again. The cycle of opening and closing, in which the vocal folds act somewhat like the vibrating lips of a brass-instrument player, feeds a train of air pulses into the vocal tract. The frequency of the vibration is determined by the air pressure in the lungs and by the vocal folds' mechanical properties, which are regulated by a large number of laryngeal muscles. In general the higher the lung pressure is and the thinner and more stretched the vocal folds are, the higher is the frequency at which the folds vibrate and emit air pulses. The train of pulses produces a rapidly oscillating air pressure in the vocal tract; in other words, a sound. Its pitch is a manifestation of the vibratory frequency. Most singers need to develop full control over a pitch range of two octaves or more, whereas for ordinary speech less than one octave suffices.

The sound generated by the airstream chopped by the vibrating vocal folds is called the voice source. It is in effect the raw material for speech or song. It is a complex tone composed of a fundamental frequency (determined by the vibratory frequency of the vocal folds) and a large number of higher harmonic partials, or overtones. The amplitude of the partials decreases uniformly with frequency at the rate of about 12 decibels per octave. The "source spectrum," or plot of amplitude against frequency, for a singer is not very different for that for a nonsinger, although the spectrum does tend to slope more steeply in soft speech than it does in soft singing.

The vocal tract is a resonator, and the transmission of sound through an acoustic resonator is highly dependent on frequency. Sounds of the resonance frequencies peculiar to each resonator are less attenuated than other sounds and are therefore radiated with a higher relative amplitude, or with a greater relative loudness, than other sounds; the larger the frequency distance between a sound and a resonance is, the more weakly the sound is radiated. The vocal tract has four or five important resonances called formants. The many voice-source partials fed into the vocal tract traverse it with varying success depending on their frequency; the closer a partial is to a formant frequency, the more its amplitude at the lip opening is increased. The presence of the formants disrupts the uniformly sloping envelope of the voice-source spectrum, imposing peaks at the formant frequencies. It is this perturbation of the voice-source envelope that produces distinguishable speech sounds; particular formant frequencies manifest themselves in the radiated spectrum as peaks in the envelope, and those peaks are characteristic of particular sounds.

The formant frequencies are determined by the shape of the vocal tract. If the vocal tract were a perfect cylinder closed at the glottis and open at the lips and 17.5 centimeters (about seven inches) long, which is about right for the average adult male, then the first four formants would be close to 500, 1,500, 2,500 and 3,500 Hz (cycles per second). Given a

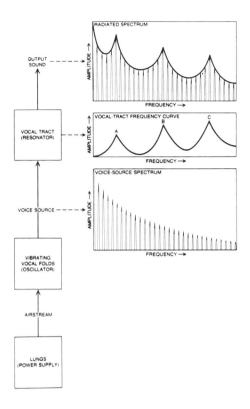

Figure 2 Voice organ is composed functionally of a power supply, an oscillator and a resonator. The airstream from the lungs is periodically interrupted by the vibrating vocal folds. The resulting sound, the voice source, has a spectrum (*right*) containing a large number of harmonic partials, the amplitude of which decreases uniformly with frequency. The air column within the vocal tract has characteristic modes of vibration, or resonances, called formants (*A, B, C*). As the voice source moves through the vocal tract each partial is attenuated in proportion to its distance from formant nearest it in frequency. The formant frequencies thus appear as peaks in the spectrum of the sound radiated from the lips; the peaks establish particular vowel sounds.

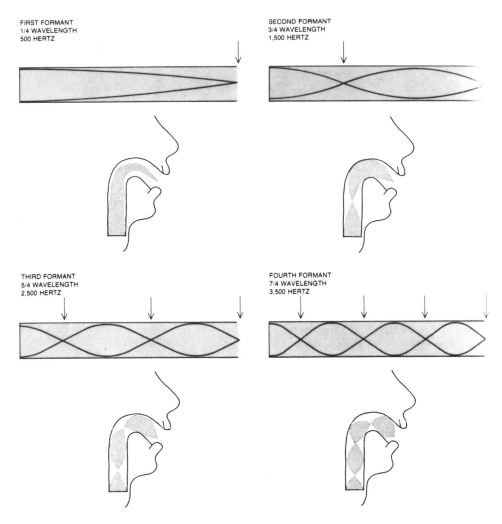

Figure 3 Formants correspond to standing waves, or static patterns of air-pressure oscillations, in the vocal tract. Here the first four formants are shown as standing waves in cylindrical tubes, the schematic equivalent of the vocal tract (*colored areas in drawings*). The sine waves represent the amplitude of the pressure differential, which is always maximal at the glottal end and minimal at the lips. For the lowest formant, a quarter of a wavelength is within the vocal tract and, if the tract is 17.5 centimeters long, the formant's frequency is about 500 Hz (cycles per second). The second, third and fourth formants are 3/4, 5/4 and 7/4 of a wavelength, and their frequencies vary accordingly. If the area of the vocal tract is decreased or increased at a place where the formant's pressure amplitude is at a minimum (*arrows*), that formant's frequency is respectively lowered or raised; the same change in area has the opposite effect if it is at a pressure maximum.

longer or shorter vocal tract, these basic frequencies are somewhat lower or higher. Each formant is associated with a standing wave, that is, with a static pattern of pressure oscillations whose amplitude is at a maximum at the glottal end near a minimum at the lip opening [*see Figure 3*]. The lowest formant corresponds to a quarter of of a wavelength, which is to say that a quarter of its wavelength fits within the vocal tract. Similarly, the second, third and fourth formants correspond respectively to three-quarters of a wavelength, one and a quarter wavelengths and one and three-quarters wavelengths.

Any change in the cross section of the vocal tract shifts the individual formant frequencies, the direction of the shift depending on just where the change in area falls along the standing wave. For example, constriction of the vocal tract at a place where the standing wave of a formant exhibits minimum-amplitude pressure oscillations generally causes the formant to drop in frequency; expansion of the tract at those same places raises the frequency.

The vocal tract is constricted and expanded in many rather complicated ways, and constricting it in one place affects the frequency of all formants in different ways. There are, however, three major tools for changing the shape of the tract in such a way that the frequency of a particular formant is shifted in a particular direction. These tools are the jaw, the body of the tongue and tip of the tongue. The jaw opening, which can constrict the tract toward the glottal end and expand it toward the lip end, is decisive in particular for the frequency of the first formant, which rises as the jaw is opened wider. The second-formant frequency is particularly sensitive to the shape of the

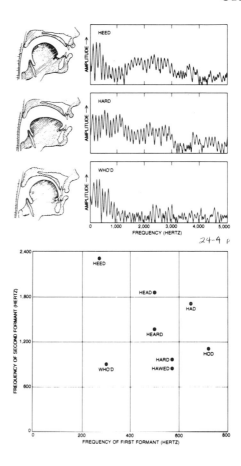

Figure 4 Movement of articulators changes the cross section of the vocal tract, shifting formant frequencies. Three articulatory configurations are shown (*top*) together with the spectrum of the vowel sound produced by each; the peaks in the spectrum envelope reflect the formant frequencies. The chart (*bottom*) gives the frequencies of the first and second formants in some English vowel sounds as spoken by an average male. For a female or a child the envelope pattern would be about the same but the peaks would be shifted somewhat higher in frequency.

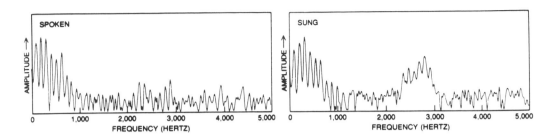

Figure 5 Vowels sound different in speech and in singing and the difference is visible in their recorded spectra. Here the spectra of the vowel in "who'd" as spoken (*left*) and as sung (*right*) by a male opera singer are compared. What is significantly different about the sung spectrum is the spectral-energy peak that appears in it between about 2,500 and 3,000 Hz. The new peak is called the singing formant.

body of the tongue, the third-formant frequency to the position of the tip of the tongue. Moving the various articulatory organs in different ways changes the frequencies of the two lowest formants over a considerable range, which in adult males averages approximately from 250 to 700 Hz for the first formant and from 700 to 2,500 Hz for the second. Moving the articulatory organs is what we do when we speak and sing; in effect we chew the standing waves of our formants to change their frequencies. Each articulatory configuration corresponds to a set of formant frequencies, which in turn is associated with a particular vowel sound. More specifically, the formant frequencies enhance voice-source partials of certain frequencies and thus manifest themselves as the peaks characterizing the spectrum envelope of each vowel sound.

All the elements and functions of the voice organ that I have been describing are common to singers and nonsingers alike. Do singers bring still other faculties into play or manipulate the voice instrument in different ways? Let us begin by comparing

normal male speech and operatic singing. Careful attention to a singer's voice reveals a number of modest but very characteristic deviations in vowel quality from those of ordinary speech. For example, the *ee* sound of a word such as "beat" is shifted toward the umlauted *ü* of the German "*für*"; the short *e* of "head" moves toward the vowel sound of "heard." The general impression is that the quality of the voice is "darker" in singing, somewhat as it is when a person yawns and speaks at the same time; voice teachers sometimes describe the effect as "covering."

These shifts in vowel quality have been found to be associated with peculiarities of articulation. In "covered" singing the larynx is lowered, and X-ray pictures reveal that the change in the position of the larynx is accompanied by an expansion of the lowest part of the pharynx and of the laryngeal ventricle, the space between the true vocal folds and the false ones. It is interesting to note that voice teachers tend to agree that the pharynx should be widened in singing, and some of them mention the sensation of yawn-

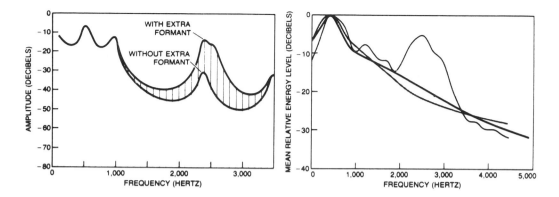

Figure 6 Singing formant's origin (*left*) and its utility in singing (*right*) are demonstrated. An extra formant was inserted between the usual third and fourth formants in an experiment with an electronic resonator that behaves like the vocal tract (*left*). The new formant increased the amplitude of the partials near it by more than 20 decibels; similarly, an extra formant (achieved by lowering the larynx) supplies the high-frequency peak in the spectrum of a sung vowel. The three curves (*right*) show the averaged distribution of energy in the sound of orchestral music (*black*), of ordinary speech (*gray*) and of the late tenor Jussi Björling singing with an orchestra (*colored*). The distribution is very similar for speech and the orchestra at all frequencies; it is the singer's voice that produces the peak in the colored curve between 2,000 and 3,000 Hz. In that frequency region a singer's voice is loud enough, compared with an orchestra's sound, to be discerned.

ing. In other words, a low larynx position and an expanded pharynx are considered desirable in singing.

What we recognize as a darkened voice quality in singing is reflected very clearly in the spectrum of a sung vowel sound. A comparison of the spectra of the vowel in "who'd" as it is spoken and sung shows that the two lowest formant frequencies are somewhat lower in the sung version and that the spectral energy, or amplitude, is considerably higher between 2,500 and 3,000 Hz [*see Figure 5*]. This spectral-envelope peak is typical of all voiced sounds sung by professional male singers. Indeed, its presence, regardless of the pitch, the particular vowel and the

dynamic level, has come to be considered a criterion of quality; the extra peak has been designated the "singing formant."

What is the origin of the singing-formant peak? The peaks in the spectrum envelope of a vowel normally stem, as I have explained, from the presence of specific formants. The insertion of an extra formant between the normal third and fourth formants would produce the kind of peak that is seen in the spectrum of a sung vowel [*see Figure 6*]. Moreover, the acoustics of the vocal tract when the larynx is lowered are compatible with the generation of just such an extra formant. It can be calculated that if the area of the outlet of the larynx into the pharynx is

24

less than a sixth of the area of the cross section of the pharynx, then the larynx is acoustically mismatched with the rest of the vocal tract; it has a resonance frequency of its own, largely independent of the remainder of the tract. The one-sixth condition is likely to be met when the larynx is lowered, because the lowering tends to expand the bottom part of the pharynx. I have estimated on the basis of X-ray pictures of a lowered larynx that this lowered-larynx resonance frequency should be between 2,500 and 3,000 Hz, that is, between the frequencies of the normal third and fourth formants and just where the singing-formant peak appears. The lowering of the larynx, in other words, seems to explain the singing-formant peak.

It also accounts for something else. Acoustically the expansion of the lower-most part of the pharynx is equivalent to an increase in the length of the vocal tract, and the lowering of the larynx adds still more to the length. The result is to shift downward all formant frequencies other than the larynx-dependent extra formant. This lowering of frequency is particularly notable in formants that depend primarily on the length of the pharynx. Two examples of such formants are the second formant of the vowels in "beat" and "head," and a drop in the frequency of those formants moves their vowels respectively toward those of "*für*" and "heard." The lowering of the larynx, then, explains not only the singing-formant peak but also major differences in the quality of vowels in speech and in singing.

To explain the singing formant's articulatory and acoustic origin is not enough, however. Why, one wonders, is it desirable for singers to lower the larynx, producing the singing formant and darkening the quality of their vowels? A plausible answer

to the question has been found. It is related to the acoustic environment in which opera and concert singers have to work: in competition with an orchestra. Analysis of the average distribution of energy in the sounds of an opera or symphony orchestra shows that the highest level of sound is in the vicinity of 450 Hz; above that the amplitude decreases sharply with frequency. Now, normal speech develops maximum average energy at about the same frequency and weakens at higher frequencies. A singer who produced sounds with the energy distribution of ordinary speech would therefore be in trouble: the orchestra's much stronger sounds would drown out the singer's. The average sound distribution of a trained singer, on the other hand, differs from that of normal speech—and of an orchestra—mainly because of singing-formant effect. We have shown that a singer's voice is heard much more easily against recorded noise that has the same average energy distribution as an orchestra's sound if the voice has a singing formant. Not only is the formant almost invariably audible, because its frequency is in a region where the orchestra's sound is rather weak, but also it may help the listener to "imagine" he hears other parts of the singer's spectrum that are in fact drowned out by the orchestra.

The singing formant is at an optimal frequency, high enough to be in the region of declining orchestral-sound energy but not so high as to be beyond the range in which the singer can exercise good control. Because it is generated by resonance effects alone, it calls for no extra vocal effort; the singer achieves audibility without having to generate extra air pressure. The singer does pay a price, however, since the darkened vowel sounds deviate considerably from what one hears in ordinary speech. In some kinds of singing that price is too high: the ideas and moods expressed in a "pop" singer's repertoire, for example, would probably not survive the deviations from naturalness that are required to generate the singing formant. And pop singers do not in fact darken their vowels; they depend on electronic amplification to be heard.

In cartoons a female opera singer is almost invariably depicted as a fat woman with her mouth opened very wide. In a study of female singers I have found that the way in which the jaw is manipulated is in fact quite different in ordinary speech and in singing. In speech the size of the jaw opening varies with the particular vowel, but in female singing it tends to depend also on the pitch of the tone that is being sung: the higher a soprano sings, the wider her jaw is opened. This suggested to me that a soprano must vary the frequency of her first formant according to the pitch at which she is singing. Analysis of formant frequencies confirmed that the articulation was being varied in such a way as to raise the first-formant frequency close to the frequency of the fundamental of the tone being sung. I noted such a frequency match whenever the frequency of the fundamental was higher than the frequency of a vowel's first formant in ordinary speech.

The reason becomes clear when one considers that the pitch frequency of a soprano's tones is often much higher than the normal frequency of the first formant in most vowels. If a soprano sang the vowel ee at the pitch of her middle C and with the articulation of ordinary speech, her first formant would be in the neighborhood of 270 Hz and the pitch frequency (the frequency of her lowest spectrum partial) would be almost an oc-

tave higher, at 523 Hz. Since a sound is attenuated in proportion to the distance of its frequency from a formant frequency, the fundamental would suffer a serious loss of amplitude. The fundamental is the strongest partial in the voice-source spectrum, and the higher its pitch is, the more important the fundamental is for the loudness of the tone, and so the singer's ee would be rather faint. Assume that her next sound was the ah sound of "father," to be sung at the pitch of high F. The fundamental, at 698 Hz, would be very close to the frequency of the first formant, about 700 Hz, and so the tone would be loud. The loudness of the singer's tones would vary, in other words, according to a rather unmusical determinant: the frequency distance between the first formant and the fundamental. In order to modulate the loudness according to the musical context, the singer would need to continually vary her vocal effort. That would strain her vocal folds. (Experiments with synthesized vowel sounds suggest that it would also produce tones more characteristic of a mouse under severe stress than of an opera singer!)

The soprano's solution is to move the first formant up in frequency to match the frequency of the fundamental, thus allowing the formant always to enhance the amplitude of the fundamental. The result is that there is minimal variation in loudness from pitch to pitch and from vowel to vowel. Moreover, changing the size of the jaw opening in this way provides maximum loudness at the lowest possible cost in vocal effort. The strategy is probably resorted to not only by sopranos but also by other singers whose pitch range includes frequencies higher than those of the first formants of ordinary speech: contraltos, tenors and occasionally even baritones.

24

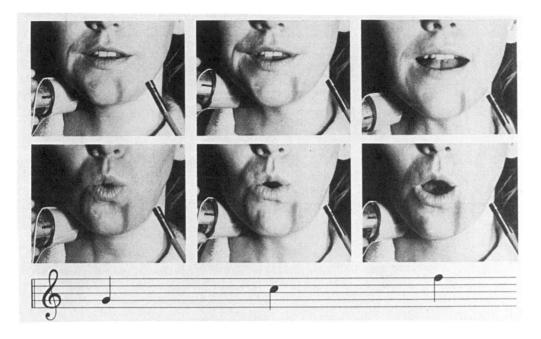

Figure 7 Sopranos and other singers of high tones tend to open their mouth wider with rising pitch. The tendency is demonstrated in these photographs of a soprano singing the vowel sounds of "heed" (*top*) and of "who'd" (*middle*) at successively higher pitches, shown in musical notation (*bottom*). When these photographs were made, the singer held a vibrator against her neck and a small microphone was placed near her lips. She began to sing each vowel at a specified pitch and then, with the vibrator turned on, she stopped singing but maintained the positions of the articulatory organs. The vibrator now supplied a steady, low-pitched sound that was influenced by the singer's vocal tract just as her own voice source would have been but that was more suitable for analysis than a high voice tone, which has few partials.

It can be hard for a student of singing to learn this special way of regulating the jaw opening, and particularly hard if the jaw muscles are under constant tension. That may explain why many singing teachers try to get their students to relax the jaw. Another frequent admonition is: "Hear the next tone within yourself before you start to sing it." That could be necessary because proper manipulation of the jaw opening requires some preplanning of articulation for particular vowels and for

the pitch at which they are to be sung. Opening the jaw, however, is not the only way to raise the first-formant frequency. Shortening the vocal tract by drawing back the corners of the mouth serves the same purpose, and that may be why some teachers tell their students to smile when the sing high tones.

Since formant frequencies determine vowel quality, shifting the first-formant frequency arbitrarily according to pitch might be expected to produce a distorted

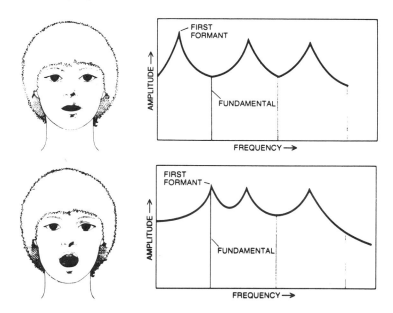

Figure 8 Need for wide jaw opening arises from the fact that a soprano must often sing tones whose fundamental (lowest partial) is far higher in frequency than the normal first formant of the vowel being sung. When that is the case (*top*), the amplitude of the fundamental is not enhanced by the first formant and the sound is weak. Opening the jaw wider raises the pitch of the first formant. When the first-formant frequency is raised to match that of the fundamental (*bottom*), the formant enhances the amplitude of the fundamental and the sound is louder.

vowel sound, even an unintelligible one. It does not have this effect, largely because we are accustomed to hearing vowels produced at various pitches in the ordinary speech of men, women and children with vocal tracts of very different lengths; if a vowel is high-pitched, we associate it with relatively high formant frequencies. The correlation is so well established in our perceptual system that we may perceive a change of vowel when we hear two sounds with identical formant frequencies but different pitches; if a singer raises her first-formant frequency with the pitch, some of that rise is actually required just to maintain the identity of the vowel. It is true that when the pitch is very high,

our ability to identify vowels deteriorates, but that seems to be the case no matter what the formant frequencies are. The soprano, in other words, does not sacrifice much vowel intelligibility specifically as a result of her pitch-dependent choice of first-formant frequency. (Incidentally, composers of vocal music are conscious of the problem of vowel identification at high pitches and generally avoid presenting important bits of text only at the top of a soprano's range; often the text is repeated so that words can be well understood at a lower pitch.)

It is clear that a good deal of the difference between spoken and sung vowels can be explained by the singer's need for

24

economy of vocal effort. The general idea is the same, whether in being heard over the orchestra or in maintaining loudness at high pitch: to take advantage of vocal-tract resonance characteristics so as to amplify sounds. The importance of these resonances, the formants, is paramount.

Confirmation of the importance of the formants was provided by a study of how male voices are classified as bass, baritone or tenor. Obviously the singer's frequency range is ultimately the determinant, but even when the true range (which is established primarily by the shape, size and musculature of the vocal folds) has not yet been developed, a good voice teacher can often predict the classification after listening to a student's voice. How is that possible? Thomas F. Cleveland, who was visiting our laboratory at the Royal Institute of Technology in Stockholm and is now at the University of Southern California, analyzed vowels sung by basses, baritones and tenors with respect to formant frequencies and the spectrum of the voice source. Then he had a jury of voice teachers listen to the vowel samples and classify the voices. The teachers tended to classify vowels in which the formant frequencies were comparatively low as having been sung by bass voices and vowels whose formant frequencies were high as having been sung by tenors. Variations in the voice-source spectrum (which varied slightly with the pitch at which a vowel was being sung), on the other hand, did not provide a basis for consistent classification. In a second test the same jury judged a series of synthesized (and therefore clearly defined) sounds and confirmed Cleveland's original impression: the lower the formant frequencies of a given vowel were, the lower the singer's voice range was assumed to be.

Cleveland found that typical bass and tenor voices differ in formant frequencies very much as male and female voices do. The formant-frequency differences between males and females are due mainly to vocal-tract length, and so the bass-tenor differences are probably also largely explained by the same physical fact. Formant frequencies are determined, however, not only by the individual's vocal-tract morphology but also by habits of articulation, which are highly variable. Be that as it may, vocal-tract morphology must set limits to the range of formant frequencies that are available to a singer.

At this point the reader who knows and cares about music may be rather disappointed. I have failed to mention a number of factors that are often cited as determinants of excellence in singing: the nasal cavity, head and chest resonances, breathing and so on. These factors have not been mentioned simply because they seem to be not relevant to the major acoustic properties of the vowel sounds produced in professional operatic singing. Our research suggests that professional quality can be achieved by means of a rather normal voice source and the resonances of the vocal tract.

Our implied model may not be perfect, to be sure. It is just possible, for example, that the nasal cavity has a role in the singing of vowels that are normally not nasalized. If that is so, we have attributed its effect to the voice source, thus compensating for error by making another. Moreover, we have dealt only with sustained vowel sounds, whose production is important but is certainly not the only acoustic event in singing.

Resonances outside the vocal tract, such as in the head or the chest, cannot contribute appreciably to the singer's acoustic output in view of the great extent to which sound is attenuated as it passes through tissues. This is not to say that such resonances may not be important to the singer, who may receive cues to his own performance not only from what he hears but also from felt vibrations. As for breathing, it is clear that the vocal folds would vibrate no matter by what technique an excess of air pressure is built up below the glottis. Breathing and laryngeal manipulation are likely to be physiologically interdependent, however, since the larynx is the gatekeeper of the lungs. Probably different ways of breathing are associated with different adjustments of the larynx, and probably some ways are effective for singing and others are inadequate or impractical.

Finally we return to the original question: What is so special about a singer's voice? The voice organ obeys the same acoustic laws in singing that it does in ordinary speech. The radiated sound can be explained by the properties of the voice-source spectrum and the formants in singing as in speech. From an acoustical point of view singers appear to be ordinary people. It is true that there is a major difference between the way formant frequencies are chosen in speech and the way they are chosen in singing, and hence between the way vowels are pronounced in singing and the way they are pronounced in speech. A man with a wide pharynx and with a larynx that will resonate at a frequency of between 2,500 and 3,000 Hz is likely to be able to develop a good singing voice more readily than a person who lacks those characteristics. And his progress may be facilitated if his vocal folds give him a range that agrees with his formant frequencies. As for a female singer, she should be able to shift the first formant to join the pitch frequency in the upper part of her range; that requirement may bar some women with a long vocal tract from having a successful career as a coloratura soprano. There are, in other words, a few morphological specifications that probably have some effect on the ease with which someone can learn to sing well. There are other conditions that may be more important, however. It is in the complex of knowledge, talent and musical instinct that is summed up as "musicality," rather than in the anatomy of the lungs and the vocal tract, that an excellent singer's excellence lies.

References

Benade, A. H. (1976) *Fundamentals of Musical Acoustics.* Oxford University Press.

Large, J. (1972) Towards an integrated physiologic-acoustic theory of vocal registers. *NATS Bulletin*, 28(3):18–25; 30–36.

Sundberg, J. (1987) *The Science of the Singing Voice.* DeKalb, IL: Northern Illinois University Press.

Sundberg, J. (1974) Articulatory interpretation of the 'singing formant'. *The Journal of the Acoustical Society of America*, 55(4):838–844.

Vannard, W. (1967) *Singing: the Mechanism and the Technic.* Carl Fischer, Inc.

Reprinted from *Scientific American*, March 1977.

24

Recovering Material Properties from Sound

Richard P. Wildes & Whitman A. Richards

Massachusetts Institute of Technology

1.0 Introduction

Physical modeling of world events occupies an important position in computational approaches to perception and motor control (Brady et al., 1982; Horn, 1970; Marr, 1982; Richards, 1988). Such models are dual in purpose. First, they lend to a precise statement of the problem under consideration. Second, they expose constraints on the solution space, which indicate how the problem can be solved. Here, we use this approach for an initial attack on a previously unsolved problem in audition: How it is possible to recover the material property of an object from the sound generated when it is struck?

Consider some examples. When you hit a drinking glass with your finger-nail it produces a distinct "ringing" sound. In comparison, if you strike a log with your knuckles it gives off a short "thud". In either case you easily identify the material of the struck object. There are other cases where the sound from striking an object leaves one with no clear impression of material type. Objects which are clamped or otherwise artificially damped often belong to this latter class. Our goal is then twofold: First, we seek to discover a physical parameter of the sound following impact which is intrinsically related to material type. Second, we desire to recognize those situations where such material identification is not possible. Guided by a model of vibrating solids we shall choose to satisfy these goals with a measure of energy dissipation during vibration—an intrinsic material property.

2.0 A Physical Model

When a solid object is subject to an impact, much of the resultant sound is due to the vibration of the object. Therefore, we study the mechanics of vibrating solids, and take that motion as analogous to the sound production. In the following presentation we do not consider the initial transient due to impact. Instead, we concentrate on the steady-state and damped behavior of the solid. We proceed in two stages. First, we introduce some basic concepts concerning the deformation of solids. Second, we develop a particular model of a vibrating solid: the standard anelastic linear solid described by Zener (1948).[1]

2.1 Basic concepts

Hooke's law states that an ideal elastic material can be described by the relation

---

[1] Many of the results in Sections 2.1, 2.2 and 3.1 are known in the literature on anelasticity. For further details see Nowick & Berry, 1972; Wert, 1986; Zener, 1948.

$$\sigma = M\epsilon \tag{1}$$

Where: σ is a stress variable (corresponding to a force); ϵ is a strain variable (corresponding to a displacement); and M is an appropriate modulus of elasticity.[2] In many situations it is convenient to define $J = \frac{1}{M}$, as the modulus of compliance. Then (1) becomes

$$\epsilon = J\sigma \tag{2}$$

Elastic behavior so defined is seen to be characterized by three conditions. First, there is a $1 : 1$ correspondence between stress and strain. Second, the stress-strain relationship is linear. Third, there is no time dependence in the mapping between stress and strain. Clearly, any real solid is only approximately characterized by these conditions. In most cases, condition three is a particularly erroneous assumption. Therefore, we proceed by considering cases where there is a time dependence between stress and strain. Solid materials characterized by such a time dependence are called anelastic solids.

Suppose a specimen is subjected to a periodic stress

$$\sigma = \sigma_0 e^{i\omega t} \tag{3}$$

Here: σ_0 is the stress amplitude; $\omega = 2\pi f$ is the angular frequency; t is time; and $i = \sqrt{-1}$. Then, our assumptions of linearity and time dependence dictate that strain has the form

$$\epsilon = \epsilon_0 e^{i(\omega t - \phi)} \tag{4}$$

with ϵ_0 the strain amplitude and ϕ a phase angle. Then, ϕ captures the notion of a time dependence between stress and strain. For subsequent operations it is convenient to separate (4) into its real and imaginary parts. Letting ϵ_1 be the component of strain in phase with stress and ϵ_2 be that component of strain $\frac{\pi}{2}$ out of phase with stress we have

$$\epsilon = (\epsilon_1 - i\epsilon_2)e^{i\omega t} \tag{5}$$

Now, in analogy with (2) we define the complex compliance

$$J(\omega) = \frac{\epsilon}{\sigma} \tag{6}$$

Then, dividing (4) by (3) gives

$$J(\omega) = \frac{\epsilon_0}{\sigma_0} e^{i\phi(\omega)} \tag{7}$$

The complex compliance can also be represented as a sum of real and imaginary parts by dividing (5) by (3) and defining

$$J(\omega) = J_1(\omega) - iJ_2(\omega) \tag{8}$$

We proceed by expanding (7) in terms of Euler's relation[3] and then equating real and imaginary parts of (7) and (8) to get

$$\begin{aligned} J_1(\omega) &= \frac{\epsilon_0}{\sigma_0} \cos\phi(\omega) \\ J_2(\omega) &= \frac{\epsilon_0}{\sigma_0} \sin\phi(\omega) \end{aligned} \tag{9}$$

From which we reach the important result that

$$\tan\phi = \frac{J_2}{J_1} \tag{10}$$

In the anelasticity literature $\tan\phi$ is referred to as internal friction. Internal friction is an intrinsic property of a given material; it measures the degree of anelasticity. We shall ultimately recover a measure closely related to internal friction as our characterization of solid materials.

---

[2]Notice that for a fine grained analysis σ and ϵ would be second order tensors. For our purposes it suffices to consider them as scalars.

[3]$e^{i\theta} = \cos\theta + i\sin\theta$

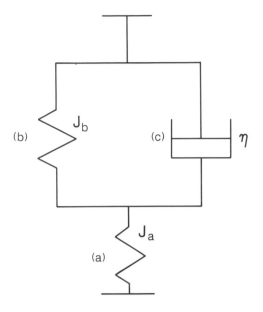

Figure 1 A mechanical model of the standard anelastic linear solid. J_a and J_b are compliances of the two springs. η is the viscosity of the "liquid" in the dashpot.

Finally, it is worth noting that analogous calculations can be carried out in terms of the modulus of elasticity. Such derivations would begin by defining

$$M(\omega) = \frac{\sigma}{\epsilon} \qquad (11)$$

with the ultimate conclusion that

$$\tan \phi = \frac{M_2}{M_1} \qquad (12)$$

2.2 The standard anelastic linear solid

The model of solids that we wish to consider is depicted as a mechanical structure in Figure 1. We refer to this model as the standard anelastic linear solid. The model consists of three elements. Elements a and b are Hookean springs; let them have corresponding compliances J_a and J_b. Element c is a Newtonian dashpot, which serves to provide internal friction. A Newtonian dashpot can be thought of as a plunger moving in a viscous liquid. Its velocity of motion is proportional to the applied force. In terms of stress and strain

$$\sigma = \eta \dot{\epsilon} \qquad (13)$$

with η the viscosity of the liquid. For our purposes we let $\eta = \frac{\tau_\sigma}{J_b}$, where τ_σ is the time required for the system to achieve equilibrium when a constant stress is applied. Notice that this model captures our intuitive notion of what happens when a force is applied to a solid: Initially the solid deforms (element a). With time further deformation takes place (element c). When the force is removed the solid returns to normal (elements a and b).[4]

In order to be more precise, we characterize the behavior of our model in terms of the differential equation

$$a_0 \sigma + a_1 \dot{\sigma} = b_0 \epsilon + b_1 \dot{\epsilon} \qquad (14)$$

where the derivatives are with respect to time. We begin by setting

$$
\begin{aligned}
\epsilon_a &= J_a \sigma_a \\
\epsilon_b &= J_b \sigma_b \\
\dot{\epsilon}_c &= J_b \frac{\sigma_c}{\tau_\sigma}
\end{aligned}
\qquad (15)
$$

We now introduce the standard rules for combining multiple stresses and strains: For series combination, stresses are equal while strains add. The reverse is true

---

[4]In some cases the solid never returns to its original configuration. This introduces the concept of visco-elasticity; we shall not consider such cases.

for parallel combinations. Applying these rules to the model of Figure 1 gives

$$\epsilon = \epsilon_a + \epsilon_b$$
$$\epsilon_b = \epsilon_c$$
$$\sigma = \sigma_a$$
$$= \frac{\epsilon_a}{J_a} \tag{16}$$
$$= \sigma_b + \sigma_c$$
$$= \frac{\epsilon_b + \tau_\sigma \dot{\epsilon}_c}{J_b}$$

We can rearrange (16) to the form (14) as

$$J\sigma + \tau_\sigma J_a \dot{\sigma} = \epsilon + \tau \dot{\epsilon} \tag{17}$$

where $J = J_a + J_b$.

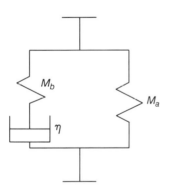

Figure 2 A second mechanical model for the standard anelastic linear solid.

We now characterize our model in terms of the standard measure of internal friction $\tan\phi$. Following methods similar to those of Section 2.1, we substitute (3) and (5) into (17) and equate real and imaginary parts to find that

$$J_1 = J_a + \frac{J_b}{1 + (\omega\tau_\sigma)^2}$$
$$J_2 = J_b \frac{\omega\tau_\sigma}{1 + (\omega\tau_\sigma)^2} \tag{18}$$

Then, upon substituting into (10) we get

$$\tan\phi = J_b \frac{\omega\tau_\sigma}{J + J_a(\omega\tau_\sigma)^2} \tag{19}$$

We continue by deriving a more convenient form for $\tan\phi$. Consider the model of Figure 2. This model can be shown to be formally equivalent to the model of Figure 1. It is customary to represent this latter model in terms of the elastic moduli and the time to strain equilibrium τ_ϵ. Following the methods used above and using analogous symbols, we can find that

$$M_1 = \frac{M_a + M_b(\omega\tau_\epsilon)^2}{1 + (\omega\tau_\epsilon)^2}$$
$$M_2 = M_b \frac{\omega\tau_\epsilon}{1 + (\omega\tau_\epsilon)^2} \tag{20}$$

Finally, to get our simpler expression for $\tan\phi$ we combine (18), (19) and (20) to arrive at

$$\tan\phi = \frac{J_b}{(J_a J)^2} \frac{\omega\tau}{1 + (\omega\tau)^2} \tag{21}$$

with τ the geometric mean of τ_σ and τ_ϵ.

We conclude this section with a recapitulation. In this section we began by introducing the concepts of stress, strain and internal friction. We proceeded to present the standard linear model of anelastic solids in terms of these three parameters. In Section 3 we make use of these relations to classify solid materials from the sound they produce following impact.

3.0 Recovery of Material Type

When an anelastic solid is struck and set into vibration its behavior, and hence the sound it generates following a brief transient, is dictated by our standard linear model. Our goal is to extract some intrinsic parameter of the solid material from this dynamic behavior. As noted earlier, internal friction, $\tan\phi$, is just such a measure. We now proceed to derive two measures of internal friction and then show how they can work together.

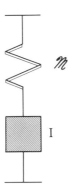

Figure 3 A lumped model of Figures 1 and 2.

3.1 Internal friction and bandwidth, Q^{-1}

We begin by relating internal friction to peak vibration of our standard linear model. To facilitate this set of derivations, we follow (Zener, 1948) and momentarily consider the mechanical system as having only one degree-of-freedom. This is depicted in Figure 3. Here we have lumped the inertia of the system into a single member I, while the anelastic and elastic components are lumped into an anelastic spring with complex modulus[5]

$$\mathcal{M} = M(1 + i\tan\phi) \qquad (22)$$

From Newton's law we observe that

$$I\ddot{\epsilon} = \sigma \qquad (23)$$

Assuming periodic motion, we also have that

$$\epsilon = \epsilon_0 e^{i\omega t} \qquad (24)$$

and as always

$$\sigma = \mathcal{M}\epsilon \qquad (25)$$

We can solve for ϵ by substituting (22), (24), and (25) into (23) to get

$$\epsilon = \frac{\frac{\sigma}{m}}{(1 - \frac{I\omega^2}{M}) + i\tan\phi} \qquad (26)$$

By inspection, we find (26) at a maximum when

$$\omega = \omega_0 = \sqrt{\frac{M}{I}} \qquad (27)$$

Further consideration shows that (26) is at $2^{-\frac{1}{2}}$ maximum amplitude when

$$\omega^2 = \omega_{\pm\frac{1}{2}}^2 = \frac{M}{I}(1 \pm \tan\phi) \qquad (28)$$

We arrive at our first measure of internal friction by noting that

$$\frac{\omega_{+\frac{1}{2}} - \omega_{-\frac{1}{2}}}{\omega_0} = Q^{-1} = \tan\phi \qquad (29)$$

where we use Q in accordance with the corresponding concept from electrical circuit theory. Thus, internal friction can be measured in terms of the sharpness of the peak around the maximum of vibration of our specimen. This will correspond to a sharpness in the peak of the acoustic signal generated by this vibration. It is this acoustic peak which we suggest measuring.

---

[5]It can be shown that an arbitrary standard anelastic linear system in vibration can always be so reduced, see (Nowick & Berry, 1972, appendix A.)

3.2 Internal friction and decay rate t_e

We now seek a measure of internal friction in terms of the decay in amplitude of a vibrating anelastic solid. Combining (22), (23) and (25) we find that

$$I\ddot{\epsilon} + M(1 + i\tan\phi)\epsilon = 0 \qquad (30)$$

describes the behavior of our standard linear system as the vibration decays. The solution to (30) is found to be

$$\epsilon = \epsilon_0 e^{-\Delta f t} e^{i\omega t} \qquad (31)$$

with $\Delta = ln(A_n/A_{n+1})$, where A_n and A_{n+1} are successive peaks in the amplitude of the decaying tone of frequency f. (Δ is called the logarithmic decrement.) We solve for the internal friction by substituting (31) into (30) and equating imaginary parts to find that

$$\frac{\Delta}{\pi} = \tan\phi \qquad (32)$$

Because of the potential difficulties of measuring two successive amplitudes, we proceed a step further. Letting t_e denote the time required for the amplitude to decrease to $\frac{1}{e}$ of its original value, we note that

$$t_e = \frac{1}{f\Delta} = \frac{2\pi}{\omega\Delta} \qquad (33)$$

Rearranging and substituting (33) into (32) then yields

$$\tan\phi = \frac{1}{\pi f t_e} = \frac{2}{\omega t_e} \qquad (34)$$

Our second measure of internal friction is then given in terms of the time it takes the amplitude of vibration (and therefore of the sound) to decrease to some fraction of the original amplitude.

3.3 Specific loss

We now have in hand two measures of internal friction (29) and (34). Examination of these relations reveals that $\tan\phi$ is a function of frequency. For our purposes, it would be more convenient to have a single characterization of anelastic behavior rather than an entire "damping spectrum". Such a measure is available in terms of loss per cycle, known as "specific loss". To motivate this measure we notice from (21) that for $(\omega\tau)^2 \gg 1$, $\omega\tan\phi$ is essentially independent of frequency. Empirical investigations of solids (Bennewitz & Rotger, 1936; Gemant & Jackson, 1937) confirm that this relation is true for a very wide range of vibrational frequencies and materials. Therefore, we define specific loss as

$$\delta = \omega\tan\phi \qquad (35)$$

as our measure of anelasticity and as our key to classifying solid materials by sound.

3.4 A constraint curve

The final task we face is to develop a method of telling when our two measures of internal friction will yield an accurate characterization of a given sample. For example, let us say an object is struck and our auditory system recognizes its pitch as $A_8 = 880$ Hz with a decay rate of 1 sec for t_e. By equation (34) we can recover a measure of internal friction, and hence characterize the material. But how do we know this answer is correct? To confirm that the material behaves as our standard anelastic linear solid, we need a second, corroborating measure. But of course, this can be obtained by recovering the bandwidth, Q^{-1}, of the sound about 880 Hz, using equation (29). In this case,

25

if each measure does not yield the same value for $\tan\phi$, then we must disregard this characterization.

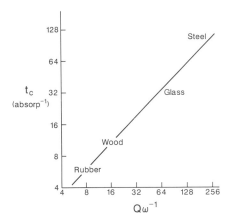

Figure 4 The constant curve relating the two measures of anelasticity for our standard linear solid model. Decay: t_e; tuning width: Q^{-1}.

By plotting t_e versus $Q\omega^{-1}$ as shown in Figure 4, we can construct a constraint line that holds for materials obeying our standard anelastic linear model. The line is independent of frequency because each measure of internal friction has been re-cast as "specific loss" (35). Clearly, all valid measurements must lie along this constraint curve. Here we show how particular material types spread out along the curve with metal at the upper right and rubber at the lower left. The data have been collected from Gemant & Jackson (1937), Berg & Stork (1982) and the *Handbook of Chemistry and Physics*. Exactly how fine a distinction can be realistically made along the constraint curve is largely an empirical question (Waller, 1938; Warren & Verbrugge, 1984).

4.0 Summary

We have described how to make auditory measures of an intrinsic parameter of solid materials. The parameter chosen is called specific loss, and is related to internal friction, a measure of anelasticity for a given material. The two measures presented are related to the width of the resonant peak of a sound and the time of its decay. Crucial to our development has been an understanding of a standard anelastic linear system, a physical model of the mechanics of solid vibration. We hope this work demonstrates the usefulness of using an explicit physical model of sound production in attempts to study sound recognition.

Acknowledgments: This study was supported by grants from ONR and NSF. We are indebted to Prof. Karl Ingard for his patience when we began to struggle with sound source recognition.

References

Bennewitz, V.K. & Rotger, H. (1936) Uber die Reibung fester Korper; Absorptionsfrequenzen von Metallen im akustischen Gebiet, *Phys. Zeitschr.*, 37:578–588.

Berg, R.E. & Stork, D. (1982) *The Physics of Sound.* New Jersey: Prentice-Hall.

Brady, M., Hollerbach, J.M., Johnson, T.L., Lozano-Perez, T. & Mason, M.T. (1982) *Robot Motion: Planning and Control.* Cambridge, MA: MIT Press.

Horn, B.K.P. (1970) Shape from shading: a method for obtaining the shape of a smooth opaque object from one view.

MIT Project MAC Internal Report TR-79 and MIT A.I. Lab. Technical Report 232.

Gemant, A. & Jackson, W. (1937) The measurement of internal friction in some solid materials, *Phil. Mag.*, 157:960 – 983.

Marr, D. (1982) *Vision: a Computational Investigation into the Human Representation and Processing of Visual Information.* San Francisco: Freeman.

Nowick A.S. & Berry, B.S. (1972) *Anelastic Relaxation in Crystaline Solids.* New York: Academic Press.

Richards, W.A. (1988) *Selections in Natural Computation*, Cambridge, MA: MIT Press.

Waller, M.D. (1938) Magneto-damping in nickel, *Phys. Soc. Proc. (London)*, 50:144 – 146.

Warren, W.H. & Verbrugge, R.R. (1984) Auditory perception of breaking and bouncing events: a case study in ecological acoustics. *Journal of Experimental Psychology: Human Perception and Performance*, 10:704 – 712.

Wert, C.A. (1986) Internal friction in solids, *J. Appl. Phys.*, 60(6):1888 – 1895.

Zener, C. (1948) *Elasticity and Anelasticity of Metals* Chicago, IL: University of Chicago Press.

Auditory Perception of Breaking
and Bouncing Events: Psychophysics

William H. Warren, Jr.*
University of Connecticut

Robert R. Verbrugge
University of Connecticut and
Haskins Laboratories, New Haven, Connecticut

Research in auditory perception has tended to emphasize the detection and processing of sound elements with quasi-stable spectral structure, such as tones, formants, and bursts of noise. In the spectral domain, these elements are distinguished by frequency peak or range, bandwidth, and amplitude. In the temporal domain, acoustic analysis has often focused on the durations of sound elements, the intervals and phase relations between them, and the influence of these on pitch and loudness perception, temporal acuity, masking, and localization. The auditory system has often been approached as an analyzer of essentially time-constant functions of frequency, amplitude, and duration, on the assumption that complex auditory percepts are compositions over sound elements having those properties, with certain temporal interactions (Fletcher, 1934; Helmholtz, 1863/1954; Plomp, 1964; see Green, 1976).

The perceptual role of *time-varying* properties of sound has received less attention. Exceptions to this are found in research on amplitude and frequency modulation, including auditory phenomena such as beats, periodicity pitch, and frequency glides. In general, research on time-varying properties has been most common in the study of classes of natural events, such as human speech, music, and animal communication, where an analysis of sound into quasi-stable elements is often problematic. In the case of speech, for example, many phonemic contrasts can be defined by differences in the direction and rate of change of major speech resonances (see Liberman et al., 1956, 1967). Some research on the perception of music has also demonstrated the perceptual significance of time-varying properties. Identification of musical instruments, for example, is strongly influenced by the temporal structure of transients that accompany tone onsets (Luce & Clark, 1967; Saldanha & Corso, 1964). In particular, the relative onset timing and the rates of amplitude change of upper harmonics have been found to be critical properties of attack transients that permit distinctions among instrument families (Grey, 1977; Grey & Gordon, 1978). Animal vocalizations are similarly rich in time-varying properties (such as rhythmic pulsing, frequency modulation, and amplitude modulation), and many of these properties have been shown to be critical for distinguishing the species, sex, location, and motivational state of the producer (e.g. Brown et al., 1978; Konishi, 1978; Petersen et al., 1978).

It is noteworthy that in each of these areas of research on natural events, the discovery or explanation of perceptually significant, time-varying acoustic properties has been motivated by an analysis of the time-varying behavior of the sound *source*. In the case of speech, for example, an analysis of speech production has been an integral part of the search for the acoustic basis for speech perception (e.g. Fant, 1960; Fowler, 1978; Fowler et al., 1980; Liberman et al., 1967; Verbrugge et al., 1985). It is also worth noting that researchers in these areas have often found it useful to characterize acoustic information in terms of *higher order structure* in sound—that is, in terms of functions over the variables of frequency, amplitude, and duration. Given the time-varying behavior of the sound sources involved, it is not surprising that many of these functions are time-dependent, defining rates of change and styles of change in lower order acoustic variables (for example, the direction, rate, and change in rate of formant frequency transitions). Finally, the example of systems capable of measuring higher order physical properties, such as area, without prior measurement of more elementary properties, such as length (Runeson, 1977), has encouraged some researchers to believe that, analogously, higher order acoustic structure may be directly detectable.

The role of time-varying properties in the perception of other familiar events in the human environment is largely unknown. Our goal in this article is to demonstrate that higher order temporal structure can be important for perceiving such events.

It is apparent from everyday experience that listeners can detect significant aspects of the environment by ear, from a knock at the door to the condition of an automobile engine and the gait of an approaching friend (see Jenkins, 1984). Such casual observations were corroborated in experiments by VanDerveer (1979a, 1979b). She presented 30 recorded items of natural sound in a free identification task and found that many events such as clapping, footsteps, jingling keys, and tearing paper were identified with greater than 95% accuracy. Subjects tended to respond by naming a mechanical event that produced the sound and reported their experiences in terms of sensory qualities only when source recognition was not possible. VanDerveer (1979a) also found that confusion errors in identification tasks and clustering in sorting tasks tended to show the grouping of events by common temporal patterns. For example, hammering was confused with walking, and the scratching of fingernails was confused with filing, but hammering and walking were not confused with the latter two events.

These results support the general claim that sound in isolation permits accurate identification of classes of sound-producing events when the temporal structure of the sound is specific to the mechanical activity of the source (Gibson, 1966; Schubert, 1974). If higher order information is found to be specific to events, whereas values of lower order variables per se are not, then it may be more fruitful to view the auditory system as being designed for the perception of source events via higher order acoustic functions, rather than for the detection quasi-stable sound elements. Schubert (1974) put this succinctly in his *source identification principle* for auditory perception: "Identification of sound sources, and the behavior of those sources, is the primary task of the [auditory] system" (p. 126).

26

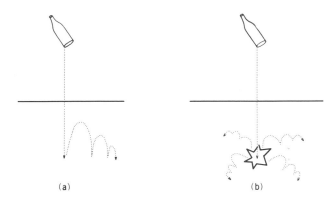

Figure 1 Caricatures of mechanical events: (a) bouncing; (b) breaking.

This general perspective on auditory perception may be called *ecological acoustics*, by analogy to the ecological optics advocated by Gibson (1961, 1966, 1979) as an approach to vision. The ecological approach combines a physical analysis of the source event, the identification of higher order acoustic properties specific to that event, and empirical tests of the listener's ability to detect such information, in an attempt to avoid the introduction of ad hoc processing principles to account for perception (Shaw et al., 1981). (*Ed. note*: the Natural Computation approach also includes these stages, but in addition requires a computationally based analysis of the inference process plus its instantiation.) In any natural event, identifiable objects may be viewed as constraining two characteristic properties of that event. The information of the event that specifies the kind of object and its properties under change is known as the *structural invariant* of an event; the information that reflects the style of change of the object's properties is known as the *transformational invariant*. These invariants may be described mathematically in terms of properties that remain constant

and those that vary systematically under change (Mace, 1977; Mark et al., 1981; Pittenger & Shaw, 1975; Shaw et al., 1974; Warren & Shaw, 1984).

The present research explores the acoustic consequences of dropping a glass object and its subsequent bouncing or breaking. Bouncing and breaking are two distinct styles of change that may be applied to a variety of objects. By acoustic and perceptual studies of these events, we hope to identify the transformational invariants specific to the two styles of change and sufficient to convey them to a listener. (Structural invariants specifying individual properties of the objects such as size, shape, and material will not be discussed here.)

Consider first the mechanical action of a bottle bouncing on a hard surface (see Figure 1a). Each collision consists of an initial impact that briefly sets the bottle into vibration at a set of frequencies determined by its size, shape, and material composition. This is reflected in the acoustic signal as an initial burst of noise followed by spectral energy concentrated at a particular set of overtone frequencies. Over a series of bounces, the collisions between object and ground occur with declining impact force and decreasing ("damped") period, although some irregularities in the pattern may occur because of the asymmetry of the bottle. The spectral components are similar across bounces, with relative overtones varying slightly because of the varying orientations of the bottle at impact. (The spectrum within each pulse is quasi-stable and is conventionally described in terms of spectral peaks in a cross section of the signal.) These acoustic consequences may be described as *a single damped quasi-periodic pulse train* in which the pulses share a similar cross-sectional spectrum (Figure 2a). We suggest that this single pulse train constitutes a transformational invariant of temporal patterning for the bouncing style of change.

Turning to the mechanical action of breaking (Figure 1b), we see that a catastrophic rupture occurs upon impact. Assuming an idealized case, the resulting pieces then continue to bounce without further breakage, each with its own independent collision pattern. The acoustic consequences appear as an *initial rupture burst* dissolving into overlapping *multiple damped quasi-periodic pulse trains*, each train having a different cross-sectional spectrum and damping characteristic (Figure 2b). We propose that a compound signal, consisting of a noise burst followed by such multiple pulse trains, constitutes a transformational invariant for the breaking style of change.

Aside from these aspects of temporal patterning and initial noise, certain crude spectral differences between breaking and bouncing can be observed by comparing spectrograms of natural cases (Figure 2). First, the overtones of breaking events

are distributed across a wider range of frequencies than are those of bouncing events. Second, the overtones of breaking are denser in the frequency domain. Both of these properties can be traced to the contrast between a single object in vibration and a number of disparate objects simultaneously in vibration.

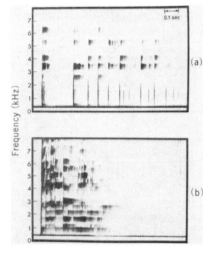

Figure 2 Spectrograms of natural tokens: (a) bouncing (BNC1); (b) breaking (BRK1).

The following experiments test the hypothesis that temporal patterning alone, without differences in quasi-stable spectral properties, provides effective information for listeners to categorize breaking and bouncing styles of change. (Spectral differences may provide important information about the nature and material of the objects involved.) By superimposing recordings of pulses from individual pieces of broken glass, artificial cases of breaking and bouncing can be constructed from a common set of pulses by varying the temporal correspondence among their collision patterns. In Experiment 1 we establish that listeners can categorize natural cases of breaking and bouncing with high accuracy. In Experiment 2, we examine performance with constructed cases that include an initial noise burst and compare it with the results for natural sound.

Experiment 1: Natural Tokens

The first experiment investigated whether natural sound provides sufficient acoustic information for listeners to categorize the events of breaking and bouncing.

Method

Subjects. Fifteen graduate and undergraduate students participated in the experiment for payment or course credit.

Materials. Natural recordings were made of three glass objects dropping onto a concrete floor covered by linoleum tile in a sound-attenuated room. The sound of each object was recorded with a Crown 800 tape deck when the object was dropped from a 1-ft (0.305 m) height (bouncing) and when it was dropped from a 2- to 5-ft (0.61-1.525 m) height (breaking). This procedure yielded three tokens of bouncing and three tokens of breaking. The objects used and the durations of the bouncing (BNC) and breaking (BRK) events are as follows: (a) 32-oz (0.946 l) jar; BNC1 = 1.600 ms, 22 collisions; BRK1 = 1,200 ms. (b) 64-oz (1.892 l) bottle: BNC2 = 1,600 ms, 15 collisions; BRK2 = 550 ms. (c) 1-liter bottle: BNC3 = 1,300 ms, 17 collisions; BRK3 = 700 ms. The recordings were digitized at a 20-kHz sampling rate using the Pulse Code Modulation (PCM) system at Haskins Laboratories. A test tape was then recorded, containing 20 trials of each natural token

in randomized order for a total of 120 test trials. A pause of 3 s occurred between trials, and a pause of 10 s occurred every six trials.

Procedure. Subjects, run in groups of 2 to 5, listened to the tape binaurally through headphones. They were told that they would be hearing recordings of objects that had either bounced or broken after being dropped but were told nothing about the nature of the objects involved. Their three-choice task was to categorize each event as a case of breaking or bouncing, with a *don't know* option, by placing a check in the appropriate column on an answer sheet. To minimize the possibility that they would choose one of the two event categories if they found the sound unconvincing, subjects were instructed to use the *don't know* category if they could not make up their minds, if they could not tell what the event was, or if it sounded like some other type of event. They were specifically instructed to ignore the nature of the object involved and attend to "what's happening to it". Subjects received no practice trials or feedback. There was a short break after 60 trials, and a test session lasted about 20 min.

Results and Discussion

Overall performance on natural bouncing tokens was 99.3% correct ("bouncing" judgments), and on breaking tokens was 98.5% correct ("breaking" judgments). *Don't know* responses accounted for 0.2% of all answers on bouncing tokens and 0.7% on breaking tokens. Experiment 1 demonstrates that sufficient information exists in the acoustic signal to permit unpracticed listeners to categorize the natural events of bouncing and breaking, at least within the limits of the three-choice task.

This successful categorization could be based on various temporal and spectral properties of the signal, as discussed in the introduction. Although the bouncing tokens were all of longer duration than were the breaking tokens, duration is a function of object elasticity and height of drop and does not provide reliable information specific to a style of change. Both spectral properties and token duration were controlled in Experiment 2 to isolate the effect of temporal patterning.

Experiment 2: Constructed Tokens

In Experiment 2 we attempted to model the time-varying information contained in natural recording by using constructed cases of bouncing and breaking, eliminating average spectral differences between the two.

Method

Subjects. Fifteen graduate and undergraduate students participated in the experiment for payment or course credit. None of them had participated in Experiment 1.
Materials. Tokens intended to model bouncing and breaking were constructed by the following method. Initially, individual recordings were made of four major pieces of glass from a broken bottle as each piece was dropped and bounced separately from a low height. These recordings were combined in two ways using the PCM system.

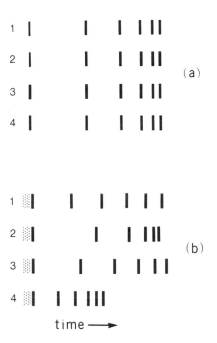

Figure 3 Schematic diagrams of constructed tokens, combining four component pulse trains: (a) bouncing, with synchronous pulse onsets; (b) breaking, with initial noise burst and asynchronous pulse onsets. (Each pulse train has unique spectral properties.)

To construct an artificial bouncing token, the temporal pattern of the recording of each piece was adjusted to match a single master periodicity arbitrarily borrowed from a recording of a natural bouncing bottle (Figure 3a). This was accomplished by inserting silence between the bounce pulses in recordings of the individual pieces. After the recordings of all four pieces had been adjusted so that their onsets matched the same pulse pattern, they were superimposed by summing the instantaneous amplitudes of the digitized recordings. The result was a combined pulse pattern with *synchronized* onsets for all bounces, preserving the invariant of a single damped quasi-periodic pulse train to model bouncing (Figure 4a).

An artificial breaking token was constructed by readjusting the recordings of the same four pieces to match four different temporal patterns (Figure 3b). As a first approximation, these master patterns were borrowed from measurements of four different bouncing bottles, because the likely patterns of individual pieces of glass in the course of natural breaking were unknown. These four patterns were initiated simultaneously, preceded by 50 ms of noise burst taken from the original rupture that produced the four pieces of glass. The result after superimposing these four independent temporal series was a combined pattern with *asynchronous* pulse onsets, preserving the temporal invariant of multiple damped quasi-periodic pulse trains to model breaking (Figure 4b). Note that the variables of temporal patterning and initial noise were confounded in this experiment. To the experimenters' ears the burst improved the quality of apparent breakage, but this assumption was later tested.

Three constructed cases of bouncing and three corresponding cases of breaking were produced by this method, each pair constructed from a unique set of recordings of original pieces and matched to a unique set of master periodicities. To help assure the generality of the method, the first three pairs constructed in this manner were used in the experiment. The original objects, and the durations of the bouncing or synchronous (SYN) and breaking or asynchronous (ASYN) tokens constructed from their pieces, were as follows: (a) 32-oz (0.946 l) jar: SYN1 = 1,000 ms, 8 collisions; ASYN1 = 950 ms. (b) 32-oz (0.946 l) jar: SYN2 = 1,400 ms, 13 collisions; ASYN2 = 650 ms. (c) 64-oz (1.892 l) bot-

tle: SYN3 = 920 ms, 9 collisions; ASYN3 = 600 ms.

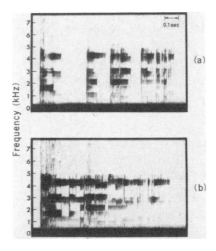

Figure 4 Spectrograms of constructed tokens: (a) bouncing (SYN1); (b) breaking (ASYN1).

Hence, the only differences between constructed bouncing and breaking tokens were in the temporal registration of pulse onsets and the presence (or absence) of initial noise. The range and distribution of spectral frequencies, averaged over time, were comparable in the two cases. Tokens SYN1, SYN3 and ASYN1 had similar durations of 920 to 1,000 ms, and thus if subjects based categorization on this factor, large errors should occur with these tokens.

There were certain problems with the constructed cases. The process of superimposing pulse patterns also summed tape hiss and hum so that background noise was increased. Moreover, using recordings of only four large pieces of glass concentrated more spectral energy in the lower frequency ranges as compared to natural tokens (cf. Figures 2 and 4), and constructing the sound of a single bouncing object by combining the spectral components of these four pieces produced two tokens that sounded more like metal than like glass material (SYN1 and SYN2). Nevertheless, the temporal invariant was preserved. Finally, the use of only four pieces of glass to model breaking, the assumption that their periodicities were akin to those of whole bouncing bottles, and the assumption of no further breakage after the initial catastrophe, were all rather arbitrary idealizations. Nevertheless, if temporal patterning constitutes sufficient information for breaking and bouncing, subjects should be able to make reliable judgments of these tokens.

Token	Bouncing	Breaking
1		
%	93.7	89.0
M	18.7	17.8
SD	1.7	2.9
2		
%	94.3	71.3
M	18.9	14.3
SD	2.0	4.3
3		
%	84.3	99.7
M	16.9	19.9
SD	3.7	0.3
Overall %	90.7	86.7

Note. Scores are based on 20 trials per subject per cell, N = 15.

Table 1 Percentage of trials in which constructed tokens of bouncing and breaking were categorized as such (Experiment 2).

Procedure. The procedure was the same as that in Experiment 1. Instructions to the subjects were the same, including the instruction to ignore object properties and concentrate on the style of change.

Results and Discussion

The results for each constructed token appear in Table 1 and are consistent with the predictions of the temporal patterning hypothesis. Bouncing judgments on synchronous tokens averaged 90.7%, and breaking judgments on asynchronous tokens averaged 86.7% (theses judgments being treated as correct). *Don't know* answers accounted for 0.1% of all responses on bouncing tokens and 1.3% on breaking tokens. Considering the artificial nature of the constructed cases and the idealizations involved, this performance may be considered quite high.

The absence of any large systematic decrement for tokens SYN1, SYN3, and ASYN1 indicates that subjects were not relying on simple duration in making their judgments. Some departures from the general pattern were found for token ASYN2, which showed markedly lower performance (71.3%), a higher intersubject standard deviation, and a relatively high rate of *don't know* responses (4.0%). These differences were primarily due to the low performance of 5 subjects who averaged 44% on this token, whereas the performance of the other 10 averaged 85%. It may be noted that the summed backround noise was greater in ASYN2 than in the other two breaking cases. The fact that overall performance in this case was well above chance indicates that even the poorest token contained usable information. It is not surprising that some tokens of constructed breaking are more convincing than others, because there are certainly some natural instances that are more compelling than others. The differences among tokens may involve both the spectral distinctiveness of the component pieces of glass and their degree of asynchrony.

In general, performance with constructed tokens was well above the chance level, similar to that found for natural tokens in Experiment 1. Performance with constructed cases was only about 10% lower than with natural cases, despite the summation of noise, the idealizations of construction, and the metallic sound of tokens SYN1 and SYN2. The data permit us to conclude that temporal patterning with initial noise provides sufficient information for listeners to categorize breaking and bouncing events. A subsequent experiment (Warren & Verbrugge, 1984) showed that, given these two types of events, the variation in temporal pattern alone without the initial noise burst is a sufficient discriminator. Further work remains to be done, however, to determine whether the initial noise is necessary for identifying breakage under conditions less constrained than those in the present experiment.

General Discussion

In the preceding experiments we have attempted to determine whether higher order, time-varying properties constitute effective acoustic information for the events of bouncing and breaking. The results show that certain damped periodic patterns provide sufficient information for listeners to discriminate the two events, without significant differences in average spectral properties.

The strength of the results is mitigated by the limitations of the three-choice categorization task. By definition, the task requires foreknowledge of the event classes and does not exclude the possibility that a token may be categorized

as *breaking* because it sounds something *like* that event, even though it would not uniquely convey breaking outside the restricted conditions of the experiment. Although a free identification task might test this possibility, the tokens were not constructed to fully simulate real events of breaking and bouncing glass, as evidenced by the metallic sound of bouncing tokens SYN1 and SYN2 and the use of only four component pieces to construct breaking tokens. Successful simulation would require still more complex manipulations of acoustic structure, including spectral information for the material composition of the object, predicated on findings such as those reported here.

The amplitude and periodicity requirements of the temporal patterns in bouncing vents were considered in two simple demonstrations worth mentioning here. Iterating a recording of one bounce pulse to match the timing of a natural bouncing sequence produced a clear bouncing event, although the usual declining amplitude gradient was absent. However, adjusting the pulse pattern to create equal 100-ms intervals between pulse onsets, thereby eliminating the damping of the periodic pattern, destroyed the effect of perceived bouncing, even with a declining amplitude gradient. The rapid staccato sound was like that produced by a machine, such as a jackhammer. A damped series of collisions, constrained by gravity and the imperfect elasticity of the system, appears necessary to the information for bouncing, as originally hypothesized. Experiments are in progress to assess the efficacy of period damping as information for elasticity or "bounciness" itself.

Further research is needed to determine the acoustic patterns necessary to specify single and multiple pulse trains. As suggested in the original hypotheses, distinct spectral properties for each asynchronous pulse train in a breaking token may be required to segregate the pulse trains and convey the existence of separate pieces of glass (although the superimposition of *synchronous* pulse trains with different frequency spectra did not yield the perception of separate pieces in the bouncing tokens). Reciprocally, it may be necessary for the successive pulses of a bouncing token to be spectrally similar in order to convey the unity of the pulse train and to cohere as the bouncing of a single object.

The present experiments exemplify an ecological approach to auditory perception, seeking to identify higher order acoustic information for environmental events. The acoustic consequences of two distinct types of mechanical events were analyzed for their temporal and spectral structure, and some time-varying properties sufficient to convey aspects of the events to a listener were empirically determined. Such work is preliminary to modeling auditory mechanisms capable of identifying acoustic events and sources in the world.

Acknowledgments: This research was supported by Grant HD-01994 from the National Institute for Child Health and Human Development, by Biomedical Research Support Grant RR-05596 to Haskins Laboratories, and by a National Science Foundation graduate fellowship to the first author. The authors wish to thank Michael Studdert-Kennedy, Michael Turvey, Robert Shaw, and Ignatius Mattingly for their comments on an earlier draft.

References

Brown, C.H., Beecher, M.D., Moody, D.B. & Stebbins, W.C. (1978) Localization of primate calls by Old World monkeys. *Science*, 201:753–754.

Fant, G. (1960) *Acoustic Theory of Speech Production*. The Hague: Mouton.

Fletcher, H. (1934) Loudness, pitch, and the timbre of musical tones and their relation to the intensity, the frequency, and the overtone structure. *Journal of the Acoustical Society of America*, 6:59–69.

Fowler, C.A. (1978) Timing control in speech production. *Dissertation Abstracts International*, 38:3927B. (University Microfilms No. 7731074).

Fowler, C.A., Rubin, P., Remez, R.E. & Turvey, M.T. (1980) Implications for speech production of a general theory of action. In *Language Production. Speech and Talk*, B. Butterworth (ed.), (Vol. 1, 373–420). New York: Academic Press.

Gibson, J.J. (1961) Ecological optics. *Vision Res.*, 1:253–262.

Gibson, J.J. (1966) *The Senses Considered as Perceptual Systems*. Boston: Houghton Mifflin.

Gibson, J.J. (1979) *The Ecological Approach to Visual Perception*. Boston: Houghton Mifflin.

Green, D.M. (1976) *An Introduction to Hearing*. Hillsdale, NJ: Erlbaum.

Grey, J.M. (1977) Multidimensional perceptual scaling of musical timbres. *Jrl. Acoust. Soc. Am.*, 61: 1270–1277.

Grey, J.M. & Gordon, J.W. (1978) Perceptual effects of spectral modifications on musical timbres. *Jrl. Acoust. Soc. Am.*, 63:1493–1500.

Helmholtz, H.L.F. von (1954) *On the Sensations of Tone as a Physiological Basis for the Theory of Music.* New York: Dover. (Original work published 1863.)

Jenkins, J.J. (1984) Acoustic information for places, objects, and events. In *Persistence and Change: Proceedings of the First International Conference on Event Perception*, W.H. Warren & R.E. Shaw (eds.), pp. 115–138. Hillsdale, NJ: Erlbaum.

Konishi, M. (1978) Ethological aspects of auditory pattern recognition. In *Handbook of Sensory Physiology, Vol. 8:Perception*, R. Held, H. Leibowitz & H.L. Teuber (eds.), pp. 289–309. New York: Springer-Verlag.

Liberman, A.M., Cooper, F.S., Shankweiler, D.P. & Studdert-Kennedy, M. (1967) Perception of the speech code. *Psychological Review*, 74:431–461.

Liberman, A.M., Delattre, P.C., Gerstman, L.T. & Cooper, F.S. (1956) Tempo of frequency change as a cue for distinguishing classes of speech sounds. *Journal of Experimental Psychology*, 52:127–137.

Luce, D. & Clark, M. (1967) Physical correlates of brass-instrument tones. *Jrl. Acoust. Soc. Am.*, 42:1232–1243.

Mace, W.M. (1977) James Gibson's strategy for perceiving: Ask not what's inside your head, but what your head's inside of. In *Perceiving, Acting, and Knowing: Toward an Ecological Psychology*, R.E. Shaw & Bransford (eds.), pp. 43–65. Hillsdale, NJ: Erlbaum.

Mark, L.S., Todd, J.T. & Shaw, R.E. (1981) The perception of growth: A geometrical analysis of how different styles of change are distinguished. *Journal of Experimental Psychology:*

Human Perception and Performance, 7:355–368.

Petersen, M.R., Beecher, M.D., Zoloth, S.R., Moody, D.B. & Stebbins, W.C. (1978) Neural lateralization of species-specific vocalizations by Japanese macaques (Macaca fuscata). *Science*, 202:324–327.

Pittenger, J.B. & Shaw, R.E. (1975) Aging faces as viscal-elastic events: Implications for a theory of non-rigid shape perception. *Journal of Experimental Psychology: Human Perception and Performance*, 1:374–382.

Plomp, R. (1964) The ear as a frequency analyzer. *Jrl. Acoust. Soc. Am.*, 36:1628–1636.

Runeson, S. (1977) On the possibility of "smart" perceptual mechanisms. *Scandanavian Journal of Psychology*, 18:172–179.

Saldanha, E.L. & Corso, J.F. (1964) Timbre cues and the identification of musical instruments. *Jrl. Acoust. Soc. Am.*, 36:2021–2026.

Schubert, E.D. (1974) The role of auditory perception in language processing. In *Reading, Perception, and Language*, D.D. Duane & M.B. Rawson (eds.), pp. 97–130, Baltimore: York Press.

Shaw, R.E., McIntyre, M. & Mace, W.M. (1974) The role of symmetry in event perception. In *Perception: Essays in Honor of James J. Gibson*, R.B. MacLeod & H.L. Pick (eds.), pp. 276–310. Ithaca: Cornell University Press.

Shaw, R.E., Turvey, M.T. & Mace, W.M. (1981) Ecological psychology: The consequence of a commitment to realism. In *Cognition and the Symbolic Processes* (Vol. 2), W. Weimer & D. Palermo (eds.), pp. 159–226, Hillsdale, NJ:Erlbaum.

VanDerveer, N.J. (1979a, June) Acoustic Information for Event Perception. Paper presented at the Celebration in Honor of Eleanor J. Gibson, Cornell University, Ithaca, NY.

VanDerveer, N.J. (1979b, June) Confusion Errors in Identification of Environmental Sounds. Paper presented at the Meeting of the Acoustical Society of America, Cambridge, MA.

Verbrugge, R.R., Rakerd, B., Fitch, H., Tuller, B. & Fowler, C.A. (1985) Perception of speech events: An ecological approach. In *Event Perception: An Ecological Perspective*, R.E. Shaw & W.M. Mace (eds.), Hillsdale, NJ: Erlbaum.

Warren, W.H. & Shaw, R.E. (1984) Events and encounters as units of analysis for ecological psychology. In *Persistence and Change: Proceedings of the First International Conference on Event Perception*, W.H. Warren & R.E. Shaw (eds.), pp. 1–27, Hillsdale, NJ:Erlbaum.

Reprinted slightly abridged from *Journal of Experimental Psychology: Human Perception & Performance*, 10:704–712 (1984).

*The first author is now at the W.S. Hunter Laboratory of Psychology, Brown University.

Perception of Melodies

H.C. Longuet-Higgins

Sussex University
Brighton BN1 9QG England

1.0 Introduction: Goal and Premises

A searching test of practical musicianship is the "aural test" in which the subject is required to write down, in standard, musical notation, a melody which he has never heard before. His transcription is not to be construed as a detailed record of the actual performance, which will inevitably be more or less out of time and out of tune, but as an indication of the rhythmic and tonal relations between the individual notes. How the musical listener perceives these relationships is a matter of some interest to the cognitive psychologist. In this paper I outline a theory of the perception of classical Western melodies, and describe a computer program, based on the theory, which displays, as best it can, the rhythmic and tonal relationships between the notes of a melody as played by a human performer on an organ console.

The basic premise of the theory is that in perceiving a melody the listener builds a conceptual structure representing the rhythmic groupings of the notes and the musical intervals between them. It is this structure which he commits to memory, and which subsequently enables him to recognise the tune, and to reproduce it in sound or in writing if he happens to be a skilled musician. A second premise is that much can be learned about the structural relationships in any ordinary piece of music from a study of its orthographic representation. Take, for example, the musical cliche notated in Figure 1.

The way in which the notes are rhythmically grouped is evident from the disposition of the bar lines and the "beams" linking the notes of the first bar. The rhythm is, in this case, a binary tree each terminal of which is a note or a rest, but more generally, such a tree may have ternary as well as binary nodes.

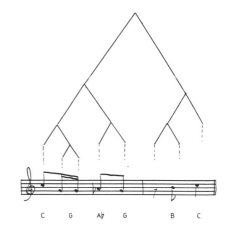

Figure 1 A well known musical cliché.

The tonal relations between the notes in Figure 1 are also indicated by the symbolism, but more subtly. It is a common mistake to suppose that the position of a note on the five-line stave (and its prefix, if any) indicates merely the approximate pitch of the note—where it would be located on the keyboard. If that were true, an equally acceptable alternative to Figure 1 would be Figure 2, in which the A♭ has been written as a G♯, with the same location on the keyboard. But a music student who offered Figure 2 as his transcription would lose marks for having misrepresented the tonal relation of the fourth note to its neighbors (though he could hardly be imagined not to have perceived it properly!)

The problems posed by melodic perception are not dissimilar to those which arise in the perception of speech. The distinction between the A♭ in Figure 1 and the G♯ in Figure 2 is analogous to the difference between the homophones "here" and "hear" in English; though these words sound exactly alike they are interpreted and spelt quite differently according to the context in which they are heard. Another problem in speech perception, which has its counterpart in the perception of melody, relates to the timing of successive acoustic events. The way in which the syllables of a poem are perceptually grouped into "feet" is largely unaffected by variations in rate of delivery, and the same applies to the rhythmic grouping of the notes in a melody. Notes which, on paper, are of equal length, will in a live performance be sounded at quite unequal intervals of time, particularly in an "expressive" performance. A change of metre from duplets to triplets, can, nevertheless, usually be distinguished quite clearly from a mere quickening of tempo, in a reasonably competent performance. Previous programs for the automatic transcription of music have required the performer to maintain a fairly constant tempo (Askenfelt, 1976; Styles, 1973); but human listeners have no difficulty in discerning the rhythms of melodies played by performers

who are free from this constraint.

The third premise of the theory is that the perception of rhythm and the perception of tonal relationships can be viewed as independent processes. This strong claim (which is not to be misunderstood as referring to the process of musical composition) may be weakly supported by two observations. First, that a given melodic sequence such as the ascending major scale will be heard as such by a Western musician regardless of the rhythm in which it is played. And conversely, that a "dotted" rhythm will be clearly recognisable for what it is, regardless of the musical intervals between the successive notes. To say this is not, of course, to deny that higher cognitive processes can and will operate on the "surface structure" generated by rhythmic and tonal perception, to reveal musically significant relations between the rhythm and the tonality. But one may reasonably suppose that such processes of musical appreciation can only begin when some structure has been created on which they can get to work.

Figure 2 A misrepresentation of the cliché of Figure 1.

2.0 Rhythm

One might imagine that to discern the rhythm of a melody the listener must

be able to perceive differences in loudness between successive notes. This may
be true on occasion but fails as a generalization for two reasons. First of all,
performers do not as a rule thump out
every note which occurs on a beat or at
the beginning of a bar; to do so would
be as tiresome as to accent, in reading a
poem, every syllable that occurred at the
beginning of a foot. But more decisively,
there are instruments such as the organ
and harpsichord on which it is physically
impossible for the performer to vary the
acoustic intensity of each individual note;
all he can control is the time of onset of
the note and its temporal duration. It is
nevertheless quite possible for a listener to
perceive correctly the rhythm of a melody
played on such an instrument; we conclude that temporal information alone is
enough for the purpose, except in special
circumstances.

The basic assumption underlying the
rhythmic component of the program is
that the first necessity in perceiving the
rhythmic structure of a melody is to identify the time of occurrence of each "beat".
Music in which the beat is irregular falls
outside the scope of the theory, which
therefore has nothing to say about the
rhythmic perception of recitative or of
music in which, for example, the beats
alternate in length. The grouping of the
beats into higher metrical units such as
"bars" raises issues which have been discussed elsewhere (Longuet-Higgins et al.,
1971; Stedman, 1973); the principal concern of the present study is with the
manner in which each beat should be subdivided, and with the problem of keeping track of the beat through unforeseen
changes in tempo.

In Western music by far the com-
monest subdivisions of the beat are into
2 and into 3 shorter metrical units; these
in turn can be further subdivided into 2
or 3. Whether a beat, or a fraction of a
beat, is perceived to be divided, depends,
according to the theory, on whether or
not it is interrupted by the onset of a
note. What counts as an "interruption"
is a matter of some delicacy, to which I
shall return in a moment.

After such a process of division, and
subdivision, every note will find itself at
the beginning of an uninterrupted metrical unit. It is the relations between
these metrical units which constitute the
rhythm of the tune; the metrical units can
be thought of as the nodes of a "tree" in
which each non-terminal node has either
two or three descendants. Every terminal
node in the tree will eventually be attached either to a rest or to a note (which
may be sounded or tied) in the manner
of Figure 1. The program does not actually draw such trees, nor print out a
musical stave; it represents the rhythm in
a nested bracketed notation. It also indicates the phrasing; if the offset of a note
occurs earlier than half-way through its
allotted time, or else appreciably before
the end of that time, the note is marked
"stc", standing for "staccato", or "ten",
for "tenuto".

We now return to the question: what
counts as an interruption? By what criterion could a listener judge whether the
onset of a note occurs "during" the current metrical unit rather than "at" its
beginning or its end? Plainly there must
be some upper limit to the temporal discrepancies he can disregard, just as there
is a lower limit to those he can detect. The
former limit—the listener's "tolerance"—
must obviously exceed the latter. It must
be small enough to permit the structuring of rapid rhythmic figures, but large

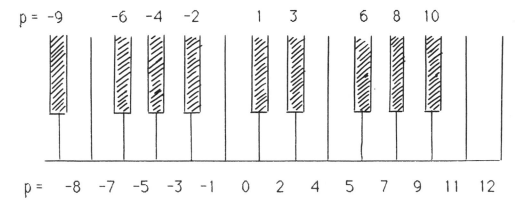

Figure 3 The positions p of the notes on a keyboard relative to "middle C".

enough to allow a reasonable degree of flexibility to the tempo. In the program the tolerance can be preset to any desired value. Experiments with the program indicate that for reasonably careful performances a tolerance of about 10 cs meets both criteria, but that for more "expressive" performances, of relatively sedate melodies, a greater tolerance is needed if an obvious rubato is not to be misconstrued as a variation in rhythm.

In order to perceive the rhythm clearly a listener must, it is assumed, take account of the precise onset time of every note within any metrical unit in predicting when the unit could end. The rule eventually adopted for making such predictions was as follows: if, in the course of a binary metrical unit, a note which terminates the first subunit begins a little less than half way through, then the expected further duration of the unit is reduced in magnitude, to the mean of its original value and the value implied by the time of onset of the note in question. Corresponding remarks apply, of course, in cases where the note is slightly late or the current metrical hypothesis assigns a ternary rather than a binary structure to

the metrical unit in question. In fact the program also allows for the termination of a metrical unit, not by the actual onset of a note, but by the anticipated end of a lower metrical unit which is itself interrupted by the onset of one or more notes. Such procedures are, unfortunately, much more difficult to specify precisely in English than in a suitably designed programming language; but this fact only underlines the value of casting perceptual theories in computational form.

Finally, it is necessary to commit oneself, in writing such a program, to a view as to what counts as good perceptual evidence for a change in metre. It is here assumed that the listener initially expects a pure binary metre, but is prepared to change his mind at any level in the metrical hierarchy. The evidence for a change in metre may be of two kinds: that the current metre implies a "syncopation", in which the beginning of the next beat, or higher metrical unit, is not accompanied by the onset of a note; or that it implies a "distortion" in which an excessively large change of tempo is required to accommodate the current metrical hypothesis. Each of these outcomes represents a flouting of the listener's expectations and either may, according to the theory, lead him to change his opinion about the metre if the other possible division of the current metrical unit (ternary instead of binary, or vice versa) does not imply a distortion or a syncopation. Lastly, it is assumed that once having changed his mind the listener does not change it back again until he encounters positive evidence for doing so.

3.0 Tonality

In committing a melody to memory the listener must not only create a rhythmic structure of the kind depicted in Figure 1; he must also identify the tonality of each note which is to be attached to it. This tonal information should ideally suffice, not only for the transcription of the melody into standard notation, but also for the purpose of evaluating the intonation of a performance on, say, the violin, which permits fine distinctions of pitch which cannot be made explicit on a keyboard instrument (see Figure 3.)

To appreciate what is involved in this task it is necessary to formalise the classical theory of tonality, as developed by Rameau (1721), Bosanquet (1876), Helmholtz (1885) and other writers. In the formal theory (Longuet-Higgins, 1962) every musical note is assigned coordinates (x, y, z) in a "tonal space" of three dimensions, corresponding to the perfect fifth, the major third and the octave, respectively. (The ideal frequency ratios of these intervals are 3/2, 5/4 and 2/1 respectively—involving the first three prime numbers—so that they are strictly incommensurable when not distorted by equal temperament.) Thus in Figure 4, if the origin is taken as "middle C", the

tonal coordinates of the various notes are as shown in the first three rows of the table. The following points may be noted: (1) It is the relative values of the coordinates (x, y, z), not their absolute values, which characterise the melodic sequence. Thus, increasing all the z values by 1 would merely put the melody up one octave. (2) The numerical values of the coordinates (x, y, z) are all small; this is evidently the result of having chosen middle C as origin. (3) The "position" p of each note on the keyboard, that is, its distance above middle C in keyboard semitones, is given by

$$p = 7x + 4y + 12z \tag{1}$$

so that there are arbitrarily many different notes (x, y, z) with the same value p. (4) The conventional name of any note is determined not by its keyboard position p but by its "sharpness" q, defined as The name N of the note is such that there are q sharps, or $-q$ flats, in the key signature of N major. Thus an "A" is a note with $q = 3$, and an "Ab" is one with $q = -4$.

$x =$	0	1	0	1	.	1	0	(0)
$y =$	0	0	-1	0	.	1	0	(2)
$z =$	1	0	1	0	.	0	1	(0)
$p =$	12	7	8	7	.	11	12	
$q =$	0	1	-4	1	.	5	0	
N	C	G	Ab	G	.	B	C	(G♯)

Figure 4 The tonal coordinates of the notes in Figure 1.

$$\delta p = \begin{array}{c} \\ \text{or} \end{array} \begin{array}{cccccccccccc} 1 & 2 & 3 & 4 & 5 & 6 & 7 & 8 & 9 & 10 & 11 & 12 \\ -11 & -10 & -9 & -8 & -7 & -6 & -5 & -4 & -3 & -2 & -1 & 0 \end{array}$$

implies that

$$\delta q = \begin{array}{c} \\ \text{or} \end{array} \begin{array}{cccccccccccc} -5 & 2 & -3 & 4 & -1 & 6 & 1 & -4 & 3 & -2 & 5 & 0 \\ 7 & -10 & 9 & -8 & 11 & -6 & -11 & 8 & -9 & 10 & -7 & \end{array}$$

Table 1 The relation between the span δp of an interval and its degree δq.

$$q = x + 4y \qquad (2)$$

The task of naming the notes of a melody played on the keyboard, or of notating them correctly on the five-line stave, therefore involves the apparently insoluble problem of determining the three coordinates (x, y, z) of each note from its keyboard position p, so as to be able to determine its sharpness q. The problem is analogous to the visual problem of adding an extra dimension to the two-dimensional image of a three-dimensional scene, except that a keyboard performance of a melody supplies the listener with only one directly audible dimension, to which he must add two more to identify each note uniquely.

There is in fact a short cut to the solution of this problem, arising from the mathematical fact that a given choice of p severely restricts the range of possible values of q. A little simple arithmetic shows that q must differ from $7p$ by a multiple of 12. If, therefore, we can find independent grounds for limiting q to one of a fairly small set of values, we can determine it uniquely from the remainder upon division of p by 12. A survey of the published scores of classical melodies reveals that the value of q (which can

be directly determined from the notation) never changes from one note to the next by more than 11 units of sharpness. As a consequence, if δp is the "span" of any interval between two successive notes, then the "degree" δq of that interval is restricted to the alternative values given in Table 1 when δp lies in the range -11 to $+12$.

By far the commonest intervals occurring in classical and traditional melodies are "diatonic" intervals, with $|\delta q| < 6$. "Chromatic" intervals, with $|\delta q| > 6$, and "diabolic" intervals, with $|\delta q| = 6$, are relatively rare. If they were nonexistent, the degree δq of each interval would be uniquely determined by its span δp, and one could infer the sharpness of each note in any melody from its position relative to its immediate predecessor. Such a "Markovian" theory of tonal perception would, as it happens, correctly predict the q values in Figure 4. It would, however, fail dismally for melodies containing chromatic scales, because each keyboard semitone in such a scale would be assigned the same value of δq, and this would lead to absurd tonal interpretations such as that shown in Figure 5.

An alternative, and musically much more plausible, hypothesis is that the

27

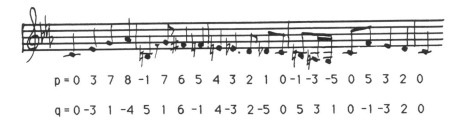

$$p = 0 \quad 3 \quad 7 \quad 8 \quad -1 \quad 7 \quad 6 \quad 5 \quad 4 \quad 3 \quad 2 \quad 1 \quad 0 \quad -1 \quad -3 \quad -5 \quad 0 \quad 5 \quad 3 \quad 2 \quad 0$$

$$q = 0 \quad -3 \quad 1 \quad -4 \quad 5 \quad 1 \quad 6 \quad -1 \quad 4 \quad -3 \quad 2 \quad -5 \quad 0 \quad 5 \quad 3 \quad 1 \quad 0 \quad -1 \quad -3 \quad 2 \quad 0$$

Figure 6 The theme of Bach's *Musical Offering* and its tonal interpretation.

listener identifies the sharpness of each note by placing it within a diatonic interval of the very first note (or perhaps an interval of degree 6 if the span indicates that the interval is diabolic.) Such a rule would account equally well for the q values of the notes in Figure 4. It would, furthermore, account very nicely for the sharpnesses of the notes in the theme of Bach's *Musical Offering* (Figure 6).

Figure 5 A "chromatic" scale composed of tonally identical intervals.

In this melody there are in fact four chromatic intervals—a diminished seventh between the 4th and 5th notes, of degree $\delta q = -9$, and three chromatic semitones, of degree -7. Such intervals could not, for obvious reasons, be correctly identified by the "Markovian" procedure.

It will not do, however, to assume that the first note is invariably the "keynote" to which every other note should be referred in order to determine its sharpness. First because melodies very often begin on notes other than the keynote, or "tonic", and

second because the tonic may very well seem to change in the course of a melody, when we speak of a "modulation" having occurred.

A good example of an indisputable modulation is to be found in the subject of the B minor fugue in the first book of Bach's *Wohltemperierte Klavier* (see Figure 7). The first three notes clearly establish the tonic as B ($q = 5$), and all the other notes in bars 1 and 2 are related to it by non-chromatic intervals ($|\delta q| < 7$). But the first note of bar 3, though in the same keyboard position as the C in bar 2, is notated differently. To have written it as a C would have produced the sequence C♯ C C♯, calling for two chromatic semitones in succession. But in unaccompanied classical melodies such an event never seems to occur, for the very good reason that if $X\ Y\ Z$ are three successive notes of a melody which, on paper, are separated by chromatic intervals $X\ Y$ and $Y\ Z$, then there is always an alternative, simpler, interpretation of the middle note Y which transforms both intervals into diatonic ones. Generally speaking, then, the tonal identity of a note cannot be finally established until the following note is heard. In Figure 7 the offending note has become transformed into a B♯, making both the neighbouring intervals into diatonic semitones, of degree 5 and -5 rather than -7 and 7 respectively. But

Figure 7 A melody that changes key (from B to F♯) in the third bar.

a B♯ is too far from the old tonic B to belong to its key, so that a modulation is perceived to occur to a new key, that of F♯, such that the value of δq for the new note B♯ is only 6, which is just close enough for comfort.

There seem to be other general restrictions upon the contexts in which chromatic intervals occur in classical melodies. The most important of these relates to four-note sequences $W\ X\ Y\ Z$ in which the middle interval is chromatic. In such a sequence not only must both $W\ X$ and $Y\ Z$ be non-chromatic, but at least one of the intervals $W\ Y$ and $X\ Z$ must be diatonic. If the interpretations of W, X, Y and Z based on the current key violate this rule, then the tonality of the note Y is reinterpreted in such a way as to make $X\ Y$ a diatonic interval, and to force a modulation into a key to which Y belongs. As implied by what has been said, a note is regarded as belonging to a given key if its sharpness relative to the tonic lies in the range −5 to +6 inclusive.

Another rule which seems to be necessary in order to account for the notation of chromatic scales, particularly in music of the period following Bach, concerns the tonal interpretation of ascending semitones. If such a semitone ends on a note whose sharpness relative to the tonic of the key is 2, 3, 4, or 5, then the first note of the semitone is to be assigned a

relative sharpness of 7, 8, 9, or 10. Though this reassignment places the note outside the key, it does not by itself precipitate a modulation; if it did, then an ascending chromatic scale of any length would trigger a whole sequence of modulations into progressively sharper and sharper keys.

Two further rules are necessary, and sufficient, for determining the relative sharpnesses of the notes in most classical melodies. The first is a rule to the effect that for the purposes of establishing tonality one may conflate repeated notes, or notes separated by an octave (the second and third notes in Figure 4 provide an example). The other rule, which is theoretically less satisfactory, is that the tonic may be determined from the first two notes, and that it will be either the first note itself or the note a fifth below it. This rule, and the absence of any more delicate tests of modulation than those already described, are undoubtedly the weakest links in the tonal section of the program.

Before I describe the program in detail, a few words of caution may be in order. First, the tonal rules outlined above must not be expected to apply to accompanied melodies, where the accompaniment supplies tonal information which may not be implicit in the melody itself. Nor must it be supposed that the rules necessarily hold for covertly polyphonic melodies

```
: printlist(cliche):
```

```
[ 12 154 227]
[ 36 285 294]
[ 31 322 327]
[ 31 336 341]   (a)
[ 32 349 383]
[ 31 384 407]
[ 35 445 453]
[ 36 484 527]
```

(c)

```
: 10->tolerance: notate(cliche):                                    (b)

[[[ 24 C STC] [[-5 G STC] [ 0 G STC]]] [[ 1 AB] [-1 G TEN]]]

[[[REST] [ 4 B STC]] [ 1 C TEN]]
```

Figure 8 Implementation: (a) the raw input, giving the keyboard position of a note, and its on and offset time; (b) the POP2 program's output, and (c) the transcription into a score.

in which, for example, alternate notes really belong to two different melodies. Further, the contextual constraints on chromatic intervals will often be violated at phrase boundaries, marked by rhythmically prominent rests, though this is not always the case. And finally, one must allow for the possibility that in a musical score a radical change of notation (such as occurs between the first and second sections of Chopin's *Raindrop Prelude*) does not signify a real change in tonality, but merely an "enharmonic change" designed to simplify the reader's task. Only if such qualifications are borne in mind can the program safely be used to indicate how a melody performed on the keyboard should be transcribed into conventional notation.

4.0 The program

The program accepts as input a list of sublists, each of which comprises three numbers. The first number is the keyboard position of the corresponding note

and lies in the range 0 to 48, there being four octaves on the organ console. The second number is the time in centiseconds at which the note was depressed, and the third number indicates the time at which the note was released. The order of the notes on the list is the order of their times of onset. The list itself is generated from a live performance of a melody on an electronic organ connected, through an analog-to-digital converter, to a high speed paper tape punch. The information on the paper tape is equivalent to the information which would be recorded on a player piano roll, and no more. The preprocessing of the paper tape is an entirely automatic matter, which simply involves constructing the above-mentioned list from the paper tape record and transferring it to disk storage.

The performer is required, by the present version of the program, to establish the initial tempo and the number of beats in a bar by prefacing his performance of the melody by a bar's worth of

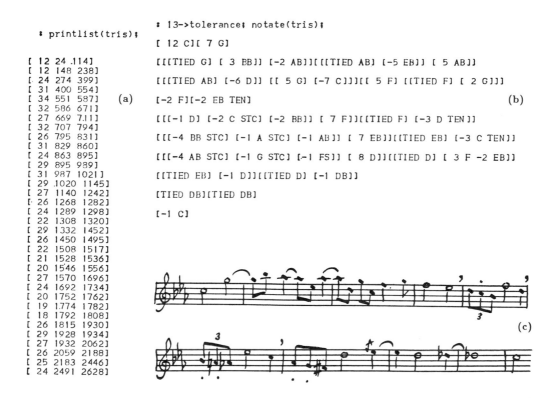

```
: printlist(tris);
```

(a)
```
[ 12  24  .114]
[ 12 148 238]
[ 24 274 399]
[ 31 400 554]
[ 34 551 587]
[ 32 586 671]
[ 27 669 7.11]
[ 32 707 794]
[ 26 795 831]
[ 31 829 860]
[ 24 863 895]
[ 29 895 989]
[ 31 987 1021]
[ 29 .1020 1145]
[ 27 1140 1242]
[ 26 1268 1282]
[ 24 1289 1298]
[ 22 1308 1320]
[ 29 1332 1452]
[ 26 1450 1495]
[ 22 1508 1517]
[ 21 1528 1536]
[ 20 1546 1556]
[ 27 1570 1696]
[ 24 1692 1734]
[ 20 1752 1762]
[ 19 1.774 1782]
[ 18 1792 1808]
[ 26 1815 1930]
[ 29 1928 1934]
[ 27 1932 2062]
[ 26 2059 2188]
[ 25 2183 2446]
[ 24 2491 2628]
```

(b)
```
: 13->tolerance; notate(tris);
[ 12 C][ 7 G]

[[[TIED G] [ 3 BB]] [-2 AB]][[[TIED AB] [-5 EB]] [ 5 AB]]

[[[TIED AB] [-6 D]] [[ 5 G] [-7 C]]][[ 5 F] [[TIED F] [ 2 G]]]

[-2 F][-2 EB TEN]

[[[-1 D] [-2 C STC] [-2 BB]] [ 7 F]][[TIED F] [-3 D TEN]]

[[[-4 BB STC] [-1 A STC] [-1 AB]] [ 7 EB]][[TIED EB] [-3 C TEN]]

[[[-4 AB STC] [-1 G STC] [-1 FS]] [ 8 D]][[TIED D] [ 3 F -2 EB]]

[[TIED EB] [-1 D]][[TIED D] [-1 DB]]

[TIED DB][TIED DB]

[-1 C]
```

(c)

Figure 9 Implementation of a part taken from Wagner's *Tristan und Isolde*. (a) The raw input, giving the keyboard position of a note and its on and offset time, (b) the POP2 program's output, and (c) the transposition into a score.

beats on some low note, which may conveniently be positioned an octave below the first note of the melody, so as not to prejudice the tonality.

The program itself is written in POP2, the high level programming language designed and developed in Edinburgh by Burstall et al., (1971). It is relatively short, and is structured as follows. First, the list of sublists is converted into a list of records, each of which has a "slot" indicating the pitch, onset time and offset time of a particular note, and further slots which are to hold the span δp and the degree δq of the interval between the note and its predecessor. The keynote is then fixed by the positions of the first two notes, and the relative sharpnesses of all the notes are determined from their keyboard positions by an algorithm based on the theory of tonality outlined in the previous section. The next stage is a rhythmic analysis (which could have been carried out first, as it is indifferent to the results of the tonal routines). Each beat is examined in turn, by a combination of "top down" and "bottom up" analysis in which the time of onset of each note is used both for establishing the structure of the rhythmic hierarchy and for correcting the estimated tempo. In the course of this analysis the time of offset of each note is used for determining how the note was phrased.

The final stage in the operation of the program corresponds to the exercise of musical literacy; it consists of displaying, on paper, the essential features of the structure created by the rhythmic and tonal analyses as a sequence of nested lists of symbols. The innermost symbols name the individual notes as, for example, 'D' (D natural), 'DS' (D sharp), or 'DB' (D flat); the word REST is self-explanatory. Each name is preceded by either the word TIED if the note is tied to its predecessor or a number indicating the span (not the degree, which is implicit in the name of the note) of the interval from the preceding note; this is needed for identifying the octave in which the note occurs. Finally, a note which is not tied may be followed by the abbreviation STC or TEN indicating that the note was played *staccato* or *tenuto*; the absence of either abbreviation implies that the note was played *legato*.

Figures 8 and 9 provide examples of the program's performance. Each figure indicates (*a*) the "raw" input, in which each set of three numbers gives the keyboard position of a note and its times of onset and offset in centiseconds, (*b*) the output generated by the program from the

input (*a*), and (*c*) the result of transcribing the output (*b*) by hand into ordinary stave notation.

The performance of the tune shown in Figure 8 was prefaced by a single low C, and the time between the onset of this note and the next was arbitrarily taken as a "minim" in adopting the note values indicated in (*c*); it will be noted that in (*b*) the outermost brackets enclose a minim's worth of notes. The interpretation (*b*) was obtained from the input (*a*) with a tolerance of 10 cs; with a tolerance of 15 cs the program would assign the two semiquavers to the same node. It is worth noting that the actual times of onset of the first four quaver units differed in the performance by 37, 27 and 35 cs respectively, the separation between the last two notes being 39 cs. The considerable discrepancy between these numbers clearly illustrates the acute difficulty which would confront any attempt to determine the rhythm without taking account of its hierarchical structure.

Figure 9 shows how the program handled a performance of part of the long *cor anglais* solo from the Prelude to Act III of Wagner's *Tristan und Isolde*. This example is interesting in two particular respects. First, it involves the perception of a change from a binary to a ternary metre in the fifth bar; and secondly, the published score indicates a grace note at the end of the seventh bar, to which it would be inappropriate to assign a separate place in the rhythmic structure. The program's output agrees fully with the score in its rhythmic and tonal indications; there are slight discrepancies in the marks of phrasing—Wagner marked all the triplet quavers as staccato—but for this the performer is clearly to blame, not the program.

5.0 Conclusions

The domain of competence of the program is, of course, very restricted: it cannot be expected to reveal significant tonal or rhythmic relations between the notes of "atonal" or "arhythmic" melodies, for example. But the perceptual theory on which it is based does seem worthy of serious consideration, in that up to the present time no detailed suggestions seem to have been offered as to how a listener builds an internal representation of a melody from a live performance. The most significant rhythmic hypothesis in the theory is that the rhythm of a melody is conceptualised as a structural hierarchy, and that the onset of each note provides important predictive information about the time of onset of the following note at every level in the hierarchy. The hypotheses underlying the tonal section of the program are presumably limited in application to the kind of music that has been developed in the West; but for such music one conclusion at least seems secure, namely that the tonality of any note cannot in general be established unambiguously until the following note has been heard. It is perhaps surprising that such a limited amount of context should usually suffice for the purpose, but it should be remembered that it is really the key of the melody which creates the tonal context in the first place.

It seems altogether possible that the principles of operation of the program's rhythmic component will apply to other temporal processes such as the perception of speech.

Acknowledgments: I thank D.C. Jeffrey, M.J. Steedman, B.C. Styles, O.P. Buneman and G.E. Hinton for practical assistance and helpful discussions, and to the Royal Society and the SRC for research support.

References

Askenfelt, A. (1976) *Quarterly Progress and Status Report, Speech Transmission Laboratory, Royal Institute of Technology, Stockholm, 1*, 1.

Bosanquet, P.H.M. (1876) *Elementary Treatise on Musical Intervals and Temperament.*

Burstall, R.M., Collins, J.S. & Popplestone, R.J. (1971) *Programming in POP2.* Edinburgh: Edinburgh University Press.

Helmholtz, H.L.F. (Ellis's translation), (1885) *On the Sensations of Tone*, 2nd ed., London.

Longuet-Higgins, H.C. (1962) *Music Review*, 224 and 271.

Longuet-Higgins, H.C. (1972) *Proc. R. Inst.*, 45, 87.

Longuet-Higgins, H.C. & Steedman, M.J. (1971) *Machine Intelligence*, 6, 221.

Rameau, M. (1721) *Traite de l'harmonie reduite a des principes naturels.*

Steedman, M.J. (1973) Thesis, Univ. Edinburgh.

Styles, B.C. (1973) Thesis, Cambridge Univ.

Reprinted from *Nature*, 263:646–653 (1976).

V

Force Sensing and Control

Force Sensing and Control

1.0 Introduction

For an animal or machine to interact successfully with its environment, the passive visual and auditory senses must be supplemented by devices which can manipulate and control objects. Because these objects have mass, their control requires the application of forces. Such actions result in a mechanical coupling between ourselves and our environment—namely an exchange of forces and movements. (No wonder our somatosensory percepts seem so direct!) Thus to sense through touch requires force interpretation; to reach, grasp, or run requires force control. To begin to understand how applied forces can be interpreted and used, we have divided our selections into three parts: 1) grasping and stable prehension; 2) force sensing—the recovery of mechanical properties of objects, and 3) reaching and walking.[1]

2.0 Grasping

Selection 28 by Rovetta presents a simple analysis of conditions for stable prehension of an object in a plane. The balancing of forces and torques (Equation 28-1,2) will generally require four friction-free contact points. Intuitively, there are two degrees of freedom for a translation (x,y), one rotation (about z), plus the need to balance one force vector caused, for example, by the mass of the object under gravity. By analogy, in the three dimensional case seven degrees-of-freedom (DOF) must be accounted for. For some objects, like spheres or cylinders, this count is reduced for friction-free contacts when "roll" can not be restricted, or for other objects, such as an ice cube, the DOF may increase because individual force vectors can not be applied independently. Salisbury & Craig in Selection 29 analyse the prehension problem in greater detail, considering the DOF reduction imposed by contact type and by segmented "fingers". Here also appears an introduction to tendon-activated joint and hand control.

Manipulators with segmented "fingers" provide an obvious advantage in stable prehension. But how many fingers and how many segments should be used? Salisbury & Craig show that a combination of three-segment fingers on a three-finger hand provides an efficient solution for grasping arbitrary objects. Although their solution does not match that chosen for a human hand, it does set a lower bound on fingers and segments. Interestingly, the same configuration can also be used to recover the shape of an object (i.e. the two principle curvatures of a uniformly curved surface) [Problem 28-1].

3.0 Touch and Torque Sensing

A hand gives us the opportunity not only to grasp and manipulate an object, but also to explore its surface. Such explorations yield data about the mechanical properties of objects, such as its rigidity or hardness (modulus of elasticity), and in Selection 30 on "Texture from Touch" Drucker presents an analysis of how surface roughness might be recovered. (See Stansfield, 1987, for a treatment of recovering Young's modulus.) The key result, conforming to experimental observations, is that surface texture is not easily estimated simply by "touching" the surface. Instead, the surface must be stroked. The fact that a dynamic analysis of the sensed strains greatly simplifies the analyses (Equation 10) is a surprise—who might expect that a seventh degree polynomial would simplify so nicely once the constraint of constant surface motion was imposed? Clearly this selection is only a start at analysing mechanical and texture properties from touch, and extensions are badly needed, particularly to clarify the precise roles of the various types of mechano-receptors found by neurophysiologists (Morely & Goodwin, 1987).

A second class of mechanical properties which can be recovered by a manipulator are the mass and moments of inertia of the grasped object. However, to recover such properties, the object must be manipulated in a controlled manner. This is a difficult problem because as the object is moved (along with one's own arm!) it is subject to inertial and gravitational forces which act back upon the manipulator. Certain conditions should be satisfied in order that these reactions do not lead to instabilities in the loaded arm movement. Similarly, when an object is grasped, some care must be given as to whether we are picking up an egg shell or a billiard ball. One can be easily crushed, the other not. If manipulators were simply driven to a position regardless of object (or skin) type, many objects or manipulators would quickly be damaged. What

is needed is a compliant grasp—one that responds to the grasped or manipulated object. Hogan addresses these problems in Selection 31. He shows that for a manipulator to exhibit compliant behavior, a sufficient condition is that the manipulator respond as a passive spring to the (re)actions of the object when subject to the imposed external forces. Our skin and fingers behave this way. So do our arms and legs when lifting objects or when they are subject to impulses imposed by feet striking the ground during running or when we hold a vibrating object, such as a jackhammer.

Although our skin may be considered as a passive compliant spring, the arm is not. While it grasps an object it must also manipulate it. One very simple proposal for a compliant arm is the Equilibrium Position Model (Asatryan & Fel'dman, 1965; Bizzi et al., 1976; Polit & Bizzi, 1978). Imagine an arm driven by muscles that act like springs as illustrated in Figure 1. In this example, elbow position is controlled by varying the relative tensions on the biceps and triceps "springs". The angular position, θ, would then be given simply by

$$Sine\ \theta = \frac{(k_t - k_b)}{(k_t + k_b)}\frac{x_0}{A} \qquad (1)$$

where k_t and k_b are respectively the spring ("stiffness") constants for the triceps and biceps and x_o/A is the ratio of muscle length for $\theta = 0$ to the distance to the pivot from its point of attachment (Sakitt, 1980). As long as these k's are held fixed, a "viscous" joint will exhibit compliant behavior—i.e. it will respond without oscillation, for example, to a novel imposed load. However the system has the further

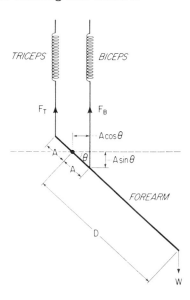

Figure 1 Two-spring model for biceps and triceps. To a first approximation, the force F_T or (F_B) assumed to follow a length-tension relation given by Hooke's Law: $F_T = k_T x_T$.

advantage of also being able to control its compliant response. Imagine holding up one's hand to receive a "punch" from a (friendly!) combatant. You automatically "stiffen" the arm prior to receiving the blow. In effect both k_t and k_b were increased together by the same percentages, thus keeping their ratio and hence *sin θ* (the arm position) the same (Figure 2). The equilibrium position scheme thus permits compliant responses independent of joint positions (Hogan, 1984).

Imagine now trying to pick up a rigid 1/2 inch, 10 foot steel rod by grabbing the rod only at one end. The torque upon the hand would be just too great. Similarly, contrast trying to wield a hammer grasped at its center of gravity versus the end of its handle. Knowledge of the inertial parameters of an object is crucial to controlled manipulation. Of course

this same knowledge tells us a lot about the object, such as is it hollow, rigid, or whether it has a fluid inside. How can this knowledge be acquired?

In Selection 32 Chris Atkeson addresses one aspect of this problem—the recovery of the (ten) inertial parameters of a rigid body. His solution requires that the object be moved in several quite different ways in order to fill out the measurement space. Although this selection demonstrates that, in principle, the inertial parameters can be recovered, it is unlikely that biological systems proceed in the same manner, in effect attempting

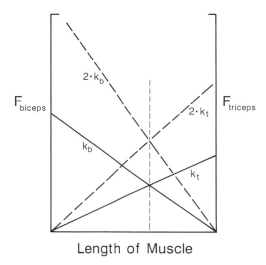

Figure 2 Equilibrium position model. Simultaneously doubling the stiffness (k) of both the biceps and triceps will not change the arm position, given a simple Hooke's Law relation between force (F) and muscle length (see Figure 1 and Equation 2).

to solve simultaneously equation (32-12). Rather, just as we proposed for the image-intensity equations, special cases which simplify the complex equations seem more plausible. For example, to estimate the mass of a rod, it is easier to simply grasp the rod at its mid-point (center of gravity) thereby eliminating gravitational torques; similarly its moments of inertia are best estimated by rotating the rod in different directions about its center-of-mass. In each of these cases $\mathbf{c} = 0$ and equations (4) and (8) simplify to two terms. Similarly, inertial moments are most easily estimated by rotations in either the horizontal plane perpendicular to gravity, or by slight perturbations from the gravity axis with $\mathbf{c} = \pm\mathbf{g}$ and aligned along one of the moments. (The directions of minimum and maximum moments can be found by exploring for the stable rotations of the object, aided by vision.) In these cases equation (12) can be reduced to at most three equations in three unknowns, and often one equation in one unknown (see Problem 32-1,2). Such simplifications seem particularly important considering that the biological arm has difficulty distinguishing between torques and forces.

To see this more clearly, consider the effect of estimating the weight of a meter stick as the grasp point is moved from the 50 cm mid-point toward the end. The apparent weight of the stick can increase by as much as 50% (see Figure 3). Clearly torques and mass are confused. The result is as if the "weight" is estimated by increasing muscle activation (i.e. the spring constants, k) to sustain the horizontal rod position, and then using these activation values as indicators of the object's weight.

Similarly, activation (stiffness) values required for compliant grasp could be used to estimate inertial moments which create counter forces upon the hand when objects are rotated at different amounts and rates about their center-of-mass. In the recovery of inertial parameters, therefore, force-sensing may in reality be torque sensing, aided by the assignment of properly set stiffness coefficients which maintain stable prehension of the object during special movements.

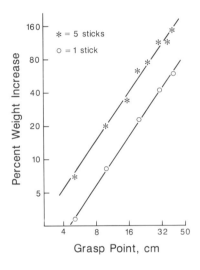

Figure 3 Apparent weight increase of a meter stick as its grasp point is moved from the center-of-gravity towards one end (solid line). For five meter sticks, the increase follows a parallel curve (dashed line), each with a slope of 1.5

4.0 Reach and Walk

When we move our limbs such as in reaching or walking, torques must be applied appropriately to the joints in order that our movements be smooth and coordinated. In the case of our legs, which usually make rather simple, pendular-like movements to be discussed later, the task seems straighforward. For our arms, however, which can execute very complicated trajectories, the control problem seems horrendous. To place this problem in better perspective, it is useful just to consider the equations of motion for a simple planar two-link manipulator (Equations 33-11,12). The inclusion of Coriolis and centripetal forces leads to a formidable result, whose inverse kinematics seem almost intractable for a biological system (Equations 33-13,15). Given such complexity, how is it possible that biological arms are so successful? We consider two cases: simplified movements and time scaling.

Any one watching an infant will note its limited repertoire of arm movements. Is it possible that these movements represent simple, special case solutions to the arm kinematics? Consider again the two-link arm (Figure 33-1) and the relations between joint angles and position (equation 33-13). If θ_2 is held fixed making the arm rigid, then executing a circular movement becomes trivial. (This corresponds to the infant's "swipe".) To complete our explorations of the plane, we then would like to make radial movements, thereby setting up a polar coordinate frame that might facilitate motor planning. Again, inspection of equations (33-13) shows this objective is easily satisfied for any movement along a ray originating at $x = y = 0$ (i.e. the shoulder) having an angle ϕ to the x-axis. Specifically, the end-point of the arm will follow radial trajectories if $\theta_1 + \theta_2/2 = \phi$, provided $l_1 = l_2$. The condition thus imposes a rather simple relation between the shoulder and elbow angles and their derivatives (Problem 33-3).

A second kind of simplification in-volves the problem of making the same movement twice as fast. How much more torque will be needed? What will happen to the velocity and trajectory profile as the torque is increased? Hollerbach's article answers both these questions. First,

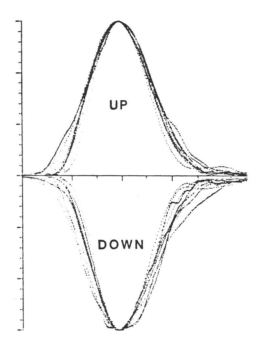

Figure 4 Tangential velocity profile shape invariance across different speeds: illustrated by normalized profiles for one subject's unloaded movements at slow, medium, and fast speeds. Downward movements are plotted as having negative tangential velocities so they can be distinguished from the upward movements. Slow and fast movements are dotted here while medium speed movements are presented as solid lines. These profiles all overlap indicating that the same shape tangential velocity profile was executed in each case. (From Atkeson & Hollerbach, 1984.)

if the constant gravity force terms can be factored out, then torques will scale as r^2, where r is the new rate desired (i.e. the effective time compression). This follows simply by applying the chain rule to scaled time in order to calculate acceleration. Note that because all terms (except the gravity one) in equations (33-11,12) are acclerations, it should not be surprising that both the Coriolus and centriptial forces also scale by r^2. What is surprising, however, is that the velocity profile along a given trajectory executed by a biological arm is the same after correcting for the time scaling. This profile of speed versus (normalized) time is roughly bell-shaped as illustrated in Figure 4 and probably serves to minimize the "jerk"—the rate of change of acceleration (Flash & Hogan, 1985). Thus, Hollerbach's analysis of how the torque limits of actuators restrict manipulator speed needs to be recast with the additional constraint of a fixed, but scalable velocity profile.

Following Hollerbach's analysis of the time-scaling of arm movements, it is now easy to see how the simpler pendular-like movements of leg-motion may also be scaled. First, however, we consider the factors which enter into simple ballistic walking. The zero-order model for walking is simply to treat the leg motion as a pendulum. (Indeed, toy manufacturers use this principle successfully to create animals or soldiers which "walk" down inclines!) Figure 5 shows the predicted stride periods for animals, assuming rigid cylindrical legs. The prediction is remarkably good (see Problem 34-1). Mochon & McMahon extend this simple ballistic model in Selection 34, exploring leg positions and torques which must be applied to explain the observed behavior. Knee flexion is, of course, critical, not just so

that the foot will clear the ground (without introducing body-sway as the toy manufacturer does), but also knee flexion reduces swing time and thus allows a walk to approach a run, aided by increased step length due to pelvic rotation.

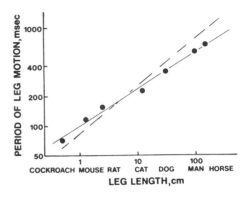

Figure 5 The relation between leg length and stride period is close to that predicted by a simple pendular motion. The dashed line has a slope of one-half. (Adapted from McMahon, 1975.)

For most animals, however, running is not simply walking at increased rates. Rather, a different pattern of footfalls is used. Beginning with Muybridge's early photos of "Animals in Motion", the different gaits of a wide variety of species have been noted. What constraints underly the observed patterns? Why does a horse walk, trot, canter and gallop, but not amble or bound? To begin to answer these kinds of questions, we need a framework for representing and manipulating gaits. McGhee & Jain in Selection 35

1 – Leg   Legs   0 = stance; 1 = swing
                  ⟶

Time ↓ |0|
            |1|

Hop

2 – Legs   L R

$\begin{vmatrix} 0 & 0 \\ 1 & 1 \end{vmatrix}$ $\begin{vmatrix} 0 & 1 \\ 1 & 1 \end{vmatrix}\begin{vmatrix} 1 & 0 \\ 1 & 1 \end{vmatrix}$ $\begin{vmatrix} 0 & 1 \\ 1 & 0 \end{vmatrix}$

Jump   Hop   Walk

4 – Legs   LF LR RR RF

$\begin{vmatrix} 0 & 0 & 0 & 0 \\ 1 & 1 & 1 & 1 \end{vmatrix}$ $\begin{vmatrix} 0 & 0 & 1 & 1 \\ 1 & 1 & 0 & 0 \end{vmatrix}$ $\begin{vmatrix} 0 & 1 & 0 & 1 \\ 1 & 0 & 1 & 0 \end{vmatrix}$ $\begin{vmatrix} 1 & 0 & 0 & 1 \\ 0 & 1 & 1 & 0 \end{vmatrix}$

Pronk   Pace   Trot   Bound

LF LR RR RF

$\begin{vmatrix} 0 & 1 & 1 & 1 \\ 1 & 1 & 1 & 0 \\ 1 & 0 & 1 & 1 \\ 1 & 1 & 0 & 1 \end{vmatrix}$ $\begin{vmatrix} 1 & 1 & 0 & 0 \\ 1 & 0 & 0 & 1 \\ 0 & 0 & 1 & 1 \\ 0 & 1 & 1 & 0 \end{vmatrix}$ $\begin{vmatrix} 0 & 1 & 0 & 0 \\ 1 & 0 & 0 & 0 \\ 0 & 0 & 1 & 0 \\ 0 & 0 & 0 & 1 \end{vmatrix}$ $\begin{vmatrix} 1 & 0 & 0 & 1 \\ 0 & 1 & 1 & 1 \\ 1 & 1 & 1 & 0 \end{vmatrix}$

Gallop   Rotary Gallop   Walk   Half-Bound

4 – Legs (Horse)   LF LR RR RF   LF LR RR RF

$\begin{vmatrix} 0 & 0 & 0 & 1 \\ 0 & 1 & 0 & 1 \\ 0 & 1 & 0 & 0 \\ 1 & 1 & 0 & 0 \\ 1 & 0 & 0 & 0 \\ 1 & 0 & 1 & 0 \\ 0 & 0 & 1 & 0 \\ 0 & 0 & 1 & 1 \end{vmatrix}$ $\begin{vmatrix} 1 & 1 & 1 & 0 \\ 1 & 1 & 1 & 1 \\ 1 & 0 & 1 & 1 \\ 1 & 0 & 0 & 1 \\ 1 & 1 & 0 & 1 \\ 0 & 1 & 0 & 1 \\ 0 & 1 & 1 & 1 \\ 0 & 1 & 1 & 0 \end{vmatrix}$

Walk   Gallop
(detailed)   (detailed)

6 – Legs   LF LM LR RR RM RF   LF LM LR RR RM RF

$\begin{vmatrix} 0 & 1 & 0 & 1 & 0 & 1 \\ 1 & 0 & 1 & 0 & 1 & 0 \end{vmatrix}$ $\begin{vmatrix} 0 & 0 & 0 & 1 & 0 & 0 \\ 0 & 0 & 0 & 0 & 1 & 0 \\ 0 & 0 & 0 & 0 & 0 & 1 \\ 0 & 0 & 1 & 0 & 0 & 0 \\ 0 & 1 & 0 & 0 & 0 & 0 \\ 1 & 0 & 0 & 0 & 0 & 0 \end{vmatrix}$

Tripod   Wave

Figure 6 Some common animal gaits presented in a matrix notation.

# LEGS	# UNCON-STRAINED GAITS	# CANONICAL CONNECTED GAITS	# REGULAR VIRTUAL-LEG GAITS	OBSERVED*
1	1	1	1	1
2	6	6	1	4
4	5040	140	3	19
6	40×10^6	2800	90	2
8	1.3×10^{12}	50000	2520	–

*These numbers are for the more common gaits.

Table 1 Observed and theoretically constrained gaits.

offer three choices: the gait matrix, the event sequence, and the event circle. Of these, the gait matrix may be the most appealing, because it is easy to see by visual inspection the pattern of footfalls. By convention a "0" indicates a foot *on* the ground, whereas a "1" indicates the *lift* or swing phase.

McGhee & Jain introduce the problem of understanding gaits by pointing out that even with the simplified two-state matrix, the number of possible patterns of footfalls is enormous. A four-legged animal, for example, in principle could have $(2k - 1)!$ or 5040 gaits. What constraints, then, can be imposed to restrict these possibilities to the observed gaits? The authors propose two important conditions: 1) regularly realizable—where the swing duration is the same for all legs, and 2) connected—where each row differs in exactly one column. A regularly realizable gait is of particular interest because each leg operates identically as if it were at its natural pendulum frequency. Unfortunately, only an upper bound can be placed upon the number of these gaits using analytic methods (see Table 1) and search is required to make the actual count. For

quadrupeds, 80 are possible, but less than one-third have been observed. Additional constraints are therefore required. Three are suggested here.

4.1 Gait-switching

Most animals exhibit several gaits, depending upon their desired speed or particular task. A cheeta may stalk his prey with a restrained walk, then gallop to overtake him, and finally may leap to bring the prey down. Similarly, horses can trot or gallop, etc., as well as simply walk. Even hand movements may exhibit similar phase transitions as the rate of movement increases (Kelso, 1984). How can the same neural machinery be reprogrammed to change from one gait to another? Perhaps here is a constraint upon allowable gait matrices: each quadraped has its own special gaits—it cannot necessarily execute any gait arbitrarily chosen from another species. As a suggestion, consider the notion of a shift matrix which changes one gait to another by simple multiplication. (This could be triggered by central command or by the muscle

GAIT
LEGS   SHIFTER   LEGS

$$\begin{vmatrix} 1 & 0 \\ 1 & 0 \end{vmatrix} \times \begin{vmatrix} 0 & 1 \\ 1 & 0 \end{vmatrix} = \begin{vmatrix} 0 & 1 \\ 0 & 1 \end{vmatrix}$$

$$\begin{vmatrix} 0 & 1 \\ 0 & 1 \end{vmatrix} \times \begin{vmatrix} 0 & 1 \\ 1 & 0 \end{vmatrix} = \begin{vmatrix} 1 & 0 \\ 1 & 0 \end{vmatrix}$$

Figure 7 Gait matrix for a biped hop and a gait-shifting matrix which changes a right to a left foot hop and vice versa.

dynamics reaching a critical point as proposed by Kugler et al., 1980.) Repeated application of the shift matrix to the current gait matrix could generate several different new gaits, but only in a fixed sequence. Figure 7 gives an example for the simple biped hop, where the shift matrix changes the hop from the left to the right leg. It would not be difficult to extend this scheme to include more complicated gaits.

4.2 Symmetry

Another constraint upon gaits follows directly from the work of Raibert described in Selection 36. Figure 36-2 shows two sequences of a cat executing a rotary gallop. One is a left-right and time reversal of the other. Yet the leg motion for each pair in the sequences is almost identical, showing that the leg motions follow the symmetry constraint proposed by Raibert to simplify the control of coordinated, balanced running. Inspecting Figure 6, we can find the gait matrix for the rotary gallop, and note that it indeed satisfies the symmetry constraint. Namely the trans-

pose of the matrix is the original matrix. Thus $n \times k$ matrices where $n > k$ such as the detailed walk or gallop in Figure 6 would not be allowed "in theory" and would have to be interpreted, either as multi-event gaits (> 2), or as algorithmic modifications. Raibert discusses some of these latter factors in his article.

4.3 Virtual Leg

The selection by Raibert not only increases our understanding of allowable gaits, but also presents an elegant solution to the

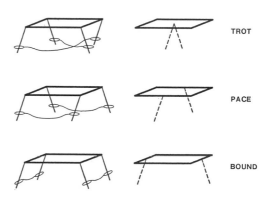

Figure 8 Three quadruped gaits move the legs in pairs. In the trot (TOP), diagonal pairs of legs act in unison, as shown by the shackles. They strike the ground at the same time, they leave the ground at the same time, and they swing forward at the same time. In the pace (MIDDLE), lateral pairs of legs act in unison. In the bound (BOTTOM), the front legs act in unison, as do the rear leg. Using the virtual leg idea, each of the gaits shown on the left reduces to the virtual biped one-foot gait shown on the right. (From Raibert et al., 1985.)

control of dynamic balance. Although the symmetry constraints are developed principally for the pogo-stick, surprisingly, the same control system can easily be adapted for multi-legged systems. The "trick" is the notion of a virtual leg, suggested by Sutherland & Ullner (1984). Figure 8 illustrates this idea.

Consider a quadruped executes either a pace, trot, or a bound. For these gaits, the legs move together in pairs, as indicated by the linkages. In effect, therefore, the number of legs is reduced by a factor of two. (For six-legged animals who use a tripod-gait, the reduction can be three-fold.) A virtual leg is simply the abstract single entity which replaces each pair. Control of the virtual leg will successfully drive the two real legs provided their linkage satisfies certain constraints (see Problem 36-2).

Using the virtual leg concept, Raibert has now built machines that "walk" using two or four legs. Each leg (or its pair-mate) are controlled just as in the single leg, pogo-stick case. In particular, their symmetric behavior in space and time permits a solution to the three central control problems: 1) body altitude (controlled by leg thrust to the ground), 2) attitude or posture of the body (controlled by hip angle) and 3) the balance (controlled by foot position). Of course, other solutions to these control problems are possible. However, Raibert's is appealling because of its simplicity and elegance, and by the fact that so many animal gaits (including our own!) obey his symmetry constraint. Consequently, the symmetry and virtual leg concepts appear excellent candidates for incorporation into a general theory of biological locomotion.

References

Asatryan, D.G. & Fel'dman, A.G. (1965) Biophysics of complex systems and mathematical models. Functional tuning of nervous system with control of movement or maintenance of steady postions. *Biophys.*, 10:925 – 935.

Atkeson, C.G. & Hollerbach, J.M. (1984) Kinematic features of unrestrained arm movements. MIT A.I. Memo 790.

Bizzi, E., Polit, A. & Morasso, P. (1976) Mechanisms underlying achievement of final head position. *J. Neurophysiol.*, 39:435 – 444.

Flash, T. & Hogan, N. (1985) The coordination of arm movements: an experimentally confirmed mathematical model. *Jrl. Neurosci.*, 5:1688 – 1703.

Hogan, N. (1984) Adaptive control of mechanical impedance by coactivation of antagonist muscles. *IEEE Trans. on Auto. Control*, AC-29:681 – 690.

Kelso, J.A.S. (1984) Phase transitions and critical behavior in human bimanual coordination. *Amer. Jrl. Physiol.*: Reg. Integ. Comp. 15.

Kugler, P.N., Kelso, J.A.S. & Turvey, M.T. (1980) On the concept of coordinated structures as dissipative structures. In G.E. Stelmach & J. Requin (eds.), *Tutorials in Motor Behavior*, Amsterdam: North-Holland, pp. 3 – 47.

McMahon, T.A. (1975) Using body size to understand the structural design of animals: quadrapedal locomotion. *J. Appl. Physic.*, 39:619 – 627.

Morely, J.W. & Goodwin, A.W. (1987) Sinusoidal movement of a grating across

---

Acknowledgment: Comments by Chris Atkeson were greatly appreciated.

the monkey's fingerpad: temporal patterns of afferent fiber responses. *Jrl. Neurosci.*, 7:2181–2191.

Polit A. & Bizzi, E. (1978) Processes controlling arm movements in monkeys. *Science*, 201:1235–1237.

Raibert, M.H., et al. (1985) Dynamically stable legged locomotion. CMU Technical Report No. CMU-LL-4-1985.

Sakitt, B. (1980) A spring model and equivalent neural network for arm posture control. *Biol. Cybernetics*, 37:227–234.

Stansfield, S.A. (1987) Visually-guided haptic object recognition. University of Pennsylvania Dept. Computer & Info. Science Report No. MS-CIS-87-93; GRASP LAB 122.

Sutherland, I.E. & Ullner, M.K. (1984) Footprints in the asphalt. *Jrl. Robotics Res.*, 3:29–36.

---

[1] For a brief overview of problems and approaches to object recognition using tactile features see Browse, R. (1987) *IEEE Trans. Pattern & Mach. Intell.*, PAMI-9:779–786.

On the Prehension of the Human Hand

Alberto Rovetta

Institute of Mechanics of Machines
Milano, Italy

Notation:

A, B contact points
a, b contact tangents
$\mathbf{T}$ external torque
$\mathbf{F}$ external force
P intersection point
R unilateral constraint
      reaction of object
V velocity

$\mathbf{n}$ moment of forces
$\mathbf{f}$ forces
π plane
ω angular velocity

1.0 Introduction

This paper deals with human hand prehension, in planar and spatial configurations, as seen from the viewpoint of mechanics. Such prehension often presents different roles for the fingers, thumb and palm when they contact an object of generic shape. The general principles of prehension are developed here with the aid of the theoretical mechanical laws. The analysis demonstrates that the human hand represents the most simple and optimal structure with automatic control for the stable prehension of generic shaped objects.

2.0 Planar Prehension

A planar rigid body is isostatic if the constraints remove its three degrees of freedom. In Figure 1 the rigid body is static because the pivot in A and the slider with pivot in B remove the $2 + 1$ degrees of freedom, with the condition that the perpendicular axis through B does not intersect A. According to dynamics laws (Cisotti, 1939) from the equations

$$\sum \mathbf{f} = 0 \tag{1}$$

$$\sum \mathbf{n} = 0 \tag{2}$$

reactions $\overline{R}_A$ and $\overline{R}_B$ in A and B may be determined: they correspond to three scalar reactions R_{A1}, R_{A2}, R_B (Figure 2). Under the kinematic point of view, the constraint system may be put into correspondence with three unilateral constraints of contact A_1, A_2, B, with rectilinear tangent segments (represented in Figure 2 with continuous or dotted lines).

Depending upon the particular dynamic conditions, values and directions of the reactions are determined; according to this determination, the constraints may be accepted as unilateral and are represented by one of the two sets of lines represented in Figure 2 with the index $'$ or $''$.

Given that one finger of the human hand may exert an unilateral constraint, it is possible to conclude that three points opportunely disposed are sufficient to ensure the prehension of an object in a plane.

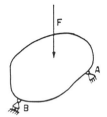

Figure 1 An external force **F** acting on a planar rigid body with restraining forces introduced by a pivot at A and a pivot plus slider at B.

The choice of the position of the constraints is conditioned by the dynamic equilibrium, according to the geometric configuration of the objects to be grasped. A kinematic consideration completes the mechanical analysis in the plane: two unilateral constraints admit a center of velocity, at the intersection P of their perpendicular axis. As a consequence, the third unilateral constraint must present a perpendicular axis which does not intersect P, in order to avoid rotation (Figure 3).

Adhesion friction will increase the stability of the prehension, because the friction cones reduce the sensitivity of constraint reactions to perturbations in the external forces.

According to the previous analysis, a thumb, a finger and a palm represents a suitable three-point contact system for grasping planar rigid bodies (Rovetta, 1979).

3.0 Spatial Prehension

A spatial force system may be reduced (Cisotti, 1939) to a force **F** and to a torque **T** in the plane π_2 (normal to the force **F** in Figure 4).

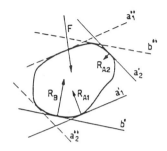

Figure 2 Scalar reaction forces R_i and contact constraints corresponding to forces illustrated in Figure 1.

For the prehension of an object in space, a control system could realize constraints which exert reactions to the force and to the torque, preventing the relative motion between the grasping system and object. The human hand, with its five fingers, performs this result, since appropriate unilateral constraints are performed by the fingertips.

In fact, if we analyze separately the force **F** in a generic plane π_1 which contains this force, it is possible to obtain, as in the case of planar prehension, a system of three suitable unilateral constraints, whose perpendicular axis are not concurrent.

The normal torque, in plane π_2, must be constrained by two equal and opposite forces, perpendicular to two parallel lines (Figure 5) according to the shape of object and to the value of **T**. (As an example, in points 4 and 5 of Figure 5 two reactions R_4 and R_5 are exerted). The two unilateral constraints give a reaction, which prevents the rotation of the section in π_2. Their disposition, depending on the geometrical shape of the section, may be chosen, on the condition that they do not violate the three previous constraints.

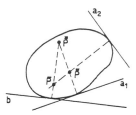

Figure 3 Placement of a third unilateral constraint (a_1) not intersecting P necessary to eliminate object rotation.

Together the unilateral constraints total five and they correspond to the fingers of the human hand, which, with the control system of sensors in fingers, muscular operations, and cerebral activity, dispose their five unilateral constraints as function of the shape of the object and of the forces on it, which are considered and computed as reduced to a force $\mathbf{F}$ and a torque $\mathbf{T}$ [perpendicular to $\mathbf{F}$ (Figure 6) or not].

Fingertip adhesion obviously makes the prehension more stable in the face of perturbations of the external forces applied to the object, and then it is not necessary to make continuous adjustments in finger positions when external actions on the object are subjected to small variations.

A mechanical analogy between forces $\mathbf{F}$ and velocities V

$$\mathbf{F} \to V \qquad (3)$$

and torques $\mathbf{T}$ and angular velocities ω

$$\mathbf{T} \to \omega \qquad (4)$$

allows one to observe that in order to prevent the rototranslatory motion in the plane three unilateral constraints are necessary and to prevent rotation two unilateral constraints suffice.

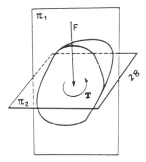

Figure 4 Reduction of a spatial force system.

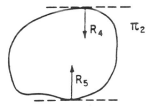

Figure 5 Reactions that constrain torque $\mathbf{T}$.

4.0 Robotics

A model of a mechanical hand was built, with fingers radially disposed with respect to the palm (Rovetta, 1977). A programmed selector controlled in an operational sequence the actuations of the various fingers. Further details appear in Rovetta (1977) and Rovetta & Casarico (1978).

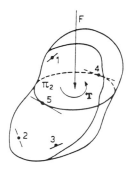

Figure 6 Stable prehension with five contact points and forces.

5.0 Conclusions

This paper demonstrates that the human hand fulfills the most simple mechanical conditions for stable prehension.

Acknowledgment: This research was developed with the support of C.N.R. (Italian National Council of Researches).

References

Cisotti, U. (1939) *Meccanica razionale.* Milano: Libreria Editrice Politecnica.

Rovetta, A. (1979) On biomechanics of human hand motion in grasping: A mechanical model. *J. of IFToMM.* (Pergamon Press), 14(1):25 – 29.

Rovetta, A. (1977) On specific problems of design of multipurpose mechanical hands in industrial robots. *Proc. 7th Int. Symp. Ind. Robots,* Tokyo.

Rovetta, A. & Casarico, G. (1978) On the prehension of a robot mechanical hand: theoretical analysis and experimental tests. *Proc. 8th Int. Symp. Ind. Robots,* Stuttgart.

Reprinted from *Mechanism and Machine Theory,* 14:385 – 388 (1979).

Articulated Hands: Force Control and Kinematic Issues

J. Kenneth Salisbury*
John J. Craig

Department of Computer Science
Stanford University

1.0 Introduction

Research activity in manipulation has been generally focused on arms with six degrees of freedom and end effectors capable of only simple grasping. Two problems with current systems are that (1) they are unable to adapt to a wide range of object shapes and (2) they are unable to make small displacements at the hand without moving the entire arm. This limits the response and fidelity of force control to that of the whole arm even for very small motions. Ironically, the most critical and necessarily accurate motions in an assembly task are of small magnitude. Once a manipulator has placed objects to be assembled in contact with each other, the subsequent partly constrained motions necessary to complete the assembly are often less than 1 cm, with angular excursions of less than 20°. Thus, joints that are designed to move through a working volume with a radius of 0.5 m or more are used to make small, critical movements.

One solution to this problem has been to use small, motion-producing devices between the end effector and the arm. The remote center compliance (RCC) device from Draper Laboratories (Drake, 1977) is an example of a passive approach. The three-axis, force-controlled assembler developed by Hill at SRI is an example of an active, small-motion device. In both these solutions, the end effectors are suited only for static grasping, not for both the moving and grasping functions. This approach limits manipulative ability in two ways. First, the lack of a stable adaptive grasp necessitates tool changes or limits the class of manipulatable objects. Second, by placing the mass of the gripper and its actuator after the small motion device, a lower bandwidth for a given input power is imposed on the motion.

Many designs for multifinger hands suited for grasping only have been developed (Childress, 1972; Crossley & Umholtz, 1977; Rovetta, 1977; Skinner, 1975). These designs have almost exclusively been aimed at approximating a subset of human grasping patterns observed to be useful in human function. A three-finger design with a total of 11 degrees of freedom has been described by Okada (1979) that uses a heuristic combination of position and force-controlled fingers to grasp objects and impart some limited motion. It does not, however, address the problem of general motion of grasped objects. Though the anthropomorphic model may be useful, we should not limit the analysis to the duplication of human motion. The process of grasping can be treated analytically with well-developed kinematic methods. We consider an object to be securely grasped when it is immobilized by contact with its surroundings (i.e. fingers). If only friction-less point contact is made with the body, seven contacts are generally needed (Lakshminarayana, 1978). This would present a formidable design problem. Furthermore, designs using only frictionless contacts could not apply moments about the axis of symmetry of common objects such as cylinders and spheres. In the analysis that follows, we will consider friction at contact points and identify several possibly acceptable designs. Of these, we will focus on a three-finger hand with 9 degrees of freedom. With this design, general forces or small motions can be imposed on securely grasped objects held in tip prehension. This hand is also capable of a variety of other prehensible patterns for securing objects, including the cylindrical, spherical, pinch, and lateral pinch grasps identified by Schlesinger (1919).

In a collaborative effort between Stanford University and Jet Propulsion Laboratory (JPL), the design and fabrication of such a hand, the Stanford-JPL hand, has been undertaken. Intended for retrofitting of existing manipulators, Stanford-JPL hand system has motors mounted on the forearm and flexible conduit that carry Teflon-coated tension cables around the wrist joints. By placing the hand actuators on the forearm of the manipulator, we reduce the gravity-loading and inertial effects of the hand actuators on the rest of the system. The hand size is greatly reduced, and durability is increased by not having the actuators inside the fingers. To ensure accurate sensing and control of forces at the fingers, a cable-tension-sensing mechanism is placed on each cable where it enters a finger. The cantilever beam shown in Figure 1 supports an idler pully around which the cable is deflected. By measuring the strain at the base of

the beam it is possible to infer the tension in the cable. This allows us to close a tension-control loop around the major sources of friction in the system (motor brushes, gears, and conduit). The sensor is the same frame reference as the actuator so that no coordinate transformation is necessary for tension control.

Degrees of Freedom	Examples
0	Glue, planar contact with friction
1	Line contact with friction, revolute joint
2	Soft finger
3	Point contact with friction, planar contact without friction
4	Line contact without friction
5	Point contact without friction
6	No contact

Table 1 Contact Types

As in some other designs (Morecki, 1980), tendon tensions are combined at the joints so as to permit use of only four actuators for each three-degrees-of-freedom finger and no pre-tensioning of the cables. A more detailed description of the mechanism design has been presented elsewhere (Salisbury & Ruoff, 1981). During grasping, the fingers and grasped object form one or more closed-loop kinematic chains. This necessitates the control architecture described later for dealing effectively with internal forces and physical constraints imposed on the cooperative motion of several fingers.

2.0 Mobility Analysis

To determine the instantaneous mobility of rigid objects grasped in various ways, we must model the constraints on object motion imposed by contacts with fingers in the gripping system. The motion of an unconstrained body is partially restricted when it is brought into contact with another object such as a finger link. Additional contacts further reduce the object's availability of motion until ultimately it is completely restrained from motion. The type and location of these contacts determine the extent to which motion is restricted. The type of contact can be classified by the degrees of freedom of relative motion it permits between two contacting bodies (in lieu of any other constraint). Degrees of freedom are listed in Table 1. The term *soft finger* (see Table 1) is used to denote a contact area with friction that is great enough to resist moments about the contact normal. In this case, rolling without slip across the contact area is possible, but translation at the contact area is precluded by frictional forces or structural restraint.

The classic kinematic approach is to consider contact without friction. In this approach, motion is limited only by structural restraint. In reality, restraint due to frictional forces is often present and necessary in common manipulative operations. Without friction, most manipulator end effectors would be unable to grasp common objects. We assume that internal or external forces in grasping will be appropriate to maintain force closure (Reuleaux, 1963) and will be sufficient magnitude so that constraints resulting from friction will be maintained (remain active).

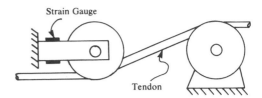

Figure 1 Cable-tension sensor.

The mobility, M, of a kinematic system is defined as the number of independent parameters necessary to specify completely the position of *every* body in the system at the instant of concern. To compute the mobility, we use Grubler's formula (Hunt, 1978) in a modified form.

$$M \geq \int f_i + \int g_i - 6L \qquad (1)$$

$$M' \geq \int g_i - 6L \qquad (2)$$

where

M = mobility of system with finer joints free to move;

M' = mobility of system with finger joints locked;

f_i = degrees of freedom in ith joint (considered to be 1 here);

g_i = degrees of freedom of motion at ith contact point (1-5);

L = number of independent loops in system.

The inequality in these relations results from the fact that constraints on the motion of a body in the system may not be independent. In this case, strict equality would indicate fewer degrees of freedom of motion than are actually possible. We are concerned with the relative motion (or lack of it) between a grasped object and the palm of the hand. The connectivity, C, between two particular bodies in a kinematic system is defined as the number of independent parameters necessary to specify completely the relative positions of the *two bodies* at the instant of concern. We will use C to denote the connectivity between the palm and the grasped object.

To illustrate the difference between mobility and connectivity, consider the mechanism in Figure 2. Two ball-and-socket joints (three degrees of freedom each) are connected by a rigid link. $M = 6$ because six parameters will locate completely all the parts of the mechanism. The connectivity between link 0 and link 2 is 5, however, because the parameter is specifying the rotation of link 1 about its "x" axis is not needed to locate link 2 relative to link 0.

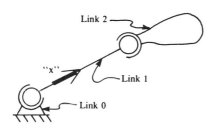

Figure 2 Ball-and-socket mechanism in which $M = 6$ and $C = 5$.

Connectivity may be derived form mobility by considering the two bodies in question as fixed and determining the mobility of each subchain connecting them. In the case of a hand, this will mean fixing the object relative to the palm and determining the mobility of each finger subchain. Subchain mobilities greater than 0 are then subtracted from overall system mobility to yield the connectivity. This procedure, worked out during conversations with Prof. B. Roth at Stanford University, has the effect of eliminating

from consideration motions in the mechanism that can be made without affecting the motion of the grasped object.

Requirements for the Stanford-JPL hand were (1) that it be able to exert arbitrary forces or impress arbitrary small motions on the grasped object when the joints are allowed to move and (2) that it be able to constrain a grasped object totally by fixing (locking) all the joints. The first requirement means that the connectivity, C, between the grasped object and the palm must be 6 with the joints active. The second requirement dictates that with the finger joints locked the new connectivity, C', must be ≤ 0.

Many different hand-mechanism designs are possible, and in each one a rigid object may be grasped in many different ways. A given link of a finger may contact an object in any of the seen ways listed in Table 1. A finger with three links, for example can touch an object in 343 (7^3) unique ways. To determine the number of different grasps possible for a hand composed of k fingers, each of which can contact an object in n ways, we use the formula for the number of combinations, with repetitions, of n things taken k at a time:

$$\binom{n + k - l}{k} = \frac{(n)(n + 1) \cdots (n + k - 1)}{k!}$$

For a three-finger hand with three links on each finger, this number is 6,784, 540. It is important to realize that this enumeration includes all one-, two-, or three-finger designs with one, two, or three links on each finger. Though all these mechanisms could be examined for acceptable designs, in designing the Stanford-JPL

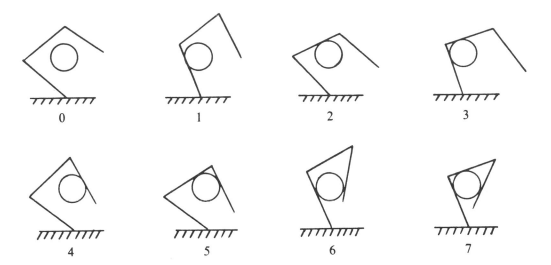

Figure 3 Contact configurations.

hand it was felt that the large number of special cases revealed would not yield significant insight into the problem. It was decided to simplify the problem by assuming that all the contacts in a given design allow the same freedom of motion (one-five degrees of freedom). With three links per finger, each finger can touch the object in one of eight configurations shown in Figure 3. We may combine these configurations for several fingers to define many different grasping situations. For example, a two-finger design with two joints on each finger touching an object only on the last link would have a 2-2-0 configuration. With three fingers the number of unique grasps (if we ignore contact type) is:

$$\binom{8 + 3 - 1}{3} = 120$$

For five different contact types (if we ignore zero- and six-degrees-of-freedom contacts), this yields 600 different designs to be investigated. The more complex hands with more links or fingers were not investigated because several acceptable designs were found within the above limitations.

Of the 600 designs considered, 39 were acceptable with $C = 6$ and $C' \leq 0$. Thirty-three of these were based on 5 degrees of freedom per contact with the grasped object, four were based on four degrees of freedom per contact with the object, and two on three degrees of freedom per contact. Designs based on five degrees of freedom per contact were rejected because with frictionless contact points it would be impossible to exert moments on common objects such as cylinders and spheres. The four acceptable designs based on four degrees of freedom per contact are as follows.

Configuration	Number of Joints	C	C'
2-2-2	6	6	0
4-2-2	7	6	0
4-4-2	8	6	0
4-4-4	9	6	0

The two designs based on three degrees of freedom at each contact are as follows.

Configuration	Number of Joints	C	C'
4-4-0	6	6	0
4-4-4	9	6	−3

Of these, the 4-4-4 design was considered best for several reasons. It is the only design in which extra joints contribute to a more secure grasp ($C' = -3$). The negative connectivity implies a degree of excess constraint and allows control of internal forces necessary to keep frictional constraints active. It was also felt that maintaining the 3-degrees-of-freedom contact type (i.e. point contact with friction) would be easier than maintaining a four-degrees-of-freedom contact type (i.e. line on a plane without friction) and would lead to more robust grasping. In the final design, the last two axes were made parallel to each other and the second axis perpendicular to the first. This allowed the fingers to curl around objects for secure, or *power* grasping. The actual placement of fingers relative to one another was based on an optimization discussed later.

3.0 Accuracy Points and Singularities

In designing a manipulator, it is important to locate its workspace in the optimum location for the anticipated tasks. This becomes increasingly important when several manipulators or fingers must cooperate to manipulate a single object. Several measures of workspace are possible. The size of reachable volume is an important performance measure. If we ignore, for the moment, limits on joint range, we can see that a point on the end of a link that rotates about a revolute joint describes a circle. Two revolute joints in series allow a point on the end of the last link to touch all points on the surface of a general toroid. Adding a third revolute joint allows a point on the last link to reach all points in the volume resulting from revolving the toroid about the third axis (Gupta & Roth, 1982; Roth, 1975). It is this volume that must be judiciously placed relative to the working volume of the other fingers on the basis of anticipated grasped-object size.

To retain full mobility throughout its range of motion, the ideal finger would have no singularities in its workspace. Singularities occur where the rank of the Jacobian matrix becomes less than full (< 3 for the fingers of the Stanford-JPL hand). At these points, it would not be possible for the tip of the finger to move in an arbitrary direction for a small distance and thus limit motion of the grasped object. If motion is not possible in a particular direction, then it is impossible to exert a controlled force in that direction. Such singularities will always occur on the boundary of the workspace described above. A three-link finger with revolute joints will also always have a locus of singular points inside the workspace (Shimano, 1978). For the finger design selected, this locus is the line passing though the first axis of revolution (see Figure 7). In selecting the placement of fingers relative to one another, we try to keep this interior locus of singularities away from the anticipated grasping points on objects so that it will be possible to make arbitrary small motions of the grasped object.

3.1 Error propagation

Another measure of workspace quality is

the accuracy with which forces can be exerted. It has been found that at certain interior points in the workspace forces may be exerted with maximum accuracy (Salisbury, 1982). By looking at the condition number of the force transformation, J^τ, it is possible to compare error propagation with different manipulator configurations. One of the anticipated uses of this hand is in force-controlled tasks, and the location of most accurate operation points is a useful design consideration.

The transpose of the Jacobian matrix, J^T, is a linear transform from joint torques, $\mathbf{n}$, to forces, $\mathbf{F}$, exerted at the fingertip. If we consider error propagation in linear systems (Strang, 1976), we note that the relative error is bounded by the product of the condition number of the Jacobian transpose matrix and the relative error in joint torque.

$$\frac{\|\delta \mathbf{F}\|}{\|\mathbf{f}\|} \geq c(J^T) \frac{\|\delta \mathbf{n}\|}{\|\mathbf{n}\|} \qquad (3)$$

where

$\delta\mathbf{f}$ = fingertip-force error vector;
$\mathbf{F}$ = fingertip-force vector;
$\delta\mathbf{n}$ = joint-torque error vector;
$c(J^T)$ = condition number $(= \|J^T\|$
  $\|J^{-T}\|)$;
$\| \cdot \|$ = norm.

Points in the workspace that minimize the condition number of the Jacobian matrix are the best conditioned to minimize error propagation from input torques to output forces. The best conditioning possible occurs when $c(.) = 1$. In general, this occurs at points in the workspace where the Jacobian matrix statisfies two conditions: (1) its columns are orthogonal and (2) its column vectors are of equal magnitude. Such best-conditioned

points, which we will call *isotropic points*, may or may not exist for a given design. For example, three mutually perpendicular prismatic joints in series would have a condition number of 1 everywhere within the range of motion. A general two-link mechanism with revolute joints that have the dimensions shown in Figure 4 will satisfy the orthogonality conditions at points within its workspace (real θ) if

$$a^2 \geq d^2 \tan^2(\alpha) + 1 \qquad (4)$$

Within the constraints of (Equation 4), mechanisms that satisfy the orthogonality and magnitude conditions simultaneously for some value of θ will have an isotropic point. Figure 5 shows the conditions number for points in the workspace of several two-revolute-joint mechanisms with axes parallel. It can be seen that the mechanism with $a = 0.707$ has a true isotropic point within its workspace. A two-link mechanism with perpendicular axes always satisfies the orthogonality constraint and allows us to place the isotropic point anywhere on the parabola shown in Figure 6 by appropriately selecting the last link length, a.

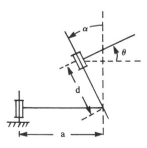

Figure 4 Linkage dimensions.

The fingers selected for the Stanford-JPL hand combine the mechanisms shown in Figures 5 and 6. The mechanism and the resulting circular locus of isotropic points are show in Figure 7. By positioning the three fingers relative to one another appropriately, the three isotropic loci may be made simultaneously to touch an object to be manipulated. A nominal object (1-in sphere) was selected as a guide in positioning these loci.

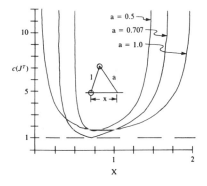

Figure 5 Condition numbers for mechanisms with two parallel revolute joints $(a = 0°)$.

We can find the best-conditioned point in the workspace of an existing manipulator design numerically. Even if strict isotropic points do not exist, one or more minima for $c(J^T)$ will exist. This may also serve as a basis for optimizing partially constrained motion. For example, if we are exerting forces on an object with symmetry about an axis (i.e. a cylinder) we may rotate it about that axis to minimize the condition number, thus improving the force-application accuracy. Ultimately, the minimization of condition numbers in the manipulator's workspace could serve as an optimization criterion in link design.

3.2 Noise propagation

Isotropic points are also points that minimize the dispersion of noise through the system. If we assume the existence of independent, identically distributed noise sources with 0 mean at each of the joint actuators resulting from quantization error, limit cycles, random friction sources, and so on), we can describe the transformation of the covariance matrix, Λ_n, from joint space to fingertip-force space, Λ_F, as

$$\Lambda_F = J\Lambda_n J^T. \tag{5}$$

The resulting multidimensional probability density function will be spherically symmetric if the eigenvalues of JJ^T are equal (the eigenvalues of JJ^T are equivalent to those of $J^T J$). Thus, the isotropic points are also points at which the likelihood of error of a given magnitude is the same in all directions.

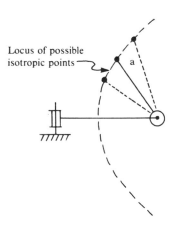

Figure 6 Mechanism with two perpendicular revolute joints $(a = 90°)$.

Again, if the eigenvalues of JJ^T are all equal (isotropic points) the maximum values of $\| \mathbf{F} \|$ will be the same in all directions.

It is assumed in the above discussions that the actuators act in joint space as do the associated noise sources. In the design selected, the actuators do not act directly in joint space but rather through a transmission system described by the matrix R^{-1} (see Section 5), which must multiply J^T. With cable tension vector, $\mathbf{T} = R^{-1}J^T\mathbf{F}$, isotropic points will actually occur where all the eigenvalues of $JR^{-T}R^{-1}J^T$ are equal.

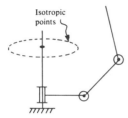

Figure 7 Three-joint finger mechanism.

4.0 Optimization of Hand Kinematics

With a kinematic structure, the problem of dimensional synthesis can be approached in several ways. In the case of spatial linkages, joint-range limits and link collisions make an analytical approach difficult. An interesting approach is to model the kinematics in software and apply parameter optimization techniques in order to choose parameter values. OPHAND is a program in which such techniques are used to choose parameter values based on maximizing a performance criterion.

An object in the hand may be controlled in 6 degrees of freedom only when held in tip prehension with grasp contact points on the last link of each finger. Because this is an important class of grasp, the performance criterion adopted in the OPHAND program considers only fingertip grasps. Potential designs are scored on the basis of *working volume*, defined as the volume within which the object may be positioned given a fixed grasp. Although this is possibly the most important criterion, it clearly does not encompass all the factors that should be considered when choosing hand designs. For example, besides *manipulative grasps*, which allow 6-degrees-of-freedom control of the object, *power grasps*, in which the object is constrained by several links and/or the palm, are important too. Thus, OPHAND results are used to supplement the design procedure rather than to guide it.

OPHAND makes use of models of the finger locations, kinematics, joint limits, object size and desired grip points. A large number of discrete positions and orientations are tested to determine the volume within which fingertip grasps are possible for a given hand design. Various parameters of the hand are adjusted by a conjugate gradient algorithm (Powell, 1964), which chooses search directions in parameter space along which one-dimensional searches are performed. This algorithm is quadratically convergent but, unlike steepest descent methods, does not require that gradient information be available at the search points.

The dimensionality of the Stanford-JPL hand's parameter space is 36. These parameters specify finger locations relative to one another, link lengths, and joint limits. Many of these parameter are selected with regard to mechanical design considerations or other criteria. OPHAND has been applied to investigation hand performance in restricted subspaces of

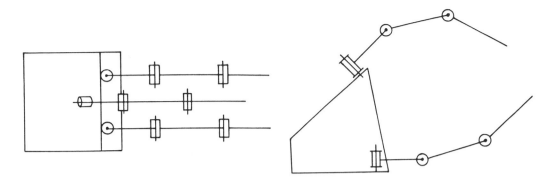

Figure 8 Top and side views of the Stanford-JPL hand showing the thumb placement determined by OPHAND.

one to five parameters. For example, if we fix the location of the two finger bases on the palm (Figure 8), we can use OPHAND to find a thumb location. By carefully choosing which parameters OPHAND is to select, we can ensure that the resulting hand design meets one of the heuristic criteria that are not reflected in the chosen performance index. The position and the orientation of the thumb base found by OPHAND more than doubled the performance index of an original heuristic design while retaining features thought to be favorable (palm area, reasonable finger placement for power grasps, and so on).

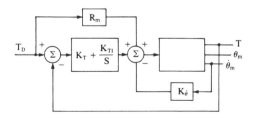

Figure 9 Tendon-control system.

Another useful design tool is a simulator with a graphic output developed at Stanford by Soroka (1980). This system

displays potential hand designs and allows the user to manipulate joints interactively and view the hand from arbitrary camera locations.

5.0 Hand Control

In active-force-control schemes for manipulators, sensing is done either at the wrist (Craig & Raibert, 1979; Raibert & Craig, 1981; Salisbury, 1980; ; Whitney, 1976) or at the joints (Paul & Wu, 1980). In wrist-based methods, the sensors are placed close to the point of interest so that force sensing is easier and more accurate, but stability problems occur due to modeling errors or simplifications, resulting in low-gain servos. Joint-based systems, in which one sensor is associated with one actuator, tend to result in high-gain, high-bandwidth servos. Use of such servos may be viewed as an attempt to make up for less-than-perfect actuator and transmission systems by use of sensing and control to remove the effects of gearing friction, backlash, an actuator nonlinearity. Joint-based systems, however, require that the effects of gravity (and possibly dynamic

29

forces) be modeled in order to extract force information at the hand form sensor data. The tendon-based actuation scheme proposed here for the Stanford-JPL hand has force sensors that are used in a servo loop that encloses the major source of friction (motor gearing and tendon conduit). The force sensors are also close to the point of interest. Thus, both control and sensing benefit.

The hand-control system in the Stanford-JPL hand is based on tendon-level control. Each tendon is controlled with a feed-forward term and a linear regulator with constant gains. The structure of the tendon controller (Figure 9) includes an integral term to remove steady-state errors due to friction. Additional feed-forward terms may be added to compensate for dynamic forces or nonlinear effects such as coulomb friction.

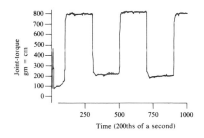

Figure 10 Response of prototype joint to steps in output torque. Units of torque are gm-cm. Time axis is in samples taken at 200 Hz.

A prototype tendon-actuated joint has been built and tested at Stanford. It makes use of active tension sensing and the control architecture described above. Figure 10 shows the response of this joint to step changes in desired torque output at the joint while it is acting on a stiff (aluminum-on-steel) environment.

The tension in the tendons determines the torques at the joints and the forces on the bearings at each joint. Determination of four tendon tensions, given three desired joint torque, is an under-specified problem. To obtain a unique solution, we specify one of the bearing forces, whose value is computed to ensure that all tendon tensions are positive. We then write the relationships:

$$[\mathbf{n} f_b]^T = R\mathbf{T} \tag{7}$$

$$\mathbf{T} = R^{-1}[\mathbf{n}\, f_b]^T \tag{8}$$

where

$\mathbf{n}$ = vector of joint torques (3×1);
f_b = scalar force on bearing of joint 1;
R = constant matrix, determined from cabling and pulley radii (4×4);
T = vector of tendon tensions (4×1).

Using (Equation 8), we can write the expression for the tension in the *ith* tendon in the form:

$$\mathrm{T}_i = G_i(\mathbf{n}) + k_i f_b. \tag{9}$$

The constants that make up the linear functions G and the constants k are the elements in R^{-1}. We determine an expression for f_b by requiring that each T_i be positive:

$$f_b = \max \frac{-G_i(\mathbf{n})}{k_i} \tag{10}$$

The value of f_b will always be positive and will ensure that all tendons are in positive tension.

In order to estimate joint position and velocity from information sensed in tendon space, we define the constant matrices A and B:

$$\boldsymbol{\theta} = A\boldsymbol{\theta}_m + B\mathbf{T} \tag{11}$$

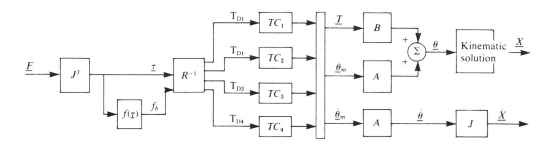

Figure 11 Four tendon controllers used to form a finger system.

$$\dot{\boldsymbol{\theta}} = A\dot{\boldsymbol{\theta}}_m \qquad (12)$$

where

$\boldsymbol{\theta}$ = vector of joint angles;

$\dot{\boldsymbol{\theta}}$ = vector of joint angular velocities;

$\boldsymbol{\theta}_m$ = vector of motor angles;

$\dot{\boldsymbol{\theta}}_m$ = vector of motor angular velocities.

Matrices A and B are determined by cabling structure and various pully radii and make use of redundant information by averaging. The B matrix allows the inclusion of tendon stretch in the joint position estimation. Figure 11 shows four tendon controllers used to form a finger system. This finger system includes transformations so that it accepts desired forces in Cartesian space and outputs Cartesian position and velocity. Below are the R, R^{-1}, A and B matrices for one finger of the Stanford-JPL hand. Note that all matrices are constant for a given finger design, and so are not calculated on line.

$$R = \begin{bmatrix} -R_1 & R_2 & R_2 & -R_1 \\ R_1 & R_2 & -R_2 & -R_1 \\ 0 & R_2 & -R_2 & 0 \\ 1 & 1 & 1 & 1 \end{bmatrix} \qquad (13)$$

$$R^{-1} =$$

$$\begin{bmatrix} \frac{-1}{2R_2+2R_1} & \frac{1}{2R_1} & \frac{-1}{2R-1} & \frac{R_2}{2R_2+2R_1} \\ \frac{1}{2R_2+2R_1} & 0 & \frac{1}{2R_2} & \frac{R_1}{2sR_2+2R_1} \\ \frac{1}{2R_2+2R_1} & 0 & \frac{-1}{2R_2} & \frac{R_1}{2R_2+2R_1} \\ \frac{-1}{2R_2+2R_1} & \frac{-1}{2R_1} & \frac{1}{2R_1} & \frac{R_2}{2R_2+2R_1} \end{bmatrix}$$

$$(14)$$

$$A = \begin{bmatrix} \frac{-R_m}{4R_1} & \frac{R_m}{4R_2} & \frac{R_m}{4R_2} & \frac{-R_m}{4R_1} \\ \frac{R_m}{4R_1} & \frac{R_m}{4R_2} & \frac{-R_m}{4R_2} & \frac{-R_m}{4R_1} \\ 0 & \frac{R_m}{2R_2} & \frac{-R_m}{2R_2} & 0 \end{bmatrix} \qquad (15)$$

$$B = \begin{bmatrix} \frac{1}{4kR_1} & \frac{-1}{4kR_2} & \frac{-1}{4kR_2} & \frac{1}{4kR_1} \\ \frac{-1}{4kR_1} & \frac{-1}{4kR_2} & \frac{1}{4kR_2} & \frac{1}{4dR_1} \\ 0 & \frac{-1}{2kR_2} & \frac{1}{2kR_2} & 0 \end{bmatrix} \qquad (16)$$

where

R_1, R_2 = radius of pulleys at joints;

R_m = equivalent radius of motor pulley (includes gearing at motor);

k = stiffness at tendons.

There is a simple control structure for a single finger that is commanded in

29

Cartesian coordinates but does not require the computation of an inverse kinematic solution or an inverse Jacobian matrix. The method also combines the best feature of previous work on active force control systems for manipulators, the hybrid position/force approach (Craig & Raibert, 1979; Raibert & Craig, 1981) and the stiffness approach (Salisbury, 1980). Figure 12 is a block diagram of such a system. Although force control appears to be open-loop at this level, there are closed force-control loops within the finger subsystem. The matrix K_x is diagonal and sets the stiffness of the fingertip in Cartesian space. K_r is calculated as a linear function of K_x in order to keep the response of the position servo approximately critically damped even as the commanded stiffness. K_x, changes. If K_x is set to 0, the finger may be operated in pure force servo mode via commands at the F_d input. By selectively zeroing elements of K_x and F_d, orthogonal Cartesian directions may be controlled in different modes.

Hand control is the problem of simultaneous control of several fingers, each with several degrees of freedom. The problem is analogous to the problem of controlling two or more manipulators cooperatively (Ishida, 1977). We are concerned here with the control of three fingers with three degrees of freedom. These nine degrees of freedom allow the specification of the six-degrees-of-freedom behavior of the grasped object relative to the palm as well as the specification of three forces within the object acting along the edges of the grasp triangle.

Control of individual fingers, as suggested in Figure 12, is useful when the fingers are not coupled, for example, for following position trajectories through space

or striking a piano key with one finger. when objects are grasped, the fingers are coupled and should be controlled differently. Control of coupled motions with uncoupled controllers is possible with some fingers in position mode and others in force-control mode, but such schemes seem to lack generality.

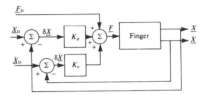

Figure 12 Cartesian finger-control system. All data paths represent (3×1) vectors.

So that all fingers can act cooperatively, we must expand the method proposed for single-finger control in Figure 12 to allow coupled control of the fingers. We wish to control parameters of position, stiffness, or force of the object in a Cartesian coordinate system. Additionally, we must specify three parameters of the grasp, for example a stiffness behavior between fingers that maintains a grasp force on the object. If fixed grasp points are assumed, this coupling between fingers may be expressed as a 9×9 *grasp matrix*, G^{-T} (inverse of G^T) (Equation 18), which relates fingertip forces to external forces on the object and internal grasp forces (Equation 17). The matrix is specified by the relationship between object grasp points and desired center of compliance, and so is computed once for a given grasp.

We may now expand the finger controller shown in Figure 12 to form a hand

$$\underline{\mathcal{F}} = G^{-T}\mathbf{F} \tag{17}$$

$$G^{-T} = \begin{bmatrix} 1 & 0 & 0 & 1 & 0 & 0 & 1 & 0 & 0 \\ 0 & 1 & 0 & 0 & 1 & 0 & 0 & 1 & 0 \\ 0 & 0 & 1 & 0 & 0 & 1 & 0 & 0 & 1 \\ 0 & -r_{1z} & r_{1y} & 0 & -r_{2z} & r_{2y} & 0 & -r_{3z} & r_{3y} \\ r_{1z} & 0 & -r_{1x} & r_{2z} & 0 & -r_{2x} & r_{3x} & 0 & -r_{3x} \\ -r_{1y} & r_{1x} & 0 & -r_{2y} & r_{2x} & 0 & -r_{3y} & r_{3x} & 0 \\ r_{12x} & r_{12y} & r_{12z} & -r_{12x} & -r_{12y} & -r_{12z} & 0 & 0 & 0 \\ r_{13x} & r_{13y} & r_{13z} & 0 & 0 & 0 & -r_{13x} & -r_{13y} & -r_{13z} \\ 0 & 0 & 0 & r_{23x} & r_{23y} & r_{23z} & -r_{23x} & -r_{23y} & -r_{23z} \end{bmatrix}$$

where

$\mathbf{r}_i$ = vectors from compliance center to *ith* grasp point;

$\mathbf{r}_{ij}$ = unit vectors pointing from *ith* to jth grasp point;

$\mathbf{F}_i$ = force vectors applied at *ith* fingertip;

$\mathbf{f}$ = force vector acting on object at compliance center;

$\mathbf{n}$ = torque vector on object at compliance center;

f_{ij} = scalar force of grasp between finger i and j;

G^{-T} = grasp matrix;

and

$\underline{\mathcal{F}} = [\underline{f}\ \underline{n}\ f_{12}\ f_{13}\ f_{23}]^T$;
$\mathbf{F} = [\underline{F}_1\ \underline{F}_2\ \underline{F}_3]^T$;
$f_{ij} = (\underline{F}_1 - \underline{F}_j) \cdot r_{ij}$.

controller. This requires that we invert the grasp matrix (once per given grasp), which is always possible if the three grasp points are not chosen to be colinear. Then, from (Equation 17), we obtain:

$$\mathbf{F} = G^T \mathcal{F} \tag{18}$$

The grasp matrix can be viewed as a Jacobian matrix relating fingertip forces to object forces (including internal forces). We can describe the desired generalized stiffness behavior of the object as

$$\mathcal{F} = K_x \delta \mathcal{H} \tag{19}$$

For small displacements and virtual work considerations.

$$\delta x = G \delta \mathcal{H} \tag{20}$$

K_x = (9×9) diagonal stiffness matrix;
$\delta \mathcal{H}$ = vector of small displacements of the object and grip joints;
δx = vector of small displacements of the fingertips.

Combining (Equations 18-20) yields the relationship needed for control:

$$\mathbf{F} = G^T K_x G \delta x \tag{21}$$

Figure 13 shows the hand controller

based on (Equation 21). It does not require any inverse kinematic or inverse Jacobian solutions. The inputs are desired position of the fingertips, which can be computed based on desired object position by straightforward Cartesian frame operations. A fingertip force input is also shown, as in the finger controller.

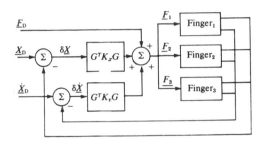

Figure 13 Cartesian hand controller. All data paths represent (9×1) vectors.

6.0 Conclusions

Several considerations related to the design of articulated hands have been introduced here: mobility, force-application accuracy, singularities, noise propagations, parameter optimization, and control-system structure. The Stanford-JPL hand has been designed with these considerations in mind. It makes use of those results that are practical when balanced against realistic design limitations. The control architecture described should allow active position and force control of a grasped object for the fine motions of automated assembly. The implementation of these ideas is in progress.

References

Childress, D.S. (1972) Artificial hand mechanisms. Paper delivered at Mechanisms Conf. and Int. Symp. on Gearing and Transmissions. San Francisco, Calif.

Craig, J.J., & Raibert, M.H. (1979) A systematic method for hybrid position/force control of manipulator. Paper delivered at IEEE COMPSAC Conf., Chicago, Ill.

Crossley, F.R.E. & Umholtz, F.G. (1977) Design for a three fingered hand. *Mechanism and Machine Theory*, 12: 85–93.

Drake, S. (1977) Using compliance in lieu of sensory feedback for automatic assembly. Laboratory Report T-657. Cambridge, Mass.: Charles Stark Draper Laboratory.

Gupta, K.C. & Roth, B. (1982) Design considerations for manipulator workspace. *Trans. ASME. J. Mechanical Design*.

Hunt, K.H. (1978) *Kinematic Geometry of Mechanisms*. Oxford: Oxford University Press.

Ishida, T. (1977) Force control in coordination of two arms. *Proceedings 5th Int. Joint Conf. on Artificial Intell.* MIT, pp. 717-722.

Lakshminarayana, K. (1978) Mechanics of form closure. Paper delivered at ASME Design Engineering Technical Conf. Minneapolis, Minn.

Morecki, A. (1980) Synthesis and control of the anthropomorphic two-handed manipulator. *Proc. 10th Int. Symp. on Industrial Robots*.

Okada, T. (1979) Computer control of multi-jointed finger system. Paper delivered at Sixth Int. Joint Conf. on Artificial Intell., Tokyo, Japan.

Paul, R.L., & Wu, C.H. (1980) Manipulator compliance based on joint torque contr. Paper delivered at IEEE Conf. on Decision and Control, Albuquerque, N. Mex.

Powell, M.J.D. (1964) An efficient method for finding the minimum of a function of several variables without calculating derivatives. *Compu. J.*, 7:152–162.

Raibert, M.H., & Craig, J.J. (1981) Hybrid position/force control of manipulators. *Trans. ASME*, 102:126–133.

Reuleaux, F. (1963) *The Kinematics of Machinery.* New York: Dover.

Roth, B. (1975) Performance evaluation of manipulators from a kinematic viewpoint. *Performance Evaluation of Programmable Robots and Manipulators.* Bethesda, Md.: National Bureau of Standards, pp. 39–61.

Rovetta, A. (1977) On specific problems of design of multipurpose mechanical hands in industrial robots. *Proc. 7th Int. Symp. Industrial Robots.*

Salisbury, J.K. (1980) Active stiffness control of a manipulator in Cartesian coordinates. Paper delivered at IEEE Conference on Decision and Conrol, Albuquerque, N. Mex.

Salisbury, J.K. (1982) "Kinematic and force analysis of articulated hands". Ph.D. dissertation, Stanford University, Dept. Mech. Engr.

Salisbury, J.K., & Ruoff, C. (1981) The design and control of a dextrous mechanical hand. *Proc. 1981 ASME Comput. Conf.*

Schlesinger, G. (1919) Der Mechanische Aufbau der Kunstlichen Glieder. *Erstzglieder und Arbeitshilfen*, part II. Berlin: Springer.

Shimano, B. (1978) The kinematic design and force control of computer controlled manipulators. Memo 313. Stanford, Calif.: Stanford University Artificial Intelligence Laboratory.

Skinner, F. (1975) Designing a multiple prehension manipulator. *Mechanical Engineering,* Sept.

Soroka, B.I. (1980) Debugging manipulator programs with a simulator. Paper delivered at Autofact West Conf. Soc. of Manufacturing Engineers, Anaheim, Calif., Nov. 17-20.

Strang, G. (1976) *Linear algebra and its applications.* New York: Academic.

Whitney. D.E. (1976) Force feedback control of manipulator fine motion. *Trans. ASME. J. Dyn. Syst. Meas. Control,* 99(2):91–97.

Reprinted from *Int. Jrl. Robtics Res.*, 1:4–17 (1982).

*Current affiliations are: J.K. Salisbury, M.I.T. Artificial Intelligence Laboratory; J.J. Craig, SILMA Corp., Los Altos, CA.

Texture from Touch

Steven M. Drucker

Artificial Intelligence Laboratory
Massachusetts Institute of Technology

1. Introduction

Although tactile sensing is usually aided by vision, many textured surfaces can be identified by touch alone. Wood, brick, fabric, leather, metal or glass all give distinctly different impressions to the touch. Of course, variations in thermal flow, or adhesion (stickiness) contribute to our judgments. But perhaps the single most important non-visual factor is the texture or roughness of the surface. Typically human observers will stroke the surface with their fingertips. Simply touching the surface is inadequate (Lederman & Taylor, 1972; Lamb, 1983; Morley et al., 1983). Here we develop a theory for tactile sensing that suggests why stroking or rubbing a surface is more profitable than simply touching it.

2.0 Goal and Givens

We begin our analysis by considering a simple one-dimensional texture illustrated in Figure 1. The texture is created by folds and undulations of a rigid sheet, which has been brought into contact with an elastic planar sensor surface (skin). Our objective is to describe the spatial arrangement of the contact points—i.e. the texture profile. Note that this is a non-trivial problem if the sensor elements are sparse and respond to strains in the elastic surface rather than to contact position.

Thus, if a single point contact force is applied to our fingerpad, its elastic skin will distribute these forces about the contact point, activating many sensors. For a one-dimensional texture where many such contact points occur at arbitrary positions, the calculation of these forces becomes difficult because of the confounding interactions between the elastic skin and the external forces (see Figure 1).

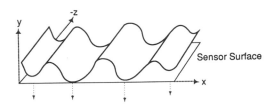

Figure 1 The contacts of an arbitrary, one-dimensional texture can be considered as point-line forces in contact with the sensor surface.

To solve this problem, additional simplifying constraints and assumptions must be introduced. First, we simplify the analysis to the case of one-dimensional textures as illustrated in Figure 1. There, the texture can be expressed as many lines pressing into the surface normal of the skin at that point. This is as if the texture is rigid with the peaks in the texture pushing into the elastic sensor surface, with no significant surface deformation in the y-direction.

Second, we assume that each sensor has a discrete sensing element, that these sensing elements lie beneath a linear elastic surface (the skin) and that the sensor detects strains in this compliant elastic surface.

Third, we use a simplification common to solid mechanical problems, namely that the surface deforms entirely in the x-y plane (we do, however, allow for stresses in the z-direction). This is commonly known as the assumption of plain strain.

Our analysis proceeds in several stages. First we show the minimal conditions for recovering a single line force in the y-direction normal to the x-z surface plane, using only one sense element. This formulation provides the framework and terminology used in the succeeding analyses. Next a single line force normal to the surface plane will be recovered using two sensor elements. Third, a single line force normal to the surface plane will be considered as before, but now the line (or sensor array) will move at some angle θ to the surface texture. It will be apparent from these cases the conditions required for our system to detect a general texture, although the mathematics for this general case will not be given. Throughout the analysis, we will contrast the biological case with the robotics application, where

the latter case has knowledge about the sensor positions and membrane elasticity.

3.0 One Force, One Sensor

The analysis presented here is based strongly on three sources (Fearing & Hollerbach, 1985; Phillips & Johnson, 1981; Timoshenko & Goodier, 1951). The steps are as follows:

1. The stresses for the given force are stated in polar coordinates.
2. These are converted to Cartesian coordinates using the appropriate tensors.
3. Using the generalized Hooke's law, these stresses are converted into strains (which the sensors can actually detect). This formulation is greatly simplified by using the plane strain assumption.
4. Finally, an equation is given that can be solved for the unknown variables (the magnitude of the force, and the place at which it contacts the sensing material).

From Timoshenko & Goodier (1951), all internal stresses σ will be in the direction of a radial line from the point application of the force $\mathbf{F}$. The stresses at the sensor will thus be

$$\sigma_r = \frac{-2\mathbf{F}\cos\theta}{\pi r}$$
$$\sigma_\theta = 0$$
$$\tau_{r\theta} = 0 \qquad (1)$$

where σ_r is the radial stress at (r, θ), σ_θ is the stress at (r, θ) normal to the radial stress, and $\tau_{r\theta}$ is the shearing stress in the r-θ plane, and $\mathbf{F}$ is the force per unit length (see Figure 2). To transform into Cartesian coordinates, the following transformations are used:

$$\sigma_x = \sigma_r cos^2\theta$$
$$\sigma_y = \sigma_r sin^2\theta \qquad (2)$$

Assuming a linear elastic medium, we can apply the generalized Hooke's law for relating stresses to strains to get:

$$\epsilon_x = \frac{1}{M}\left(\sigma_x - \nu(\sigma_y + \sigma_z)\right)$$

$$\epsilon_y = \frac{1}{M}\left(\sigma_y - \nu(\sigma_x + \sigma_z)\right)$$

$$\epsilon_z = \frac{1}{M}\left(\sigma_z - \nu(\sigma_x + \sigma_y)\right) \qquad (3)$$

where M is the modulus of elasticity and ν is Poisson's ratio which equals $\frac{1}{2}$ for mediums that do not change volume upon compression, and ϵ is the strain along a single dimension. Using the plane strain assumption, the last of these three equations must be equal to 0 thus making the following true:

$$\sigma_z = \frac{1}{2}(\sigma_x + \sigma_y)$$

$$\epsilon_x = \frac{1}{M}\left(\sigma_x - \frac{1}{2}\left(\sigma_y + \frac{\sigma_x + \sigma_y}{2}\right)\right)$$

$$\epsilon_y = \frac{1}{M}\left(\sigma_y - \frac{1}{2}\left(\sigma_x + \frac{\sigma_x + \sigma_y}{2}\right)\right) \quad (4)$$

The last two equations simplify to:

$$\epsilon_x = \frac{3}{4M}(\sigma_x - \sigma_y)$$

$$\epsilon_y = \frac{3}{4M}(\sigma_y - \sigma_x). \qquad (5)$$

Finally, substituting in for the stresses that we calculated earlier:

$$\epsilon_y = \frac{-3P}{2\pi r M}\cos\theta(cos^2\theta - sin^2\theta) \quad (6)$$

With the following true from Figure 2:

$$\cos\theta = \frac{x}{r}$$

$$\sin\theta = \frac{d}{r}$$

$$r = \sqrt{d^2 + x^2} \qquad (7)$$

we finally obtain:

$$\epsilon_y = \frac{-3Fx(d^2 - x^2)}{2\pi M(d^2 + x^2)^2} \qquad (8)$$

This gives one equation with four unknowns: F, the magnitude of the force; x, the distance of the force from the sensor; M, the modulus of elasticity; and d, the depth of the sensor below the surface. Thus there are an infinity of solutions to this problem, corresponding physically to larger forces at greater distances which appear exactly the same as smaller forces closer to the sensor (unless, of course, M and d are known as in a robotics situation). To show the ambiguity more clearly, we can relate F to x for a constant strain:

$$F = -\frac{2\pi M\epsilon_y(d^2 + x^2)^2}{3x(d^2 - x^2)} \qquad (9)$$

Note that this equation becomes linear in x in the case where the sensor lies near the surface such that $d \ll x$.

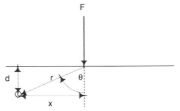

F = force
r = radial distance from contact
θ = angle from normal
d = distance below surface
x = distance from contact

Figure 2 Basic layout for analysis.

4.0 One Force, Multiple Sensors

The second stage of the analysis presented here is simply an extension of the previous analysis for two and three sensors.

Referring to the diagram shown in Figure 3, and using the same derivations as before, we can generate the following three equations for two sensors:

$$\epsilon_{y_1} = \frac{-3Fx_1(d^2 - x_1^2)}{2\pi M(d^2 + x_1^2)^2}$$

$$\epsilon_{y_2} = \frac{-3Fx_2(d^2 - x_2^2)}{2\pi M(d^2 + x_2^2)^2}$$

$$x_1 = x_2 - b \qquad (10)$$

These are three equations in six unknown variables, x_1, x_2, d, b, M and F. If $d \simeq 0$, then x_1, x_2 and also F can be recovered up to the (unknown) factor b which is, as mentioned before, known in the robotics situation. However, if $d \gg 0$, then the solution for x_1 is a seventh degree polynomial equation, and hence in general there is not a unique solution (Bennett et al., 1987; Richards et al., 1982). Thus only with rather implausible simplifying assumptions about d and b (in the biological case) can two sensors recover the force F and its position.

If we now assume constant receptor spacing and add a third sensor at distance b from the second (see Figure 3), we obtain two more equations of the form (10)

$$\epsilon_{y3} = \frac{+3F}{2\pi Mx_3}$$

$$x_1 = x_3 - 2b \qquad (11)$$

where we also impose the simplifying condition that $d \ll x$. There are now five equations in six unknowns. However, because the array spacing term b always appears together with x and F, we have an incomplete set of linear equations.

Thus for biological static tactile sensing, at least two sensors are required to recover the force F up to a scale factor b, assuming the sensors "are on the surface" (i.e. $d \ll x$), and that they are spaced in a regular array. Adding information from more sensors does not eliminate this unknown factor b. To solve for b would require the full polynomial solution, which is regarded as biologically implausible, with no guarantee of uniqueness. From this analysis, it should be clear that static tactile sensing is probably impractical for a biological system, especially one like ours where the sensors lie beneath the elastic surface. We therefore explore the effect of adding a temporal dimension.

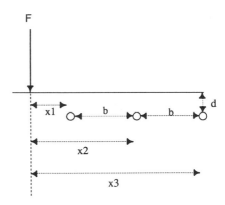

Figure 3 Basic layout for analysis of stage 2.

5.0 Single Line Force in Motion

Let us move the line force tangentially relative to the sensor surface at a known velocity and a constant pressure in a direction perpendicular to the sensor. Now we will show that the texture profile can be recovered trivially and that the magnitude of the force can be determined, and thus the location of the force can be identified at any time. This seems to be the method by which humans detect texture, rubbing their fingers along a surface. The greatest advantage of this method is that only one sensor need be used, though that can still give false targets which will be explained later.

The first step in the analysis is to use the equation derived earlier for the strain in the y-direction at some distance from a point source:

$$\epsilon_y = \frac{-3Fx(d^2 - x^2)}{2\pi M(d^2 + x^2)^2} \qquad (12)$$

If x varies as a linear function of time, then $x = vt$, and this equation becomes:

$$\epsilon_y = \frac{-3Fvt(d^2 - (vt)^2)}{2\pi M(d^2 + (vt)^2)^2} \qquad (13)$$

To find the time at maximum strain, we differentiate this equation and set it equal to 0:

$$0 = \frac{3Ft^2v^3}{\pi M(t^2v^2 + d^2)^2}$$

$$\frac{3Fv(d^2 - t^2v^2)}{2\pi M(t^2v^2 + d^2)^2} +$$

$$\frac{6Ft^2v^3(d^2 - t^2v^2)}{\pi M(t^2v^2 + d^2)^3} \qquad (14)$$

and then solve for t_{max}:

$$t_{max} = \pm\frac{\sqrt{2\sqrt{2} \pm 3}d}{v} \qquad (15)$$

Thus the scaled texture profile is found trivially by simply noting the time between maximum strains.

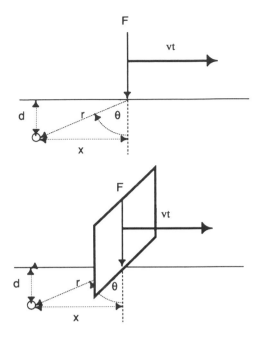

Figure 4 Basic layout for analysis of stage 5.

As a bonus we can also recover F up to a scale constant by substituting t_{max} back into the expression for strain and getting the maximum strain.

$$F = -\frac{(16\sqrt{2} + 24)\pi M\,d\epsilon_{y\,max}}{\sqrt{2\sqrt{2} + 3}(3\sqrt{2} + 2)} \qquad (16)$$

or numerically:

$$F = -15.071\,M\,d\epsilon_{y\,max} \qquad (17)$$

Note that unlike the polynomial solutions to equations (10) encountered for the static sensing, our dynamic solutions (15,17) is linear in the unknowns F and (dM). Hence at the very least, the texture profile of the surface can be determined unambiguously by using stroking movements. Recent physiological data support this solution, showing

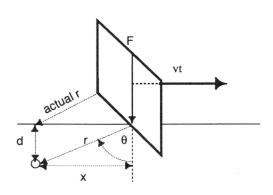

Figure 5 Basic layout for analysis of stage 6.

that certain response characteristics of afferent mechano-receptors are independent of stroking velocity (Goodwin & Morley, 1987; LaMotte & Srinivasan, 1987).[1]

6.0 Arbitrary Direction of Force-Sensor Motion

Taking this analysis one step further, we can examine what happens if the line is not moving in a direction exactly perpendicular to the sensor. (See Figure 5.) All we are really concerned about is the strain in the y direction. The determination of the force can proceed exactly as before, since again, it is only the time that the force is directly above the sensor that is important for the maximum force. There is however some confounding produced by having the line at an angle to the sensor. This situation effectively changes the minimum distance to the sensor, as illustrated in Figure 5. This is simply

a scale change in v. Thus if the angle were known, then the distance could be determined, but the angle can not be determined by using only one sensor. We can imagine a configuration such as that shown in Figure 6 that would help determine the angle by comparing the times when the maxima occur at each sensor (assuming sensors are spaced in an array of known distances), but this will not be analyzed here.

7.0 Noise

A final bit of analysis needs to be done concerning how small variations in the readings of the sensors will affect our results. In the first analysis, there is a fairly straightforward relationship between the force and the distance from the sensor. Any noise in the sensor can not be disambiguated from changes in force or distance. However, if the force and distance are constant, the strain readings can be filtered and a fairly accurate force or distance value may be

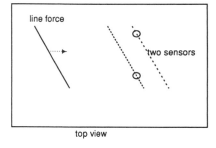

Figure 6 Configuration for determining angle at which a line is moving tangential to the surface.

---

[1]Note that for rigid textures if we allow the observer the ability to sense the maximum counterforce to F (i.e. through joint torques), then Md can be estimated and then used for subsequent measurements of textural elasticity.

obtained. Noise in the sensor becomes much more problematic when the force is moving. Since we are essentially taking the derivative of the signal, we will probably need more than one sensor to filter the noise from the signal, each sensor having a different response time. A solution to the problem is produced by the fact that we are using an array of tactile sensors to measure the force. The maximum strain reading for each sensor can be compared and averaged thus yielding a more accurate value for the force. Given a two dimensional array of sensors, we can also determine the angle at which the line is moving, and the speed at which it may be traveling as discussed before. Thus with enough sensors, each processing the information in parallel, and averaging the results, any noise problem should be greatly decreased.

8.0 Summary

Fingerpads contain a rich array of mechano-receptors, each of which is exquisitely sensitive to forces applied in their neighborhood (Andres & von Düring, 1973; Loewenstein, 1960). Afferents from these receptors send their signals upstream to the sensory cortex, which is faced with the task of separating out the confounding effects of spatial structure, rate (and direction) of movement, and the contact force between the finger and surface.

We have shown that by using stroking motions rather than merely touching the surface, the identification of the spatial structure of a material can be quite straightforward in principle. Further analysis can be done, similar to that already performed, for more than one line force. The mathematics will become more complex, but the concepts remain essentially the same since the principle of superposition can be applied. That is, the strain at some point in the sensor is due to the sum of the stresses from various line forces. This permits each line force to be treated as it was in the first part of the analysis and the strain to be the sum of all individual strains. Because of this principle, we expect no real surprises in extending the results of this paper. A texture might also be dependent on the compliance of the material and that too must be investigated at some separate time. The analysis presented here should permit a tactile sensor with a fine enough resolution to distinguish the geometry that makes up the texture of a material.

Acknowledgment: This problem was suggested by W. Richards for a term paper in "Natural Computation", and his criticisms of the original analysis were appreciated, as were Chris Atkeson's.

References

Andres, K.H. & von Düring, M. (1973) Morphology of cutaneous receptors. In *Handbook of Sensory Physiology*, Vol. 2, (ed.) A. Iggo, pp. 1–28, Berlin: Springer-Verlag.

Bennett, B., Hoffman, D. & Prakash, C. (1987) Perception and computation. *Proc. First Int. Conference on Computer Vision*, pp. 356–364.

Fearing, R.S. & Hollerbach, J.M. (1985) Basic solid mechanics for tactile sensing. *Int. J. Robotics Research*, 4(3):40–54

Goodwin, A.W. & Morley, J.W. (1987) Sinusoidal movements of a grating across the monkey's fingerpad: representation of grating and movement features in afferent responses. *Jrl. Neurosci.*, 7:2168 – 2180.

LaMotte, R.H. & Srinivasan, M.A. (1987) Tactile discrimination of shape: responses of slowly adapting mechanoreceptive afferents to a step stroked across the monkey fingerpad. *Jrl. Neurosci.* 7;1655 – 1671.

Lamb, G.D. (1983) Tactile discrimination of textured surfaces: psychophysical performance measurements in humans. *J. Physiol. (Lond.)*, 338:551 – 565.

Lederman, S.J. & Taylor, M.M. (1972) Fingertip force, surface geometry, and the perception of roughness by active touch. *Percept. & Psychophys.*, 12:401 – 408.

Loewenstein, W.R. (1960) Biological transducers. *Sci. Amer.*, 202:98 (August).

Morley, J.W., Goodwin, A.W. & Darian-Smith, I. (1983) Tactile discrimination of gratings. *Exp. Brain Res.*, 291 – 299.

Phillips, J.R. & Johnson, K.O. (1981). Tactile spatial resolution III: A continuum mechanics model of skin predicting mechanoreceptor responses to bars, edges and gratings. *Journal of Neurophysiology*, 46(6):1204 – 1225.

Richards, W., Rubin, J. & Hoffman, D. (1982) Equation counting and the interpretation of sensory data. *Perception*, 11:557 – 576.

Timoshenko, S. & Goodier, J.N. (1951). *Theory of Elasticity.* New York: McGraw-Hill.

30

Physical Systems Theory and Controlled Manipulation

Neville Hogan

Department of Mechanical Engineering
Massachusetts Institute of Technology

1.0 Introduction

The work presented here is part of an effort to develop a unified approach to the control of a system which may interact dynamically with its environment. The principal perceived problem is that when a controlled system interacts with its environment, its performance may be drastically altered. Even if the controlled system is stable in isolation, when it interacts with dynamic objects in its environment that stability may be jeopardised. This problem is particularly acute for a manipulator. Manipulation has been succinctly described as a series of collisions between the manipulator and the objects in its environment (Goertz, 1963). Every time a manipulator grasps or releases an object, the dynamic behavior of the physical system interfaced to the controller undergoes an abrupt change, and this change may have a profound effect on the manipulator's behavior.

The approach discussed here is based on physical systems theory and has been developed from an investigation of the strategies used to control the primate upper extremities (Bizzi et al., 1984; Hogan, 1985a; Hogan, 1984a; Mussa-Ivaldi et al., 1985), and the application of similar strategies to the control of robot manipulators (Hogan, 1985b,c,d; Hogan, 1984c; Hogan, 1980). It may be sufficiently general to have application for controlling other complex biological systems. The ultimate goal of this work is to develop a class of controlled systems which could be dynamically coupled to or isolated from a wide variety of environments without serious degradation of performance and stability. This paper will show that the preservation of stability in the face of changing environmental dynamics can be achieved through a control strategy which ensures that a manipulator's behavior is compatible with the physical behavior of its environment.

2.0 Physical Equivalence

The basis of the approach is the concept of physical equivalence (Hogan, 1985b). Any controlled system will consist of "hardware" components (e.g. sensors, actuators and structures) combined with controlling "software" (e.g. a neural network, brain or computer). A unified approach to the analysis and design of both the controller and the physical hardware can be developed by postulating that, taken together, the hardware and software is still a physical system in the same sense that the hardware alone is.

The value of this conjecture is its implication that no controller need be considered unless it results in a behavior of the controlled system which can be described as an equivalent physical system. Several well developed formalisms exist for describing physical systems, the most notable being Paynter's bond graphs (Paynter, 1961; Rosenberg & Karnopp, 1983), which have been applied successfully to a broader class of systems than any other formalism. The postulate of physical equivalence justifies using the same technique to describe control systems. This provides a powerful and intuitive way of thinking about control action in physical terms, and may provide an effective vehicle for promoting communication between control system theorists and those working in other disciplines.

However, if this conjecture is to be of anything more than philosophical interest, it is necessary to clarify the definition of a physical system. What (if anything) distinguishes the differential equations used to model a physical system from any other general system of differential equations? No complete definition is attempted here, but some key issues are considered. One of the important differences lies in the structure of the equations.

3.0 Structure

What is meant by structure and why does it matter? Consider the differential equations for a general second order linear system driven by a single input.

$$\begin{bmatrix} \dot{x}_1 \\ \dot{x}_2 \end{bmatrix} =$$

$$\begin{bmatrix} a_{11} & a_{12} \\ a_{21} & a_{22} \end{bmatrix} \begin{bmatrix} x_1 \\ x_2 \end{bmatrix} + \begin{bmatrix} b_1 \\ b_2 \end{bmatrix} u \qquad (10)$$

x_1, x_2 = state variables

u = input variables

$a_{11}, a_{12}, a_{21}, a_{22}, b_1, b_2$ = system parameters

or

$$\dot{\mathbf{x}} = A\mathbf{x} + B\mathbf{u} \qquad (2)$$

One important property of a system is its controllability, and this system is controllable if and only if the matrix $[\mathbf{B}|\mathbf{AB}]$ is of full rank.

One way of imposing structure on these equations is by restricting the values of some system parameters, and this can have a profound effect on system properties. Suppose, for example, that the parameters a_{12} and b_1 are identical to zero.

$$a_{12} \equiv 0 \qquad (3)$$

$$b_1 \equiv 0 \qquad (4)$$

The resulting system is structurally uncontrollable; it is always uncontrollable for all values of the remaining system parameters because

$$\det[\mathbf{B}|\mathbf{AB}] = \det \begin{bmatrix} 0 & 0 \\ b_2 & a_{22}b_2 \end{bmatrix} = 0 \qquad (5)$$

If the differential equations are a mathematical model of a physical system then that system will determine their structure. For example, dynamic interaction between a spring and a mass subject to external forces can be modelled by a second order linear system of state equations. In this case the state variables can be given a physical meaning and the equations may be written in phase variable form in which one state variable is the displacement of the mass and the other its velocity.

$$\begin{bmatrix} \dot{x}_1 \\ \dot{x}_2 \end{bmatrix} =$$

$$\begin{bmatrix} 0 & 1 \\ -k/m & 0 \end{bmatrix} \begin{bmatrix} x_1 \\ x_2 \end{bmatrix} + \begin{bmatrix} 0 \\ 1/m \end{bmatrix} F \qquad (6)$$

x_1 = displacement of mass

x_2 = velocity of mass
k = spring constant
m = mass
F = external force

This system is structurally controllable. Aside from the trivial case $1/m = 0$ (corresponding to infinite mass) this system is always controllable for all values of its parameters. This is seen because

$$\det[\mathbf{B}|\mathbf{AB}] = \det \begin{bmatrix} 0 & 1/m \\ 1/m & 0 \end{bmatrix} = -1/m^2 \tag{7}$$

This example shows that the structure imposed on the equations by the physical system they describe leads to useful restrictions on the behavior they may exhibit.

4.0 Interaction

Another important characteristic of physical systems is the way they may interact. Consider two general first order open linear systems. Each system receives an input from and delivers an output to its environment.

$$\dot{x}_1 = a_1 x_1 + b_1 u_i \tag{8}$$

$$y_1 = c_1 x_1 \tag{9}$$

$$\dot{x}_2 = a_2 x_2 + b_2 u_2 \tag{10}$$

$$y_2 = c_2 x_2 \tag{11}$$

u_1, u_2 = input variables
y_1, y_2 = output variables
c_1, c_2 = system parameters

The stability of each system in isolation is determined by the eigenvalues of its system matrix, in this simple case a scalar. A necessary and sufficient condition for asymptotic stability of each system is that it eigenvalue(s) be less than zero.

$$a_1 < 0 \tag{12}$$

$$a_2 < 0 \tag{13}$$

When the two systems are coupled the output of one becomes the input to the other.

$$u_1 = y_2 \tag{14}$$

$$u_2 = y_1 \tag{15}$$

The equations for the complete system are obtained by substitution.

$$\begin{bmatrix} \dot{x}_1 \\ \dot{x}_2 \end{bmatrix} = \begin{bmatrix} a_1 & b_1 c_2 \\ b_2 c_1 & a_2 \end{bmatrix} \begin{bmatrix} x_1 \\ x_2 \end{bmatrix} \tag{16}$$

A condition for stability of the coupled system is:

$$a_1 a_2 - b_2 c_1 b_1 c_2 > 0 \tag{17}$$

Although the product $a_1 a_2$ is greater than zero if the two systems are stable in isolation, stability of the coupled system requires that $a_1 a_2$ be greater than $b_2 c_1 b_1 c_2$. In general, stability of individual systems in isolation provides no guarantee of the stability of the system formed when they are dynamically coupled.

However, if the equations represent physical systems, then useful restrictions can be placed on the form of the coupling. In the formalism of bond graphs, dynamic interactions between physical systems are described (essentially by generalising Kirchoff's current and voltage laws) as an instantaneous exchange of energy without loss or storage (Paynter, 1961). Instantaneous energetic interaction or power flow between a physical system and its environment may always be described as a product of two variables, an effort (generalised voltage or force) and a flow (generalised current or velocity).

Energetic interaction between two systems also impose a causal constraint on the forms of their input/output relations. One system must be an impedance, accepting flow (e.g. motion) input and producing effort (e.g. force) output while the other must be an admittance, accepting effort (e.g. force) input and producing flow (e.g. motion) output.

A mechanical spring and a frictional element experiencing a common force (i.e. in series) provides an example of an impedance; a mass and a frictional element sharing a common velocity provides an example of an admittance.

$$\dot{x}_1 = -(k/b_1)\,x_1 + V_1 \qquad (18)$$

$$F_1 = k\,x_1 \qquad (19)$$

x_1 = spring displacement
V_1 = input velocity
F_1 = output force
k = spring constant
b_1 = viscous friction constant

$$\dot{x}_2 = -(b_2/m)\,x_2 + (1/m)F_2 \qquad (20)$$

$$V_2 = x_2 \qquad (21)$$

x_2 = velocity of mass
F_2 = input force
V_2 = output velocity
m = mass
b_2 = viscous friction constant

Assuming the usual convention (Paynter, 1961; Rosenberg & Karnopp, 1983) that power is positive into a dynamic element or system, a sign constraint on the coupling equations is imposed. For example, if the coupling imposes a common velocity (flow) on the two systems,

then to satisfy conservation of energy, the forces (efforts) must be equal but opposite (Newton's third law).

$$V_1 = V_2 \qquad (22)$$

$$F_1 = -F_2 \qquad (23)$$

The equations for the coupled system are again obtained by substitution:

$$\begin{bmatrix} \dot{x}_1 \\ \dot{x}_2 \end{bmatrix} = \begin{bmatrix} -k/b_1 & 1 \\ -l/m & -b_2/m \end{bmatrix} \begin{bmatrix} x_1 \\ x_2 \end{bmatrix} \qquad (24)$$

A condition for stability of the coupled system is:

$$(k/b_1)(b_2/m) + k/m > 0 \qquad (25)$$

In this case, if the individual systems are stable in isolation, the coupled system is also stable. Physically, this makes sense as the stability of each system in isolation guarantees that its energy is always decreasing. Coupling the two systems does not generate any energy, therefore the total energy of the coupled system is also decreasing and the coupled system is stable. Again, a knowledge of the structure of the equations for a physical system permits stronger statements about its behaviour.

5.0 Impedance Control

The same concepts may usefully be applied to more complex systems. If a manipulator (biological or artificial) is to interact dynamically with its environment then it is important to understand the structure of the environmental dynamics and to ensure that the behavior of the manipulator is compatible. In the vast majority of cases, the environment which a manipulator grasps consists of inertial objects, possibly kinematically constrained, and may include some elastic and frictional elements. An environment of this class can be described using Lagrange's equations in the following form.

$$L(\underline{q}, \underline{\dot{q}}) = E_\kappa^*(\underline{q}, \underline{\dot{q}}) - E_p(\underline{q}) \qquad (26)$$

$$\frac{d}{dt}[\partial L/\partial \underline{\dot{q}}] - \partial L/\partial \underline{q} = -\underline{P}(\underline{q}, \underline{\dot{q}}) + \underline{P}(t) \quad (27)$$

$\underline{q}$ = vector of generalised coordinates

$L(\underline{q}, \underline{\dot{q}})$ = Lagrangian

$E_\kappa^*(\underline{q}, \underline{\dot{q}})$ = kinetic co-energy

$E_p(\underline{q})$ = potential energy

$\underline{P}(\underline{q}, \underline{\dot{q}})$ = generalised frictional forces

$\underline{P}(t)$ = generalised input forces

The coupling between manipulator and environment is typically such that a set of points on the manipulator have the same position and velocity as a corresponding set of points on the environmental object. These points define an interaction port. The position and velocity of the interaction port of the environment are functions of its generalised coordinates.

$$\underline{X} = \underline{L}(\underline{q}) \qquad (28)$$

$$\underline{V} = \mathbf{J}(\underline{q})\underline{\dot{q}} \qquad (29)$$

$\underline{X}$ = interaction port coordinates

$\underline{L}(\underline{q})$ = kinematic transformatin equations

$\underline{V}$ = interaction port velocities

$\mathbf{J}(\underline{q})$ = Jacobian of kinematic transformation

As the transformation from generalised coordinates to interaction port coordinates is non-energic, the generalised input force is related to the interaction port force through the transposed Jacobian.

$$\underline{P} = \mathbf{J}(\underline{q})^t \underline{F} \qquad (30)$$

$\underline{F}$ = interaction port forces

Thus the input/output relation at the interaction port is:

State equations:

$$\frac{d}{dt}[\partial L/\partial \underline{\dot{q}}] - \partial L/\partial \underline{q} = -\underline{P}(\underline{q}, \underline{\dot{q}}) + \mathbf{J}(\underline{q})^t \underline{F} \qquad (31)$$

Output equations:

$$\underline{V} = \mathbf{J}(\underline{q})\underline{\dot{q}} \qquad (32)$$

These equations show that this class of environments accepts input forces and produces output motions in response. Note that in these equations the vector of generalised coordinates may be of any order and the Jacobian need not be square. It is not, in general, possible to reformulate the equations in the dual form with velocity as the input and force as the output; this system is a generalised mechanical admittance.

Accordingly, to be compatible with this class of environments, the manipulator should be a generalised impedance, accepting motion inputs and producing force outputs in response. As the behavior of the manipulator or the demands of the task vary, that impedance may need to be modulated or controlled, and the approach outlined in this paper and elsewhere (Hogan, 1985b,c,d; Hogan, 1984b,c; Hogan, 1980) has therefore been termed impedance control. The principal distinguishing feature of this approach is in the objective of the controller. Conventional controllers are usually structured so as to make some selected time function of the system state variables (e.g. position, velocity, force, etc.) converge to a desired time function. For example, almost all of present robot control technology is focused on the problem of making the robot end effector follow a desired trajectory in space (Paul, 1981). An impedance controller attempts the more demanding task of making the entire dynamic behavior of the manipulator converge to some desired dynamic function relating input motions to output forces.

The feasibility of imposing a desired impedance on a robot manipulator has been demonstrated and discussed in detail elsewhere (Hogan, 1985c; Hogan, 1984c). It has been shown that if a robot controller is designed with an impedance as the target behavior some of the more prominent computational problems associated with control—inversion of the kinematic equations and computation of the inverse Jacobian in the vicinity of singular points—can be eliminated. However, it is not the intent of this paper to discuss computational techniques as their relevance to the general problem of control of complex systems is unclear. For example, in a biological system, computational complexity may not be a major issue.

Instead a more fundamental question will be addressed: Is it useful for manipulator to assume the behaviour of a generalised mechanical impedance? As detailed elsewhere (Hogan, 1985b,c,d; Hogan, 1984c) impedance control provides a unified framework for coordinating free motions, obstacle avoidance, kinematically constrained motions and motions involving dynamic interaction. In this paper a further benefit of impedance control is considered: the preservation of stability in the face of changes in the dynamic environment in which a manipulator is coupled. One simple (but versatile) class of impedances produces an output force as a function of only the position and velocity of the interaction port. In the following it will be shown that if the manipulator has the behavior of this general class of impedances then a sufficient condition for the manipulator and the environment to be stable in isolation from one another is also sufficient to guarantee that the coupled system formed by dynamic interaction between manipulator and environment is also stable.

6.0 Preservation of Stability

To prove this result, it is convenient to express the behavior of the environment in generalised Hamiltonian form (Stiefel & Scheifele, 1971). The Hamiltonian is formed by defining the generalised momentum as the velocity gradient for the kinetic co-energy and applying a Legendre transformation.

$$\underline{p} \overset{\Delta}{=} \partial L / \partial \underline{\dot{q}} \tag{33}$$

$$E_\kappa(\underline{p}, \underline{\dot{q}}) = \underline{p}^t \underline{\dot{q}} - E_\kappa^*(\underline{q}, \underline{\dot{q}}) \tag{34}$$

$$H(\underline{p}, \underline{q}) = \underline{p}^t \underline{\dot{q}} - L(\underline{q}, \underline{\dot{q}}) = E_\kappa + E_p \tag{35}$$

$$\underline{p} = \text{generalised momentum}$$
$$E_\kappa(\underline{p}, \underline{q}) = \text{kinetic energy}$$
$$H(\underline{p}, \underline{q}) = \text{Hamiltonian}$$

The displacement equations are obtained from the momentum gradient of the Hamiltonian.

$$\partial H / \partial \underline{p} = \underline{\dot{q}} \tag{36}$$

Substituting into the Lagrangian form yields the Hamiltonian form of the momentum equations.

$$\underline{\dot{p}} + \partial H / \partial \underline{q} = -\underline{P}(\underline{p}, \underline{q}) + \mathbf{J}(\underline{q})^t \underline{F} \tag{37}$$

Rearranging these into the usual causal form:

$$\underline{\dot{q}} = \partial H / \partial \underline{p} \tag{38}$$

$$\underline{\dot{p}} = -\partial H / \partial \underline{q} - \underline{P}(\underline{p}, \underline{q}) + \mathbf{J}(\underline{q})^t \underline{F} \tag{39}$$

31

This formulation has several advantages. The system equations are now in first order form (in contrast to the fundamentally second order Lagrangian form). In addition, the structure of the Hamiltonian form of the equations is preserved under a very broad class of transformations known as canonical transformations (Stiefel & Scheifele, 1971). In addition, for this system the Hamiltonian is identical to the total mechanical energy. This latter property can be used to assess system stability because the total mechanical energy of a stable system may not grow without bound and the total mechanical energy of an asymptotically stable system must decrease. The rate of change of the mechanical energy may be expressed as follows:

$$\underline{H}_q \overset{\Delta}{=} \partial H / \partial \underline{q} \tag{40}$$

$$\underline{H}_p \overset{\Delta}{=} \partial H / \partial \underline{p} \tag{41}$$

$$dH/dt = \underline{H}_q^t \dot{\underline{q}} + \underline{H}_p^t \dot{\underline{p}} = \\ \underline{H}_q^t \underline{H}_p - \underline{H}_p^t \underline{H}_q - \underline{H}_p^t P + \underline{H}_p^t \mathbf{J}^t \underline{F} \tag{42}$$

In the absence of external forces, $\underline{F}$ is zero and this system is isolated. A sufficient condition for stability is then:

$$\underline{H}_p^t \underline{P} > 0 \tag{43}$$

or

$$\dot{\underline{q}}^t \underline{P} > 0 \tag{44}$$

Now consider a manipulator with the behaviour of the following simple class of impedances:

$$\underline{F} = \underline{K}(\underline{X} - \underline{X}_o) + \underline{B}(\underline{V}) \tag{45}$$

$\underline{K}(\dot{\ }) = $ force-displacement relation
$\underline{B}(\dot{\ }) = $ force-velocity relation

$\underline{X}_o$ is the vector of desired positions of the manipulator end-effector. In the following it will be assumed to be a constant, corresponding to the maintenance of a fixed posture. If the function relating force to displacement from that posture is restricted so that it has no curl, then a potential energy function can be defined and this simple impedance can be expressed in the following Hamiltonian form:

$$\underline{q} = \underline{X} - \underline{X}_o \tag{46}$$

$$\partial E_p / \partial \underline{q} \overset{\Delta}{=} \underline{D}(\underline{q}) \tag{47}$$

$$H(\underline{p}, \underline{q}) = E_p(\underline{q}) \tag{48}$$

State equations:

$$\dot{\underline{q}} = \underline{V}(t) \tag{49}$$

$$\dot{\underline{p}} = \partial H / \partial \underline{q} + \underline{B}(\underline{V}(t)) \tag{50}$$

Output equations:

$$\underline{F} = \partial H / \partial \underline{q} + \underline{B}(\underline{V}(t)) \tag{51}$$

The rate of change of the system energy is:

$$dH/dt = \underline{H}_q^t \underline{V} \tag{52}$$

In the absence of imposed motions, $\underline{V}(t)$ is zero and this system is isolated. The rate of change of its total energy is then zero. Although the mechanical energy is non-increasing, no statement can be made about its asymptotic stability. However, one of the assumptions underlying impedance control is that the manipulator is at least capable of stably positioning an arbitrarily small unconstrained mass (i.e. a rigid body) (Hogan, 1985b). In Hamiltonian form the equations of motion for a rigid body are:

$$H(\underline{p}, \underline{q}) = E_\kappa(\underline{p}) = 1/2 \underline{p}^t \mathbf{I}^{-1} \underline{p} \tag{53}$$

$\mathbf{I} = $ rigid body inertia tensor

State equations:

$$\underline{\dot{p}} = \underline{F}(t) \qquad (54)$$

$$\underline{\dot{q}} = \partial H/\partial \underline{p} \qquad (55)$$

Output equations:

$$\underline{V} = \partial H/\partial \underline{p} \qquad (56)$$

Note that the rate of change the energy of this system is:

$$dH/dt = \underline{H}_p^t \underline{F} \qquad (57)$$

Thus, in common with the simple impedance above, this environmental system has the property that when the force $\underline{F}(t)$ is zero and the system is isolated, its mechanical energy is non-increasing but no statement can be made about its asymptotic stability.

When the rigid body and the impedance are coupled according to (22) and (23), the equations for the resulting closed system become:

$$H(\underline{p}, \underline{q}) = E_\kappa(\underline{p}) + E_p(\underline{q}) \qquad (58)$$

$$\underline{\dot{p}} = -\partial H/\partial \underline{q} - \underline{B}(\underline{P}) \qquad (59)$$

$$\underline{\dot{q}} = \partial H/\partial \underline{p} \qquad (60)$$

The rate of change of the total system energy is:

$$dH/dt = \underline{H}_q^t \underline{H}_p - \underline{H}_p^t \underline{H}_q - \underline{H}_p^t \underline{B} \qquad (61)$$

A sufficient condition for stability of the manipulator grasping the rigid body is:

$$\underline{H}_p^t \underline{B} > 0 \qquad (62)$$

or

$$\underline{\dot{q}}^t \underline{B} > 0 \qquad (63)$$

Now consider the stability of the system formed when the simple impedance described by (49), (50) and (51) is coupled to the more general environment described by (29), (38) and (39) through the coupling equations (22) and (23). In the following, subscript 1 refers to the manipulator and the subscript 2 refers to the environment. The total system energy is:

$$H_{\text{total}} = H_1 + H_2 \qquad (64)$$

Its rate of change is:

$$dH_{\text{total}}/dt = \\ \underline{H}_{1p}^t \underline{\dot{p}}_1 + \underline{H}_{1q}^t \underline{\dot{q}}_1 + \underline{H}_{2p}^t \underline{\dot{p}}_2 + \underline{H}_{2q}^t \underline{\dot{q}}_2 \qquad (65)$$

$$= \underline{H}_{1q}^t \mathbf{J} \underline{H}_{2p} - \underline{H}_{2p}^t \underline{H}_{2q} - \underline{H}_{2p}^t \underline{P} - \\ \underline{H}_{2p}^t \mathbf{J}^t \underline{H}_{1q} - \underline{H}_{2p}^t \mathbf{J}^t \underline{B} + \underline{H}_{2q}^t \underline{H}_{2p} \qquad (66)$$

Eliminating terms:

$$dH_{\text{total}}/dt = -\underline{H}_{2p}^t \underline{P} - \underline{H}_{2p}^t \mathbf{J}^t \underline{B} \qquad (67)$$

Using (29) and (38) the last term in (67) can be written in terms of the velocity at the interaction port.

$$dH_{\text{total}}/dt = -\underline{\dot{q}}_2^t \underline{P} - \underline{\dot{q}}_1^t \underline{B} \qquad (68)$$

Thus the sufficient conditions (44) and (63) for stability of each of the two individual systems are also sufficient to guarantee stability of the coupled system. Intuitively, this makes physical sense because the non-energic coupling does not generate energy, thus there is no mechanism through which the total mechanical energy could grow without bound, and the frictional elements, however small, ensure that the total mechanical energy always decreases.

Summarizing briefly, this discussion has shown that structuring the dynamic behavior of a manipulator to be causally

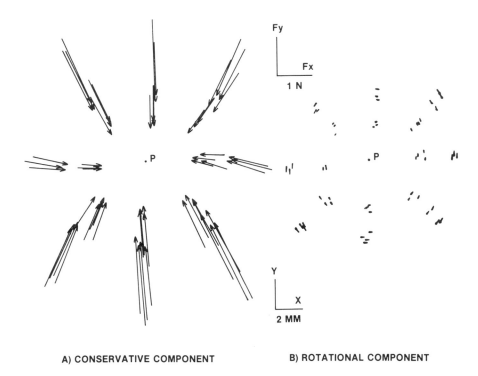

A) CONSERVATIVE COMPONENT   **B) ROTATIONAL COMPONENT**

Figure 1 While human subjects maintained a fixed posture of the upper extremity, a series of small (approximately 4 to 8 mm in magnitude) displacements were imposed on the hand and the steady state postural restoring force generated by the neuromuscular system in response was measured. The postural stiffness matrix was estimated by multivariable regression of between 50 and 60 observations of the force vectors onto the corresponding displacement vectors. This figure shows graphical representations of the symmetric (conservative or spring-like) component and the antisymmetric (rotational or curl) component of the postural stiffness. In these diagrams the two components are represented by drawing the force vectors obtained by multiplying each of the imposed displacement vectors by the symmetric (part a) and antisymmetric (part b) components of the postural stiffness. Each force vector is drawn with its tip at the tip of the corresponding displacement vector. For clarity, the displacement vectors are not shown. The nominal hand posture is at point P in each diagram.

compatible with its environment has desirable stability properties. Note that the proof can be extended to more general forms of the target impedance without losing the fundamental result.

7.0 Application to a Biological System

Because of the generality of the physical equivalence conjecture these concepts can be applied to complex biological systems.

How well do they describe observed behavior? If the skeleton is modelled as a collection of kinematically constrained rigid bodies, then it is properly described as an admittance. Consequently, by the reasoning above, the neuromuscular system should behave as an impedance (Hogan, 1985a).

Despite the complexity of the thermodynamically non-conservative physiological processes underlying muscle contraction, under normal physiological conditions the external behavior of a single muscle exhibits a relation between force and displacement similar to that of a spring (Gordon et al., 1966; Rack & Westbury, 1969). A growing body of literature in the neurosciences (Bizzi et al., 1976; Bizzi et al., 1984; Cooke, 1979; Feldman, 1966; Hogan, 1984a; Kelso, 1977; Kelso & Holt, 1980; Mussa-Ivaldi et al., 1985; Polit & Bizzi, 1979; Schmidt & McGown, 1980) has investigated the influence of this "spring-like" behaviour on the control of movement. Indeed, one prominent and (to date) successful hypothesis (Crago et al., 1976; Hoffer & Andreassen, 1961; Nichols & Houk, 1975) explains one of the principal functions of the spinal reflex arcs (involving muscle spindles and Golgi tendon organs) as preserving the spring-like behaviour of an individual muscle in the face of perturbing effects. Furthermore, the relation between force and velocity produces a behaviour similar to that of a frictional element (Bigland & Lippold, 1954; Hill, 1938; Joyce et al., 1969; Katz, 1939) and thus a single muscle does, in fact, exhibit the behaviour of an impedance of the form (45).

When muscles act in coordinated synergy, there is no guarantee that the behavior of the complete neuromuscular system will be equally simple. For example, the presence of intermuscular spinal reflex arcs could introduce a relation between force and displacement with non-zero curl, or a relation between force and velocity with non-zero curl (Hogan, 1985a). Such a system would still be an impedance, but would not enjoy the stability properties discussed above. However, recent experiments by the author and colleagues (Mussa-Ivaldi et al., 1985) have investigated the patterns of postural stiffness of the human upper extremity. Under steady state postural conditions, the anti-symmetric component of the stiffness was negligible in comparison to the symmetric component of the stiffness (see Figure 1) verifying that under these conditions the entire neuromuscular system of the upper extremity behaves as a simple impedance of the form of (45). Note that this behavior requires that either the intermuscular reflex feedback is non-existent or that it is exquisitely balanced (Hogan, 1985a). For example, the gain of the reflex pathways relating torque about the elbow to rotation of the shoulder must be identical to that relating torque about the shoulder to rotation of the elbow. These results suggest that despite the evident complexity of the neuromuscular system, coordinative structures in the central nervous system go to some lengths to preserve the simple "spring-like" behaviour of the single muscle at the level of the complete neuromuscular system.

If such finely tuned coordinative structures exist, what is their purpose? The analysis presented in this paper offers one explanation of the benefits of imposing the behaviour of a generalised spring on the neuromuscular system. If the curl of the force displacement relation is zero then the stability of the isolated limb is guaranteed with even the most modest frictional effect. Furthermore, when the limb grasps an external object—even an object as complicated as another limb on another human—then if that object is stable in the sense described above, the stability of the coupled system is again guaranteed.

8.0 Conclusion

The approach outlined in this paper offers a new perspective on the control of complex systems such as the primate upper extremity. An unique feature of the approach is that it is firmly based in physical systems theory. One important aspect of the dynamic equations of a physical system is their structure. If a manipulator is to be physically compatible with its dynamic environment then its behavior should complement that of the environment. In the most common case in which the environment has the behavior of a generalised mechanical admittance, the manipulator must have the behavior of a generalised mechanical impedance, and its controller should not attempt to impose any other behaviour.

Imposing appropriate structure on the dynamic behavior of a manipulator can result in superior stability properties. It must again be stressed that in general the stability of a dynamic system is jeopardised when it is coupled to a stable dynamic environment. In contrast, in this paper it was shown that if the force displacement behaviour of a manipulator has the structure of a generalised spring then the stability of the manipulator is preserved when it is coupled to a stable environment. Experiments to date indicate that the behaviour of the neuromuscular

system of the human upper extremity has precisely this structure.

Control of a complex system is not exclusively a matter of preserving stability; acceptable performance must also be achieved. A clear definition of "acceptable performance" may prove to be elusive, but one desirable feature is that the manipulator should have a sufficiently rich repertoire of behaviour. In that context it is interesting to note that the impedance control strategies discussed in this paper give the manipulator the behaviour of a set of coupled nonlinear oscillators. Coupled nonlinear oscillators exhibit a prodigious richness of behavior, and recent research has shown that some of their behavioural peculiarities are qualitatively similar to aspects of coordinated human movement (Kelso, 1984; Kelso & Tuller, 1984).

Acknowledgment: This work was supported in part by National Science Foundation Research Grant ECS 8307641, National Institute of Neurological Disease and Stroke Research Grant NS 09343, and National Institute of Handicapped Research Grant 900 820 0048.

References

Bizzi, E., Accornero, N., Chapple, W. & Hogan, N. (1984) Posture control and trajectory formation during arm movement. *Jrl. Neurosci.*, 4:2738 – 2744.

Bizzi, E., Polit, A. & Morasso, P. (1976) Mechanisms underlying achievement of final head position. *Jrl. Neurophysiol.*, 39:435 – 444.

Bigland, B. & Lippold, O.C.J. (1954) The relation between force, velocity and integrated electrical activity in human muscles. *Jrl. Physiol.*, 123:214 – 224.

Cooke, J.D. (1979) Dependence of human arm movements on limb mechanical properties. *Brain Res.*, 165:366 – 369.

Crago, P.E., Houk, J.C. & Hasan, Z. (1976) Regulatory actions of the human stretch reflex. *Jrl. Neurophysiol.*, 39:925 – 935.

Feldman, A.G. (1966) Functional tuning of the nervous system with control of movement or maintenance of a steady posture. III. Mechanographic analysis of the execution of man of the simplest motor tasks. *Biophysics*, 11:766 – 775.

Goertz, R.C. (1963) Manipulators used for handling radioactive materials. Chapter 27 in *Human Factors in Technology*, (ed.) E.M. Bennett. New York: McGraw-Hill.

Gordon, A.M., Huxley, A.F. & Julian, F.J. (1966) The variations in isometric tension with sarcomere length in vertebrate muscle fibers. *Jrl. Physiol.*, 184:170 – 192.

Hill, A.V. (1938) Heat of shortening and the dynamic constants of muscle. *Proc. Roy. Soc. Lond. B*, 126:136 – 195.

Hoffer, J.A. & Andreassen, S. (1961) Regulation of soleus muscle stiffness in premammillary cats: Intrinsic and reflex components. *Jrl. Neurophysiol.*, 45:267 – 285.

Hogan, N. (1985a) The mechanics of multi-joint posture and movement control. *Biological Cybernetics*, 53:1 – 17.

Hogan, N. (1985b) Impedance control: an approach to manipulation: Part I—Theory. *ASME Journal of Dynamic Systems, Measurement and Control*, 107:1 – 7.

Hogan, N. (1985c) Impedance control: an approach to manipulation: Part II—Implementation, *ASME Journal of Dynamic Systems, Measurement and Control*, 107:8 – 16.

Hogan, N. (1985d) Impedance control: an approach to manipulation: Part III—Applications. *ASME Journal of Dynamic Systems, Measurement and Control*, 107:17 – 24.

Hogan, N. (1984a) An organising principle for a class of voluntary movements. *Jrl. Neurosci.*, 4:2745 – 2754.

Hogan, N. (1984b) Adaptive control of mechanical impedance by coactivation of antagonist muscles. *IEEE Transactions on Automatic Control*, AC-29:681 – 690.

Hogan, N. (1984c) Impedance control of industrial robots. *Robotics and Computer Integrated Manufacturing*, 1:97 – 113.

Hogan, N. (1980) Mechanical impedance control in assistive devices and manipulators, paper TA 10-B. In *Proceedings of the 1980 Joint Automatic Control Conference*, (eds.) B. Friedland & H.A. Spang, American Automatic Control Council.

Joyce, G., Rack, P.M.H. & Westbury, D.R. (1969) The mechanical properties of cat soleus muscle during controlled lengthening and shortening movements. *Jrl. Physiol.*, 204:1-474.

Katz, B. (1939) The relation between force and speed in muscular contraction. *Jrl. Physiol.*, 96:45 – 64.

Mussa-Ivaldi, F.A., Hogan, N. & Bizzi, E. (1985) Neural, mechanical and geometric factors subserving arm posture in humans. *Jrl. Neurosci.*, 5:2732 – 2743.

31

Nichols, T.R. & Houk, J.C. (1975) Improvement in linearity and regulation of stiffness that results from actions of stretch reflex. *Jrl. Neurophysiol.*, 39:119–142.

Paul, R.P.C. (1981) *Robot Manipulators: Mathematics, Programming and Control.* Cambridge, Mass.: MIT Press.

Paynter, H.M. (1961) *Analysis and Design of Engineering Systems.* Cambridge, Mass.: MIT Press.

Polit, A. & Bizzi, E. (1979) Characteristics of the motor programs underlying arm movements in monkeys. *Jrl. Neurophysiol.*, 42:183–194.

Rack, P.M.H. & Westbury, D.R. (1969) The effects of length and stimulus rate on tension in the isometric cat soleus muscle. *Jrl. Physiol.*, 204:443–460.

Rosenberg, R.C. & Karnopp, D.C. (1983) *Introduction to Physical System Dynamics.* New York: McGraw Hill.

Schmidt, R.A. & McGown, C. (1980) Terminal accuracy of unexpectedly loaded rapid movements: Evidence for a mass-spring mechanism in programming. *Journal of Motor Behaviour*, 12:149–161.

Kelso, J.A. Scott (1984) Phase transitions and critical behaviour in human bimanual coordinations. *Amer. Jrl. Physiol.*, 246:R1000–R1004.

Kelso, J.A. Scott (1977) Motor control mechanisms underlying human movement reproduction. *Jrl. Exper. Psychol.*, 3:529–543.

Kelso, J.A. Scott & Tuller, B. (1984) Converging evidence in support of common dynamical principles for speech and movement production. *Amer. Jrl. Physiol.*,, 246:R923–R925.

Kelso, J.A. Scott & Holt, K.G. (1980) Exploring a vibratory system analysis of human movement production. *Jrl. Neurophysiol.*, 43:1183–1196.

Stiefel, E.I. & Scheifele, G. (1971) *Linear and Regular Celestial Mechanics.* Berlin: Springer-Verlag.

Reprinted from *Complex Systems – Operational Approaches in Neurobiology, Physics, and Computers.* H. Haken (ed.), Proceedings of the International Symposium on Synergetics at Schlob Elmau, Bavaria, May 6-11, 1985. Berlin: Springer-Verlag.

Rigid Body Load Inertial Parameter Estimation

Christopher G. Atkeson
Chae H. An
John M. Hollerbach

Massachusetts Institute of Technology

1.0 Introduction

This chapter presents a method of estimating all of the inertial parameters of a rigid body load using a wrist force-torque sensor. These parameters include the mass, the moments of inertia, the location of its center of mass, and the object's orientation relative to a force sensing coordinate system. Identifying such parameters is useful for many applications. These include: (1) The accuracy of path following and general control of manipulators moving external loads can be improved by incorporating a model of the load into the controller, as the effective inertial parameters of the last link of the manipulator change with the load. (2) The mass, the center of mass, and the moments of inertia constitute a complete set of inertial parameters for an object; in most cases, these parameters form a good description of the object, although they do not uniquely define it. The object may be completely unknown at first and an inertial description of the object may be generated as the hand picks up and moves the object. (3) The data may also be used in a verification process, in which the desired specification of the object is known and the manipulator examines the object to verify if it is within the tolerances. (4) Recognition, finding the best match of a manipulated object to one among a set of known objects, may also be desired.

(5) Finally, the estimated location of the center of mass and the orientation of the principal axis can be used to verify that the manipulator has grasped the object in the desired manner.

A key feature of our approach is that no special test or identification movements are required. Therefore we can continuously interpret wrist force and torque sensory data during any desired manipulation. Previous methods of load identification were restricted in their application. Paul (1981) described two methods of determining the mass of a load when the manipulator is at rest, one requiring the knowledge of joint torques and the other forces and torques at the wrist. The center of mass and the load moments of inertia were not identified.

Coiffet (1983) utilized joint torque sensing to estimate the mass and center of mass of a load for a robot at rest. Moments of inertia were estimated with special test motions, moving only one axis at a time or applying test torques. Because of the intervening link masses and domination of inertia by the mass moments, joint torque sensing is less accurate than wrist force-torque sensing.

Olsen & Bekey (1985) assumed full force-torque sensing at the wrist to identify the load without special test motions. Mukerjee (1984, 1985) developed an approach similar to ours, again allowing general motion during load identification. Nevertheless, neither paper simulated or experimentally implemented their procedures to verify the correctness of the equations or to determine the accuracy of estimation in the presence of noise and imperfect measurements.

Our algorithm requires measurements of the force and torque due to a load and also measurements or estimates of the position, velocity, acceleration, orientation, angular velocity, and angular acceleration of the force sensing coordinate system. The algorithm can handle incomplete force and torque measurements by simply eliminating the equations containing missing measurements. The necessary kinematic data can be obtained from the joint angles and, if available, the joint velocities of the manipulator. The inertial parameters of a hand can be identified using this algorithm and then the predicted forces and torques due to the hand can be subtracted from the sensed forces and torques.

The procedure has three steps:

1. A Newton-Euler formulation for the rigid body load yields dynamics equations linear in the unknown inertial parameters, when the moment of inertia tensor is expressed about the origin of the wrist sensor coordinate system.

2. These inertial parameters are then estimated using a least squares estimation algorithm.

3. The location of the load's center of mass, its orientation, and its principal moments of inertia can be recovered from the estimated parameters.

In principle, there are no restrictions on the movements used to do load identifi-cation, except that if accurate estimation of all the parameters is desired the motion must be sufficiently rich (i.e. occupy more than one orientation with respect to gravity and contain angular accelerations in several different directions). In practice, however, special test movements must sometimes be used to get accurate estimates of moment of inertia parameters.

2.0 The Newton-Euler Approach To The Load Identification Problem

2.1 Deriving the parameter equation

To derive equations for estimating the unknown inertial parameters, the coordinate systems in Figure 1 are used to relate different coordinate frames and vectors.

O is an inertial or base coordinate system, which is fixed in space with gravity pointing along the $-z$ axis. **P** is the force reference coordinate system of a wrist force-torque sensor rigidly attached to the load. **Q** represents the principal axis of the rigid body load located at the center of mass. The x axis of **Q** is along the largest principal moment of inertia, and the z axis along the smallest. **Q** is unique up to a reflection in bodies with 3 distinct principal moments of inertia. In the derivation that follows all vectors are initially expressed in the base coordinate system **O**.

The mass, moments of inertia, location of the center of mass, and orientation of the body (a rotation $_{QP}\mathbf{R}$ from the principal axes to the force reference system) are related to the motion of the load

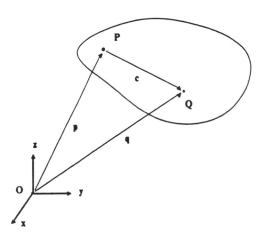

p = position vector from the origin of the base coordinate frame to the origin of the wrist sensor coordinate frame.

q = position vector from the origin of the base coordinate frame to the center of mass of the load.

c = position vector from the origin of the wrist sensor coordinate frame to the center of mass of the load.

Figure 1 Coordinate frames.

and the forces and torques exerted on it by the Newton-Euler equations. The net force $_q\mathbf{f}$ and the net torque $_q\mathbf{n}$ acting on the load at the center of mass are:

$$_q\mathbf{f} = \mathbf{f} + m\mathbf{g} = m\ddot{\mathbf{q}} \qquad (1)$$

$$_q\mathbf{n} = \mathbf{n} - \mathbf{c} \times \mathbf{f} = {_q}\mathbf{I}\dot{\omega} + \omega \times ({_q}\mathbf{I}\omega) \qquad (2)$$

where:

f = the force exerted by the wrist sensor on the load at the point **p**,

m = the mass of the load,

g = the gravity vector ($\mathbf{g} = [0, 0, -9.8$ meters/sec^2]),

$\ddot{\mathbf{q}}$ = the acceleration of the center of mass of the load,

n = the torque exerted by the wrist sensor on the load at the point **p**,

c = the unknown location of the center of mass relative to the force sensing wrist origin **p**,

$_q\mathbf{I}$ = the moment of inertia tensor about the center of mass,

ω = the angular velocity vector, and

$\dot{\omega}$ = the angular acceleration vector.

We need to express the force and torque measured by the wrist sensor in terms of the product of known geometric parameters and the unknown inertial parameters. Although the location of the center of mass and hence its acceleration $\ddot{\mathbf{q}}$ are unknown, we follow Symon (1971) and relate $\ddot{\mathbf{q}}$ to the acceleration of the force reference frame $\ddot{\mathbf{p}}$ by

$$\ddot{\mathbf{q}} = \ddot{\mathbf{p}} + \dot{\omega} \times \mathbf{c} + \omega \times (\omega \times \mathbf{c}) \qquad (3)$$

Substituting (3) into (1),

$$\mathbf{f} = m\ddot{\mathbf{p}} - m\mathbf{g} + \dot{\omega} \times m\mathbf{c} + \omega \times (\omega \times m\mathbf{c}) \qquad (4)$$

Substituting (4) into (2),

$$\begin{aligned} \mathbf{n} = {}& {_q}\mathbf{I}\dot{\omega} + \omega \times ({_q}\mathbf{I}\omega) + m\mathbf{c} \times (\dot{\omega} \times \mathbf{c}) \\ & + m\mathbf{c} \times (\omega \times (\omega \times \mathbf{c})) \\ & + m\mathbf{c} \times \ddot{\mathbf{p}} - m\mathbf{c} \times \mathbf{g} \qquad (5) \end{aligned}$$

Although the terms $\mathbf{c} \times (\dot{\omega} \times \mathbf{c})$ and $\mathbf{c} \times (\omega \times (\omega \times \mathbf{c}))$ are quadratic in the unknown location of the center of mass **c**, these quadratic terms are eliminated by expressing the moment of inertia tensor about the force sensor coordinate origin ($_p\mathbf{I}$) instead of about the center of mass ($_q\mathbf{I}$). Equation (5) can be rewritten as:

$$\mathbf{n} = {_q}\mathbf{I}\dot{\omega} + \omega \times ({_q}\mathbf{I}\omega) \; +$$

$$m[(\mathbf{c}^T\mathbf{c})\mathbf{1} - (\mathbf{cc}^T)]\dot{\boldsymbol{\omega}} \ +$$
$$\boldsymbol{\omega} \times (m[(\mathbf{c}^T\mathbf{c})\mathbf{1} - (\mathbf{cc}^T)]\boldsymbol{\omega}) \ +$$
$$m\mathbf{c} \times \ddot{\mathbf{p}} - m\mathbf{c} \times \mathbf{g} \qquad (6)$$

where $\mathbf{1}$ is the three dimensional identity matrix. Using the three dimensional version of the parallel axis theorem

$$_p\mathbf{I} = \ _q\mathbf{I} + m[(\mathbf{c}^T\mathbf{c})\mathbf{1} - (\mathbf{cc}^T)] \qquad (7)$$

expression (6) can be simplified to

$$\mathbf{n} = \ _p\mathbf{I}\dot{\boldsymbol{\omega}} + \boldsymbol{\omega} \times (_p\mathbf{I}\boldsymbol{\omega}) + m\mathbf{c} \times \ddot{\mathbf{p}} - m\mathbf{c} \times \mathbf{g} \quad (8)$$

We now express all the vectors in the wrist sensor coordinate system $\mathbf{P}$, since then the quantities $\mathbf{c}$ and $_p\mathbf{I}$ are then constants. Moreover, the wrist force-torque sensor measures forces and torques directly in the $\mathbf{P}$ coordinate frame.

In order to formulate the above equations as a system of linear equations, the following notation is used:

$$\boldsymbol{\omega} \times \mathbf{c} = \begin{bmatrix} 0 & -\omega_z & \omega_y \\ \omega_z & 0 & -\omega_y \\ -\omega_y & \omega_x & 0 \end{bmatrix} \begin{bmatrix} c_x \\ c_y \\ c_z \end{bmatrix} \overset{\triangle}{=} [\boldsymbol{\omega}\times]\mathbf{c} \qquad (9)$$

$$\mathbf{I}\boldsymbol{\omega} = \begin{bmatrix} \omega_x & \omega_y & \omega_z & 0 & 0 & 0 \\ 0 & \omega_x & 0 & \omega_y & \omega_z & 0 \\ 0 & 0 & \omega_x & 0 & \omega_y & \omega_z \end{bmatrix} \begin{bmatrix} I_{11} \\ I_{12} \\ I_{13} \\ I_{22} \\ I_{23} \\ I_{33} \end{bmatrix} \overset{\triangle}{=} [\bullet\boldsymbol{\omega}] \begin{bmatrix} I_{11} \\ I_{12} \\ I_{13} \\ I_{22} \\ I_{23} \\ I_{33} \end{bmatrix} \qquad (10)$$

where

$$\mathbf{I} = \mathbf{I}^T = \begin{bmatrix} I_{11} & I_{12} & I_{13} \\ I_{12} & I_{22} & I_{23} \\ I_{13} & I_{23} & I_{33} \end{bmatrix} \qquad (11)$$

Using these expressions, Equations (4) and (8) can be written as a single matrix equation in the wrist sensor coordinate frame:

$$\begin{bmatrix} f_x \\ f_y \\ f_z \\ n_x \\ n_y \\ n_z \end{bmatrix} = \begin{bmatrix} \ddot{\mathbf{p}} - \mathbf{g} & [\dot{\boldsymbol{\omega}}\times] + [\boldsymbol{\omega}\times][\boldsymbol{\omega}\times] & 0 \\ 0 & [(\mathbf{g} - \ddot{\mathbf{p}})\times] & [\bullet\dot{\boldsymbol{\omega}}] + [\boldsymbol{\omega}\times][\bullet\boldsymbol{\omega}] \end{bmatrix} \begin{bmatrix} m \\ mc_x \\ mc_y \\ mc_z \\ I_{11} \\ I_{12} \\ I_{13} \\ I_{22} \\ I_{23} \\ I_{33} \end{bmatrix} \qquad (12)$$

or more compactly,

$$w = A\phi \quad (13)$$

where w is a 6 element wrench vector combining both the force and torque vectors, A is a 6×10 matrix, and ϕ is the vector of the 10 unknown inertial parameters. Note that the center of mass cannot be determined directly, but only as the mass moment mc. But since the mass m is separately determined, its contribution can be factored from the mass moment later.

2.2 Estimating the parameters

The quantities inside the A matrix are computed by direct kinematics computation (Luh, Walker, & Paul, 1980) from the measured joint angles. The elements of the w vector are measured directly by the wrist force sensor. Since (13) represents 6 equations and 10 unknowns, at least two data points are necessary to solve for the ϕ vector, i.e. the force and the position data sampled at two different configurations of the manipulator. For robust estimates in the presence of noise, we actually need to use a larger number of data points. Each data point adds 6 more equations, while the number of unknowns, the elements of ϕ, remain constant. w and A can be augmented with n data points:

$$A = \begin{bmatrix} A[1] \\ \vdots \\ A[n] \end{bmatrix}, \quad w = \begin{bmatrix} w[1] \\ \vdots \\ w[n] \end{bmatrix} \quad (14)$$

where each $A[i]$ and $w[i]$ are matrix and vector quantities described in (12). Formulated this way, any linear estimation algorithm can be used to identify the ϕ vector. A simple and popular method is the least squares method. The estimate for ϕ is given by:

$$\hat{\phi} = (\mathbf{A}^T\mathbf{A})^{-1}\mathbf{A}^T\mathbf{w} \quad (15)$$

Equation (15) can also be formulated in a recursive form (Ljung & Soderstrom, 1983) for on-line estimation.

2.3 Recovering object and grip parameters

The estimated inertial parameters (m, mc, $_p\mathbf{I}$) are adequate for control, but for object recognition and verification we also require the principal moments of inertia I_1, I_2, I_3, the location of the center of mass $\mathbf{c}$, and the orientation $_{qp}\mathbf{R}$ of $\mathbf{Q}$ with respect to $\mathbf{P}$.

The parallel axis theorem is used to compute the inertia terms translated to the center of mass of the load.

$$\hat{\mathbf{c}} = \frac{\widehat{m\mathbf{c}}}{\hat{m}} \quad (16)$$

$$_q\hat{\mathbf{I}} = {}_p\hat{\mathbf{I}} - \hat{m}[(\hat{\mathbf{c}}^T\hat{\mathbf{c}})\mathbf{1} - (\hat{\mathbf{c}}\hat{\mathbf{c}}^T)] \quad (17)$$

The principal moments are obtained by diagonalizing $_q\hat{\mathbf{I}}$.

$$_q\hat{\mathbf{I}} = {}_{QP}\hat{\mathbf{R}} \begin{bmatrix} \hat{I}_1 & 0 & 0 \\ 0 & \hat{I}_2 & 0 \\ 0 & 0 & \hat{I}_3 \end{bmatrix} {}_{QP}\hat{\mathbf{R}}^T \quad (18)$$

This diagonalization can always be achieved since $_q\hat{\mathbf{I}}$ is symmetric, but when two or more principal moments are equal the rotation matrix, $_{QP}\mathbf{R}$, is no longer unique.

Figure 2 PUMAwith a test load.

3.0 Experimental Results

3.1 Estimation on the PUMA robot

The inertial parameter estimation algorithm was originally implemented on a PUMA 600 robot equipped with an RTI FS-B wrist force-torque sensor (Figure 2). The PUMA 600 has encoders at each joint to measure joint angles, but no tachometers. Thus, to obtain the joint velocities and accelerations, the joint angles are differentiated and double-differentiated, respectively, by a digital differentiating filter (Figure 3). The cutoff frequency of 33 Hz for the filter was determined empirically to produce the best results. Both the encoder data and the wrist sensor data were initially sampled at 1000 Hz. It was later determined that a sampling rate of 200 Hz was sufficient, and the data were resampled at the lower rate to reduce processing time. A least squares identification algorithm was implemented as an off-line computation, but an on-line

implementation would have been straight-forward.

3.1.1 Static estimation using the PUMA

To test the calibration of the force sensor and the kinematics of the PUMA arm a static identification was performed. The forces and torques are now due only to the gravity acting on the load, and equations (4) and (8) simplify to

$$\mathbf{f} = -m\mathbf{g} \qquad (19)$$

$$\mathbf{n} = -m\mathbf{c} \times \mathbf{g} \qquad (20)$$

As seen in (19) and (20), only the mass and the center of mass can be identified while the manipulator is stationary.

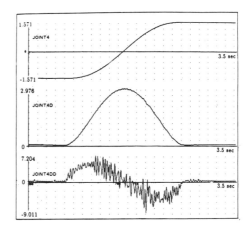

Figure 3 Measured angle θ, calculated angular velocity $\dot{\theta}$, and calculated angular acceleration $\ddot{\theta}$ for joint 4.

To avoid needing to determine the gripper geometric parameters, the center of mass estimates are evaluated by the estimates of the changes in the center of mass as the load is moved along the y-axis from the reference position by known amounts. The results of estimation are shown in the second column of Table 1 for an aluminum block ($2 \times 2 \times 6$) inches with a mass of 1.106 Kg. Only the changes in c_y are shown in Table 1; the estimates of c_x and c_z remained within 1 mm of the reference values ($c_x = 1$ mm and $c_z = 47$ mm). Each set of estimates were computed from 6 sets of data, i.e. data taken at 6 different positions and orientations of the manipulator, where each data point is averaged over 1000 samples to minimize the effects of noise. The results show that in the static case the mass of the load can be estimated to within 10 g of the actual mass. The center of mass can be estimated to within 1 mm of the actual values for this load.

Parameters	Actual Values	Static Estimates	Dynamic Estimates
Mass (kg)	1.106	1.103	1.067
Change in $c_y(m)$	0.037	0.037	0.039
Mass (kg)	1.106	1.107	1.084
Change in $c_y(m)$	-0.043	-0.043	-0.042
Mass (kg)	1.106	1.100	1.073
Change in $c_y(m)$	-0.021	-0.020	-0.021
Mass (kg)	1.106	1.099	1.074
Change in $c_y(m)$	0.018	0.018	0.020

Table 1 Mass and the center of mass estimates.

Static load estimation only tests the force sensor calibration and the position measurement capabilities of the robot the sensor is mounted on. In order to assess the effects of the dynamic capabilities of the robot on load estimation and to be able to estimate the moments of inertia of the load we must assess parameter estimation during general movement.

3.1.2 Dynamic estimation using the PUMA

In the dynamic case, the joint position encoder and the wrist sensor data are sampled while the manipulator is in motion. A fifth order polynomial trajectory (a minimum-jerk time function) in joint space was used to minimize the mechanical vibrations at the beginning and the end of the movement, and to improve the signal to noise ratio in the acceleration data (Figure 3). For more popular bang-coast-bang type trajectories, the joint accelerations are zero except at the beginning and the end of the movements, resulting in a poor signal to noise ratio in the acceleration data for most of the movement.

We found that the PUMA robot lacked the acceleration capacity necessary to estimate the moments of inertia of the load. It also lacked true velocity sensors at the joints, which made estimation of the acceleration of the load difficult. The dynamic estimates of mass and center of mass for the previous load are shown in the last column of Table 1. The data used in these estimates were sampled while the manipulator was moving from $[0°, 0°, 0°, -90°, 0°, 0°]$ to $[90°, -60°, 90°, 90°, 90°, 90°]$ degrees on a straight line in joint space in 2 seconds. Joint 4 of the PUMA has a higher maximum acceleration than the other joints, and thus, a longer path was given for it. This movement was the fastest the PUMA can execute using the fifth order trajectory without reaching the maximum acceleration for any of its joints. The estimates used all 400 data points sampled during the 2 second movement. The results show slight deterioration in these estimates when compared to the static estimates; but they are still within 40g

Parameters $(kg \cdot m^2)$	Actual Values	PUMA[1] Estimates	PUMA[2] Estimates	DDA[1] Estimates
I_{11}	0.0244	0.0192	0.0246	0.0230
I_{12}	0	-0.0048	0.0006	0.0006
I_{13}	0	0.0019	0.0008	0.0005
I_{22}	0.0007	0.0021	0.0036	-0.0002
I_{23}	0	-0.0016	-0.0004	-0.0002
I_{33}	0.0242	0.0176	0.0199	0.0241

Table 2 Actual and estimated moments of inertia, either for all joints moving[1] or special test motions[2].

and 2mm of the actual mass and displacement, respectively. However, the signal to noise ratios in the acceleration and the force-torque data were too low for accurate estimates of the moments of inertia for this load (0.00238 Kg $\cdot m^2$ in the largest principal moment). In this case, the torque due to gravity is approximately 40 times greater than the torque due to the maximum angular acceleration of the load. Thus, even slight noise in the data would result in poor estimates of **I**.

Therefore, experiments with a larger rotational load were performed for the estimates of the moments of inertia. The new experimental load is shown in Figure 2. This load has large masses at the two ends of the aluminum bar, resulting in large moments of inertia in two directions ($\sim 0.024 kg \cdot m^2$) and a small moment in the other. A typical set of estimates of the moments of inertia at the center of mass frame for the load with the gripper subtracted out are shown in Table 2 for the above all-joints-moving trajectory. They contain some errors but are fairly close to the actual values.

3.1.3 Special test movements using the PUMA

In order to improve the estimates by maximizing the rotational accelerations in the trajectories, a series of special test movements were generated. The data was sampled while the robot was following three separate 2-second rotational trajectories around the principal axes of the load. Such trajectories used joints 4 and 6 only, and resulted in higher acceleration data than the previous trajectory, thus improving the signal to noise ratio in both the acceleration and the force-torque data. Typical estimates for these special movements show improvements over the estimates with the previous trajectory (Table 2). Although the estimate of I_{22} is slightly worse than before, all the other terms have improved; the cross terms, especially, are much smaller than before. However, these estimates of **I** are not as accurate as the estimates of the mass and the center of mass shown in Table 1.

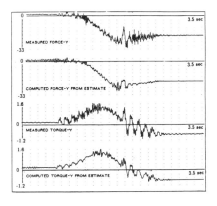

Figure 4 Measured force-torque data and computed force-torque data from the estimates using the PUMA.

Figure 4 shows the comparison of the measured forces and torques, and the computed forces and torques from the estimated parameters and the measured joint data using the simulator for the original trajectory. The two sets of figures match very well even in the mechanical vibrations, verifying qualitatively the accuracy of the estimates. This suggests that for control purposes even poor estimation of moment of inertia parameters will allow good estimates of the total force and torque necessary to achieve a trajectory. This makes good sense in that the load forces with the PUMA are dominated by gravitational components, and angular accelerations experienced by the load are small relative to those components.

4.0 Discussion

4.1 Did the algorithm work?

This paper describes an attempt to characterize the usefulness of wrist force-torque sensing for estimating the inertial parameters of rigid body loads for control and recognition/verification/grasping. Our conclusion is that prediction of forces for control can be good and seems to work well in our implementations. Identifying parameters well enough for recognition of the object may require large accelerations or special test movements in order to accurately identify the moment of inertia parameters.

It is important to realize that there are two distinct uses of an identified model. For control what matters is matching the input-output behavior of the model (in this case the relationship of load trajectory to load forces and torques) to reality, while for recognition/verification what matters is matching estimated parameters to a set of parameters postulated for reality.

We find that our implementations of load inertial parameter estimation successfully match the input output behavior of the load, although we have not yet used this information in a control scheme. However, we find that the limited acceleration capacity of the PUMA robot and its limited sensing do not permit us to estimate the moments of inertia of the load accurately without the use of special test motions. (Subsequent experimments with the M.I.T. Serial Link Direct Drive Arm which is capable of higher velocities and accelerations improved these estimates— see last column of Table 2.) In all cases the mass and the location of the center of mass could be accurately estimated from both a series of static measurements, and measurements taken during movements.

4.2 Sources of errors

This work is preliminary in that an adequate statistical characterization of the errors of the estimated parameters or the predicted forces has not been attempted. Nevertheless, we have gained insight into the sources of such errors.

4.2.1 Sensor errors

The ultimate source of error is the random noise inherent in the sensing process itself. The noise levels on the position and velocity sensing are probably negligible, and could be further reduced by appropriate filtering using a model based filter such as the Extended Kalman Filter (Gelb, 1974). The force and torque measurement process involve measuring the strains of structural members in the sensor with strain gauges. The random noise involved in such measurements is also probably negligible.

However, strain gauges are notoriously prone to drift. We feel that periodic recalibration of the offsets (very often) and the strain to force calibration matrix (often) may be necessary to reduce load parameter estimation errors further. Before using the force sensors we allowed the system to warm up and we recalibrated the offsets before each data collection session and checked for a change in the calibrated offsets afterward.

4.2.2 Unmodelled dynamics

A further source of noise is unmodelled structural dynamics. Neither the robot links nor the load itself are perfectly rigid bodies. A greater source of concern is the compliance of the force sensor itself. In order to generate structural strains large enough to be reliably measured with strain gauges, a good deal of compliance is introduced into the force sensor. The load rigidly attached to the force sensor becomes a relatively undamped spring mass system. The response of the Astek force sensor to a tap on an attached load is shown in the "undamped impulse response" record of Figure 5. The effect of robot movement on this spring mass system is shown in the "undamped movement response" record.

The most successful approach we found to this problem is to mechanically damp out the vibrations by introducing some form of energy dissipation into the structure (see Hogan, Selection 32). We added hard rubber washers between the force sensor and the load, and the "damped impulse response" of Figure 5 illustrates the response of the force sensor to a tap on the load. We see that the oscillations decay much faster. The "damped movement response" indicates that this

mechanical damping greatly reduces the effect of movement on the resonant modes of the force sensor plus load. The conclusion we draw is that appropriate damping should be built into force sensors, just as accelerometers are filled with oil to provide a critically damped response for a specified measurement bandwidth. Failing that, energy dissipation must be introduced either into the structural components of the robot or into the gripper either structurally or as a viscous skin. Appropriate mechanical damping may also be useful when using a force sensor in closed loop force control.

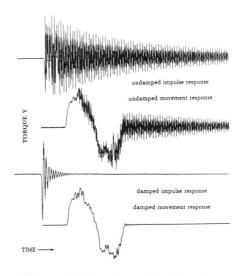

Figure 5 Vibration of load on force sensor.

4.2.3 Optimal filtering

The need to numerically differentiate the velocity to find the acceleration, or worse yet, double differentiate positions, greatly amplifies whatever noise is present. One can avoid the need to explicitly calculate accelerations by symbolically integrating

$$\begin{bmatrix} \cos(\theta) & -\sin(\theta) \\ \sin(\theta) & \cos(\theta) \end{bmatrix} \begin{bmatrix} \lambda_1 & 0 \\ 0 & \lambda_2 \end{bmatrix} \begin{bmatrix} \cos(\theta) & \sin(\theta) \\ -\sin(\theta) & \cos(\theta) \end{bmatrix} \tag{21}$$

equations (4) and (8) (Atkeson, An & Hollerbach, 1985). However, we feel that an effort to characterize the various noise sources and an attempt to "optimally" filter and differentiate/integrate the data will result in better estimates. If there is substantial low frequency noise or bias in the data the integration will amplify that noise relative to the signal frequencies of the data. What is needed is a problem formulation that gives us guidance as to how to design data processing filters for estimation and how to handle the need to differentiate or integrate some of the data to supply missing measurements.

4.2.4 Kinematic errors

Part of the error may be due to inaccuracies in the current kinematic parameters of the manipulator. Experiments have shown that the actual orientation of the robot can be up to 4° off from the orientation computed from the encoder data.

4.3 Why estimating moment of inertia parameters is hard

One of the factors that makes it difficult to accurately identify moments of inertia is the typically large contribution of gravitational torque, which depends only on the mass and the relative location of the center of mass to the force sensing coordinate origin. A point mass rotated at a radius of 5 cm from a horizontal axis must complete a full 360° rotation in 425 milliseconds for the torque due to angular acceleration to be equal to the gravitational torque, if a 5th order polynomial trajectory is used.

A way to avoid gravitational torques is to rotate the load about a vertical axis, or to have the point of force-torque sensing close to the center of mass.

A simple example will illustrate the difficulty of recovering principle moments of inertia, given the moment of inertia tensor about the force sensing origin. The principle moment of inertia of a uniform sphere is only 2/7 of the total moment of inertia when it is rotated about an axis tangent to its surface, so that the effects of any errors in estimating the mass, the location of the center of mass, and the grip moments of inertia are amplified when the principle moment of inertia is calculated. This problem can be reduced by having the point of force sensing as close to the center of mass as possible.

It still may be difficult to find the orientation of the principle moments of inertia even when the moment of inertia tensor about the center of mass has been estimated fairly accurately. This occurs when two or more principle moments of inertia are approximately equal. Finding the orientation of the principle axis is equivalent to diagonalizing a symmetric matrix, which becomes ill-conditioned when some of the eigenvalues are almost equal. A two dimensional example illustrates the problem: Consider the diagonalized matrix in (21) with eigenvalues $\{\lambda_1, \lambda_2\}$ and whose first principle axis is oriented at an angle θ with respect to the x axis. By substituting $\lambda_1 - \lambda_2 = \epsilon$ into the matrix (21),

$$\begin{bmatrix} \lambda_2 + \epsilon \cos^2(\theta) & \epsilon \cos(\theta) \sin(\theta) \\ \epsilon \cos(\theta) \sin(\theta) & \lambda_2 + \epsilon \sin^2(\theta) \end{bmatrix} \tag{22}$$

we see that when the two eigenvalues are almost equal, the terms of the matrix dependent on the angle, θ, become very small. All terms that contain angle information are multiplied by the difference of the principle moments of inertia, ϵ. With a fixed amount of noise in each of the entries of the identified moment of inertia matrix, the orientation of the principle axis, θ, will become more and more difficult to recover as the principle moments of inertia approach equality and therefore ϵ approaches zero.

Acknowledgment: This paper describes research done at the Artificial Intelligence Laboratory of the Massachusetts Institute of Technology. Support for the laboratory's artificial intelligence research is provided in part by the Systems Development Foundation and the Defense Advanced Research Projects Agency under Office of Naval Research. Partial support for C. Atkeson was provided by a Whitaker Fund Graduate Fellowship and an NSF Graduate Fellowship, for C. An by an NSF Graduate Fellowship, and for J. Hollerbach by an NSF Presidential Young Investigator Award.

References

An, C., Atkeson, C. & Hollerbach, J. (1985a) Estimation of inertial parameters of rigid body links of manipulators. *Proc. 24th Conf. Decision and Control*, December 11-13, Fort Lauderdale, Florida.

Atkeson, C.G., An, C. & Hollerbach, J. (1985) Rigid body load identification for manipulators. *Proc. 24th Conf. Decision & Control*, Dec. 11-13, Fort Lauderdale, Florida.

Coiffet, P. (1983) *Robot Technology: Interaction with the Environment*. Englewood Cliffs, N.J.: Prentice-Hall.

Gelb, A. (1974) *Applied Optimal Estimation*. Cambridge, Mass.: MIT Press.

Ljung, L. & Soderstrom, T. (1983) *Theory and Practice of Recursive Identification*. Cambridge, MA: MIT Press.

Luh, J.Y.S., Walker, M. & Paul, R.P. (1980) On-line computational scheme for mechanical manipulators. *J. Dynamic Systems, Meas., Control*, 102: 69–76.

Mukerjee. A. (1984) Adaptation in biological sensory-motor systems: A model for robotic control. *Proc., SPIE Conf. on Intelligent Robots and Computer Vision, SPIE Vol. 521*, Cambridge.

Mukerjee, A. & Ballard, D.H. (1985) Self-calibration in robot manipulators. *Proc. IEEE Conf. Robotics and Automation*, St. Louis, pp. 1050–1057.

Olsen, H.B. & Bekey, G.A. (1985) Identification of parameters in models of robots with rotary joints. *Proc. IEEE Conf. Robotics and Automation*, St. Louis, pp. 1045–1050.

Paul, R.P. (1981) *Robot Manipulators: Mathematics, Programming, and Control*. Cambridge, Mass.: MIT Press.

Symon, K.R. (1971) *Mechanics*. Reading, Mass.: Addison-Wesley.

Adapted from C.G. Atkeson, Chapter 4, "Roles of knowledge in motor learning", Ph.D. dissertation, Dept. Brain and Cognitive Sciences, M.I.T., 1986. Also presented at the 24th IEEE Conferences on Decision and Control, 1985. For more recent work, see *Model-based Control of a Robot Manipulator*, C.H. An, C.G. Atkeson & J.M. Hollerbach, MIT Press, 1988.

Dynamic Scaling of Manipulator Trajectories

J.M. Hollerbach

Massachusetts Institute of Technology

1.0 Introduction

Trajectory planning algorithms seldom incorporate extensive knowledge of the interaction between inverse dynamics and actuator torque limits into the planning process. Past efforts have typically used fixed velocity limits of the joints as a way of determining how fast a trajectory may be executed (Paul, 1975). Due to the complex relationship between joint velocities and dynamics, such a procedure is at best a very coarse approximation of the true influence of actuator limits on trajectory speed. An exact method for determining the optimal velocity distribution for a fixed path has been proposed in (Vukobratovic & Kircanski, 1982), where dynamic programming was straightforwardly applied to minimize energy under actuator and dynamic constraints. The computational cost of such optimization approaches however may prevent their useful application.

We develop a fundamental time-scaling property of manipulator dynamics that allows trajectory planning and inverse dynamics to be exactly and efficiently coupled. The dynamic realizability of a proposed trajectory can be readily determined, and a simple procedure to modify the movement speed can be applied to render proposed trajectories realizable.

We presume that a time sequence of joint angles $\underline{\theta}(t) = (\theta_1(t), \theta_2(t), \ldots, \theta_n(t))$ for an n-joint manipulator has been proposed by the trajectory planner, where t represents the time in the interval $0 \leq t \leq t_f$. Because of fast recursive formulations of inverse dynamics (Hollerbach, 1980; Luh et al., 1980; Silver, 1982) for each sampling time t the joint torques $\mathbf{n}(t) = (n_1(t), n_2(t), \ldots, n_n(t))$ corresponding to $\underline{\theta}(t)$ can be efficiently found. The comparison of $\mathbf{n}(t)$ against motor torque limits is therefore readily accomplished, and it is straightforward to determine whether the proposed trajectory can be realized by the actuators.

A more difficult task is to ascertain how to change the trajectory in case motor torque limits are violated. Here we consider only changing the speed at which a manipulator follows a path, where by speed change is meant a constant scaling of the velocity profile so that the total movement duration is scaled without changing the actual path through space. It is not sufficient merely to slow down a trajectory, with the hope that a slower trajectory requires lower motor torques, because some trajectories can only be realized at higher speeds, and some trajectories may not be realizable at any speed. Moreover, unless one is careful to employ an algorithm such as is presented here, then modifying the movement speed requires that the inverse dynamics be recomputed from scratch.

The algorithm presented here determines what speed range is permissible for the proposed trajectory given actuator torque limits. At the same time the nominal dynamics for the proposed trajectory can be simply modified for the new trajectory, without dynamics recomputation.

2.1 Time scaling and trajectories

Suppose that some trajectory plan $\underline{\theta}(t)$ has been fashioned. A new trajectory $\underline{\tilde{\theta}}(t)$ will be defined such that $\underline{\tilde{\theta}}(t) = \underline{\theta}(r)$, where $r = r(t)$ is a monotonically increasing function of time with $r(0) = 0$ and $r(t_1) = t_f$ for some $t_1 > 0$. The function $r(t)$ can be considered a time warp which moves the arm along the same path but with a different time dependence, perhaps going slower along some points of the path and faster along others. $r(t)$ must increase monotonically because time cannot reverse itself, and $r(0) = 0$ because the movement must start at the same point.

To determine how the dynamics of the arm changes for the new trajectory, the time derivatives of the joint angles are required. From the chain rule,

$$\frac{d\underline{\tilde{\theta}}(t)}{dt} = \frac{d\underline{\theta}(r)}{dr}\frac{dr}{dt}$$

or, using the dot notation for time derivatives,

$$\dot{\underline{\tilde{\theta}}}(t) = \dot{\underline{\theta}}(r)\dot{r} \qquad (1)$$

where $d\underline{\theta}(r)/dr$ has been written $\dot{\underline{\theta}}(r)$ because it takes the value $\dot{\underline{\theta}}$ evaluated at $r(t)$. Similarly,

$$\ddot{\underline{\tilde{\theta}}}(t) = \ddot{\underline{\theta}}(r)\dot{r}(t)^2 + \dot{\underline{\theta}}(r)\ddot{r}(t) \qquad (2)$$

The dynamic equations of motion can be compactly written (Hollerbach, 1980) as

$$\mathbf{n}(t) = \mathbf{I}(\underline{\theta}(t))\ddot{\underline{\theta}}(t) + \\ \dot{\underline{\theta}}(t) \cdot \mathbf{C}(\underline{\theta}(t)) \cdot \dot{\underline{\theta}}(t) + \mathbf{g}(\underline{\theta}(t)) \qquad (3)$$

where

$\mathbf{n}(t) =$ is the n-dimensional vector of net joint torques corresponding to the movement point,

$\mathbf{I}(\underline{\theta}(t)) =$ is the $n \times n$ generalized inertia tensor of the manipulator,

$\mathbf{C}(\theta(t)) =$ is the $n \times n \times n$ position-dependent tensor in the formulation of the Coriolis and centripetal torques, and

$\mathbf{g}(\underline{\theta}(t)) =$ is the position-dependent n-dimensional vector of gravity torques.

The notation for the velocity product term $\dot{\underline{\theta}} \cdot \mathbf{C} \cdot \dot{\underline{\theta}}$ is slightly unconventional, but has been adopted for compactness. The product $\mathbf{C} \cdot \dot{\underline{\theta}}$ is an $n \times n$ matrix with element ij as $\sum_k C_{ijk}\dot{\theta}_k$, which in turn is multiplied against $\dot{\underline{\theta}}$ to yield an $n \times 1$ vector.

In the following derivations, the acceleration and velocity dependent torques are treated separately and are designated as $\mathbf{n}_a(t) = (n_{a1}(t), n_{a2}(t), \ldots, n_{an}(t))$, so that $\mathbf{n}(t) = \mathbf{n}_a(t) + \mathbf{g}(\theta(t))$. For the new trajectory $\underline{\tilde{\theta}}(t)$,

$$\tilde{\mathbf{n}}_a(t) = \mathbf{I}(\underline{\tilde{\theta}}(t))\ddot{\underline{\tilde{\theta}}}(t) + \dot{\underline{\tilde{\theta}}}(t) \cdot \mathbf{C}(\underline{\tilde{\theta}}(t)) \cdot \dot{\underline{\tilde{\theta}}}(t) \quad (4)$$

Substituting from (1) and (2),

$$\tilde{\mathbf{n}}_a(t) = \left[\mathbf{I}(\underline{\theta}(r))\ddot{\underline{\theta}}(r) + \dot{\underline{\theta}}(r) \cdot \mathbf{C}(\underline{\theta}(r)) \cdot \dot{\underline{\theta}}(r)\right] \\ \dot{r}^2 + \mathbf{I}(\underline{\theta}(r))\dot{\underline{\theta}}(r)\ddot{r} \qquad (5)$$

Rearranging and substituting from (3),

$$\tilde{\mathbf{n}}_a(t) = \dot{r}^2\mathbf{n}_a(r) + \ddot{r}\mathbf{I}(\underline{\theta}(r))\dot{\underline{\theta}}(r) \qquad (6)$$

This is a potentially significant reformulation of dynamics, indicating how the underlying dynamics changes when the time dimension of a trajectory changes. The new torque $\tilde{\mathbf{n}}_a(t)$ is related to the old $\tilde{\mathbf{n}}_a(r)$ by the scaling factor $\dot{r}^2$ plus a term proportional to the generalized momentum $\mathbf{I}(\underline{\theta}(r))\dot{\underline{\theta}}(r)$ of the manipulator. Note that the gravity torque $\mathbf{g}(\underline{\tilde{\theta}}(t)) = \mathbf{g}(\underline{\theta}(r))$ is not scaled since it is position dependent only, which is the reason for the separation between $\mathbf{n}_a(t)$ and the gravity torques.

2.1 Constant Time Scaling

The simplest instance of (7) is when $\ddot{r}(t) = 0$, i.e. $r(t) = ct$ for some constant $c > 0$. If $c > 1$ the movement is sped up; if $c < 1$ the movement is slowed down. Then

$$\tilde{\mathbf{n}}_a(t) = c^2 \mathbf{n}_a(ct) \qquad (7)$$

Interestingly, movement speed can be proportionally changed without affecting the underlying dynamics very much, so long as the gravity contribution is separated from the acceleration and velocity term contributions. The relation was also noted by Bejczy (1979). Humans apparently adopt such a strategy when changing movement speed, perhaps to simplify the dynamics computation (Hollerbach & Flash, 1982).

This relation also shows that the velocity and acceleration terms of the dynamics would have the same significance relative to each other for all speeds of movement. For, the acceleration term $\mathbf{I}(\underline{\theta}(t))\ddot{\underline{\theta}}(t)$ is scaled by c^2 from (2), and the velocity term $\dot{\underline{\theta}}(t) \cdot \mathbf{C}(\underline{\theta}(t)) \cdot \dot{\underline{\theta}}(t)$ receives a c factor for each $\dot{\underline{\theta}}(t)$. Thus both terms change equally with differing movement speeds. This contradicts the normal assumption in the robotics literature, where in designing control systems workers typically throw out the velocity terms because they are a nonlinear product, with the presumption that they are significant only at higher speeds of movement (Bejczy, 1979; Paul, 1981). For the slow movement speeds of most manipulators, and hence because of the predominance of frictional and gravitational effects, this is a reasonable assumption (Brady et al., 1983). But for consistency the acceleration terms should be thrown out as well since they share the same significance as the velocity terms, yet this is not done. In any case, future generations of robots will contain

examples of fast manipulators with low joint friction where dynamic effects, both acceleration and velocity terms, are highly significant (Brady et al., 1983).

In the remainder of this paper, we assume the special case (7) and use it to determine allowable speeds of movement for a given trajectory. By allowable speed it is meant that the trajectory is stretched or compressed uniformly to fit the allotted duration without changing the path or the velocity profile shape. Constant scaling of velocity is a simple but important method of bringing a trajectory within actuator constraints. Certainly there are many classes of manipulator trajectories where an exact path through space must be followed, as in straight-line Cartesian motions of the manipulator hand (Paul, 1979; Taylor, 1979), but where the time dependence along the path is not strongly restricted. While non-uniform time scaling may yield a realizable trajectory where a constant scaling would not, results for the general case (6) are not yet available while other approaches (Vukobratovic & Kircanski, 1982) may be too computationally inefficient for routine use. Even more difficult is path modification under actuator and dynamic constraints, for which no general results are yet available [see however (Kahn & Roth, 1971) for an approximate time-optimal trajectory planning solution].

3.0 Time Scaling of Trajectories to Satisfy Torque Limitations

Torque limits of actuators restrict how fast a manipulator may move along a trajectory. In order to determine whether a proposed trajectory $\underline{\theta}(t)$ violates actuator limits, the inverse dynamics must be solved and the computed torques compared to these limits. Suppose we have computed the acceleration and velocity dependent torques $\mathbf{n}_a(t)$ separately from the gravitational torques $\mathbf{g}(\underline{\theta}(t))$. Suppose further that the maximum and minimum torque limits, $\mathbf{n}^+ = (n_1^+, n_2^+, \ldots, n_n^+)$ and $\mathbf{n}^- = (n_1^-, n_2^-, \ldots, n_n^-)$ respectively, are constant throughout a movement. (Ordinarily one would presume $\mathbf{n}^+ = -\mathbf{n}^-$.) Later we consider velocity dependencies as in electric torque motors.

At a given position $\underline{\theta}(t)$ of the manipulator, some of the actuator torque is required for postural support of the manipulator only. In terms of what torque capability is remaining to actually generate a movement, we formulate new effective torque limits by absorbing the gravitational torques into the torque limits, i.e.

$$\begin{aligned} \mathbf{n}^+(t) &= \mathbf{n}^+ - \mathbf{g}(\underline{\theta}(t)) \\ \mathbf{n}^-(t) &= \mathbf{n}^- - \mathbf{g}(\underline{\theta}(t)) \end{aligned} \qquad (8)$$

Note that the torque limits are now position dependent, and hence have been written as functions of time.

Because we are looking for a time scaling value c that brings the trajectory within the torque limits, a slight alteration of (7) is required. Since (7) holds for all times, we can write $\tilde{\mathbf{n}}_a(t/c) = c^2 \mathbf{n}_a(t)$ and the torque limits for the new trajectory as $\tilde{\mathbf{n}}^\pm(t/c) = \mathbf{n}^\pm(t)$. We require that for the new trajectory $\tilde{\mathbf{n}}_a(t/c)$ be bounded by $\tilde{\mathbf{n}}^\pm(t/c)$, which is done by finding the c that bounds $c^2 \mathbf{n}_a(t)$ by $\mathbf{n}^\pm(t)$ according to the following procedure.

For each time t and joint i, we find the minimum and maximum scaling values of c^2 that satisfy the torque limits by solving (7) together with the computed torques $n_{ai}(t)$ and the torque limits $n_i^-(t)$ and $n_i^+(t)$. The result will be denoted by the interval $[c_i^{2-}(t), c_i^{2+}(t)]$, where any scaling value within this interval is a permissible movement speed for this joint at this point in the trajectory. This scaling interval, however, may violate constraints at other joints and times, and the permissible range of c^2 values for the whole movement is found by intersecting all such intervals:

$$[c^{2-}, c^{2+}] = \bigcap_{i,t} [c_i^{2-}(t), c_i^{2+}(t)] \qquad (9)$$

We can then choose any value in the final interval $[c^{2-}, c^{2+}]$ to generate a movement which satisfies the actuator constraints.

To determine $[c_i^{2-}(t), c_i^{2+}(t)]$, there are three cases.

Case 1: $n_i^+(t) > 0$, $n_i^- < 0$.

Condition	$c_i^{2-}(t)$	$c_i^2(t)$
$n_{ai}(t) > 0$	0	$n_i^+(t)/n_{ai}(t)$
$n_{ai}(t) = 0$	0	∞
$n_{ai}(t) < 0$	0	$n_i^-(t)/n_{ai}(t)$

Case 2: $n_i^+(t) > 0$, $n_i^-(t) > 0$.

Condition	$c_i^{2-}(t)$	$c_i^2(t)$
$n_{ai}(t) > 0$	$n_i^-(t)/n_{ai}(t)$	$n_i^+(t)/n_{ai}(t)$
$n_{ai}(t) \leq 0$	unrealizable	

Case 3: $n_i^+(t) < 0$, $n_i^-(t) < 0$.

Condition	$c_i^2(t)$	$c_i^{2+}(t)$
$n_{ai}(t) \geq 0$	unrealizable	
$n_{ai}(t) < 0$	$n_i^+(t)/n_{ai}(t)$	$n_i^-(t)/n_{ai}(t)$

To explain these cases, consider first Case 1. The minimum value of c^2 is zero because $n_{ai}(t) = 0$ falls within actuator bounds and c^2 must be non-negative. If $n_{ai}(t) > 0$, then the appropriate torque limit for comparison is $n_i^+(t)$, because time scaling can change a torque magnitude but not a sign. The maximum value of c^2 is then determined by the ratio $n_i^+(t)/n_{ai}(t)$. Note that when $n_{ai}(t) < n_i^+(t)$, then $c^2 > 1$ and it is possible to speed the movement up and still satisfy actuator constraints. When $n_{ai}(t) > n_i^+(t)$, $c^2 < 1$ and the movement must be slowed down. To complete case 1, if $n_{ai}(t) < 0$, the appropriate torque limit is $n_i^-(t)$ and the maximum value of c^2 is $n_i^-(t)/n_{ai}(t)$.

In Case 2, if $n_{ai}(t) \leq 0$, then this movement is unrealizable at any speed. The actuator can produce only a positive torque, but a non-positive torque is required by the movement. Put simply, the manipulator cannot even hold itself up at this position. Of course manipulator actuation is ordinarily designed to counteract gravity, but this actuation may become inadequate if too heavy a load is picked up. For $n_{ai}(t) > 0$, the maximum movement speed is determined by the ratio $n_i^+(t)/n_{ai}(t)$ and the mini-

mum by $n_i^-(t)/n_{ai}(t)$. It is possible that $c_i^{2-}(t) > 0$, which says that there is a minimum non-zero speed at which the movement is realizable. Also it is possible that $c_i^{2-}(t) > 1$, so that the movement can be realized only by speeding up. Case 3 is analogous to case 2, except that the roles of $n_i^+(t)$ and $n_i^-(t)$ are reversed due to sign change.

The intersection of all the intervals $[c_i^{2-}(t), c_i^{2+}(t)]$ may be null, with incompatible scaling requirements at different parts of the trajectory. This movement is then unrealizable at any speed. If $c^{2-} > 1$, then the movement should be speeded up by at least a factor c^{2-}, while if $c^{2+} < 1$ the movement should be slowed by at least a factor c^{2+} in order to produce a realizable trajectory. Having chosen a c^2 value, the inverse dynamics can be simply recomputed from the old values of $\mathbf{n}_a(t)$ and $\mathbf{g}(\underline{\theta}(t))$ as follows:

$$\tilde{\mathbf{n}}(t) = c^2 \mathbf{n}_a(ct) + \mathbf{g}(\underline{\theta}(ct)) \qquad (10)$$

The acceleration and velocity torques are amplitude scaled, the gravity torque is added in separately, and both together are time scaled. Speed change can therefore be accomplished without dynamics recomputation.

33

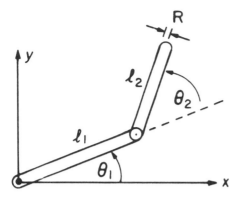

Figure 1 A planar two-link manipulator

4.0 Examples

This algorithm will be illustrated for straight-line movements by a two-link planar manipulator (Figure 1); the algorithm is quite easily applied to manipulators with more degrees of freedom. This manipulator has two rotary joints with joint angles θ_1 at the shoulder and θ_2 at the elbow. The axes of rotation are both directed along the z-axis, so that the manipulator only generates movement in the x-y plane. Gravity is presumed to act in the negative y direction with magnitude g. The length, mass, and moment of inertia about the proximal joint for each link are designated as l_i, m_i, and I_i respectively, where $i = 1$ refers to the upper arm link and $i = 2$ refers to the forearm link. Each link is a uniform cylinder with radius R.

The equations of motion are (Brady et al., 1983):

$$n_2 = \ddot{\theta}_1 \left(I_2 + \frac{m_2 l_1 l_2}{2} \cos\theta_2 + \frac{m_2 l_2^2}{4} \right) +$$
$$\ddot{\theta}_2 \left(I_2 + \frac{m_2 l_2^2}{4} \right) +$$
$$\frac{m_2 l_1 l_2}{2} \dot{\theta}_1^2 \sin\theta_2 +$$
$$\frac{m_2 l_2 g}{2} \cos(\theta_1 + \theta_2) \tag{11}$$

$$n_1 = \ddot{\theta}_1 \left(I_1 + I_2 + m_2 l_1 l_2 \cos\theta_2 + \frac{m_1 l_1^2 + m_2 l_2^2}{4} + m_2 l_2^2 \right) +$$
$$\ddot{\theta}_2 \left(I_2 + \frac{m_2 l_2^2}{4} + \frac{m_2 l_1 l_2}{2} \cos\theta_2 \right) -$$
$$\frac{m_2 l_1 l_2}{2} \dot{\theta}_2^2 \sin\theta_2 - m_2 l_1 l_2 \dot{\theta}_1 \dot{\theta}_2 \sin\theta_2 +$$
$$\left(\frac{m_2 l_2}{2} \cos(\theta_1 + \theta_2) + l_1 \left(\frac{m_1}{2} + m_2 \right) \cos\theta_1 \right) g \tag{12}$$

A common class of manipulator trajectories are straight line movements of the tip, i.e. $y - y_0 = (x - x_0)(y_1 - y_0)/(x_1 - x_0)$ for beginning and end positions of the tip (x_0, y_0) and (x_1, y_1) respectively. To solve the inverse dynamics, it is required to transform from the position, velocity, and acceleration of the tip to the position, velocity and acceleration for each joint angle. These inverse kinematic equations are presented below (Brady et al., 1983):

$$\cos\theta_2 = \frac{x^2 + y^2 - l_1^2 - l_2^2}{2 l_1 l_2}$$
$$\theta_1 = \tan^{-1}\left(\frac{y}{x} \right) - \tan^{-1}\left(\frac{l_2 \sin\theta_2}{l_1 + l_2 \cos\theta_2} \right) \tag{13}$$

$$\begin{bmatrix} \dot{\theta}_1 \\ \dot{\theta}_1 + \dot{\theta}_2 \end{bmatrix} = \frac{1}{l_1 l_2 \sin\theta_2} \begin{bmatrix} l_2 \cos(\theta_1 + \theta_2) & l_2 \sin(\theta_1 + \theta_2) \\ -l_1 \cos\theta_1 & -l_1 \sin\theta_1 \end{bmatrix} \begin{bmatrix} \dot{x} \\ \dot{y} \end{bmatrix} \tag{14}$$

$$\begin{bmatrix} \ddot{\theta}_1 \\ \ddot{\theta}_1 + \ddot{\theta}_2 \end{bmatrix} = \frac{1}{l_1 l_2 \sin\theta_2} \begin{bmatrix} l_2 \cos(\theta_1 + \theta_2) & l_2 \sin(\theta_1 + \theta_2) \\ -l_1 \cos\theta_1 & -l_1 \sin\theta_1 \end{bmatrix} \begin{bmatrix} \ddot{x} \\ \ddot{y} \end{bmatrix} +$$
$$\frac{1}{l_1 l_2 \sin\theta_2} \begin{bmatrix} l_1 l_2 \cos\theta_2 & l^2 \\ -l_2^2 & -l_1 l_2 \cos\theta_2 \end{bmatrix} \begin{bmatrix} \dot{\theta}_1^2 \\ (\dot{\theta}_1 + \dot{\theta}_2)^2 \end{bmatrix} \tag{15}$$

Three different movements are illustrated in the examples below: one that must be slowed down, one that must be sped up, and one that is unrealizable at any speed. For the link parameters, we have set $l_1 = l_2 = 0.5$ meters, $m_1 = m_2 = 1$ kg, $I_1 = I_2 = m_1 l_1^2/12 + m_1 R^2/4$, $R = 0.1 l_1$, and $g = 9.8$ m/sec^2.

4.1 A movement whose speed is scaled down

A straight line motion from $(x_0, y_0) = (0.5, -0.5)$ to $(x_1, y_1) = (0.5, 0)$ is to be generated at a constant velocity of 4 meters/second. The torque limits for the actuators are set at $n_1^+ = -n_1^- = 6.9$ kg-m, and $n_2^+ = -n_2^- = 2$ kg-m. A comparison between $\mathbf{n}^+(t)$, $\mathbf{n}^-(t)$, and $\mathbf{n}_a(t)$ is presented in Figure 2.

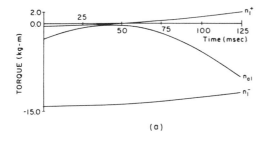

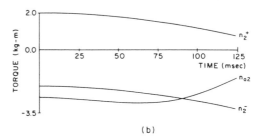

(a)   (b)

Figure 2 Torque profiles for a constant-velocity, straight-line trajectory of 4 m/sec from $(x, y) = (.5, -.5)$ to $(.5, 0)$ when $n_1^+ = -n_1^- = 6.9$ kg-m and $n_2^+ = -n_2^- = 2$ kg-m. (a) Joint 1 minimum and maximum torques, $n_1^-(t)$ and $n_1^+(t)$, and the velocity and acceleration torque $n_{a1}(t)$ are shown versus time; (b) corresponding torque profiles for joint 2.

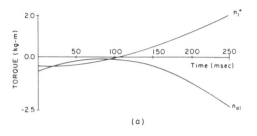
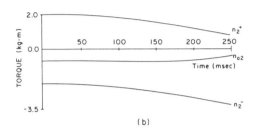

Figure 3 Torque profiles for a constant-velocity, straight-line trajectory of 2 m/sec with other conditions the same as in Figure 2.

Joint 1 is represented by Figure 2a, where the torque requirements $n_{a1}(t)$ for the complete movement fall within the modified actuator constraints $n_1^-(t)$ and $n_2^+(t)$. For joint 2 in Figure 2b, however, the required torque $n_{a2}(t)$ falls below the lower actuator bound $n_2^-(t)$ for the initial movement segment. This suggests that the movement must be slowed down. By scaling the torque $n_{a2}(t)$ by a factor $c^2 < 1$, the elements of the new torque $\tilde{n}_{a2}(t)$ become larger (i.e. less negative). The $\tilde{n}_{a2}(t)$ curve could then be made to lie completely above the $n_1^-(t)$ curve, as if it had been shifted upwards.

Carrying out the computations in (9), it is found that $[c^{2-}, c^{2+}] = [0.582, 0.745]$. The value $c^{2+} = 0.745$ arises from joint 2 at time $t = 0.035$ sec., while the value $c^{2-} = 0.582$ arises from joint 1 at the same time. Thus the fastest speed at which this movement can be executed is determined by $4\sqrt{0.745} = 3.45$ m/s. On the other hand, there is a non-zero lower speed limit, $4\sqrt{.582} = 3.05$ m/s. Examining Figure 2a, if the movement is slowed too much,

then the $n_{a1}(t)$ curve is displaced upwards, intersecting the $n_1^+(t)$ curve and exceeding that upper torque limit.

4.2 A movement whose speed is scaled up

As shown above, if the movement speed falls under 3.05 m/s, then the actuator limits are exceeded. This condition is verified here by considering the same movement but executed at 2 m/s and by working through the algorithm. Figure 3a shows that the shoulder torque $n_{a1}(t)$ exceeds the upper actuator bound $n_1^+(t)$ at the beginning of the movement. Calculations show that for joint 1, $c^{2-} = 2.329$ at $t = 0.035$ s, so that the movement must be sped up by $2\sqrt{2.329} = 3.05$ m/s as predicted. This would push the $n_{a1}(t)$ curve down until it is completely beneath $n_1^+(t)$. The curve $n_1^-(t)$ is the same as in Figure 2a, but has been left out here to allow an expanded scale.

There is an upper limit of $c^{2+} = 2.981$ at $t = 0.035$ s as well, determined this

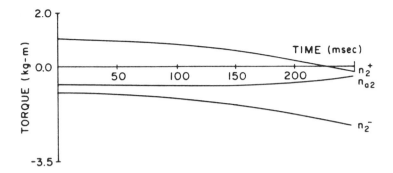

Figure 4 Joint 2 torque profiles for the same movement as in Figure 3 except with $n_2^+ = -n_2^- = 1$ kg-m.

time by joint 2 (Figure 3a). If the curve $n_{a2}(t)$ is pushed down too far, it will violate the lower bound $n_2^-(t)$. Thus the fastest this movement can be executed is $2\sqrt{2.981} = 3.45$ m/s, in agreement with the first movement analysis.

4.3 An unrealizable movement

For the third movement, the conditions are the same as for the second movement, but the second actuator limits are now changed to $n_2^+ = -n_2^-(t) = 1$ kg-m. As before, the actuator limits on joint 1 (Figure 3a) require that the minimum speed for this movement be determined by $c^{2-} = 2.329$. But Figure 4 shows that the joint 2 actuator limits prevent any higher speed scaling than $c^{2+} = 1.522$, because $n_{a2}(t)$ would fall below $n_2^-(t)$. Thus there are incompatible scaling requirements, and this movement cannot be realized at any speed.

5.0 Conclusion

Trajectory planning and inverse dynamics may be efficiently coupled to reflect the exact influence of actuator torque limits on execution capability. By factoring out gravity, a time-scaling property of manipulator dynamics readily allows a realizable speed of movement for the whole trajectory to be determined if there exists one. Rather than recomputing the dynamics corresponding to a new trajectory speed from scratch, the dynamics of the new trajectory is obtained by a simple linear combination of components of the original trajectory dynamics.

An important side effect of the dynamic time scaling property is that a ubiquitous assumption in manipulator control, namely that the velocity-product dynamic terms are significant only at high speeds of movement, is false: these terms have the same significance relative to the acceleration dynamic terms for all speeds of movement.

Acknowledgments: This report describes research done at the Artificial Intelligence Laboratory of the Massachusetts Institute of Technology. Support for the laboratory's artificial intelligence research is provided in part by the Office of Naval Research under contract N00014-81-0494 and in part by the Advanced Research

Projects Agency under Office of Naval
Research contracts N00014-80-C-0505 and
N00014-82-K-0334.

References

Bejczy, A. K. (1979) Dynamic models and control equations for manipulators. *Jet Propulsion Laboratory, California Institute of Technology, Report No. 715-19.*

Brady, J.M., Hollerbach, J.M., Johnson, T.L., Lozano-Perez, T. & Mason, M.T. (1983) *Robot Motion: Planning and Control.* Cambridge, Mass.: MIT Press.

Electro-Craft Corp. (1980) *DC Motors, Speed Controls, Servo Systems.* Hopkins, Minn.

Hollerbach, J.M. (1980) A recursive formulation of Lagrangian manipulator dynamics. *IEEE Transactions on Systems, Man, and Cybernetics*, SMC-10, 11:730–736.

Hollerbach, J.M. & Flash, T. (1982) Dynamic interactions between limb segments during planar arm movement. *Biol. Cybernetics*, 44:67–77.

Kahn, M.E. & Roth, B. (1971) The near-minimum-time control of open-loop articulated kinematic chains. *J. Dynamic Systems, Measurement, Control*, 93:164–172.

Luh, J.Y.S., Walker, M.W. & Paul, R.P.C. (1980) On-line computational scheme for mechanical manipulators. *Journal of Dynamic Systems, Measurement, and Control*, 102:69–76.

Paul, R.P.C. (1975) Manipulator path control. *Proc. IEEE Int. Conf. Cybernetics and Society*, New York, September, pp. 147–152.

Paul, R.P. (1979) Manipulator Cartesian path control. *IEEE Trans. Systems, Man, Cybernetics*, SMC-9:702–711.

Paul, R.P. (1981) *Robot Manipulators: Mathematics, Programming, and Control.* Cambridge, Mass.: MIT Press.

Silver, W. (1982) On the equivalence of Lagrangian and Newton-Euler dynamics for manipulators. *Robotics Research*, 1(2):60–70.

Taylor, R.H (1979) Planning and execution of straight-line manipulator trajectories. *IBM J. Research and Development*, 23:424–436.

Vukobratovic, M. & Kircanski, M. (1982) A method for optimal synthesis of manipulation robot trajectories. *J. Dynamic Systems, Measurement, Control*, 104:188–193.

Reprinted from MIT A.I. Lab. Memo 700 (1983).

A Ballistic Model for Walking

Simon Mochon
Thomas A. McMahon

Division of Applied Sciences
Harvard University, Cambridge, MA

1.0 Introduction

Human walking is a very complicated activity in which the cyclic movements of the lower extremities translate the body in the forward direction. These movements are due to the action of muscles, which in turn are coordinated by the nervous system.

In walking at low and moderate speeds, the kinetic and potential energies of the center of mass of the body change approximately in opposite phase, so that the total energy is kept at a relatively constant level. This means that gravity is used to minimize the work that the muscles have to do to translate the center of mass of the body (external work).

In addition to the movement of the center of mass, there are also changes in the relative positions and velocities of each limb of the body. The net action of the muscles tending to change the angles of the joints is given by the moments applied to each of these joints during the walking cycle. Relatively strong moments are applied to the hip, knee and ankle joints during the stance phase, but during most of the swing phase these moments are relatively small (see for example Zarrugh, 1976). Electromyographic traces also show that the muscles of the swing leg are reasonably silent during the whole swing

period, except just at the beginning and end (Basmajian, 1976).

Thus, on electromyographic as well as dynamic grounds it seems plausible that the swing phase of the human gait may be described as a ballistic motion. Based on this, a theoretical model for human waking has been developed, which proceeds from the assumption that no muscular moments are provided to any of the joints of the extremities after the initial positions and velocities of the joints have been established at the beginning of the swing phase. Therefore this ballistic model moves through its stride under the influence of gravity alone, and finishes in a position which allows direct entry into the next step. In an earlier paper (Mochon & McMahon, 1980), a simple ballistic walking model was analyzed. The next section gives a quick review of that paper. In the present paper, an improved model is presented.

Previous theoretical works are mainly optimal type approaches based on the hypothesis that walking is performed in a way that requires the least expenditure of energy. Among them are the works by Beckett & Chang (1968) and Chow & Jacobson (1971). Our model is essentially different from these, since we assume zero muscular torques acting during the swing and therefore the total energy is kept constant.

34

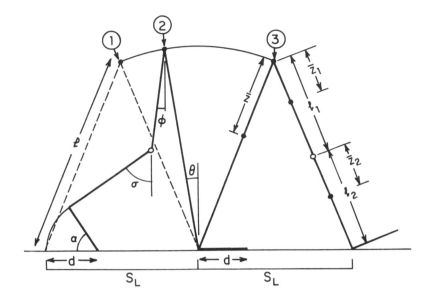

Figure 1 Schematic representation of the stiff-stance-leg model. The numbers (1), (2), and (3) give respectively the position of the model at heel strike, toeing off, and following heel strike. The angles, lengths, and positions of the centers of mass of each limb are shown in the figure. For meaning of symbols see Appendix.

2.0 Summary of Previous Model

This section contains a brief summary of our previous model. For further details the reader should consult the paper by Mochon & McMahon (1980).

The model, shown schematically in Figure 1, consists of three links: one representing the stance leg and two representing the thigh and shank of the swing leg. The foot of the swing leg is rigidly attached to the distal link, and therefore does not constitute a separate link. Each link is assumed to have a distributed mass. The moment of inertia and location of the center of mass of each link are taken from the anthropometric data of Dempster (given in Williams & Lissner, 1974). The mass of the trunk, head, and arms is represented by a point mass at the hip joint.

Since, by assumption, no muscular torques are applied at any of the joints, the total energy is conserved. Thus, the equations of motion were obtained by applying Lagrange's equations for conservative systems.

A number of initial and final conditions were imposed to specify the motion. At toeing off (2) the condition that the toe is still in contact with the ground and a distance $S_L - d$ from the ankle of the other leg imposes two geometric conditions. Another condition specifies the distance that the center of mass of the body moves during the double support phase. This is taken from the experimental data of Cavagna et al. (1976). We also required that at heel strike (3) the knee angle should arrive at zero and the heel of the swing leg should contact the ground.

Additionally we imposed two kinematic constraints: one requires that the foot must clear the ground at all times. The other is that the vertical force applied at the ground must always remain positive; otherwise the model will fly off the ground.

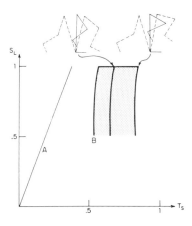

Figure 2 The range of possible times of swing (shaded) for the model shown in Figure 1. The upper diagrams show the moment of toeing off (left broken configuration), maximum knee flexion (continuous configuration), and maximum hip flexion (right broken configuration) for a step length of 1.0 and a maximum knee flexion of 90° (left diagram) and 125° (right diagram).

Before solving the equations on a computer, we transformed them to dimensionless form using the length l of the leg and its natural half period (with rigid knee) $\tau_n = \pi(I_l/m_l g \bar{Z})^{1/2}$ as the scales for length and time. With this, then, the step length S_L is normalized with respect to the length of the leg, and time of swing, T_S is normalized with respect to the natural half-period of the leg.

The constraints imposed on the model will set limits on the possible range of the variables. The results of the analysis are shown in Figure 2. The time of swing is varied in this model by changing the initial angular velocity of the stance leg (higher values of this initial angular velocity correspond to smaller times of swing). The initial angular velocities of the thigh and shank of the swing leg are then adjusted to satisfy the final conditions imposed. The leftmost heavy line (B) in Figure 2 represents those swings in which the toe of the swing leg grazes the ground in mid stride. When the time of swing is made smaller than this limit (to the left of this line), the toe will strike the ground at mid swing. For a fixed step length, higher values of the time of swing are found to correspond with higher maximum knee flexion angle. The next two heavy near-vertical lines in Figure 2 correspond to those swings in which the knee has flexed to a maximum of 90° and 125°, respectively. This 125° limit seems to us a reasonable physiological limit for knee flexion. The boundaries of $S_L = 0.5$ and $S_L = 1.0$ represent the range of step lengths most commonly used in normal walking (Grieve, 1968).

A light line (A) is also shown in Figure 2. This line divides those swings during which the model will fly off the ground (to the left of this line) from those in which it will not. Note, then, that the condition of positive vertical force at the ground is not a determining factor in setting a lower limit to the time of swing.

Typical histograms of force and angles against time during the swing phase are given in Figure 3. Forces are normalized with respect to body weight. For comparison, experimental traces of the vertical and forward forces on the ground

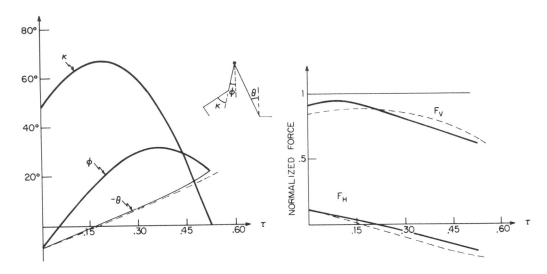

Figure 3 Solid lines: calculated angles and ground reactions as a function of time during the swing phase for a limiting case where the foot just clears the ground. Broken lines: F_V, F_H, and θ for a simple inverted pendulum which starts with the same initial angle and velocity.

reproduced from Cavagna & Margaria (1966) are presented in Figure 4 (the portion between the arrows is the swing phase). Figure 3 shows that the predicted angles and ground reactions have the same general shape as those found experimentally for normal walking during the swing phase, except for the vertical force, which resembles the vertical force due to an inverted pendulum swinging freely through its position of unstable equilibrium.

Figure 5 shows a comparison of the range of times of swing predicted by this model (shaded area) with the experimental results of Grieve & Gear (1966). The three heavy lines are the same as shown in Figure 2. Each vertical line represents the range of possible times of swing for a subject. We can see that the range of times of swing predicted by the ballistic model encompasses most of the times of swing found experimentally. The dis-

crepancy for small statures suggests that young children have a different mechanism of walking; this is discussed further in Mochon & McMahon (1980).

3.0 Improved Models of Walking

3.1 Walking with knee flexion of the stance leg

We saw that the simple model presented in the last section predicts reasonably well the time course of the angles of the limbs and the horizontal ground force, but fails to give an accurate description of the vertical force. Improvements to this model may be made in two directions: one is to investigate the effects that the determinants absent from the previous model have on walking, when added progressively; the other is to correct the lack of agreement between the vertical ground force and the experimental results by adding an appropriate mechanism. These two directions are not mutually exclusive, and in fact we expect that if our assumption of ballistic walking is correct and if the six determinants given by Saunders et al. (1953) provide the unifying principles of walking, the addition of all of them to the model will bring the vertical force into agreement with experimental data.

One possible mechanism for raising the vertical ground force at the end of the swing phase is the lifting of the heel of the stance leg. Very crudely, we can model this as follows (see Figure 6): after toeing off [(1) in Figure 6] the stance leg rotates about the ankle until it reaches 90° at the middle of the swing phase. After this, the heel begins to rise, rotating around the middle of the foot and keeping the ankle at a constant angle (90°) until heel strike.

This mechanism by itself cannot improve the results obtained before, because in the second part of the swing, with constant ankle angle, we have only redefined the length of the leg as $(l^2 + r^2)^{1/2}$. This will raise the vertical force in mid swing, but at the end of this phase the force will again decrease with time. We then also added knee flexion of the stance leg to the model to see if these two mechanisms together will lift the center of mass enough to bring the vertical force to higher values at the end of the swing. With these additions, then, a further determinant is included in the model: this is knee and ankle interaction.

The model is shown schematically in Figure 6. It consists of four links representing the thighs and shanks of both legs, and a point mass at the hip representing the mass of the rest of the body. All the inertial properties of the

links are the same as in the model with stiff stance leg. The only difference is that the mass of the foot is not lumped within the mass of the shank. Instead, the mass of the foot is represented as a point mass at the ankle joints. This is done because the mass of the foot should enter the dynamics only if the heel is raised from the ground.

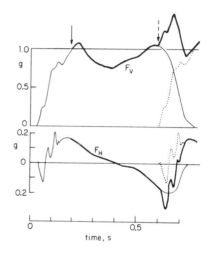

Figure 4 Experimental traces of the vertical and forward forces on the ground in normal walking (from Cavagna & Margaria, 1966). The solid arrow shows the time of toeing off; the broken arrow, the moment of heel strike. The forces have been normalized by body mass. The thin and broken lines show the normalized force for the two feet separately; the thick line shows the sum.

The division of the stance leg into two links introduces a problem if we want to continue with our ballistic assumption that no muscular moments should be applied at any of the joints. If no further restrictions are imposed, the model will collapse at mid swing because the knee of the stance leg is unstable.

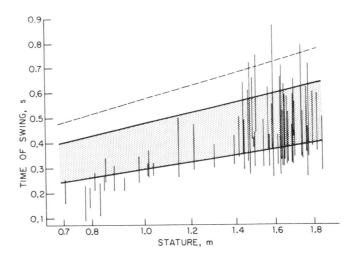

Figure 5 The range of times of swing observed in each subject is represented by a vertical line plotted against stature. Superimposed is the range of times predicted by the model with stiff stance leg (shaded area). The lower line corresponds to the limit where the toe just clears the ground. The upper solid line represents the boundary when a maximum of 125° of knee flexion is allowed. The broken line gives the half natural period of the leg considered as a compound pendulum with a joint at the knee.

This problem is solved without violating the ballistic assumption if we assume that the angles of the thigh and shank of the stance leg are functionally related in the form $\theta = \theta(\alpha)$. This constraint is equivalent to prescribing the trajectory of the hip of the model. The point mass at the hip is then constrained to move in the same way as a bead is constrained to move along a wire under the action of gravity, and therefore the total energy of the system will be conserved. Note that this would not be true if instead α and θ were prescribed as a function of time (this would give not only the trajectory but also the velocity and acceleration). The details of this modification to the original "stiff-stance leg" model are given elsewhere (Mochon & McMahon, 1980). Surprisingly, only minor improvements are obtained. Thus neither raising the

heel nor flexing of the knee of the stance leg is the mechanism responsible for the shape of the vertical force found in normal walking.

3.2 Walking including pelvic rotation

If we wanted to investigate rigorously the effect that pelvic rotation has on walking, we would have to add to our model another link which joins the hips of both legs to represent the pelvis (Winter, 1979). Fortunately, this is not necessary, and in fact it is very simple to add the dynamics of the rotation of the pelvis. From Lamoreux's data (Lamoreux, 1971), it can be seen that curves of pelvic rotation during the swing phase for different speeds can be approximated well by straight lines. This means that during the swing period the pelvis rotates at a nearly constant angular speed and therefore the forward displacement of one hip relative to the other is performed at almost constant speed.

If we assume that during the swing phase the hips move at a constant speed relative to each other, then adding another link to the model to simulate the rotation of the pelvis will not change its dynamics at all. The only change that this addition will produce on the model is to increase the step length by an amount equal to the relative horizontal displacement of the hips (this is given by the sum of the horizontal distances between the hips at toeing off and at heel strike). The time of swing will be unaffected.

This change can be very easily included in the model. The effect of pelvic rotation is to allow the body to reach a higher step length without changing the minimum time of swing. This will increase the speed of walking. Generally, then, the use of pelvic rotation allows for a decrease of the excursion of the limbs to achieve the same step length.

4.0 Discussion

In this paper, we have analyzed the contribution of four of the determinants of gait to the mechanics of walking. We started with the stiff-legged walking model, which includes only one determinant (hip flexion), and we have added progressively three other determinants (knee flexion, knee and ankle interaction, and pelvic rotation) to study their effects on walking.

Only two determinants have not been explored. These are pelvic tilt and lateral pelvic displacement. We do not expect lateral pelvic displacement to have a significant influence on any of the variables

investigated here, provided that the amplitudes of the lateral movements are small, because the lateral displacements would have to be quite large to change the effective length of the limbs. In any case, the addition of a lateral degree of freedom to our model would complicate it substantially, as there would be coupling between the lateral- and saggital-plane motions.

Pelvic tilt reaches a maximum shortly after toeing off. At this point, the hip of the stance leg is higher than the hip of the swing leg. After this, the hip of the swing leg is raised until mid swing, where both hips reached the same vertical position and continue so until heel strike. From this we see that pelvic tilt is significant only in the first part of swing phase.

Although we have studied the interaction between knee and ankle of the stance leg, the angular movement of the ankle was modeled very crudely by assuming that this joint was locked at 90° in the second part of the swing. This is not exactly true, and in fact plantarflexion is observed in this period until heel strike (Murray, 1967).

We expect, then, that the introduction of pelvic tilt and stance-leg ankle plantarflexion into the model will improve agreement between the calculated and observed vertical-force traces. Pelvic tilt would be responsible for the first maximum found in the vertical force immediately after toeing off, and ankle plantarflexion would be the mechanism for bringing the vertical force back above body weight before heel strike. This view is supported by Cavagna & Margaria's (1966) findings on the external positive work in walking. They observed that this work is due to two contributions at distinct moments of the step cycle. One vertical thrust is necessary to complete

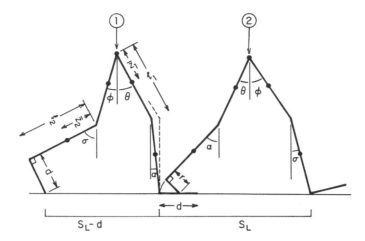

Figure 6 Schematic representation of the model with knee flexion of the stance leg. The numbers (1) and (2) give respectively the positions of the model at toeing off and heel strike. The angles, lengths, and positions of the centers of mass of each limb are shown. See Appendix for meaning of symbols.

the lift of the center of the body (pelvic tilt) which ends when the center of gravity is at its highest level. The other is due to the forward and upward push of the foot leaving the ground (ankle movement).

We can say then that the mechanisms absent from the models considered in this paper can plausibly account for the discrepancies between theory and experiment found in the vertical force traces. To prove this, a more complicated model which includes the remaining missing determinants of gait is needed.

5.0 Conclusions

Summarizing then, the most important conclusions of this paper are:

1. The constraint that the foot of the swing leg must clear the ground was found to be a limiting factor in going to higher speeds for each step length.

2. Knee flexion of the stance leg and pelvic rotation were found to be mechanisms for increasing the speed of walking, the former by decreasing the time of swing and the latter by increasing the step length.

3. Within the context of the ballistic walking models considered in this paper, neither the raising of the heel nor flexion of the knee of the stance leg is the mechanism responsible for increasing the vertical force in the second part of the swing phase.

4. This work also suggests that the remaining two determinants of gait, pelvic tilt and ankle dorsi-plantar-flexion, are the mechanisms responsible for the two maxima seen in the vertical force during the swing phase of normal walking.

Appendix: List of Symbols

m_T, m_l, m_1, m_2, m_f	Mass of body, leg, thigh, shank, and foot
l, l_1, l_2, d	Length of the leg, thigh, shank and foot
r	Length of the part of the foot of the stance leg which is raised at mid swing, $= d/2$
$\bar{Z}$, $\bar{Z}_1$, $\bar{Z}_2$	Distance of the center of mass of the leg, thigh, and shank to proximal end
I_l, I_1, I_2	Moment of inertia of the leg, thigh, and shank around proximal end
g	Gravitational constant
S_L	(Step length)/(leg length)
τ	Normalized time $= t/\tau_n$
T_s	Normalized time of swing
τ_n	$\pi(I_l/m_l g\bar{Z})^{1/2} =$ time of swing (half period) for the leg with rigid knee
θ, α, ϕ, σ	Angle that the thigh and shank of stance leg and thigh and shank of swing leg make with the vertical
κ, β	Knee angles: $\kappa = \phi - \sigma$, $\beta = \alpha - \theta$

References

Basmajian, J.V. (1976) The human bicycle. In P.V. Komi (ed.), *Biomechanics V-A*, University Park Press, pp. 297–302.

Beckett, R. & Chang, K. (1968) An evaluation of the kinematics of gait by minimum energy. *J. Biomech.* 1:147–159.

Cavagna, G.A. & Margaria, R. (1966) Mechanics of walking. *J. Appl. Physiol.* 21:271–278.

Cavagna, G.A., Thys, H. & Zamboni, A. (1976) The sources of external work in level walking and running. *J. Physiol.* 262:639–657.

Chow, C.K. & Jacobson, D.H. (1971) Studies of human locomotion via optimal programming. *Math. Biosci.* 10:239–306.

Grieve, D.W. & Gear, R.J. (1966) The relationship between the length of stride, step frequency, time of swing and speed of walking for children and adults. *Ergonomics* 9:379–399.

Grieve, D.W. (1968) Gait patterns and the speed of walking. *Bio-Med. Eng.* 3:119–122.

Lamoreux, L.W. (1971) Kinematic measurements in the study of human walking. *Bull. Prosthetics Res.* BPR 10-15:3–84.

Mochon, S. & McMahon, T.A. (1980) Ballistic walking. *J. Biomech.* 13:49–57.

Murray, M.P. (1967) Gait as a total pattern of movement. *Amer. J. Phys. Med.* 46:290–333..

Saunders, J.B., Inman, V.T. & Eberhart, H.D. (1953) The major determinants in normal and pathological gait. *J. Bone Jt. Surg.* 35-A:543–558.

Williams, M. & Lissner, H.R. (1974) *Biomechanics of Human Motion.* W.B. Saunders.

Winter, D.A. (1979) *Biomechanics of Human Movement.* New York: Wiley, p. 48.

Zarrugh, M.Y. (1976) "Energy and power in human walking". Ph.D. dissertation, University of California, Berkeley.

Adapted from Ballistic walking: An improved model. *Math Biosci.*, 52:241–260 (1980).

Some Properties of Regularly Realizable Gait Matrices

R.B. McGhee
A.K. Jain

Department of Electrical Engineering
Ohio State University

Introduction

One of the generally recognized features of natural legged locomotion is that animals typically employ their limbs in a number of distinct periodic modes. Thus we say that a man walks, runs, or leaps and a horse trots, canters, gallops, etc. Such modes are identified by characteristic patterns of footfalls ordinarily called *gaits* (Hildebrand, 1965; Muybridge, 1955, 1957).

In an earlier paper by one of the authors (McGhee, 1968), it is shown that some concepts taken from finite-state machine theory can be used to establish a formal mathematical basis for the study of gaits for legged locomotion in animals or machines. The notion of a "gait matrix" is central to this work. Briefly, a *gait matrix*, G for a k-legged locomotion system is an n-row, k-column binary matrix whose rows represent the n successive phases of one period of a particular gait. By convention, a zero entry in column j indicates that leg j is in contact with the ground (support phase) while a 1 entry means that it is not (transfer phase). Several examples of gait matrices can be found in (McGhee, 1968) and (McGhee & Frank, 1968) and others will be presented in subsequent sections of this paper.

As explained in McGhee (1968), a gait matrix does not completely specify leg states (1 or 0) as functions of time. This is because it displays only the successive phases of a gait without assigning durations to any of them. To complete the description of a particular gait, it is therefore necessary to append to G an n-row *duration vector*, t, whose successive rows denote the duration of the corresponding phase of the gait. The only requirement placed on t is that every component be strictly greater than zero (McGhee, 1968; McGhee & Frank, 1968).

Much of the development in McGhee (1968) and McGhee & Frank (1968) is concerned with the definition and identification of gait matrices possessing various special properties. One of the motivations for investigating these properties is a desire to account for the gait preference of animals. That is, while the number of theoretically possible gaits is very large (McGhee, 1968; McGhee & Kuhner, 1969), only a small fraction of these have been observed in use by any animal. In McGhee & Frank (1968), an optimality criterion is defined that leads to a unique choice of gait for low speed quadruped locomotion. This gait corresponds to the gait preferred by natural quadrupeds for grazing and other very low speed activities. The present paper represents an attempt to find an explanation for gait selection in other circumstances. The property proposed is that of "regular realizability". A gait matrix is said to be *regularly realizable* (McGhee, 1968), if and only if there exists at least one duration vector, **t**, such that the duration of the 1-state is the same for all legs (columns).

It is easily shown (McGhee, 1968) that the regularly realizable gait matrices are a proper subset of the set of all gait matrices. They are of particular interest since they involve the use of every leg in a fashion identical to every other leg. That is, in a *regular gait* (McGhee, 1968), the "duty factor" (fraction of a cycle spent in the support phase) is the same for all legs. This is what one would expect if every leg of an animal or machine were mechanically identical and were to be operated at its natural pendulum frequency while sharing equally in the task of supporting the propelling the animal.

The remainder of this paper consists of a formal statement of the regular realizability property followed by the development of some necessary conditions and a sufficient condition for a given matrix to be regularly realizable. The cases of biped and quadruped locomotion are studied exhaustively and the results obtained are compared to available knowledge regarding animal and human locomotion. It is found that only two gaits which are not regularly realizable have been observed in nature.

Problem Statement

Theorem 7 of (McGhee, 1968) presents a necessary and sufficient condition for regular realizability in terms of the solution of a quadratic programming problem. For convenience, this theorem is restated here.

THEOREM. *If T denotes the half-open unit n cube defined by $0 < t_i \leq 1$, $i =$* $1, 2, \ldots, n$, *then an n-row, k-column gait matrix G is regularly realizable if and only if there exists a point $\mathbf{t} \in T$ such that*

$$\min_{\mathbf{t} \in T} \sum_{j=1}^{k} \left[\left(\sum_{i=1}^{n} t_i g_{ij} \right) - 1 \right]^2 = 0 \quad (1)$$

where t_i are the components of $\mathbf{t}$ and g_{ij} are the elements of G.

Examination of (1) shows that this condition can be restated as a linear programming problem (Jain, 1970).

DEFINITION 1. *A binary matrix G is regularly realizable if and only if there exists at least one feasible solution (Hadley, 1962) to the following linear programming problem:*
Objective function:

$$\tau = \sum_{i=1}^{n} t_i \quad (2)$$

Inequality constraints: $t_i > 0$, $i = 1, \ldots n$
$$(3)$$

Equality constraints: $\qquad G^T \mathbf{t} = \mathbf{1} \quad (4)$

where $\mathbf{1}$ is a column vector of ones.

In (McGhee, 1968), it is assumed that G has the property that no two successive rows are identical and that every column of G consists of a single sequence of ones followed by a single sequence of zeros (taking into account the cyclic nature of a gait). These conditions will again be imposed at a later point in this paper, but are unnecessary in Definition 1. Thus, the regular realizability test furnished by this definition can be applied to any binary matrix.

In (McGhee, 1968), the objective function given by (2) is called the gait *cycle time.* It will be seen that the minimum and maximum value of this particular objective function provide useful information concerning a given regularly realizable gait. However, since the regular realizability property depends only on the existence of a *feasible solution*, any other linear combination of the components of **t** could be substituted for (2) without altering the outcome of the test for regular realizability.

Given Definition 1, it is natural to wonder if the regular realizability of a given matrix can ever be confirmed or rejected without solving the associated linear programming problem. The next two sections of this paper show that this is indeed sometimes possible.

A Necessary Condition for Regular Realizability

While the successive phases of any gait are represented unambiguously by a gait matrix, an equivalent but more compact description is provided by the following definition suggested by the work of Roberts (1967).

DEFINITION 2. *The event sequence for a k-column gait matrix G is a sequence in which each of the integers* 1, 2, ... 2k *appears exactly once. For* $1 \leq i \leq k$, *the position of i in the sequence is determined by the order of occurrence of the event of placing leg i in contact with the ground during one complete gait cycle. Likewise, the position of any integer j, where* $j = i + k$, *is determined by the event of lifting leg i. If two or more events occur simultaneously, the event sequence is a partial ordering in which simultaneous events are enclosed in parentheses.*

Figure 1 illustrates the derivation of an event sequence for the quadruped walk (McGhee, 1967). The gait matrix for this gait is an example of a *connected matrix* (McGhee, 1968) in which exactly one placing or lifting event produces each successive gait phase. Obviously, the event sequences for such gaits always are free of parentheses; i.e. the 2k events are *totally ordered.* Figure 2 illustrates a "singular crawl" (McGhee & Frank, 1968) quadruped gait and its associated event sequence. In this case, the event sequence is a partial ordering rather than a total ordering of the gait events.

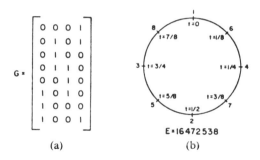

Figure 1 Gait matrix and event sequence for a quadruped walk, (a) gait matrix and (b) event sequence.

Roberts (1967), suggests that the periodic nature of a gait is clarified by placing the event sequence on a circle. If the circumference of the circle is normalized to unity, then the time of occurrence of each event can also be shown on this diagram as a fraction of the gait cycle time. This has been done in Figures 1 and 2. In both cases, the components of **t** have been chosen to achieve a regular realization.

In (McGhee, 1968), yet another representation of a gait is defined. This representation, called a *gait formula*, is a vector whose components specify a duty factor, β_i, for each leg and which also specifies a *phase variable*, ϕ_i, for each $i > 1$. The phase of leg i is just the fraction of a gait cycle by which the contact of leg i with the ground lags the contact of leg 1. Thus, taking $t = 0$ at the contact of leg 1, every other leg, i, contacts the ground at $t = \tau\phi_i$ and is lifted at $t = \tau(\phi_i + \beta_i)$. As will be seen, the concept of a gait formula will be useful in proving the possibility or impossibility of a regular realization for certain gait matrices.

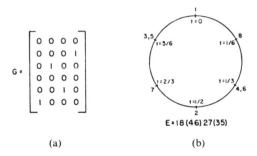

$$E = 18\,(46)\,27\,(35)$$

(a)   (b)

Figure 2 Gait matrix and event sequence for a singular crawl, (a) gait matrix and (b) event sequence.

The above discussion permits the definition of a relationship between the columns of a gait matrix which bears upon a necessary condition for regular realizability.

DEFINITION 3. *A pair of columns i and j, of a k-column gait matrix G are compatible if, when the event sequence associated with G is presented on a circle, the arc from event i to event $i + k$ does not overlap the arc from event j to event $j + k$, and conversely, where $i, j = 1, 2, \ldots k$.*

Examination of the event sequence of Figures 1 and 2 shows that this condition is satisfied for all pairs of events on each of these figures. Since both of these gaits are known to be regularly realizable (McGhee & Frank, 1968; McGhee, 1967), the following theorem is suggested.

THEOREM 1. *A necessary condition for the regular realizability of a gait matrix G is that every column of G be compatible with every other column of G.*

Proof. Let i and j be an incompatible pair of columns and let i be the overlapping column. This means that either the placing of leg i precedes the placing of leg j, or the lifting of j precedes that of i, or both. In the first case, from the definition of compatibility, if G is regularly realizable it must be true that

$$\phi_i < \phi_j \quad \text{and} \quad \phi_i + \beta \geq \phi_j + \beta, \qquad (5)$$

while in the second case the corresponding conditions are

$$\phi_i \leq \phi_j \quad \text{and} \quad \phi_i + \beta > \phi_j + \beta. \qquad (6)$$

In either case, the stated inequalities cannot be satisfied by any pair of real numbers ϕ_i and ϕ_j, so the condition of the theorem must hold for any regularly realizable G. ∎

While the event sequence provides a very compact representation of a gait matrix, and was therefore used in the definition of compatibility, when the gait matrix itself is explicitly available, an easier test for compatibility is possible. Specifically, from Definition 3, it is evident that two columns i and j of a gait matrix G are compatible if and only if the rows of i containing ones are not a proper subset of the rows of j containing ones. That is, the ones of neither column may overlap the ones of any other column. This observation permits the following equivalent statement of Theorem 1.

COROLLARY 1. *A necessary condition for the regular realizability of a gait matrix G is that no column of G may be such that its one entries overlap the one entries of any other column.*

While Theorem 1 provides a necessary condition, the condition is not sufficient. This is shown by the following quadruped example.

$$G^T = \begin{bmatrix} 0 & 0 & 0 & 1 & 1 & 1 & 1 & 1 \\ 1 & 0 & 0 & 0 & 0 & 0 & 1 & 1 \\ 1 & 1 & 1 & 1 & 0 & 0 & 0 & 1 \\ 0 & 0 & 1 & 1 & 1 & 0 & 0 & 0 \end{bmatrix} \quad (7)$$

It is easy to see that the rows of G^T (columns of G) satisfy the condition of Corollary 1. For this particular matrix, the equality constraint condition (4) can be written in expanded form as

$$t_4 + t_5 + t_6 + t_7 + t_8 = 1 \quad (8)$$
$$t_1 + t_7 + t_8 = 1 \quad (9)$$
$$t_1 + t_2 + t_3 + t_4 + t_8 = 1 \quad (10)$$
$$t_3 + t_4 + t_5 = 1 \quad (11)$$

Adding (8) to (10) produces the result

$$\mathbf{t}_4 + t_8 = 2 - \tau \quad (12)$$

where τ is the objective function defined by (2). Adding (9) to (11) yields

$$-(t_2 + t_6) = 2 - \tau \quad (13)$$

Combining (12) and (13), any solution to the equality constraint equation for G must satisfy the relation

$$(t_2 + t_6)/(t_4 + t_8) = -1 \quad (14)$$

But this is impossible if the inequality constraint (3) is satisfied. Consequently G is not regularly realizable and, in general, Theorem 1 is merely necessary, not sufficient.

A Sufficient Condition for Regular Realizability

It is obvious that if a gait matrix for G has the property that every column contains the same number of ones as every other column, then no column can overlap another column and Corollary 1 is automatically satisfied. The following theorem shows that this condition is also sufficient for regular realizability.

THEOREM 2. *Let G be an n-row, k-column binary matrix with the property that every column G contains m ones. Such a G is always regularly realizable.*

Proof. Let $t_i = 1/m$, $i = 1, 2, \ldots n$. Then for any column j of G, it must be true that

$$\sum_{i=1}^{n} g_{ij} t_i = 1 \quad (15)$$

Thus both the inequality constraints (3) and the equality constraints (4) are satisfied by this choice of $\mathbf{t}$ and G is regularly realizable. ∎

While Theorem 2 is sufficient, it is not in general necessary. For example, the following matrix does not satisfy this theorem:

$$G^T = \begin{bmatrix} 0 & 0 & 0 & 1 & 1 & 1 & 1 & 1 \\ 1 & 0 & 0 & 0 & 0 & 1 & 1 & 1 \\ 1 & 1 & 0 & 0 & 0 & 0 & 1 & 1 \\ 1 & 1 & 1 & 1 & 0 & 0 & 0 & 1 \end{bmatrix} \quad (16)$$

However, it is easy to see that both conditions (3) and (4) are satisfied by

$$\mathbf{t} = (\tfrac{1}{4}, \tfrac{1}{4}, \tfrac{1}{8}, \tfrac{1}{8}, \tfrac{1}{8}, \tfrac{1}{4}, \tfrac{1}{4}, \tfrac{1}{4})^T \quad (17)$$

so G is in fact regularly realizable.

Equivalence Classes of Connected Gait Matrices

While a necessary condition and a sufficient condition for regular realizability have been found, no condition which is both necessary and sufficient has been established other than that given by Definition 1. Thus, to determine exactly which k-legged gaits are regularly realizable, it is necessary to solve a linear programming problem for all k-column gait matrices satisfying the necessary condition (Theorem 1) but not satisfying the sufficient condition (Theorem 2). The magnitude of this task is substantially reduced by considering only connected gait matrices. This is justified by the fact that these matrices, which are all $2k \times k$ in dimension, are the only matrices possessing *nonsingular* gait formulas (McGhee, 1968). That is, they represent the only class of gaits which can be utilized as a strictly periodic sequence of leg states by a real legged locomotion system. The reader is referred to McGhee (1968) and McGhee & Frank (1968) for a fuller discussion of this point.

The enumeration of the regularly realizable gait matrices is further simplified by noting that the regular realizability property is preserved under arbitrary row and column permutations. In McGhee (1968) a canonical row form for gait matrices is defined. In the present paper, this definition is extended for connected gait matrices to a *canonical row and column* form as follows.

DEFINITION 4. *A connected gait matrix, G, is transformed to canonical row and column form by first cyclically permuting the rows so that the first row begins with a 0 and the last row begins with a 1 and* then permuting columns $2, 3, \ldots k$, so that the order of the placing events in the event sequence becomes $2, 3, \ldots k$. The event sequence associated with the canonical row and column form of a connected gait matrix will be called the canonical event sequence.

The matrix given by (16) is already in canonical row and column form. the corresponding event sequence is

$$E = 12345678. \tag{18}$$

The quadruped walk illustrated in Figure 1 is in canonical row form, but is not in canonical column form. It is transformed to canonical column form by moving column 2 to column 3, column 3 to column 4, and column 4 to column 2. The event sequence then becomes

$$E = 17283546. \tag{19}$$

Consideration of these two examples should make it clear that the column permutations allowed in Definition 4 partition the set of all connected matrices into a set of equivalence classes. The number of distinct canonical row matrices in each such class is evidently

$$N = (k - 1)! \tag{20}$$

Since there are $(2k-1)!$ canonical row connected gait matrices [4], the total number of equivalence classes to be examined for regular realizability is

$$M = \frac{(2k - 1)!}{(k - 1)!} \tag{21}$$

The next section of this paper provides an upper bound on the number of such equivalence classes which satisfy the necessary condition of Theorem 1.

An Upper Bound on the Number of Equivalence Classes of Regularly Realizable Connected Gait Matrices

In order to test all equivalence classes of connected gait matrices satisfying Theorem 1 for regular realizability, it is necessary to have an algorithm for generating at least one member of each class. the following definition and theorem provide a basis for one such algorithm.

DEFINITION 4. *An event sequence, E, for a k-column connected gait matrix, G, is column comparable, if, when E is presented on a circle, the lifting events occur in the same order as the placing events.*

It might appear that column comparability amounts to the same thing as column compatibility. However the example of Figure 3 shows that this is not the case. While the lifting sequence of this gait (5678) corresponds to the placing sequence (1234) and the event sequence is therefore column comparable, examination of the associated matrix, also shown on this figure, reveals that the ones of column 3 overlap the ones of column 4.

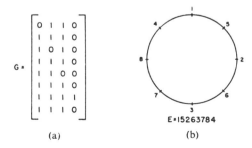

(a)   (b)

Figure 3 A column comparable gait matrix which is not column compatible, (a) gait matrix and (b) event sequence.

Thus while it is clear that compatibility

of every pair of columns of a gait matrix ensures column comparability, the converse is not necessarily true. The event sequences for all connected matrices satisfying Theorem 1 form a subset of the column comparable event sequences. the present example shows that this is a proper subset for $k = 4$.

It is relatively straightforward to generate all column comparable canonical event sequences. Each of these can then be tested to see if the condition of Theorem 1 is satisfied. The following theorem establishes the number of column comparable canonical event sequences as a function of the number of columns in the associated gait matrices and suggests a specific algorithm for obtaining the comparable sequences.

THEOREM 3. *The number of column comparable canonical event sequences for k-column connected gait matrices is given by*

$$N = \frac{(2k-1)!}{[(k-1)!]^2} \qquad (22)$$

Proof. Every row and column canonical form connect gait matrix possesses the placing sequence $1, 2\,3, \ldots k$. Event 1 occurs in row 1 by definition. The other $k-1$ placing events can be associated with the other $2k-1$ rows in C_{k-1}^{2k-1} distinct ways. The lifting of leg 1, event $k+1$, can occur in any of the remaining k rows. When the location of this event has been chosen, all of the remaining lifting events must occur in sequence in the remaining $k-1$ rows. Therefore

$$N = kC_{k-1}^{2k-1} = \frac{k(2k-1)!}{k!(k-1)!} = \frac{(2k-1)!}{[(k-1)!]^2} . \blacksquare$$
$$(23)$$

Since the above proof is essentially

constructive in nature, it is easy to write a computer program to generate all N column comparable canonical event sequences for any specified k. Because every matrix satisfying Theorem 1 is column comparable, (23) provides an upper bound on the number of equivalence classes of regularly realizable connected gait matrices.

Complementary Gait Matrices

A further reduction in the number of equivalence classes of column comparable canonical event sequences is made possible by the use of matrix complementation. The following theorem shows that, for gait matrices, regular realizability is preserved under matrix complementation. Some useful relationships between the maximum value of the objective function (2) for a gait matrix and its complement are also established.

THEOREM 4. *Let G be a binary matrix such that every column of G contains at least one 1 and at least one 0. Let H be the binary complement of G and let τ_G and τ_H be the maximum value of the objective function, $\tau = \sum_{i=1}^{n} t_i$, for G and H respectively. Then H is regularly realizable if and only if G is regularly realizable. Furthermore, if β_G is the duty factor for a regular realization of G, then*

$$1/\tau_H \leq \beta_G \leq -1/\tau_G \qquad (24)$$

Proof. Let $\mathbf{t}$ be any feasible solution for a regular realization of G and let τ be the corresponding value for the objective function. Let $\mathbf{t}^*$ be defined by

$$\mathbf{t}^* = \mathbf{t}/(\tau - 1). \qquad (25)$$

Because every column of G contains at least one zero, τ is strictly greater than one

and $\mathbf{t}^*$ always exists. Since the equality constraints imply that the total duration of the one states in any column is equal to 1, the duration of the zero states of G must be $\tau - 1$. It therefore follows that

$$H^T \mathbf{t}^* = \frac{1}{\tau - 1} H^T \mathbf{t} = \frac{\tau - 1}{\tau - 1} \mathbf{1} = \mathbf{1} \qquad (26)$$

so H is regularly realizable. Now form the above arguments

$$\beta_G = (\tau - 1)/\tau \leq (\tau_G - 1)/\tau_G. \qquad (27)$$

Finally if τ^* is the objective function associated with $\mathbf{t}^*$ and H, and the zeros of G are the ones of H, then

$$\beta_G = 1/\tau^* \geq 1/\tau_H. \quad \blacksquare \qquad (28)$$

Taking into account the fact that (24) must hold for H as well as G, algebraic manipulations reveal that for any two complementary matrices, H and G, if $\beta_{\min} < \beta_{\max}$, then

$$\beta_{\max}(H) + \beta_{\min}(G) = 1. \qquad (29)$$

Using this relationship, both the regular realizability and the range of allowable duty factors can be determined for every gait matrix satisfying the necessary condition by solving the linear programming problem defined by (2), (3), and (4) while maximizing the objective function in each case.

Computational Results

For bipeds, (23) shows that the number of column comparable canonical event sequences for connected gait matrices is

$$N = 3!/(1!)^2 = 6 \qquad (30)$$

These event sequences and their corresponding gait matrices are all shown on Figure 4. As can be seen, gaits 1 and 6

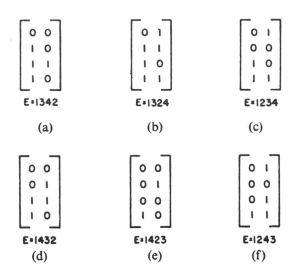

Figure 4 Connected biped gait matrices, (a) gait 1, (b) gait 2, (c) gait 3, (d) gait 4, (e) gait 5, and (f) gait 6.

fail to satisfy Corollary 1 and are therefore not regularly realizable. On the other hand, gaits 2, 3, 4, and 5 satisfy Theorem 2 so they are all regularly realizable. Since Figure 4 displays all possible connected biped gait matrices (McGhee, 1968), it follows that either Theorem 1 or Theorem 2 can be used as a necessary and sufficient condition for regular realizability for connected biped gait matrices.

Complementation followed by cyclic row permutation shows that gait 2 is the complement of gait 5 while gaits 3 and 4 are self-complementary. Solution of the linear programming problem for each regularly realizable gait shows that β may take on any value from 0 to 1 for gaits 3 and 4 while for gait 2

$$0 < \beta_2 < \frac{1}{2} \qquad (31)$$

Consequently, for gait 5

$$\frac{1}{2} < \beta_5 < 1. \qquad (32)$$

For quadrupeds, (23) yields the result

$$N = 7!/(3!)^2 = 140. \qquad (33)$$

To determine which of these 140 equivalence classes of gait matrices are actually regularly realizable, a computer program was written to generate the canonical row and column form matrix for each of the 140 classes. Examination of these matrices showed that 82 satisfied Theorem 1 (Corollary 1) and 16 satisfied Theorem 2. The linear programming problem was solved for each of the 82 matrices satisfying the necessary condition and it was found that all but the matrix given by (7) and its complement are in fact regularly realizable. This result is summarized in the following theorem (Jain, 1970).

THEOREM 5. *A 4-column connected gait matrix G is regularly realizable if and only if no column of G overlaps any other column of G and if the canonical event sequence for G is not one of the two sequences 12853467 or 17823564.*

CANONICAL EVENT SEQUENCES AND DUTY FACTOR RANGES FOR REGULARLY REALIZ-
ABLE QUADRUPED GAITS

Equivalence class number	Canonical event sequence	Maximum duty factor	Minimum duty factor	Complementary event sequence
1	12345678*	1	0	—
2	12354678	$\frac{1}{2}$	0	18234567
3	12356478	$\frac{1}{2}$	0	12834567
4	12356748	$\frac{1}{2}$	0	12384567
5	12385467	1	$\frac{1}{2}$	18235674
6	12385647	1	$\frac{1}{2}$	12835674
7	12385674*	1	0	—
8	12534678	$\frac{1}{2}$	0	17823456
9	12536478	$\frac{1}{2}$	0	17283456
10	12536748	$\frac{1}{3}$	0	17238456
11	12563478*	$\frac{1}{2}$	0	12783456*
12	12563748	$\frac{1}{3}$	0	12738456
13	12738546	1	$\frac{1}{2}$	18256374
14	12738564	1	$\frac{1}{2}$	12856374
15	12783546	1	$\frac{1}{2}$	18256347
16	12783564	1	$\frac{1}{2}$	12856347
17	12785346	1	$\frac{1}{2}$	17825634
18	12785364	1	$\frac{1}{2}$	17285634
19	12785634*	1	0	—
20	12835467	$\frac{2}{3}$	$\frac{1}{2}$	18235647
21	12835647*	$\frac{2}{3}$	$\frac{1}{3}$	—
22	12853647	$\frac{1}{2}$	$\frac{1}{3}$	17283564
23	12853674	$\frac{1}{2}$	0	17238564
24	15234678	$\frac{1}{3}$	0	16782345
25	15236478	$\frac{1}{3}$	0	16728345
26	15236748	$\frac{1}{3}$	0	16723845
27	15263478	$\frac{1}{3}$	0	16278345
28	15263748*	$\frac{1}{2}$	0	16273845*
29	16273854	1	$\frac{2}{3}$	18526374
30	16278354	1	$\frac{2}{3}$	18526347
31	16278534	1	$\frac{1}{2}$	17852634
32	16723854*	1	$\frac{1}{2}$	18523674*
33	16728354	1	$\frac{1}{2}$	18523647
34	16728534	1	$\frac{1}{2}$	17852364
35	16782354	1	$\frac{1}{2}$	18523467
36	16782534	1	$\frac{1}{2}$	17852346
37	16785234*	1	0	—
38	17238546	1	$\frac{1}{2}$	18253674
39	17283546*	$\frac{1}{2}$	$\frac{1}{2}$	18253647*
40	17285346	$\frac{2}{3}$	$\frac{1}{2}$	17825364
41	17285364*	$\frac{2}{3}$	$\frac{1}{3}$	—
42	17823546	$\frac{2}{3}$	$\frac{1}{2}$	18253467
43	17825346*	$\frac{2}{3}$	$\frac{1}{3}$	—
44	18235467*	$\frac{2}{3}$	$\frac{1}{3}$	—

Note: Event sequences labeled with * are those which satisfy the sufficient condition of Theorem 2.

Table 1

OBSERVED CONNECTED QUADRUPED GAITS

Gait number	Gait name	Source	Event sequence	Canonical sequence
1	slow walk (H1)	3, 9, 11	18462735	16273845
2	H2	3, 11	18642753	16723854
3	H3	3, 11	14672358	12783456
4	walk (H4)	2, 3, 9, 11	16472538	17283546
5	H6	3, 11	17632854	16723854
6	H8	3, 11	16382547	17283546
7	amble (H9)	2, 3, 9, 11	17452836	18253647
8	pace (H10)	2, 3, 9, 11	17542863	18523674
9	trot (H11)	2, 3, 9, 11	14582367	12563478
10	H13	3, 11	18352746	18253647
11	trot (H14)	3, 11	18532764	18523674
12*	elephant amble	9	16742583	17823564
13	slow canter	2, 9	16754238	17852346
14*	fast canter	9	18765423	16875234
15	transverse gallop	2, 9	16543827	18523647
16	rotatory gallop	2, 9	17256438	18256347
17	cat gallop	9	16453872	18253674
18	dog gallop	9	15264387	15263478
19	cheetah gallop	12	15438726	15236748

Note: The designations H1, H2, etc. refer to a numbering scheme introduced by Hildebrand [11]. The numbers appearing under the column headed "Source" refer to the list of references associated with this paper. The two non-regularly realizable gaits are marked with an asterisk.

Table II

Table 1 lists the eighty regularly realizable event sequences along with the maximum and minimum duty factor for one of the gaits of each complementary pair. The duty factor range for the other gait is of course determined by (29). As can be seen, eight of the eighty regularly realizable quadruped gait equivalence classes are self complementary.

Some Applications

Among the six possible connected biped gaits shown on Figure 4, only gaits 2 and 5 are commonly encountered in nature. These two gaits correspond to the normal biped run and walk, respectively (Muybridge, 1955). Gaits 3 and 4 are sometimes used by children at play, especially while imitating a galloping quadruped. To the authors' knowledge, gaits 1 and 6 are never used by any biped. It thus appears that regular realizability does account for biped gait preferences.

A number of individuals have studied the gaits actually used by quadruped animals. Prominent among such investigators are E. Muybridge (1957), M. Hildebrand (1960; 1965; 1966) and T.D.M. Roberts (1967). The connected gaits reported in the referenced publications are all listed in Table II. Comparison of the canonical event sequences of this table with those of

Table I shows that all but gaits 12 and 14 of Table II are regularly realizable. Gait 14 fails to satisfy the necessary condition of Theorem 1. This was noted specifically by Roberts who recognized that the "fast canter" was in some sense an anomalous gait (Roberts, 1967). Gait 12, the "elephant amble", corresponds to one of the two counter-examples of Theorem 5. The reasons for the use of these two non-regularly realizable gaits is not clear at present.

Gaits 1 through 11 in Table II are not only regularly realizable, but are also symmetric (Hildebrand, 1965, 1966). That is, these gaits are capable of execution with the right and left legs of either the front or rear pair striking the ground at evenly spaced intervals. It is interesting to note that these eleven gaits (as well as an additional five theoretically possible regular symmetric gaits recognized by Hildebrand) reduce to just four equivalence classes under the column permutation and matrix complementation operations associated with Table I.

Summary and Conclusions

A condition, called "regular realizability", has been found which accounts for the gait preferences of bipeds and, with two exceptions, of quadrupeds. Of the six possible non-singular (connected) biped gaits, four are regularly realizable. Two of these four correspond the the common biped "walk" and "run" respectively. Of the 5040 theoretically possible non-singular quadruped gaits, 480 are regularly realizable. A total of 19 of these have been observed in use by some animal. Only two quadruped gaits which are not regularly realizable have been reported.

Simple necessary and sufficient conditions for the regular realizability of biped and quadruped gait matrices have been derived. For animals or machines with more than four legs, a necessary condition, a sufficient condition, and an upper bound on the number of regularly realizable gaits has been obtained. A general relationship between the ranges of allowable duty factors for complementary matrices has been found. The allowable duty factor range has been tabulated for every regularly realizable biped and quadruped gait.

Hopefully, this paper sheds additional light on the reasons for the gait preferences of animals. The results obtained certainly have a bearing on the design of legged vehicles. Additional work is needed to extend the applications of the theoretical results obtained here to insect and arachnid locomotion. It would also be interesting to attempt to find additional conditions to apply to the 480 regularly realizable quadruped gait matrices to further account for the particular gaits favored by various species of animals.

Acknowledgments: This research was sponsored in part by the U.S. Air Force Office of Scientific Research under Grant No. AFOSR-70-1901 and in part by the National Science Foundation under Grant No. GK-25292.

References

Hadley, G. (1962) *Linear Programming.* Reading, Mass.: Addison-Wesley Publishing Co.

Hildebrand, M. (1966) Analysis of the symmetrical gaits of tetrapods. *Folia Biotheoretica,* 4:9 – 22.

Hildebrand, M. (1965) Symmetrical gaits of horses. *Science*, 150:701–708.

Hildebrand, M. (1960) How animals run. *Sci. Amer.*(May):148.

Jain, A.K. (1970) "A Study of Regularly Realizable Gait Matrices". M.S. dissertation, College of Engineering, The Ohio State University, Columbus, Ohio.

McGhee, R.B. (1968) Some finite state aspects of legged locomotion. *Math. Biosci.*, 2:67–84.

McGhee, R.B. (1967) Finite state control of quadruped locomotion. *Simulation*, 9:135–140.

McGhee, R.B. & Frank, A.A. (1968) On the stability properties of quadruped creeping gaits. *Math. Biosci.*, 3:331–351.

McGhee, R.B. & Kuhner, M.B. (1969) On the dynamic stability of legged locomotion systems. *Proceedings of the Third International Symposium on External Control of Human Extremities*, Dubrovnik, Yugoslavia, August.

Muybridge, E. (1957) *Animals in Motion.* New York: Dover Publications.

Muybridge, E. (1955) *The Human Figure in Motion.* New York: Dover Publications.

Roberts, T.D.M. (1967) *Neurophysiology of Postural Mechanisms.* London: Plenum Press.

Reprinted from *Math. Biosciences*, 13:179–193 (1972).

Balance and Symmetry in Running

Marc H. Raibert

Department of Computer Science
Carnegie-Mellon University

1.0 Introduction

Running is a series of bouncing and ballistic motions that exert forces on the body during every stride. The bouncing motions are caused by the vertical rebound of the body when the legs push on the ground. The ballistic motions occur between bounces when the body is airborne (Cavagna, 1970). For a legged system to run at a fixed speed with its body in a stable upright posture, then the net acceleration of the body must be zero over each entire stride. This requires that the torques and horizontal forces exerted on the body by the legs must integrate to zero over each stride and that the vertical forces integrate to the body's weight times the duration of the stride. This is equally true for running machines and for running animals. Here we show how a control system can satisfy these constraints by using body and leg motions that obey a simple set of symmetries. The symmetries apply to a variety of legged models running with a variety of gaits, and they describe the behavior of running animals.

Hildebrand first recognized the importance of symmetry in legged locomotion nearly two decades ago when he observed that the left half of a horse often did the same thing as the right half, but 180° out of phase (Hildebrand 1965, 1966, 1968). He devised a very simple and elegant characterization of the symmetric walking and running gaits using just two parameters; the phase angle between the front and rear legs, and the duty cycle of the legs. By mapping each observation of symmetric behavior into a point in phase/duty cycle space, Hildebrand was able to systematically classify gaits for over 150 quadruped genera.

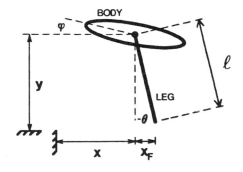

Figure 1 Definition of variables used in symmetry equations. Positive hip torque τ acts to accelerate the body in the positive ϕ direction. Positive leg thrust f pushes the body away from the ground.

Here we use this symmetry notion to define a class of body and leg motions that permit accelerations of the body within each stride, but that don't change the average forward running speed throughout the stride. However, rather than look at relationships between the footfalls of the

36

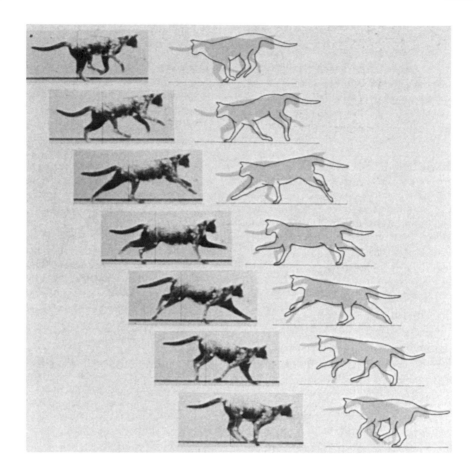

Figure 2 Galloping cat. (Left) The photographs show a cat running on a treadmill with a rotary gallop. Each photograph is separated by 50 msec. (Right) The shaded figures repeat the normal running behavior illustrated in the photographs. The super-imposed outlines were made from the same photographs, but their left-right orientation was reversed, $x = -x$, and their sequential order was reversed, $t = -t$. Therefore, the outline at the top was made from the photograph at the bottom after reversing its orientation. The pattern of footfalls for the normal running cat and the *reverse* running cat are nearly identical, as predicted by symmetry (Diagram Construction). The relative placement of the figures within each of the three sequences accurately reflects the forward progress of the cat with respect to the surface of the treadmill. After the figures in each sequence were assembled according to the forward movement, the assembled set of figures for the reverse running sequence (outlines) was positioned relative to the assembled set for the normal running sequence (shaded). Photographs are from a film described by Wetzel et al. (1976). The frames shown here correspond to the vertical dashed lines in Figure 9.

left and right legs, as Hildebrand did, we consider symmetry in the trajectories of the feet with respect to the body, and in the trajectory of the body through space. The key idea is that symmetric motions facilitate the control task because when the behavior deviates from symmetry, the resultant net accelerations deviate from zero in a manageable way.

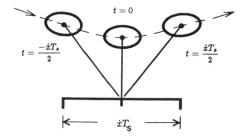

Figure 3 Symmetric motion used by one-legged system in running. The left-most drawing shows the configuration just before the foot touches the ground, the center drawing shows the configuration half way through stance when the leg is maximally compressed and vertical ($t = 0$, $\theta = 0$, $\phi = 0$), and the right-most drawing shows the configuration just after the foot loses contact with the ground. T_S is the duration of the stance phase.

We first recognized the value of symmetric motions when exploring control for machines that run by hopping on one leg (Raibert et al., 1984). Like an inverted pendulum, a one-legged system tips and accelerates when its point of support is not located directly below the center of mass. It undergoes no net forward acceleration when the trajectory of the support point, the foot, is symmetric about the center of mass. In this case, the forces and torques acting on the body when the leg extends forward during the first half of the support interval, are equal and opposite to those acting when the leg extends backward during the second half of the support interval (see Figure 3). The average running speed remains constant because the integral of the horizontal force acting on the body is zero. When motion of the foot with respect to the center of mass is skewed either forward or backward, the forces acting on the body become unbalanced and the body accelerates.

First we introduce motion symmetry in the context of one-legged systems, and then generalize to more complicated systems. Symmetry is particularly simple for one-legged machines, because only one leg provides support at a time, each support interval is isolated in time by periods of ballistic flight, and the hip is located at the center of mass. To generalize the symmetries we consider motions that span several support intervals, and motions of several legs that provide support during a single support interval. We find that the same symmetry equations apply for models that have one, two, and four legs, and for gaits that use legs singly and in combination.

2.0 Model for Motion Symmetry

2.1 Preliminaries

A number of simplifications ease the analysis of symmetry. Our basic model consists of a body and one or more legs that are restricted to move in a plane, with massless legs and no losses anywhere in the system. The body is a rigid object that moves fore and aft and up and down, and that pitches in the plane with position

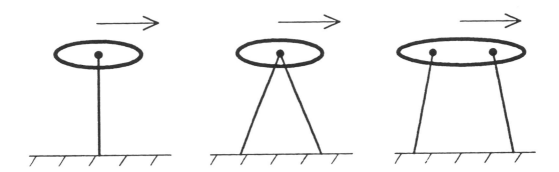

Figure 4 Symmetric configuration during support. Configuration of models half way through the support interval, when they have fore/aft symmetry (left/right as shown in diagram), as well as symmetry moving forward and backward in time. In each case the vertical velocity is zero and the center of support is located directly under the center of mass.

and orientation given by $[x\,y\,\phi]$. For models with four legs, two hips are located equal distances fore and aft of the body's center of mass. Models with two legs may have either of these hip configurations.

Each leg is a single massless member that pivots about its hip at a hinge-type joint and that lengthens and shortens by telescoping. The length of the leg and its angle with respect to the vertical are given by $[\ell\ \theta]$. At the end of each leg is a foot that can provide a point of support. Friction between a foot and the ground prevents the foot from sliding on the ground whenever there is contact. A foot in contact with the ground acts mechanically like a hinge joint. A leg actuator exerts a force f along the leg's axis between the body and the ground. Positive f accelerates the body away from the ground, and because the feet are not sticky, $f \geq 0$. This force is zero when there is no contact between the foot and the ground. Normally, the leg is springy in the axial direction, in which case f is a function of leg length. A second actuator

acts at the hip, generating a torque τ between the leg and the body. Positive τ accelerates the body in the positive ϕ direction. Equations of motion for this sort of system are given in Appendix A.

In normal operation the models follow a regular pattern of activity, alternating between periods of support and periods of flight. We call the transition from flight to support is called *touch-down* and the transition from support to flight is called *lift-off*. During support a foot remains stationary and the leg exerts a combination of vertical and horizontal forces on the body. Because legs are springy, the body's vertical motion is an elastic rebound that returns the system to the flight phase after each collision with the ground. Once airborne, the body follows a ballistic trajectory. Depending on the number of legs in the system and the gait, the body may derive support from one or more legs during a single support interval. Because the legs have no mass and the entire system is lossless, bouncing motions continue undiminished, without an external source of energy.

2.2 Symmetric motion with one leg

Imagine that at time $t = 0$ the foot of a one-legged system is located directly below the center of mass, the body is upright, and the velocity of the body is purely horizontal: $\theta = 0$, $\phi = 0$ and $\dot{y} = 0$ (see Figure 3). Because the system has left-right symmetry of motion and there are no losses, the expected behavior proceeding forward in time is precisely the same as its past behavior receding backward in time, but with a reflection about the line $x = 0$. This behavior is described by the following body-symmetry equations, which state that $x(t)$ and $\phi(t)$ are odd functions of time and $y(t)$ is an even function.

$$\text{Body Symmetry} \quad \begin{cases} x(t) = -x(-t) & (1) \\ y(t) = y(-t) & (2) \\ \phi(t) = -\phi(-t) & (3) \end{cases}$$

Because the body moves along a symmetric trajectory with respect to the origin and because the foot is located at the origin during support, the body-symmetry equations imply that the foot's motion is symmetric with respect to the body, which gives the following leg-symmetry equations:

$$\text{Leg Symmetry} \quad \begin{cases} \theta(t) = -\theta(-t) & (4) \\ \ell(t) = \ell(-t) & (5) \end{cases}$$

Finally, symmetric motion of the body and legs requires symmetric actuation, which is given by:

$$\text{Actuator Symmetry} \quad \begin{cases} \tau(t) = -\tau(-t) & (6) \\ f(t) = f(-t) & (7) \end{cases}$$

From the equations of motion (Appendix A) we see that hip torque τ is the only influence on body pitch angle ϕ, so odd ϕ implies odd τ. With the evenness and oddness of the other variables specified, f must be even to satisfy the equations of motion.

Symmetric body and leg motion results in *steady-state locomotion*.[1] For the forward speed to remain unchanged from stride to stride, the horizontal force f_x acting on the body just integrate to zero over a stride. From the equations of motion for the one-legged case (see Appendix A) we see that the horizontal force exerted on the body during stance is:

$$f_x = f \sin\theta - \frac{\tau}{\ell} \cos\theta \qquad (8)$$

Since f and ℓ are even while τ and θ are odd, f_x is an odd function of time during the support interval. Therefore:

$$\dot{x}(t_{lo}) - \dot{x}(t_{td}) = \int_{t_{td}}^{t_{lo}} f_x(t) = 0 . \qquad (9)$$

This merely affirms our earlier conclusion that symmetric motion provides no net horizontal force on the body, and average running speed does not change from stride to stride.

The vertical position and velocity also proceed in steady state for a symmetric motion. The elevation of the body is an even function of time during stance, so $y(t_{\ell o,i}) = y(t_{td,i})$ and $\dot{y}(t_{\ell o,i} =$

---

[1] A trajectory that provides steady-state locomotion is one that provides a nominal motion that would repeat from cycle to cycle if there were no disturbances. It does not mean that there are restoring forces that will return the system to the trajectory if it deviates as a result of a disturbance. Restoring forces are also required for stability once the nominal trajectory has been determined. Asymmetry in the motion is a source of such restoring forces.

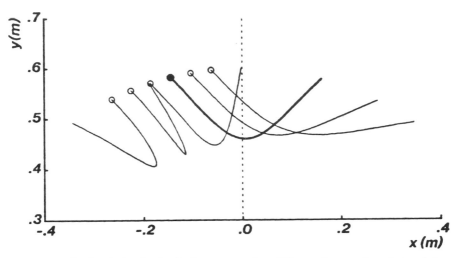

Figure 5 Path of the body during stance for different leg angles at touchdown. The forward position of the foot at touchdown influences the symmetry of the body's motion during support. For a given forward velocity, only one position (shown bold) results in a symmetric body trajectory. Other trajectories are skewed. In each case the foot is positioned at (0, 0) with body velocity $[\dot{x}(t_{td}) = 1$ m/sec, $\dot{y}(t_{td}) = 1$ m/sec$]$. Bullets indicate location of body at touchdown. Adapted from (Stentz, 1983).

$-\dot{y}(t_{t_{td},i})$. During flight, the body travels in a parabolic trajectory that is also even. If we specify $t = 0$ halfway through the flight, then $y(t_{td,i+1}) = y(t_{\ell o,i})$ and $\dot{y}(t_{td,i+1}) = -\dot{y}(t_{\ell o,i})$. Consequently $y(t_{td,i}) = y(t_{td,i+1})$ or $y(t_{td}) = y(t_{td+T})$, which is the steady state condition on y for the stride period T. A similar condition applies to $\dot{y}$.

The torque acting on the body is zero during flight and an odd function during stance, so the body pitch rate $\dot{\phi}$ undergoes zero net acceleration during stance, i.e. $\dot{\phi}(t_{\ell o}) = \dot{\phi}(t_{td})$. This satisfies the steady-state condition on $\dot{\phi}$. For the pitch angle of the body to proceed in steady state, its value at the end of flight must be equal and opposite to its value at the beginning of the flight phase. Assuming that symmetry holds during stance so $\phi_{\ell o} = -\phi_{td}$ and that no torques act on the body during flight,

then a repeating pattern requires that

$$\frac{\dot{y}(t)}{-g} = \frac{\phi(t)}{\dot{\phi}(t)} \qquad (10)$$

where g is the acceleration of gravity. This constraint ensures that the pitch angle of the body negates itself during flight, so that behavior repeats from cycle to cycle. It is trivially satisfied if there is no pitching motion, namely when $\phi(t) = 0$ and $\dot{\phi}(t) = 0$. Note also that Equation (10) also satisfies a second symmetric configuration about $\dot{y} = 0$ and $\phi = 0$ occuring during flight where $f = 0$.

So far we have described a class of body motions that satisfies the requirements for steady state locomotion. $x(t)$ is an odd function of time permitting the forward running speed to remain unchanged. $y(t)$ is even, allowing the vertical acceleration during support to compensate for the acceleration of gravity during flight. $\phi(t)$ is an odd function during support, compensating for the fixed rotation rate of the body during flight. These motions of the body require symmetric motions of the leg.[2] $\theta(t)$ must be odd, so the leg sweeps the foot in a symmetric pattern under the center of mass during support, and $\ell(t)$ is even. These symmetries are important because they result in accelerations of the body that are odd functions of time throughout a stride, and hence integrate to zero over symmetric limits, leaving the forward running speed, body elevation and body pitch unchanged from one stride to the next.

2.3 Controlling symmetry

The symmetries suggest *what* motions the legged system should use to proceed in steady state, but they do not prescribe *how* to produce them. What action must a control system take to produce symmetric behavior? Recall that a legged system moves with symmetry if θ, $\dot{y}$ and ϕ all equal zero when the foot is located directly under the body during support. However, the control system must commit the foot to a position on the ground before touchdown when neither $\dot{y}$ nor ϕ is zero. The task of orchestrating such a rendezvous is to predict where the center of mass will be when the body's vertical velocity and pitch angle are both zero. Similarly, during the support phase, the pitch angles and rate and the vertical velocity at lift-off must be coordinated to ensure an odd set of body angles during flight. At present, general closed-form solutions to these problems are not known.

Despite the lack of a general solution, approximate solutions exist for gaits that use just one leg for support at a time. The simplest approximate solution assumes that forward speed is constant during support and that the period of support T_s is constant, depending only on the spring mass characteristics of the leg and body. The normal foot position is then based on an estimate of the path of the body will travel during the next support interval. The vertical projection of this path onto the ground is called the *CG-print*. The length of the *CG-print* is then approximately equal to the product of the forward speed and the duration of support, $\dot{x}T_s$. Specifically, the length of the *CG-print* will be

$$x_f = \frac{\dot{x}T_s}{2} - k(\dot{x} - \dot{x}_d) \qquad (11)$$

where

$x_f =$ is the forward displacement of the foot with respect to the projection of the center of mass,

$\dot{x}, \dot{x}_d =$ are the measured and desired forward velocities of the body,

$T_S =$ is the duration of a support period, and

$k =$ is a gain

The first term in Equation (11) is the neutral (nominal) foot position that provides symmetry. The second term introduces asymmetry that accelerates the system to correct for errors in running speed (see Figure 7). It displaces the foot from the neutral point to skew the pattern of body motion. A set of systematically skewed motions is shown in Figure 5. These displacements accelerate the body

---

[2]For a one-legged system, symmetric body motion can be obtained *only* from symmetric leg motion (see Appendix B).

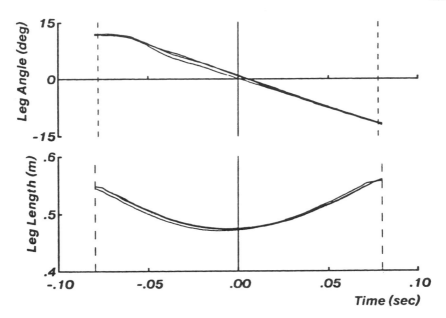

Figure 6 Symmetry data from physical one-legged hopping machine. The behavior of a one-legged hopping machine obeys the symmetry equations when the foot is placed in the center of the CG-print. Data for the leg are plotted when the foot is in contact with the round on three successive strides. The difference in leg length at touchdown and at lift-off is due to thrust delivered by the leg during support to compensate for losses. The time axes were adjusted so that $t(t = 0)$. Dashed vertical lines indicate touchdown and liftoff.

to stabilize its motion against disturbances and can change running speed.

We find our approximation provides good symmetry at low and moderate running speeds. Control systems have been built along these lines for one-, two- and four-legged machines. Data recorded from a three-dimensional one-legged machine running at about 1.6 m/sec are shown in Figure 6. Kinematics determine the leg angle that satisfies (11), $\theta = \arcsin(x_f/\ell)$, and a servomechanism positions the leg. To control the pitch angle of the body, the control system servos the torque about the hip during support, when friction holds the foot in place. Because the moment of inertia of the body was substantially

larger than that of the leg, the attitude of the body changed very little. This method produces leg and body motions with a good degree of symmetry. Raibert, Brown & Chepponis (1984) give more details about the one-legged control algorithms and their experimental results and two- and four-legged machines are described in Raibert (1986) and Raibert et al. (1986).

2.4 Pairs of balanced steps with anti-symmetry

Motion symmetry need not be confined to just one step. Although we have concentrated on symmetry that applies on

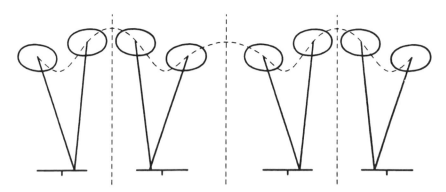

Figure 7 Pairs of balanced steps. If the foot is positioned behind the center of the CG-print on one step, and in front of it on the next step, then the pair of steps may have symmetry that stabilizes the forward running speed, even though motion during each step is no longer symmetric. We redefine the stride to include the symmetric pair of steps. The body and leg are drawn once for each touchdown and lift-off. The vertical dashed lines indicate the planes of symmetry, which occurs half way through the strides and between the strides.

a step-by-step basis, symmetries apply equally well when a pair of steps produce complementary accelerations, with the symmetry distributed over more than one support interval.

Suppose motion during a single support period does not have symmetry, but that two sequential support periods deviate from symmetry in a complementary fashion. Figure 7 shows a sequence of such anti-symmetric steps. Since the foot is not positioned in the center of the CG-print, the trajectory of the body during each step is skewed and the system accelerates because the foot is displaced from the neutral point. However, if the foot is positioned on the next step to compensate, then the body motions on successive steps balance with equal and opposite accelerations. Equations $(1)-(7)$ continue to describe the behavior of the body and leg, provided that we define $t = 0$ at the point halfway between the two steps. We can rationalize this definition by suggest-

ing that the two asymmetric steps taken together determine the support interval, and the time origin is still half way through support.

Antisymmetric pairs of steps can be used when running in place. So far we have assumed that the forward running speed is non-zero, but it need not be. For instance if the foot were placed so that the horizontal component of the body velocity is just reversed during support and this were done on each step, then the average forward running speed would be zero and the system would bounce back and forth on each step. This is just the sort of behavior observed in the frontal plane of the human biped or a pacing quadruped.

3.0 Symmetry with More Legs

A system with two legs can run with a variety of gaits. The two legs can operate precisely in phase, precisely out of phase, or with intermediate phase. Figure 8

36

shows several examples that differ in with regard to the amount of body pitching, the variation in forward running speed within a stride, and the degree of temporal overlap in the support provided by the two legs. In each case, however, symmetric body and leg motions result in steady state locomotion.

The body symmetries for a system with several legs are the same as for one leg, but the leg and actuator symmetries are modified slightly. Each leg and actuator variable, θ, ℓ, τ, and f has the same meaning as before, but with subscripts distinguishing among the individual legs:

$$\theta_j(t) = -\theta_k(-t) \qquad (12)$$

$$\ell_j(t) = \ell_k(-t) \qquad (13)$$

$$\tau_j(t) = -\tau_k(-t) \qquad (14)$$

$$f_j(t) = f_k(-t). \qquad (15)$$

For a system with two legs $j = 1$ and $k = 2$. For four legs $j = [1\ 4]$ and $k = [2\ 3]$ or $j = [1\ 4]$ and $k = [3\ 2]$, depending on the gait, where 1-left front, 2-left rear, 3-right rear, 4-right front. These equations reduce to the one-legged case when $j = k = 1$.

Symmetric body motion no longer requires an individual leg to move with a symmetry of its own. Instead, the behavior of one leg is linked to the behavior of another leg, so that they operate with reciprocating symmetry. This frees θ, ℓ, τ and f for any one leg to take on arbitrary functions of time, while preserving the symmetric forces and moments impinging on the body during support. These motion symmetries apply (i) when a pair of legs located symmetrically about the center of mass share the same support phase and act in unison (Sutherland, 1983), (ii) when legs have different but overlapping

support periods, and (iii) when the legs provide support separately. As before, the equations that describe leg motion only apply when $f(t) > 0$. This means that it does not matter how the legs move when they are not touching the ground.

The arguments for symmetry are as before, except that the support symmetry configuration need not place any feet under the center of mass. For instance, Figure 4 shows two two-legged symmetric configurations that have no feet directly under the center of mass. In both of these cases, however, the *center of support* is located under the center of mass. It is also possible to have no support in the symmetric configuration. The bottom figure of Figure 8 suggests such a gait. The antisymmetric activity of the two legs operating as a pair produces symmetric motion of the body when measured over the stride. This is very much like the behavior of the one-legged system discussed in the previous section, that uses pairs of steps to achieve motion symmetry.

An important characteristic of such locomotion is that the individual feet need not be placed in the center of the CG-print to achieve steady state behavior. The feet may not be able to reach far enough under the center of mass to provide symmetry when the hips are located at the extremes of a long body. This situation arises in the sagittal plane for the quadruped bound and gallop, and to a lesser extent in the frontal plane for the quadruped pace.

4.0 Galloping Cat

Can the motion symmetries given in the previous sections describe the behavior of running animals? To explore this question we examined film records of a galloping

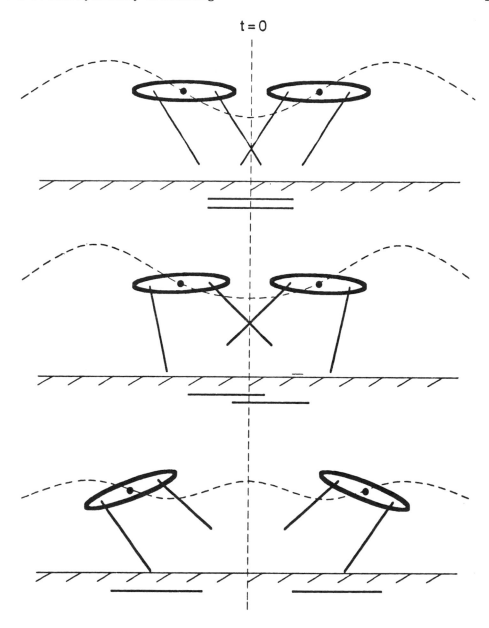

Figure 8 Running with two legs separated by a long body. Symmetry can be achieved when both feet provide support simultaneously, when there is partial overlap in the support periods, and hen the legs provide support in sequence. It may be difficult to place the feet in the centers of the CG-prints when the hips are widely separated. The displacement of the feet from the centers of the CG-prints will influence pitching of the body and the durations of each flight phase.

36

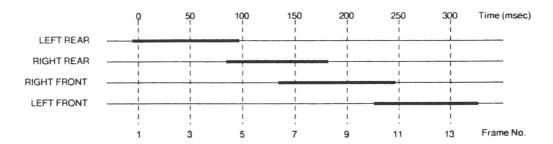

Figure 9 Pattern of foot contacts in the rotary gallop of a cat. Horizontal bars indicate that foot is in contact with the support surface. The duration of an entire stride is 350 msec. Data taken from high speed film of cat on treadmill, made by Wetzel, Atwater & Stuart (1976). Vertical dotted lines indicate the seven frames used in Figure 2.

cat, made by Wetzel, Atwater & Stuart (1976). Digitized data from this film are shown in several forms in Figures 2, 9, 10, and 11. Figure 10 plots the behavior of the body, x, y, and ϕ, as functions of time during the support interval of one stride, while Figure 11 gives data from the legs, θ_i and ℓ_i.

All plots show data that are in general agreement with the symmetries expected from (1)–(3), (12) and (13). Only the leg length data of Figure 11 deviate substantially from the expected pattern. This deviation could be due to a number of factors. One explanation may be that we consistently misestimated the location of the front shoulder in each frame. There were no clear markings that moved with the front shoulder in the film we used, so we had to estimate the pivot point in each frame. Another potential factor may be that the mass of the head causes uneven loading of the front and rear legs. Such an uneven distribution of mass would violate the assumption that the body has a symmetric mechanical structure.

One way to interpret the symmetries described in this paper, is that if we reverse the direction of forward travel and if we also reverse time $x(t) = -x(-t)$, then the pattern of footfalls should not change. Figure 2 demonstrates this invariance, at least qualitatively, for the galloping cat. It compares the patterns of body and leg motion of the *forward running cat* to the *reverse running cat*. The shaded figures in Figure 2 show the normal running sequence. The outlines are from the same photographs, but they are presented in reverse sequential order, $-t$, and they are reflected about the vertical axis, $-x$. The close correspondence between the locations of the shaded and outlined feet indicate that motion of the support points with respect to the body agrees quite well with the predicted symmetry.

5.0 Discussion

Symmetric running motions may have great generality. In principle, a wide variety of natural running gaits can be

fect symmetry in the behavior of physical legged robots and animals. One reason for asymmetry is that legs are not loss-less. The arguments used to motivate the

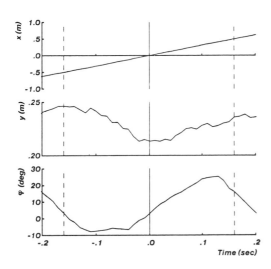

Figure 10 Motion of body in gallop-ing cat. Data digitized from film of a cat running on a treadmill with a ro-tary gallop. One frame every 10 msec. Dashed vertical lines indicate touch-down and lift-off. Solid vertical line indicates the point half way between touchdown and lift-off. The data are in reasonably good correspondence with the even and odd symmetries predicted by the theory.

achieved using body and leg motions that exhibit the symmetries we describe. These include the trot, the pace, the canter, the gallop, the bound, and the pronk, and the intermediate forms of these gaits. Al-though we have plotted symmetry data only for the galloping cat and examined data casually for the human, horse and dog, we expect to find that a wide vari-ety of natural legged systems use nearly symmetric motions when they run.[3]

There are several reasons, however, why one shouldn't expect to see per-

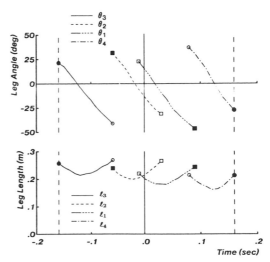

Figure 11 Leg motion of galloping cat. Same stride as Figure 10. (Top) the sweeping motion of the legs has the expected odd symmetry. Symbols indicate pairs of points that should have a symmetric relationship about the origin. (Bottom) The length of the legs were expected to have an even symmetry bout $t = 0$. An odd compo-nent is clearly present, indicating that the front legs are shorter than the hind legs. Part of this odd component is probably due to a systematic error in estimating the location of the shoul-der in each frame. Symbols indicate pairs of points that should have a sym-metric relationship about the center of support, $t = 0.51$. Data for each leg are shown only when foot touches the ground. Dashed vertical lines indicate touchdown and lift-off. Solid vertical line indicates the center of support.

---

[3]For other, more recent examples, including human data, see Raibert (1986).

relationship between symmetric motion and steady state behavior do not apply in the presence of friction. In particular, the behavior of the system moving forward in time is no longer symmetric to its behavior backward in time. The details of the discrepancy depend on the details of the losses and on the geometry of the system. Another energy loss contributing to asymmetric motion is due to unsprung mass in the legs. Each time a foot strikes or leaves the ground, the system looses a fraction of its kinetic energy. The ratio of the unsprung mass of the leg to the mass of the entire system determines this ratio (Raibert, 1984a). In order to maintain stable locomotion, the control system must re-supply energy on each cycle to compensate for these losses. For instance, we lengthen the leg during the support interval, and shorten it during flight to maintain a stable hopping height. This can only be done by delivering asymmetric forces and torques through the actuators.

Another reason for asymmetric behavior is asymmetry in the mechanical system. Most animals have large heavy heads at one end of their bodies that are not counter balanced by large heavy tails at the other end. Front and rear legs often vary in size, and the hips may not be equally spaced about the center of the mass. Each of these factors induces asymmetry in the class of motions that can provide steady state behavior. This is less of a problem for laboratory machines, since we design them to conform to have whatever mechanical symmetry we require.

Naturally, we shouldn't expect to see symmetric motion when the control system purposely skews the symmetry to change forward running speed. In this case asymmetric motion provides the forces that accelerate the body. An external load such as that produced by wind resistance or a draw-bar load, would also require a component of asymmetry in motion of the body and legs. A runner at the start of a short foot race and the driver of a jinrikisha demonstrate these sorts of asymmetric behavior.

We can interpret the symmetries described in this paper in several ways. Firstly, they help us to control legged machines. The strategy we used to control running machines was built around the symmetry ideas expressed in this paper, and similar strategies may play a role in controlling more complicated running behaviors. For instance, reciprocating leg symmetry is important in making a quadruped leg gallop.

Symmetry also helps us to characterize and understand the behavior we observe in animals. Our analysis of the galloping cat shows that symmetry describes how the cat moves when it gallops, and we expect to find that the same symmetries describe the motions of other animals running with other gaits. Perhaps most important is the idea that symmetry and balance give us tools for dealing with a dynamic system, without requiring detailed solutions to intractable formulations. Symmetry implies that there are two parts that have opposing characteristics, just as balance requires equal and compensating forces and torques.

Finally, we should note that the symmetry approach splits the responsibility for the control of running into two parts. One relies solely on the intrinsic properties of the mechanical system. The other adjusts the leg position just once per stride, rather than using a servo to move each joint of the legged system along a prescribed trajectory. Once the foot has been positioned on each step, the mechanical system passively determines the details of the motion for the remainder of the stride. This approach depends upon having a passive nominal motion that is close to the desired behavior. In the present context, symmetry is a means of achieving the nominal motion. This sort of approach is most applicable to systems that perform repetitive behaviors, such as juggling and handwriting (Hollerbach, 1980).

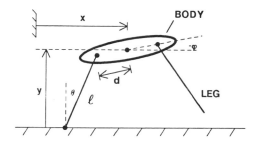

Figure 12 Model of two-legged planar system with separated hips. It can represent the lateral half of a quadruped viewed in the sagittal plane, or a biped viewed in the frontal plane.

6.0 Summary

Our main point is that symmetric motions of the body in space, and of the feet with respect to the body provide nominal motions for steady state locomotion. A control system for running can produce steady state behavior by choosing motions of the legs that give $x(t)$ and $\phi(t)$ odd symmetry, and $y(t)$ even symmetry. The leg motions chosen are themselves described by odd and even symmetries. This method applies to a number of sim-

ple legged configurations, and helps to describe the behavior of running animals.

The conditions for symmetric body motion can be stated simply: At a single point in time during the support period, the center of support must be located under the center of mass, the pitch angle of the body must be zero, and the vertical velocity of the body must be zero, $[\theta_j(t_0) + \theta_k(t_0) = 0,\ \phi(t_0) = 0,$ and $\dot{y}(t_0) = 0]$. When these conditions are satisfied the body follows a symmetric trajectory during the support interval.

The significance of these symmetric motions is that they permit a control system to manipulate the symmetry and skewness of the motion, rather than the detailed shape of the motion. When a system's behavior deviates from symmetry, the net acceleration of the system over one stride deviates from zero in a manageable way. The control task becomes one of manipulating these deviations.

In principle, a wide variety of natural running gaits can be achieved using body and leg motions that exhibit the symmetries described. These include the trot, the pace, the cantor, the gallop, the bound, the pronk, as well as intermediate forms of those gaits. Although we have plotted symmetry data only for the cat, we expect to find a wide variety of natural legged systems using nearly symmetric motions when they run.

Acknowledgements: This research was sponsored by a contract from the Defense Advanced Research Projects Agency (DoD), Systems Sciences Office, ARPA Order No. 4148, and by a grant from the System Development Foundation. I am grateful to Mary Wetzel for providing me with the cat film, and to Jeff Koechling for writing the computer programs used to digitize and process the data.

7.0 Appendix A: Equations of Motion for Planar Model

Equations of motion for planar model with two massless legs, and hips located a distance d from the body's center of mass, as shown in Figure 12:

$$m\ddot{x} = f_1 \sin\theta_1 + f_2 \sin\theta_2 - \frac{\tau_1}{\ell_1}\cos\theta_1 - \frac{\tau_2}{\ell_2}\cos\theta_2 \quad (16)$$

$$m\ddot{y} = f_1\cos + f_2\cos\theta_2 + \frac{\tau_1}{\ell_1}\sin\theta_1 + \frac{\tau_2}{\ell_2}\sin\theta_2 \quad (17)$$
$$- mg$$

$$I\ddot{\phi} = f_1 d\cos(\theta_1 - \phi) - \frac{\tau_1 d}{\ell_1}\sin(\phi - \theta_1) + \tau_1 + f_2 d\cos(\theta_2 - \phi) - \frac{\tau_2 d}{\ell_2}\sin(\phi - \theta_2) + \tau_2 \quad (18)$$

where

$x, y, \phi =$ are the horizontal, vertical, and angular positions of the body,

$\ell, \theta =$ are the length and orientation of the leg,

$\tau =$ is the hip torque, (positive τ accelerates body in positive ϕ direction),

$f =$ is the axial leg force (positive f separates body and ground),

$m =$ is the body mass,

$I =$ is the body moment of inertia, and

$g =$ is the acceleration of gravity.

8.0 Appendix B: Proof of Symmetric Leg Motion

In order to prove that symmetric body motion requires symmetric leg motion for one-legged case, we rewrite the equations of motion expressing each element of the leg motion as the sum of an even and odd part. For instance, the angle of the leg with respect to the vertical is $\theta = {}^e\theta + {}^o\theta$, where ${}^e\theta$ represents the even part, and ${}^o\theta$ the odd part. Also, replace ℓ with $1/({}^ez + {}^oz)$:

$$m\ddot{x} = ({}^ef + {}^of)\sin({}^e\theta + {}^o\theta) - \tau({}^ez + {}^oz)\cos({}^e\theta + {}^o\theta) \quad (19)$$

$$m\ddot{y} = ({}^ef + {}^of)\cos({}^e\theta + {}^o\theta) + \tau({}^ez + {}^oz)\sin({}^e\theta + {}^o\theta) - mg. \quad (20)$$

$$I\ddot{\phi} = {}^o\tau + {}^e\tau \quad (21)$$

From (21) τ must be odd, and because ϕ is odd, we assume $\ddot{\phi}$ is odd. In order to constrain the leg motion according to the symmetry of the body motion, set the even part of the right hand side of (19) to zero, and the odd part of the right hand side of (20) is also set to zero:

$$0 = {}^ef\sin{}^e\theta\cos{}^o\theta + {}^of\cos{}^e\theta\sin{}^o\theta + \tau{}^ez\sin{}^e\theta\sin{}^o\theta - \tau{}^oz\cos{}^e\theta\cos{}^o\theta. \quad (22)$$

$$0 = -{}^ef\sin{}^e\theta\sin{}^o\theta + {}^of\cos{}^e\theta\cos{}^o\theta + \tau{}^ez\sin{}^e\theta\cos{}^o\theta + \tau{}^oz\cos{}^e\theta\sin{}^o\theta. \quad (23)$$

A solution to (22) and (23) requires that

$$\tan{}^e\theta = \frac{\tau\,{}^oz}{{}^ef}$$

and

$$\tan{}^e\theta = -\frac{{}^of}{\tau\,{}^ez} \quad (24)$$

During the support interval the foot remains stationary with respect to the ground, so motion of the body with respect to the round dictates motion of the foot with respect to the body. Therefore, the symmetries of Equations (1)–(3) and the solutions to (24) also govern the trajectory of the foot with respect to the body, requiring that $x_f(t) - x_f(0) = -x_f(-t) + x_f(0)$ and $y_f(t) = y_f(-t)$, where (x_f, y_f) are the coordinates of the foot with respect to the body. The leg motion is symmetric if $x_f(0) = 0$. Since odd functions equal zero when $t = 0$, (24) requires that $^e\theta(t = 0) = 0$, implying that $x_f(0) = 0$. Hence $^e\theta = {}^o\ell = {}^of = 0$, leaving θ odd and ℓ and f even. They obey the leg symmetries given by (4) and (5).

References

Cavagna, G.A. (1970) The elastic bounce of the body. *Jrl. Appl. Physics*, 29:279–282.

Hildebrand, M. (1965) Symmetrical gaits of horses. *Science*, 150:701–708.

Hildebrand, M. (1966) Analysis of the symmetrical gaits of tetrapods. *Folia Biotheoretica*, 4:9–22.

Hildebrand, M. (1968) Symmetrical gaits of dogs in relation to body build. *Journal of Morphology*, 124:353–359.

Hildebrand, M. (1976) Analysis of tetrapod gaits: general considerations and symmetrical gaits. In: R.N. Herman, S. Grillner, P.S. Stein & D.G. Stuart (Eds.), *Neural Control of Locomotion*, NY: Plenum Press, pp. 203–236.

Hollerbach, J.M. (1980) "An oscillation theory of handwriting". Ph.D. dissertation, Artificial Intelligence Laboratory, Massachusetts Institute of Technology.

Raibert, M.H. (1984) Hopping in legged systems—modelling and simulation for the 2D one-legged case. *IEEE Transactions on Systems, Man, and Cybernetics*, 14(3):451–463.

Raibert, M.H. (1986) *Legged Robots that Balance*. Cambridge, MA: MIT Press.

Raibert, M.H. & Brown, H.B., Jr. (1984) Experiments in balance with a 2D one-legged hopping machine. *ASME Jrl. Dynamic Systems, Measurement, and Control*, 106(1):75–81.

Raibert, M.H., Brown, H.B., Jr. & Chepponis, M. (1984) Experiments in balance with a 3D one-legged hopping machine. *International Journal of Robotics Research*, 3(2):75–92.

Raibert, M.H., Chepponis, M. & Brown, H.B. Jr. (1986) Running on four legs as if they were one. *IEEE J. Robotics & Automation*, 2:70–82.

Raibert, M.H., Brown, H.B., Jr. & Murthy, S.S. (1984) 3-D balance using 2-D algorithms. *First Int'l. Symposium on Robotics Res.*, 1:279–301.

Stentz, A. (1983) Behavior during stance. In M. Raibert et al. (eds.), *Dynamically Stable Legged Locomotion—Third Annual Report*, Robotics Institute, Carnegie Mellon University, CMU-RI-TR-83-20, pp. 106–110.

Sutherland, I.E. (1983) *A Walking Robot*. The Marcian Chronicles, P.O. Box 10209, Pittsburgh, PA. 15232.

Wetzel, M.C., Atwater, A.E. & Stuart, D.G. (1976) Movements of the hindlimb during locomotion of the cat. Analysis of tetrapod gaits: general considerations and symmetrical gaits. In: R.N. Herman, S. Grillner, P.S. Stein, D.G. & Stuart (Eds.), *Neural Control of Locomotion*, New York: Plenum Press, pp. 99–136.

Adapted from "Running with symmetry", *Int. Jrl. Robotics Research*, 5:3–19, 1986.

VI

Future Directions

Future Directions

Natural Computation is an approach to understanding intelligent behavior that provides a bridge between the Cognitive and the Neural Sciences. Anatomy and morphology take on meaning only with insight as to function—what is being represented and how this representation may be computed and manipulated. Similarly, solutions to cognitive problems in perception, motor control, or reasoning must not remain in their abstract state, but should be certified by experiments that demonstrate their applicability to machine or biological systems. Computation, psychophysics and neurophysiology are among the most useful tools needed to build such bridges. So perhaps the single most important direction for future work is to continue to show how cognitive objectives can be explicitly translated into hardware. This will require many more examples than the present few selections, not only in vision, but also in sound and force interpretation as well as language and reasoning.

One can also ask what specific issues are the most pressing? Where are our lacunae? I have chosen seven areas:

1.0 Sound Interpretation.

2.0 Temporal-Spatial Integration of Knowledge.

3.0 Scene Parsing.

4.0 Category Formation.

5.0 From Pictures to Language.

6.0 Space-frames.

7.0 Neural Architectures.

In advance, apologies must be made for the vagueness of the discussion. However, if each topic could have been presented more concisely, and coherently, then there would be no lacunae.

1.0 Sound Interpretation

Understanding the competences of auditory systems is one of the most neglected and virgin areas of study. We have too easily cast our ideas about hearing in terms of algorithms and mechanisms. Consequently, we lack a full understanding of the conditions and constraints that will allow successful inferences and those conditions that will not. Even our selections suffer this failing. Understanding the competence of the inference process requires knowledge about the world, its laws and constraints, much of which has not yet been incorporated into auditory theory. Performance can be duplicated without an understanding of the system or its environment. Competence can not. More effort should be made to understand the constraints upon acoustical processes in the world which permit the reliable inference of sounds from signals, thereby deepening our understanding of hearing.

2.0 Temporal-Spatial Integration of Knowledge

Almost all animals have foveae—a region of high acuity and complex visual processing. Unlike a camera, which records the en-

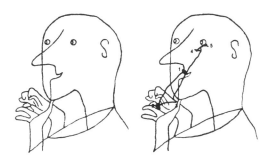

Figure 1 Sequence of fixation positions when an observer first inspects an adaptation of Klee's drawing. During recognition, a similar sequence is also used, suggesting that the cartoon may be encoded by a particular sequence of sub-patterns and their relative dispositions. (From Noton & Stark, 1971.)

tire landscape with equal fidelity, our fovea darts from region to region inspecting only certain portions of the scene. The visual input thus is a super-imposed sequence of small disconnected snapshots, which are somehow integrated into a coherent picture.

Noton & Stark (1971) illustrate this point with their measurements of eye movement positions when a subject inspects drawings such as Klee's cartoon (Figure 1). Remarkably, the sequence is similar for most observers. What directs the eye to these particular regions? How are these regions then put together to create an internal effigy? Or, more generally, how can a sequence of snapshots or partial descriptions of an object or scene be unified to yield a more complete description?

A key ingredient to the unification of a collection of snapshots must certainly be the exploitation of constraints about the

world. This point is illustrated by one particular example: Parks' slit phenomenon. Imagine looking from your office to the corridor when your door is only slightly ajar. There is no problem in recognizing the people who pass, although only a very small fragment of the person is visible at any one instant (Figure 2). The result is as if we had tracked the object all along (Morgan et al., 1982; Rock, 1981). Our ability to integrate the temporal-spatial information is remarkable—a hyperacuity (Burr, 1979; Fahle & Poggio, 1984). But the accomplishment succeeds only when the input satisfies constraints such as objects moving at constant velocity (Shimojo & Richards, 1986).

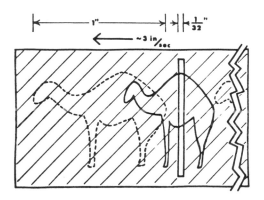

Figure 2 Passing a camel through the eye of a needle. A simple outline figure (dashed line) is passed behind a slit in an opaque screen. If it passes in approximately 1/2 sec., it will be seen briefly in the region of the slit, to move slightly, and to be foreshortened (solid line). The foreshortening increases with the speed of its passage until only a blur is seen. At slow speeds, the figure may be identified but will not be seen as a whole. (From Parks, 1965.)

Even very mundane "unconscious" inferences about the shape of objects and their material composition are achieved by collecting pieces of information via a sequence of eye contacts (see Chapter 2), and not by one single direct regard. The need for multiple inspections of the simple vase to determine its composition becomes obvious when we recognize that the complexity of the image-intensity equation (24-1) prohibits solution in its full blown form. Instead, pieces of this equation are first solved for simplified conditions by looking at special regions of the scene, such as highlights or occluding contours. Each of these partial descriptions is then somehow integrated into a more complete and coherent description. How can this be done? What are the general properties of such a unification framework?

Integrating a sequence of spatially "disconnected" images into a coherent whole is not necessarily a problem confined to vision. The auditory system transforms the acoustic input into a spatial pattern of spectral bands. Objects represented in this spatial acoustic-image come and go, and hence their pieces may also appear as a discontinuous pattern, embedded in competing patterns. Touch sensing also often suffers the same problem, for example, when we change our grasp of an object. Thus, even if we assume that the observer has successfully parsed the input so he can "track" one object while disregarding others (see Section 3), there still remains the problem of integrating partial, often discontinuous, spatial-temporal fragments of information.

At the level of algorithm and implementation, the problems raised by integrating a sequence of spatially disconnected, partial descriptions are perhaps still more obvious. Returning to the two special cases of inspecting Klee's drawing and slit viewing, we are drawn immediately to two kinds of mechanistic solutions: First, the sequence of incoming spatial information might simply be shifted over time through a shift register, with the readout triggered by beginning and end markers—such as a saccade or a novel input. The similarity between the results of eye movements or "attentional" shifts in recovering fragmental shapes in slit viewing experiments would then easily be explained. The registers also could provide a mechanism for "attentional" shifts directed to one side or the other of the midline or horizontal meridian (in consideration of the anatomy of V2 and MT). The second proposed implementation is more abstract. Rather than a physical shift in neural activity propagating through a register, each fragment of spatial input between two markers could be given directional tags showing its topological relation to the preceding and succeeding fragment. These tags would allow a network description to be built, similar to the "ring" proposed by Noton & Stark (1971). Obviously in vision, the directional tags would have to accept either eye movement or retinal position as inputs. Whether either of these proposals has merit or not is almost irrelevant at this stage of our understanding. My point is that here is an extremely important problem which is effortlessly solved every instant or our active lives. Yet we have no understanding of this competence, and only some feeble ideas about mechanisms.

3.0 Scene Parsing

The preceding section assumed that an object or event had somehow been identified as its own entity. Yet in practice, optical and acoustic images contain a clutter and complex assortment of "objects", most partly hidden or obscured (Fischler & Firschein, 1987). How do we define an "object" and then identify one object as distinct from another? Or, given that distinct "objects" have been identified, how do we assign relations between objects, such as when we attach the rotating wheel to the translating cart, or the hand or foot to a person's face. This problem is not one of image segmentation, such as identifying each region of the scene and completing occluded contours. Rather, it is a kind of grouping problem, but not one which explicitly links all blue patches of the sky seen through a tree. Successful grouping operations should capture the meaningful relations[1] between objects or surface properties. Linking patches of blue tells us nothing about the sky, for the image structures of these patches are governed by the tree- or cloud-process.

Such arguments suggest a constraint-based approach to scene parsing, where the constraints are meaningful world properties, processes or relations. Barrow & Tenenbaum's (1978) intrinsic images and Marr's (1978) 2 1/2 D sketch sketch is a step in this direction. Let each intrinsic image conduct its special grouping operations, collecting data that satisfied a common constraint. The scheme is more obvious in hearing. Consider the classical cocktail party problem. One speaker's voice is isolated (in part) from another by its pitch and modulations, perhaps aided by visual observations of mouth movements. Just as the auditory system locks onto a feature common to all sequences

of an acoustic signal, so may the visual system (especially when integrating foveal snapshots!). A material assertion is made by combining information from contiguous regions that share the same color, for example. Or the slit viewing problem is "solved" by imposing a constant velocity constraint upon the sequence of fragmented inputs. Similarly, explorations by touch sensing with one hand may use as a unification constraint the fact that the object is grasped by the other hand (or simply is viewed!). In each case the perceptual system appears to use the occurrence of a particular (measurable) world property as the basis for choosing a framework that selects and integrates incoming information. Let me call such a framework a "constraint space".

Perhaps one hint as to the nature of these constraint spaces comes from recent neurophysiology. There are as many as a dozen different, anatomically distinct visual areas beyond the primary cortical receiving area 17 (Van Essen & Maunsell, 1983). One of these seems especially partial to movement (MT), another to color (V4) and still another for shape (IT) (Allman et al., 1985; Gross et al., 1972; Schein et al., 1982; Zeki, 1983). However, rather than simply encoding motion or color as a feature, is it possible that these areas are the constraint spaces we seek? In particular, if areas such as these each act as a constraint space, then a response would be contingent upon the occurrence of a constraint (such as directional motion) appearing in conjunction with other features (such as orientation, color, size or whatever). In effect, each area could then serve as a unifying framework for

---

[1]The definition of a "meaningful relation" is elusive, and, of course constitutes part of the problem. My intent is to imply the goals or processes underlying an object's structure or behavior (Witkin & Tenenbaum, 1983).

straint rule. It is then not difficult to imagine building a hierarchy of increasingly complex constraint rules, each of which would be embodied in a higher cortical area. At times, these higher cortical areas may in their turn impose their particular specifications selectively upon lower level inputs.[2] Activity in each area, therefore, would occur when proper conjunctions of features were present, with the constraint rule being shared by all. The principal difference between the proposal here and the earlier ideas about intrinsic images is that each image (or area) would allow for a range of feature responses outside its intrinsic property, which would serve principally as a 2 1/2 D constraint upon grouping.

Imagine now the problem of interpreting and parsing the scene as a whole. Is it possible that there exist areas which serve as representations for more cognitive entities, such as faces, crowds, or even action-based flow fields? A hint of evidence that we indeed have such areas appears in the literature. "Face detectors" and other high-level shapes have been noted in the temporal areas by neurophysiologists (Baylis et al., 1985; Gross et al., 1972) and action-based hallucinations or illusions have been reported by neurologists (Teuber et al., 1960). In our dynamic world, it is not difficult to see that high level cognitive features or events could be organized into "flow fields" or "flow lines". Such "flow lines" would have sources and sinks which could serve to characterize the relations between events and actions. For example, people entering (or leaving) the main entrance to a mall not only move toward (or away) from

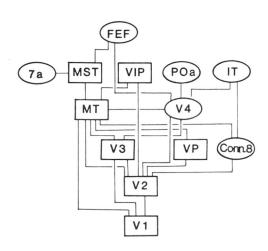

Figure 3 The hierarchy of macaque cortical visual areas based on the laminar distributions of projections. Each visual area is assigned to the level immediately above the highest area from which it receives a forward projection. *Rectangles* indicate well established visual areas. This scheme is likely to be modified since there are undoubtedly more connections which have yet to be identified, and levels containing two or more areas may ultimately be split. Projections that are weak or inconsistent have not been included. The connections shown and the laminar distributions used to assign levels in the hierarchy are from Maunsell & Van Essen, 1983. For a more complex map and a review, see Maunsell & Newsome, 1987.

coordinating and integrating fragments of the scene which shared the same con-

[2] In effect, such feedback would constitute "constraint satisfaction" (see Mackworth, 1987). Note that the constraint-space role proposed for the cortical areas greatly facilitates recognition because exponential search times for "matches-to-models" could be eliminated (Grimson, 1987).

this entrance along established routes, but also face that way. Flow (or postures) outside these routes are immediately noticed. Such cognitive maps often have very simple image correlates, which could serve as constraints imposed upon representations built in the more cognitive cortical areas.

To recap, the primary goal of perception should be to understand the significance of the scene, not to identify each flower, shrub, or patch of blue. To accomplish this task, we need a better understanding of how objects should be defined and represented and how (partial) object descriptions can be related to one another. In this regard, does the notion of an integrating framework based upon constraints (regularities) of the world have merit? Need such a framework be tied to a pre-formed model (such as the ODL or a velocity space), or can a more flexible scheme be devised which includes generative models also (Johnson, 1987; Smith, 1984; Tidhar, 1987)? If so, what principles underly such generative models, and how do they allow new integrating frameworks to be built using new constraint rules?

4.0 Category Formation

Implicit in scene parsing and understanding is that there exists a framework within which the scene can be interpreted. One ingredient of this framework must be a categorical representation. We don't just perceive things; rather, we perceive trees, dogs, people, cars, houses, etc. Much evidence suggests that object recognition begins a particular level of detail—at the so-called Basic Level Category (Rosch, 1978). Recently, Bobick (1987) has shown why there is an advantage in beginning at this level: it represents a compromise between being able to identify an object, given a list of features as inputs, versus being able to specify an object's features given its category. For example, if we began object recognition at the level of our dog "Pluto", we would know a lot about the object, but would also require many more features to identify this category than simply to know the object was an animal or specifically a dog.

Category formation presents two difficult problems. First, how should the features be selected in the first place? We encountered a similar problem in the earlier discussion of Scene Parsing. Second, how are new categories formed? To date, neither of these problems has adequate answers (However, see Bobick, 1987.) Perhaps one insight to feature selection is the Principal of Natural Modes, appealed to earlier in this book. A clustering of objects in the world might satisfy a particular set of constraints which lead to a preferred set of features that successfully categorize these objects initially. (See Richards & Bobick, 1988.) On the other hand, it is also clear that we have the ability to create new features for categorization in special tasks—such as identifying corals, enemy airplanes, or cars.

Regarding the second problem of learning new categories, I am intrigued by the Bongard Problems (see Figure 4). Here, after reviewing the six examples, once one realizes the difference between the two sets, the conclusion seems inevitable, very strong and unique. But this need not be the case. Rather, our "solution" matches that of Bongard's only because we share the same feature language. What is its grammar? Clearly new categories must obey these constraints. Need this imply that our selection of possible constraint rules is limited?

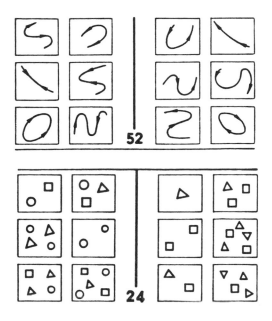

Figure 4 Two Bongard Problems. How do each of the left set of six panels differ from each of the right set of six? Is there more than one solution? (From Bongard, 1970.)

5.0 From Pictures to Language

Visual Imagery drives language (Berger, 1972). For a child, a word rarely has meaning independent of a pictorial representation. Words are simply tokens attached to perceptual representations. This would imply that the structure of our perceptual representations also provides a framework for language, through which we communicate our observations and thoughts (Jackendorf, 1987). Such arguments underlie Selection 12, From Waltz to Winston, which develops an Object Description Language (ODL) from visual representations. Such a language is model-based, rather than one based upon meaning.

Therefore it is still an incomplete bridge from vision to language, where thematic and contextual constraints are routine in everyday linguistic interpretation. How then can we move from visual representations to others more abstract and suitable for arbitrary cognitive descriptions? Such a bridge seems extremely worthwhile, for then the different expressive powers of such higher level languages, for example the incorporation of quantification, could be utilzed for manipulating and interpreting pictorial descriptions (Genesereth & Nilsson, 1987; Pylyshyn, 1980). What kinds of such high-level conceptual languages might be useful? What are their tokens and data structure? Perhaps some insight can be obtained from art and aesthetics. Aesthetics, it seems to me, is a very high-level, conceptual language. Art is one form of its instantiation. When we view a painting (or listen to music) one of our objectives is to understand the intent of the composer. The organization and structure of the art is critical to this interpretation process. Again, like the Bongard problems, the artist and observer must share a common set of rules or grammar for a unique and "correct" interpretation. The artist aids the interpretation process by creating cognitive lines of flow, sources and sinks which emphasize his key objects and their relation to one another and to the scene as a whole. A dynamics is implied, such as by the horrified or curious expressions on the faces of a crowd all focused together at a suffering Christ. If the Christ is now painted out of the scene, the painting becomes imbalanced, strange, and incomprehensible (Cerillo, 1972). Something is missing. Thus, the objects of our attention are not simply sculptures, but rather seem more likely to be dynamic entities whose potential for action and reaction are much more important than their actual structure. Is meaning drawn from the intensities of these potentials? If so, then our earlier problem of Scene Parsing becomes quite difficult and perhaps intractable for decades. Yet, on the more positive side, an effort in this direction may bear fruit and fill several lacunae, many still unknown.

6.0 Space-Frames

We move freely about our world, yet few rarely are lost. How is this map created and updated? Our eyes can move independently of our heads, our heads independently of our bodies, yet we have no trouble whatsoever in coordinating our retinal, auditory, vestibular and egocentric frames, not only with each other, but also to the external world even as we move about. Many have worked on this problem [see Arbib & House (1987) and Howard & Templeton (1966) for overviews], and there is a wealth of both psychophysical and physiological data. But we have no computational theory of how the separate, disjoint space-frames are integrated into one stable structure. Perhaps the earliest are the reafferance proposals of MacKay (1956), Teuber (1960), and Von Holst & Mittelstaedt (1950). But in retrospect, these seem to me too much like the brute force approach adopted for weapons systems like the cruise missile. Can nature be so clumsy?

Many very simple biological systems seem to solve the space-frame problem with ease. Consider the wasp, who finds his nest after a seemingly haphazard tour. How does he do it? Perhaps one solution would be to identify key features as "landmarks" to which other signs could be related. The memory would store a network or graph of landmarks, indicating the expected direction of one from its neighbors, each carrying its own local coordinate frame presumably based on its distinctive features (plus gravity?). Such a network would be similar to the one proposed by Koenderink & van Doorn (1977, 1979, 1987b) for shape. Adjacent nodes represent the next expected "view" or landmark if one were to move in that particular direction (see Chapter 2). Viewed in this light, the Space-Frame problem then becomes identical to that of Temporal-Spatial Integration, where successive fixations must be spatially encoded. Imagine walking into a room. Why shouldn't the door of entry be the landmark to which the structures of primary interest in the room are related? Or, if not, then perhaps an unusual permanent fixture of the room, such as a picture window or fireplace? At a larger spatial frame, the entry of the room would then be the link to its relation to other rooms in the dwelling. Whoever would spatially relate the fireplace in one room to the faucet in a friend's kitchen down the block? Or who provides clear directions without landmarks? Our spatial frames seem organized primarily through a tangled (hierarchical?) network of local, topologically correct relations between significant and unusual landmarks (Lynch, 1960). These in turn provide a useful way of linking the nodes of the net in space or time (see Levitt et al., 1987). This would imply that the coordination of our separate space-frames should be by registration of common landmarks (perhaps at parent nodes), not by metrical transformations.

Figure 5 A wasp appears to find its nest by noting significant landmarks, in this case the pattern formed by the twig and three pine cones (upper left). As this pattern is altered, the wasp's approach becomes disturbed, depending upon the rearrangement of the landmark's features. (From Tinbergen, 1972.)

Demonstrating this point, if true, will also impact several other problem areas in perception, and perhaps even language, and reasoning.[3]

7.0 Neural Architectures

The above lacunae are presented largely as problems of understanding competence, although of course their resolution will require aid from psychophysics, neuro-

physiology and computer science. Here I point out an open problem at the level of mechanism and implementation. (For other problems at this level, see Reichardt & Poggio, 1981.)

The cortex is not randomly wired. It has a structure which restricts how neurons can communicate with one another. For example, it is not a 3D tesselation or array, but rather a stack of 2D layers with interpenetrating columns. Many structures in the brain, including the retina, have this general type of organization. What does such a geometry imply for the complexity of its computations? What kind of input-output relations are possible? Is there the possibility of creating a calculus of connectivity which will guide the functional interpretation of neural architectures?

Sutherland & Oestreicher (1973) were among the first to address this issue. They showed that the number of crossings made by wires on a printed circuit board indicates the rough size of the board. More generally, the problem can be viewed as one in Graph Theory (Temperley, 1981), a tack taken recently by Roe (1987) in an analysis of the connectivity of the visual cortex. To illustrate her approach, consider the effect of imposing the constraint that the number of crossings per volume of striate cortex be minimized, and that all connections lie in a plane and are either along the 2D layers or vertical to them. How many networks are possible? Figure 6 illustrates her solution.

A second potential constraint upon neural architectures may be the need to reconnect the network, such as during attentional gating or simply as a basis for learning. Earlier, in our discussion of ani-

---

[3]A still more complicated, but more general representation, using a network of "threads" has been proposed by Vaina, 1987. See also Langacker (1986) for linguistic analogues.

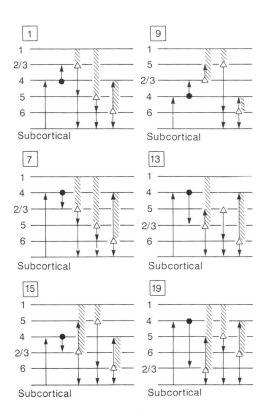

Figure 6 Six of 24 possible arrangements of the five distinctly different layers of the striate cortex. The fewest crossings of lamina are for the first network which is the observed arrangement. (From Roe, 1987.)

mal gaits, we saw the need to reprogram the spinal networks which control the sequence of footfalls when the animal wishes to go from a walk to a trot or gallop, for example. In vision, the tremendous richness of discrimination capabilities suggests also that each early visual network might be able to compute at different times quite different properties (such as curvature or separation), depending upon the task (Koenderink, 1987a; Tsotsos, 1987). This

seems especially true for hyperacuities (Wilson & Richards, 1988). How does this need affect the neural architecture and its connectivity pattern?

The above two examples are only meant to be illustrative, to point out the potential richness of exciting problems in theoretical neuroanatomy.

References

Allman, J., Miezin, F. & McGuiness, E.L. (1985) Directions and velocity-specific responses from beyond the classical receptive field in the middel temporal visual area (MT). *Perception*, 14:105–126.

Arbib, M.A. & House, D.H. (1987) Depth and detours: an essay on visually guided behavior. In M.A. Arbib & A.R. Hanson (eds.) *Vision, Brain and Cooperative Computation*, Cambridge, Mass.: Bradford Books, MIT Press, chapter 3.

Barrow, H.G. & Tenenbaum, J.M. (1978) Recovering intrinsic scene characteristics from images. In A. Hanson & E. Riseman (eds.), *Computer Vision Systems*, New York: Academic Press.

Baylis, G.C., Rolls, E.T. & Leonard, C.M. (1985) Selectivity between faces in the responses of a population of neurons in the cortex in the superior temporal sulcus of the monkey. *Brain Res.*, 342:91–102.

Berger, J. (1972) *Ways of Seeing.* London: British Broadcasting Corp.

Bobick, A. (1987) "Natural object catigorization". Ph.D. dissertation, Massachusetts Institute of Technology (to appear as MIT A.I. Lab. TR 1001).

Bongard, M. (1970) *Pattern Recognition.* New York: Spartan Books.

Burr, D.C. (1979) Acuity for apparent vernier offset. *Vis. Res.*, 19:835–837.

Cerillo, M. (1972) Personal communication.

Fahle, M. & Poggio, T. (1984) Visual hyperacuity: spatio-temporal interpolation in human vision. In S. Ullman & W. Richards (eds.), *Image Understanding 1984*, Norwood, N.J.: Ablex.

Fischler, M.A. & Firschein, O. (1987) *Readings in Computer Vision: Issues, Problems, Principles, and Paradigms.* Los Altos, Calif.: Morgan Kaufman.

Genesereth, M.R. & Nilsson, N.J. (1987) *Logical Foundations of Artificial Intelligence.* Los Altos, Calif.: Morgan Kaufman.

Gross, C.G., Rocha-Miranda, C.E. & Bender, D.B. (1972) Visual properties of neurons in inferotemporal cortex of the monkey. *J. Neurophysiol.*, 35:96–111.

Howard, I.P. & Templeton, W.B. (1966) *Human Spatial Orientation.* London: Wiley.

Jackendorf, R. (1987) On Beyond Zebra: the relation of linguistic and visual information cognition. *Cognition*, 26:89–114.

Johnson, M. (1987) Attribute-value logic and the theory of grammar. Dept. of Linguistics, Stanford University. (To appear as CSLI Lecture Notes Series.)

Koenderink, J. (1987a) Geometry of the front-end of a visual system. Presented at Harvard College, November 1987. (See also Koenderink, J.J. & van Doorn, A.J., Representation of local geometry in the visual system. *Biol. Cyberntics*, 55:367–375.)

Koenderink, J. (1987b) The internal representation of solid shape. In W. Richards & S. Ullman (eds.), *Image Understanding 1985- 86*, Norwood, N.J.: Ablex.

Koenderink, J.J. & van Doorn, A.J. (1977) How an ambulant observer can construct a model of the environment from the geometrical structure of the visual inflow. In G. Hauske & E. Butenandt (eds.), *Kybernike*, Munich: Oldenburg.

Koenderink, J.J. & van Doorn, A.J. (1979) The internal representation of solid shape with respect to vision. *Biol. Cybern.*, 32:211–216.

Langacker, R. (1986) An introduction to cognitive grammer. *Cognitive Science*, 10:1–40.

Levitt, T.S., Lawton, D.T., Chelberg, D.M. & Nelson, P.C. (1987) Qualitative landmark-based path planning and following. *Proc. AAAI'87*, Los Angeles, Calif.: Morgan Kaufman.

Lynch, K. (1960) *The Image of the City.* Cambridge, Mass.: MIT Press.

MacKay, D.M. (1956) Towards an information-flow model of human behavior. *Int. Jrl. Psychol.*, 47:30–43.

Mackworth, A.K. (1987) Constraint satisfaction. In S. Shapiro (ed.) *Encyclopedia of Artificial Intelligence*, New York: J. Wiley & Sons, pp. 205–211.

Marr, D. (1978) Representing visual information. *Lectures on Mathematics in the Life Sciences*, 10:101–

Acknowledgment: Mark Johnson provided an excellent bangboard that helped to hone these directions, and he also provided a critical contribution regarding the Landmark ideas, and their value to scene parsing and spatial-temporal integration, as well as to the more obvious space-frame problems.

180. Reprinted in A.R. Hanson & E.M. Riseman (eds.), *Computer Vision Systems*, New York: Academic Press (1979).

Maunsell, J.H.R. & Newsome, W.T. (1987) Visual processing in monkey extrastriate cortex. *Ann. Rev. Neurosci.*, 10:363–401.

Maunsell, J. & Van Essen, D. (1983) Connections of the middle temporal visual area (MT) and their relationship to a cortical hierarchy in the macaque monkey. *Jrl. Neurosci.*, 12:2563–2587.

Morgan, M.J., Findley, J.M. & Watt, R.J. (1982) Aperture viewing: a review and synthesis. *Quart. Jrl. Exp. Psychol.*, 34A, 211–233.

Noton, D. & Stark, L. (1971) Eye movements and visual perception. *Sci. Amer.*, June.

Parks, T.E. (1965) Post-retinal visual storage. *Amer. Jrl. Psychol.*, 78:145–148.

Pylyshyn, Z.W. (1980) *Computation and Cognition: Toward a Foundation for Cognitive Science.* Cambridge, Mass.: Bradford Books, MIT Press.

Reichardt, W.E. & Poggio, T. (1981) *Theoretical Approaches in Neurobiology.* Cambridge, Mass.: MIT Press.

Richards, W. & Bobick, A. (1988) Playing Twenty Questions with Nature. In Z. Pylyshyn (ed.), *Computational Processes in Human Vision*, Norwood, N.J.: Ablex.

Rock, I. (1981) Anorthoscopic perception. *Sci. Amer.*, 244(3):145–153.

Rosch, E. (1978) Principle of categorization. In *Cognition and Categories*, E. Rosch & B. Lloyd (eds.), Hillsdale, N.J.: Erlbaum Assoc., pp. 28–49.

Roe, A.W. (1987) "Constraints determining the laminar organization of primary visual cortex (Area 17)". Term paper in Natural Computation, MIT.

Schein, S.J., Marrocco, R.T. & DeMonasterio, F.M. (1982) Is there a high concentration of color-selective cells in Area V4 of monkey visual cortex? *J. Neurophysiol.*, 47:193–213.

Shimojo, S. & Richards, W. (1986) "Seeing" shapes that are almost totally occluded: a new look at Parks's camel. *Percept. & Psychophys.*, 39:418–426.

Smith, A.R. (1984) Plants, fractals and formal languages. *Computer Graphics*, 18:1–10 (SIGGRAPH'84).

Sutherland, I.E. & Oestreicher, D. (1973) How big should a printed circuit be? *IEEE Trans. on Computers*, C-22(5):537–542.

Temperley, H.N.V. (1981) *Graph Theory and Application.* New York: Halsted Press.

Teuber, H.-L. (1960) Perception. In J. Field, H.W. Magorn & V.E. Hall (eds.), *Handbook of Physiology*, Vol. III, Chapt. LXV, Baltimore: Williams & Wilkins.

Teuber, H.-L., Battersby, W.S. & Bender, M.B. (1960) *Visual Field Defects After Penetrating Missle Wounds of the Brain.* Cambridge, Mass.: Harvard Univ. Press.

Tidhar, A. (1987) Using a structured world model in flexible recognition of two dimensional patterns. Univ. Penn. Dept. Computer & Info. Science Report MS-C15-87-104 GRASP LAB 125.

Tinbergen, N. (1972) *The Animal in Its World.* Cambridge, Mass.: Harvard Univ. Press.

Tsotos, J.K. (1987) A "complex level" analyis of vision. *Proc. ICCV'87*, The Comp. Society of the IEEE, Order No. 777, pp. 346–355.

Vaina, L. (1987) Towards a computational theory of semantic memory. In L. Vaina & J. Hintikka (eds.), *Cognitive Constraints on Communication*, Dordrecht, Holland: Reidel, pp. 97–113.

Van Essen, D.C. & Maunsell, J.H.R. (1983) Hierarchical organization and functional streams in the visual cortex. *Trends in Neurosci.*, 6:370–375.

von Holst, E. & Mittelstaedt, H. (1950) Das Reafferenzprinzip. *Naturwissenschaften*, 37:464–476.

Witkin, A.P. & Tenenbaum, J.M. (1983) On the role of structure in vision. In J. Beck, B. Hope & A. Rosenfeld (eds.), *Human and Machine Vision*, New York: Academic Press, pp. 481–543.

Wilson, H. & Richards, W. (1988) In preparation.

Zeki, S.M. (1983) The distribution of wavelength and orientation selective cells in different areas of monkey visual cortex. *Proc. Roy. Soc. Lond. (Biol.)*, 217:449–470.

Problems
in Natural Computation

1-1   A British cryptologist has sent you a communication whose intensity values are given below. What is the message? Important! Show how you proceeded to solve this problem. What assumptions did you make along the way? How did you know your assumptions were correct? The signal: 0, .1, .2, 1.2, .5, 0, 2.3, .1, 1.9, 0, .9, 0, .5, 1.8, .5, 0, .9, 0, 1.9, .1, 2.3, 0, .5, 1.2, .2, .1, 0 . . .

1-2   The following signal is received from outer space. What is the message? Again, as in problem 1-1, state why you think your answer is correct. The signal is 00000000101010011101001010100000000. What is the probability of this being a random event? (Hint: the number of events in the message is important.)

1-3   How many narrow-band acoustic channels are needed to isolate a known narrow-band signal heard against a background of noise? Did you impose any constraint on the nature of the noise spectrum?

1-4   Given a problem in Euclidian plane geometry, such as determining the area of a triangle, identify the components at each of the three different levels of your solution: Theory of Competence; Representation & Algorithm; and Mechanism. Is there any part of your answer which is analogous to conducting a psychophysical experiment? If not, can you develop an analog? (Hint: consider the importance of your tools for measurement.)

1-5   What is the significant difference between "seeing" with the eye + brain versus "seeing" by television, each of which "takes a picture of the world".

1-6   How many cylindrical branches of a tree are needed to recover the direction of the sun? Assume that each branch is in a plane containing the axis to the trunk.

1-7   Label an impossible triangle using the Waltz set of edges.

1-8   Enumerate all possible junctions for the edge of a folded or wrinkled sheet, such as a curtain. Use the same labels as in the primitive Waltz set, plus necessary supplements (Huffman, 1971).

1-9   In Chapter 1, Section 4, there are two simple degenerate viewing conditions. What are they?

2-1   Your are viewing one vertex of a cube. Graph the observed image-intensities along a line that cuts through one of the visible edges of the cube. Similarly, graph the image-intensity profile along a line that cuts through a sphere. Consider both a point illuminant (such as the sun) as well as lighting typical of a cloudy day. Assume matter surfaces.

2-2   You are a cockroach and cracks are your shelter. Your goal is to find "cracks" using image intensity information. To solve this problem, first attempt to define what a crack is in the world. Then consider how the properties or 3D shape of a crack will

P

affect the observed image intensities. Draw a plot of the image intensities versus position as seen by the roach. Is there something distinctive about a crack that makes this image different from a shadow or surface marking, such as a scratch. Can multiple views or forward motion be the cockroach be useful? (See Walker, 1986.)

3-1   Prepare a table like that of Chapter 2, Figure 7, illustrating the types of edges which show hits (correct identification), misses, false alarms, and correct rejections for the accretion-deletion algorithm.

3-2   A flying object casts a shadow on the ground. Will the accretion-deletion method detect the moving shadow? Why? What will be the behavior of the algorithm if presented with a moving transparent object? How would you modify the algorithm to distinguish between moving shadows, transparent objects and opaque objects?

4-1   Show all the different-shaped profiles resulting from the convolution of a balanced 1D difference-of-gaussian filter with a bar-shaped (rectangular) intensity profile. What if your filter is a rectified version so its values are either $-1/2$, 0 or 1?

4-2   An interior shadow (as opposed to an exterior one) is defined as a shadowed region surrounding a relatively small illuminated patch, such as when sunlight reaches the ground after passing through dense foliage. What 2D image intensity profile will be common to many interior shadows? (Hint: consider a camera.)

4-3   What is the maximum difference in percent between a balanced difference-of-Gaussian filter (with excitatory and inhibitory space constants differing $3\times$) and the nearest equivalent second-derivative of a Gaussian filter? (Consider only one-dimensional filters.) An estimate based on a graph of the filters is acceptable.

4-4   Show that in the limit as the space constant of the Gaussian approaches zero, the two operators of problem 4-3 become identical.

4-5   Describe three algorithms for identifying an image contour as arising from an occluding edge.

5-1   Construct a neural network that will respond both to a solid occluding edge and to an edge created by phase-shifting a grating, as illustrated in Figure 5-3A. Use simple on-center-off-surround type units (or their complements) as inputs.

5-2   An illusory Kaniza contour need not be straight (see Figure 5-1A). If the straight edges of the Pacman mouths are to create a curved illusory contour, certain restrictions must be placed on the angles the separate Pacman edges make to one another. Propose a plausible constraint that will apply to curved illusory contours and derive the conditions the two visible "contour inducing" edges must satisfy. Does your solution specify a unique illusory contour? (Hint: one answer is related to mechanisms for computing curvature and symmetry. Consider the angles made between the two inducing edges and the chord joining their endpoints.)

5-3   In the previous problem, calculate the locus (equation) of an ellipse tangent to two separate Pacman edges such that the ellipse is a slanted view of a circle whose chord is the line to the mid-points of the two edges, with the direction of slant lying along this chord. How does this scheme compare with that of Brady & Yuille (Selection 8)? (See also Horn, 1981.)

6-1   Prove that there are only five possible codon types.

6-2   Prove that the binary codon representation is complete (almost!).

6-3   What are the transformation rules for converting the binary version of a smooth codon string to its mirror image?

6-4   Construct a table of the allowable smooth joins of strings having three codons. (Omit the infinity codon.) How many smooth, closed codon triples are there?

7-1   Modify Hoffman's finite state machine to include the (infinity) straight-line codon type.

7-2   There are three different scale problems that arise when implementing curvature-based descriptions of image contours. What are they?

8-1   A bunch of leaves have fallen on the ground, and have been blown in a turbulent gust so their orientations are random. What is the distribution of the orientations of their major axes as seen a) from directly above, b) from a 45 degree angle of slant, c) from a very shallow angle of grazing view? (Witkin, 1981.)

8-2   Show that there is a unique orthographic projection into the image plane of a trapezoid slanted in space. Do all quadrulaterals have a unique planar interpretation as a trapezoid?

9-1   Calculate the 3D part-boundary locus for the parallel sinusoids of Figure 3 (or Figure 7). Is this locus along the extrema of curvature of the 2D projections of the sinusoids?

9-2   As the amplitude of the parallel sinusoids in Figure 5 increases, eventually the perceived depth of the surface collapses. Suggest a constraint which imposes a limitation on the observed depth for these images. (Hint: note that the left panels of Figure 5 can be interpreted as two oppositely inclined ridges divided at the locus of inflection points of the sinusoids.)

9-3   Given a cylindrical surface with lines of curvature drawn in that intersect at angle (β) in the image plane. What is the allowable range of tilts for any given (β) which ranges from $\pi/2$ to π? What are the allowable slants over the same range of (β)?.

9-4   Calculate the relation between the virtual binocular image of a specularity and the curvature of the surface. Simpler version: show the relation between the sign of observed disparity relative to the surface and the convex/concave curvature.

10-1   Identify the rim, contour, and outline for the simple arch shown in Figure 12-3.

10-2   Show all different topological views of a pear-shaped object, drawing in the rim for each view. (Hint: there are seven basic views.)

11-1   For problem 10-2, draw a graph (or network) showing the transition from one topologically different view to the next as the pear is rotated.

P

11-2   Let n be the number of parabolic (flexional) points on a silhouette. How many possible non-generic pairings of these points are there? How many (generic) pairings are there if none of the curves connecting the points are allowed to cross another? (Beusmans et al., 1987.)

11-3   Consider the Gauss map of shape Q12. What will be the maximum number of coverings (i.e. how many different surface normal vectors can map into the same point on the Gaussian sphere)?

11-4   Extend the taxonomy of 3D parts begun in Section 7 by defining a "knob" and a "cavity", or a "tongue" and a "groove". Are their Gauss maps unique?

12-1   Write a description for a wedge in the ODL. Is this description unique? (i.e. will any other blocks-world shapes fit this description?)

12-2   Add a "less-than" definition to the ODL and describe a tetrahedron whose base is smaller than the sides.

12-3   Calculate the weight function W for the arch illustrated in Figure 12-3. How do the weights of the three possible CT's agree with your perceptual preference for describing an arch?

12-4   Construct a canonical connection table for the rooms in your house. Does the first entry in this table have any special significance? (See Chapter 6-6.)

13-1   Consider Figure 13-2 depicting an illumination gradient across a Mondrian display. What is the relation between the observed intensity gradient dI/dx and the reflectance of the surface? At the edge between two Mondrian patches, what is the relation between the ratio of intensity gradients on each side of the edge, and the reflectances? (Ullman, 1976.)

13-2   Assume a two-percent error in measuring intensities at an edge. In Figure 13-5, what will be the average cumulative error after traversing the path from top to bottom? How can you reduce this error?

13-3   In Figure 13-4, how many patches are required to recover the direction of an extended source of illumination? Can this information aid the retinex computation? If so, how?

14-1   How many different wavelength samples are needed to distinguish a shadow edge from an edge created by a change in pigment density?

14-2   How many different wavelength samples are needed to distinguish shadows from highlights?

14-3   A green leaf seen from below is illuminated from above by the sun and transmits half the sunlight. A similar leaf of the same tree is seen from above, and appears much darker, yet has the same hue. This is surprising because for many materials (such as dichoics), the transmitted and reflected colors are complementary, as if those wavelengths not transmitted are reflected. What constraint is required for the hue of a leaf to be similar for both transmitted and reflected light? (Hint:

consider the internal reflections of the light reflected off the bottom surface of the leaf, and how these contribute to the observed transmittance and reflectance.)

14-4 Assume a highlight desaturates the appearance of a surface patch by an additive mixture of reflected light (see Equation 14-6). Plot on Figure 14-4 the position of a pure highlight and a flat matte surface patch. Variations of the highlight on this patch now will lie on the straight line joining these two points. In general, however, any given highlight on a surface will yield points lying only on a small portion of this line. Then how many surface patches will be needed to recover the color of the illuminant? (Lee, 1986).

14-5 Consider the distribution of color of an interior shadow cast on a flat textured surface such as grass or pebbles which have matte and specular reflectance components (see Problem 4-2). Show that if the 3D elements of the texture have a random distribution of orientation, then the solution to Problem 14-4 applies. Will the spatial scale of the imaging filter have any effect?

15-1 Many rocky, dusty surfaces (such as the moon) have a reflectance function equal to $\cos i / \cos e$ where i is the incident angle between N and L and e is the emergent angle between N and V. For a fixed viewing and illuminant direction, what will be the perceived intensity of a spherical surface?

15-2 What is the reflectance function for a retro-reflect surface?

15-3 Plot the range of the Phong model in the reflectance representation proposed in Chapter 3, Figure 5.

16-1 Given that the index of refraction of water is 1.3, at what angular range of incidence will the reflection fall below 0.1 for a point source of strength 1.0?

16-2 Many surfaces have oily films which reflect part of the light and transmit the balance, causing "gloss". Assume this film is smooth ($G = D = 1$). Describe the resultant image intensity equation for a planar matte surface with such a film (i.e. wood). Choose an albedo fraction, and an illuminant whose spectral content differs from the albedo spectral reflectance function. Now graph the observed intensities reflected off the surface at two different wavelengths, plotting for each viewing and illumination geometry the intensity seen at one wavelength versus the intensity seen at the other. How will the graph change if the surface is a cylinder? (Shafer, 1985).

17-1 How many line segments with (perpendicular) velocity known are needed to recover the correct translation vector of motion? How do you know the obtained vector is correct? How many moving line segments are needed to recover a rotation? (Kanade, 1985).

17-2 A rigid contour of arbitrary shape translates behind a slit so that only the contour angle (tangent), the change in this angle, and its speed along the slit can be recovered. How many views of the contour are needed to recover the direction of translation in the image plane (Shimojo & Richards, 1985)?

P

18-1 How many line segments are needed to determine whether a patch of a flow field is a rotation or a dilation? Why? Show an indeterminate configuration of three segments. What if the patch has a spiral flow? (Consider orientation of line segment only, not its length.)

18-2 How many points are required in Problem 18-1? Is the problem unique? Is correspondence required? Consider both orientation and distance between pairs of points (Richards, 1984).

18-3 A flow field may be decomposed to first order into a rotation, dilation, stretch or shear. The stretch is equivalent to deforming a circle into an ellipse, thus changing the spacing between equally spaced radial lines (or spokes) on a circle. Given an initially uniform spacing of radial lines, how many pairs of lines on the ellipse (yielding $\Delta\theta_i$ at θ_i) are needed to recover the axes of deformation?

19-1 Derive the relation between the (horizontal) angular disparity of two points separated by a distance d at a fixation distance F. Consider sagittal plane approximation only.

19-2 What is the relation between the slant of a line segment and its binocular disparity in retinal orientation (i.e. the angular difference between the projection of a line in 3-space onto the two image planes)?

19-3 How many stereo views of two points are required to remove the ambiguity in their true 3D configuration that results when fixation distance is not known? What if the head motion causes the points to appear to move, and that their instantaneous velocities in the image plane are now given?

20-1 Prove that the fractal dimension of a fractal Brownian function is invariant over transformations of scale.

20-2 A Koch curve may be created by replacing the middle third of each side of an equilateral triangle with a smaller equilateral triangle with sides one-third those of the larger triangle, and continuing this process for *all* edge segments. By what factor does the distance along the outside of the figure increase at each step? What is the fractal dimension of the silhouette?

20-3 Calculate the fractal dimension of the image contour created by shadow of a horizontal planar surface with a Koch curve edge. Use either triangular or rectangular bases elements for the edge. Consider only one illuminant position such as $\sigma_L = \pi/4$, $\tau_L = \pi/4$ and at least one non-trivial orientation of the edge and viewer position with respect to the (horizontal) ground onto which the shadow has been cast. Assume orthographic projection.

20-4 Consider an object having a fractal surface viewed stereoscopically, with the edge of the object visible. Show how the roughness of the surface can be used to obtain the correct 3D configuration of the object, independent of fixation distance.

20-5 Consider a surface such as water which has only a specular reflectance function. If the surface is a fractal Brownian function, show that the image intensities will also have a fractal distribution.

21-1 Your hearing ranges from 100 to 10,000 Hz. What acoustic frequencies are the most effective for communicating precise temporal information? Why?

21-2 A cricket communicates by sending coded trains of short pulses which have a rise time of about 2 msec. What minimum bandwidth would you predict for the cricket's auditory tuning curve?

22-1 A moth has two simple "ears" separated by about 5 mm. What is the maximum interaural delay of a sound? (Sound travels at about 330 m/sec.) Write down an equation relating the difference of arrival time of a sound at the two ears, as a function of azimuth angle, α, in degrees. Let D be the interaural distance between the ears. What is the solution when the sound source is quite distant relative to D.

22-2 A source located anywhere on a cone of fixed angle α to the head will result in equal interaural delays. A head rotation through a known angle will give a different "view" of a stationary sound source. How many "views" are required to determine the sound source direction? Is the solution unique? What are the false targets?

22-3 How many "views" are needed to recover the direction of motion of a translating sound source? Are there any degenerate movements of the source?

23-1 Why is a reversed sound track of speech impossible to interpret? Would you expect the same difficulty with music? What other natural sounds would also be difficult to interpret if reversed? Can you identify another class of natural sounds which would be easy to interpret regardless of whether played forward or backward? Why?

23-2 MacAdams (1984) has demonstrated that a single sound source can be isolated from several if it has a distinctive FM modulation (i.e. a vibrato). Write an equation for the FM modulation of a sinusoid.

23-3 How are the observed formants of a speaker affected by the echoes in a room? Consider each formant as a pure sinusoid. To simulate the echoes add together delayed sinusoids having the same frequencies. Will the formant frequency be altered?

24-1 Identify the four components of a sound source and give two examples—one percussive, the other non-percussive.

24-2 At MIT the infinity corridor is roughly 3×4 meters in width and height and 300 meters long. What are the fundamental resonant modes of this corridor? What are the first three harmonics? (Sound travels in air at about 330 m/sec.)

24-3 How many harmonics are needed to tell an open from a closed cylinder, assuming their fundamental frequency is identical? How does this number change if a bell is also included, whose first harmonics are 1, $\sqrt{2}$, 2, 3?

24-4 Why does a violin "A" string sound different from the ring of a tuning fork having

P

the same note?

25-1 What is the, $wQ - 1$ constraint curve for materials that are perfectly elastic?

25-2 Note that $J2/J1 = M2/M1$ (not $J1/J2$). Why?

25-3 As a wine glass is filled with water, it is struck with a spoon. Will the pitch increase or decrease as the glass is filled? Why? What will happen to the duration of the "ring" during active pouring, as compared to the case when there is no liquid in motion?

25-4 Why does a clap made with the palms of one's hand have a lower pitch than the snap of one's fingers? Derive a relation for the frequency of these impulsive sounds versus the area of the impacting surface.

26-1 Calculate the intervals between bounces for an elastic bouncing ball. Next consider the case where energy is dissipated. What if the struck surface is inclined by 15 degrees?

26-2 Calculate the expected distribution of pulses between raindrops hitting an inelastic surface.

26-3 Design a fractal model for the sound made by crunching up a paper sheet, or for a twig snap.

27-1 Write a grammar showing the relations between half, quarter, eighth notes, etc. Then label the nodes in Figure 27-1 to show the structure of the clichè.

27-2 Show the grammatical structure of the theme illustrated in Figure 27-6.

27-3 Let the meter of all songs be represented in terms of a 2 or 3 meter base unit, or their combination. How many possible descriptions are there for meters from 4 to 12? Graph the result—i.e. number of descriptions versus meter. Can you introduce a plausible constraint which will reduce the allowable descriptions?

28-1 How many points of contact are needed to determine the Gaussian curvature of a smooth surface? What constraints must be imposed on the surface normals? (Courtesy of Marilyn Matz.)

28-2 How many friction-free points of contact are needed to hold a cylindrical rod in an arbitrary position?

29-1 What is the minimum number of two-segment fingers (two joints) needed to grip a rod to be held rigidly in an arbitrary configuration? Assume tangential contact with friction. Justify your answer by an analysis of the degrees-of-freedom (DOF) required and imposed by each finger. Draw a sketch of the resultant "hand".

29-2 Show all possible contact configurations for a two-finger hand, where one finger has two links and the other one, and where the motion of each finger is opposite to the other (i.e. the "object" is grasped between the two fingers). What is the connectivity of this system?

30-1 Show that two sensors can recover the direction of motion of an 1D texture (see Figure 30-6). What assumptions are necessary?

30-2 What plausible biological assumptions might be invoked to permit the recovery of the skin's modulus of elasticity, M, using contact without motion?

31-1 Derive Equation (1) of the introduction to the readings comprising Chapter 5.

31-2 Show that the equilibrium model described in the introduction to Chapter 5 is a controllable physical system.

32-1 Simplify Equations (3-7) and the derivation of Equation (12) of Selection 32 by considering movement restricted to the horizontal plane.

32-2 Repeat 32-1 for movement restricted to the sagittal (vertical) plane containing the **g** vector.

33-1 To perform the same arm movement three times as fast, how much more torque should you apply to your joints? Why this value?

33-2 Refer to Figure 33-1, showing a planar two-link manipulator. Assume $l_1 = l_2$ and that the range of elbow angle θ_2 is -0 to $+180$ degrees, and that the range of the shoulder angle θ_1, is -90 to $+135$ degrees. (i) Describe the set of points the wrist can reach (i.e. the end of link l_2). This is the work-space of the arm. A graph is acceptable. (ii) Write an equation for the position of the wrist, relating x, y coordinates to θ_1, θ_2. (iii) For any given wrist position in the x, y plane how many possible arm positions are there? (In other words, how many arrangements of θ_1, θ_2 will yield the same x, y position of the wrist?) (iv) Solve for the relation between any x, y position and the θ_1, θ_2 joint angles needed to reach this position. (v) graph the values of θ_1, and θ_2 for a trajectory of wrist motion parallel to the x-axis, say for $y = l$.

33-3 Referring to Problem 33-2, graph the values of θ_1, θ_2 for a trajectory of wrist motion along a path where $y = Ax$, with "A" an arbitrary constant. Is there a simple relation between θ_1 and θ_2 for this trajectory?

34-1 What should be the mass ratio of the upper to lower leg in order that the entire leg has a natural period equivalent to a one-meter pendulum? Assume the thigh and lower leg are each one-half a meter long with their center-of-mass one-quarter meter from the knee joint.

34-2 Using a model similar to that of Figure 1 in the introduction to Chapter 5, show that the least muscle tension exerted about an ankle joint during toeing-off is when the foot-to-leg angle is near $90°$.

35-1 Construct a gait matrix for bird flight. Show the event sequences.

35-2 A cockroach has six legs. Construct a symmetric, regularly-realizable gait matrix for this beast.

36-1 Show that Raibert's symmetry equations are consistent with the equations of motion for a simple leg by labeling the symmetry for each term in these equations.

36-2 Use Raibert's equations of motion to prove the virtual leg condition.

References

Beusmans, J.M.H., Hoffman, D.D. & Bennett, B.M. (1987) Description of solid shape and its inference from occluding contours. *Jrl. Opt. Soc. Amer. A*, 4:1155–1167.

Horn, B.K.P. (1981) The curve of least energy. MIT A.I. Lab. Memo 610.

Huffman, D.A. (1971) Impossible objects as nonsense sentences. *Machine Intell.*, 6:295–323.

Kanade, T. (1985) Motion from line correspondence and trioculor stereo. *Jrl. Opt. Soc. Amer. A*, 2(13):4.

Lee, H.-C. (1986) Method for computing the scene illuminant chromaticity from specular highlights. *Jrl. Opt. Soc. Amer. A*, 3:1694–1699.

MacAdams, S. (1984) Spectral fusion, spectral parsing and the formation of auditory images. Ph.D. dissertation, Speech and Hearing Sciences, Stanford University.

Richards, W. (1984) Grouping without prior correspondence. *Jrl. Opt. Soc. Amer. A*, 1:1265(A).

Shafer, S.A. (1985) Using color to separate reflection components. *COLOR Research and Application*, 10(4):210–218. Univ. Rochester TR 136, 1984, Computer Science Dept.

Shimojo, S. & Richards, W. (1986) "Seeing" shapes that are almost totally occluded: a new look at Parks's camel. *Percept. & Psychophys.*, 39:418–426.

Ullman, S. (1976) On visual detection of light sources. *Biol. Cybernetics*, 21:205–212.

Walker, J. (1986) The amateur scientist. *Sci. Amer.*, 222(4, Oct.):204–209.

Witkin, A.P. (1981) Recovering surface shape and orientation from texture. *Artif. Intell.*, 17:17–47.

Glossary

A_4 — A note of 440 Hz, just above middle C.

Accretion-deletion — The appearance or disappearance of image features adjacent to moving object boundaries (see Chapter 4).

Albedo (ρ) — Ratio of reflected to incident radiant flux as function of wavelength for a matte surface.

Areas 17 & 18 — The primary cortical receiving areas for visual information. Location of first orientation and disparity-sensitive neurons. In monkey, Area 18 receives its principal input from Area 17.

C — Connectivity between two bodies, such as the palm and a grasped object, defined as the number of independent parameters needed to specify completely the relative positions of the two bodies at a given instant.

CG-print — The vertical projection onto the ground of the estimated path the center-of-gravity will travel during the next support interval.

Cochlear — The sense organ for hearing, which is shaped like a snail shell.

Codon — A primitive part descriptor based on the relations between the three singularities of curvature (namely the zeros and the positive and negative extrema).

Condition number — A number associated with a matrix indicating the convergence or stability of the matrix (see Chapter 29).

Correct rejection — Correctly asserting that no target signal was presented, when indeed none was.

Critical band — The bandwidth within which acoustic tones will raise the threshold for detecting a reference tone.

Crosspoint — A relation between the spectral reflectance across an edge (see Chapter 14).

cs — Centiseconds, or 1/100 second.

CT — Connection Table, which is a graph representation for an object showing the spatial relations between its parts.

Cylinder	A surface with one of the principle curvatures equal to zero, the other being non-zero.
Δ	See Logarithmic decrement.
$\nabla^2 G$	Laplacian of the Gaussian $\partial^2 G/\partial x^2 + \partial^2 G/\partial y^2$.
d	Fraction of reflectance that is diffuse.
D	Fractal dimensions.
D	Distribution of microfacets (see Chapter 15).
dB	Decibels, a logarithmic measure of signal strength relative to a baseline of 0.0002 dynes/cm². Hence a ratio scale.
Disparity	The difference in retinal angle between two points as viewed by the two eyes.
$E(\lambda)$	Illuminant strength—a function of wavelength, λ.
E_k, E_p	Kinetic and potential energy.
ϵ, σ	Strain and sress variables.
Elliptic patch	A surface region of positive Gaussian curvature. (The patch lies entirely on one side of the tangent plane.)
Explicit naming (Principle of)	Whenever a collection of data is to be described or manipulated as a whole, it should first be given a name, thus becoming an explicit symbolic object, rather than existing only implicitly in the data (Marr, 1976).
F	Fresnel reflection coefficient (see Chapter 15 & 16).
$\mathbf{F}, \mathbf{f}, \underline{F}$	Force vector.
False alarm	Asserting the presence of a target signal when none was presented.
Fifth	A 'perfect fifth' is a frequency ratio of 3/2 in an octave scale.
Flexional line	See parabolic line.
Flux	Short form for radiant flux (watt) or its psychophysical correlate, or luminous flux (lumen), according to context.
Formant	A resonant frequency determined by the shape of the vocal tract, with the lowest formant corresponding to a quarter-wavelength. See Chapter 24.

Fourier Transform	See Chapter 21.
Fractal	A word invented by Mandelbrot to describe the non-Euclidean, space-filling property of irregular curves, surfaces or volumes (see selection 20).
Frontal plane	The plane perpendicular to the line of sight.
G	Gait matrix (see Chapter 35).
G	Facet shadowing factor (see Chapter 15 & 16).
g	Gravitational force.
Gauss map (or sphere)	The parallel mapping of surfaces normals onto the unit sphere.
Gaussian curvature	The product of the two principal curvatures.
General position	A generic view of a surface or object such that the topology of the features and their relations does not change when the viewpoint is slightly perturbed.
Geodesic	The shortest distance between two points on a smooth surface.
Glottis	A space at the base of the larynx between the two vocal folds (or "cords").
Graceful degradation (Principle of)	Degradation of data should not prevent one from delivering at least some of the answer (Marr, 1976).
Gradient space	A two-dimensional representation of three-dimensional surface orientation using the partial derivatives of x and y with respect to distance z $(\frac{\delta x}{\delta z} = p; \frac{\delta y}{\delta z} = q)$.
H	Fractal scaling parameter.
H	Surface orientation for maximum specular reflection.
H	Hamiltonian (see Horn, 1986).
$\overline{h}$	One minus the Hausdorf dimension (see Chapter 20).
Hamming window	A filter which truncates a Fourier series by smoothly tapering the N samples to a near-zero valve about a maximum of $(N-1)/2$, as opposed to a rectangular window where side lobe effects can become objectionable. See Oppenheim & Schafen, *Digital Signal Processing*, 1975, Chapters 5 and 10.
Hit	The correct identification of a target signal.

G

Hyperbolic patch   A surface region of negative Gaussian curvature. (The patch
                          will cut the tangent plane).

Hz   Hertz, temporal frequency, $\sec^{-1}$.

I   Moment of inertia.

$I(x, y)$ Image intensity.

Illuminance   Luminous flux incident per unit surface area (lumen/meter^2).

Imbalanced mask   An image filter created by the difference of two Gaussians,
                          usually with space constraints differing by a factor of three.
                          When the areas (or volumes) of the two Gaussians are unequal,
                          the mask is "imbalanced". This technique serves to eliminate
                          noise.

Intensity (E, I) Short for radiant intensity (watts/steradian) or luminous in-
                          tensity (lumens/steradian), according to context.

Internal friction   A measure of the degree of damping of anelastic materials,
$(\tan \phi)$ analogous to the viscocity measure for a Newtonian dashpot.
                          See Chapter 25.

Isoclastic   See elliptic.

Isotropy, Isotropic   The same in all directions, such as the uniform distribution of
                          3D surface orientation in 3D or contour orientation in 2D.

J   Modulus of compliance, equal to the reciprocal of the modulus
                          of elasticity. The complex modulus is denoted J.

$J^{\top}$ The transpose of the Jacobean matrix.

κ Curvature.

K_x Stiffness matrix.

L   Illuminant direction unit vector.

ℓ leg length.

λ Wavelength; or, length of measuring stick.

Larynx   A short tube in the vocal tract. See Chapter 23.

Least commitment   Never do something that may later have to be undone (Marr,
(Principle of)   1976).

Legato   The smooth connected playing of notes without breaks.

Lightness	The subjective correlate of achromatic reflectance, such as the Munsell Value scale from black to gray to white.
Lines of curvature	A locus of principal curvatures.
Logarithmic decrement (Δ)	A decay rate measure for tones, defined as the natural log of the ratio of two adjacent amplitude peaks.
LPC	Linear predictive coding.
Lumen	Psychophysical correlate of one watt of radiant flux.
Luminance	Luminous flux per unit solid angle emitted per unit projected surface area (lumens/steradian $\times$ meter^2).
M	Modulus of elasticity, which equals the spring constant or σ/ϵ for an ideal elastic material. The complex modulus is denoted $\mathcal{M}$.
M	Mobility of a kinematic system, defined as the number of independent parameters necessary to specify completely the position of every body in the system at given instant.
m	Mass.
Matte	A diffusing surface where the flux reflected per unit solid angle is proportional to the cosine of the angle to the surface normal.
Mel (scale)	A scale for pitch that spaces tones in equal subjective intervals. The pitch of a 1000 Hz tone 40 dB above threshold is defined as 1000 mels.
Middle C (C_4)	A tone of 261.6 Hz, four octaves above C_0.
Minim	A half-note
Miss	Stating that the target signal was not present, when indeed it was.
Modular design (Principle of)	Any large computation should be split up and implemented as a collection of small sub-parts that are nearly as independent of one another as the overall task allows (Marr, 1976).
η	Viscosity of a liquid, related to stress (σ) and strain (ϵ) by $\tau = \eta\dot{\epsilon}$.
N	Surface normal unit vector.

G

n	Torque vector.
n	Index of refraction (see Chapters 15 & 16).
Null-space	For surfaces (or space of possible velocity fields), it is the set of surfaces that cannot be distinguished by the functional from the surface (or velocity) which is zero everywhere.
$\underline{\theta}(t)$	Joint angle vector, specifying a trajectory for a manipulator.
Octave	A separation equivalent to eight full notes, or a factor of two in frequency.
ODL	Object Description Language, which is a formal specification for an object satisfying certain structural and grammatical properties.
Opposite slope sign	A relation between the spectral reflectances across an edge (see Chapter 14).
Overtone	An harmonic frequency.
$\underline{P}$	Generalized input forces (see Chapter 32).
p, q	Position vectors.
p, q	Generalized momentum.
$\underline{p}, \underline{q}$	Generalized momentum ($\underline{p}$) and coordinate ($\underline{q}$) vectors.
P, Q	Force coordinate frame.
Parabolic line	The locus of zero Gaussian curvature on a smooth surface (also called a flexional line).
Parallel axis theorem	The moment of inertia at a point other than at the center of mass is simply greater by the mass times the square of the distance to that point.
Parallelogram Law	Let θ be a function of two variables u, v. Then the parallelogram law is satisfied if $[\theta(u+v)]^2 + [\theta(u-v)]^2 = 2[\theta(v)]^2 + 2[\theta(w)]^2$.
Place token	A token that marks a point of interest in an image. Such tokens have a position, usually possess other properties, and are useful in the analysis of spatial arrangements in the image.

Plane curve	Any curve confined to lie in a plane (as opposed to a curve or trajectory in 3-space).
Primal sketch	An intensity-based representation of sensory data (e.g. zero-crossings, line elements, blobs, short-term Fourier Transform). Note that this representation is entirely descriptive and makes no commitment to the physical origin of the features represented.
Principal curvature	Of a smooth surface, is either the greatest or the least curvature at a point. (Note that the directions of the greatest and least curvatures are perpendicular.)
Q	The quality or ability of a resistance to produce resonance effects, hence inversely related to bandwidth.
Quaver	An eighth note.
Radiance	Radiant intensity per unit projected angle (watts/steradian $\times$ meter^2).
Radiant flux	Rate of transfer of radiant energy (watts).
Reflectance	Ratio of reflected to incident radiant flux.
Reflectance function	Ratio of reflected to incident radiant flux as a function of light direction, surface normal, and viewer position.
Representation	A representation is a formal scheme for describing a set of entities together with rules which specify how these entities are related and can be manipulated. A *description* is a particular instantiation.
Retinex	A term invented by Edwin Land (retina + cortex) to describe his scheme for removing the confounding effects of illumination when recovering spectral reflectances. See Chapter 13.
$\rho\,(\lambda)$	Albedo function over wavelength.
Rim	The curve on a surface that divides the potentially visible from the non-visible regions (see-thru is allowed). Thus, it is a locus of points where the visual ray just grazes the surface.
RMS	Root-means-square, i.e. square-root of the sum of the squared distances from the mean, divided by the number of entries.
Rubato	A tempo in which some notes are shortened (robbed) that others may be lengthened.

s	Fraction of reflectance that is specular.
Semi-norm	A function p on a vector space $\{v\}$ which satisfies the following scaling and additivity properties: (i) $p(\alpha v) = |\alpha| p(v)$ and (ii) $p(v_i + v_j)S \leq p(v_i) + p(v_j)$.
Semi-quaver	A sixteenth note.
Slant (σ)	The angle between the visual ray to a point and the surface normal at that point.
SNR	Signal-to-noise ratio.
Sone (scale)	A scale for loudness that spaces acoustic intensities in equal subjective intervals. One sone is the loudness of a 1000 Hz tone, 40 dB above threshold.
Specific loss (δ)	A frequency-independent measure of the damping of anelastic materials due to internal friction.
Specular	A surface reflection where the incident and reflected angle are equal.
Staccato	The short, clear-cut playing of notes.
Strain (ϵ)	A displacement (e.g. an elongation or contraction of a material under stress).
Stress (σ)	A force which causes a displacement (e.g. an elongation or contraction of a material).
Synclastic	See hyperbolic.
τ	Time (normalized to $1/2\pi f$). [Also tilt of a plane.]
T	Topological dimension.
T	A tension vector (see Chapter 29).
3D model	An object-centered representation, such as the stick-figure model of Marr & Nishihara, or the topological model of Koenderink, both of which provide a framework for specifying the relations between the components of an object.
T_s	Duration of stance phase.
Tenuto	A note held to its full value, as opposed to being cut short, as in staccato.

Terminator	The edge where self-shading occurs. Hence $N \cdot L = 0$.
3D-skeleton	A base feature representation analogous to Marr's 2 1/2 D sketch, which makes explicit 3D structure.
Third	A "major third" is a frequency ratio of 5/4 in an octave scale.
Tilt (τ)	The angle in the frontal plane between the chosen vertical and the projection of the surface normal.
Token	See place token.
Tonic	The keynote to which other notes are referred.
2 1/2 D sketch	A viewer-centered representation of visible world properties such as surface orientation or material type (e.g. reflectance functions, surface micro-structure).
V	Viewer direction (unit vector).
$\underline{V}$	Velocity vector.
w	A wrench vector of forces and torques.
ω	Angular frequency or velocity $(2\pi f)$.
$\underline{X}$	Coordinate or position vector.
Zero-crossing	Generally refers to a zero in the convolution of the second derivative of a Gaussian with image intensity. (Equivalent to locating a maximum in intensity change, such as occurs at a step edge.)

G

Name Index

Italics refer to entries in the references.

N

N

N

N

N

N

Subject Index

S

S

S

S

S